Fighting the Merchants of Hate: The War for America's Soul

By

William C. McConkey, Ph.D.

For Tecumseh and Sitting Bull, Frederick Douglas and Martin Luther King, Abigail Adams and Susan B. Anthony, Rachel Carson and Erin Brockovich, for Oprah, for Angie and Di, for Ellen Lee DeGeneres and David Kopay, for Ken Marcus, for Harvey Milk, for Lester Pines, Tamara Packard, Edward Marion, for Tim Gill, for Barney Frank and Tammy Baldwin

Dedicated to my mother, Betty McConkey Carr

1919-1999

Fighting The Merchants of Hate

ISBN 9780971449756
Library of Congress 2010902073
Quiet Side Publishing, 2009
Baileys Harbor, WI
March 01, 2010

Special Thanks

There are always people to thank and the words, from those of us who write, are strangely inadequate, but we try. I thank my wife, Sandy, once again, for the hours, days, weeks, months, years I spent on this task. I thank Karl McCarty for his chapter, for an immense amount of research, and for his reading the rest, and though paid for his work, it was not enough. I thank Stewart and Jilly Sweet for her cover graphics and his web page assistance. I thank Kristin Lange for formatting assistance. I thank Lisa Wedekind with Lightning Source for her technical assistance. I must thank Lester Pines, Tamara Packard and Edward Marion for their legal assistance, all the way to the Wisconsin Supreme Court. I thank my daughters for teaching me so much.

A Note: My errors of omission and commission are never intentional, always accidental, and I apologize in advance.

The Power of the Spoken Word

I have been privileged to know and work with Professor of Communication, Lori Carrell. I have heard her talk, several times, of the power of the spoken word. The power of the spoken word is absolutely under estimated and under discussed in this world of sound bites and visual images. Yet, the spoken word, from strong and passionate people, delivered to those who want to hear those words, can have major influences upon the listener. That power has the potential for an awesome impact for good or evil; indeed even to create acts of good or evil.

There is much being said that leads to evil. Our nation needs voices for goodness, kindness, equality, "life, liberty and the pursuit of happiness', for safety from hatred and harm.

I hope this book makes a case for voices for equality for all our citizens.

Table of Contents

Introduction

In 2006, the State of Wisconsin passed a Constitutional Amendment that made it possible, by a simple majority vote of even one vote, to strip any group of people in Wisconsin from their Constitutional protections, rights and privileges. It was falsely labeled a "Defense of Marriage Amendment".

I was, in 2006, a straight, married, overweight, white, conservative Republican. I am still straight, married, overweight, white, and conservative. The Republican Party has left me and became a Party of anti-democratic authoritarian ideologues teamed with a group of equally greedy radio talk show hosts and televangelists, and hate mongers disguised as clergy. These people use hatred and ignorance to line their wallets, fill their pews and stuff their ballot boxes.

The members of this right-wing conspiracy, and it is just that, want to destroy any one different than they see themselves. They are the American Taliban. There are merchants of hatred in our nation, as well as other nations, who would prevent Americans from realizing their rights and possibilities simply because Group A does not like or agree with Group B. These people sell hatred and acts of unkindness for gain. That gain may be financial, political, ideological, or even a warped psychological kick.

I have been guilty of ignoring the teaching of hatred for far too long. If my silence has condoned those who spread hatred, I am guilty of the reckless endangerment of members of my own family, as well as friends and people I do not even know. This sincerely shames me.

I was also raised in a religious family. I am sorely disappointed in the hatred I see spread by far too many churches. It is unfathomable to me that "Men of God", pastors and preachers are actively opposing hate crime legislation. Certainly others see the incongruity of Christians opposing hate crime laws. These "Men of God" are giving Jesus a bad name.

I also read, in the daily news, of violent hate crimes against people. I read in business and academic publications of the impacts of hateful speech and acts in the workplace: the cost, the ruined careers, and the humiliation. And, I see people who are afraid of these merchants of hatred, whether politicians, preachers or neighborhood or office bullies.

I understand fear; it is a real emotion, with a powerful impact. I believe, to my very core, that people who are not afraid have a moral responsibility to fight for those people who are. I am not afraid of these bullies, these politicians, these preachers, these thugs and criminals. I have a moral obligation to fight them on behalf of those who are afraid. I hope and pray that those who are abused and afraid will find the strength to fight back and fight to claim their position as full and equal citizens of this nation. I hope and pray that those who are not abused will fight for those who are.

Chapter One: A Definition of Terms

Love: Acts of kindness from a human being or group of human beings toward and/or for the benefit of other humans, animals, plants or living things of any kind. Love is as love does.

Hate: Any action, statement or lack of either, that is in its effect, an act of unkindness from a human being or group of human beings toward and/or for the harm of other humans, animals, plants or living things of any kind. Hate is as hate does.

Hate is as hate does. You enslave the American Indians, the Africans. That is an act of hatred. You enforce Jim Crow laws and condone the lynching of 3437 Afro-Americans and 1293 whites in 86 years, including 11 Italian-Americans on one day in New Orleans, that is hatred. You sterilize people, against their will, because they are mentally deficient, regardless of whether their problem was genetic or not, that is hatred. You give prisoners, in our prisons, syphilis so you can test serums, without their permission, thereby killing them, that is hatred. When you deny people of different races the right to marry, that is hatred. When you deny equal pay for equal work and opportunities through the glass ceiling, that is hatred. In 39 states, an unmarried couple—gay or straight—is denied the same constitutional and statutory protections and benefits of those who are in the voting majority and who created the situation. That is hatred**.**

Neo-con Republicans: Republicans who are supporters of the very wealthy at the cost of the nation's infrastructure, who wish to interfere in the lives of private citizens, who talk and vote as if they wish to abolish the separation of Church and State tradition and wish to impose a "Christian" order of their liking on the nation, who oppose equal rights, protections and benefits for all American citizens, and who think Rush Limbaugh is something besides an overweight, rightwing, radio entertainer and windbag.

Merchants of Hatred: Those who teach and encourage hatred by their words and actions. Although speech is protected, reckless endangerment is not; neither is public policy that harms people and robs them of equal protections of the law. Specifically, Neo-con Republicans and other politicians in search of absolute power, the money-grubbing religious zealots and their henchmen and women, hate-groups and hateful individuals, inciting their fellows and/or committing unkind acts, and unfortunately, millions of parents who teach their children to hate.

Theocratic Evangelical and/or "Dominionists": People who wish to establish the United States as officially a "Christian" nation; of course, with their definition of "Christian".

Mugwumps: To paraphrase William Safire, people who sit on the fence concerning issues of public policy, with their mug on one side and their wump on the other.

Chapter Two:
The Freedom of Speech- Let The Sun Shine In

The freedom of speech is an incredible protection. It allows us to know the hearts and minds of people and may save us from truly unholy alliances.

Robert Frost wrote these powerful words, "Before I'd build a wall, I'd know what I was walling in and what I was walling out."

Before I'd follow any of the following groups or people, I would certainly know where they were going to take me. It is astonishing that any thinking person would listen more than once to or pay attention to any of these folks. Read at your own peril.

Speaking of "peril", the other side of the coin is the evil that can be and is often perpetuated by the professional communicator. Just as Joseph Goebbels served Hitler as his head propagandist, modern day professionals of the Big Lie, sew an equally kind of evil. Goebbels said,"If you tell a lie big enough and keep repeating it, people will eventually come to believe it. The lie can be maintained only for such time as the State can shield the people from the political, economic and/or military consequences of the lie. It thus becomes vitally important for the State to use all of its powers to repress dissent, for the truth is the mortal enemy of the lie, and thus by extension, the truth is the greatest enemy of the State."[1]

That so-called "Christians" like Pat Robertson attack hate crimes legislation by comparing homosexuals to men who might want to "have sex with ducks", and I am not making that up, is utterly contemptuous. He targets the know-nothings, Skinheads and morons such as Scott P. Roeder, of Merriam, Kansas, and helps nudge them into acts such as murder during a church service.

There is no hiding behind some kind of my God is better than your God argument. I will always defend free speech but there is no acceptable free speech excuse here. These demagogues must at least have the personal integrity to admit that they walk in the footsteps of Goebbels and enflame hatreds and actions. Bill O'Reilly, of Fox News, singled out Dr. George Tiller as an abortionist 29 times on his show prior to Tiller's murder while in church and claimed that Dr. Tiller was guilty of "Nazi stuff," a moral equivalent to NAMBLA and al-Qaida, and said that Tiller "has blood on his hands." Then O'Reilly denied any responsibility for Scott Roeder's actions, thereby denying any legitimacy for television or his own skills. Roeder gunned down Tiller while Tiller was serving as an usher in Sunday morning services. That is such a cowardly sack of crap. Come on O'Reilly, you plan on firing up the masses, you are paid to do so; so why hide when some nut case kills a man in church?

The Reverend Pat Robertson…

"Many of those people involved in Adolf Hitler were Satanists, many were homosexuals - the two things seem to go together."[2]

"How can there be peace when drunkards, drug dealers, communists, atheists, New Age worshipers of Satan, secular humanists, oppressive dictators, greedy money changers, revolutionary assassins, adulterers, and homosexuals are on top?"[3]

"You say you're supposed to be nice to the Episcopalians and the Presbyterians and the Methodists, and this and that and the other thing. Nonsense! I don't have to be nice to the spirit of the Antichrist."[4]

In regard to Planned Parenthood, Robertson said, "It is teaching kids to fornicate, teaching people to have adultery, every kind of bestiality, homosexuality, lesbianism - everything that the Bible condemns."[5]

When discussing Gay Day at Disney World, Robertson said, "I would warn Orlando that you're right in the way of some serious hurricanes and I don't think I'd be waving those flags in God's face if I were you. This is not a message of hate; this is a message of redemption. But a condition like this will bring about the destruction of your nation. It'll bring about terrorist bombs, it'll bring earthquakes, tornadoes, and possibly a meteor."[6]

"The key in terms of mental ability is chess. There's never been a woman Grand Master chess player. Once you get one, then I'll buy some of the feminism."[7]

The Reverend D. James Kennedy...

"As the vice-regents of God, we are to bring His truth and His will to bear on every sphere of our world and our society. We are to exercise godly dominion and influence over our neighborhoods, our schools, our government... our entertainment media, our news media, our scientific endeavors – in short, over every aspect and institution of human society."[8]

Julaine Appling, CEO Wisconsin Family Council...

"I think we've been extremely tolerant in allowing them [lesbians and gays] to live wherever they choose."[9]

Reverend Jimmy Swaggart...

"I've never seen a man in my life I wanted to marry. And I'm going to be blunt and plain: if one ever looks at me like that, I'm going to kill him and tell God he died."[10]

Rush Limbaugh...

"...Feminism was established so as to allow unattractive women easier access to the mainstream of society."[11]

Dr. Albert Mohler...

Southern Baptist Theological Seminary president Dr. Albert Mohler, in a 2000 Interview: "As an evangelical, I believe that the Roman Catholic Church is a false church...It teaches a false gospel. And the Pope himself holds a false and unbiblical office."[12]

Reverend Fred Phelps, Westboro, Kansas Baptist Church...

From a Westboro Baptist Church news release in March 2004:

> "Gen. [Wesley] Clark opposed fags & dykes in the military—BUT—when he decided to run for President on the Democratic ticket he groveled like a mangy dog to the FagiNazis running the Democratic Party, and promised to lift the ban on gays in the military. His Christ-rejecting, God-hating Jew blood bubbled to the surface. Yes, like his boss [John] Kerry, Clark is a Jew...That these two turds are Jews would not matter—except when they ask for supreme political power & spit in the Face of God, pushing for same-sex marriage, threatening to bring down God's wrath on us as on Sodom—then some inquiries are in order. Beware! 'Jews killed the Lord Jesus, and their own prophets, and have persecuted us; and they please not God, and are contrary to all men; forbidding us to speak to the Gentiles that they might be saved, to fill up their sins always; for the wrath is come upon them to the uttermost." 1 Thess. 2:14.' Apostate fags & Jews certain to bring God's wrath."[13]

Bob Jones Jr., Bob Jones University...

"Romanism is a pagan counterfeit of the Christian religion, ancient paganism and idolatry, claiming to be the church which Christ founded...The Roman Church is not another Christian denomination. It is a satanic counterfeit, an ecclesiastic tyranny over the souls of men, not to bring them to salvation but to hold them bound in sin and to hurl them into eternal damnation. It is the old harlot of the book of the Revelation--'the Mother of Harlots.'...Threats and fear have been her weapons. Her wealth has dazzled, her ceremonies blinded the eyes of her devotees to the blackness of her purpose and the rottenness of her heart."[14]

The Mormons point of view...

Joseph Smith stated: "This [the LDS] Church...is the only true and living church upon the face of the whole earth" (Doctrine and Covenants 1:30). "If it had not been for Joseph Smith and the restoration, there would be no salvation. There is no salvation outside. The Church of Jesus Christ of Latter-day Saints."[15]

The Reverend Jerry Falwell...

"Billy Graham is the chief servant of Satan in America."[16]

"I listen to feminists and all these radical gals... These women just need a man in the house. That's all they need. Most of the feminists need a man to tell them what time of day it is and to lead them home. And they blew it and they're mad at all men. Feminists hate men. They're sexist. They hate men; that's their problem."[17]

James Dobson, Focus on the Family...

"Because homosexuals are rarely monogamous, often having as many as three hundred or more partners in a lifetime — some studies say it is typically more than one thousand — children in those polyamorous situations are caught in a perpetual coming and going."[18]

The Reverend Steven L. Anderson of the Faithful Word Baptist Church in Tempe, Arizona...

> "You want to know who the biggest hypocrite in the world is? The biggest hypocrite in the world is the person who believes in the death penalty for murderers and not for homosexuals. Hypocrite. The same God who instituted the death penalty for murderers is the same God who instituted the death penalty for rapists and for homosexuals - sodomites, queers! That's what it was instituted for, okay? That's God, he hasn't changed. Oh, God doesn't feel that way in the New Testament ... God never "felt" anything about it, he commanded it and said they should be taken out and killed... Why? Because each sodomite recruits far more than one other sodomite because his whole life is about recruiting other sodomites, his whole life is about violating and hurting people and molesting 'em. So how many sodomites is one sodomite going to produce? A lot, and that's why it's just exploding. The only way to stop it, you say "how do we stop it?" ... You want to know why sodomites are recruiting? Because they have no natural predators."[19]

Anderson also has stated he wants President Obama to die of a brain tumor, "like Ted Kennedy." A member of his church, carrying a firearm, showed up at an event featuring President Obama.

And the mainstream churches, the rest of the Evangelicals, the priests, what do they say about Anderson's call for the execution and murder of all homosexuals? Nothing.

I'm not a psychiatrist, but I think he is deeply disturbed. The silence of the mainstream churches is terribly wrong.

Please Note, from The Psychology of Hate: When churches attack churches....

"Religions, which proclaim love but at the same time almost always identify other religions as false and as the wrong way to worship God, have been both a frequent basis of differentiating us and them and a source of hate for those of other faiths." (Staub, p.52)

Chapter Three:
Some few words on the causes and psychology of hate

The human infant, the newborn homo sapient, is totally dependent upon others for survival. It will not live without constant care. It depends upon others for food, drink, shelter, warmth, protection from the elements and beast. It stays in that condition longer than any other mammal on earth.

When born, that infant hates no one.

****

"Hate", my mother said, "is an awful ugly word, and try not to use it." There was wisdom in that.

Tolerance is almost as ugly; it may infer superiority. I am no position to tolerate you. Perhaps you should be the decision maker and decide to tolerate me.

We should seek sincere care, compassion, and understanding. Toleration falls far short of that.

If we have no personal, direct, experiential reason to hate, why should we? How can people hate groups of people who have committed no acts of aggression or harm? We are certainly not carrying such baggage when we slide out of the womb.

How is it that I grew from zero to sixty-eight without catching or developing a hatred of any people? Not the Germans, Japanese, Chinese, Koreans or Vietnamese, all of with whom we were at war during my childhood and college years; not the Russians, who we were supposed to hate; not the Blacks, Catholics, Jews, or gays. I didn't even develop a hatred of white young Illinois men, even though one of them shot and killed my father, a state policeman doing his duty.

Hatred is not genetic. Nothing in my conscious or subconscious taught me to hate groups of people.

Yes, I heard racial and religious slurs, anti-Afro-American, anti-Semitic, and anti-Catholic sidebar comments. And, being raised in very political families, anti-Democrat and anti-Republican comments were common. In spite of what ever motivated such comments in a small rural community, in spite of being raised in a part of Illinois with many sun-down towns, in spite of hearing such, hatred was not handed down in a manner that infected me.

Even the hate mongering political, religious, ideological and sociopathic merchants I discuss in this book, with whom I disagree and are the subject of an expose, I cannot hate. I can work to undo their work and I can battle for the rights of others, but I will not hate them.

I will write below of self-loathing and of the relationship between love and hate. And, people can be taught to hate and led to hate, if they are harboring a need for it, or if they are young, or if they are stupid.

I think, actually believe, that hatred can be defeated. People's hatreds must be exposed, publicly examined and dissected and even ridiculed, and otherwise combated if their hatred is acted out against others.

But, have no doubts, it will be a never-ending war; it must be fought with truth, courage, persistence, imagination, and a love of the fight.

Afro-Americans, women, environmentalists, gays and lesbians, consumers have fought and are still fighting. Any group that sees wrong and evil must fight it, every individual must fight and fight hard.

Some professional views on the psychology of hate, with editorial comment

To prepare for this chapter I went to Amazon, found The Psychology of Hate, edited by Robert J.Sternberg, Ph.D., published by The American Psychological Association in Washington, DC., in 2005. I highly recommend it. I will summarize a few relevant subjects, giving full credit to the authors and encouraging those interested to purchase the book.

Some definitions to consider:

"...hate could be viewed as a compound of anger and fear (e.g.,McCauley,2002); the object of hate not only is blamed for some past maltreatment of oneself or someone one cares about but is recognized as a source of future threat." (Royzman, et al, in Sternberg, 2005, p.7)

Gaylin (2003) proposed that real hate is a mental abnormality (p.14) that exhibits obsessive-paranoid ideation and whose emotional core is rage (p.34): 'Hatred is a neurotic attachment to a self-created enemy that has been designed to rationalize the anxiety and torment of a demeaning existence.' (p. 240) Gaylin also suggested that 'the hate-driven people live in a distorted world of their own perceptions.' (p. 202)" (Royzman in Sternberg, 2005, p.8)

"Religions, which proclaim love but at the same time almost always identify other religions as false and as the wrong way to worship God, have been both a frequent basis of differentiating us and them and a source of hate for those of other faiths." (Staub, in Sternberg, 2005, p.52)

The devaluation of the Jews in Germany, African slaves in the United States, the Armenians in Turkey, Christians in present day Iran, Roma's throughout Europe, and gays in many parts of the world lead to hatred and often violence, if not genocide such as seen in Darfur, Kosovo, and Rwanda.

Unchecked hatred can often and does often lead to violence. Violence breeds more violence. The perpetrators feed off their violent acts. In mobs, groupthink takes over, a desire to fit in or not becomes a goal. For a lack of courage or whatever the reason, people will act out the group hatreds, often with tragic results.

In research with a student at UW-Oshkosh, we discovered that peer pressure was not pressure from others as much as it was pressure from self because of a desire to belong. (Jennifer Dagel, 2000) When the group has attributes the individual seeks, accepting hatred, even embracing hatred of others, is often part of the package, and the evil grows.

What is frightening to me is the cloaking of evil in a robe of "goodness". People may actually believe that their acts are acts of necessity. Perhaps the murderers of doctors who perform legal abortions believe they are doing "good."

> "Hate is almost certainly a factor in idealistic violence. If God and goodness are on our side, then those who oppose us must have embraced the cause of evil, and therefore it is appropriate (perhaps even obligatory) to hate them."
>
> (Baumeister and Butz in Sternberg, 2005, p.97)

Religious and other cultural prejudices often lead to hatred of an individual. Allport defined prejudice as "an aversive or hostile attitude towards a person who belongs to a group, simply because he belongs to that group, and is assumed to have the objectionable qualities ascribed to the group... Without some generalized belief concerning a group as a whole, a hostile attitude could not long be sustained... the belief system has a way of slithering around to justify a more permanent attitude..." (Allport in Lerner et al in Sternberg 2005, p. 106)

I have often heard that people who are vocal and or active bigots are full of self-loathing. Baumeister and Bushman claim the opposite and that it is actually the "over estimation of self" that is the key to aggression and mistreatment of others. "Violent men, these researchers contend, 'have a strong sense of personal superiority, and their violence often seems to stem from a sense of wounded pride. When someone else questions or disputes their favorable view of self, they lash out in response.'" (Baumeister et al in Sternberg, 2005, p.177) Such behavior has been seen in terms of verbal and other non- physical, yet harmful, behavior by narcissistic spouses, when confronted with a significant other who stands his/her ground and questions inappropriate behaviors.

When one considers the above in terms of egocentric and narcissistic politicians, preachers, media mouthpieces, and assorted groupies, it is not difficult to comprehend their hateful words and actions and the evil they do.

They may be doing it for money and power, or they just might be a tad nuts, or both. Their unthinking followers require a more difficult analysis. I think people do what they do because of what happens to them when they do it. Some need is being met, whether rational or not.

The problem with concentrating on the academic view of all of this is that it can ignore the suffering of the victim. Hate crime legislation, on the other hand, brings four important possibilities:

1.) Decreasing the amount of acts of violence against people because of who they happen to be.
2.) An elevation of social discourse about crimes of violence.
3.) A better understanding of one another.

4.) A recognition that there are real persons who are the victims of hatred, not just another anonymous person whose home has been bombed, bones broken or child murdered.

In the beginning of this book I described hate as simply hate is as hate does, in terms of unkind acts. I stick by that definition. I am not really as concerned with explaining the emotional or psychological reasons for hateful behavior as I am in preventing it.

Losing something... Another basis for fear... and therefore hatred...

It is a widely accepted premise that people will fight harder to keep something they have than they will to get something they do not have. Basic human freedoms and liberties, and Maslow's basic needs are perhaps the exceptions.

The drive to acquire and the drive to defend are seldom at odds with one another, but it is my premise, from years of observation, that a challenge to the status quo, the loss of something, or even change, may create tension, fear and even hatred.

Loss of or even the fear of the loss of wealth, personal jealousies over fear of loss of affection, change in social status, change in political power, even change in working methods or organizational re-organization, all may cause immense emotional reactions, leading often to hateful words and actions.

It is not healthy to hate one's self, or others, but self-loathing is particularly destructive. Accordingly, others are often used for transference. This is true personally and it is true in large social movements. Out of this mass transfer of fear, blame, anger, and even hatred comes hateful speech and hateful actions. We have seen it in the murder of civil rights workers, "liberals", and immigrant workers.

We see this hysterical fear of change fed over mass media, in pamphlets, over talk radio and television, in political speeches, by individuals and by organizations. Serious debate gives way to clichés, slogans, and name calling, chanting and yelling. It has and can get worse. In the electronic world, in the United States, there seems to be no way to calm the storm and seek peace and rational thought. I hear conservatives saying they hate liberals, and recommending great harm to them.

Where this phenomena may take us is frightening and dangerous to a free society.

Chapter Four:
Current Hatred: USA and Others

Hate can damage the life of all people, it does not, itself, discriminate. Hateful people decide whom to hurt, and for adults, it is a purposeful decision. LGBT references lesbian, gay, bisexual and trans-gender people. Human beings. Although my book focuses on the racial, Native American, lesbian and gay issues facing our national community, I, in no way, want to diminish the difficulties and damage suffered by the bisexual and transgender people in our nation and others. The lack of understanding of and compassion for bisexual and transgender people is as great a tragedy as the hatreds based upon race, gender, religion, age, disability, national background, or being a lesbian or gay.

As this book points out, many times, there have been many victims of "group hatred", in our nation. Native Americans, Afro-Americans, Asian-Americans, the Irish, Italian, Jews, Catholics, the young, the old, women, and now, the gay community. A sad phenomenon is the hatred that these groups suffered has often been visited upon a subsequent group, by the very people who just paid the price.

It is so sad and ironic to see many members of the Afro-American community now attack the gay community for wanting the equal protections and opportunities that the Afro-American community fought for during the Civil Rights Era.

A June 19, 2009, post on the *Anchorage Daily News* web site by Jo Malley stated the following: "I went back inside just as Pastor Alonzo Patterson headed for the podium. He's from Shiloh Baptist, maybe the biggest black church in town. He and my grandparents worked on civil rights issues in Anchorage 30 years ago…. Patterson was getting worked up. He was outraged that anyone would compare the civil rights movement to the gay rights movement. Gays weren't beaten down, he said. They weren't lynched. I thought about Matthew Shepard, the gay kid beaten to death and tied to a fence in Wyoming in 1998. I thought of gays sent to concentration camps when my grandmother was a girl in Italy."

From my 20+ years in Alaska, I know Reverend Patterson, I have attended church services in his church. I was shocked and appalled to read of his position. <u>Do we now have a "lynch factor or lynch quota" that has to be met in America?</u> We are all well aware of hate crimes, beatings, murder and desecration of the homes of gays. We know that Hitler and Muslim nations have executed thousands of gays, just because they were gay. Rev. Patterson's position deeply saddens me.

Nevertheless, the gay and lesbian community currently gains much attention from those who hate. And, the cost of homophobia can be tragic. Gay youth attempt suicide at about four times the rate as non-gay youth and gay youth rejected by their parents are 8.4 times more likely to attempt ending their lives. (See Massachusetts 2006, *Youth Risk Survey* and Ryan, *"Family Rejection as a Predictor of Negative Health Outcomes"*, San Francisco State University, 2009)

Proposition 8

Please note: I go into great detail about the Proposition 8 battle. It is a learning exercise for the battles ahead.

California History

California has been a pacesetter on marrage issues. It was two decades after a California court ruled a ban on interracial marriage unconstitutional that the U.S. Supreme Court concurred, in 1967.[20]

The Prop 8 battle came eight years after 61 percent of California voters favored Prop. 22, which banned same-sex marriage in the state.[21] Even the *San Francisco Chronicle* noted (11.5.2008), "In 2004, San Francisco Mayor Gavin Newsom set off a political and social explosion when he ordered marriage licenses issued to same-sex couples in the city. Gay and lesbian couples flocked to the city, showing up in wedding dresses and tuxes for the chance to be legally married. Despite outraged reaction from across the state and nation, Newsom didn't back down until a court ordered the city to stop issuing the same-sex licenses."[22]

In 2005, San Francisco County Superior Court Judge Richard Kramer ruled denying same-sex couples the right to marry violated the equal-protection clause; his ruling read: "Simply put, same-sex marriage cannot be prohibited solely because California has always done so before."[23]

When the Legislature passed bills allowing same-sex marriage in 2005 and 2007, Gov. Arnold Schwarzenegger vetoed them both.[24] The California Supreme Court overturned Proposition 22 in May 2008.[25] Prop.8 was constructed in retaliation against legalizing gay marriage. In November 2008, Prop. 8 asked voters to affirm that "only marriage between a man and a woman is valid or recognized in California," which was a concept backed with the approval of Proposition 22 in 2000.[26]

About 110,000 same-sex couples lived in California, according to census data.[27]

The Republican Supreme Court Supported Gay Marriage

The ruling allowing gay marriage in May 2008 was a 4-3 decision.[28] In that decision, 4 of the 7 justices concluded gays and lesbians have the right to marry, and also said preventing gays from marrying amounted to discrimination under the California Constitution.[29] With the May ruling, legalization of gay marriage in California would start June 17.[30] In comparison, same-sex marriages were also legal in Massachusetts and Connecticut.[31]

Ronald George, a Republican appointee and the California Court's Chief Justice, told the *San Diego Union-Tribune* (June 2008): "When the court is faced with the responsibility of having to declare a measure unconstitutional, it's not thwarting the will of the people...It's really adhering to the ultimate expression of the people's will, namely the constitution that the people have adopted."[32]

It's important, in light of 2006-2008 debates, to note how huge of an upset it was that the Republican-dominated California Supreme Court declared marriage a constitutional right for homosexuals.[33] Six of the seven justices were Republican appointees, including Chief Justice Ronald George, who was appointed by Gov. Pete Wilson in 1991.[34] George largely borrowed from that historic 1948 decision in which the California Supreme Court became the first state to overturn a ban on interracial marriages.[35] George wrote in his opinion that the voter-approved state law against same-sex marriages effectively suggested "gay individuals and same-sex couples are in some respects 'second-class citizens.'"[36]

The California Supreme Court ruling (5.15.2008) also elevated sexual orientation to the constitutional status of race and gender, an elevation that provided strong legal protection from discrimination.[37]

The three dissenting justices in the ruling said voters or the Legislature, not the court, should make the decision to permit same-sex marriage.[38] This was a view quickly taken up by opponents of the ruling and the Yes on Prop.8 campaign.

California's first couple married by Mayor Newsom

In June 2008, Newsom presided over the wedding ceremony of Del Martin and Phyllis Lyon, lesbians who had been partners more than 50 years. They became the first same-sex couple to be legally married in California.[39] Mayor Newsom said, "What we want, the narrative coming out of it, is about them and what they represent—their story, their history. This is really where it all started."[40] Martin and Lyon were among the first to line up at City Hall in 2004 when Newsom began issuing same-sex marriage licenses.[41] However, within months, California's Supreme Court invalidated almost 4,000 same-sex marriage licenses after the court cited a state law defining marriage as that between one man and one woman.[42]

Protectmarriage.com

Protectmarriage.com was set up for Prop.8 supporters. The website had the "Take the Marriage Pledge" form in which respondents were asked six questions:

> Do you believe that marriage should be between a man and a woman?
> Do you believe that traditional marriage is the foundation of society?
> Do you believe that children are entitled to a mother AND a father?

> Do you believe that four judges on the California Supreme court were wrong to overturn the decision of over four million voters who decided that marriage is reserved for a man and a woman?
> Do you support putting the definition of traditional marriage into the California constitution where judges will not be able to change it?
> Finally, do you pledge to vote Yes on Proposition 8 declaring that only marriage between a man and a woman is valid or recognized in California?[43]

After each question, "defenders" of marriage could respond "I Do," then give their contact number to volunteer for their campaign.

What were other arguments of the Prop.8 supporters? Here are seven:

1) The will of Californians had been overturned. In 2000, over 60 percent of California voters approved a measure banning same-sex couples from marrying, only to see the state's Supreme Court rule the law unconstitutional in 2008. [44]

2) Religious Discrimination was coming. One overlooked court decision may have occurred in August, as social conservatives perceived that there was no choice but to accept gays. The California Supreme Court ruled doctors couldn't refuse treatment for gays and lesbians for religious reasons; thus, the right to exercise religion was trumped by the state law forbidding discrimination.[45]

This was the background of the case: a lawsuit had been filed by Guadalupe "Lupita" Benítez, who said her doctors and their employer (a San Diego-based fertility clinic) refused her a standard fertility treatment because of her sexual orientation.[46] The doctors were Christian, and claimed treatment denial because Benítez was unmarried, and they argued they could do so under the First Amendment's guarantee of freedom of religion.[47] It was disputed what violated the doctor's beliefs: the doctor said it was Benitez's marital status, Benitez said it was her sexual orientation.[48]

According to the *Washington Post*, "A trial court sided with Benítez in 2004, ruling that doctors in a for-profit medical group must comply with California's anti-discrimination laws. An appeals court overturned that decision one year later, finding that the previous ruling had denied the doctors' religious rights. Monday's decision voided that ruling."[49]

3) Freedom of Religion was leaving. "This vote on whether we stop the gay-marriage juggernaut in California is Armageddon…We lose this, we are going to lose in a lot of other ways, including freedom of religion," said Charles W. Colson, the founder of Prison Fellowship Ministries and an evangelical voice, speaking to pastors in a video promoting Proposition 8. The comment was quoted in the *New York Times*.[50]

The Yes on 8 campaign brought over the Swedish Pastor, Ake Green, who had been sentenced to a month in prison under Sweden's law that banned hate speech because he gave a speech denouncing homosexuality.[51] Green's testimony was featured in "Yes on 8" simulcasts to churches throughout California.[52] For the record, Green's conviction and sentence were overturned.[53] But Prop 8 supporters were convinced Green's story was the future if Prop 8 failed and suggested ministers will be jailed if they preach against homosexuality.[54]

Another Prop.8 website posting said, "Ministers who preach against same-sex marriages may be sued for hate speech and risk government fines. It already happened in Canada, a country that legalized gay marriage. A recent California court held that municipal employees may not say: 'traditional marriage,' or 'family values' because, after the same-sex marriage case, it is 'hate speech.'"[55]

In truth, Religious leaders would NOT loose their right to turn away gay couples. *The New York Times* reported (5.16.2008) that California "Chief Justice George took pains to emphasize the limits of the ruling. It does not require ministers, priests or rabbis to perform same-sex marriages, he said."[56] George also went out of his way to cancel the slippery slope argument of the social conservatives. He said the California Supreme Court decision did "not affect the constitutional validity of the existing prohibitions against polygamy and the marriage of close relatives."[57] But Prop.8 supporters continued to whip up as much fear as they could. Name the last time you heard of a Catholic Church forced to marry someone who had been divorced, or a rabbi forced to perform an interfaith marriage.

4) Churches will lose tax exempt status. A pro-Prop.8 website posting said, "Churches may be sued over their tax exempt status if they refuse to allow same-sex marriage ceremonies in their religious buildings open to the public. Ask whether your pastor, priest, minister, bishop, or rabbi is ready to perform such marriages in your chapels and sanctuaries."[58] The fear of churches losing their tax exempt status was unrealistic.

5) Education would be infiltrated with gay support. The Mormon Church suggested if Proposition 8 wouldn't pass, then schoolchildren would be indoctrinated about gay marriage.[59] Parents were told they would have no right to prevent their children from being taught in school about same-sex marriage.[60]

In a Yes on Prop 8 ad, the narrator said, "Proposition 8 opponents claim gay marriage has nothing to do with school instruction. But then a public school took first-graders to a lesbian wedding calling it a teachable moment and now a liberal politician claims schools aren't required to teach about marriage."[61] The ad also said teaching marriage is required in 96 percent of all California schools, according to the State Public School superintendent's website.[62]

But the superintendent set it straight: "Prop 8 has nothing to do with schools or kids. Our schools aren't required to teach anything about marriage and using kids to lie about that is shameful."[63] Furthermore, the parents let their children see their teacher getting married. The kids were not a prop for gay groups, but rather used as a scare tactic by Yes on Prop 8.

A pro-Prop.8 website posting convinced voters gay marriage would be taught aggressively throughout Califonia public schools: "Children in public schools will have to be taught that same-sex marriage is just as good as traditional marriage.The California Education Code already requires that health education classes instruct children about marriage. (§51890) Therefore, unless Proposition 8 passes, children will be taught that marriage is between any two adults regardless of gender. There will be serious clashes between the secular school system and the right of parents to teach their children their own values and beliefs."[64]

6) "We" won't survive if the institution is lost. Prop 8 was more important than the presidential race in social conservative's eyes. Tony Perkins, president of the Family Research Council, a conservative Christian lobby based in Washington, was quoted in the *New York Times* about the crucial outcome in California: "It's more important than the presidential election…We've picked bad presidents before, and we've survived as a nation…But we will not survive if we lose the institution of marriage."[65]

7) Gay Marriage will cost you money. A pro-Prop.8 website posting said, "This change in the definition of marriage will bring a cascade of lawsuits, including some already lost (*e.g.*, photographers cannot now refuse to photograph gay marriages, doctors cannot now refuse to perform artificial insemination of gays even given other willing doctors). Even if courts eventually find in favor of a defender of traditional marriage (highly improbable given today's activist judges), think of the money – your money – that will be spent on such legal battles. And think of all the unintended consequences that we cannot even foresee at this time. Where will it end? It's your children, your grandchildren, your money, and your liberties. Lets work together to protect them. Join with us in walking precincts and phoning voters to vote Yes on Prop 8."[66]

Economic Benefit in California

A paper posted by the Williams Institute at the UCLA School of Law suggested (June 2008) that same-sex marriages would bring nearly $700 million to the California wedding industry and another $65 million in state budget revenue over the following three years.[67] The authors felt over 100,000 same-sex couples would marry within three years, and another 70,000 would come to California to marry.[68]

Even Gov. Arnold Schwarzenegger implied an economic benefit: (5.21.2008), "You know, I'm wishing everyone good luck with their marriages, and I hope that California's economy is booming because everyone is going to come here and get married." Though Schwarzenegger's spokesmen said the governor's remark was meant to be "tongue in cheek."[69]

Up And Down Campaign

What is clear during the campaign is that both sides, at some point, were winning. After Proposition 8 was put on the ballot for November 2008, initial polls suggested it was going to be defeated.[70] However, a Sept. 18 poll by the San Francisco-based Field Poll found the measure losing 55-38 among likely voters.[71]

But a Survey USA poll (from N.J.) had the measure favored 48-45 on October 17, a statisitical tie.[72] A general attitude was that Prop 8 was going to fail, then by September it seem it was going to pass, and by mid-October it was too-close-to-call.[73]

Final Results

As the *New York Times* reported, "While the battle over same sex marriage has been all but invisible in the presidential race this year, it is raging like a wind-whipped wildfire in California."[74]

With 3 million votes left to be cast, the gay supporters conceded the 500,000 vote lead on the "Yes" side could not be overturned.[75] At the time of the concession, the margin of victory was 52.5 percent in favor to 47.5 percent of votes against Prop.8.[76] The *San Francisco Chronicle* reported, "Prop. 8 supporters won a surprisingly widespread victory Tuesday, winning almost everywhere in the state but in the Bay Area and a few other counties."[77]

A Big Money Race

The battle for Prop.8 used up tons of cash. The amount raised by both sides combined in California was as much as what was raised in all 24 states that had same-sex marriage initiatives on their ballots since 2004.[78] As Frank Schubert, campaign manager for "Yes on 8" stated, "This is the ballgame. There is no other battle than this one, with all due respect to my colleagues in Arizona and Florida...If you are concerned about marriage and how it gets to be defined, this is where it will be decided."[79]

It's noteworthy that those against Prop 8 were loosing in the money race. As of mid September, backers of the measure were "still winning the money game, out raising the No on 8 campaign $17.8 million to $12.4 million."[80] As recently as second week in October, Yes on 8 was out raising No on 8 by a 3-to-2 ratio. [81] The *New York Times* noted (10.27.08), "the ranks of those who oppose same-sex marriage were surpassing the supporters' side — at least until gay-rights groups sounded the alarm this month. Each side had raised more than $25 million by mid-October, but new figures due out on Monday are likely to show big jumps in the final stretch."[82]

Where was the support for gays and lesbians?

1) Public Education. The California Teachers Association Issues political action committee, which in July donated $250,000 to No on 8, upped their support for marriage equality on October 15 by $1 million.[83] By late October, the California Teachers Association raised $1.3 million to fight the initiative.[84] Jack O'Connell, the California superintendent of public instruction, also voiced his opposition to the ban and condemned TV ads that implied that supporting the rights of gay couples to marry will affect what's taught in public schools: "Proposition 8 has nothing to do with schools or kids...Our schools aren't required to teach anything about marriage, and using kids to lie about that is shameful."[85]

2) Democratic leaders. Joe Biden told Ellen DeGeneres, "If I lived in California, I'd clearly vote against Proposition 8…I think it's regressive, I think it's unfair, and so I'd vote no."[86] *USNews.com* noted Obama was more on the fence (10.29.08): "Obama has stayed mum on the subject, though he has indicated in the past that while he personally believes marriage should be between a man and a woman, he does not support efforts like the one in California to amend state constitutions to ban same-sex unions."[87]

New York Governor David Paterson attended a $5,000 per-person fundraiser in New York with S.F. Mayor Gavin Newsom.[88] Sen. Dianne Feinstein (D) seemed to be less vocal. In late October, she appeared in a tv ad for the first time.[89] Los Angeles Mayor Antonio Villaraigosa contributed $25,000 to the No on Prop. 8 campaign.[90]

In August 2008, the Democratic National Committee gave $25,000 to Equality for All, a leading homosexual activist group in the state seeking to keep "gay marriage" legal.[91]

3) Jerry Brown.

Another Democratic figure, helped the perception of Prop.8 and how it read to voters. The *San Francisco Chonicle* noted a week before the election that if the same-sex supporters won, "it will largely be due to state Attorney General Jerry Brown."[92] Brown's office had the final ballot description for the proposed constitutional amendment to ban homosexual weddings.[93]

Recognizing the state's support for traditional marriage, and with the May 2008 California Supreme Court decision already legalizing same-sex marriage, Brown changed the words of Prop.8's ballot description. The original title for Prop.8 was "Limit on Marriage," but the final title was "Elminates Right of Same-Sex Couples to Marry."[94] When Prop.8 supporters went to court against Brown's wording, they lost.[95]

There was proof Brown's actions helped. According to the *San Francisco Chronicle* (10.26.2008), after the wording official switched, "pollsters said support for the ban dropped by eight points - with the most recent PPIC survey showing 52 percent of likely voters now opposing the ban."[96]

<u>Logically, there is a difference between asking someone what they support (first version) versus voting on taking something away (second, final version).</u> For the record, with a week to go in the campaign, Brown took no official position on Prop.8.[97] But Brown joined San Francisco Mayor Gavin Newsom, Los Angeles Mayor Antonio Villaraigosa and Lt. Gov. John Garamendi at a Hollywood fundraiser against Prop.8 in October.[98]

4) Many Republicans leaders in California. *Protectmarriage.com* listed the major public officials who endorsed Prop 8, and as of October 26, 2008, the list of major public officials who Endorsed Prop.8 was rather thin: 15 California State

Senators, 19 California Assembly Members, and handful of local mayors and councilmen.[99]

Not all Republicans backed Prop.8. Arnold Schwarzenegger, twice vetoed marriage equality against the will of the state legislature, but stated at the Log Cabin Republicans convention (4.11.2008) his opposition to Prop. 8.[100] Specifically, he was asked if he could be counted on to oppose Prop. 8: "Well, first of all, I think that it will never happen in California, because I think that California people are much further along with that issue. And number 2, I will always be there to fight against that, because it should never happen."[101]

5) Hollywood actors and TV personalities. Ellen DeGeneres starred in her own commercial, and purchased an initial $100,000 in airtime for the ad, and *YouTube* postings of the PSA already racked up 80,000 views and counting by mid October.[102] Steven Spielberg and his spouse, Kate Capshaw, donated $100,000.[103] Brad Pitt donated $100,000. [104] *Will & Grace* star Eric McCormack donated $5,000.[105] *Desperate Housewives*' Dana Delany donated $5,000.[106] Real estate tycoon and Hollywood producer Steve Bing donated $500,000, marking the largest non-LGBT gift to the No on 8 campaign.[107]

6) Big Companies. Levi Strauss & Co pledged $25,000 to Equality for All.[108] Levi Strauss was the first Fortune 500 company to ever offer health benefits to the domestic partners of gay employees. [109] Pacific Gas & Electric, a public utilities company, donated $250,000 to the No on 8 campaign.[110]

Noteworthy here is how the human resources department of companies were bogged down. Employers spend a lot of time on HR dealing with different benefits under domestic-partnership rules versus married employees.[111] Gay marriage in California would have save companies time and money.

Who was campaigning for Prop.8?

1) Rick Warren. Warren's credentials: "Warren is considered one of the most respected and influential pastors in America and his support of Proposition 8 is unequivocal. He was named one of *TIME*'s 100 Most Influential People in the World and 15 World Leaders Who Matter Most and was called one of America's Top 25 Leaders by U.S. News and World Report."[112] By 2005, Warren's *The Purpose Driven Life* had sold over 20 million copies.[113]

Rick Warren's support came late in the campaign; he said, "For 5,000 years, every culture and every religion—not just Christianity—has defined marriage as a contract between men and women...There is no reason to change the universal, historical definition of marriage to appease 2 percent of our population."[114] Warren referenced the State Supreme Court's decision in May to overturn Proposition 22: "The courts threw out the will of the people...I never support a candidate but on moral issues I come out very clear."[115]

After the 2008 elections, Rick Warren said, "I have many gay friends. I've eaten dinner in gay homes. No church has probably done more for people with

AIDS than Saddleback Church."[116] But in the same interview, he compared the "redefinition of a marriage" to legitimizing incest, child abuse, and polygamy.[117]
2) Republicans. Alaska Gov. Sarah Palin suggested (Oct.2008) she would support a constitutional amendment to ban gay marriage nationwide.[118] John McCain supported California's Prop 8,[119] but Palin was more vocal. "He's not helping, and he's not being helped by the support for the marriage amendment," Mr. Perkins said of the McCain-Palin campaign in contrast to the campaigns of President Bush.[120]
3) Religious organizations and churches. The Knights of Columbus, a Connecticut based Catholic fraternal organization, donated $1.4 million.[121] Focus on the Family (Colorado Springs-based ministry led by James C. Dobson) also donated to Yes on 8,[122] as did the American Family Association, based in Mississippi and led by the Rev. Donald E. Wildmon.[123]

The *New York Times* concluded, "The fight for Proposition 8 was initiated in San Diego by evangelical Christian megachurch ministers like Mr. Garlow. But they have brought together an impressive statewide coalition that will not disappear with this election: Hispanic, Asian and black evangelicals; Roman Catholics; Mormons; conservatives within mainline Protestant churches; and a smattering of Orthodox Jews."[124]
4) Mormons. Californians Against Hate, who were opposed to Proposition 8, claimed at least 59,000 Mormons contributed more than a combined total of $19.15 million to the Yes on 8 campaign.[125] *USNews* said by late October, roughly 40 percent of the campaign's overall donations came from members of the LDS Church.[126] The *Christian Science Monitor* concluded Mormons gave around $15 million.[127] The *Chronicle* reported (11.10.2008) Mormons made 40 percent of the individual donations made to the Yes on 8's $30 million-plus campaign. [128]

Other percentages were higher. Of the Prop.8 money with two weeks left in the campaign, *The Advocate* concluded Mormons accounted for an estimated 77% (17,.67 million of $22.88 million).[129] Other numbers were less, a *Wall Street Journal* op-ed suggested (10.22.2008), "Between 30% and 40% of the $25.5 million in donations raised as of last week by the 'Yes' campaign has come from the Utah-based Church of Jesus Christ of Latter Day Saints, supporters of the measure say. 'Yes' campaigners say the Mormons are just one of many religious groups that support the ban."[130] Mormons contributed $6.9 million to pass a similar law, Proposition 102, in Arizona.[131]

Latter Day Saints Church estimated 770,000 members in California, accounting for about 2% of California's population.[132] "Senior church elders broadcast a call to Mormons October 8 for increased volunteer efforts and donations for the marriage fight. The hour-long message went out to churches in Utah, Hawaii, and Idaho as well as California"[133]

Mormon Call For intervention

In June 2008, the top three leaders of the LDS sent a letter strongly urging members to donate time and money.[134] According to the *Salt Lake Tribune*, "The LDS Church in a statement this summer urged members to support the ballot measure; the church since has encouraged active campaigning by members in California and until this week, Californians living in Utah and other states."[135] The paper also concluded (October 2008) LDS action "represents its most vigorous and widespread political involvement since the late 1970s, when it helped defeat the Equal Rights Amendment."[136] (emphasis mine)

The Tribune's portrayal of the LDS's zealotry was disturbing:

> ... Many California members consider it a directive from God and have pressured others to participate. Some leaders and members see it as a test of faith and loyalty. Those who disagree with the campaign say they feel unwelcome in wards that have divided along political lines. Some are avoiding services until after the election; others have reluctantly resigned. Even some who favor the ballot measure are troubled by their church's zeal in the matter.[137]

During the campaign, the Mormon leadership sent a letter urging members to get involved: "The Church's teachings and position on this moral issue are unequivocal...We ask that you do all you can to support the proposed constitutional amendment by donating of your means and time to assure that marriage in California is legally defined as being between a man and a woman."[138]

The Mormons Experience With Traditional Marriage

Complete hypocrisy. As Michelangelo Signorile stated, "They are a group of people who have experienced bigotry and religious bigotry in this country... They should understand what it is like to be a minority in this country and to know that other people are trying to take your rights away."[139]

Michael Otterson, a spokesman for the LDS, clarified: "Well, let's not fudge the issues here. We're not talking about what kind of marriages that Mormons were involved in, in the 1800s. That's not the issue. Let's keep focused on where we are with marriage today."[140] The LDS spokesman minimized history: "This is not about being anti-gay. This is not about being unfair to another minority. This is about protecting an institution that has been the bedrock of society for millennia, and the idea of having that redefinition of marriage on the part of a minority forced on the majority of our society was just not palatable to many people in California, including our own members."[141] Traditional marriage was not a bedrock of Mormon history. Otterson said it was wrong to target a place of worship for speaking out.[142] But it was okay to target $30 million to bash homosexuals in California. The incident was a sad commentary on the LDS Church. The Mormons hijacked campaigns in California and Arizona. A religion that had suffered persecution in the eastern U.S. and fled to Illinois and finally settled in Utah, now bashed homosexuals in California.

I cannot help but think much of the Mormon intervention was an effort to build files, databases, and organizational strength for a 2012 Mitt Romney race for the Presidency. He needs to strengthen his base with the neo-cons. This marriage of Mitt Romney and the neo-con soldiers of hatred helps his attempts to become the bride of the far right.

Opponents of Mormons

The church is on record in support of domestic partnerships – just not marriage – for same-sex couples.[143] But the church rejects sex outside marriage, effectively forcing gay Mormons to stay celibate singles.[144]

Critics of the LDS said the church should not have organized their members to donate time and money. In response, Mormonsfor8.com was started to list the name and hometown of each Mormon donor.[145] And petitions were circulated to call for the LDS church's tax-exempt status to be revoked.[146] This was an unlikely request, given that the LDS didn't spend money itself – its members did – so the church was unlikely to be penalized.[147]

Who helped the Mormons?

For the record, Prop.8's passage wasn't all due to Mormons: other larger demographic groups – including Catholics and African-Americans – made up more of the 'Yes' vote.[148]

Exit polls showed: 84 percent of those who attend church weekly voted yes, 81 percent of white evangelicals voted yes, 65 percent of white Protestants voted yes, and 64 percent of Catholics voted yes. [149]

The Catholics may be the most important, given that Catholics accounted for 30 percent of all voters.[150] The *San Francisto Chronicle* noted a Field Poll conducted in late October showed "weekly churchgoers increased their support in the final week from 72 percent to 84 percent. Catholic support increased from 44 percent to 64 percent - a jump that accounted for 6 percent of the total California electorate and equivalent to the state's entire African American population combined."[151]

In addition, a neglect of reaching out to other groups by the anti-Prop 8 campaign had a particularly profound effect on Latinos and African Americans, who hold strong religious views.[152]

Why would Mormons support Prop 8?

The Mormons needed to legitimize themselves, politically. The LDS were accused of attempting to boost the church's social standing among other churches, especially after being looked down upon by other Christians, Catholics, and evangelicals.[153] So they teamed up with Catholics and other evangelicals. Months before the first ads ran, San Francisco Catholic Archbishop George Niederauer reached out to the Mormons. It was an easy campaign marriage, for

Niederauer improved Catholic-Mormon relations while he was Bishop of Salt Lake City for 11 years. In June 2008, he asked the LDS for help, and it turned out to be the cementing of a multi-religious coalition. By bringing together Mormons and Catholics, Niederauer would align the two most powerful religious institutions in the Prop. 8 battle. The LDS-Catholic marriage may have been well beyond 2008, as a 1997 memo from the LDS Church noted if the Mormons got into the gay marriage battle Catholics "are the ones with which to join."[154]

In addition, if the Mormons could become part of the political mainstream, so would Mitt Romney. In September 2007, Romney claimed he had schemed with Jerry Falwell: "Several months ago, not long before he died, I had the occasion of having the Rev. Jerry Falwell at our home. He said that when he was getting ready to oppose same-sex marriage in California, he met with the president of my church in Salt Lake City, and they agreed to work together in a campaign in California. He said, 'Far be it from me to suggest that we don't have the same values and the same objectives.'"[155]

Without proof, but from years of experience, Romney now has all the records of who donated how much and who actually worked in California. Do not be surprised to see their names show up in the 2011-2012 nomination and election activities of candidate for President, Mitt Romney. In my opinion, this is the major reason the Mormons got involved and certainly hides Romney's earlier hypocrisy and flip-flopping on the issue.

Are Mormons victims?

After the Prop 8 victory, Mormons and other religious groups had to endure protests. Some, such as Family Research Council leader Tony Perkins, said gays were rioting. Mormons then acted like "victims" here.

As Dan Savage told CNN (11.13.2008):

> "Part of the democratic process is if you're going to throw a punch you're going to have a punch thrown back. You don't get to march in the public square, slime people, malign people and demagogue against people and then jump behind a bush and say, no God we're a church. You can't criticize us. You can't bring it back to our front doors and say we have a problem with what you've been saying about us in public and doing to us in the public square. The Mormon Church has politicized itself with this movement and -- in California to ban same-sex marriage. And it wasn't just the Mormon Church encouraged its followers. The first prophet of the Mormon Church had a letter read from every temple, every Mormon temple in the land instructing its members as a religious duty to donate time and money to this campaign. You cannot campaign against the vulnerable minority group in this country in the political arena without expecting some sort of response."[156]

What were some points from the Prop.8 campaign?

The following points are important: 1) Prop.8's campaign made history; 2) Asian Americans supported Gays; 3) Fight for those who fear; 4) African Americans lean toward homophobia; 5) Scare tactics work; and 6) Polls in gay marriage usually undercount.

1) It was historic. Prop. 8 was "the most expensive social issue race the nation has ever seen."[157] *US News* concluded (11.5.08), "In total, more than $70 million was spent on television ads and get-out-the-vote efforts by both sides, making this the most expensive social policy initiative in history. Only the presidential candidates spent more money on an election this year."[158]

After the presidential and Prop 8 campaigns, the next highest campaign spending numbers was the Minnesota U.S. Senate race between Norm Coleman and comedian Al Franken, who together spent $35 million combined with less than a week left in the campaign.[159]

2) Asian-Americans Supported Gays. Asian-Americans in California overwhelmingly opposed Prop 8, according to a groundbreaking survey part of a national poll released by researchers at the University of California-Berkeley, UC-Riverside, the University of Southern California and Rutgers University.[160] Almost 1,900 Asian Americans were interviewed using 8 different languages (Aug/Sep.2008), and "was the largest scientific poll of Asian-American voters ever done — both nationally and in California." The national survey cost $300,000.[161]

Of likely Asian-American voters, 57 percent opposed Prop 8, 32 percent planned to vote yes, and 11 percent were undecided.[162] Nine percent of California voters are Asian Americans.[163]

This was the *San Jose Mercury News* evaluation (10.15.08): "In some ways, the lopsided opinion of Proposition 8 was surprising because many Asian-Americans have traditionally been less tolerant of homosexuality. One big reason: Many emigrated from countries where homosexuality is less tolerated. Although Asian literature is sprinkled with centuries-old allusions to men having sex with men, or women having sex with women, many Asian societies tend to ignore homosexuality or even deny that it exists — although those attitudes are beginning to change in countries undergoing rapid Westernization such as Vietnam and China. Experts in Asian-American voting trends attribute the unfavorable opinion of Proposition 8 to the ability of gay-marriage proponents to frame it as a major civil rights issue."[164] If there is one group who would be sensitive to taking rights away from a group, it would be Asian-Americans. Japanese-Americans were interned during World War II, and in the first half of the 1900s, many Asian-Americans were banned from marrying whites.[165]

3) Fight for those who fear. Once again, remember that the gay community needs all the political support it can get. It is outnumbered. As the *San Francisco Chronicle* wrote, "This was a classic case of a majority using its power of numbers to discriminate against a minority group."[166]

4) Afro-American votes for Obama killed gay marriage. Exit polls indicated over two-thirds of Afro-American voters and a large majority of Latino voters favored Prop.8.[167] In the Survey USA poll (10.17.2008), "...two Democratic constituencies -- African-Americans and Latinos -- are leaning toward the ban. Among likely black voters, 58% supported Proposition 8 compared with 38% who opposed it in the most recent Survey USA poll. Among Latinos, 47% supported the proposition while 41% opposed it; white voters were nearly evenly split. The reason, "Yes" officials say, is that church attendance is strong in many minority communities."[168] There were three groups the Survey USA poll found to support Prop 8 by more than 50% within the group; Over half of Afro-Americans, men, and those "over 50" supported Prop 8 by those 50-plus margins.[169]

It was a historic irony: a symbolic victory over discrimination by Barack Obama's win in the state was overshadowed in California continued gay-bashing. The push for Obama actually hurt gay-marriage supporters. *USNews.com* also concluded (11.5.08), "in addition to widespread support among conservatives in the state, huge turnout among African-Americans may have played a role in the defeat of same-sex marriage. Seventy percent of blacks told pollsters they voted for the ban."[170]

Research About Afro-American Views On Gays. Pew found (May 2008), "…nearly as many African Americans oppose civil unions as oppose gay marriage. By more a margin of more than two-to-one (56% to 26%), more blacks oppose gay marriage than favor it. The balance of opinion among African Americans regarding civil unions is only modestly less negative (53% oppose vs. 34% favor)."[171] That is a telling comparison, because other races have different results when comparing support for gay marriage and support for civil unions (civil unions are usually supported by a noticeable margin over gay marriage).

A report released by the National Black Justice Coalition and Freedom to Marry showed (May 2008) Afro-Americans are more likely than whites — by a 65 percent-to-53 percent margin — to oppose marriage equality for gays and lesbians.[172] The report said, "Nearly three-quarters of blacks say that homosexual relations are always wrong, and over one-third say that AIDS might be God's punishment for immoral sexual behavior…. Overall, blacks are 14 percentage points more likely to hold both positions than whites."[173] A study by the University of Chicago concluded Afro-American youth think just as negatively over gay marriage than older Afro-Americans. Fifty-five percent of Afro-American youth "believe that homosexuality is always wrong;" a huge difference than youth among Latinos (36 percent) or whites (35 percent).[174]

What are the stumbling blocks in the Afro-American community? The Church plays a major political role in the Afro-American community. These churches are more likely to have evangelical roots.[175] Even though Afro-American leaders may logically push for social reforms, they are being held back from supporting gay rights by their church community.[176] In addition, the black family is already a weak institution, and church leaders have a hard time arguing that gay marriage will strengthen marriage. Finally, some blacks still perceive homosexuality as a "white issue."[177]

Andrew Sullivan notes (10.2.2008):

"The rampant homophobia in urban black culture also cannot be denied, as well as the role of the black church in fomenting and entrenching homophobia, even as so many black men and women have died of HIV and AIDS. I've been following this issue since I first raised the issue of black indifference to HIV and the awful isolation of gay black men as far back as 1990. There are many black heroes in this, with John Lewis and Coretta Scott King standing out; and the Congressional Black Caucus has been very supportive, as has the black civil rights leadership. But it helps no one to deny that the leadership knows how deeply hostile to gay equality many in the African-American community are. I'm surprised that some would seek to deny this rather than confront it."[178]

5) Scare tactics work. Conservative and religious groups "blanketed the state with television ads urging families to vote in favor of the initiative, warning that if the measure is defeated, children would be taught about gay marriage in schools."[179] In one ad, a girl came home from school and showed her mom a picture book about a prince who married another prince, and the girl declares she wants to marry a princess.[180] Prop 8 supporters also took advantage of the story when first graders made a trip to San Francisco's City Hall to witness a lesbian wedding (with parent permission).[181] For the record, *USNews.com* reported (11.3.08), "The state's education code does not require schools to offer comprehensive sex education if parents opt to take their children out of the instruction."[182]

Another scare tactic was the pedophilia issue. Gay rights supporters need to figure out how to answer how pro-gay rights is pro-family and good for children. The No on 8 campaign's talking points initially didn't have language to address religious groups, and their campaigners were told by strategists not to talk about children, and the campaign was afaid it would be tied to pedophilia.[183] It was a noteworthy campaign tactic, eventhough gays are just as capable of being good parents. Meanwhile Yes on 8 talked about kids, which appealed to churchgoers.[184]

6) Polls historically undercount. The *New York Times* noted both sides agreed on one thing: "Polls in every other state that has had a marriage amendment on the ballot have consistently undercounted voters who oppose same-sex marriage by significant percentages."[185]

What should be done with the existing gay marriages?

The day after the loss, same-sex couples and the city of San Francisco filed lawsuits to overturn Prop.8. In addition, Attorney General Jerry Brown (representing California in court) said he would defend the legality of the thousands of same-sex marriages conducted in the 5 1/2 months leading up to election day, and the *San Francisco Chronicle* noted "That controversy is also likely to end up before California's high court and could reach the U.S. Supreme

Court."[186] Brown said, "It is my belief that the courts will hold that these same-sex marriages entered into are valid," though he also said he would defend Prop. 8 against legal challenges.[187] Brown's position was that Prop.8 was not retroactive.[188]

A research institute at UCLA has estimated 18,000 same-sex couples married in California since the state's court's rulling took effect (June 2008).[189] (The California Supreme Court later upheld the legality of the 18,000 marriages.)

And now, on to the Federal Courts of the United States...

Republican heavyweight attorney Ted Olsen and equally strong Democrat David Boies, in May of 2009, filed suit in U.S. District Court in Northern California, against Proposition 8, even though it passed and was upheld by the California Supreme Court. Citing the well known and understood status that the US Constitution and US Suprme Court trumps state consititions and courts, Olsen and Boies cited the US Fourteenth Amendment. Olsen told the Washington Examiner, on May 26, "It is our position in this case that Proposition 8, as upheld by the California Supreme Court, denies federal constitutional rights under the equal protection and due process clauses of the constitution. The constitution protects individuals' basic rights that cannot be taken away by a vote. If the people of California had voted to ban interracial marriage, it would have been the responsibility of the courts to say that they cannot do that under the constitution. We believe that denying individuals in this category the right to lasting, loving relationships through marriage is a denial to them, on an impermissible basis, of the rights that the rest of us enjoy...I also personally believe that it is wrong for us to continue to deny rights to individuals on the basis of their sexual orientation."

Constitutional issues will be covered, in depth, in chapter nine.

Don't Ask, Don't Tell

Gays are second-class in the military like Afro-Americans once were. This is unacceptable in a democratic society. But barring service was and is acceptable to many, including many former 2008 presidential candidates. President Obama has stated he would repeal it, but it has not been repealed as of the publication of this book.

1948 Integration of the Military

It wasn't until 1948 that President Truman ordered the end to racial discrimination in the armed forces.[190] The military has long stereotyped its servicemen. In regard to Afro-Americans, in 1937, a report from senior officers in the U.S. Army War College noted, "As an individual the Negro is docile, tractable, lighthearted, care free and good natured. If unjustly treated he is likely to become surly and stubborn, though this is usually a temporary phase. He is careless, shiftless, irresponsible and secretive. He resents censure and is best handled with praise and by ridicule. He is unmoral, untruthful, and his sense of right doing is relatively inferior."[191] The military not only had to deal with racism, they perpetuated it. In the year of Truman's decision to integrate the military, a Gallop Poll showed only 26% favored integration of the military (63% opposed).[192]

Gay Integration v. Afro-American Integration

Like homosexuals today, minorities were seen as a culprit weakening the military. Sen. Richard B. Russell said the "mandatory intermingling of the races throughout the services will be a terrific blow to the efficiency and fighting power of the armed services.... It is sure to increase the numbers of men who will be disabled through communicable diseases. It will increase the rate of crime committed by servicemen."[193]

However, there are obvious differences with gays and blacks serving in the military. Homosexuality isn't a visible as skin color. And there are smaller numbers. Three to six percent of people are homosexual, with a slightly lower ratio of lesbians among females.[194] Blacks make up 13 or 14 percent of the US population. These differences may help explain the lack of support for gays serving in the military.

It's important to note gay military service is not a new issue. In the 1980s, colleges and universities banned military recruiters and Reserve Officers Training Corps (ROTC) programs from campuses because of the treatment of gays in the military.[195]

Why do we ban gays?

Dr. Gregory Herek from University of California-Davis notes, "In 1778, Lieutenant Gotthold Frederick Enslin became the first soldier to be drummed out of the Continental Army for sodomy. Throughout U.S. history, campaigns have purged military units of persons suspected of engaging in homosexual acts."[196] However, simply excluding homosexuals from the military was not rampant, and the attitude against keeping homosexuals in the military did not heighten until after WWII.[197] When the military was short on personnel at the height of the war, the rules in baring homosexuals from serving loosened; those rules tightened when the need for recruits diminished.[198]

Biased Discharge

Dr. Gregory Herek at University of California-Davis found, "In 1981, the DOD formulated a new policy which stated unequivocally that homosexuality is incompatible with military service (DOD Directive 1332.14, January 28, 1982, Part 1, Section H). According to a 1992 report by the Government Accounting Office (GAO), nearly 17,000 men and women were discharged under the category of homosexuality in the 1980s. The Navy was disproportionately represented, accounting for 51% of the discharges even though it comprised only 27% of the active force during this time period. Statistical breakdowns by gender and race revealed that, for all services, White women were discharged at a rate disproportionate to their representation. Overall, White females represented 6.4% of personnel but 20.2% of those discharged for homosexuality"[199]

Blame Clinton for selling out?

As *Time* concluded (3.13.2007), "Ultimately, many military officers believe, openly gay men and women will be allowed to serve in uniform, but it's just not going to happen very quickly. And for that, ironically, you can blame the most gay-friendly President ever: Bill Clinton."[200] Critics note President Clinon underestimated the military's opposition, the strength of the Christian conservaties, and the amount of split on the issue within his own party.[201]

Before Clinton took office, the rule barring gays from the military was within the power of the President, who could lift the ban.[202] Clinton came to office pledging to get rid of the ban, while opposition from Colin Powell, chairman of the Joint Chiefs, initiated the public debate.[203] When DADT was hammered out by Congress, Congress "took the extraordinary step of removing the policy from the President's hands and writing it into law."[204]

Powell Cop-out

Colin Powell was arguably the strongest voice against having gays in the military. Although widely respected across partisan lines, his support among gays is historically lukewarm at best. Powell's opposition legitimized the views of social conservatives within the Republican Party. At the time, Phyllis Schlafly deferred the gays in the military issue to Gen. Colin Powell and other Pentagon members who opposed admitting gays to the military.[205] Also worth considering is Powell's ambitions. By 1994 and 1995, there was speculation that he would seek the GOP nomination for president in 1996. Privately, at least, he was likely considering his ambitions at the time DADT was passed.

Congressional Testimony

To balanced criticism of Bill Clinton, understand that DADT was partially passed on the assumption that heterosexuals would overcome their prejudices toward gays.[206] Dr. Herek testified before Congress when DADT was being debated; Herek noted roughly one American adult in three already knew someone openly gay or lesbian. Herek even had to tell Congress that previous testimony was inaccurate (opponents of gays testified that gays were child molesters, gays preyed on heterosexuals, and gays were obsessed with sex).[207]

The Compromise

After his inauguration, Clinton asked the Secretary of Defense to draft a policy to end the discrimination against gays; but Clinton was opposed by the Joint Chiefs of Staff, many in Congress, and a significant block of the American public.[208] From the Congress came a compromise. Sam Nunn (D-GA) chaired the Senate Armed Services Committee and the compromise was called Don't Ask, Don't Tell, Don't Pursue.[209] Don't ask military personnel about their sexual orientation, but military personnel would not be kicked out simply for being gay (so personnel shouldn't tell their homosexuality to others).

The Pentagon's justification stems from the belief that homosexual personnel would interfere with the military's mission.[210] Straights have such animosity toward gays that they wouldn't want to serve with them.[211] Critics argue the issue isn't homosexuals, but rather heterosexual service members and military leadership.[212] Others defend gays by suggesting strong military leadership should enforce nondiscrimination.[213] Commanders also are barred from asking about a service member's orientation.[214]

McCain in 1998

Sen. John McCain (R-AZ), in 1998, said, "My view is that in the case of the military, the 'don't ask, don't tell' policy was appropriate. And I also believe that gays should not be in the military, and I know that's a problem that a lot of people would have. At the same time, I don't believe that we should discriminate against anyone, and that includes because of their sexual orientation. That may get me in trouble, but I don't believe that should be the case."[215]

DADT by the Numbers

A Government Accountability Office report in February 2005 said $30 million annually was spent to train replacements for homosexuals discharged though DADT, and $200 million total since the statute's beginning.[216] The 2005 GAO study showed 54 of the 10,000 released personnel were Arabic specialists.[217]

A Blue Ribbon Commission sponsored by the University of California said the policy cost the Pentagon over $360 million to implement in it's first decade, and concluded the GAO's estimate was only half of what the true cost was.[218] Former Clinton Secretary of Defense William J. Perry was on the commission.[219]

The Urban Institute estimated according to the 2000 census, there were 65,000 gay and lesbian members serving in the military, and over 1 million homosexual veterans.[220] And women were nearly a third of the DADT charges despite that they only made 14% of the military.[221]

Likewise, elsewhere it has been clearly shown DADT disproportionately affects lesbians. Indeed, the *New York Times* reported (6.23.2008), "While women make up 14 percent of Army personnel, 46 percent of those discharged under the policy last year were women. And while 20 percent of Air Force personnel are women, 49 percent of its discharges under the policy last year were women. By comparison for 2006, about 35 percent of the Army's discharges and 36 percent of the Air Force's were women, according to the statistics."[222] Over 11,000 homosexuals had been dismissed from 1993-2005.[223] In 2005, 726 service members were dismissed for DADT.[224] *"But most Americans should be shocked to know that while the country's economy is going down the tubes, the military has wasted half a billion dollars over the past decade chasing down gays and running them out of the armed services."* Barry Goldwater

According to an Annenberg Public Policy study, about two thirds of the public thought gays and lesbians should be able to serve openly;[225] half in the military thought they should not. [226]

Copas provided an interesting dilemma.

Bleu Copas was discharged from the Army in January 2006, for being gay. His discharge reopened questions about Don't Ask, Don't Tell.[227] Copas claimed he never told his superiors of his orientation, and as of August 2006 still did not know his accuser.[228] He told the *AP* his sexuality was made known because of anonymous emails to his superiors within the 82nd Airborne Division at Fort Bragg, North Carolina.[229]

Copas suggested he was inquired about his sexuality (rather than serving as openly gay). Copas description of the questioning of his sexuality by his supervisors was interrogative. "So the leaders of the chorus brought us into the hallway and asked us, or let us know, 'We know one of you is gay, who is it?'"[230] Copas said he did not initially admit he was gay, but then he and his peers were questioned about emails. They asked, "'Do I know of any one who thinks I am homosexual, or do I associate with others who are homosexual, and am I involved in the community theatre?'"[231] The superviors asked about community theatre because it came up in emails.[232]

Copas said, "the gay ban punishes every single member, even those who never tell and the straight troops who lose trusted, and trained, fellow soldiers."[233] Indeed, Copas' argument focused more on that his outing was not in line with DADT, rather than being against the DADT policy.[234] After all, Copas suggested his director brought everyone in the hallway and asked 'Which one of you are gay?" and Copas himself noted "Even with the policy we have, it should never have happened."[235] His commanding officer told the AP "the evidence clearly indicated" Copas "had engaged in homosexual acts," and military investigators wrote Copas had "at least three homosexual relationships" and was dealing with "at least two jealous lovers, either of whom could be the anonymous source proving this information."[236]

Adding more credibility to Copas, he was given full benefits with his discharge and had no intention to sue. Copas noted the DADT "policy hurts the war on terror."[237] If he was so "guilty," it's odd the military gave him full benefits. More importantly, Copas' discharge may exemplify how the US hurts itself when it comes to the war in Iraq, and the War on Terror.

Creating a Military Weakness

If finding translators to help the military in Iraq was a problem, it certainly was no surprise. The GAO found (2002) the Army's goal to recruit Arabic interpreters met only 50% of the intended result.[238] But it wasn't as if the administration was hiding the issue. Near the fall of 2003, President Bush blamed the translator shortage as a reason why WMD had not been found in Iraq.[239] Critics were left questioning the President's effort to get more translators, or if he showed any effort at all.

The February 2005 GAO report noted the Pentagon fired 322 who had "skills in a foreign language that DoD had considered to be especially important."[240] Fifty-five of those were fluent in Arabic, including Bleu Copas.[241]

In 2003, potential presidential candidates from Retired Gen. Wes Clark to John McCain decried the lack of translators in Iraq. McCain warned: "...linguists we're running short of." Would Clark and McCain soften their position against gays and lesbians to fight the war on terror?

Newt Gingrich said (12.7.03), "we should have gone into Iraq with Iraqis who live in America who are American citizens who are fluent in Arabic with every unit."[242] Other Senators, too, questioned our ground intelligence in Iraq. Sen. Cornyn (R-TX) appeared in the same interview with Evan Bayh on *Late Edition* (12.19.04). "But the problem is there are porous borders, and people who can just flow across those borders literally at will. One of the problems we have, Wolf, is we don't have adequate human intelligence. This has been a chronic problem, and we don't really know exactly what is happening in so many parts of the Middle East because we don't have the trained human intelligence sources in order to get that information."[243]

As neo-conservative and Bush ally Ken Adelman said after the Iraq Study Group report:

> This Iraqi report gives an example,... that just breaks your heart. In the thousand-person U.S. Embassy in Baghdad today, there's six people, six people who speak fluent Arabic. Now, this is not Chiluba, this is not, you know, an obscure language. This is one of the great languages of the world. And out of 1,000, we don't have any more than six people who can speak the language where they are? How can you, how can the president hear that, how can anybody in the U.S. government hear that and not be totally ashamed by the unserious-ness of this effort? It also makes the point that in the Defense Intelligence Agency, less than 10 analysts have been looking at this insurgency for two years or so. Less than 10. And this is what's killing 100 Americans a month, and 100 Iraqis a day. I mean, it is just—it just breaks your heart.[244]

Newt Gingrich later stressed (Dec.2006) good points from the Iraq Study Group, such as the amount of linguists:

> ...it's a failure [the administration's Iraq policy] because the instruments of national power don't work. And it's important to understand we all focus on Maliki's government. The, the Baker-Hamilton Commission reports that out of 1,000 people in the American Embassy, 33 speak Arabic, eight of them fluently. Now, at some point we have to have a national conversation about the fact that, outside of the uniform military, none of the instruments of national power work, and they need to be fundamentally overhauled. This isn't about policy. It's as though you wanted to go to Boston, I wanted to go to Los Angeles, and the car standing outside was broken. Doesn't matter what our policy agreement is, the car doesn't run.[245]

Some suggest the amount of linguists in Iraq was unrelated to DADT. For example, Bill Clinton's Executive Order 13166 mandated services provided by the federal government be provided in all languages requested.[246] Put in effect in August 2000, the directive said, "Each Federal agency shall also work to ensure that recipients of Federal financial assistance provide meaningful access to their LEP [Limited English Proficiency] applicants and beneficiaries."[247] Perhaps the U.S. would have more linguists in Iraq if not for this Executive Order, but it's noteworthy that President George W. Bush, too, avoided rescinding the order.

General Pace ignited DADT Discussion

Chairman of the Joint Chiefs of Staff General Peter Pace told the *Chicago Tribune* (3.12.07), "homosexual acts between two individuals are immoral and…we should not condone immoral acts."[248] "I do not believe the United States is well served by a policy that says it is OK to be immoral in any way," said Pace.[249] He also likened homosexual behavior to adultery, which is also prohibited in the military.[250] "As an individual, I would not want (acceptance of gay behavior) to be our policy, just like I would not want it to be our policy that if we were to find out that so-and-so was sleeping with somebody's else's wife, that we would just look the other way, which we do not. We prosecute that kind of immoral behavior."[251]

At the time of Pace's remarks, it was estimated about 65,000 homosexuals were serving in the military.[252]

A Republican Defended Gays

A Republican, not Democrats, stood up for gays. Sen. John Warner (R-VA) criticized Pace and "strongly"[253] disagreed with the general that the behavior was immoral.[254] As one observer wrote, "The first significant response to Pace's comment from a political leader came not from one of the frontrunners for the Democratic presidential nomination, but from the ancient Republican Senator from Virginia."[255]

CNSNews.com reported (3.15.07) Obama and Clinton had "both quietly announced that they also disagree with Pace's view."[256] Obama and Clinton said homosexuality was not immoral "only after they were criticized for failing to do so by a homosexual advocacy group."[257] In fact, Obama, Clinton and McCain "initially dodged the question of whether they agreed with Pace, which critics said illustrates just how uncomfortable politicians are addressing gay issues."[258] Two days passed before Clinton and Obama answered questions on Pace's comments.[259]

Clinton finally clarified on Mach 15, she "completely" disagreed with Pace and told *Bloomberg News* homosexuality was not immoral.[260] On March 13 she was asked if was immoral and said "Well, I am going to leave that to others to conclude."[261] Clinton hid her (eventual) support behind Warner: "I should have echoed my colleague Senator John Warner's statement forcefully stating that homosexuality is not immoral because that is what I believe."[262] Before her statement of regret, Clinton had been "widely assailed by gay rights supporters and bloggers."[263]

Obama's initial response was also indirect, as he first stated General Pace had previously restricted his public comments to military issues, which was "probably a good tradition to follow."[264]

Mitt Romney went as far to say Pace's comments were "inappropriate for public discourse," and "…in a governmental setting, the right way to go is to show more of an outpouring of tolerance."[265] Romney's statement was shocking given that his presidential campaign previously spent 2006 distancing himself from his past support of gays.

Then there were those indifferent. Defense Secretary Robert Gates said (3.18.07) he did not think it was an "issue where personal opinion has any place," and as far as Pace apologizing, "...we should just move on from this point."[266] McCain declined to answer whether homosexuality was immoral.[267] On his Straight Talk Express campaign bus, he said morality judgments were not "a purview of public policy."[268]

Brownback Defended Pace

U.S. Senator Sam Brownback (R-KS) circulated a letter to his colleagues to show support for Pace.[269] In the letter, Brownback said the criticism of Pace was "unfair and unfortunate," but was also "duty-bound to support the policies of the United States."[270] When asked if he agreed with Pace, Brownback said, "I do not believe being a homosexual is immoral, but I do believe homosexual acts are. I'm a Catholic and the Church has clear teachings on this."[271] Brownback actually made Pace the victim, instead of gays in the military: "The moral behavior of members of the Armed Forces is of the highest importance, particularly during this time of war. The question is whether personal moral beliefs should disqualify an individual from positions of leadership in the U.S. military? We think not."[272] Brownback was less specific on *who* exactly was demanding Pace to resign. Brownback said Pace's comments "do not deserve the criticism they have received, in fact, we applaud General Pace for maintaining a personal commitment to moral principles."[273]

Still posturing for the 2008 presidential primaries, Brownback received the headlines he wanted, and *Yahoo! News* posted the *AP* report: "Brownback supports Pace's remark on gays."[274]

Ann Coulter

In this whole debate on DADT, it is noteworthy to emphasize conservatives continued to re-evaluate their image towards gays and lesbians, especially after Ann Coulter's comments. In early March, at the Conservative Political Action Conference (C-PAC), the conservative pundit called John Edwards a "faggot."[275] "I was going to have a few comments on the other

Democratic presidential candidate John Edwards, but it turns out you have to go into rehab if you use the word 'faggot,' so I—so kind of an impasse, can't really talk about Edwards."[276] Coulter was callous in reacting to Republican critics, and in an email said, "C'mon, it was a joke. I would never insult gays by suggesting that they are like John Edwards. That would be mean."[277]

Even though Coulter "all but endorsed" Romney at the conference,[278] Mitt Romney's spokesman said Coulter's remark was "offensive," and "Romney believes all people should be treated with dignity and respect."[279] McCain did not go to C-PAC, but his spokesman called the comments "wildly inappropriate."[280] (Which was noteworthy given McCain did not even attend the conference). Giuliani said they "were completely inappropriate and there should be no place for such name-calling in political debate."[281]

Edwards used the incident to raise $100,000 of what his campaign called "Coulter Cash" to "fight back against the politics of bigotry."[282] Elizabeth Edwards blogged about "Miss Coulter," as she apparently implied the 46 year old had not yet married.[283]

Should DADT be reviewed?

The question was asked after Pace's comments. The reason Pace said his "immoral" comment was because he was expressing his support for Don't Ask, Don't Tell, and in his quasi-apology said "I should have focused more on my support of the policy and less on my personal moral views."[284] Even for supporters of DADT, Pace's comments were unfortunate because it appeared he supported the policy because of his moral beliefs rather than for the best interest of the U.S. military.

Defense Secretary Gates said he was not reviewing it.[285] McCain said DADT was "working,"[286] and Romney wanted to maintain the policy.[287] In the *Chicago Tribune* article covering McCain, Romney, and the Democratic presidential candidates view on the policy, Rudy Giuliani was entirely left out.[288]

But the clue for reviewing DADT came from Sen. Warner, who did not make a statement on DADT, but did say he would "decline comment on the current policy until after such hearings [Armed Services Committee] are held."[289]

GOP Presidential Primary Debate

In the June 2007, GOP debate, Wolf Blitzer said, "recently we've learned that several talented, trained linguists — Arabic speakers, Farsi speakers, Urdu speakers trained by the U.S. government to learn those languages to help us in the war on terrorism — were dismissed from the military because they announced they were gays or lesbians."[290]

Rudy Giuliani said (6.5.07) "…in time of war…I don't think this would be the right time to raise these issues."[291] Romney, who advocated gays to openly serve in 1994, said he initially thought DADT would not be "effective."[292] [Actually, in a letter to Log Cabin Republicans, Romney complimented "Don't

Ask, Don't Tell" as a "step in the right direction," and the first steps toward gays serving "openly" in the military.[293]] But in 2007, Romney agreed with Giuliani: "this is not the time to put in place a major change, a social experiment, in the middle of a war going on."[294] McCain said the policy was "working."[295] How could it be working when McCain preceded his comments on DADT by noting he was proud of the military, "There just aren't enough of them."[296] Everyone was saying nothing.

Republican Presidential Candidates Ducking the Issue

Jon Stewart stated (sarcastically in the GOP logic) the only thing worse than a terrorist attack was a gay man stopping it.[297] Marine Eric Alva, was the first U.S. service member injured in the Iraq conflict.[298] Howard Dean's response to the GOP was one of the more effective: "How many of you know that the first soldier who was wounded in the line of duty in Iraq was a gay man? We need leadership at the top that understands the sacrifices of the troops in the field."[299]

Also in the debate, Giuliani also passed the issue, and wanted to "rely on the judgment of our commanders in a situation like this."[300] McCain, too, relied on "our military leadership" to make the decision.[301] McCain previously said (10.18.06):

> We have to have the most effective and professional military that we can possibly obtain. I listen to people like General Colin Powell, Former Chairman of the Joint Chiefs of Staff and literally every military leader that I know. And they testified before Congress that they felt the "don't ask, don't tell" policy was the most appropriate way to conduct ourselves in the military. A policy that has been effective. It has worked...And I understand the opposition to it, and I've had these debates and discussions, but the day that the leadership of the military comes to me and says, Senator, we ought to change the policy, then I think we ought to consider seriously changing it because those leaders in the military are the ones we give the responsibility to.[302]

Ron Paul was somewhat indifferent, he called DADT "a decent policy," and "...If there is homosexual behavior in the military that is disruptive, it should be dealt with. But if there's heterosexual sexual behavior that is disruptive, it should be dealt with. So it isn't the issue of homosexuality, it's the concept and the understanding of individual rights."[303] So in the common libertarian view, why did the military need a policy for gays at all?

Some Democratic Views on Reviewing DADT

Clinton, Edwards, and Obama all favored repeal of DADT.[304] New Mexico Governor Bill Richardson too, said DADT should be repealed and President Bush should reject Pace's comments. [305] So did President Clinton's chairman of the Joint Chiefs, Gen. John Shalikashvili, who served when the policy was adopted in 1993 and changed his mind in January 2007.[306] Shalikashvili said he met with gay servicemen at the beginning of the year, and "These conversations showed me just how much the military has changed, and that gays and lesbians can be accepted by their peers."[307] The Democrats were in agreement about ending DADT.

Mike Gravel took bold stand for the LGBT community.

Gravel hadn't been the U.S. Senator for Alaska in decades, but his longshot bid for the Democratic nomination occasionally made some excellent points. Gravel's website said (12.10.06):

> Since 1993, more than 11,000 talented, skilled men and women have been dismissed from the armed forces under the "Don't Ask, Don't Tell" ban on lesbian, gay and bisexual service personnel. It is time to place national security ahead of federal bigotry and repeal this un-American law once and for all. The law flies in the face of common sense, and undermines our nation's commitment to equal opportunity. As commander-in-chief, I will welcome every qualified American, regardless of sexual orientation, who wants to serve in our fighting forces.[308]

In a presidential debate, Gravel said DADT "should have been gotten rid of 20 years ago," despite that it did not come into existence until 1993.[309] Gravel also said (June 2007) how in the 1950s, while serving in the military, a fellow officer told Gravel he was gay:

> ...I almost fell off my barstool. All my life I had been told that all gays were effeminate, silly creeps—but here was Vic—a big, tough, true-blue military type. How could he be gay? In that one moment I experience a total reeducation. ....I often think about Vic when I talk about the injustice of Don't Ask. Here's a guy who was much more dedicated to the army than I was, but because he liked men, his life long military career has been in constant jeopardy.[310]

The Clinton History, Revised

Senator Hillary Clinton, who was first lady when Congress wrote DADT into law, wanted it repealed.[311] Brian Todd of CNN reported (3.13.07) "An aide to Bill Clinton tells CNN the former president always felt openly gay people should be allowed to serve in the military, but he got the best deal he could nearly 14 years ago, when against strong opposition, he got the don't ask, don't tell law passed."[312] President Clinton now wanted it repealed and sided with his wife.[313] "We have thousands of loyal, patriotic Americans who have been discharged from the military in a time of war. That to me, does not make sense," said Sen. Clinton.[314]

Attitudes Changing Worldwide

The issue in the U.S. military is not over the right of marriage; it is over of the right to serve. Two dozen militaries no longer have gay bans, including Great Britain, Canada, France, and Germany.[315] There were coalition members in Iraq who allowed gays to serve openly, "And back in 1993, the same year that Congress refused to let gays serve openly...the Israeli Defense Forces, decided to drop the last of its own restrictions" and let gays serve openly for Israel.[316] Open gays serve in the CIA, DIA, FBI and the NSA.[317] To ban them from serving their country in the armed military but not from serving in other government service branches is inconsistent.

More Recent DADT Study

In July 2008, a California based research center released a study suggesting Congress should repeal DADT because gay presence in the military is unlikely to undermine the ability to fight and win.[318] Four retired military officers conducted the study, including "the three-star Air Force lieutenant general who in early 1993 was tasked with implementing President Clinton's policy that the military stop questioning recruits on their sexual orientation."[319] That officer concluded evidence showed letting gays serve openly was unlikely to pose any significant risk to morale, discipline or unit cohesion.[320] The study was sponsored by the Michael D. Palm Center at the University of California at Santa Barbara, which picked the panel members to portray bipartisan representation.[321] Undermining unit cohesion was a determining factor when Congress passed the 1993 law.[322] Despite a 35 year military career, Navy Vice Adm. Jack Shanahan had no opinion on the issue when he joined the study panel; Shanahan, a Republican opposed to the Bush administration's handling of the Iraq war, said he was struck by the loss of personal integrity required by individuals to carry out DADT.[323]

What has changed the perception of DADT?

Numerous changes have helped homosexual's odds of serving openly. There is a rejection of the religious right and Republicans, who historically supported DADT or didn't want gays to serve the military. Also, the fact that more military personnel were needed after 9/11, along with the Iraq invasion of 2003, helped focus on the needs of more troops in the military, not the policy of banning gays. Over 612 homosexuals were kicked out of the military in 2006, and another 627 in 2007, although, "Those figures represent a drop of about 50 percent from a peak in 2001, before the wars in Iraq and Afghanistan."[324] The number of annual discharges peaked at 1,273 in 2001.[325]

Polls are also favorable. NYT/CBS found (Feb. 2010) 70% of U.S. adults (and over two-thirds of conservatives) favored allowing lesbians and gay men to serve openly.[326]

According to a Quinnipiac poll (April 2009), 56% of Americans believed the ban on openly gays and lesbians should be overturned.

Indifference is Not Progress

The Servicemembers Legal Defense Network, a gay advocacy group, reported (Jan.2008) that 500 gay troops were serving openly without consequences, the highest number the group had ever been aware of.[327] However, the *LA Times* reported (2002) the U.S. Supreme Court has "refused repeatedly to hear challenges to the military's policy of excluding openly gay men and women."[328]

Shalikashvili changed his mind

In 2007, Gen. John M. Shalikashvili, who was chairman of the Joint Chiefs of Staff when DADT was adopted, argued for its repeal citing conversations with military personnel brought him a change of heart.[329] General Shalikashvili wrote in *The New York Times* on Jan. 2, 2007: "I now believe that if gay men and lesbians served openly in the United States military, they would not undermine the efficacy of the armed forces…Our military has been stretched thin by our deployments in the Middle East, and we must welcome the service of any American who is willing and able to do the job."[330]

Opposing Obama on DADT

Retired Air Force Gen. Merrill McPeak, who backed Obama early in the 2008 primaries, said he did not support Obama's plan to get rid of DADT: "The issue is unit cohesion in combat units…I think with combat units the question of cohesion is crucial. It is a war-winner. . . . My judgment is declared homosexuality in combat units will not contribute to unit cohesion. In fact, as near as I can tell, it would be inimical to it."[331]

McPeak argued that DADT and Integration in the 1950s is different. He compared racially integrating the armed forces after World War II and trying to sell the ranks on accepting openly gay colleagues:

> "We've only had mixed races in combat units for 50 years or so…The first mixing of races was by the Army in Korea in 1950. It was done because service leaders, generals, chiefs of staff, were able to get ahead of it, were able to go to the lunch at black history week and talk about American values that include equal opportunity for everybody no matter what color their skin is. So the service leadership made a commitment to racial equality and made it happen. Otherwise it wouldn't have happened…If you want to do something like racial integration or the integration of openly homosexual soldiers, sailors and marines, airmen, the service leadership will have to get ahead of it. Service leadership will have to go to the gay and lesbian annual ball and lead the first dance. I've spoken many, many times at black history week and am proud to do it. . . . But I couldn't see how I could become an advocate for open homosexuality in Air Force combat units. I don't see how people can do it today."[332]

Obama the Candidate

In November 2008, over 100 retired generals and admirals asked for DADT to be repealed.[333] Among the signatories was Clifford Alexander, Army secretary under former President Jimmy Carter.[334] Only 28 former generals and admirals signed a similar statement the year before.[335]

Obama's spokesman declined to comment on the signatories, but in September 2008, Obama told *Philadelphia Gay News*, "Although I have consistently said I would repeal 'don't ask, don't tell,' I believe that the way to do it is make sure that we are working through a process, getting the Joint Chiefs of Staff clear in terms of what our priorities are going to be."[336]

DADT… real people, real tragedy:

Private Winchell

Private Barry Winchell was in the 101st Airborne Division (the "Screaming Eagles"), who have played historic roles in service since D-Day. He enlisted in 1997 and wanted to be an Army helicopter pilot.[337] In Fort Benning, Ga., during his basic training, he had a girlfriend. But after transferring to Fort Campbell, Kentucky (May 1998) he spent time with a man.[338] Winchell did tell a wife of a fellow soldier he was gay.[339] Many in Winchell's company were all but sure he was gay, including Calvin Glover, who murdered Winchell.

Winchell v. Glover

Time concluded (1999), "If it had been anyone else who stood up to Private Calvin Glover about his outrageous, macho bragging that summer night, things might have turned out differently. But it may have been just too humiliating to be challenged by Private First Class Barry Winchell, of all people."[340] According to *Time*, Winchell got sick of Glover's antics. Glover tried unsuccessfully to knock a beer out of Winchell's hand, Winchell still did not want to fight, but Glover kept provoking.[341] Finally, trying to end it, Winchell hit Glover several times, then grabbed Glover by the waist and threw him.[342] *Time* said, "That should have been the end to an ordinary fight, but for Glover the stakes were higher. He had just been beat by a man whose suspected homosexuality had preoccupied the barracks for months."[343] Glover then said he would kill Winchell.[344] After the fight, Glover told fellow soldiers, "I can't believe it. I won't let a faggot kick my ass."[345] Winchell asked a fellow soldier, "Why do people have to push me like that?"[346]

The murder

It was Independence Day, and about a dozen soldiers had a cookout and blared music; they played wiffle ball and drank (even though many were under the age limit, like Glover, who was 18).[347] The staff sergeant on duty in the barracks did nothing to stop the illegal drinking among Glover and Winchell's company.[348] Glover and Winchell apparently stayed away from each other and there was no outward hostility between them. Eventually Winchell went to watch the company's mascot, an Australian blue heeler.[349]

When Winchell was asleep, Glover beat him with a baseball bat. "Winchell struggled to breathe, gurgling on his own blood. Both his eyes were blackened and swollen shut. Blood poured, and brains oozed, from the left side of his head. An Army investigator said it had been shattered 'like an eggshell.'"[350] He was airlifted to Vanderbilt and didn't die until 30 hours later.[351]

Glover's Punishment

Glover claimed he left the keg party to avoid Winchell's gay passes, and that he didn't want to kill Winchell but instead just teach him a lesson.[352] Glover pleaded not guilty to the murder charge in November 1999.[353] Glover came from

Sulphur, Okla.[354] Prevailing Oklahoma culture is seriously anti-gay. Oklahoma is home for anti-gay leaders such as televangelist Oral Roberts, former U.S. Rep. Steve Largent, and U.S. Sen. James Inhofe.

Leaders on Winchell

Upon the Winchell murder, Vice President Al Gore, and both Hillary Rodham Clinton and President Bill Clinton labeled DADT a policy failure.[355] President Clinton described DADT as "out of whack."[356]

The New York Times reported the Winchell murder "has permeated the presidential campaign."[357] Bill Bradley (D-NJ) and Gore, both campaigning for the 2000 Democratic presidential nomination, promised to reverse the DADT policy.[358]

Not surprisingly, the Republican presidential candidates took a different stand. Sen. John McCain (AZ) and Gov. George W. Bush (TX) supported DADT. Farther-right GOP candidates such as Gary Bauer, Alan Keyes, and Steve Forbes said they would bar gays from serving.[359]

The Lesson's of Winchell's Murder

1) DADT wasn't being followed. Remember that under the DADT policy, the military cannot inquire into a soldier's sex life unless there is clear evidence of homosexual conduct.[360] And homosexuals who volunteer the information can be discharged.[361]

Rumors spread that Winchell was gay, so a sergeant launched his own informal probe.[362] That sergeant's actions are against DADT policy.[363] Winchell denied being gay.[364] The sergeant dropped his pursuit.[365] But the damage was done. Gossip spread in Winchell's midst. The company's first sergeant claimed he wanted to "get that little faggot" when Winchell showed up for duty one day smelling of alcohol.[366] One fellow soldier noted, almost everybody in the company called him derogatory names.[367] In addition, Winchell's "sergeant let the [gay] trash talking continue, contrary to Army policy."[368]

2) DADT legitimizes and increases harassment. *Time* reported in 1999, "The Army is haunted by the fear that it may be seen as …[an]…accomplice for fumbling the military's policy on gays in uniform, not just in this case, but on a more widespread basis."[369] Winchell's murder showed how DADT could create a dangerous atmosphere in the ranks.[370]

Time noted the death of Winchell showed DADT was more like an "unfulfilled promise, not a functioning policy."[371] In fact, DADT traps gays. Winchell couldn't say anything. If he went to his superiors to complain about the slurs, it would be suggesting he was gay. If he acknowledged he was a homosexual, he'd have to leave the army. So Winchell kept taking the demeaning comments.[372]

Keith Meinhold, a former Navy officer and the first openly gay person to serve in the U.S. Armed Forces, said (1999), "Absolutely," the DADT policy was responsible for Winchell's death, "Not just the policy, but the lack of proper implementation of the policy is responsible for his death. I think what has happened out of the policy is that the Pentagon has perpetuated this anti-gay sentiment and hasn't done anything to prevent this."[373]

3) Further Evidence of Homophobia in Army Report. In 2000, *The New York Times* reported of "a survey [after Winchell's death] of 38 military bases and 11 warships that concluded that anti-gay remarks and harassment were commonplace in the American military, and that most service members believed their superiors and colleagues tolerated such behavior 'to some extent.'"[374] The survey suggested hostile attitudes toward gays remained pervasive in military culture.[375] But, "Despite the evidence of anti-gay behavior, the report exonerated all officers of blame in the murder of Private Winchell and concluded that there was no general climate of homophobia at the base, home of the 101st Airborne Division."[376]

The report gave examples of how the Army failed to educate service personnel. Indeed, less than five percent of commanders, command sergeant majors and leaders interviewed received training on the DADT policy in their units.[377]

By 1999, according to the Servicemembers Legal Defense Network, it was clear antigay harassment was on the rise in the military's ranks.[378] *Time* reported, "virulent antigay bigotry remains an accepted prejudice in much of the U.S. military."[379] The Army denied the family's claim for $1.4 million in damages under the Military Claims Act in May 2001.

According to the *New York Times* in May 2003, "An investigation by the Army's inspector general exonerated all officers, including General Clark, and said no climate of homophobia existed at the base. But the investigation also found that some members of the unit in which the killing took place, a company within the 101st Airborne Division, held antigay attitudes."[380]

In 2000, when Patricia Kutteles, Private Winchell's mother, said the Army was covering up a gay-bashing atmosphere on Winchell's base, General Eric Shinseki (then the Army Chief of Staff and now Secretary of Veterans Affairs for the Obama Administration) said, "I will tell you this, if this were a cover-up I wouldn't be standing here today."[381]

4) Sen. Warner, a Republican, was influenced. Maj. Gen. Robert T. Clark was commander of Fort Campbell, Ky., in 1999.[382] Years later, the Senate Armed Services Committee had to vote on General Clark's nomination to lieutenant general.[383] Private Winchell's mother said Clark should not be promoted: "He doesn't have the command authority or responsibility…The promotion would be another obstacle in the way of everything we have tried to do to honor our son."[384]

The Servicemembers Legal Defense Network, the Democratic National Committee, the Human Rights Campaign, the National Gay and Lesbian Task Force, the National Organization for Women and People for the American Way were all against Clark's promotion.[385] Executive director of the Servicemembers Legal Defense Network, C. Dixon Osburn, said, "General Clark demonstrated a profound lack of leadership...He failed to take even the most basic steps to improve conditions on the base."[386]

In the spring of 2003, Sen. John Warner (R-VA), the chairman of the Senate Armed Services Committee, delayed for the second time a vote on the promotion of this Army general who commanded the base where Winchell was killed.[387] The delay gave the committee more time to consider the general's responsibility in Winchell's death. [Clark's initial nomination expired at the conclusion of the previous Congressional session after the committee could not get the votes to support it, but in March 2003, President George W. Bush renominated Clark.[388]] The committee was expected to vote on General Clark's promotion to lieutenant general in May 2003, but Warner postponed the vote after meeting with Private Winchell's parents.[389]

Warner's postponement explained how this elder statesman—a Republican—would eventually support the repeal of Don't Ask, Don't Tell.

5) A vague new policy for homosexuals... In July 2000, the Pentagon announced an "anti-harassment action plan" that required military commanders to discipline service members who engaged in, condoned or ignored anti-gay behavior.[390] Still, *The New York Times* said the plan was "short on details," and an under secretary of the Air Force who drafted the plan said it was going to take "some work" to get the four military branches to actually carry it out.[391]

6) Suspected homosexuals were still treated badly in the military. In a 1999 *60 Minutes* report, CBS News Correspondent Ed Bradley uncovered new evidence of anti-gay sentiment and harassment on base after Winchell's murder.[392] Javier Torres concealed his homosexuality at Fort Campbell, and heard fellow soldiers remarking, "Hey, it's just one less fag to deal with. I mean, they don't really belong here."[393] According to CBS News, "One day his entire platoon went on a five-mile run around Fort Campbell, and, he says, the sergeant led them in a chant that went: 'Faggot, faggot down the street. Shoot him, shoot him, till he retreats.'"[394]

7) White supremacists in the military... According to *The New York Times*, "After Private Winchell's murder and reports of white supremacists in the Army, President Bill Clinton signed an executive order in 1999 that amended the court-martial manual to allow judges to weigh hate-crime factors in sentencing."[395] There is little debate that a faction of the military has white supremacists. The question is how much.

In 2008, the blog *crooksandliars.com* reported on the neo-Nazis in the military as exposed by the the Southern Poverty Law Center. The military has downplayed the issue.[396] In 2008, the SPLC's David Holthouse published a follow-up report and found the neo-Nazis problem was dragging on, particularly as the Iraq War continued.[397] According to *Crooks and Liars*:

> The July 2006 report by the SPLC found this infiltration occurring at an alarming rate. Neo-Nazis "stretch across all branches of service, they are linking up across the branches once they're inside, and they are hard-core," Department of Defense gang detective Scott Barfield told the SPLC. "We've got Aryan Nations graffiti in Baghdad," he added. "That's a problem." The source of the problem, as the report explained, was the extreme pressure military recruiters were under to fill their recruitment quotas. "Recruiters are knowingly allowing neo-Nazis and white supremacists to join the armed forces," said Barfield, "and commanders don't remove them . . . even after we positively identify them as extremists or gang members." The military downplayed a neo-Nazi presence in the ranks, Barfield added, "because then parents who are already worried about their kids signing up and dying in Iraq are going to be even more reluctant about their kids enlisting if they feel they'll be exposed to gangs and white supremacists." The FBI's assessment in the "White Supremacist Recruitment of Military Personnel Since 9/11" report found that the numbers of identifiable neo-Nazis within the ranks was quite small (only a little over 200)....[398]

The Federal Gay Marriage Amendment: 2006

The Gay Marriage amendment to the Constitution was debated on the Senate floor in early June, 2006. Only 27 amendments had successfully passed in U.S. history. There was absolutely no reason to believe why a gay marriage ban would pass in 2006. Two thirds-support for a constitutional amendment in both Houses of Congress, then ratified by 38 state legislatures, would be improbable if not impossible. However, polls did show a majority of Americans opposed same sex marriages.[399] Indeed, an ABC poll released the first week of June showed 58% of Americans thought gay marriage should be illegal, however, only 42% favored to amend the constitution for it.[400]

However, as the *Wall Street Journal*'s John Hardwood pointed out, "people under 40 just don't care about gay marriage at all in a large sense. And so Republicans know that this is a losing argument, you know, five, 10, 20 years down the road. But right now, it still has some utility for them."[401] According to Gallup, in 1977, only 56% felt homosexuals should have equal rights in terms of job opportunities (89% in 2006); and in 1982, only 34% felt homosexuality was an acceptable alternative lifestyle (54% in 2006).[402]

A March 2006 Pew found 58% of those age 18-29 favored allowing gays to adopt children, in no other age bracket was the favor of such action above 50%.[403] Forty eight percent of those age 18-29 favored gay marriage, as only a third over age 30 favored it.[404] Though Pew concluded "the social liberalism of the young" did not span to abortion, as 31% of those age 18-29 believed abortion should be "generally available," 6 points lower than those over thirty.[405] Even if gay marriage was an issue worth playing in 2006, it was losing its potency.

The U.S. Senate Debate

Sen. Sam Brownback (R-Kansas) released a statement (June 7) citing his European example: "…if we allow activist judges to redefine marriage it will dramatically alter our society, as it has done in the European countries who are embracing same-sex marriage."[406] On the Senate floor, Brownback said, "You can raise good children in other settings, but the best—the optimal setting—is in the union between a man and a woman, bonded together for life…That's something we've got social data on, but we also know that in our hearts."[407] He had so many charts in his floor presentation, the *The Daily Show* (June 6), it it's closing Moment of Zen segment, sarcasticly showed Brownback refering to his charts.[408] He argued "the institution of marriage has been weakened in this country."[409]

Sen. Bill Frist (R-Tennessee) went as far to suggest "marriage is under attack."[410] If marriage was under attack, such attacks must have occurred only in even years, election years. As the Senate had not voted on the topic in 2005.

Still, Brownback said, "We're not going to stop until marriage between a man and woman is respected."[411] "It is not bigotry to define marriage as a union of a man and a woman," said Brownback, who was quoted in the *New York Times*.[412] What Brownback and his friends won't admit is that wedlock often ruins great relationships.

Mike Huckabee's comments, were, at best homophobic: "marriage has historically never meant anything other than a man and woman. It has never meant two men, two women, a man and his pet, or a man and a whole herd of pets."[413] Being gay was just like having intercourse with dogs, a remarkable stupid statement from the Governor of Arkansas?!?

Rick Santorum said senators faced "potentially the greatest moral issue of our time"—the "integrity of the family in America."[414] President Bush said the amendment was to prevent "activist judges" from redefining marriage.[415]

Russ Feingold (D-WI) and Ted Kennedy (D-Mass.) were the only two senators who supported gay marriage.[416] Feingold said the amendment would make homosexuals "permanent second-class citizens."[417] Feingold's Senate colleague from Wisconsin, Herb Kohl, unlike Feingold, supported the 1996 Defense of Marriage Act that said marriage was between a man and a woman for federal law purposes and stated it did not have to recognize same-sex marriages from other states.[418]

Sen. Inhofe (R-OK) Stated Case

1) Inhofe was proud of his "recorded" straight family. Sen. Inhofe (R-OK) defended his position on a constitutional ban on gay marriage in June 2006. On the Senate floor (6.6.06), Inhofe stood before a large family photograph to share his wisdom: "As you see here, and I think this is maybe the most important prop we'll have during the entire debate, my wife and I have been married 47 years. We have 20 kids and grandkids. I'm really proud to say that in the recorded history of our family, we've never had a divorce or any kind of homosexual relationship."[419]

How many grandchildren thank grandparents for their sexuality? Inhofe's words were powerful. Numerous children have said, "Gramps, I'm so proud you and Grandma turned out to be heterosexual. Thanks!" In addition, Inhofe implied sex is sinful if it does not produce children. Married couples who have sex but bear no offspring are an insult to God? If a loving couple can't have kids, it shouldn't mean the marriage has no meaning. Lastly, Inhofe is proud of the recorded history of his family. Did the "unrecorded" portions included homosexuals, polygamists, and cousins who matriculated in college and were thesbians?

2) There is not just a gay lobby, there's a polygamist lobby! Inhofe said, (6.6.06), "The homosexual marriage lobby, as well as the polygamist lobby, they share the same goal of essentially breaking down all state-regulated marriage requirements to just one, and that one is consent. In doing so, they're paving the way for illegal protection of such practices as homosexual marriage, unrestricted sexual conduct between adults and children, group marriage, incest, and, you know, if it feels good, do it."[420]

3) There will be no parents, and numerous kids will have to be raised by the state. Steve Benen wrote for the *Washington Monthly* and commented on other ridiculous comments by Inhofe. "My personal favorite came when Inhofe explained his belief that gay marriage will, for reasons he never quite explained, lead to more children being born out of wedlock. With this in mind, Inhofe believes the whole gay-marriage effort may be some kind of big-government conspiracy."[421] Indeed, Sen. Inhofe was convinced (6.6.06), thru gay marriage, more kids would become wards of the state. "Now, stop and think. What's going to be the results of this? The results are going to be that it's going to be a very expensive thing, all these kids, many of them are going to be ending up on welfare. So it goes far beyond just the current emotionals [sic]. I think that my colleague, Senator Sessions, said I believe yesterday, 'If there are not families to raise children, who will raise them? Who will do the responsibility? It will fall on the state.' Clearly it will be a state."[422] The irony of Inhofe's ignorance is the answer could be used to justify abortion.

The Senate Vote

The vote to end the debate and move on was 49-48 in favor, still 11 short of the 60 needed to send the issue to an up-or-down vote.[423] Although the votes in favor was 48-50 in 2004, and Republicans made one vote gain in 2006, the reality was two Republicans who supported a ban in 2004 (Arlen Specter [PA] and Judd Gregg [NH]) voted no in 2006; and a third previous ban supporter, Chuck Hagel (R-NE), was traveling with the President and could not vote.[424] Bush visited

Nebraska to discuss Immigration Reform, an indication of the potency of the issue in Nebraska.[425] Hagel said he would have voted for cloture like in 2004.[426]

Hagel's counterpart in Nebraska, Ben Nelson was the only Democrat who supported the amendment (not just cloture, like Byrd had).[427] Republicans such as George Allen, Brownback, Frist, Santorum voted yes; and Democratic presidential contenders voted no, along with John McCain, who was the only Republican who voted 'no' that was not from the Northeast.[428]

Besides Hagel's missing vote, Chris Dodd attended a ceremony in Rhode Island for his sister's volunteering in public schools, and did not vote, though he said he "would have voted no on the motion for cloture."[429] Where as Russ Feingold was steadfast for gay marriage, Chris Dodd (D-CT) said it was an issue for the states to address,[430] and would have voted against cloture just like he did in 2004.[431] Sen. Jay Rockefeller (D-WV) was recuperating from back surgery, but if all three Senators had voted accordingly, the vote would have been 50-50.[432]

The Fight Must Go On! To the States?

Brownback said, "We're not going to stop until marriage between a man and a woman is protected."[433] "We have 45 states that have defined marriage as the union of a man and a woman. Since the last time we voted in the Senate, we've seen a total of 14 states take this issue up on a ballot—on the ballot—and you've got another seven set for this fall."[434] This was a bit ironic, because such comments supported the states rights mentality of leaving choice to the states, defeating the purpose of a federal amendment.

George Allen (R-VA), at the time a contender for the GOP presidential nomination for 2008, made similar statements. Allen called marriage "the most important institution in our society. It's from families that you learn right from wrong and certain principles of living."[435] CNN asked Allen why a Republican was bringing the issue up even though it had little chance of success, Allen answered, "Because it is a key issue. In Virginia this fall will be an amendment proposed to the Virginia constitution recognizing marriage as between a man and a woman. This is important throughout the country. The fact that we'll have a majority vote but not a two-thirds vote doesn't mean that you don't try."[436]

If Virginia was proposing a constitutional ban, it defeated the purpose of the federal government to have to make one. Also, there was the perception if Virginia had an amendment for gay marriage in the November 2006 election, it would bolster Allen's turnout for his Senate reelection bid. That is the true reason why Republicans put such measures on ballots in Virginia and Wisconsin in 2006. They played election politics at the expense of the U.S. Constitutional rights of American citizens. They are not only neo-con theocratic dominionists, they are hypocrites and liars.

The U.S. Senate vote on a ban occurred the day after Alabama became the 20th state to amend its constitution to ban gay marriage.[437] This wasn't a reason to pass a federal ban, but a reason to show why it was unnecessary. The states that would have ratified a federal ban would likely have already passed a state ban.

Meanwhile, President Bush spun the issue and said history showed "it can take several tries before an amendment builds the two-thirds support it needs…"[438]

McCain Boldly Against Party

In contrast, McCain said, "Most Americans are not yet convinced that their elected representatives or the judiciary are likely to expand decisively the definition of marriage to include same-sex couples." Arlen Spector paraphrased Barry Goldwater and said the government "ought to be kept off our backs, out of our pocketbooks and out of our bedrooms."[439] Such a position made Specter criticized as a RINO (Republican In Name Only), but in truth, Specter, Goldwater, and McCain represented the old Republican Party that used to prevent government from interfering in private lives.

"Activist Judges": New York, Georgia Rulings in July

On July 6, 2006, the state supreme courts of New York and Georgia both ruled same-sex couples were not entitled to marry, and delivered "a double setback to gay rights advocates" that left Massachusetts the only state in which such unions were legal.[440] The New York decision suggested it was "not for us [judges] to say whether same-sex marriage is right or wrong" and essentially deferred the issue to the legislature.[441]

USA Today reported New York Governor George Pataki, at the time considering a GOP presidential bid, "said he was pleased the court upheld marriage between only a man and a woman."[442] But New York was not anti-gay. Gubernatorial candidate and then-Attorney General Eliot Spitzer announced (July 6) he would propose legislation to legalize gay marriage.[443] In addition, Joseph L. Bruno, the state senate majority leader who stood in the way of Spitzer, had tolerated his stance against gays.[444] Bruno became majority leader in 1994 and undid domestic partner benefits for Senate staffers and blocked hate crimes legislation from floor votes but later brought back the benefits and supported hate crime legislation.[445] The *New York Times* reported gay groups were giving New York Republicans more money.[446]

On July 14, the 8th Circuit Court of Appeals reinstated Nebraska's voter-approved ban on gay marriage, and the Tennessee Supreme Court tossed out an attempt to keep a proposed ban off the ballot.[447] Those weren't the type of activist court's Bush warned about, illustrating more hypocrisy.

The background of an anti-gay Senator…

The *Washington Post* reported of Brownback's religious ties in an article (June 7) titled "Faith Based Initiative."[448] "He sometimes sounds as though he's quoting the Bible even when he isn't," wrote the Post.[449] And when Brownback spoke to the Denver Archdiocese in 2003 he called for the conversion of culture:

"When we walk up to the McDonald's counter, what if we looked at that person in the eye…and we said, 'God bless you for that Big Mac?!'"[450] (And God bless you for the heart attack.) The *Post* said Brownback once washed the feet of a staffer at a farewell party to show humility and respect, periodically gave staffers index cards with Scripture, and said he practiced prayer when he found himself in heated situations.[451]

The *Post* story piecemealed Brownback's religious background succinctly. Until 2002, Brownback had been a Protestant all his life but then decided to be Catholic.[452] Brownback would not "talk much about this aspect of his religious life…perhaps conscious of his many evangelical supporters."[453] He would not even call it a 'conversion' ("a conversion is if I became a Buddhist.")[454]

As a youth, Brownback was a Methodist, and then later belonged to a nondenominational evangelical church.[455] Brownback said becoming Catholic "was joining the early Church. This is the mother church."[456] He was sponsored by Rick Santorum, in a ceremony presided by an Opus Dei member who had also converted columnist Bob Novak and former abortion provider Bernard Nathanson.[457]

In summation: Brownback was not satisfied with Methodist or nondenominational evangelicals, and became a Catholic through the help of a man connected to the group even some Catholics viewed as a cult. Nor did the release of *The Da Vinci Code* weeks earlier help the Opus Dei stereotype. However, Brownback did go to Church twice on Sundays—a Catholic Mass and a nondenominational service with the rest of his family who did not convert.[458]

Flag Burning & Gay Rights: Seriously

And so having a debate on gay marriage that solved nothing, and having debated the Iraq war with simplistic overtones, the U.S. Senate decided to finally discuss flag burning at the end of June 2006. Flag burning became a political issue after the 1989 ruling by the Supreme Court which protected the act as a form of political expression.[459]

Pew found (June 2006) flag burning, abortion, the inheritance tax and gay marriage were the last four issues (out of 19) that both Democrats and Independents rated as "very important."[460] But it vindicated why the Republicans were spending Senate time because, for Republicans, flag burning ranked 9th, followed by the Inheritance tax (11th), abortion (13), and gay marriage (15).[461]

Frist on both amendments: Where are the priorities?

In an interview with *Late Edition* (5.14.06), Bill Frist said he would introduce legislation banning same-sex marriage around early June.[462] He was asked about the gay-marriage amendment and flag-burning amendment on *Fox News Sunday*.

> Securing America's values — and I hope tomorrow and today, as people see that American flag — and I'm going to Arlington Cemetery tomorrow, and I'm going to see that American flag waving on every single grave over there. And when you look at that

> flag and then you tell me that right now people in this country are saying it's OK to desecrate that flag and to burn it and to not pay respect to it — is that important to our values as a people when we've got 130,000 people fighting for our freedom and liberty today? That is important.It may not be important here in Washington where people say well, it's political posturing and all, but it's important to the heart and soul of the American people.[463]

Was that really the heart and soul of the American people? Frist then stated, "Right now, why marriage today? Marriage is for our society — that union between a man and a woman is the cornerstone of our society. It is under attack today. Right now there are 13 states who passed constitutional amendments in the 1.5 years to protect marriage. Why? Because in nine states today, activist judges, unelected activist judges, are tearing down state laws in nine states today. That's why I will take it to the floor of the Senate — simply define marriage as the union between a man and a woman."[464] His prepared Senate remarks began with the belief that "Throughout human history and culture, the union between a man and woman has been recognized as the essential cornerstone of society."[465]

Not surprisingly, Matt Lauer mentioned to Frist that critics "say you are pandering to the conservative base" as the Tennessee Senator prepared a White House bid.[466]

Chapter Five:
AROUND THE GLOBE:
How is the LGBT community treated elsewhere?

The nations' status summarized below may not be entirely up to date. LGBT issues are rapidily moving targets. The following, however, will give some impression on how the LGBT community is treated in the respective countries. The nations are grouped by those which allow gay marriage, civil unions and domestic registeries; civil tolerance; and those places, to quote Dante's *Inferno*, "Abandon hope, all ye who enter here."

Countries Allowing Gay Marriage, Civil Unions and Domestic Registeries

For same-sex marriage: Belgium, Canada, Netherlands, Norway, South Africa, Spain and Sweden.

For civil unions and registered partnerships: Andorra, Austria, Colombia, Czech Republic, Denmark, Ecuador, Finland, France, Germany, Greenland, Hungary, Iceland, Luxembourg, New Caledonia, New Zealand, Slovenia, Switzerland, Wallis and Futuna, United Kingdom and Uruguay.

New Zealand

In December, 2004, New Zealand's parliament passed legislation recognizing civil unions between gay couples.[467] New Zealand's parliament passed the controversial legislation which recognized civil unions between gay couples by a vote of 65 votes to 55, and also recognized unions between men and women who do not want to marry.[468] The new law gave unmarried couples the same rights as married couples in child custody, tax and welfare.[469]

Australia

Edge-Boston described the Aussie success of Olympic swimmer Matthew Mitcham, "This 20-year-old overcame huge obstacles to take the 10-meter platform Gold Medal from the Chinese with the single most highly rated dive in Olympics history. Mitcham was the first Aussie to win gold since 1924 and became a hero at home. He also caused controversy when NBC edited out shots of his partner, whom he hugged and kissed during media interviews. NBC Sports later apologized."[470]

Argentina

Argentina had its first gay civil union in July 2003; their unions give legal rights similar to those for heterosexual couples, but excluded adoption and inheritance rights.[471] Argentina was the first country in Latin America to allow such unions.[472]

Canada

Andrew Sullivan summarized Canada's accomplishment (6.22.2003), "Canada's federal government decided last week not to contest the rulings of three provincial courts that had all come to the conclusion that denying homosexuals the right to marry violated Canada's constitutional commitment to civic equality. What that means is that gay marriage has now arrived in the western hemisphere. And this isn't some euphemism. It isn't the quasi-marriage now celebrated in Vermont, whose 'civil unions' approximate marriage but don't go by that name. It's just marriage — for all. Canada now follows the Netherlands and Belgium with full-fledged marital rights for gays and lesbians."[473]

In July 2005, the Canadian government passed a bill to legalize same-sex marriage, but by that time gay marriage was already legal in eight of 10 provinces and one of Canada's three territories.[474]

Europe: Civil Unions All Over

In summary, Northern European countries first recognized same-sex unions, and this trend quickened in the 1990s and eventually crossed to the United States by 2004.[475] In a "number of countries in Europe," the "registered partnership" status has been established.[476]

For example, in 1989, Denmark became the first country to institute legislation granting registered same-sex partners the same rights as married couples, but church weddings were not allowed.[477] Norway, Sweden and Iceland all enacted similar legislation by the mid 1990s, and Finland followed in 2002.[478]

In 1999, France introduced a civil contract called the Pacs that gives some rights to cohabiting couples, regardless of sex; but the Pacs don't include full rights of marriage, notably over taxes, inheritance and adoption.[479] When a mayor conducted France's first gay marriage in 2004, it was later voided by a court.[480] Luxembourg had a similar law (2004) on civil partnerships like the French model.[481]

Germany has allowed same-sex couples to register for "life partnerships" since 2001, but the law only gives couples the same inheritance and tenants' rights as married heterosexuals.[482] British legislation (2005) gave same-sex couples in registered partnerships similar rights to married couples (such as pensions, property, social security, and housing).[483]

Some European Nations Have Marriages

The Netherlands became the first country to offer full civil marriage rights to gay couples in 2001.[484] Belgium was the second EU country to offer full civil marriage rights to gay couples in 2003.[485]

Spain legalized gay marriage in June of 2005, despite fierce opposition from the Roman Catholic Church.[486] Gay married couples can also adopt children in Spain.[487] As of April 6, 2009, the Netherlands, Norway, Belgium, Spain and Sweden all allow gay marriage.

South Africa is Changing Africa's Attitudes

Compared to the continent of Africa, South Africa is generous toward gay rights. The post-apartheid constitution included a clause which made sexual identity discrimination illegal; and homosexual couples are allowed to adopt.[488] By December 2005, South Africa's high court said it was unconstitutional to deny gay people the right to marry, and instructed parliament to amend marriage laws to include same-sex unions within a year.[489] Already South Africa's constitution allowed gay couples to adopt, but not to marry.[490]

Tutu on South Africa, Gays, & Anglican Church

Desmond Tutu has fought against homophobia. He is the former Archbishop of Cape Town, and former head of the Anglican Church in Southern Africa; he also won a Nobel Peace Prize.[491] He has been a strong leader for gays on a continent that has made them an outcast.

Tutu is proud of South Africa's constitution. "And I am proud that in South Africa, when we won the chance to build our own new constitution, the human rights of all have been explicitly enshrined in our laws," Tutu said, but "…We treat them as pariahs and push them outside our communities. We make them doubt that they too are children of God - and this must be nearly the ultimate blasphemy. We blame them for what they are."[492]

Homosexuality is controversial and an ongoing conflict threatening to split the global Anglican Communion, especially in Africa. Indeed, "The current head of the Anglican Church in Southern Africa, Njongonkulu Ndungane, has been an outspoken supporter of including homosexuals in the Church community, putting himself in a strong-worded conflict with other African Church leaders."[493] Tutu has regretted the dominant view among his church colleagues: "Churches say that the expression of love in a heterosexual monogamous relationship includes the physical, the touching, embracing, kissing, the genital act - the totality of our love makes each of us grow to become increasingly godlike and compassionate. If this is so for the heterosexual, what earthly reason have we to say that it is not the case with the homosexual?"[494]

When it comes to gay violence and gay loathing, Archbishop Tutu notes such "destructive forces" of "hatred and prejudice" are an evil: "A parent who brings up a child to be a racist damages that child, damages the community in which they live, damages our hopes for a better world. A parent who teaches a child that there is only one sexual orientation and that anything else is evil denies our humanity and their own too."[495]

U.S. States in Step with the March for Equality:

Those states which have legal same-sex marriages are Connecticutt, Iowa, Massachusetts, New Hampshire, Vermont. Washington D.C is on the list too, but is subject to Congressional override. Finally, the Coquille Native Americans of Oregon allow gay marriage.

Those states which have civil unions or registered partnerships include California, Colorado, Maine, New Jersey, Neveda, Oregon, Washington and Wisconsin.

There are 36 U.S. states that ban any recognized same-sex relationship, they join such nations…..

"Abandon hope, all ye who enter here."

Jamaica & the Caribbean

In April 2006, *Time* reported unlike its idolized vacationing, "Jamaica is hardly idyllic. The country has the world's highest murder rate. And its rampant violence against gays and lesbians has prompted human-rights groups to confer another ugly distinction: the most homophobic place on earth."[496] In the previous two years, Jamaica's most prominent gay activist (Brian Williamson and Steve Harvey) were murdered. In 2004, a father learned his son was gay and invited a group to lynch the boy at his school. They did.[497] Meanwhile, police egged on a mob, which stabbed and stoned a gay in Montego Bay.[498] In 2006, a Kingston man drowned after gay-bashers chased him off a pier.[499]

What caused all this homophobia? Reggae. Including Jamaica's reggae Star Buju Banton; One of Banton's first hits, 1992's *Boom Bye-Bye,* brags of killing gays with Uzis and burning their skin with acid "like an old tire wheel."[500] Banton has been accused of beating a homosexual. Banton refused to be interviewed by *Time*, and even the judge warned Banton to avoid violence toward gays in the future.[501] Banton's manager told *Time* Banton was innocent: "Buju's lyrics are part of a metaphorical tradition. They're not a literal call to kill gay men."[502]

Sadly, Banton isn't the only Jamaican reggae artist who is gay bashing. According to *Time*, "Elephant Man (O'Neil Bryant, 29) declares in one song, 'When you hear a lesbian getting raped/ It's not our fault ... Two women in bed/ That's two Sodomites who should be dead.' Another, Bounty Killer (Rodney Price, 33), urges listeners to burn 'Mister Fagoty' and make him 'wince in agony.'[503] Politically, the country's major political parties have passed some of the world's toughest anti-sodomy laws and include such homophobic music in their campaigns.[504]

Little is different elsewhere in the Caribbean. Barbados still criminalizes homosexuality (2006).[505] In St. Martin, two Americans were beaten (2006) with tire irons by a gay-hating mob.[506] One of the victims had a fractured skull.[507]

Fidel Castro's Cuba

When Fidel Castro took power, the Cuban government ordered the internment of gay people in prison labor camps where they were either killed or worked to death for alleged "counterrevolutionary tendencies."[508] Castro's brother and fellow Cuban ruler, Raul Castro, is known for executing political opponents, including those whose only crime was their sexual orientation.[509]

Peter Tachell wrote (2002), "While Castro challenged many backward ideas as remnants of the old society, he embraced with enthusiasm the homophobia of Latin machismo and Catholic dogma, elevating it into a fundamental tenet of Cuba's new socialist morality. Idealizing rural life, he once claimed approvingly that 'in the country, there are no homosexuals.'"[510] Communism also has homophobic roots, for Stalin re-criminalized gay sex in 1934 (in the effort to promote the Soviet "socialist family").[511] Homophobia was common in Latin America in the 1960s and 1970s: the Pinochet dictatorship in Chile also oppressed gays.[512]

In Castro's Cuba of the 1960s, homosexuality usually earned four years of imprisonment, and if parents did not inform the government of their gay children, that too was a crime.[513] When gays were rounded up (often without trial), they were put into labor camps and "re-educated."[514]

When Cuba softened towards gays in the 1990s, it was more for the government's benefit—not homosexuals. For example, with the threat of AIDS, Castro figured out that safer sex education wouldn't occur if gays felt threatened by the government.[515] And detention of gays, economically speaking, was expensive.[516] Though Cuba's penal code de-criminalized homosexuality in 1979, gay activities could still get the offenders a year in prison if they caused a "public scandal." Gays still aren't allowed to join the Communist Party, a big factor in blocking career advancement in a communist nation.[517] As of 2009, the government still bans gay organizations.[518]

Africa

Homosexuality is illegal in Zimbabwe, Kenya, Uganda, Nigeria, and most sub-Saharan countries .[519] According to the BBC, "homosexuality remains a taboo subject in many African societies."[520] Homosexuality is punishable by death in Sudan, Mauritania and some Northern Nigerian states.[521] Zimbabwe President Robert Mugabe's has protested that homosexuality is "against African traditions."[522]

As *Edge-Boston* reported for 2008, "The list of nations that took it upon themselves to oppress, harass, exile, beat, imprison or even execute gay men (and some lesbians) is depressingly long, but includes Cameroon, Gabon, Nigeria, Uganda, Egypt and Kenya. In South Africa, the nation's president's past refusal to acknowledge HIV as the cause of AIDS was estimated to contribute to the death of 350,000--and counting. The country enshrines gay rights in its constitution, but still roving bands managed to gang rape a lesbian, among other atrocities."[523]

Senegal: One Step Forward, Two Steps Back

One month after gay activists from around the world gathered at the International African AIDS conference in Dakar, a Senegalese judge sentenced

(Jan.2009) nine men to eight years in prison for their homosexuality.[524] The legal action was a surprise, given Senegal was a progressive country in AIDS, being the first to address HIV in gay communities.[525] Nonetheless, Senegal's penal code states "an impure or unnatural act with another person of the same sex" is punishable by a maximum of five years in prison; even worse, the judge in this case added an extra three years for criminal conspiracy.[526]

Influential religious leaders in Senegal supported the court's action, such as the president of JAMRA, an Islamic organization in Dakar, who said homosexuality is "revolting" and the judge's decision to add three years to the sentence emphasized the seriousness of the offense.[527] Such actions will actually hurt the AIDS prevention in Africa, as it forces activists into hiding and virtually kills HIV/AIDS programs.[528]

The Middle East

The region is sexist, so if a man is deemed effeminate that man has lowered himself to the status of a women.[529] When it comes to politics, the governments crack down on gays because the government is defending Islam.[530] Homosexuality is rarely covered on television in the Middle East region.[531] In addition, Arabic terms widely used to describe 'gay' closely translate to "pervert."[532]

Iraq & Homosexuals

CNN reported (6.2.2006), "...nowhere more than in Iraq is homophobia becoming a socio-political weapon that is making life for gay men nearly impossible."[533] Not until 2006 did Grand Ayatollah Ali Al Sistani lift a fatwa calling on the killing of gays in Iraq.[534]

Newsweek reported (Aug.2008) how militia men from the Shiite Muslim Mahdi Army hunts down homosexuals (instead of Sunni Muslims): "Now that Iraq's sectarian war has cooled off, it's open season on homosexuals and others who infuriate religious hardliners."[535]It's a lonely world for homosexuals in Iraq:

> Iraqi authorities scoffed at the subject [homosexuality in Iraq]--when not scolding a reporter for even asking about it. Some of NEWSWEEK's own local staff were wary of the story. Virtually no government officials would sit for an interview. And the United Nations human-rights office, which has a big presence in Iraq, dodged the subject like a mine field. As with a number of Muslim societies where homosexuality is officially nonexistent but widely practiced, the policy in Iraq during Saddam Hussein's rule was "don't ask, don't tell." But that has changed. Iraqi LGBT, the London NGO that Nadir works for, says more than 430 gay men have been murdered in Iraq since 2003. For the country's beleaguered gays, it's a friendless landscape.[536]

Newsweek noted (Aug.2008), "An adviser to the government of Prime Minister Nuri al-Maliki said that of all the meetings he has attended, none ever touched on the rights--or even the existence--of homosexual Iraqis."[537] It also comes down to religion: "Persecution of gays will stop only if Iraqis can abandon centuries-old prejudices. They would have to acknowledge that human rights don't cover only the humans they like. Insisting that gays are just a few undesirable perverts who 'should be killed'--as one Iraqi who works in journalism put it--encourages an atmosphere of impunity no matter the offense. Killing gays becomes 'honorable.' And raping them is OK because it isn't considered a homosexual act--only being penetrated or providing oral sex is."[538]

Iran Doesn't Have Homosexuals—But Kills Them

In September 2007, Iranian President Mahmoud Ahmadinejad spoke at Columbia University and denied the existence gay Iranians.[539] In the question-and-answer portion of Ahmadinejad's appearance, the moderator asked why Iran executes gays. The response: "…In Iran, we don't have homosexuals, like in your country. We don't have that in our country. In Iran, we do not have this phenomenon. I don't know who's told you that we have it."[540]

Those comments were edited out of official Farsi transcripts for Ahmadinejad's website and Iran's official news agency, IRNA.[541] The AP reported (9.26.2007), "…homosexuality, which remains highly sensitive in Iran, is rarely discussed in Farsi-language official media. Gay sex is prohibited, and in some circumstances, people convicted of it can be sentenced to death."[542]

Amnesty International claims Iranians have been arrested and harassed for allegedly committing homosexual acts.[543] But in 2005, a more vivid story exemplified Iranian persecution.

In July 2005, two gay teenagers were publicly executed in Iran for the crime of homosexuality. Before their execution, they were held in prison for 14 months and severely beaten with 228 lashes.[544]

Iranian penal code allows girls as young as nine and boys as young as 15 to be hanged.[545] Iran enforces Islamic Sharia law, which dictates the death penalty for gay sex.[546] According to Iranian human rights campaigners, over 4,000 lesbians and gay men have been executed since the Ayatollahs seized power in 1979.[547] Another estimated 100,000 Iranians have been executed over the last quarter century because of clerical rule, as the victims include women who have sex outside of marriage and political opponents of the Islamist government.[548]

Lebanon

In 2006, CNN reported on a man in Beirut, Lebanon who was openly gay; his name was Youssef, a 21-year-old man from a conservative Shia Muslim family.[549] When CNN's reporter interviewed Youssef, a driver yelled out "fag."[550] When Youssef came out to his family, two of his brothers kidnapped him at gunpoint and he was held hostage in the family home for weeks, because his relatives felt their honor was trashed.[551] CNN reported that for interviews for the story, "Most gays and lesbians in the region would only agree to speak to us anonymously. It took months to find willing participants. Often, we would meet in hotel lobbies and film interviews in silhouette, hiding identities and distorting voices."[552]

Egypt's Queen Boat Incident

In 2001, Egyptian authorities raided a gay hangout on the Nile, as dozens were arrested in the Queen Boat then jailed on charges of "debauchery."[553] Before the end of the year, 52 men were tried in Cairo for having gay sex.[554] The BBC described (11.14.2001) as "a pleasure boat moored in the Nile off an affluent Cairo area where there are five-star hotels and embassies.... the Queen Boat was known as a popular gay venue, though it was also frequented by a heterosexual clientele."[555]

Homosexuality was not explicitly in the Egyptian penal code, but implied in a wide range of laws covering obscenity, prostitution and debauchery.[556] Many of those accused were not even on the boat when they were arrested, as some were arrested in their homes and others picked off the streets of Cairo.[557] After the raid of the Queen Boat, dozens of men without women partners were detained, and, while in custody, "were subjected to internal medical examinations to see if they had had gay sex."[558]

The hearing of the 52 men came before an Emergency State Security Court, convened under 1981 laws designed to protect national security, and 23 men were convicted and jailed for one to five years.[559] Worse yet, as the BBC reported (11.14.2001), "The verdicts of Egyptian state security courts are final which means that the 23 convicted men will not be able to appeal against their sentences."[560]

Critics argued bashing gays was an effort by the government to divert attention from the real problems that Egypt faced, like a bad economic situation.[561] Egyptian authorities also used matchmaking websites to find gays and arrest them.[562] Fear was used to frighten the closet gays to shut up. Others attacking homosexuals called them agents of Israel,[563] which fit into many Egyptian's foreign policy viewpoints of the Jewish state.

French President Jacques Chirac came out against Egyptian criminalization of gay sex.[564] But when Chirac told Egyptian President Hosni Mubarak that hopefully the 2001 convictions would be overturned,[565] the pro-government *Rose El-Youssef* weekly described the complaints from those around the globe as "an international homosexual campaign against Egypt."[566] Weeks after the Queen Boat aftermath, in January 2002, eight more men were arrested on suspicion for being gay and the Egyptian press labeled it a crackdown on a "network of perverts."[567] The Egyptian media was a joke. The BBC reported (8.15.2001), "There were lurid accounts of what was alleged to have happened on the Queen Boat, including false reports of a gay wedding on board. The names and workplaces of the defendants were also put into print."[568]

The BBC reported (2.11.2002), "Homosexuality is so detested in Egypt that the country's largest rights group says it cannot campaign against persecution of gay men despite international concern."[569] At the time of the Queen Boat incident, there was no human rights group in Egypt that defended homosexuals.[570] The Director of the Egyptian Organization for Human Rights, Hisham Kassem, was incredibly weak: "What could we do? Nothing. If we were to uphold this issue, this would be the end of what remains of the concept of human rights in Egypt…We let them [homosexuals] down, but I don't have a mandate from the people, and I don't want the West to set the pace for the human rights movement in Egypt."[571]

United Arab Emirates

In the UAE, similar arrests like the Queen Boat incident in Egypt occurred after authorities saw what they felt was a "gay wedding."[572] In 2001, Dubai authorities shut down a nightclub after it hosted a gay night featuring a transvestite DJ from Britain.[573] The BBC reported (April 2001), "Like all the Gulf Arab states, Dubai officially frowns on homosexuality."[574] The Diamond Club was closed after Dubai's Crown Prince, General Sheikh Mohammed al-Maktoum, was notified of thousands of flyers inviting residents of the Gulf emirate to come out of the closet.[575] Having been notified by the fliers, government officials went to the club to watch and they closed the evening down and filed a report.[576]

The Not So Good But Not So Bad

Greece

Greece serves as an asterisk to homosexual acceptance in Europe. According to *Reuters*, when it comes to legislation recognizing gay marriage, "Greece's traditional society has preferred to turn a blind eye to homosexuality."[577] In September 2008, Greece's Justice Ministry tried to overturn two marriages (one lesbian, one gay) after they took advantage of Greek civil law which failed to specify gender in matrimony.[578] The marriages drew strong criticism from the powerful Orthodox Church, which officially represents more than 90 percent of the 11 million-strong population.[579]

Asia

Asia is seeing increases in gay acceptance. Though not as accepting as Western Europe, Asia is certainly in better shape than the Middle East and Africa. The year 2008 was a particularly good one for Nepal, who overthrew its ancient monarchy and recognized gay rights.[580]

Turkey: Troubling in Rural Areas

In general, homosexuality is taboo in Turkey. But Turkish gays have much more freedom in Germany. In fact, approximately 15,000 homosexuals with Turkish roots are living in Germany.[581] One Germany media said (2004) Turkish gays were in "A game of hide-and-seek," because "Turkish gays often prefer to stay in the immigrant scene and the majority of immigrants in Germany don't come from the big Turkish cities, where there is more tolerance for people who live alternative lives. They mostly come from rural areas of Anatolia, where homosexuality is at best seen as a sickness."[582]

India Improves

The penal code is from 1860.[583] According to Section 377 it states: ''Whosoever has carnal intercourse voluntarily against the order of nature with any man, woman or animal shall be punished with imprisonment for life, or imprisonment for a term which may extend to 10 years, and shall be liable to fine."[584] The BBC reported (2005), "The 145-year-old colonial Indian Penal Code clearly describes a same sex relationship as an 'unnatural offence.'"[585] The irony is that the British made the section to replace the tolerant Indian attitude on sexuality with an oppressive one; meanwhile the British repealed their code in 1967.[586]

India is just as gay as other regions of the world. In an article publishing in the Times of India, it was reported, "A recent study conducted by the UNFPA in rural India has found that male-to-male sex is not uncommon. 'In fact, a higher percentage of men reported male-to-male sex than sex with sex-workers. Close to 10 per cent of unmarried men and 3 per cent of married men reported sex with other men in the past 12 months,' says the study."[587]

Lesbians are worse off than gays in India.[588] Many lesbians are still forcibly married off by their parents.[589] Parents may have their gay children who are lesbians go to a doctor, who still tell the girls to swim, cook and knit to become a girl again.[590]

Bigger cities like Calcutta are more open to gays than the rural areas. And the eastern West Bengal state alone has some nine gay and lesbian support groups.[591] Still, India has a way to go. In an April 2008 meeting of the UN Human Rights Council in Geneva, India underwent harsh questioning on their homosexuality stances.[592] In 2008, India began the process of decriminalizing private, consensual gay sex.[593]

China Takes Steps Forward

AFP has reported in China, gays often have "their ignorance and guilt instead reinforced by scant information in the media that tends to connect homosexuals with ...AIDS or crime. While long-term jail sentences for homosexuals on 'hooliganism' charges have become rare in recent years, police continues to promote fear in the cowed community by occasionally rounding gays up and fining them or detaining them for several days. With so many negative factors preventing gays from nurturing a stable relationship, many instead resort to sordid, 'unsafe' encounters in public toilets. Afterwards, they return home to their wives and resume pretence of a heterosexual life."[594] It is common that after the age of 30, most gays get married because of social pressure.[595]

In general, some major universities are starting to openly have classes about homosexuality, such as Fudon University in Shanghai.[596] China's leaders have admitted AIDS exists there, and that gay men would have to become part of the solution, not just blamed.[597]

Hong Kong

Time reported (12.14.2008), Although the area had already demonstrated against homophobia, Hong Kong's first official gay-pride parade occurred in December 2008; "in fact, for a country that rarely acknowledges homosexuality, let alone celebrates it, it was downright revolutionary."[598] Over 1,000 parade-goers stopped traffic and filled the streets.[599] The protest marked "the first large-scale event of its kind in any major Chinese city (only Taipei has hosted similar events)."[600]

The road to gay tolerance in Hong Kong has taken a while. An inspector of the Royal Hong Kong Police Force committed suicide in 1980, before other officers were about to arrest him for homosexual activities; the ordeal started a discussion on legalizing homosexuality, which was decriminalized a decade later.[601] Until 2005, the legal age of consent for gays was 21, but 16 for heterosexuals; even in 2008, this law was not yet formally repealed. And non-heterosexuals rarely appear in Hong Kong media, and if they do they are viewed as effeminate, flamboyant, perverted or as AIDS carriers.[602] There is also a lot of pressure in Hong Kong to conform to parental expectations so as to not disappoint.[603] Old Chinese thinking should not be blamed for Chinese homophobia. In fact, Victorian colonial laws (not Chinese) were the first in the area to criminalize homosexuality.[604] In 1901, the British threatened homosexuals with life imprisonment for sodomy and two-years for indecent acts between two men.[605]

Please note: I felt it important to include a chapter that would inform some and re-inform others of some events and spoken words of our past. They speak for themselves. This chapter was researched and written by Karl McCarty, a university honors graduate and a former student of mine.

Chapter Six: A Trail of Tears: Earlier, Wider, Longer and Meaner

Karl McCarty

The following is an overview of various types of hatred, bigotry, and violence in the United States from Columbus to the 1960s. It is a brief synopsis on major events and people signifying the worst cases of cultural hatred.

Described below are historical events. The quotes of leaders mentioned below are offensive, but are included to illustrate the degree at which prejudice and hatred has dominated U.S. History.

COLUMBUS

Columbus "Discovers" America

On Columbus's first voyage to what would become known as the Americas, he landed in the Caribbean (1492).[606] The Caribbean islands' natives were Arawaks. Columbus kidnapped several to take back to Spain, few of which survived the trip.[607]

In 1493 he intended to plunder Haiti.[608] Accordingly, in his second voyage back, he went to Haiti and intensified his aggression. Columbus's appalling activities have been well-documented in James W. Loewen's national bestseller *Lies My Teacher Told Me*. The Spaniards took what they wanted from the natives (from food to sex).[609] Columbus's subordinates were rewarded with the ability to rape native women.[610] Ears and noses were cut off to teach a lesson.[611]

During this time frame, Columbus put down Arawak rebellions by using dogs to hunt the locals and tear them apart.[612] In Ferdinand Columbus's biography of his father, the Arawak-killing dogs were described.[613]

Hatred Justified By Greed

Rather than a noble quest for new land, Columbus's foray into the Western Hemisphere was primarily selfish. Today, textbooks still downplay wealth as a major, if not *the*, reason Columbus set sail in 1492.[614] Documents from those who actually accompanied Columbus suggest wealth was the main goal. Indeed, Michele de Cuneo wrote (1495) about Columbus's Haiti expedition for gold the year before, "which was the main reason he [Columbus] had started on so great a voyage of so many dangers."[615]

Worse yet, the economic justification was cloaked in religion. Some argue Columbus and his royal sponsors were devout Catholics.[616] After the Spaniards would come to a "new" island and met a new native tribe, the Spaniards read the Requirement. The Requirement asked the natives to recognize the Catholic Church, "If you do not do it, I tell you that with the help of God I will enter powerfully against you all...I will take your women and children and make them slaves...."[617] The Requirement was Grade-A cruelty. It was read out loud in Spanish.[618] Second, it was a classic example of self-delusion. The Spanish Catholics were absolved from guilt. They had offered natives a chance for conversion. Given the natives didn't listen (when in fact they couldn't understand), the Spaniards and Columbus could do whatever they pleased.

Hatred was masked in divinity and cognitive dissonance. Accordingly, Columbus initially said the natives were "well built" and had "good customs," then needing to justify their enslavement, he later called them "cruel," "stupid" and "warlike."[619]

Columbus started raiding the Caribbean of its locals to sell into slavery on a mass scale, and sent 500 Arawaks to Spain in 1495.[620] By the end of his life, Columbus may have sent as many as 5,000 slaves across the Atlantic,[621] making him one of the worst slave traders in the Americas.

LESSONS FROM MASSACHUSETTS

Puritans Kicked Out Roger Williams

The Puritans settled in Massachusetts in search of religious freedom, but did not offer that freedom to non-Puritans.[622] Baptists and Quakers were forced to leave the colony,[623] as was Roger Williams, who preached for separation between church and state.[624] Williams also said colonists shouldn't settle on land unless it was purchased from Native Americans.[625] He was banished from the colony, and in 1636 Williams started the colony of Rhode Island, which was land purchased from Native Americans.[626] All Christians were allowed in Rhode Island, and so were Jews.[627] There, church remained separate from government,[628] but not in Massachusetts.

Hutchinson Forced Out From Massachusetts Bay Colony

By the time Williams left Massachusetts, Anne Hutchinson became another problem for the Puritans. Hutchinson (1591-1643)[629] was born in England and came to Massachusetts with her family in 1634.[630] She married William Hutchinson in 1612, and had 14 children.[631] Their firstborn led them to move from England to Boston.[632]

Her intelligence was respected in the community, but she ran into trouble when she was considered outspoken.[633] Fascinated by theology, Hutchinson began to hold discussion groups after Sunday services.[634] The meetings she organized were for Boston women, but many community leaders eventually attended,[635] such as Governor Henry Vane.[636]

She started to openly criticize Puritan ministers' interpretation of the Bible. Her following grew, so authorities put her on trial.[637] Attitudes on

Hutchinson divided. She lost a great deal of support when Governor Vane lost his position to John Winthrop.[638] Winthrop was a colonial Puritan statesman who was the first governor of Massachusetts Bay from 1629 to 1634, then later served again three different times.[639]

Where Hutchinson got into trouble was her logic on faith. She started to openly suggest that the efficacy of faith and grace would bring salvation.[640] This belief struck at the heart of the Puritanical principal that good works was the key to salvation.[641] Indeed, because of grace, her opinion seemed to negate the need for institutionalized religion and law.[642] Thus, opponents said she was attacking the rigidity of Puritanical code in New England.[643]

Hutchinson was a threat to the major powers of Massachusetts Bay: the Puritan Clergy and the civil authorities.[644] In her realm, God could be revealed without the clergy.[645] Thus, she was bashed publicly as a threat to God's virtues, but privately the religious establishment of Massachusetts was really worried about their potential loss of power. Accordingly, her opponents labeled her an Antinomian because she "rejected" moral laws, and branded her immoral.

She believed beliefs and conduct were between that person and God.[646] If Hutchinson was correct, who needed John Winthrop or the local government?[647] Not surprisingly, John Winthrop said women could do irreparable damage to themselves if they kept thinking about such theological matters.[648] John Cotton also led the opposition claiming Hutchinson was a heretic.[649] Cotton was a Puritan deacon, priest and author, who initially was quite liberal in his teachings and supported Hutchinson, but then supported her excommunication.[650]

Winthrop presided over the General Court of Massachusetts' trial against Hutchinson.[651] She was charged for "traducing the ministers."[652] Winthrop's cohorts had her excommunicated and kicked out of the Massachusetts Bay Colony.[653] Ordered to leave, she went to Rhode Island and started a new settlement (Portsmouth).[654] She was later killed in a Native American attack.[655]

Hatred Masked By Fear: Salem Witch Trials (1690s)

A witchcraft craze expanded Europe from the 1300s to the 1600s.[656] In Europe, the "hundreds of thousands of supposed witches—mostly women—were executed." The hysteria briefly occurred in the U.S. in the 1690s in the village of Salem, Massachusetts.[657] The peak came around 1693 when about 150 people were accused of witchcraft.[658] The accused witches were both male and female, and twenty of the accused were killed.[659]

In Salem, Reverend Samuel Parris' daughter Elizabeth (age 9) and his niece started odd behaviors such and screaming, throwing objects and contorting themselves is strange positions.[660] Another girl had similar issues.[661] Meanwhile, a local doctor blamed the supernatural.[662]

Within a month, magistrates pressured for a cause and the girls blamed three women: a homeless beggar (Sarah Good); Reverend Parris' slave, a

Caribbean by the name of Tituba; and a poor elderly woman (Sarah Osborne).[663] Though Good and Osborne said they were innocent, Tituba said, "The Devil came to me and bid me serve him."[664] All three women were put in jail, and paranoia spread and by June 1893 supposed "witches" were being hanged.[665]

A respected minister, Cotton Mather, said the local courts should not be using vague evidence in the testimonies, but by September another 18 were hanged.[666] Cotton's father, Increase Mather, the president of Harvard, famously said, "It were better that ten suspected witches should escape than one innocent person be condemned."[667] When Governor Phipps' wife was accused of witchcraft, he listened to the Mathers and abolished the courts set up for witch trials.[668] By May of 1693, Phipps pardoned all who were imprisoned of witchcraft charges.[669] But 200 had been jailed.[670] None of the accused witches were burned at the stake, one was pressed to death and the remaining 19 were hanged.[671]

The *History Channel*'s research has found that accusers were "always young girls not puritanical men," as many have previously believed.[672] And surviving family members of the victims were given some financial restitution about 20 years after the trials.[673]

What caused the witch trials?

There are many reasons for the hysteria, including the notion that the young accusers enjoyed the publicity from their accusations. In addition, a 1976 article in *Science* claimed the rye and wheat-based fungus ergot contaminated foods leading to the muscle spasms, vomiting and delusions.[674] Because Salem was near swampy meadows, the fungus thrived.[675] The trials serve as a strong reminder of how quick religious zealotry can be misused to hate those being incorrectly blamed. They also remind us science might provide a legitimate answer to the unexplained.

NATIVISM IN THE MID-1800s

The Know Nothings

The American Party originated as a major third party in the 1850s, but it had its roots a decade prior.[676] They were commonly known as Know-Nothings, because secret party regulations required members to respond they "knew nothing" when asked about their party.[677] They were anti-immigrant, particularly anti-German and anti-Irish.[678] The American Party supported the position that foreigners shouldn't vote until having lived in the U.S. for 21 years.[679]

The American Party had initial success in Massachusetts, and then spread to other northern states in 1854.[680] The new third party was aided by the dissolution of the Whig Party, who ran their last credible presidential candidate in the 1852 election.[681] By 1860, the Whigs, as the opposition to the present-day Democratic Party established by Andrew Jackson, were fully replaced by the new Republican Party. The American Party served as go-between the Whig's demise and rise of the Republican Party. When the Republicans ran their first presidential candidate in 1856, they lost. John C. Fremont won only 33% of the national vote in 1856.[682] The bigoted Know-Nothings, represented by former Whig and former President Millard Fillmore, finished in third but with substantial support.

Nativist Popularity

Know-Nothings were secretive partially because their beliefs initially went against the traditional U.S. attitudes toward immigration.[683] The colonies' success was based on foreign exploration and immigration. But European issues made many cross the Atlantic by the mid-1850s (which by that time three million Germans and Irish came to America because of political unrest and famine).[684] It's estimated the influx of Germans and Irish accounted for ten to fifteen percent of the U.S. population at the time.[685]

The base of Know Nothings was broad. Many disaffected wage-earners thought immigrants were taking jobs.[686] Others concluded immigrants were a tax burden who simultaneously offended Protestants.[687] Prohibitionists appalled by their version of the stereotypical drunken-Irish clung to this nativist party. In addition, strategically, Southerners feared the continued influx of Irish and Germans to the North would eventually weaken the political power of the South.[688]

Because slavery was such a divisive issue by the 1850s, some in the political realm thought the anti-immigration beliefs of the Know-Nothings would actually override the slavery issue and unite the country by using anti-immigrant racism.[689] To some extent, that almost happened in the 1856 presidential election.

Irish Suffered Worse

The Irish suffered more because they tended to settle in the cities. For example, according to *American Heritage*, "The Irish made up 30 percent of New York's population and accounted for 70 percent of the city's charity recipients and half its arrests."[690] The Irish Catholics were the outsiders, as the U.S. in the 1850s was fundamentally Protestant.[691] The Germans had a tendency to settle on farms in the frontier,[692] and politically and perceptually, may have been seen as less intrusive.

Some have concluded the hatred for Irish was rooted in political hacking. For example, the Democratic Party was known to exchange jobs for the Irish votes, and some states even ignored naturalization laws and let the Irish vote.[693] Thus, Republicans and anti-slavery Northerners became disgusted because Irish who settled in northern cities voted Democrat, giving the South an advantage in Congress with northern support for the party.[694]

Nativists also joined gangs (sometimes named after Native American tribes) and, more specifically street gangs, particularly in New York. Anti-Irish attitudes were so heated churches were burned and Catholic clergy were brutalized.[695] Gangs continued to persecute Catholics even after the fall of the Know Nothings. Indeed, anti-Irish riots occurred in Baltimore and a cathedral was burned in Philadelphia.[696] Meanwhile, Massachusetts voters went as far to endorse literacy tests to vote.[697]

Who chastised Know-Nothings?

There were leaders with bold opinions against them. Abraham Lincoln wrote, "I am not a Know-Nothing. That is certain.... As a nation, we began by declaring that '*all men are created equal.*' We now practically read it 'all men are created equal *except negroes.*' When the Know-Nothings get control, it will read 'all men are created equal except negroes *and foreigners and Catholics.*'"[698] However, "Abraham Lincoln and the future secretary of state William Seward were practically alone among the Republican leadership in their abhorrence of the Know Nothings."[699]

Nativism Not Just For Know-Nothings

The American Party nominated former President Millard Fillmore, who was pro-slavery,[700] a position not accepted by all in the party in 1856. Indeed, their party convention decided to support the Kansas-Nebraska Act and eventually "split the party in two."[701] But Fillmore won over a fifth of the votes in the country and carried Maryland's electoral votes.[702] The Know-Nothings fizzled out from a party perspective, yet its bigotry was converted to other issues and parties over the next 100 years.

Furthermore, John C. Fremont was the Republican candidate in 1856 who had nativist tendencies, but won many Midwestern German immigrants because his "handlers cleverly kept his nativism quiet."[703] This is an important fact because the bigotry represented in Know-Nothings is not limited to the 1850s or just to Know Nothings. Fremont was nativist, and James Buchanan won the 1856 election by winning the South, a bastion for white supremacy.

NATIVE AMERICANS

The Declaration Against "Indian Savages"

The cultural hatred towards Native Americans is evident in early U.S. historical documents. The Declaration of Independence warns: "The history of the present King of Great Britain is a history of repeated injuries and usurpations, all having in direct object the establishment of an absolute tyranny over these states. To prove this, let facts be submitted to a candid world."[704] One of those facts was that the King "...has excited domestic insurrections amongst us, and has endeavored to bring on the inhabitants of our frontiers, the merciless Indian savages, whose known rule of warfare, is undistinguished destruction of all ages, sexes and conditions."[705]

Andrew Jackson's Eclectic Group

In the War of 1812, General Andrew Jackson's militia in the Battle of New Orleans was one of the most diverse units in US military history. It included Germans, Irishmen, Spaniards, Cajuns, Italians, and Portuguese and Norwegian seamen.[706] Jackson also fought with a pirate (Jean Lafitte), along with some slaves, and some freed slaves; even Jackson's drummer boy was a teenager and former Georgian slave.[707] Stephen Ambrose concluded "Jackson put together the first multiracial army," with the exception that it had no women.[708] As multicultural as Jackson was in the War of 1812, he was just the opposite with his treatment of Native Americans.

Andrew Jackson vs. Cherokee

In the first half of the 1800s, many Americans believed the area from the Missouri River to the Rocky Mountains (at the time known as "The Great American Desert") would be a sufficient reservation for the Native Americans.[709] Andrew Jackson and Martin Van Buren supported the so-called "Indian removal," and sold it as an effort to protect Native Americans from fraud and said the government policy for removal was humane,[710] a complete contradiction given that many in the U.S. concluded where the Native Americans were to be displaced was a desert.

The Cherokee were from Georgia, and were even considered highly developed by then-contemporary standards. They had schools, mills, and even turnpikes.[711] The Cherokee National Council even adopted a constitution (1827) to govern itself.[712] Their convention used principles of the U.S. Constitution, established a representative government, and outlined the boundaries of the Cherokee Nation.[713] Their 1827 constitution also showed Cherokee desire to protect their lands.[714] They pushed for a strong centralized government.[715]

The Georgia government threatened to take Cherokee lands in the 1820s, so they hired lawyers and sued in a trial that reached the U.S. Supreme Court.[716] Chief Justice John Marshall actually sided with the Cherokee instead of Georgia.[717] But President Jackson refused to follow out the decision: "Marshall has made his opinion, now let him enforce it."[718] Jackson sent the army to kick them out of their homes and into Arkansas and Oklahoma (at the time called Indian Territory).[719] The U.S. enforced the Treaty of Enchota with the Cherokees in 1838, thus evicting 17,000 Cherokees to present-day Oklahoma.[720] About 4,000 Cherokees died in the process,[721] either from starvation and sickness during this "Trail of Tears."[722]

Other tribes were relocated or killed as well. By 1840, the only Native Americans living east of the Mississippi River was the Seminoles hiding in the Everglades of Florida, but their Chief Osceola was eventually tricked into being captured and died in prison.[723]

Treaty of Ghent Precedent

Very few publicly opposed what Jackson did to Native Americans. Henry Clay said Jackson's attitude was a stain on the nation's honor, and many Methodists and Quakers opposed the relocation.[724]

In December 1829, Jackson used his annual message to Congress to ask for legislation to remove Native Americans west of the Mississippi River.[725]

Congress responded by passing the Indian Removal Act in 1830.[726] Clay responded to Jackson's plea on December 17, 1829 in a speech given in his home state of Kentucky.[727] Clay said Native Americans were inferior to Whites, but he defended their legal rights and said the federal government should treat them humanely.[728]

Clay based his legal justification from the Treaty of Ghent, which ended the War of 1812.[729] Clay helped negotiate the treaty with the British, and claimed Jackson's proposal would be against previous U.S. policy.[730] Clay spoke of the short history of the US and its treatment of Native Americans:

> Hitherto, since the United States became an independent power among the nations of the earth, they have generally treated the Indians with justice, and performed towards them all the offices of humanity. Their policy, in this respect, was vindicated during the negotiations at Ghent, and the principles which guided them in their relations with the Indians, were then promulgated to all Christendom. On that occasion, their representatives, holding up their conduct in advantageous contrast with that of Great Britain, and the other powers of Europe, said: ". . . . the Indians residing within the United States are *so far independent*, that they live under their *own customs and not under the laws of the United States*; that their rights upon the lands where they inhabit or hunt, are *secured* to them by boundaries defined in *amicable treaties* between the United States and themselves; and that whenever those boundaries are varied, it is also by *amicable and voluntary treaties*, by which they receive from the United States ample compensation for every right they have to the land ceded by them…." Such was the solemn annunciation to the whole world, of the principles and of the system, regulating our relations with the Indians, as admitted by us and recognized by them. There can be no violation of either, to the disadvantage of the weak party, which will not subject us, as a nation, to the just reproaches of all good men, and which may not bring down upon us the maledictions of a more exalted and powerful tribunal.[731]

Jackson's position on the Cherokees is appalling. Not only was it inhumane, it was unconstitutional. The President didn't listen to the U.S. Supreme Court. Not only was it arrogant, it was worthy of impeachment. Certain limits of civil rights have been approved during a time of war (as we see in WWI and WWII), what makes Jackson's position on Native Americans so astonishing is that the justification for racism can't be cloaked in "national security."

Clay never became president, and Jackson was put on the twenty dollar bill.

Previous Thoughts On Native American Treatment

Minister Roger Williams (who founded Rhode Island after being removed from Massachusetts Bay because of his religious beliefs) said Native Americans should be fairly compensated for their lands.[732] Likewise, William Penn (1644-1718), who founded the colony of Pennsylvania, was a Quaker who insisted on fair dealings with Native Americans.[733] Thus, Andrew Jackson's disregard for Native American rights was not the only viable solution in the 1830s. Respect for natives was shown by leaders two hundred years before Jackson became the seventh president.

California Natives Abused

The Spanish missionaries in California elminated California native lifestyle as it was known. The Roman Catholic Priests, known as Padres, demanded heavy labor from the natives and even separated them from their children.[734] Coastal California tribes had to abandon their lands in exchange for horrid labor camps at the request of the missionaries.[735] Resistance among natives did occur, as a San Diego Padre was poisoned in 1804.[736] A third of the California aboriginal population died because of the missions.[737] It is estimated that present-day California had 300,000 natives living in the region before the 1500s and European exploration.[738]

By the 1820s, Spain was losing control of South America, so the new nation of Mexico controlled California, which then became a U.S. territory after the U.S.-Mexican War in the 1840s. As the U.S. went into the territory, the U.S. Army killed natives. Indeed, in 1846, John C. Fremont commanded U.S. Army forces, which murdered and attacked native villages near the Sacramento River.[739] Fremont later won the 1856 Republican nomination for president.

Government and settler treatment of Native Americans worsened after gold was discovered in California. Within the first year of the gold rush, 100,000 new settlers came at the price native livelihood.[740] Vigilante groups sprung up in the effort to kill Native Americans for the miners.[741] Within a couple of years, another estimated 100,000 Indians were killed by miners in California.[742] By the mid 1850s, there were only 70,000 natives left in California.[743]

The Natives of the Plains

There were some bright spots of heroics among natives against the U.S. government. The Nez Perce marched 1,500 miles under Chief Joseph in 1877, but their capture was bound to happen.[744] When he surrendered, Chief Joseph said "Our chiefs are killed…The little children are freezing to death. My people…have no blankets, no food."[745]

The result was worse in the Dakotas. Gold was discovered in the Dakota Territory in the mid 1870s, and miners came into traditional areas of the Sioux and Cheyenne.[746] The Sioux were led by Chiefs Sitting Bull and Crazy Horse, who both began attacking settlers by 1876.[747] These conflicts were a tipping point at Little Bighorn River, where a large group of Sioux and Cheyenne were camped, then attacked, and responded by killing General George Custer and his men.[748] The Sioux only won brief breathing room, and by 1881 they surrendered to the Army.[749] Then in December 1890, nearly 200 unarmed Native Americans were killed at Wounded Knee, South Dakota.[750]

***The Wonderful Wizard of Oz* & Native Americans**

L. Frank Baum published a weekly newspaper in Aberdeen, South Dakota from January 1890 to March 1891.[751] The *Saturday Pioneer* was obscure,[752] but Baum's comments on Native Americans are vivid. A decade later, he would start his rise to legendary status as the child book author of *The Wonderful Wizard of Oz*.

His racism has been validated by mainstream media. NPR reported (Aug.2006), "In the late 1800s, L. Frank Baum, author of *The Wizard of Oz*, wrote racist editorials in a South Dakota newspaper, calling for the extermination of Native Americans."[753]

Baum responded to actions of the Sioux twice (December 1890 and January 1891).[754] The first Baum editorial was reaction to the murder of Sioux leader Sitting Bull in mid-December 1890.[755] It was published just days after Sitting Bull was killed. In this initial editorial, Baum called for the total destruction of the Sioux.[756] Specifically, Baum suggested the saftey of White settlers was dependent on exterminating the remaining Native Americans:

> The Whites, by law of conquest, by justice of civilization, are masters of the American continent, and the best safety of the frontier settlements will be secured by the total annihilation of the few remaining Indians. Why not annihilation? Their glory has fled, their spirit broken, their manhood effaced; better that they die than live the miserable wretches that they are. History would forget these latter despicable beings, and speak, in later ages of the glory of these grand Kings of forest and plain that Cooper loved to heroism.[757]

Baum added, "We cannot honestly regret their extermination…"[758] Some claim the Baum editorial "sparked the Wounded Knee massacre of 1890."

Baum's Opinion on Wounded Knee

On December 28, 1890, the Sioux were captured at Wounded Knee Creek in southwestern South Dakota.[759] When they were surrendering their weapons the next day, a shot was fired and the U.S. Seventh Calvary opened fire.[760] Just how many Sioux were killed has been disputed (at least 150, maybe as much as 350).[761] Baum's editorial on Wounded Knee was very critical of the US military. But not because their effect on the Sioux, but because it was poorly executed:

> The peculiar policy of the government in employing so weak and vacillating a person as General Miles to look after the uneasy Indians, has resulted in a terrible loss of blood to our soldiers, and a battle which, at its best, is a disgrace to the war department. There has been plenty of time for prompt and decisive measures, the employment of which would have prevented this disaster.[762]

In this second editorial on Native Americans (published January 3, 1891), Baum restated his support for extermination:

> The Pioneer has before declared that our only safety depends upon the total extirmination [sic] of the Indians. Having wronged them for centuries we had better, in order to protect our civilization, follow it up by one more wrong and wipe these untamed and untamable creatures from the face of the earth. In this lies future safety for our settlers and the soldiers who are under incompetent commands. Otherwise, we may expect future years to be as full of trouble with the redskins as those have been in the past.[763]

This editorial was separated by a line, under which read a quote: "An eastern contemporary, with a grain of wisdom in its wit, says that 'when the whites win a fight, it is a victory, and when the Indians win it, it is a massacre.'"[764] It is unclear whether this quote was cryptic, sarcastic, or both, but it is most certainly an additional commentary on Wounded Knee.

In 2006, Baum's family offered a public apology.[765]

TR Thought Natives were Inferior

In *The Winning of the West*, Teddy Roosevelt discussed the necessity of the conquest, writing, "All men of sane and wholesome thought must dismiss with impatient contempt the plea that these continents should be reserved for the use of scattered savage tribes, whose life was but a few degrees less meaningless, squalid, and ferocious than that of the wild beasts with whom they held joint ownership."[766]

TR concluded: "The most ultimately righteous of all wars is a war with savages, though it is apt to be also the most terrible and inhuman. The rude, fierce settler who drives the savage from the land lays all civilized mankind under a debt to him."[767] He reaffirmed his belief with his perception of history: "American and Indian, Boer and Zulu, Cossack and Tartar, New Zealander and Maori,—in each case the victor, horrible though many of his deeds are, has laid deep the foundations for the future greatness of a mighty people."[768]

TR's belief that natives were inferior is surprising, given his amicable relationship with African-American leader Booker T. Washington (see below).

CHINESE AMERICANS

Chinese Come to America

After gold was discovered in California in 1849, a subsequent demand for cheap labor brought the Chinese to work in gold fields and then construction on the Central Pacific Railroad.[769] The Chinese were often given harsh treatment while working on the railroad, and were more likely to be given difficult tasks, like using dynamite. In the early 1850s, there were 25,000 Chinese on the Pacific Coast, who in the 1860s came at a rate of 4,000 annually.[770] By the 1870s, there were over 75,000.[771]

California Response to Chinese

In the 1850s California Supreme Court ruling, *People v. Hall*, it was determined that Chinese immigrants had no rights to testify against white citizens. The ruling was based on an earlier act passed which stated, "No Black, or Mulatto person, or Indian, shall be allowed to give evidence in favor of, or against a white man."[772]

Labor leaders in California reinforced racism against the Chinese. Denis Kearney and H.L. Knight both represented the California's Workingmen's Party in the 1870s.[773] They gave an address in which they concluded the Chinese were a race of "cheap working slaves," [774] and:

> These cheap slaves fill every place. Their dress is scant and cheap. Their food is rice from China. They hedge twenty in a room, ten by ten. They are wipped curs, abject in docility, mean, contemptible and obedient in all things. They have no wives, children or dependents....They are imported by companies, controlled as serfs, worked like slaves,

and at last go back to China with all their earnings. They are in every place, they seem to have no sex. Boys work, girls work; it is all alike to them.[775]

Of course, Kearney and Knight said they were calm and rational: “Do not believe those who call us savages, rioters, incendiaries, and outlaws. We seek our ends calmly, rationally, at the ballot box. So far good order has marked all our proceedings. But, we know how false, how inhuman, our adversaries are.”[776]

Chinese Exclusion Act

In 1882, Congress suspended Chinese immigration from China for a decade,[777] as the act made a 10-year moratorium on Chinese labor immigration.[778] The Chinese Exclusion Act of 1882 effectively banned the entrance of Chinese immgrants to the U.S., a policy later reinforced and lasting until the 1940s. The 1882 bill was signed by Republican President Chester A. Arthur.[779]

The Democratic Party on Chinese

The 1876 Democratic Party Platform stated, “We, the delegates of the Democratic party of the United States . . . demand such modification of the treaty with the Chinese Empire, or such legislation within constitutional limitations, as shall prevent further importation or immigration of the Mongolian race.”[780] This was backed up in 1880, when the platform demanded, “No more Chinese immigration, except for travel, education, and foreign commerce, and that even carefully guarded.”[781]

In 1884, the Democratic platform said, “American civilization demands that against the immigration or importation of Mongolians to these shores our gates be closed.”[782] Nearly a generation later in 1900, the Democratic Party was still defiant against the Chinese, with its platform stating, “We favor the continuance and strict enforcement of the Chinese exclusion law, and its application to the same classes of all Asiatic races.”[783] Then in 1908, with William Jennings Bryan as their presidential nominee, the platform stated, “We are opposed to the admission of Asiatic immigrants who can not be amalgamated with our population, or whose presence among us would raise a race issue and involve us in diplomatic controversies with Oriental powers.”[784]

THE WAR WITH SPAIN

Where are the Philippines?

When President William McKinley signed the war resolution with Spain, it was the only time in history Congress voted for war without presidential request.[785] Teddy Roosevelt said, perhaps appropriately, McKinley “has no more backbone than a chocolate éclair.”[786]

Eventually McKinley succumbed to the pressures of war. McKinley didn’t even know where the Philippines were located before the Spanish-American War (1898), and said he could not place the islands on a map:[787] “I could not have told where those darned islands were within two thousand miles.”[788]

By the end of the Spanish American War, the U.S. had taken over Cuba, Guam, Puerto Rico and the Philippines—all from the Spanish Empire. In addition, during the imperialistic fervor, the U.S. annexed Hawaii. But during the post-war phase, a major focus came on what to do with the Filipinos. Should they be given independence? Or should the U.S. control the archipelago? The Spanish American War, after all, started as an effort to liberate the Cubans from harsh Spanish rule. The war ended in Filipino suppression courtesy of the U.S.

***Civilized* U.S. Should Expand**

The support for the U.S. expansionism movement in the late 1800s was significant, as it included many in government, clergy, and military.

Some felt the U.S. was the most civilized. Sen. Albert Beveridge said God made Americans "the master organizers of the world," to rule over "savage and senile" people.[789] He said the Philippines should be the United States forever.[790] These attitudes were reinforced by Rev. Josiah Strong from Ohio, a Social Darwinist who wanted church missions all over the world. Strong said America would dominate South America, Mexico, and Africa because U.S. domination would represent the survival of the fittest in the ensuing race competition.[791]

McKinley's Divine Intervention

After the Spanish-American War, President McKinley wrestled with the issue of what to do with the islands. McKinley said it would be "criminal aggression" to annex the Philippines.[792] He changed his mind, and told the story of his conversion to the Methodist Episcopal Church's missionary committee (who were imperialists).[793]

McKinley said he "went down on my knees and prayed to Almighty God for light and guidance."[794] Guidance came. McKinley said there were four main points that came to him. First, it would be cowardly to give the Philippines back to Spain; second, the islands couldn't be given to "commercial rivals" like the French or Germans in the Orient; third, "we could not leave them to themselves—they were unfit for self-government—and they would soon have anarchy and misrule over there worse than Spain's was." This third point was remarkably ethnocentric. The Philippines, *them*, couldn't be left to *themselves*.[795] The President's logic was incredibly ignorant. *Them* Filipinos were not a homogenous group: the archipelago was 7,100 islands of seven million people who spoke 87 different languages and dialects.[796]

With all of McKinley's divine logic, his fourth point spoken to the missionary committee was most disturbing: "...there was nothing left for us to do but to take them all, and to educate the Filipinos, and uplift them and civilize and Christianize them, and by God's grace do the very best we could for them, as our fellow-men for whom Christ also died."[797] Harold Evans has aptly pointed out "the small detail that nearly all the nontribal population of about 7 million were already members of the Roman Catholic Church."[798] Christianizing attempts of the islands had started in the 1500s.[799]

Mark Twain Recognized Christian Hypocrisy

The shortsideness of the likes of McKinley was recognized by contemporaries. In an essay titled "Greetings from the Nineteenth to the Twentieth Century," Mark Twain was sarcastic toward imperialist powers, including the U.S.: "I bring you the stately nation named Christendom, returning bedraggled, besmirched, dishonored, from pirate raids into KiaoChou, Manchuria, South Africa, and the Philippines, with her soul full of meanness, her pocket full of boodle, and her mouth full of pious hypocrisies. Give her soap and a towel, but hide the looking glass."[800]

Filipino "Insurrection"

Soon the Filipinos recognized they weren't going to get independence, and fighting broke out between Filipinos and the U.S. by February of 1899.[801] A military effort that began to liberate the Cubans from the oppressive Spanish ended as a U.S. war against Filipinos who wanted independence. Mark Twain said the U.S. flag should be black with skull and crossbones.[802] Three years and 60,000 U.S. soldiers were required to put down the Filipino's revolt led by Emilio Aguinaldo.[803]

Andrew Carnegie told a friend in the government, "You seem to have finished your work civilizing the Filipinos; it is thought about 8,000 of them have been completely civilized and sent to heaven. I hope you like it."[804] Historian Stephen Ambrose later concluded, "the tactics the American army used in suppressing the Philippine 'Insurrection' of 1898 to 1901 were almost Nazi-like."[805]

Nonetheless, McKinley, before being assassinated, was convinced there would be no exploitation: "The Philippines are ours, not to exploit but to develop, to civilize, to educate, to train in the science of self-government."[806] After the insurrection was quelled on the islands, English replaced Spanish, and American businesses sold their goods tariff-free in the foreign archipelago.[807] No exploitation, of course.

Even Anti-Imperialist Thought Filipinos Were Inferior

The 1896 and 1900 Democratic presidential nominee, William Jennings Bryan, spoke for the Filipinos and their independence: "The Filipinos cannot be citizens without endangering our civilization; they cannot be subjects without imperiling our form of government."[808] Thus, ironically, Bryan supported the islands independence not because they knew best, but because they were inferior. This was a poor rhetorical argument for Bryan. Bryan's opposition (the imperialists) said if it appeared the Filipinos could use an education in democracy, the U.S. should be the islands' mentor.[809] Now, with Bryan's help, both imperialists and anti-imperialists were convinced the Filipinos were inferior. Of all people, Bryan—McKinley's two-time opponent—helped the warmongers justify the colonization of the Philippines.

Meanwhile, In Cuba

Meanwhile, Cuba was not given independence either after the 1898 war with Spain. Cuba was made a protectorate controlled by the US. As William Allen White editorialized in Kansas's *Emporia Gazette*, "Only Anglo-Saxons can govern themselves. The Cubans will need despotic government for many years to restrain anarchy until Cuba is filled with Yankees."[810] Accordingly, General Leonard Wood directed military rule on Cuba for four years.[811]

Filipino Ending

It seems the anti-U.S. attitude on the islands started to change after 1901, when future President William Howard Taft was appointed the islands' Governor by President Teddy Roosevelt.[812] Taft has been described as "genuinely devoted to the interests of the island people."[813] He was also devoted to improving the treatment of Afro-Americans in the U.S.

ANTI-SEMITISM

General Grant Clears Out Jews

In late 1862, General Ulysses Grant issued General Order No. 11, which expelled Jews from Kentucky, Tennessee and Mississippi.[814] The order said: "The Jews, as a class violating every regulation of trade established by the Treasury Department and also department orders, are hereby expelled … within twenty-four hours from the receipt of this order."[815] Grant's order attacked an entire race and tied them to the illegal black market cotton trade when only a handful of the illegal traders were in fact Jewish.[816] Grant said, "the Israelites" were "an intolerable nuisance."[817]

There were about 30 Jewish families in Paducah, Kentucky ordered to leave in 24 hours; all of these Paducah Jews were long-term residents, none of them speculators, and two were Union Army veterans.[818] Within weeks President Lincoln asked Gen. Grant's order be revoked.[819]

The brief expulsion of Jews serves as a vivid reminder of the ease at which discrimination occurs during war.

Louis Brandeis

On January 28, 1916, Louis Brandeis became the first Jewish judge on the US Supreme Court.[820] The vacancy occurred because Associate Justice Joseph Rucker Lamar died.[821] Brandeis was more progressive than the justice he replaced, as he opposed the same railroad trusts Lamar defended.[822]

Why was Brandeis nominated?

President Wilson's reelection was coming up in 1916. Brandeis was of German heritage and could appease German-Americans anxious of anti-Germany feelings in the U.S. due to World War I.[823] Perhaps President Wilson knew Dembitz was Brandeis' middle name.[824] And Brandeis completed his secondary education in Germany.[825] Nominating a progressive could also win over Teddy

Roosevelt supporters from 1912 and address the growing support for organized labor.[826]

Was Brandeis Qualified?

His resume was very impressive. When Brandeis graduated from Harvard Law School in 1877, he did so at the head of his class "with the highest marks of any student ever to have attended the school until that time."[827] He had a great legal mind, and was also one of the founders of the Harvard Law Review.[828]

In Boston, he was known as "the people's attorney" because he took cases pro bono.[829] Early in his legal career, Brandeis helped establish minimum wages for women workers.[830] Also in private practice, he helped enact a state law providing low-cost insurance through savings banks.[831] He also defended municipal control of Boston's subway system.[832] He developed the "Brandeis Brief," which was an appellate report analyzing cases on economic and social evidence instead of just legal precedents. [833] He often pursued cases mixed with politics, and represented small companies against big corporations.[834] Thus, Brandeis fought the social ills brought on by the industrialization of the country, and was an appropriate nominee to the Supreme Court during the Progressive Era.

Brandeis met Wilson during the 1912 presidential campaign.[835] Brandeis was a fitting pick for Wilson and his approach to "New Freedom" policies: they both had liberal views on social policy, but they both thought the federal government should not over-regulate the economy.[836] The major difference was that Wilson's opponent in 1912, Teddy Roosevelt, wanted to rid monopolies by direct regulation; Wilson and Brandeis wanted to make economic competition possible rather than regulating monopolies.[837]

Could a Jew be on the Supreme Court?

Brandeis' main opposition came from former President William Howard Taft and former Secretary of State Elihu Root.[838] Taft's opposition was more ideological. In addition, Harvard President A. Lawarence Lowell (who eventually helped Sacco and Vanzetti to their deaths) opposed Brandeis.[839]

Rumors spread Brandeis was actually a socialist.[840] The *New York Press* called the appointment President Wilson's "worst mistake."[841] The *New York Sun* said he was "ridiculously unfit" to be on the Court.[842] And the *New York Times* questioned the nominee's temperment.[843]

The nominee's ties to Judiasm was the real issue. *The New York Times* noted Brandeis would be the first member of the Court with "Jewish blood."[844] Jeff Kiselhoff has blogged for *The Nation:* "Even *The Nation* wasn't immune to such prejudices. One wishes that the magazine's editor had taken a blue pencil to *The Tattler*'s observation that Brandeis's nose was his most 'obviously Hebraic feature.'"[845] Brandeis wasn't on a hell-bent mission to have Jews control the United States. In a speech given to rabbis in 1915, Brandeis spoke on the issue of Zionism and US patriotism:

Let no American imagine that Zionism is inconsistent with Patriotism. Multiple loyalties are objectionable only if they are inconsistent. A man is a better citizen of the United States for being also a loyal citizen of his state, and of his city; for being loyal to his family, and to his profession or trade; for being loyal to his college or his lodge. Every Irish American who contributed towards advancing home rule was a better man and a better American for the sacrifice he made. Every American Jew who aids in advancing the Jewish settlement in Palestine, though he feels that neither he nor his descendants will ever live there, will likewise be a better man and a better American for doing so."[846]

Brandeis added: "There is no inconsistency between loyalty to America and loyalty to Jewry. The Jewish spirit, the product of our religion and experiences, is essentially modern and essentially American."[847] Furthermore, the Brandeis family was tolerant of Jewish and Christian rituals.[848] And later in life some have described him as a secular humanist.[849]

Brandeis was confirmed in executive session of the Senate by a vote of 47-22 with one Democrat against his confirmation (Francis Newlands of Nevada).[850] However, three Republicans voted in favor.[851] Retired, Brandies died in Washington, D.C. in 1941, after more than two decades of serving on the Court.[852]

Henry Ford's Anti-Semitic Campaign

Henry Ford made great cars at a cheap price, courtesy of his assembly line. In the early 1920s, he considered running for president,[853] and although he decided not to, it's important to understand his notoriety as a businessman in a business era. In the 1910s, Ford was against labor, immigrants, liquor and Jews, and by the end of the decade he bought the *Dearborn Independent* newspaper.[854]

Ford's initial editor refused to run anti-Jewish articles and resigned, but when Ford got a new editor, the *Independent* ran (1920) "The International Jew: The World's Problem," which ran as a continuing series.[855] An August 1921 edition of the *Independent* featured an article: "Jewish Jazz - Moron Music - Becomes our National Music--the Story of Popular Song Control in the United States."[856]

Ford's investigators even claimed Woodrow Wilson took secret orders from Justice Brandeis.[857] In 1927, due to public dissent on his anti-Semitism, Ford had to admit error and publicly ask forgiveness.[858]

AFRO-AMERICANS

Jefferson's View

Thomas Jefferson said (1787) Afro-Americans "are inferior to the whites in the endowments of both of body and mind."[859]

In *Notes on the State of Virginia,* Jefferson wrote Negroes had not produced any scholars or poets, without mentioning it was illegal down South to teach a slave.[860] Jefferson also said the Negroes smelled different, always had sex—but always without love.[861] Stephen Ambrose wrote: Jefferson "said things about these fellow human beings that would make members of a nineteenth- or twentieth-century lynch mob feel comfortable."[862]

The Early Presidents & Slavery

Nine Presidents owned slaves: George Washington (1st), Thomas Jefferson (3rd), James Madison (4th), James Monroe (5th), Andrew Jackson (7th) William Henry Harrison (9th), John Tyler (10th), James K. Polk (11th) and Franklin Pierce (14th).[863] Only Washington freed his slaves.[864] It is customary to defend these early presidents because of current social traditions. That is a poor defense.

Of the first 11 presidents, three did not own slaves. These include John Adams (2nd), his son John Quincy Adams (6th), and Martin Van Buren (8th).

John Adams' son, John Quincy Adams, served in the U.S. House of Representatives for 17 years after serving in the nation's highest office.[865] For years, Adams fought the Gag Rules, which were House resolutions used to keep abolitionist petitions from being read on the floor.[866] John Quincy Adams was also the first congressmen to assert the government's right to free slaves during a time of war, an argument President Lincoln based his Emancipation Proclamation on.[867] Adams' words were very telling (1836): "From the instant your slave-holding states become a theater of war—civil, servile, or foreign—from that instant the war powers of the Constitution extend to interference with the institution of slavery in every way that it can be interfered with."[868]

Adams also openly attacked John Tyler in 1841 on the slavery issue: "Tyler is a political sectarian, of the slave-driving, Virginian, Jefferson school, principled against all improvement, with all the interests and passions and vices of slavery rooted in his moral and political constitution—with talents not above mediocrity."[869]

Martin Van Buren served only one term as president (1837-1841), but ran for president in 1848 for the anti-slavery Free Soil Party.[870] The third party nominated Charles Francis Adams (John Quincy Adam's son) as Vice President, and took ten percent of the popular vote, enough to swing the election.[871]

The Adams family and Van Buren are solid reminders that slavery was not accepted by all.

Andrew Jackson's Cabinet & Afro-Americans

Andrew Jackson's cabinet was racist. For example, John C. Calhoun served as Vice President for both John Quincy Adams and Andrew Jackson.[872] In 1837, Sen. John C. Calhoun said, "I hold that the present state of civilization, where two races of different origin, and distinguished by color, and other physical differences, as well as intellectual, are brought together, the relation now existing in the slaveholding states between the two, is, instead of an evil, a good—a positive good."[873]

Jackson was also instrumental in the promotion of Roger Taney. Courtesy of Jackson, Taney was appointed Attorney General (1831), then Secretary of the Treasury (1833), and finally to the Supreme Court (1836).[874] As Chief Justice of the Supreme Court during the disasterous *Dred Scott v. Sandford* case (1856),

Taney said blacks are "a subordinate and inferior class of beings who had been subjugated by the dominant race."[875]

Abolitionist Persecution

By the 1830s, the anti-slavery cause grew, as leaders like William Lloyd Garrison increased efforts against the southern institution. He started publishing *The Liberator* to get out his message.

Unfortunately, the more boisterous abolitionists were also persecuted—in the North. Garrison was dragged through the streets of Boston.[876] Richard Hofstadter once noted, "Public opinion stigmatized the abolitionists as a band of misguided bigots whose activities would destroy the Union if they were left unchecked."[877] Accordingly throughout the middle of the 1830s, abolitionists were heckled, stoned, tarred and feathered, and lynched.[878] In 1837, an anti-slavery editor in Alton, Illinois was murdered by a mob.[879]

Democratic Party Racism Before And After Civil War

Rep. Andrew Johnson, (D., Tenn.) said (1844) if blacks were given the right to vote it would "place every splay-footed, bandy-shanked, hump-backed, thick-lipped, flat-nosed, woolly-headed, ebon-colored Negro in the country upon an equality with the poor white man."[880] He replaced Lincoln as President in 1865.[881]

Sen. Stephen A. Douglas (D-Ill) declared in 1858, "I hold that a Negro is not and never ought to be a citizen of the United States. I hold that this government was made on the white basis; made by the white men, for the benefit of white men and their posterity forever, and should be administered by white men and none others."[882] He was the Democratic Presidential nominee in 1860.[883]

In 1868, Francis P. Blair Jr of Missouri accepted the Democratic nomination for Vice President: "My fellow citizens, I have said that the contest before us was one for the restoration of our government; it is also one for the restoration of our race. It is to prevent the people of our race from being exiled from their homes—exiled from the government which they formed and created for themselves and for their children, and to prevent them from being driven out of the country or trodden under foot by an inferior and barbarous race."[884] Blair served in the U.S. Senate (1869-1872).[885]

In 1869, Sen. Thomas Hendricks (D-Indiana) said, "While the tendency of the white race is upward, the tendency of the colored race is downward."[886] Hendricks became the Democratic nominee for Vice President in 1876 as Samuel Tilden's running mate.[887] He later became Vice President for President Grover Cleveland (1885).[888]

Press Confirmed Afro-American Inferiority

In 1900, the *New York Times* editorialized:

> "It has of late become the custom of the men of the South to speak with entire candor of the settled and deliberate policy of suppressing the negro vote. They have been forced to choose between a policy of manifest injustice toward the blacks and the horrors of negro

rule. They chose to disfranchise the negroes. That was manifestly the lesser of two evils. . . . The Republican Party committed a great public crime when it gave the right of suffrage to the blacks. . . . So long as the Fifteenth Amendment stands, the menace of the rule of the blacks will impend, and the safeguards against it must be maintained."[889]

Taft Defended Afro-Americans

President William Howard Taft, Teddy Roosevelt's handpicked successor, deserves a lot of respect for his treatment toward Afro-Americans.

In his inaugural address (3.4.1909), President Taft spoke of the South and freed slaves: "The thirteenth amendment secured them freedom; the fourteenth amendment due process of law, protection of property, and the pursuit of happiness; and the fifteenth amendment attempted to secure the negro against any deprivation of the privilege to vote because he was a negro. The thirteenth and fourteenth amendments have been generally enforced and have secured the objects for which they are intended. While the fifteenth amendment has not been generally observed in the past, it ought to be observed, and the tendency of Southern legislation today is toward the enactment of electoral qualifications which shall square with that amendment."[890]

In addition, Taft added: "The negroes are now Americans. Their ancestors came here years ago against their will, and this is their only country and their only flag. They have shown themselves anxious to live for it and to die for it. Encountering the race feeling against them, subjected at times to cruel injustice growing out of it, they may well have our profound sympathy and aid in the struggle they are making. We are charged with the sacred duty of making their path as smooth and easy as we can."[891]

Compared to Taft's replacement (Wilson), Republicans were more favorable to Afro-Americans. Presidents occasionally appointed Afro-Americans as postmasters.[892] And Republican presidents appointed Afro-Americans the port collector for New Orleans and Washington D.C.[893] Afro-Americans had even taken part in the GOP presidential conventions.[894]

Booker T: A Friend of TR, Taft

While Teddy Roosevelt and Taft held the presidency, Booker T. Washington was an unofficial adviser on racial matters and Afro-American political appointments.[895] Roosevelt's attention to Afro-American troubles is noteworthy. In contrast, when TR met with Booker T. Washington, Sen. Ben Tillman (D-S.C.) said, "The action of President Roosevelt in entertaining that nigger will necessitate our killing a thousand niggers in the South before they learn their place again."[896]

Not surprisingly, TR's successor, worked well with Booker T. Washington, who wrote to Taft:

> It was very kind of you to send me word that you wished to consult with me fully and freely on all racial matters during your administration. I assure you I shall be glad to place myself at your service at all times. . . . The greatest satisfaction that has come to me during the administration of President Roosevelt is the fact that perhaps I have been of

some service to him in helping to raise the standard of the colored people, in helping him to see that men holding office under him were men of character and ability. . . .[897]

Likewise, William Howard Taft is considered one Tuskegee's "most influential backers."[898] Tuskegee was Booker T. Washington's institute created to educate Afro-Americans and improve their skills.

Woodrow Wilson Takes Office

When Wilson took office on March 4, 1913, there were many ominous signs for Afro-Americans. Bands all over D.C. played 'Dixie.'[899] The Chief Justice who swore in Wilson was a former KKK member.[900]

In the context of Wilson, one can better appreciate the potential of Strom Thurmond's Dixiecrat candidacy in 1948. Rather than Thurmond enacting a radical racial policy, he would have merely imitated President Wilson from thirty years earlier.[901] Likewise, George Wallace's Independent and racist presidential campaign of 1968 won five southern states. But, like Thurmond, Wallace lost. Wilson actually won, and implemented the policies Thurmond and Wallace could have only dreamed of.

Examples of Wilson's Bigotry

While president at Princeton, Wilson led the only major Northern university to refuse black students.[902] Wilson turned away Afro-American applicants because he regarded their requests for higher education as "unwarranted."[903]

Wilson was a Southerner raised in a climate where the assumption was former slaves were less evolved than Anglo-Saxons.[904] When it came to electoral politics, outside the South, Wilson only won a majority of votes in one state (Arizona) during the 1912 election.[905] Racism was a way of life for Wilson, whose wife told "darky" stories at cabinet meetings.[906]

During Wilson's first term, the U.S. House passed a law making racial intermarriage a felony in Washington D.C.[907] Congress eventually refused to pass Wilson's recommendations to take rights away from Afro-Americans.[908] Because Congress did not validate his position, Wilson did so in his executive bureaucracy.

After the Civil War, Republicans made it possible for Washington's large Afro-American population to work in the federal government.[909] Wilson segregated the federal bureaucracy in the nation's capital.[910] Wilson's Postmaster General made his capital offices to be segregated, as the Navy and Treasury followed.[911] Wilson's segregation was justified by health: under the belief that white government workers had to be protected from diseases from blacks, like venereal diseases.[912]

Wilson required pictures of all applicants for federal jobs. Wilson spun the bigoted logic to black leaders: "The purpose of these measures was to reduce the friction... It is as far as possible from being a movement against the Negroes. I sincerely believe it to be in their interest."[913] Blacks could rightfully infer Wilson was caustic, arrogant, or both. Wilson once told a black delegation: "segregation is not a humiliation but a benefit, and ought to be so regarded by you gentlemen."[914]

Wilson's Democrats

Wilson was backed by his Democratic Party contemporaries. Sen. James Vardaman (D-Miss.) said (1914), "The Negro as a race, in all the ages of the world, has never shown sustained power of self-development. He is not endowed with the creative faculty. . . . He has never created for himself any civilization. . . . He has never had any civilization except that which has been inculcated by a superior race. And it is a lamentable fact that his civilization lasts only so long as he is in the hands of the white man who inculcates it. When left to himself he has universally gone back to the barbarism of the jungle."[915]

Wilson appointed many racists to high positions. As editor of the *Raliegh News & Observer* in 1912, Josephus Daniels said, "The South is serious with regard to its attitude to the Negro in politics. The South understands this subject, and its policy is unalterable and uncompromising. We desire no concessions. We seek no sops. We grasp no shadows on this subject. We take no risks. We abhor a Northern policy of catering to the Negro in politics just as we abhor a Northern policy of social equality."[916] The following year, President Wilson appointed Daniels as Secretary of the Navy.[917] Daniels was widley respected among Democratic circles for years, as FDR appointed him Ambassador to Mexico (1933), and LBJ named the *USS Josephus Daniels* in his honor (1965).[918]

The Birth of a Nation

D.W. Griffith's *The Birth of a Nation* cries out at the fall of the South, justifies the rise of the KKK, and characterizes Afro-Americans as violent, simple-minded and obsessed with sex.

In 1998, the American Flim Institute rated it 44 on the "Top 100 American Films" list.[919] Some consider it the first true blockbuster in US film history.[920] It is hard to officially tabulate the film's profits, but it is believed it held the world record for two decades.[921]

The film covered the issues of miscegenation and the effects of empowering blacks.[922] Major black roles in the film "were stereotypically played and filled by white actors - in blackface. [Afro-American actors in the film only played in minor roles.]"[923]

There is a scene when a character in blackface is in the front of the scene as real Afro-Americans work in the field behind him.[924] Griffith used white actors in blackface to depict the black villains.[925] Most conclude Griffith made the blackface purposely noticeable because white audiences wouldn't have accepted the film if it had real interracial acting in the sexually motivated scenes.[926]

One of the most audacious scenes is set in the 1870s South Carolina Legislature as text on the screen introduces the material as drawn from "historic incidents."[927] Courtesy of Reconstruction, Afro-American legislators are shown as lazy and barefoot while drinking whiskey, eating chicken and checking out white women in the gallery.[928]

What caused the hatred?

The film revived the self-loathing whites of the South, and gave them an excuse to use violence. Some point to the loss of power as the reason for this hatred. More specifically, the white rural male had lost his manhood. Male southerners lost the Civil War, lost their Southern currency, and lost some of their land to blacks; they also felt like their franchise was devalued because African Americans could supposedly now vote.[929] *The Birth of a Nation* brought power and prestige back to Southern males, and the South.

This loss to the Southerner may be real to the director of the movie, given D.W. Griffith was the son of the Confederate War cavalry officer who returned after the Civil War and suffered "the disgrace of Reconstruction."[930]

President Wilson's Reaction

The film was based on the white religious view in the South through Baptist Rev. Thomas Dixon's 1905 racist play, *The Clansman.*[931] Dixon was from North Carolina.[932] President Wilson was an old Princeton classmate of Dixon.[933] Dixon was a Wilson friend who wanted Wilson in the White House.[934] Dixon's writing career focused on white supremacy, and the KKK's use of violence for "Lost Cause" redemption.[935] Now President Wilson validated this Southern white position.

Wilson's writings from *A History of the American People* were cited in the movie.[936] Not only was the film the first one screened and previewed at the White House,[937] but Wilson helped get preview screenings for his cabinet, Congress, and the Supreme Court.[938]

Wilson's comments aren't exactly clear, some claim the quote was reportedly said.[939] Key word, *reportedly*. Others fully attribute Wilson's comments to the President. Whatever the case, Wilson is credited with stating, "It's like writing history with lightning. And my only regret is that it is all terribly true."[940]

A letter from Wilson's secretary to Boston's branch of the NAACP said, "...the President was entirely unaware of the nature of the play before it was presented and at no time has expressed his approbation of it."[941] (Given that Mr. Dixon was Wilson's friend, that secretarial comment was likely manufactured.) Roger Ebert surmised of Wilson's infamous comments: "My guess is that Wilson said something like it in private, and found it prudent to deny when progressive editorialists attacked the film."[942]

Even if Wilson didn't say the comment, it doesn't matter. His whole administration's action in the executive bureaucracy validated his approval of the beliefs of the film.

NAACP Reaction

The National Association for the Advancement of Colored People (NAACP) was an organization created in 1909. They organized opposition, given the film endorsed slavery and the KKK. Riots occurred in Boston and Philadelphia, and the film wasn't allowed to be released in Chicago, Pittsburgh, St. Louis, Denver and Minneapolis.[943]

The NAACP reacted by publishing a 47-page pamphlet, "Fighting a Vicious Film: Protest Against *The Birth of a Nation.*"[944] The NAACP was joined in opposition by social activist Jane Addams and many Ivy League presidents.[945] W.E.B. Dubois was successful in using *The Crisis* to make those in New York consider whether the film should be shown.[946] Despite Du Bois efforts, the film had a public opening in New York with huge publicity, as Times Square's Liberty Theater charged two dollars a ticket.[947]

Dubois v. Washington: Unnecessary Bickering

Wilson had to deal with more militant Afro-American leaders (compared to Taft working with Booker T. Washington) such as W.E.B. Dubois, Marcus Garvey and Monroe Trotter.[948] Garvey was in his prime of popularity when Wilson was president. Garvey "led the largest black organization Americans had ever known. His Universal Negro Improvement Association."[949] Garvey was deported in 1927 "after a vicious campaign by the federal government and other black leaders to discredit him."[950]

Sadly, Dubois and Booker T. Washington did not get along. Privately, Washington was involved in court cases opposing Afro-American exclusion from juries.[951] This is in significant contrast to what Dubois led the public and his followers to believe about Washington. Thus, Washington was aggressively attacking the institutional structures Dubois wanted Washington to fight; it's just that Washington didn't want a medal for it.

Worse yet, William Monroe Trotter claimed Booker T. Washington was not a true leader on race, claiming Washington had really been elevated by whites.[952] Trotter worked for the *Boston Guardian*,[953] and led non-violent protests against *The Birth of a Nation.*[954]

The fight between Booker T. Washington and the more militant factions of the black civil rights movement is a debate still played out in various civil rights causes. Should you work with the elitist establishment to get rights, or should you fight the establishment in more aggressive fashion? The answer is difficult, but one of the results of the division may have been the empowerment of President Wilson, who managed to divide his opposition.

Wilson & Afro-American Leaders

Trotter also led criticism against Wilson. When Wilson allowed his cabinet to segregate their government offices, Trotter led a delegation to meet Wilson.[955] Wilson explained: "segregation was caused by friction between the colored and white clerks, and not done to injure or humiliate the colored clerks, but to avoid friction."[956] Trotter grew irate, a shouting match occurred, and he was ushered out of the White House.[957]

Trotter tried to return the favor. He stood on the White House grounds and told the press everything that just occurred.[958] Dubois supported President Wilson in 1912, but now sided with Trotter.[959] Dubois said Wilson, by birth, was "...unfitted for largesse of view or depth of feeling about racial injustice."[960]

When peace talks began in Paris in 1919, Du Bois went to Europe via his position in the press; but Trotter couldn't get a passport from Wilson's State Department.[961] Trotter got to Paris as a cook on a trans-Atlantic steamer.[962]

Booker T. Washington, although differing from Trotter on black issues, concurred with Trotter on President Wilson. During Wilson's first term, Booker T. Washington wrote: "I have recently spent several days in Washington and I have never seen the colored people so discouraged and bitter as they are at the present time."[963]

In the 1910s and 1920s, the Afro-American community was divided on the political strategy of how to help their people, but they were not divided in their disappointment of President Wilson.

Wilson's Legacy

While examining Wilson's effects, there are many results of his treatment of Afro-Americans. First, the Democratic Party would shut out Afro-Americans for 20 years.

Second, the federal government remained segregated past the 1950s.[964] Wilson's bigotry is credited with partially causing violence during and after his presidency. With *The Birth of a Nation,* and with Wilson's backing, the KKK rose from the ashes. The North became more racist; even Duluth had an Afro-American lynched.[965] The film has been credited as a cause of the race riots of the north, especially in 1919.[966] The KKK had somewhat dissolved by the 1870s.[967] *The Birth of a Nation* and President Wilson brought the KKK back in full force.

Wilson's racism affected Wilson at Versailles. Ho Chi Minh wanted self determination for Vietnam; Wilson sided with the French. Wilson, who told the U.S. he wanted to fight in WWI to spread democracy, hypocritically supported French colonialism in Vietnam. Ho Chi Minh was rejected because Wilson hated communism—even though Minh was a nationalist first. And of course, Wilson's perception wasn't helped by his opinion on Asians. Adding more to Wilson's hypocrisy in fighting WWI, Wilson "personally vetoed a clause on racial equality in the Covenant of the League of Nations."[968]

Historians typically rate Wilson as an idealist progressive who fought valiantly for the League of Nations against isolationist Republicans.[969] "Wilsonian" ideals have become synonymous with extending democracy and justice.[970] Textbooks and historians continue to give Wilson credit as a legendary figure who fought for democracy around the world. In truth, Wilson advocated democratic principles for privileged white men.

Why historians have demoted Wilson's bigotry to minor coverage is unclear. His domestic actions toward Afro-Americans are certainly important. George Wallace (1968) and Strom Thurmond (1948) ran racist presidential campaigns, but their failed bids pale to actually having the racist President in power from 1913 to 1921. President Wilson's misused power is a valuable lesson in civil rights, as his policies helped perpetuate Jim Crow laws until the 1960s.

Virginia's Racial Integrity Act of 1924

By 1915, over half the states invalidated marriages between blacks and whites, including a half dozen who put it in their constitution.[971] This act is important because it is an example of anti-miscegenation laws derived from eugenicists.[972]

Madison Grant was a leading eugenicist convinced miscegenation was "a social and racial crime," as he warned of the eventual disappearance of white civilization.[973] In his view the higher races were, for example, the Nordic Whites.[974] If a white married a lower race, the offspring was the race of the parent of the less desired race. For example, Grant wrote in his 1916 book *The Passing of the Great Race*, "The cross between a white man and an Indian is an Indian; the cross between a white man and a negro is a negro..."[975]

Madison Grant and Harry Laughlin consulted with three local Virginia eugenicists, including John Powell.[976] John Powell was a pianist who founded the Anglo-Saxon Clubs of America, which has been described as an "elitist version" of the KKK.[977]

The Virginia Racial Integrity Act of 1924 had provisions which required racial registration certificates and stringent qualifications for members of the white race.[978] Oddly, the law made a stipulation in the definition of Caucasian, as "persons who have one-sixteenth or less of the blood of the American Indian and have no other non-Caucasic blood shall be deemed to be white persons...."[979] This was because over a dozen members of the Virginia General Assembly claimed to be descendents of Pocahontas.[980]

The U.S. Supreme Court, in *Loving v. Virginia* (1967), finally declared the Virginia law unconstitutional.[981]

But 50 years earlier such bigotry was endorsed by Vice President Calvin Coolidge, who became our 30th president (1923-1929); Coolidge said, "Biological laws tell us that certain divergent people will not mix or blend."

Sen. Heflin Fights Miscegenation

As a U.S. Representative, Tom Heflin shot and seriously wounded an Afro-American man who confronted him in a Washington streetcar in 1908.[982] Heflin was indicted, but had his charges dismissed.[983] In later Alabama campaigns he said his shooting was one of his major career accomplishments.[984]

In 1929, the Afro-American captain of the New York University track team, married a white girl. When notified by a friend, Sen. Heflin wrote: "Shame upon those in authority who will permit such a humiliating, disgraceful and dangerous thing to happen! Where are the white men of self-respect, of race pride? The great white race is the climax and crowning glory of God's creation…The present disgusting and deplorable situation in New York State is not new under the modern Roman-Tammany system. Scores of Negroes in Harlem have been permitted to marry white wives with licenses granted by and with the hearty approval of the state and city government…"[985]

In 1930, Heflin got permission to have his letter reprinted in the Congressional Record's appendix so his letter could be reprinted by the government printing office and franked everywhere with no postage having to be paid by Heflin.[986] When New York's Senator Royal S. Copeland found out about the letter in the Congressional Record, he asked that it be expunged.[987] Heflin objected and, according to *Time* (1930), "warned Senator Copeland that he might be lynched if he ever went South on a Presidential campaign." *Time* even published Heflin's caustic comments:

> "They will ask 'Is he the fellow who tried to have Tom's letter expunged from the Record when he protested against the marriages of Negroes and Whites?' It will be said 'Yes, he's the same fellow.' 'Well,' they will say, 'We'll give it to him' "— here Senator Heflin executed an encircling gesture with his hand as if tying a rope tight around his throat— "'in the neck.'"[988]

Heflin Removed From Senate

In April 1932, in an exceptionally rare instance, the U.S. Senate allowed one of their former members to address their body.[989] The privilege was given to former Senator Heflin by a one-vote margin.[990] Heflin endorsed Herbert Hoover in 1928, but outraged leaders in Alabama's Democratic Party.[991] In retaliation, the state's Democratic Party denied Heflin the party nomination in 1930 to run again for Senate.[992] Heflin decided to run as an independent, but lost to John Bankhead.[993] Having lost but still in office, Heflin asked for a Senate investigation for voting fraud in the election; the investigation cost $100,000 and lasted 15 months.[994]

In April 1932, Sen. Bankhead was already seated but the Senate was about to vote on a committee recommendation not in Heflin's favor.[995] So Heflin was given two hours to speak before the Senate, but took five as the Senate gallery was filled with his supporters.[996] His speech included "vehement gestures and offensive racist jokes."[997] The Senate overwhelmingly dismissed the former

Senator's claim.[998] Heflin's career ended, but not Southern support opposing racial intermarriage.

Later Thoughts on Miscegenation

Herman E. Talmadge was a U.S. Senator from Georgia (1957-81), in 1955 he said, "The decline and fall of the Roman empire came after years of intermarriage with other races. Spain was toppled as a world power as a result of the amalgamation of the races. . . . Certainly history shows that nations composed of a mongrel race lose their strength and become weak, lazy and indifferent."[999]

William Jennings Bryan's Base

One of the biggest ironies of the Progressive Era (1900-1917) was that in all its efforts to help the poor and disadvantaged, minority rights weren't included. We have seen this with President Wilson, but it was also common for Progressive leaders (Progressive Republicans, Progressive Democrats and Socialists) to oppose civil rights for minorities.

This was the case for Williams Jennings Bryan. Bryan was the moral crusader for rural Protestant America for the first quarter century of the 1900s. A three-time Democratic nominee (1896, 1900 and 1908) who served as Wilson's Secretary of State, Bryan led the Prohibitionist movement and defended his fundamentalist interpretation of the bible in the Scopes Evolution trial. To his supporters, Bryan was the voice standing up for God.

One supporter of Bryan was Benjamin "Pitchfork" Tillman, who has been described as an "inveterate white supremacist."[1000] Tillman (D-S.C.) said (1906), "Republicanism means Negro equality, while the Democratic Party means that the white man is supreme. That is why we Southerners are all Democrats."[1001] Tillman served in the U.S. Senate from 1895 to 1918.[1002] Tillman was a populist who supported William Jennings Bryan and progressive limits on monopolies.[1003] Although an advocate for public education, Tillman felt it should only be for whites: "When you educate a negro you educate a candidate for the penitentiary or spoil a good field hand."[1004]

Sen. Hoke Smith (D-Georgia) said (1912), "I am opposed to the practice of having colored policemen in the District [of Columbia]. It is a source of danger by constantly engendering racial friction, and is offensive to thousands of Southern white people who make their homes here."[1005] This qoute validates a similar position taken by President Wilson on the implication of "friction" between the races. Hoke Smith was appointed Secretary of the Interior by Grover Cleveland in 1893.[1006] Smith left the Cleveland Administration in 1896 to support William Jennings Bryan's presidential campaign.[1007]

Of course, it wouldn't be fair to kill Bryan's zealotry through death by association. So here is the three time presidential nominee in his own words. In 1923, Bryan said, "Slavery among the whites was an improvement over independence in Africa. The very progress that the blacks have made, when—and only when—brought into contact with the whites, ought to be a sufficient argument in support of white supremacy—it ought to be sufficient to convince even the blacks themselves."[1008]

Bryan had a huge following in 1923, speaking against evolution being taught in public schools, as he would eventually attack Charles Darwin theories in the Scopes Trial (1925).[1009] Today, Bryan's statue stands in the U.S. Capitol.[1010]

Progressive Era Killed Civil Rights

The racism that killed the self-esteem of Afro-Americans heightened with President Wilson and extended into the 1960s. It's important to understand "progressives" allowed this bigotry to occur, thus prolonging it well past the first half of the 1900s.

Westminster College historian David W. Southern has noted the odd correlation of progressive reform during the early 1900s running simultaneously with bigotry. Southern has commented: "At college, budding progressives not only read exposés of capitalistic barons and attacks on laissez-faire economics by muckraking journalists, they also read racist tracts that drew on the latest anthropology, biology, psychology, sociology, eugenics, and medical science."[1011]

Madison Grant's bestseller *The Passing of the Great Race* (1916) considered "race suicide," the belief inferior races were out-breeding the best races.[1012] Many Progressives agreed, such as Teddy Roosevelt, who opposed voting rights for blacks (even though it was granted in the 15th amendment).[1013]

Carter Glass was a state Senator from Virginia who became a U.S. Senator.[1014] While in the U.S. House, he chaired the Committee on Banking and Currency and grafted the Federal Reserve Act of 1913.[1015] Progressive as he was, he supported taking away civil rights. He told a journalist, "Discrimination! Why that is exactly what we propose. To remove every negro voter who can be gotten rid of, legally, without materially impairing the numerical strength of the white electorate."[1016]

Socialist Didn't Help Afro-Americans Either

Another example of arrogant progressivism came with the socialists. Eugene Debs declared in his 1912 Socialist presidential campaign: "We have nothing special to offer the Negro."[1017] Victor Berger, another leading socialist writing in the *Socialist Democratic Herald*, said, "there can be no doubt that the negroes and mulattoes constitute a lower race—that the Caucasian and even the Mongolian have the start on them in civilization by many years."[1018]

Eleanor Takes A Stand

In February 1939, the First Lady Eleanor Roosevelt resigned from the Daughters of the American Revolution to show her support for Marian Anderson, an African American contralto opera singer.[1019] Initially, Anderson was to perform at Constitution Hall in the nation's capital owned by the D.A.R., who didn't allow black performers.[1020] The First Lady had already invited Anderson to perform at the White House in 1936.[1021] And Anderson was able to sing in many famous European concert halls.[1022]

The First Lady used her weekly column to announce her withdrawal from the D.A.R:[1023] "I belong to an organization in which I can do no active work. They have taken an action which has been widely talked of in the press. To remain as a member implies approval of that action, and therefore I am resigning."[1024]

FDR On Anti-lynching:

As a Representative from South Carolina in 1919, James F. Byrnes said, "This is a white man's country, and will always remain a white man's country."[1025] He was appointed to the Supreme Court by Franklin Delano Roosevelt in 1941, and became Secretary of State for Harry Truman.[1026]

When the U.S. House debated the proposed federal anti-lynching bill, a Wisconsin representative rebuked a Mississippi colleague who blamed lynching on black criminality.[1027] Afro-Americans in the gallery cheered. White southern politicians shouted back: "Sit down, niggers."[1028] Senator Byrnes criticized Senate Majority Leader Alben Barkley for placing anti-lynching legislation on the agenda in 1938.[1029] Byrnes blamed Barkley for being influenced by NAACP official Walter White; Byrnes said Barkley "can't do anything without talking to that nigger first."[1030]

Sadly, civil rights was not FDR's speciality. His First Lady fought for a federal anti-lynching bill, but the President let it die in Congress. Thus, FDR sided with white Southernors, like Sen. Pepper. In 1938, During a six-hour speech against the antilynching bill, Sen. Claude Pepper (D-Fla.) said, "… the crime of lynching . . . is not of sufficient importance to justify this legislation."[1031]

Afro-Americans' Ugly Doll

Psychologist and Educator Kenneth Clark, together with his wife Mamie, originated the famous doll studies on the harmful effects of racism on Afro-American children that brought victory for civil rights in *Brown v. Board of Education* (1954).[1032]

Clark found Afro-American children thought black dolls were the ugly dolls when compared to white dolls. The psychological test was simple. Its lesson was profound. When we tell someone they are inferior, they will eventually believe it.

Brown v. Board of Education

After the U.S. Supreme Court ruling in *Brown v. Board of Education,* public schools were to be desegregated. The unanimous decision was based largely on Clark's doll experiment: separating blacks was unequal because it made them inherently unequal. In response, 101 southern members of Congress offered their Southern Manifesto which called the Supreme Court's decision "a clear abuse of judicial power," and pledged to use "all lawful means to bring about a reversal."[1033]

Afro-Americans still had a long way to go. Besides adequate public schooling, they were denied ballot access. In 1960, less than 6% of potential Afro-American voters in Mississippi were registered to vote.[1034]

Attitudes like Georgia governor Eugene Talmadge still followed. Talmadge said "the niggers will never go to a school which is white while I am governor."[1035]

LBJ, RFK Weak on Civil Rights

The reason Talmadge had a voice was because he was a governor. There were Democrats (and Republicans for that matter) elsewhere in the country who should have publically opposed and corrected the man.

Lyndon B. Johnson has been credited with passing the Civil Rights Act in the 1960s. But we shouldn't forget that as a Representative from Texas in 1948, LBJ said President Truman's civil rights program "is a farce and a sham—an effort to set up a police state in the guise of liberty. I am opposed to that program. I have voted against the so-called poll tax repeal bill… I have voted against the so-called anti-lynching bill."[1036] Johnson then served as a US Senator (1949 to 1961), including half the time as Majority Leader (1955-1961).[1037]

In 1957, Sen. Johnson (D-Texas) said, "These Negroes, they're getting pretty uppity these days and that's a problem for us since they've got something now they never had before, the political pull to back up their uppityness. Now we've got to do something about this, we've got to give them a little something, just enough to quiet them down, not enough to make a difference. For if we don't move at all, then their allies will line up against us and there'll be no way of stopping them, we'll lose the filibuster and there'll be no way of putting a brake on all sorts of wild legislation. It'll be Reconstruction all over again."[1038]

Looking at the beginning of JFK's Administration, both his Vice President (LBJ) and Attorney General (Bobby Kennedy) were lukewarm on civil rights. In 1961, Attorney General Robert F. Kennedy said, "I did not lie awake at night worrying about the problems of Negroes."[1039] Later on, RFK authorized bugging Martin Luther King Jr.'s hotel rooms.[1040]

WWI AND THE ROLLBACK OF RIGHTS

Creel Committee

The Committee on Public Information was made during WWI. It was led by George Creel, an author and journalist.[1041] His committee played a huge role in WWI propaganda, including the pro-war organization of advertising, artists, authors, songwriters, speakers, and the motion picture industry.[1042] Creel reinforced President Wilson's moral crusade for the war while uniformly promoting "widespread intolerance."[1043] Creel even organized Loyalty Leagues, which told Americans to spy on neighbors and report disloyalty.[1044] Under this umbrella of fear and hatred for WWI opposition, many were arrested for criticizing President Wilson, questioning the U.S. government, and opposing WWI.[1045]

Wilson's position on "Hyphenated Americans" was also ignorant and stereotypical: "Any man who carries a hyphen about with him carries a dagger that he is ready to plunge into the vitals of this Republic whenever he gets ready."[1046]

Espionage Act & Sedition Acts

During WWI, Congress passed the Espionage and Sedition Acts that brought legal approval of the intolerance for anti-war opinions.[1047]

Due to the Espionage Act of June 1917 and Sedition Act of 1918, President Wilson's postmaster general suppressed socialist, anti-British, and pro-Irish mail.[1048] Wilson's also halted civil liberties after WWI, when he vetoed a bill that would have abolished both the Espionage and Sedition Acts.[1049]

Eugene Debs

Not surprisingly, when Eugene Debs told an audience to "resist militarism, wherever found," he was given a decade in prison.[1050] Debs also said WWI was about economic interests and claimed the Espionage Act was undemocratic.[1051] Having been convicted, Debs called the Espionage Law "a despotic enactment in flagrant conflict with democratic principles and with the spirit of free institutions…"[1052] In his statement to the court (Sept.1918), Debs sounded like a elderly, wise grandfather—not an evil traitor:

> I am thinking this morning of the men in the mills and the factories; of the men in the mines and on the railroads. I am thinking of the women who for a paltry wage are compelled to work out their barren lives; of the little children who in this system are robbed of their childhood and in their tender years are seized in the remorseless grasp of Mammon and forced into the industrial dungeons, there to feed the monster machines while they themselves are being starved and stunted, body and soul. I see them dwarfed and diseased and their little lives broken and blasted because in this high noon of Christian civilization money is still so much more important than the flesh and blood of childhood. In very truth gold is god today and rules with pitiless sway in the affairs of men….[1053]

Wilson didn't even consider pardoning the elderly socialist, that good deed was done by Warren G. Harding. Some have blamed Wilson's frail health for his attacks on civil liberties, but this has been refuted. Indeed, the Attorney General A. Mitchell Palmer asked Wilson to pardon Debs.[1054] Wilson said "Never!"[1055]

Even when Debs died, the press was disrespectful. The *New York Times* headline (1926) was "EUGENE V. DEBS DIES AFTER LONG ILLNESS; Socialist Leader Succumbs to Heart Ailments After Month in Illinois Sanitarium. ONCE LEADER OF RAIL UNION He Led Pullman Strike In 1895 -- Served Nearly Three Years In Prison for Opposing War."[1056] *Sanitarium* had to be included the socialist's obituary.

Helen Keller's Only Handicap: The Press

Helen Keller (1880-1968) was the blind and deaf girl Anne Sullivan helped educate. She spent a lot of her lifetime raising funds for the American Foundation for the Blind.[1057]

She was also a socialist. She used her fame to bring attention to liberal causes, such as advocating for women's suffrage. She supported the Russian Revolution, praised the USSR, supported Eugene V. Debs presidential candidacy, and joined the IWW—a radical union Wilson criticized. This white Alabaman supported the NAACP and *The Crisis* in the 1920s.

Unfortunately, she was dropped by the press when she got political. Her political activism has also been forgotten by U.S. History textbooks. As James W. Loewen wrote, "Keller, who struggled so valiantly to learn to speak, has been made mute by history."[1058] Historians focus on her physical handicaps instead of her vocal socialist position.

Initially the media reaction to Keller towards her handicap was immensely popular, but after her socialism was apparent, she was criticized. The editor of the Brooklyn *Eagle* wrote her "mistakes spring out of the manifest limitations of her development."[1059] Keller had previously met with the editor. She said she was complimented many times by him, "But now that I have come out for socialism he reminds me and the public that I am blind and deaf and especially liable to error."[1060]

Keller concluded President Wilson was "the greatest individual disappointment the world has ever known!"[1061]

THE KKK RISES

The 1920s Racist Rebirth

In the 1920s, with the help of *The Birth of a Nation* in 1915, the KKK rebounded—and not just in the south. Oregon and Indiana, for example, are just two of the many states whose politics were influenced by the racist organization. It set the tone for a bigoted 1920s, as the KKK was anti-Catholic, anti-Jew, anti-Afro-American. The only thing it was supportive of was white, rural Protestantism.

KKK Alumni

Speaking of Alabama U.S. Senators, Hugo Black, D-Ala., accepted a life membership in the Ku Klux Klan upon his election to the U.S. Senate in 1926: "This passport which you have given me is a symbol to me of the passport which you have given me before. I do not feel that it would be out of place to state to you here on this occasion that I know that without the support of the members of this organization I would not have been called, even by my enemies, the 'Junior Senator from Alabama.'" Black was appointed to the Supreme Court by Franklin D. Roosevelt in 1937.

Sen. Robert C. Byrd was a former Ku Klux Klan recruiter.[1062] In 1946, Byrd said, "I am a former Kleagle [recruiter] of the Ku Klux Klan in Raleigh County. . . . The Klan is needed today as never before and I am anxious to see its rebirth here in West Virginia. It is necessary that the order be promoted immediately and in every state in the union."[1063] Byrd has been the Democratic Senator from West Virginia since 1959, and has served as Majority Leader (1977-1980, 1987-1988).[1064] In 2004, Sen. Chris Dodd (D-Conn.) said, "I do not think it is an exaggeration at all to say to my friend from West Virginia that he would have been a great senator at any moment. . . . He would have been right during the great conflict of civil war in this nation."[1065] Dodd ran for president in 2008.

THE 1928 PRESIDENTIAL ELECTION

Thomas J. Heflin Recalled 1924 Convention

Heflin was elected to the Senate in 1920.[1066] He was also known as "Cotton Tom" because his efforts for Alabama's cotton industry.[1067] He also went by the nickname "Tom-Tom."[1068] Heflin has been described as "an unremitting opponent of equal rights for black Americans, women, and Roman Catholics."[1069]

As Senator, Heflin opposed federal child labor legislation arguing it might create a shortage of field hands in agriculture.[1070] Although he voted against giving women the right to vote, he thought women would be grateful for his efforts to make Mother's Day a national holiday.[1071]

Heflin spoke (Jan.18.1928) before the Senate on Al Smith and Catholicism as the 1928 presidential election approached.[1072] Smith was the 1928 Democratic nominee, and a Catholic. Heflin used the speech to blame his fellow Democrat John W. Davis' 1924 defeat on Roman Catholics and Al Smith's demand for the Democratic Party to denounce the KKK.[1073]

Heflin had a bold recollection of the 1924 Democratic Convention. Heflin said, "I saw Roman Catholic delegates in the corridors of the hotels noisily demanding that the Ku-Klux-Klan be denounced by the Democratic convention."[1074] He said he told the Catholic delegates "you have got no business trying to get a National Democratic Convention to denounce" the KKK.[1075] The rhetorical question he supposedly asked them in 1924: "What would you think if I sought to denounce the Knights of Columbus by the convention?"[1076]

Heflin concluded Catholics at the convention "put Roman Catholic government above everything, above the Democratic Party, and above their country. That is plain talk, but it is the plain truth."[1077] Heflin said, "John W. Davis [the 1924 Democratic nominee] denounced it [the Klan] after this group of Catholics from Tammany, New York City, Al Smith's crowd, insisted that he denounce it . . . . And in an evil hour Davis denounced the Klan and lost four States by that action . . . ."[1078]

Heflin warned the Senate of the upcoming election on Smith in 1928: "The Roman Catholics of every country on the earth are backing his campaign.

Already they are spending money in the South buying up newspapers, seeking to control the vehicles that carry the news to the people. They are sending writers down there from New York and other places to misrepresent and slander our State, all this to build a foundation on which to work for Al Smith for President. The Roman Catholic edict has gone forth in secret articles, "Al Smith is to be made President."[1079]

Heflin was one of the most bigoted anti-Catholics in the country. *Time* said (1930) Heflin "mortally hates and fears the Roman Pope."[1080] In the end, Heflin was a great "poster child" for those representing the Klan.

Smith & Hoover

The 1928 presidential election pitted New York Democratic Governor Al Smith against Republican Herbert Hoover, the Commerce Secretary during the Roaring 20s. Hoover was popular and Republican in an election high on "Coolidge Prosperity." He would have been hard to beat anytime, but it was particularly easy because Smith was Catholic. The traditionally Democratic South clung to their rural Protestant roots instead of voting for an anti-Prohibitionist Irish Catholic from New York.

During the 1928 campaign, a periodical known as the *Fellowship Forum* said, "The real issue in this campaign is PROTESTANT AMERICANISM VERSUS RUM AND ROMANISM."[1081] Smith lost by a landslide.

Smith Supported Separating Church & State

When he accepted the Democratic nomination, Smith said, "I will not be influenced in appointments by the fact that a man is either rich or poor, whether he comes from the North, the East, the South or the West, or by what church he attends in the worship of God."[1082] Though his speech was meant to reassure doubters, his obvious New York accent reinforced prejudices.[1083]

Smith responded to the criticisms that he'd let the Catholic Church run the country: "I recognize no power in the institutions of my Church to interfere with the operations of the Constitution of the United States or the enforcement of the law of the land. I believe in absolute freedom of conscience. . .in the absolute separation of church and state…I believe that no tribunal of any church has any power to make any decree of any force in the law of the land, other than to establish the status of its own communicants within its own church."[1084]

Kennedy Supported Separation of Church & State

Massachusetts U.S. Senator John F. Kennedy was criticized for his Catholicism in the 1960 presidential campaign against Vice President Richard M. Nixon. Kennedy replied: "I believe in an America where the separation of church and state is absolute - where no Catholic prelate would tell the President (should he be Catholic) how to act. . .where no public official either requests or accepts instruction on public policy from the Pope, the National Council of Churches or any other ecclesiastical source - where no religious body seeks to impose its will directly or indirectly upon the general populace or the public acts of its officials."

Kennedy added, "Whatever issue may come before me as President - on birth control, divorce, censorship, gambling or any other subject - I will make my decision...in accordance with what my conscience tells me to be the national interest, and without regard to outside religious pressures or dictates. And no power or threat of punishment could cause me to decide otherwise."[1085]

When to Separate Church & State Depends On Popularity

Catholic leaders' positions on political involvement shadows whether they are in sync with the dominant side of public opinion in the country. That position of relative strength is determined by the strength of the agreement with the public on public policy issues.

When a religion is in a minority position in the United States (Smith in 1928, Kennedy in 1960), they push for religious tolerance and separation of church and state. When a religion and/or their position is considered mainstream, they push their religious views in the political sector and blur the lines between church and state.

In fact, when the Catholic hierarchy was trying to withhold communion to New York politicians in the 1990s, Arthur Schlesinger Jr. made the comment "If they [Bishops] had spoken then as they speak now, John F. Kennedy would never have been elected President."[1086] Yet, contrary to how Catholics won political power in the U.S., many bishops deny politicians communion as a litmus test for their political views, making the Catholic politician theocratic.

EUGENICS, STERILIZATION & *BUCK V BELL*

Galton's Eugenics

Eugenics originated in the 1880s with Sir Francis Galton's focus on encouraging healthy capable people of above-average intelligence to have more kids to improve the human race.[1087] This view has been termed "positive eugenics."[1088] The eugenics that took hold in the U.S. and Germany has been codified as "negative."[1089] The latter version emphasized certain races as degrading. In the early 1900s, the poor were reproducing faster than the middle- and upper-class, so there was ample support for the negative version.[1090]

U.S. Eugenics

Eugenics had popular support. President Teddy Roosevelt warned that if Anglo-Saxon couples failed to produce large families, the result would be "race suicide." [1091] Eugenics was popular not only in Virginia (as we see in *Buck v. Bell)*. Great schools like Harvard, Cornell and Columbia had courses in eugenics.[1092]

The American Eugenics Society had eugenics exhibits at state fairs throughout the country and encouraged "high-grade" people to reproduce at a greater rate for the benefit of society.[1093] The AES even sponsored Fitter Family contests.[1094]

Harry Laughlin

The Eugenics Record Office is considered the center of the U.S. eugenics movement.[1095] Harry Hamilton Laughlin was superintendent of the (ERO) of the Department of Genetics of the Carnegie Institute from 1910 to 1921, after which he fully directed almost until 1940.[1096]

Laughlin was one of the most influential U.S. leaders of eugenics during the 20th century,[1097] and dedicated his whole life to eugenics until he died in 1943.[1098] Not surprisingly, Laughlin was a member of the Galton Society.[1099]

Harry Laughlin worked on immigration issues, and helped pass the Immigration Restriction Act of 1924.[1100] He also played a leading role in developing the nation's compulsory sterilization policy.[1101]

Laughlin's Model Sterilization Law

By 1922, Laughlin concluded many state-laws on compulsory sterilization were flawed (not in purpose, but in wording).[1102] Thus, to address constitutional concerns (many state courts had deemed the laws unconstitutional), Laughlin published his "Model Eugenical Sterilization Law," so it would be constitutionally approved and used often.[1103] This model spawned the law passed in Virginia in 1924.[1104] It was found constitutional by the U.S. Supreme Court in *Buck v. Bell* (1927).[1105]

His model law (Chapter 15) was published in *Eugenical Sterilization in the United States* (1922).[1106] Laughlin had backing from the Carnegie Institute, whose name was also on the 1922 publication.[1107]

Laughlin wrote the "State's Motive" was to be "Purely eugenic, that is, to prevent certain degenerate human stock from reproducing its kind. Absolutely no punitive element."[1108] *No punitive element*?

In Laughlin's model law, he covered all potential subjects as "All persons in the State who, because of degenerate or defective hereditary qualities are potential parents of socially inadequate offspring, regardless of whether such persons be in the population at large or inmates of custodial institutions, regardless also of the personality, sex, age, marital condition, race, or possessions of such person." Therefore, by adding "regardless," such laws could be deemed unbiased.

In his model law, Laughlin described the "socially inadequate classes" who could be sterilized:

> The **socially inadequate classes**, regardless of etiology or prognosis, are the following: (1) Feeble-minded; (2) Insane, (including the psychopathic); (3) Criminalistic (including the delinquent and wayward); (4) Epileptic; (5) Inebriate (including drug-habitués); (6) Diseased (including the tuberculous, the syphilitic, the leprous, and others with chronic, infectious and legally segregable diseases); (7) Blind (including those with seriously impaired vision); (8) Deaf (including those with seriously impaired hearing); (9)

Deformed (including the crippled); and (10) Dependent (including orphans, ne'er-do-wells, the homeless, tramps and paupers).[1109]

The laws were also under the presumption of guilty before innocent. This was primarily due to the fact that the descriptions of those who could be sterilized covered just about anybody. In his model law, Laughlin even said "a potential parent of socially inadequate offspring" could be sterilized.[1110]

Laughlin was an epileptic and would have been suitable to be sterilized under his version of the law.[1111]

Laughlin's Model Sterilization Law: Hitleresque

Laughlin's Model Sterilization Law was so detailed it became persuasive in its "logic." They were used by many states which passed sterilization laws.[1112] The Nazi's 1930s sterilization laws were "modeled after Laughlin's."[1113]

The data retrieval of Nazis was preceded by Laughlin's idea for a state-employed eugenicist, "To conduct field-surveys seeking firsthand data concerning the hereditary constitution of all persons in the State who are socially inadequate personally or who, although normal personally, carry degenerate or defective hereditary qualities of a socially inadequating nature…."[1114] The state eugenicist was also "To preserve as property of the State complete records of all investigations and transactions of the office of State Eugenicist, and annually to render to the Governor in writing a true and complete report thereof."[1115] The state eugenicist, in Laughlin's view, should also have the legal power "to administer oaths, to subpoena and to examine witnesses under oath, and to make arrests."[1116]

And like the Nuremburg Trials when leading Nazis said they were "just following orders," Laughlin added a section (19) on liability, in which "Neither the State Eugenicist, nor any other person legally participating in the execution of the provisions of this Act, shall be liable either civilly or criminally on account of said participation."[1117]

In the same chapter for a model state law, Laughlin also commented on the need for a federal eugenicist. Here, a proposed bill was explicitly used to address the immigration issue. Laughlin noted additional potential subjects: "Immigrants who are personally eligible to admission but who by the standards recommended in the model state law are potential parents of socially inadequate offspring…. All persons below the standards of parenthood set in the model state law who are beyond the jurisdiction of state laws, including the inhabitants of the District of Columbia, unorganized and outlying territories, Indian reservations, inmates of federal institutions, and soldiers and sailors."[1118]

Philanthropy Backed Sterilization

Eugenical-backed sterilization and the push for "selective breeding" came courtesy of the elites, such as the Rockefeller Foundation and the Carnegie Institution of Washington, who funded the movement in the U.S. and abroad.[1119]

The Rockefeller Foundation is credited with the founding of Germany's eugenics program.[1120] The Rockefeller Foundation also founded Josef Mengele's program before he worked at Auschwitz.[1121] In addition, Carnegie backed a 1911 report called the "Preliminary Report of the Committee of the Eugenic Section of the American Breeder's Association to Study and to Report on the Best Practical Means for Cutting Off the Defective Germ-Plasm in the Human Population," which considered euthansia.[1122]

It is entirely possile the acceptance of eugenics was bought thru the charitable donations of philanthropists.[1123] Besides Carnegie and Rockefeller, the Harriman railroad money fostered eugenic research.[1124] The Harriman railroad fortune paid local charities to find Jews and Italians to deport.[1125]

Indiana: First In The Nation

Indiana enacted the world's first eugenic sterilization law in 1907.[1126] It's no surprise Indiana passed the first law, given it became a haven for the KKK in the early 1920s. Indiana's law (1907) was passed "to prevent procreation of confirmed criminals, idiots, imbeciles, and rapists…WHEREAS, heredity plays a most important part in the transmission of crime, idiocy, and imbecility…"[1127] Indiana's Supreme Court declared it unconstitutional by the 1920s, at which point a revised bill was enacted in 1927.[1128]

The second version applied to "inmates of state institutions, who are insane, idiotic, imbecile, feebleminded, and epileptic, and who by the laws of heredity are the probable potential parents of socially inadequate offspring likewise afflicted."[1129] The law was in place until repealed in 1974, and after 2,500 forced sterilizations.[1130]

The Virginia Colony

The Virginia Colony was officially described as the "Virginia Colony for the Epileptic and Feebleminded."[1131] Located in Lynchburg, Virginia, it opened in 1910 and was the largest asylum in the United States.[1132] The Virginia Colony was for epileptics, mentally retarded and the severely disabled; but by 1912, it's Supt. Albert Priddy pushed the state's General Assembly to expand the Colony for the "feebleminded."[1133]

The Virginia Colony (a.k.a. Lynchburg Colony or The Colony) grew because it was a dumping ground for low-class white Virginians considered uneducated, and, thus "unfit."[1134] The population was growing too much, so Priddy came up with an idea (around 1914) to sterilize feebleminded Virginians so patients would be less likely to have to be segregated from the population.[1135] Priddy was sterilizing at the Virginia Colony well before the passage of Virginia's Eugenical Sterilization Act of 1924.[1136] Evidence suggests Priddy was caught up in his own moralism, and started justifying his duty to determine who could have kids—and by his evaluation, that list didn't include "anti-social morons," and "non-producing and shiftless persons, living on public and private charity."[1137]

Should Carrie Buck be sterilized?

The Virginia Colony deemed Carrie Buck and her mother Emma as feebleminded and sexually promiscuous, both of which were considered hereditary.[1138] Given Emma and Carrie were already institutionalized, it was easier to argue Carrie's daughter Vivian was going to be an "imbecile."[1139]

Supt. Priddy pushed for passage of the Virginia sterilization law validating procedures he was already using; now Priddy thought a challenge to the law in the case of Carrie Buck would actually make it a stronger law.[1140]

When the case finally had reached the U.S. Supreme Court, Priddy had died and was replaced by Dr. J.H. Bell, who also replaced the name in the suit.[1141] At Carrie's trial, Dr. Priddy said Emma Buck had "a record of immorality, prostitution, untruthfulness and syphilis."[1142] In reference to the Buck family, Priddy said, "These people belong to the shiftless, ignorant, and worthless class of anti-social whites of the South."

Laughlin, Eugenics & Buck

Carrie Buck's sterilization can be faulted on a sham diagnosis based on eugenics.[1143] Harry Laughlin drew out Buck's pedigree in his notes according to the standard ERO format used to demonstrate the hereditary passage of undesirable traits.[1144] While the court process was going on in Virginia, Laughlin didn't even appear at Carrie Buck's initial trial, but he was convinced she should be sterilized. Laughlin had never met any members of the Buck family,[1145] which is only more evidence that Laughlin used stereotypes to come to "medical" conclusions.

The U.S. Supreme Court

The U.S. Supreme Court took up the case and judged in favor of sterilization. Supreme Court Justice Oliver Wendell Holmes, Jr. wrote, "It is better for all the world, if instead of waiting to execute degenerate offspring for crime or to let them starve for their imbecility, society can prevent those who are manifestly unfit from continuing their kind...Three generations of imbeciles are enough."[1146] Holmes wrote for the majority in the Supreme Court's decision and described Carrie Buck as a "probable potential parent of socially inadequate offspring, likewise afflicted," and added, "her welfare and that of society will be promoted by her sterilization."[1147]

Justice Holmes was also a student of eugenics.[1148] He used the assertions made by the "expert" witnesses at Carrie Buck's original trial to make his case.[1149] She was sterilized in October of 1927.[1150]

Holmes: A Well-qualified Judge

Holmes graduated from Harvard (1861), served and was wounded in the Civil War, went back to get his law degree from Harvard, then taught there.[1151] He edited the *American Law Review*, and was appointed to the Massachusetts Supreme Court (1882) and eventually served the last three years of his tenure as

Chief Justice until he was appointed to the U.S. Supreme Court in 1902.[1152] Holmes life was long and his accomplishments were impressive: he served two decades on the Massachusetts Supreme Court and almost three decades on the U.S. Supreme Court.[1153] He left the U.S. Supreme Court in 1932 and died three years later, two days short of his 94th birthday.[1154]

Holmes was qualified to be on the Supreme Court. The opinion of *Buck v. Bell* came from someone seen as a dignified judge and honorable veteran. For his time, he was the cream of the crop when it came to intellect. His resume was remarkable. And he had no problem with forced sterilization.

Bad Evidence Courts Missed

Carrie Buck's biological mom, Emma Buck, had previously been committed.[1155] But the institutionalization of the mother is worthy of questioning. In all likelihood, Emma was institutionalized because of alleged sexual promiscuity and, likewise, Carrie was diagnosed similarly as a single mother at age 17.[1156] However, evidence suggests although Emma Buck was accused of having Carrie illegitimately, a marriage license existed between Emma and Carrie's father.[1157]

Carrie's sterilization and subsequent court battles were flawed for various reasons. First, she was unfairly represented, for her defense attorney conspired with a Virginia Colony lawyer to rule in favor of sterilization.[1158] Second, Carrie Buck's foster parents had committed her after Carrie gave birth to an illegitimate child.[1159] The suggested moral failings and promiscuity were grossly inaccurate: she was raped by the relatives of her foster parents.[1160] The rape was not brought up in court.[1161] Third, Harry Laughlin gave a written deposition validating Carrie's "moral delinquency."[1162] Not only was Laughlin not at the trial, he "never met Carrie."[1163]

Carrie's six-month old daughter Vivian was diagnosed as "not quite normal" in the effort to sterilize Carrie.[1164] Specifically, while in the Virginia court system, Vivian was examined by a nurse who stated, "there is a look about it that is not quite normal."[1165] The tests for Vivian's intelligence were invalid. Vivian's foster mother was pictured flashing a coin past Vivian's face and the child did not follow the coin with her eyes, therefore she was deemed an imbecile.[1166] Completely neglected was the fact that Vivian may have been distracted by the camera taking a picture.[1167] Vivian was not "feebleminded." She turned out to be an honor roll student.[1168]

With the true background of the Bucks, one can validate the ignorance of Justice Holmes's quote: "Three generations of imbeciles are enough."[1169]

***Buck v. Bell* Aftermath**

The consequence of the 1927 ruling was simple but profound. It increased the passage of sterilization laws and eugenic sterilization use.[1170] State sterilization programs sterilized over 64,000 mentally ill and developmentally disabled patients until most stopped by the mid-1960s.[1171]

Eugenics also surfaced in another U.S. Supreme Court case during WWII.[1172] A 1935 Oklahoma law called for forced sterilization for repeated criminals.[1173] This wasn't a solution for sex-offenders, but theft. Jack Skinner was convicted of armed robbery and chicken stealing.[1174] The law was struck down by the U.S. Supreme Court in *Skinner v. Oklahoma* (1942), but not before a dozen states had legalized criminal sterilization.[1175] Even still, the precedent *Buck v. Bell* set for sterilizing the feebleminded was never overruled. [1176]

U.S. Sterilization Facts

By the 1920s, sterilization was sold as a cost-effective means of strengthening and improving American society.[1177] In general, the forced sterilization occurred up to WWII, though some states (Virginia), continued into the 1970s.[1178] The push pre-WWII was largely due to *Buck v. Bell*, and by the early 1930s over half the states adopted eugenic laws.[1179] The eugenics push also influenced mixed-marriage bans.[1180]

California and Virginia had the most sterilizations performed per state during the reign of forced sterilizations in the U.S.[1181] Of the 7,500 sterilized in Virginia, one was a woman who was told her appendix was going to be removed, but she did not discover the truth until years after she tried to have a child.[1182] In the beginning, California usually sterilized women under the classification of "bad girls," and "oversexed."[1183] Women in Sonoma were sterilized due to "what was deemed an abnormally large clitoris or labia."[1184]

North Carolina was unique in that most of their sterilizations occurred after WWII, when they also became more minority focused.[1185] Indeed, "almost 80% of North Carolina's cases occurred after 1945. By the late 1960's over 60% of those sterilized in North Carolina were black and 99% were female."[1186]

In addition, forced sterilization of patients was not the only product of patient treatment courtesy of eugenics. In Lincoln, Illinois, one institution gave patients milk from tubercular cows with the logic that a eugenically strong individual would be immune.[1187]

Nazis "Improve" U.S. Sterilization Laws

The focus on forced sterilizations went from the U.S. to Nazi Germany, who evolved it into euthanasia. Clearly there was commitment to eugenics in the U.S., where scientists played a "vanguard role."[1188] Then the University of Heidelberg awarded Harry Laughlin with an honorary doctorate for his "services on behalf of racial hygiene"[1189] and his efforts on the "science of racial cleansing."[1190]

Dr. J.H. Bell (of *Buck v. Bell*) wrote, "The fact that a great state like the German Republic, which for many centuries has helped furnish the best that science has bred, has in its wisdom seen fit to enact a national eugenic legislative act providing for the sterilization of hereditarily defective persons seems to point the way for an eventual worldwide adoption of this idea."[1191]

In addition, others in Virginia were embarrassed by so-called Nazi success. In 1934, the superintendent of Virginia's Western State Hospital, Joseph DeJarnette said, "The Germans are beating us at our own game."[1192] Dr. DeJarnette said (1938), "Germany in six years has sterilized about 80,000 of her unfit while the United States with approximately twice the population has only sterilized about 27,869 to January 1, 1938 in the past 20 years... The fact that there are 12,000,000 defectives in the U.S. should arouse our best endeavors to push this procedure to the maximum."[1193]

Some have argued not only did the U.S. influence Nazi policy, but the Nazis flat out copied the U.S. In fact, Germany borrowed Harry Laughlin's Model Sterilization Law for states when they made their 1933 Law for the Prevention of Hereditary Defective Offspring.[1194] The eugenics version in the U.S. promoted the Nordic stereotype.[1195] When it came to Germany, nazis simply replaced the Nordic preference with "Germanic" or "Aryan."[1196]

Hitler told a Nazi colleague: "I have studied with great interest the laws of several American states concerning prevention of reproduction by people whose progeny would, in all probability, be of no value or be injurious to the racial stock."[1197] Madison Grant was a U.S. leader in eugenics. Hitler called Grant's book, *The Passing of the Great Race*, his "bible."[1198]

The Germans were, like the U.S., aided by philanthropy. By the mid-1920s, Rockefeller gave over $400,000 to German researchers.[1199] Most damning, the Nazis at the Nuremberg trials defended themselves by quoting U.S. Supreme Court Justice Oliver Wendell Holmes.[1200]

IMMIGRATION

Racist Immigration Policy

Senator Henry Cabot Lodge (Mass.) had a reactionary philosophy toward immigration.[1201] He wanted to exclude immigrants from southern and eastern Europe.[1202] In 1896, Lodge wanted a bill to exclude immigrants if they couldn't read or write twenty five words of the U.S. Constitution is some language, and that test would "bear most heavily upon the Italians, Russians, Poles, Hungarians, Greeks, and Asiatics… races most affected by the test are those who[m] emigration has… swelled rapidly…and who are most alien to the great body of the United States."[1203] Lodge's ideas on Southern Europeans became law in the 1920s.

Harry Laughlin on Immigration

Eugenicist Harry Laughlin testified before Congress to support immigration restriction of those from Eastern and Southern Europe.[1204] He was very active in immigration policy. Laughlin served as the eugenics expert for the Committee on Immigration and Naturalization for the U.S. House of

Representatives (1921-1931).[1205] He was the U.S. immigration agent to Europe for the Department of Labor (1923-1924) and was a member of the permanent Immigration Commission of the International Labor Office of the League of Nations in 1925.[1206] Laughlin's immigration studies supported the idea that Southern and Eastern European immigrants were more likely to be "socially inadequate" than other immigrants.[1207] With the focus on Southern and Eastern Europeans, the immigration quotas disproportionately had a bigger impact on Jews (in Eastern Europe) and Italians (in Southern Europe). Laughlin's positions led to the highly restrictive immigration quota system of 1924, which, accordingly, was more sympathetic to Northern European immigrants.[1208] The Northern Europeans, by the 1920s, were clearly more accepted.

Laughlin gave "skewed data to support his assertion that the percentage of these immigrant populations in prisons and mental institutions was far greater than their percentage in the general population would warrant."[1209] Laughlin's ideas were reinforced by President Calvin Coolidge. When he signed the 1924 Immigration Restriction Act, President Coolidge said, "America must remain American."[1210]

Japanese Excluded

The National Origins Act of 1924 completely excluded Japanese immigrants from the U.S. Thus, moderate Japanese politicians lost an argument to stay pro-U.S., and reactionary militarists in Japan were given an excuse to hate America.[1211] The 1924 act became one of the many justifications for bombing Pearl Harbor in 1941. So devastated were the Japanese by this national insult of exclusion, the day the National Origins Act went into effect was a Japanese national day of public mourning and national humiliation.[1212]

Franklin D. Roosevelt Supported Japanese Exclusion

In 1925, FDR justified Japanese Exclusion:

> Anyone who has traveled to the Far East knows that the mingling of Asiatic blood with European or American blood produces, in nine cases out of ten, the most unfortunate results. . . . The argument works both ways. I know a great many cultivated, highly educated and delightful Japanese. They have all told me that they would feel the same repugnance and objection to have thousands of Americans settle in Japan and intermarry with the Japanese as I would feel in having large numbers of Japanese coming over here and intermarry with the American population. In this question, then, of Japanese exclusion from the United States it is necessary only to advance the true reason—the undesirability of mixing the blood of the two peoples. . . . The Japanese people and the American people are both opposed to intermarriage of the two races—there can be no quarrel there.[1213]

THE RADIO PRIEST

Father Coughlin

Father Charles E. Coughlin was actually Canadian born, but his outreach in the U.S. in the 1930s was widespread. He served as a Roman Catholic priest in Royal Oak, Michigan at the National Shrine of the Little Flower Church.

In 1933, *Time* reported his broadcasts reached 10 million.[1214] The *Detroit News* later (1995) concluded his coast-to-coast following was 30 million at its peak, and he received 80,000 letters a week.[1215] Perhaps it was only FDR who had a bigger audience. But Coughlin received more mail than FDR.[1216] Coughlin also had a newspaper (*Social Justice*).[1217]

A Clear Demagogue By 1933

In late 1933, *Time* had already covered his demagoguery in an article implicating Coughlin's cynicism and political strategy (instead of being a priest). Here is the news magazine's report on Coughlin's criticism of New York Gov. Al Smith, who Coughlin criticized for not supporting FDR:

> Meanwhile statements were flying thick & fast over Spellbinder Coughlin's accusation that Alfred Emanuel Smith, foe of the Roosevelt program, had gone with two Catholic bishops to the House of Morgan to arrange a loan for his Empire State Building. Al Smith warmly denied this, adding: "From boyhood I was taught that a Catholic priest was under the divine injunction to 'teach all nations' the word of God. That includes the divine Commandment: 'Thou shalt not bear false witness against thy neighbor.'" Father Coughlin countered by issuing a series of verbose statements in which he called Al Smith "the outstanding lay Catholic in the country." Declaring "I am not hedging at all," he hedged a little, toned down his story, hung it on one bishop, unnamed. He also said his own Bishop stood by him.[1218]

Some in the Church spoke up. By 1933, Monsignor John L. Belford of Brooklyn went after the Radio Priest: "The man is an infernal nuisance. He has gone mad with popularity. . . . Members of his Church despise him. . . . His Bishop is even worse than he is. The Bishop [of Detroit] has it in his power to stop him and he has not done so, although appeals have been made to him by the most outstanding ecclesiastics in this country. I believe that the time has come when the Apostolic Delegate should step in and stop this wild ranting that is disgracing religion."[1219] This was a bold, accurate statement. Within a week, Belford apologized to Coughlin and said, "No Christian, and certainly no clergyman, should express such uncharitable views."[1220] Coughlin later bragged he was expecting an apology from Al Smith.[1221]

Coughlin remained grotesquely stereotypical in his rhetoric (March 1934): "I believe that when a banker speaks, you can go the opposite way and be right. That has been proved in recent years."[1222]

Coughlin's Switch

Coughlin was so fond of FDR he said (1933) the U.S. had a choice between "Roosevelt or Ruin."[1223] But the new anti-FDR Coughlin said FDR was "the great liar and betrayer."[1224] By 1934, Coughlin opposed FDR and worked to create a new political party, the National Union of Social Justice.[1225] Louisiana Governor Huey Long would likely have been the party's presidential candidate in 1936, but he was killed in 1935.[1226]

Coughlin changed his mind so much that he now said FDR should be impeached because he was "leaning toward international socialism or sovietism."[1227] Coughlin said (August 1935), "Roosevelt has a poor brand of Russian communism ... I think it is significant the leaders among the communists of the world never once attacked international bankers. Roosevelt will not touch that subject."[1228] Coughlin also hit a journalist who asked him for proof that communists influenced FDR.[1229]

Monsignor John A. Ryan also had a radio show. The attacks by Coughlin were so negative the Democratic National Committee prodded Ryan to speak up; Ryan was reluctant.[1230] In 1936, Ryan told his listeners to reject Coughlin's ideas and vote for FDR in the presidential election.[1231]

Coughlin weakened his downright opposition to FDR in late 1936: "The people have spoken and the only American thing to do is abide by the will of the people."[1232] After the election, Coughlin softened his blows to maintain his version of credibility, given FDR's popularity.

Fascist Priest

The National Union for Social Justice was organized in 1934, fizzled out after the 1936 presidential elections, then was molded into his Christian Front and "was even more ardent in its support of fascism and became a mouthpiece for Nazi propaganda."[1233] Coughlin was greatly influenced by Italian Fascism, and concluded democracy and capitalism were not the answers for the U.S.[1234]

Coughlin rationalized the fascist policies of Mussolini and Hitler. The Nazi press in Germany said Coughlin was "America's most powerful radio commentator."[1235] Coughlin used Nazi propaganda minister Joseph Goebbels' speeches.[1236]

Anti-Semite

He called Jews "Christ-killers and Christ-rejecters."[1237] In November 1938, Coughlin said, "If Jews persist in supporting communism directly or indirectly, that will be regrettable. By their failure to use the press, the radio and the banking house, where they stand so prominently, to fight communism as vigorously as they fight Nazism, the Jews invite the charge of being supporters of communism."[1238] In 1938, roughly the time of the previous comments, a public opinion poll suggested one in every four supported all or most of his ideas.[1239]

In January 1939, Coughlin asked: "Must the entire world go to war for 600,000 Jews in Germany who are neither American, nor French, nor English citizens, but citizens of Germany?"[1240]

Coughlin was an isolationist as WWII approached, and claimed Jewish financiers were trying to get the US in the war.[1241] But Coughlin made sure to point out he was not an anti-Semite.[1242]

Priest Until Death

The Bishop of Detroit is credited with allowing Coughlin to continue a national career as long as he did.[1243] Coughlin was quieted not so much because of the bigotry, but more so because a sedition trial seemed possible, as Coughlin remained an isolationist even after Pearl Harbor.[1244] Coughlin was quieted because of being anti-war, not for hating communists, Jews, and capitalists.

Still, even more disturbing, the Roman Catholic Church never defrocked Coughlin for his hate speech. Coughlin was the pastor at the Shrine of the Little Flower until his retirement in 1966; he died in 1979.[1245] But he continued his blunt speech until the end. In 1973, Coughlin said, "On this earth you must belong to the church militant or get the hell out of it. That's the right word. You're either with me or against me. There is no middle ground in this battle between Christ and the anti-Christ. If you step out of (the battle), you're worse than those boys who ran off to Norway, Sweden, those boys who deserted the government. You're deserters, rotten deserters."[1246]

Coughlin Hurt His Own Church

Coughlin is an important figure who rose to fame because he masked his hatred in the name of God. Furthermore he completely discredited Catholicism in the political realm. Al Smith tried to get himself, a Catholic, in the White House by supporting separation of church and state. Instead, Coughlin was a bigoted, theocratic Catholic who validated some of the anti-Catholicism fears of the 1928 election. In Coughlin's own bigoted quest, he allowed his fellow Catholics to be stigmatized.

JAPANESE AMERICANS

After Pearl Harbor, the U.S. government had to figure out how to handle the Japanese threat in the United States. The decision was a tragic one for Japanese-Americans.

Fear Mongering, Courtesy of...

Army General John DeWitt reported upon investigation: "The Japanese race is an enemy race and while many second and third generation Japanese born on United States soil have become, 'Americanized,' the racial strains are undiluted...It, therefore, follows that along the vital Pacific Coast over 112,000 potential enemies of Japanese extraction are at large today."[1247] DeWitt was responsible for West Coast defenses.[1248] DeWitt is an easy figure to blame in the fear mongering, but he was aided by the Hearst press.[1249]

Earl Warren also heightened hatred against the Japanese-Americans. As the California Attorney General preparing to run for governor, he said, "It is quite significant that in this great state of ours we have no fifth column activities and no sabotage reported...That was the story of Pearl Harbor. I can't help believing that something is planned for us."

Safety or the Constitution?

FDR's cabinet didn't seem bothered by civil rights issues. Hatred of the Japanese promoted this ignorance during WWII. Even FDR has been described as "receptive" to ideas of Dr. Ales Hrdlicka.[1250] Hrdlicka was a Smithsonian curator who argued that due to evidence such as skull size, the Japanese race was linked to deceit and cruelty.[1251]

Some have argued the issue of internment was deferred by FDR because of his eyes on WWII, therefore he left the internment issue up to the Secretary of War, Henry Stimson, who handed the issue off to his assistant.[1252] Stimson admitted Japanese American internment would "make an awful hole in our constitutional system," but he saw the constitution more as a hurdle than rights to be defended.[1253] This position was validated by Assistant Secretary of War John J. McCloy, who said, "...if it is a question of the safety of the country or the Constitution of the U.S., why, the Constitution is just a scrap of paper to me."[1254] McCloy's support for internment was "supported by high-ranking and distinguished members of the Administration and Congress, including Milton Eisenhower, Abe Fortas, Henry Stimson, and Hugo Black."[1255] (Like McCloy's logic, the U.S. Supreme Court upheld internment in two court cases based on the grounds of national security during war.[1256])

FDR signed Executive Order 9066 for internment on February 19, 1942, without holding any cabinet meetings.[1257] Besides being ripped out of their homes, those interned forfeited their investments and bank accounts.[1258] Camps were set up in the inner West (Utah, Wyoming, and Arizona).[1259] Those in government relabeled the camps "residence control centers."[1260] But these Japanese-American detention centers were surrounded by barbed wire and patrolled by soldiers until the end of the war.[1261]

Internment Criticisms

The first criticism of those interned was the fact that 70,000 of them were American-born Japanese descendents (Nisei).[1262] They were Americans.

The Japanese-Americans who were interned were not given individual review.[1263] This is noteworthy given that immediately after Pearl Harbor, the FBI rounded up and arrested about 2,000 male Japanese in the U.S. considered "bad risks" who were given individual review.[1264]

J. Edgar Hoover, head of the FBI, opposed internment because the executive order inherently implied the FBI's previous roundup of Japanese nationals (immediately after Pearl Harbor) was ineffective.[1265] More ironic, as Harold Evans wrote, "Japanese Americans went unmolested in Hawaii."[1266] Nine out of every ten Japanese Americans (excluding Hawaii) lived in the Pacific Northwest and California.[1267] The government cared less about the Japanese-Americans in Hawaii, even though Hawaii was actually attacked by Japan.

The Supreme Court decided in *Korematsu v. United States* (Dec.1944) to uphold the government policy because of national security.[1268] But three Supreme Court justices opposed internment in the 1944 decision, and one of those said internment was the "legalization of racism."[1269]

Honorable Japanese-Americans

An army unit was recruited from the Japanese internment camps and fought in the Italian campaign of WWII and "was the army's most decorated unit in American military history."[1270] In addition, Daniel Inouye was a Japanese American who volunteered to serve from his home state of Hawaii.[1271] After he lost his right arm in Italy, he received a Distinguished Service Cross.[1272] But when he was in uniform in San Francisco, he was refused a haircut.[1273]

During all of WWII, there was not a case recorded of sabotage, subversion or spying by a Japanese American.[1274] Yet ignorance prevailed. By March 1942 alone, there were three dozen anti-Japanese crimes in the US, seven of which were murders.[1275] Adding to the ignorance, some victims of the crimes were actually Chinese.[1276]

WOMEN

Women have been treated as second class citizens throughout U.S. history. But here are two telling examples of cultural bias.

Al Smith & Frances Perkins

Frances Perkins became the first woman appointed to a president's (FDR's) cabinet in 1933.[1277] Al Smith, the 1928 Democratic presidential nominee, questioned President Franklin D. Roosevelt's decision. He told the President: "Men will take advice from a woman, but it is hard for them to take orders from a woman."[1278] Labor unions opposed her appointment to Labor Secretary.[1279] Male columnists said she was tearful and hysterical.[1280] Accordingly, she wasn't even invited to the Gridiron dinner (all the other male cabinet members were).[1281] Hate groups called her another Jew in the "Jew Deal," even though she was actually Episcopalian.[1282]

Helen Gahagan Douglas

Helen Douglas (1900-1980) was a Broadway musical star in the 1920s who married actor Melvyn Douglas in 1931 and moved to California, where she was elected to the U.S. House of Representatives in the 1940s.[1283] She served three terms in the House and had an affair with Lyndon Johnson.[1284] She lost by almost 20 points to Nixon for Senate, and was also hurt by the new struggle against communism in Korea.[1285]

In 1972, Henry Fonda was asked why he disliked Richard Nixon. Was it Nixon's position on Vietnam or the economy? Fonda responded: "No, I think he's trying to end the war as fast as he can, and I don't think the President has that much impact on the economy. But I would go anywhere and do anything I could to stop Richard Nixon because I will never forget or forgive what he did to Helen Gahagan Douglas."[1286]

In the 1950 Senate campaign, Nixon earned his nickname "Tricky Dick," and Douglas was labeled the "Pink Lady."[1287] She was one of Nixon's earliest victims. Mixing sexism and anti-communism, Nixon used one of the most vitriolic campaign slanders of all-time by calling Douglas "pink down to her underwear."

Hypocrisy Everywhere

History is filled with hypocrisy, contradictions and unjustified hatred, especially when it comes to civil rights.

The Puritans set out to America for religious freedom, but kicked Roger Williams and Anne Hutchinson out of Massachusetts Bay Colony.

Thomas Jefferson penned the Declaration of Independence, but owned slaves.

Andrew Jackson may have fought with one of the most diverse military units in U.S. history during the Battle of New Orleans, but did more than anyone to remove Native Americans from their lands.

Martin Van Buren opposed slavery, but supported "Indian Removal."

President Grant tried to support freed-slaves' rights during Reconstruction, but he evicted Jews from Kentucky in the Civil War.

Teddy Roosevelt let Booker T. Washington into the White House, but called the Native Americans savages.

President William Howard Taft stood up for blacks in his inaugural address, but was Chief Justice of the US Supreme Court in *Buck v. Bell.*

Woodrow Wilson appointed the first Jew to the Supreme Court, but was thrilled and supportive of *The Birth of a Nation.*

William Jennings Bryan was seen as the moral crusading Protestant voice for God fighting Prohibition and Evolution, but he was a white supremacist.

Al Smith endured anti-Catholic hatred, but was convinced Frances Perkins would be an ineffective Labor Secretary because she was a woman.

California Attorney General Earl Warren interned the Japanese, but was the voice for desegregation as Chief Justice of the US Supreme Court during *Brown v. Board of Education.*

Lesson From Lincoln

Abraham Lincoln freed the slaves. But Lincoln, while previously debating Stephen Douglas, said, "I am not, nor ever have been in favor of bringing about the social and political equality of the white and black races," to which there was applause and Lincoln continued, "that I am not nor ever have been in favor of making voters or jurors of Negroes."[1288]

This quote is embarrassing, but it is not included to discredit the 16th president. This quote may be the most important of all those included in this chapter because it should make us examine ourselves. If the author of the Emancipation Proclamation can so speak, what lapses in logic do we have? What blind spots are we unaware of?

What breeds hatred?

Bigotry survives because our leaders, however great or small, close or distant, validate it. The reasons for allowing hatred to continue are numerous. But there are common themes. Here are four recurring historical reasons for hating or denigrating a group of people.

1) Unexplainable Fear Rationalized. Whenever there is something to be feared, the fear needs an explanation. Some locals in Salem were acting strange. There had to be *some* reason. The fear was erroneously put on "witches."

Japanese-American internment is another example. Pearl Harbor occurred, and the U.S. couldn't let it happen again. Internment was a horrid idea, because it was the imprisonment of *Americans*. Even J. Edgar Hoover opposed it. But Pearl Harbor was a shock, and the nation's fears had to be quelled.

2) Economic Interests. Columbus raped and pillaged "his" New World. Gold was his major priority, not the treatment of natives. Miners killing California Native Americans in the 1850s is another example. By justifying the killing of "savages," the natives could be killed. Like Columbus, the California miner's pockets were full. But their character was stained.

The Indian Removal Act was the result of conjured up excuses to rip Native Americans off their land so settlers could selfishly keep moving west. Hating "Indians" is easier when the are dehumanized, labeled warlike and considered inferior.

Immigration issues latent with racism seems to always revolve around jobs. Whether that was the Irish in the 1850s, the Chinese in the 1880s, the Italians in the 1920s or today's Latinos.

3) Loss of Power. If Anne Hutchinson was right in Massachusetts, there would have been no need for John Winthrop's leadership. So Winthrop removed Hutchinson.

If Afro-Americans were allowed to vote in the South, the white man's voice would be less powerful. If women are allowed to succeed at work or in government, men have more competition.

Of course, political power and risks is always a factor in allowing bigotry to continue. Examples here would include FDR's silence on an anti-lynching bill, or JFK's and LBJ's initial inaction on civil rights. In those cases, the Democratic Presidents did not want to infringe on the power their party had on the South.

4) Weakness of those who can make change. Weakness is what allows bigotry to continue. FDR couldn't pass an anti-lynching bill but his wife had the courage to leave the D.A.R.

The bishop of Detroit should have quieted Fr. Coughlin in 1933. Instead, Coughlin maintained his radio fame and nationwide influence for almost another decade. The inability to quiet Coughlin promoted fascism, hurt Jews, and perhaps most importantly, discredited a Catholic Church with many sincere followers.

Those in power, those in leadership roles, and those in the majority have a moral obligation to speak for those who fear to talk. William Howard Taft and Eleanor Roosevelt's leadership on Afro-American issues is important because they were in the white majority. Eugene Debs' right to socialist beliefs were given some credibility because Warren G. Harding, a conservative Republican critical of labor unions, pardoned him.

Please speak for those who can't defend themselves.

Chapter Seven:
The totally bear scat homophobic logic being used and a response to that nonsense.

"War. Rape. Murder. Poverty. Equal rights for gays. Guess which one the Southern Baptist Convention is protesting?"[1289]

I encourage all the readers to study the issues and responses in this chapter and to use them vigorously. The issues discussed below, with the illogical and indefensible arguments being used, cover the following: being gay, gay marriage, gays and children, gay adoption, reparative therapy, and the sky is falling.

Many, if not most, of the common myths, misconceptions, and misunderstandings of the LGBT community and the desire of lesbians and gays to be covered by the Constitutional provisions guaranteed by the 14th Amendment come from the public ravings of two groups and their subsidiaries, The Family Research Council of James Dobson and the Family Research Institute of Paul Cameron.

The Family Research Institute (FRI) has its origins in the early 1980s in Colorado Springs. It was originally known as the Institute for the Scientific Investigation of Sexuality (ISIS). It was founded by Cameron. Though Cameron claims to be a doctor, some have argued the American Psychological Association (APA) dropped Cameron from its membership because of his research methods; supporters claimed Cameron resigned from the APA before they dropped him from membership.

According to Sourcewatch, "The FRI is a homophobic hate group that presents itself as a Think Tank and chaired by Paul Cameron, a former psychologist who has been kicked out of and censored by professional associations for his misrepresentations of scientific data to advance his homophobic views. Information on who funds the institute is conspicuously absent from the organizations web site."[1290]

Research used by Focus on the Family and the Family Research Institute is paid for by people who want results that prove their point. It is "peer reviewed" by philosophical fellow travelers, it is based on qualitative research that is not valid or reliable. It is a sham. It is Lucky Strike telling you that smoking is good for you. I have a Ph.D.. I know what valid, reliable, honest research is, Cameron's work doesn't come close.

Myths on Homosexuality

1) Homosexuality is a public health risk. Mike Huckabee said (1992) he felt "homosexuality is an aberrant, unnatural, and sinful lifestyle, and we now know it can pose a dangerous public health risk."[1291] Unprotected sex, straight or gay, is a health risk.

2) Homosexuality is a disease. Homosexuals were once thought to be mentally ill. Perhaps one of homosexual's biggest burden was being labeled a disorder into the 1960s. Ronald Gold aptly stated, "The diagnosis of homosexuality as a 'disorder' is a contributing factor to the pathology of those homosexuals who do become mentally ill.... Nothing is more likely to make you sick than being constantly told that you are sick."[1292]

So gays should call in sick. Robin Tyler once said, "If homosexuality is a disease, let's all call in queer to work: 'Hello. Can't work today, still queer.'"[1293]

3) Homosexuals focus on sex. By that logic almost all teenage boys are gay. Boy George has also countered: "There's this illusion that homosexuals have sex and heterosexuals fall in love. That's completely untrue. Everybody wants to be loved."[1294] There isn't a cap on love. By granting gay rights, the love of one heterosexual couple does not lose love.

4) Homosexual sympathy will mean more homosexuals. For example, gay bashers say if straight kids understand and are more compassionate and accepting of gay kids, then more kids will "turn" gay. The anti-gay lobby fears if straight kids see gays as real people (not so-called freaks), the anti-gay lobby will lose support for their anti-gay political agendas. The ever increasing understanding, tolerance and acceptance of the gay community drives the homophobe nuts; so, they use this argument. I like vampire movies, will I bite people in the neck and drink their blood? I am 67, haven't done it yet.

5) Acting gay makes you gay. Perry King once said, "People sometimes think I'm gay because I once played a gay in a movie. It's funny. Audiences don't think you're a murderer if you play a murderer, but they do think you're gay if you play a gay."[1295]

6) Pride parades aren't necessary. Hell, neither is St. Patrick's Day. Rob Nash once said, "I get sick of listening to straight people complain about, 'Well, hey, we don't have a heterosexual-pride day, why do you need a gay-pride day?' I remember when I was a kid I'd always ask my mom: 'Why don't we have a Kid's Day? We have a Mother's Day and a Father's Day, but why don't we have a Kid's Day?' My mom would always say, 'Every day is Kid's Day.' To all those heterosexuals that bitch about gay pride, I say the same thing: Every day is heterosexual-pride day! Can't you people enjoy your banquet and not piss on those of us enjoying our crumbs over here in the corner?"[1296]

I think the solidarity shown in the parade is very important. I think showing your ass is not. Extremely counter-productive.

7) Homosexuals are not real people. There are people who are straight. We do not call them straight people. I am not called a straight man. I am called a man. There are homosexuals, heterosexuals, bisexuals, and transsexuals. So why do we say, “He is a gay man?” He is a man, who happens to be gay. Don’t over focus on labels. As Martina Navratilova said, “Labels are for filing. Labels are for clothing. Labels are not for people.”[1297] Labels hurt society’s perception of gays, because heterosexuals see gays as abnormal and as a separate culture. So, the society becomes more anti-gay. And, like Joseph Francis once said, “As long as society is anti-gay, then it will seem like being gay is anti-social.”[1298]

8) Homosexuals are bad co-workers. Dr. Gregory Herek’s research at UC Davis concludes, “Scientific research provides no evidence that homosexual people are less likely than heterosexuals to exercise good judgment and appropriate discretion in their employment settings.”[1299]

9) Homosexuals don’t live in committed relationships. The American Psychological Association noted, “Research indicates that many lesbians and gay men want and have committed relationships. For example, survey data indicate that between 40% and 60% of gay men and between 45% and 80% of lesbians are currently involved in a romantic relationship. Furthermore, data from the 2000 U.S. Census indicates that of the 5.5 million couples who were living together but not married, about 1 in 9 (594,391) had partners of the same sex. Although the census data are almost certainly an underestimate of the actual number of cohabiting same-sex couples, they indicate that there are 301,026 male same-sex households and 293,365 female same-sex households in the United States.”[1300]

10) Homosexual couples have different goals and values as heterosexual couples. The American Psychological Association notes a “common misconception is that the goals and values of lesbian and gay couples are different from those of heterosexual couples. In fact, research has found that the factors that influence relationship satisfaction, commitment, and stability are remarkably similar for both same-sex cohabiting couples and heterosexual married couples.”[1301]

11) Homosexuals are unhappy, dysfunctional. The American Psychological Association says, “…one stereotype is that the relationships of lesbians and gay men are dysfunctional and unhappy. However, studies have found same-sex and heterosexual couples to be equivalent to each other on measures of relationship satisfaction and commitment.”[1302]

12) Homosexuals are only in San Francisco …

The *Milwaukee Journal Sentinel* reported (8.22.2001) the U.S. census counted 594,391 households headed by same-sex couples, [1303] about one-half of 1% of the 105.5 million U.S. homes.[1304] During the census, people could check off ‘unmarried partner” living with them, and they also said they were living with someone of the same sex.[1305]

Individuals in the census aren’t asked about their orientation, and the census doesn’t count gay couples who do not live together.[1306] The numbers are a low estimate, given the amount of homosexuals unwilling to publicize their sexuality. When the numbers were released in 2001, Gary Glenn, president of the American Family Association's Michigan affiliate, said "Clearly this tiny percentage does not justify . . . passage of local or state laws that grant special protected-class status to such behavior...It's obviously in the political interests of homosexual activists to artificially inflate the number of people who engage in homosexual behavior."[1307]

California, New York, Texas and Florida led the country in the number of same-sex-led households, but in terms of percentage, Washington D.C. led (with 1.48% of all D.C. households); California and Vermont tied for second at 0.80%.[1308]

San Francisco County led all other counties in the U.S. when it came to percentage of same-sex household (2.70%), followed by Monroe County, Florida (1.59%), Hampshire County Massachusetts (1.53%); DeKalb County, Georgia (1.38%); and Arlington County, Virginia (1.34%). [1309]

California had over 92,000 gay couples in the 2000 census.[1310] It is true that Midwestern states have fewer gays. Illinois had 22,887; Indiana, 10,219; Iowa, 3,698; Michigan, 15,368; and Minnesota, 9,147. The 2000 data was more reflective of homosexual population realities, but the 2010 census will actually attempt to count same-sex households.

Myths About Gay Marriage

Marriage Equality would harm existing marriages. I have searched and searched hard through the records of all 50 states, the District of Columbia, Puerto Rico, Guam, and our military bases scattered world-wide. In all that work, examining records since 1787 until now, nationwide and world wide, I have not found one single divorce filed because the United States or or any state did not have a Constitutional Amendment banning gay marriage.

The Government would be sponsoring "unethical" behavior. First, the government cannot regulate every "unethical" behavior. Defining what unethical behavior that the U.S. government should regulate is not always easy. Murder, stealing, fraud...they are all unethical. They also are behaviors of one individual that negatively impact another individual. Homosexual behavior between consenting adults is constitutionally protected behavior (*Lawrence v. Texas*). Furthermore, governments allow "unethical" behavior that many churches or citizens think are evil: the lottery, favoring certain forms of pollution, corrupt sourcing of defense hardware. Allowing is not sponsoring. State governments do not actively prosecute adultery, even in states where it is a felony, which it is in Wisconsin.

The Government would be sponsoring disease causing behavior. Actually, encouraging monogamy among same-sex couples is a public health benefit, with marriage comes social responsibility and increased monogamy, and less disease.

Marriage will be ruined as an institution and redefined. When 50% of marriages end in divorce, it is hard to say the institution of marriage is rock solid. Half of marriages end before death, and it's not because of gayness. The institution of heterosexual marriage is broken and we have millions of children of divorced parents suffering through this trauma daily to prove it. Furthermore…

a. Gays don't want to redefine the institution; they just want to participate in the already existing one.
b. The working definition of marriage is two people united as one pledging themselves to stay together and form a family. Whether those two people are two men, two women, or one man and one woman doesn't really "redefine" the base of the institution.
c. Nothing is redefined for heterosexual couples. Even if we allow two gay men to marry, heterosexuals will still be able to marry, so nothing has been "redefined" about heterosexual marriage.

Gay Marriage will destroy family structure. If you want to encourage stability and family structure, let people get married! In February 2004, Mayor Richard M. Daley said he would have "no problem" with Cook County issuing marriage licenses to same-sex couples.[1311] He said, "Marriage has been undermined by divorce…So don't tell me about marriage. People should look at their own life and look into their own mirror."[1312]

Banning gay marriage will preserve the human race. As one blogger argued, "We are not banning any activity [gay marriage] but promoting an activity ["traditional marriage"] that is not only good for society but necessary for the preservation of the human race."[1313] With about 40 percent of all births in the United States being out-of-wedlock births, who claims it is necessary? Biologically, it just isn't so. Banning gay marriage will not stop a flu epidemic or nuclear war.

Gay Marriage would ruin the natural way of having kids. What is "natural"? Adopting kids isn't natural? Inutero planting an embryo isn't natural? So adoptive parents mean less to society than heterosexual-biological parents? When anti-gay groups think marriage only legitimizes children, they demean adoptive families. One doesn't have to share genetic material to have "parents."

Gay Marriage will erase traditional marriage. Nobody is proposing to outlaw 'traditional' marriage. This is the biggest fallacy. A man and a woman can get married before the justice of the peace, there's nothing traditional about it. Gays deserve that same right. This isn't about forcing the Catholic Church to let two men get married at St. John's Cathedral and a priest forced at gunpoint to consecrate the union.

President George W. Bush gave speeches on how marriage is "sacred." Civil institutions regulated by government are not "sacred." Religious institutions regulated by churches are, by definition, "sacred." Thus, Bush is explicitly advocating government regulation of what he himself asserts to be a religious institution, which is a clear violation of the First Amendment, and blatant theocracy. Civil institutions regulated by government are not "sacred." How many of these religious right fanatics bashing gay marriage would be proud to have their son married by the justice of the peace? The ridiculous assertion that churches are going to be forced/sued into marrying gay people is absurd.

Not allowing churches to legally marry a gay couple is a violation of the First Amendment just as forcing them to would be. Obtaining, paying for, signing and witnessing, and filing a marriage license is not sacred.

The marriage of one man and one woman may be considered the traditional marriage in the United States, possibly, since they are the only ones ever allowed. Totally weird circular logic.

Gay Marriage is an assault on the Bible Belt and the portion of the country that respects marriage. In 2005, the old Confederacy, the present "Bible Belt" had a combined average of 4.35 divorces per 1000 population. Oklahoma had 5.6. The national average was only 3.6. And how about Massachusetts where gay marriages are allowed? Only 2.2.[1314]

Gay Marriage has never existed, and it's always been one woman and one man. Rick Santorum said (4.7.2003), "Every society in the history of man has upheld the institution of marriage as a bond between a man and a woman. Why? Because society is based on one thing, children. Monogamous relationships. In every society, the definition of marriage has not ever to my knowledge included homosexuality."[1315] Monogamy is relatively new to the planet and is certainly not universal. And last time I looked, not all marriages have children.

Gay marriage is a subset for tax and other material advantages. To not be at the death bed of your lover is not a material advantage. You shouldn't be banned from a hospital visit by your lover's parents, or from inheriting what other heterosexuals rightfully inherit.

Gay Marriage would lead to polygamy. Polygamy would have to require a new line of thinking on custody, taxes, and social benefits, and more importantly, it's not a form of household that's at all common in the U.S. To suggest gay marriage would be a slippery slope is pushing it. The slippery slope argument can just as easily be applied to straight marriages. If we allowed one man to marry one woman, what's to stop one man from marrying two women? The polygamist threat of gay marriage is a straw man. But, if society decided to expand men and women's freedom to so choose, would it not be their choice. It was so in the Bible.

And if there is a problem with polygamy, it's because heterosexual marriage (NOT Gay marriage) already led to polygamy. The Bible, which is an apparent wealth of truth against homosexuality, is also a wonderful history of polygamy. Polygamy is feared as a branch of gay marriage, but polygamy already exists, and fermented during the reign of heterosexual marriage. We've had polygamy for millennia, far longer than we've had the idea of gay marriage. It's illogical that gay marriage would be more likely to lead to polygamy when straight marriages have already included polygamy.

As comedians point out, we actually have polygamy, a chronological version that includes two, three, or even more spouses.

People are almost unanimously opposed to gay marriage. Pew concluded (June 2008), the balance of public opinion regarding gay marriage was "more positive in 2008 than what it was during the 2004 campaign."[1316] Pew found (May 2008), "49% of Americans said they oppose allowing gay and lesbian couples to marry while 38% favored gay marriages."[1317] It was the first time (in over a decade of asking the question) that a majority (over 50%) did not oppose gay marriage.[1318]

In July 2004, 56% opposed gay marriage while only 32% supported it.[1319] However, gay marriage had increased in importance in mid 2008 from the fall of 2007, specifically among Republicans and white evangelical Protestants.[1320] Pew noted, "While there is somewhat greater support for gay marriage than four years ago, overwhelming majorities of Republicans (75%) and white evangelical Protestants (81%) oppose allowing gays to marry, and about half in each group strongly opposes gay marriage (48% of Republicans, 54% of white evangelicals). Opinions about gay marriage in both groups are virtually unchanged from July 2004."[1321]

In comparison from four years earlier, Pew concluded the opposition towards gay marriage weakened among women, college graduates, and those 65 and older.[1322] The ten point decrease in elderly opposition did not swing entirely to support of gay marriage, but rather a higher proportion of elderly respondents who did not offer an opinion.[1323]

The numbers swing month to month. Pew found the following views on same-sex marriage and civil unions during 2009:

	Same sex marriage			Civil unions		
	Favor	Oppose	DK	Favor	Oppose	DK
	%	%	%	%	%	%
Total	39	53	8	57	37	6

According to a Washington Post-ABC News Poll (Feb.2010), 47 percent of respondents thought gay marriage should be legal, and 50 percent said it should be illegal. The same poll also found 75 percent of respondents supported repealing DADT.[1324]

Gay marriage is against the natural way of love. Gay-basher's wrapped in religion confuse love of spirit with love focused on genitalia. When gay-bashers are saying marriage is between a man and a woman, they really mean marriage requires a penis and a vagina. The zealot's version of "God's image" focuses on genitalia rather than love. This is one of the saddest ironies: the religious conservatives and their political supporters, wrapping themselves in the flag of God, ignore His love and concentrate on the genitalia of human beings. Such a sad almost sick tunnel vision way of looking at the world. Are they all suffering from penis-envy? I actually think they might be.

Paul Newman once said, "I'm a supporter of gay rights. And not a closet supporter either. From the time I was a kid, I have never been able to understand attacks upon the gay community. There are so many qualities that make up a human being... by the time I get through with all the things that I really admire about people, what they do with their private parts is probably so low on the list that it is irrelevant."[1325]

After gay marriage, homesexual will want more rights. Women could finally vote for president in 1920; then they got greedy and still wanted to be paid fairly and be free from harassment and groping at work. Give me a break.

Gay marriage and gay rights is different than Afro-American civil rights. On *The View*, Mike Huckabee said (Nov.2008), "People who are homosexuals should have every right in terms of their civil rights, to be employed, to do anything they want. . . . But when we're talking about a redefinition of an institution, that's different than individual civil rights. . . . Here is the difference. Bull Connor was hosing people down in the streets of Alabama. John Lewis got his skull cracked on the Selma Bridge."[1326] Segregation was institutional. So is homophobia, as for the rest, ask Matt Shepherd.

Hate the sin but love the sinner... What is the sin, being a homosexual? Then God created a sinner. So we love the homosexual, a sinner. See. None of this makes sense.

Then why are you prohibiting the homosexual to marry the person of their choice or to have civil union types of benefits and protection? Is marriage the sin? No. After all, the proponents of DOMA are trying to "save marriage." Is a civil union a sin? Nonsense. So, where is the sin? Ah, we know, sex is the sin. What people do with their private parts is a sin. Sex is a sin if you are single; if you are enjoying it with someone who is not your spouse, it is a sin; and sex during menstrual periods is a sin. Finally, sex with your right hand is a sin. We do not prosecute or enforce these sins. So, what makes this "sin" so special for these folks? Why are they so fascinated by it?

It is all about protecting the family.

A 2007 Pew Research Center Report found "children had fallen to eighth out of nine on a list of factors that people associate with successful marriages," reports the AP. In fact, sharing in household chores and having a satisfying sex life were seen as more essential than children to a good marriage. What's more, 65 percent of Americans say the purpose of marriage is "mutual happiness and fulfillment";

only 23 percent say it instead services the "bearing and raising of children."

A new 2008 Census Bureau report shows more women in their 40s are childless, while those who are having children are having fewer than ever before. The same report shows more than 28 percent of children born in the year preceding the 2006 survey were born to mothers who had never been married. According to the Census Bureau's report "Fertility of American Women: 2006," over the last 30 years the number of women aged 40 to 44 with no children has doubled from 10 percent to 20 percent. If it is all about family, is the sin having no children?

Speaking of Families.... Gay Adoption

"Arkansas's Child Welfare Agency Review Board established a policy in 1999 that banned gay people from serving as foster parents, and the Arkansas Supreme Court struck it down after a seven-year legal battle between the state and the ACLU."[1327] The decision occurred in June 2006.[1328] The Arkansas Supreme Court was convinced "the driving force behind adoption of the regulations was not to promote the health, safety and welfare of foster children but rather based upon the board's views of morality and its bias against homosexuals."[1329]

The Arkansas Supreme Court pointed to the findings of a lower court overturning the ban and criticized the Review Board's reasoning: "These facts demonstrate that there is no correlation between the health, welfare, and safety of foster children and the blanket exclusion of any individual who is a homosexual or who resides in a household with a homosexual."[1330] The Court said the state's argument "flies in the face" of the scientific evidence about gay parenting.[1331]

Next, a bill barring unmarried couples from adopting was taken up by the legislature. At the time, Gov. Mike Beebe suggested there were constitutional problems with the bill and the legislation died (although Beebe would not say if he intended to veto it if it were passed).[1332]

In 2008, a socially conservative group which spearheaded the Arkansas constitutional ban on same-sex marriage organized the signatures for the adoption referendum, which was similar to a bill that died in the legislature earlier that year.[1333] In August, proponents submitted over 85,000 valid signatures from registered voters, which was 23,000 more valid names than required.[1334]

In November 2008, Arkansas voters decided whether to bar unmarried couples from fostering or adopting children.[1335]

The results in Arkansas

The Associated Press concluded (11.6.08), "Rural counties and evangelical voters fueled by a pulpit campaign pushed Arkansas into adopting one of the nation's strictest bans on unmarried couples serving as foster or adoptive parents."[1336] It passed with nearly 57% of the vote.[1337] Only Pulaski County (Little Rock included) had a strong margin of opposition, and Washington County (home of the University of Arkansas) rejected the ban by over 2,000 of the 65,000 cast.[1338]

Gov. Mike Beebe opposed the ban because of the lack of foster homes in the state.[1339] Opponents were surprised, including Arkansas Families First which ran TV ads for gay adoption.[1340] In contrast, the Arkansas Family Council painted the proposal to battle against a "gay agenda" and concentrated their support through pulpit sermons, not television ads.[1341] No surprise, the initiative's passage was credited to "those identifying themselves as evangelical or born-again Christians."[1342]

Arkansas children needing and wanting the love, safety, and nurturing a home with parents lost that possibility. It was taken from them by the preachers. In God's name. Morons.

There are 500,000 foster care kids in the country who need stable homes.[1343] There's no surprise the American Academy of Pediatrics supports gay adoption.[1344]Gay adoption bans immediately nullify the child's best interest. By not allowing a child to have the opportunity to have gay parents, a ban immediately is limiting a child's choice.

Nationwide Gay Adoption Status

In short, as 2008 came to a close; 3 states effectively banned gay couples from adoption; a dozen more allowed same-sex couples to adopt, and another 35 states were unclear what would happen if a gay adoption petition were presented.[1345]

Arkansas joined Utah as the only two states banning unmarried straight or gay couples from fostering or adopting children.[1346] Utah prohibits both adoption and fostering by unmarried partners who live together, a de facto ban for gay couples; in general, Utah's ban is like Arkansas's.[1347]

Mississippi bans gay couples, but not single gays, from adopting children.[1348]

Florida is the only state in the nation to ban gay adoption outright and explicitly.[1349] The Florida law was passed in 1977.[1350] It is noteworthy that gays can foster children. *USNews.com* reported how one gay raised two boys in Miami from 2004 to 2008, but couldn't finalize adoption[1351]

Confusing options for homosexuals?

Michigan is a good example of the confusion of where potential gay adoption supporters could go; the state's attorney general had a nonbinding 2004 opinion against gay couples adopting.[1352] Because Michigan courts have a tendency to be conservative (and unlikely to support gay adoption), gay advocates are leery of fighting a court battle.[1353]

Likewise, if gays are in a state where the outcome for gay couples adoption is unclear, it may be better to adopt as an individual.[1354] However, problems arise if the second person in the couple can't adopt. As of 2008, it was unclear in 22 states whether the second person in a gay couple could adopt their partner's adopted or biological child.[1355] The child is left vulnerable if the gay parent dies, and the remaining partner has no legal rights.

At the same time, gay advocates are cautious in trying to increase legal rights and clarifying the issue. *USNews.com* gave the example in Florida, where a state senator wanted to overturn the state's gay adoption ban, but she was warned her attempt would cause conservative groups to counter with a ban on gay foster parents.[1356] If the status quo is left alone, gay parented families may be better off if family judges see them in individual court cases rather than a set of overt state laws.

In general, gay adoption is not a social hot-button yet because it is overshadowed by gay marriage.[1357] Gay supporters may want to keep it that way. Once social conservatives think gay marriage is "solved," they will work against gay adoption.

Correcting Myths On Homosexual Parents

The American Psychological Association notes, "In the 2000 U.S. Census, 33% of female same-sex couple households and 22% of male same-sex couple households reported at least one child under the age of 18 living in the home. Although comparable data are not available, many single lesbians and gay men are also parents, and many same-sex couples are part-time parents to children whose primary residence is elsewhere."[1358] There are plenty of gay parents in the United States, and it important to defend them.

Myth: Lots of evidence shows gays are bad parents. The American Psychological Association notes, "social science has shown that the concerns often raised about children of lesbian and gay parents—concerns that are generally grounded in prejudice against and stereotypes about gay people—are unfounded. Overall, the research indicates that the children of lesbian and gay parents do not differ markedly from the children of heterosexual parents in their development, adjustment, or overall well-being."[1359]

Myth: Children of gay parents will have sexual identity problems. An example would be anti-gays suggest children will develop problems in gender identity or their gender role. The American Psychological Association notes: "The answer from research is clear: sexual and gender identities (including gender identity, gender-role behavior, and sexual orientation) develop in much the same way among children of lesbian mothers as they do among children of heterosexual parents. Few studies are available regarding children of gay fathers."[1360]

Myth: Children of gay parents will have more mental breakdowns, behavior issues. The American Psychological Association states, ".... studies of personality, self-concept, and behavior problems show few differences between children of lesbian mothers and children of heterosexual parents."[1361] There have been fewer studies on gay fathers.[1362]

Myth: Gay parents will molest children. The American Psychological Association observes, "There is no scientific support for fears about children of lesbian or gay parents being sexually abused by their parents or their parents' gay, lesbian, or bisexual friends or acquaintances."[1363]

IS HOMOSEXUALITY GENETIC?

"If God had wanted me otherwise, He would have created me otherwise."
~Johann von Goethe

Does the question matter?

By proving gays are born gay, homosexuals likely would have wider social acceptance because they don't have a "choice" and therefore would get better protection from discrimination.[1364] As the biological argument is more accepted, as it has in recent years, many supporters argue it has made Americans more accepting of homosexuals.[1365]

Proving homosexuality is genetic is a threat to social conservatives. *The Boston Globe* reported how the Family Research Council, a Christian based conservative think tank, argued in the book *Getting It Straight.* The book admits if people found gays were born that way, it "would advance the idea that sexual orientation is an innate characteristic, like race; that homosexuals, like African-Americans, should be legally protected against 'discrimination;' and that disapproval of homosexuality should be as socially stigmatized as racism. However, it is not true."[1366]

Gay marriage advocates will have an easier time with their debate if they play it as civil rights, since they are equal citizens under the Constitution. The science on the question is important. Indeed, "if the long-overdue national debate on homosexuality took place, the poverty of the anti-homosexual case would become readily apparent."[1367]

Michael Bailey and Richard Pillard, who studied twins and homosexuality, noted (1991), "Despite many attempts, there has been no clear demonstration that parental behavior, even a parent's homosexuality, affects children's sexual orientation. Cultures tolerant of homosexuals do not appear to raise more of them than do less permissive societies. Homophobes sometimes justify their prejudice against homosexuals by alleging that homosexuality is contagious -- that young homosexuals become that way because of older homosexuals and that homosexuality is a social corruption. Such beliefs form the core of the organized anti-homosexual movement. If homosexuality is largely innate, this would prove that these claims are groundless."[1368]

To this author I have to ask what difference does it make. A man and a woman are who they say they are. Regardless of reason. It is the worst kind of elitism to challenge someone's identity.

Homosexuality May Be Genetic Because…

With no particular preference, here is list of theories and research indicating homosexuality is a predisposition.

1) Men with older brothers are more likely gay. A study released in the Proceedings of the National Academy of Sciences in late June 2006 showed men who had multiple older brothers from the same mother, whether raised together or not, had an increased chance of being homosexual.[1369]

The Big-Brother effect comes from Canadian researchers who found that the chances of a boy being gay increase with each additional older brother he has.[1370] In contrast, birth order does not seem to determine lesbian orientation.[1371] The more older brothers a boy has, the more likely they will be gay. This theory holds there is a complex interaction with hormones (antigens) and the mother's immune system.[1372] Though don't overanalyze the numbers, because there still is a 90% chance the boy with older brothers will be straight.[1373]

Homosexuality runs in families, as studies show 8 to 12 percent of brothers of gay men are also gay, compared with the 2 to 4 percent of the general population.[1374]

2) LeVay: Hypothalamuses are different. In the early 1990s, a study by Simon LeVay, a neurobiologist at the Salk Institute, found a difference among gay and straight men in the hypothalamus, a brain part that develops at an early age.[1375] LeVay, who was from San Diego, announced (1991) he found a major difference in straight and gay men he studied.[1376] He could show a tiny clump of neurons of the anterior hypothalamus, believed to control sexual behavior, was usually twice the size in straights rather than gays.[1377] LeVay's research did not prove the nature over nurture debate, because the clumps could have changed size because of homosexual behavior; but nature supporters argue that is unlikely.[1378]

3) Homosexuals can act different before puberty. Homosexuals often act differently from heterosexuals in early childhood, before they ever heard of sex.[1379] Sometimes pre-pubescent children will have qualities of the opposite sex. For example, a boy who insists he is a girl and wants to play with dolls exhibits behavior called childhood gender nonconformity (CGN).[1380] This isn't a stereotypical tomboy, but rather consistent exhibition of strongly feminine traits in a male while avoiding typical boy behaviors.[1381] In a *Boston Globe* story (2005), it was suggested that much CGN research has been done with males, and of the boys who show CGN, 75 percent of them turn out to be gay or bisexual.[1382]

The *Globe*'s story focused on identical twins who were very different: one male was the typical boy on the playground, the other was clearly feminine.[1383] This is a case were environment clearly wasn't a factor: both were fed, clothed, and nurtured the same way, and the odds were the feminine acting boy was going to be gay.[1384]

Some discussions claim of the children who self-identify as a member of the opposite sex are transgendered.

4) Even conservative religions argue gays are born gay. The Catholic Church concedes you're born gay. The Roman Catholic bishops within the U.S. drafted guidelines for ministry to homosexuals said gays had "no moral obligation to attempt" therapy.[1385] Thus, by its own definition the Church admitted homosexuality was a genetic trait. You couldn't fix it. When the new guidelines for gay outreach came out (Nov.14.06), they were meant to be welcoming but still said gays should be celibate because the church considered such sexuality "disordered."[1386] Although many gay supporters would be disappointed in the Church's positions on gay sex, at least they are starting to concede homosexuality's predisposition. If other religions started to acknowledge the possibility of a genetic root, there would be less push for reparative therapy.

Likewise, in 2005, evangelist Rev. Rob Schenk said he believed homosexuality is not a choice and something "deeply rooted" in people.[1387] Schenk said his conclusion was rendered after speaking to genetic researchers and psychologists.[1388] He still said his followers should oppose homosexuality, but admitted "many evangelicals are living in a sort of state of denial about the advance of this conversation."[1389] Schenk seemed to admit the science was in favor of a biological cause of homosexuality: "If it's inevitable that this scientific evidence is coming, we have to be prepared with a loving response. If we don't have one, we won't have any credibility."[1390]

5) Twin studies. In late 1991, a study of male twins was released by Boston University psychiatrist Richard Pillard and Northwestern University psychologist J. Michael Bailey.[1391] Bailey and Pillard found "male sexual orientation is substantially genetic. In short: Pillard and Bailey found that in identical twins, if a twin was gay, the other had a 50 percent chance of also being gay; for fraternal twins, the rate was about 20 percent.[1392] Identical twins share their entire genetic makeup, but fraternal twins only share about half, so genes were the difference in causing more identical siblings to be gay.[1393]

Even if fraternal twins split with different orientations, genetics still may be involved. Indeed, if a parent feels they raised two kids in a set of twins the same way, it's hard to fathom how one son could be gay because of his environment and the other one not.

6) Why are there still gays? Others have wondered why homosexuality continues. Logically, natural selection should wipe out gays. It doesn't.

7) Jody Huckaby. Jody Huckaby was named the executive director of PFLAG in 2005.[1394] Huckaby's family was strongly Catholic and devoutly Republican. Jody attended a divinity school and one of his sisters is a nun.[1395] The Huckabys grew up in rural Louisiana, and of Jody's seven siblings, three of his brothers, in addition to himself him, are gay.[1396]

The four boys came out during four separate Christmas seasons in the 1980s.[1397] Jody told *On Top Magazine* (2008): "I knew I was gay at an early age. I also knew it was a bad thing, affirmed by my faith and family… It was a big challenge for my family. It took a lot of education. Like many families they moved from tolerance, to acceptance, then finally celebration."[1398] Oprah Winfrey featured the Huckaby family on her show.[1399]

The Huckabys serve as a reminder of the high possibility (proof) that homosexuality is a predisposition.

REPARATIVE THERAPY & THE BELIEF GAYS CAN CHANGE

Family Research Council's Advice

At the FRC website, a question is posted: "I am struggling with homosexuality. Will you please refer me to organizations that can help me?"[1400] The FRC's answer is "Many people, including Christians, struggle with unwanted same-sex attractions. There are support groups that help persons such as yourself deal with those feelings in a way that pleases God. We recommend contacting the organizations at the below links: Love Won Out[,] Exodus International [,and] Parents and Friends of Ex-Gays and Gays."[1401]

How does it come to the point that a gay man might go to the FRC's website? The answer is religion. The following is brief story a gay man shared with my research team. The name of Shaun is cover to insure privacy. The story helps explain why a religious follower may want to "repair" his gay thoughts.

Shaun's Early Catholic Days

The following is a verbatim transcript from a gay Catholic, Shaun. Shaun went to Catholic school for six years, and served mass for his priest for 15 years. After puberty started kicking in, Shaun realized he had homosexual thoughts. He wasn't gay in his mind, although he occasionally had gay thoughts. Being in his teens, and missing no more than five Sunday masses his whole life up to age 22, Shaun was convinced he could pray his way out of it:

"Every weekend I went to confession. I'd ask the priest to forgive me for my sins. I believed if I prayed hard enough my gayness would go away. If it didn't, it was my fault because I didn't have enough faith. I was trapped."

"Another neighboring parish priest suggested reparative therapy, others did not. I remember my priest at college, Fr. Bob, told me my sexual thoughts was my 'cross to carry.' That statement implied that we all have a cross to carry (like Jesus Christ had before he was crucified). Fr. Bob told me God loved me, and I should take up that 'cross and follow' God's will. In addition, Fr. Bob once told me that as you get older, 'The blood runs cold," implying that twenty years later I wouldn't have as many sexual thoughts and my homosexuality would be easier to 'handle' some day."

Shaun added, "Not until I was 23 did I finally breakaway from thinking my homosexuality could be changed. I still cringe at the ten years I lost. Of course, the real shit-kicker was when I found out my archbishop had gay sex when he was younger. Not only had I developed a sense of worthlessness, but the ones who developed my belief were f******g hypocrites. Yes I gave up my cross. And it feels great. And my Maker is okay with it. After all, what type of Father gives his children unbearable crosses to carry. That's not love, it's child abuse. A loving Father wouldn't make you feel like shit every time you think a sexual thought, but that's what the Catholic Church did to me."

Gays Can Change

Various terms are synonymous with the programs initiated to change homosexuals: ex-gay therapy, reparative therapy, conversion therapy. And many organizations exist, such as NARTH and Exodus. NARTH stands for National Association for Research and Therapy of Homosexuality. In addition, there are other groups like Homosexuals Anonymous, Courage (Roman Catholic), JONAH (Jews Offering New Alternatives to Homosexuality), Evergreen (Mormon) and others.[1402]

The Founder of Exodus thinks…

Randy Thomas, Executive Vice-President of Exodus International, says schools are "being co-opted by a worldview that is undermining a child's ability to actually learn how to be a responsible citizen…Teenagers are confused enough about their identity; they don't need gay activists or 'transgendered' activists going into their schools confusing them even further. Gender identity, sexual identity, sexuality are all very complex issues. They should originate from the home."[1403]

Past Treatments

In the past, it was more common in reparative therapy to use electric shock or nausea-producing drugs.[1404] The purpose of the drugs was to induce vomiting while homoerotic material was presented.

The Paulk: Ex-gays

John Paulk was once featured on the cover of *Newsweek* magazine for going straight.[1405] Paulk appeared on the cover of *Newsweek* in 1998, then released his book, and appeared on *Oprah* and *60 Minutes*.[1406] Before the year was over, Paulk was featured prominently in a national advertising campaign funded by ex-gay ministries and conservative religious groups.[1407] The ad usually featured Paulk, ex-gays, and Reggie White.[1408] John Paulk's book was titled *Not Afraid to Change; The Remarkable Story of How One Man Overcame Homosexuality*.[1409]

His wife Anne is a self-described ex-lesbian; she too appeared in nationwide advertisements claiming their conversion thru prayer.[1410]

John Paulk was also on staff for Focus on the Family and managed its Homosexuality and Gender Department.[1411] He was also tied to Exodus. The *Southern Voice* noted (Sept.2000), "[John] Paulk's Exodus International cites about 100 ministries in 35 states, as well as Latin America, the South Pacific and Europe. Two of Exodus' founders, Gary Cooper and Michael Bussee, left their wives for each other in 1979, and remained together until Cooper died of AIDS several years ago."[1412]

Anne Paulk Ad (1998)

A national syndicated advertisement included Anne Paulk in a huge picture gazing at the reader with her hand holding up her head (she, of course, had her wedding ring on). The brief caption by Anne's picture said "Anne Paulk-wife, mother, former lesbian." Her story in the ad used bold heading to reinstitute stereotypes toward gays. For example, the reason she was a lesbian was because she was molested when she was 4 years old. That paragraph was titled "One boy's sin and the making of a lesbian."

The ad's bottom included the line "If you really love someone, you'll tell them the truth." This, like many of the other ads, defended Trent Lott, Reggie White, and Angie and Debbie Winans' then-recent comments calling homosexuality a sin.[1413] Lott, White, and the Winans all were national stories (Lott arguably the biggest) giving attention to their belief that homosexuality could be changed.

Isn't it wonderful when the sun shines and we know the truth!

In September 2000, the "ex-gay" John Paulk was patronizing a Washington DC gay bar.[1414] Paulk admitted to being at Mr. P's, but claimed his intention was just to use the bathroom.[1415] A gay who works for the Human Rights Campaign recognized Paulk.[1416] *Southern Voice* aptly pointed out, "Mr. P's is well known to Washingtonians as the city's longest standing gay bar, operating in the same location since 1976. The bar is located in a block with several establishments offering public restrooms, including two major hotels, a coffee shop, and a number of restaurants."[1417] John said, "I thought I'll go in and go to the bathroom…I wandered back, thinking it was weird to be in a gay bar again. I got a glass of water, sat down and chatted with patrons, including a gentleman who was married."[1418] Paulk told *Southern Voice* he had not been inside a gay bar since 1987.[1419]

John Paulk said, "I want to make it clear that there was no sexual, homosexual intention of any kind…That was not my intention. Focus on the Family is supportive of me and I have the support of my wife Anne, who I love very much."[1420]

Reggie White Shocks Wisconsin: "Nuke the Feminist Unborn Gay Whales"

Reggie White was an "ordained fundamentalist Christian minister,"[1421] known as the "Minister of Defense" for leading the NFL in quarterback sacks, and helping the Green Bay Packers win Super Bowl XXXI.

In March of 1998, the Green Bay Packers' defensive end was invited to speak to the Wisconsin Legislature.[1422] He gave a nearly-hour long speech discussing homosexuality, race and slavery. The speech "turned the Assembly's applause to stunned silence."[1423]

White claimed the country veered from God, partially because homosexuality, a sin, was allowed to "run rampant."[1424] He said gay's plight should not be compared to blacks.[1425] White also stated homosexuality is "one of the biggest sins in the Bible."[1426] "Homosexuality is a decision, it's not a race…People from all different ethnic backgrounds live in this lifestyle. But people from all different ethnic backgrounds also are liars and cheaters and malicious and back-stabbing."[1427]

White explained why there were different races. They are worth mentioning because it gives insight to his logic on homosexuality. "If you go to a black church, you see people jumping up and down because they really get into it."[1428] When it comes to whites, "You guys do a good job of building businesses and things of that nature, and you know how to tap into money."[1429] "Hispanics were gifted in family structure, and you can see a Hispanic person, and they can put 20, 30 people in one home."[1430] In this speech, White said Caucasians could not enslave American Indians because they "knew the territory, and the Indians knew how to sneak up on people."[1431] Indians had spirituality, and Asian were so inventive they "can turn a television into a watch."[1432] And "When you put all of that together, guess what it makes: It forms a complete image of God."[1433] White stood by his comments. He claimed he did not mean to stereotype, but rather talk about society coming together.[1434]

All walks of politics found his speech divisive. The Wisconsin Assembly Minority Leader, Walter Kunicki, D-Milwaukee, noted the tension in the room and concluded most were offended.[1435] State Assembly Speaker Scott Jensen, R-Waukesha said Whites remarks on homosexuals was "disappointing," and said homosexuality was a genetic predisposition.[1436] Rep. Tammy Baldwin, a Madison Democrat who at the time was the Legislature's only openly gay member, was rather reserved and said she hoped there could be a healthy debate.[1437] Baldwin now serves in the U.S. House of Representatives.

CBS, particularly their sports division, had to react. At the time in March of 1998, White had already auditioned for a job at CBS, who fired football analyst Jimmy "The Greek" Snyder in 1988.[1438] Snyder said blacks had been "bred from slavery" to make better athletes.[1439] The *USA Today* eventually reported CBS officials indicated White would not be considered for an NFL commentator position.[1440]

White discussed the criticism he received with the *New York Times*: “I didn't start a ministry to please everybody. I'm getting tired of people patting me on the back, anyway…People are saying they're going to have to re-evaluate me. I said: 'Don't re-evaluate me. Forget about me. I don't need your money.’”[1441]

Trent Lott

In June 1988, Senate Majority Leader Trent Lott (R-Miss.) equated homosexuality with alcoholism, sexual addiction and kleptomania.[1442] Specifically, an interviewer said, “The act of homosexuality in and of itself was a sin. It is a sin.”[1443] Lott responded, “It is. My father had that problem, as I said, with alcoholism. Other people have sex addiction. Other people, you know, are kleptomaniacs. I mean, there are all kinds of problems and addictions and difficulties and experiences with things that you—that are wrong, but you should try to work with that person.”[1444] Lott added: "You still love that person and you should not try to mistreat them or treat them as outcasts. You should try to show them a way to deal with that.”[1445]

The GOP response varied. There were a few Republicans who defended gays. Richard Tafel, executive director of Log Cabin Republicans, said “Senator Lott has insulted every gay person in the Republican Party…It was an insult to Congressman Jim Kolbe of Arizona, an Appropriations subcommittee chairman in the House, and to the dedicated and loyal gay and lesbian Republican activists across the country that helped the GOP win its majority."[1446]

Others worked the middle ground for the GOP. During this saga, John McCain said, “It's a very tough issue…We have a large party, a majority party. We have lots of facets to our party and lots of interests. The Log Cabin Republicans [a gay and lesbian organization] should be part of our party. The Christian Right should be part of our party."[1447]

Many Republican leaders hid behind their bibles. Assistant Majority Leader Don Nickles (R-Okla.) said Lott was "biblically correct" in describing gays; House Majority Leader Dick Armey (R-Texas) said, "My faith is based in the teachings of the Lord God Almighty, as found in the Holy Bible, and I do not quarrel with the Bible on this subject.”[1448] Then there was former Seattle Seahawk wide receiver turned Congressmen Steve Largant (R-OK). In a then-recent fundrasing letter, Largent said, “As a father of four children, I am not about to allow liberal bureaucrats or irresponsible judges, who believe in everything from abortion to homosexuality to [hand] out condoms to 10-year-olds, to usurp my God-given rights."[1449]

As PBS noted, “Following Lott’s comments, a coalition of conservative religious groups started a major lobbying and advertising campaign aimed at stopping Congress from passing what it considers gay rights legislation. The coalition spent $200,000 for ads in *The New York Times*, *The Washington Post*, and *USA Today*, focusing on Senator Lott's opinion that the lifestyle is a sin and that gays can be cured and become straight by having counseling."[1450] That brings this chapter back to reparative therapy and the ads which included the Paulks.

As a sidenote, some have argued Trent Lott is gay, and his past experiences with gay escorts was the true reason he abruptly announced his resignation/retirement from the US Senate in late 2007.[1451]

American Psychiatric Association Against Reparative Therapy

In 1998, the American Psychiatric Association officially opposed "all forms of therapy based on the assumption that homosexuality per se is a mental illness."[1452] In December 1998, the American Psychiatric Association Board of Trustees unanimously endorsed a position statement opposing reparative therapy:

> The potential risks of 'reparative therapy' are great, including depression, anxiety and self-destructive behavior, since therapist alignment with societal prejudices against homosexuality may reinforce self-hatred already experienced by the patient. Many patients who have undergone 'reparative therapy' relate that they were inaccurately told that homosexuals are lonely, unhappy individuals who never achieve acceptance or satisfaction. The possibility that the person might achieve happiness and satisfying interpersonal relationships as a gay man or lesbian is not presented, nor are alternative approaches to dealing with the effects of societal stigmatization discussed.[1453]

Overall Criticisms of Reparative Therapy

1) Success is poorly defined. Sometimes ex-gay believers think success is defined as a suppression of a homosexual response. Others argue if the "ex-gay" engages in heterosexual intercourse, victory is achieved. But that isn't heterosexual orientation. In the end, what really occurred was a reduction in homosexual behavior; not an increase in heterosexual attraction.[1454]

Lack of sexual contact is considered success for some of the religious groups backing reparative therapy.[1455] To use Trent Lott's comparison…if a repeating kleptomaniac is put in jail, is the prisoner no longer a kleptomaniac because he can't commit what he desires?

2) Bisexual's heterosexual experiences make them ex-gay. Reparative "doctors" labeled bisexuals homosexuals. If the bisexuals subjects enjoyed having sex with the opposite sex, that didn't mean a homosexual had become a heterosexual.[1456]

"A finding that bisexual men can be taught to strengthen their heterosexual behavior is not equivalent to changing sexual orientation."[1457] It's a lot easier to strengthen a bisexual's tendencies for the opposite sex than it is to make an exclusive homosexual an exclusive heterosexual.

3) Unscientific science. Most studies which "prove" ex-gay therapy work are biased. Many lack control groups, and usually are from the doctors who have the agenda of wanting to change their subjects to straight.[1458] One pro-reparative doctor (Spitzer) told the *New York Times* his subjects for ex-gay therapy have been "unusually religious," and success rate was "pretty low."[1459]

Why is it important for homosexuals to become heterosexual? The real problem lies in society's hostility toward homosexuals and bisexuals. Those who support reparative therapy oppose homosexuality's declassification as a mental illness and blame it on lobbying from gay activists. In truth, it was a "mental illness" because of a prevailing social prejudice.[1460] This social prejudice propels reparative therapy.

There is little reason to believe that anecdotal reports of people recruited through Exodus and NARTH are non-biased; those organizations exist to change homosexuals. Paul Cameron's research posted on the Family Research Institute website in Colorado Springs asked for donations based on the amount of pamphlets ordered.[1461] Piss off homophobes so they'll donate to the Family Research Institute. After all, they are merchants of hate.

4) The change may have occurred without therapy. Another criticism is that gays who changed from the therapy may have changed anyway.[1462]

Indeed, "claims by the Family Research Council, Charles Socarides, Joseph Nicolosi, and others of 'successful' conversions through reparative therapy are filled with methodological ambiguities and questionable results"[1463] The American Psychiatric Association's official web site notes that: "There is no published scientific evidence supporting the efficacy of 'reparative therapy' as a treatment to change one's sexual orientation, nor is it included in the APA's Task Force Report, *Treatments of Psychiatric Disorders*."[1464]

5) The research is biased toward gay men rather than lesbians. Douglas C. Haldeman, Ph.D has noted, "...it should be noted that almost all published research on conversion therapy deals with male homosexuals, not lesbians. Presumably, this reflects a general devaluation of women in clinical research agendas, as well as a greater tolerance on the part of some heterosexual males for lesbians than for gay men. Nevertheless, conversion therapists continue to apply their findings to women, even though their own studies do not support that extension."[1465]

6) The result is heavily wanted by the subject. Therapists incorrectly think a homosexual intrinsically wants to change, and can neglect the influence of social pressure, which is often a central factor in an individual's attempts to change their sexual orientation.[1466] When homosexuals are subjected to harassment, violence, and discrimination; its no surprise they want to "change."[1467] That climate of change is heightened by pressure from family and society. Social factors are what force someone into reparative therapy; and it also blinds homosexuals into thinking they are 'cured.' If the end goal of conversion therapy is inherently a "cure," the patient is more likely to tell the doctor he/she is "cured."[1468]

7) Asexual is not heterosexual. Some gays who underwent reparative therapy were shamed and made asexual, not changed to heterosexuals.[1469]

8) Reinforces Stereotypes. The American Psychological Association states, "All major national mental health organizations have officially expressed concerns about therapies promoted to modify sexual orientation. To date, there has been no scientifically adequate research to show that therapy aimed at changing sexual orientation (sometimes called reparative or conversion therapy) is safe or effective. Furthermore, it seems likely that the promotion of change therapies reinforces stereotypes and contributes to a negative climate for lesbian, gay, and bisexual persons. This appears to be especially likely for lesbian, gay, and bisexual individuals who grow up in more conservative religious settings."[1470]

False information only enhances prejudice and discrimination. The ad campaign for reparative therapy in 1998 only devalued homosexuals.

9) Unethical. With religions and "ex-gay ministries" involved, subjects are already depressed over their homosexuality. This depression is even worse when the sense of shame over having failed at conversion therapy is added.[1471] The American Psychological Association noted, "lesbians and gay men who feel they must conceal their sexual orientation report more frequent mental health concerns than do lesbians and gay men who are more open; they may even have more physical health problems."[1472]

10) Reparative therapy is bullying. Gays are being bullied into silence because they are told they can change. We should not allow gays to be victimized and defined by others. When gays are told to apologize for being gay, they are apologizing for something out of their control.

11) Church is a business: they need gays broken. These "Christians" create and reinforce an environment and a society that treats gays as "broken" people who need to be fixed. The pastors can get people to pay for that. Its about the money.

12) Doesn't validate "hate the sin, not the sinner." If you are taught by Christian churches to "hate the sin, not the sinner," it means you accept the homosexual for who he is. The Church just doesn't like sex. It is the actions, not thoughts, that make the gay go to hell. Then what are you trying to repair? Is castration on the agenda?

The sky is falling.

The nation will not survive with gay marriage. Tony Perkins, president of the Family Research Council, a conservative Christian lobby based in Washington, was quoted in the *New York Times* about the crucial outcome in California: "It's more important than the presidential election...**We've picked bad presidents before, and we've survived as a nation...But we will not survive if we lose the institution of marriage."**[1473]

This must be news to the Canadians, Europeans, and the people of Massachusetts, Connecticut, Iowa, Vermont, New Hampshire, Vermont, Washington D.C., Mexico City...

The Conservative Argument for Gay Marriage

The following is a list of how conservative Republicans can argue for gay marriage from a conservative standpoint.

1) Gay Marriage is good for conservatives because it gives gays the goal of family. Andrew Sullivan has aptly wrote the move toward gay marriage seemed:

> "...an eminently conservative one — in fact, almost an emblem of "compassionate conservatism." Conservatives have long rightly argued for the vital importance of the institution of marriage for fostering responsibility, commitment and the domestication of unruly men. Bringing gay men and women into this institution will surely change the gay subculture in subtle but profoundly conservative ways. When I grew up and realized I was gay, I had no concept of what my own future could be like. Like most other homosexuals, I grew up in a heterosexual family and tried to imagine how I too could one day be a full part of the family I loved. But I figured then that I had no such future. I could never have a marriage, never have a family, never be a full and equal part of the weddings and relationships and holidays that give families structure and meaning. When I looked forward, I saw nothing but emptiness and loneliness. No wonder it was hard to connect sex with love and commitment. No wonder it was hard to feel at home in what was, in fact, my home."[1474]

2) Religious freedom will remain with gay marriage. As Andrew Sullivan noted:

> "As for religious objections, it's important to remember that the issue here is not religious. It's civil. Various religious groups can choose to endorse same-sex marriage or not as they see fit. Their freedom of conscience is as vital as gays' freedom to be treated equally under the civil law. And there's no real reason that the two cannot coexist. The Roman Catholic Church, for example, opposes remarriage after divorce. But it doesn't seek to make civil divorce and remarriage illegal for everyone. Similarly, churches can well decide this matter in their own time and on their own terms while allowing the government to be neutral between competing visions of the good life. We can live and let live."[1475]

The conservatives warn of a slippery slope of the government sanction continuing to devalue marriage. However, the slippery slope goes downhill both ways. If the government can decide who partakes in the religious ceremony of marriage, what other religious activities will government regulate? And what other restrictions will government put on marriage?

There are those who support gay marriage and are in support of freedom of religion.

3) Marriage will be ruined by making half-marriages such as partnerships and civil unions. As Andrew Sullivan wrote, "Give gays domestic partnerships and marriage-lite and straights will demand them as well. And so marriage becomes less special and less constructive an institution." It was the heterosexuals, in thinking they were preserving marriage, whom have weakened the institution.[1476] The anti-gay reaction of piecemeal marriage actually reduced the power of what marriage used to be. The "sanctity of marriage" will be thoroughly eroded when straight couples forego marriage and opt for civil unions and partnerships, or as they are doing now, just living together.

Likewise, the social conservatives are presently worried about "cheapening" marriage. But what cheapens the value of marriage is denying the committed couples the opportunity to marry.

4) Gay Marriage stabilizes young adults. The purpose of marriage is not just to raise children, it is also to stabilize and settle young adults. Marriage is not just for children, it's a great stabilizer. Author Jonathan Rauch noted, "If you hope to get married, and if your friends and peers hope to get married, you will socialize and date more carefully... you will reach for respectability. You will devote yourself to work, try to build status, and earn money to make yourself more marriageable... Because you aspire to marry, you prepare to marry. You make yourself what people used to call marriage material."[1477] Homosexual couples currently can't strive to be marriage material. Rauch noted, "from society's point of view, an unattached person is an accident waiting to happen."[1478]

I strongly prefer the increase of responsibility for ourselves and others, albeit presently counter-cultural by the neo-conservatives.

5) Children cannot be the only disqualification of marriage. If it were, we should deny marriage to the infertile and post-menopausal women. That would be ludicrous—just as is opposing gay marriage.

6) Conservatives should want to build the Republican Party. However, the Republicans are watching the demise of their party. This is not opinion. It is fact. A poll from October 2003 for the *USA Today* found that 67% of the 18-29 age group believed that gay marriage would benefit society. [1479] And more recent polling is similar. Old voters vote well. They also die. As time goes on, the higher percentage of voters will exist who find the conservative homophobic comments of "mainstream" Republicans as repulsive.

As Andrew Sullivan wrote (Oct.2003), "When the daughter of the vice president is openly gay, it's hard to treat homosexual citizens as some permanent kind of Other, as a threat to civil order and society."[1480]

7) As mankind progresses… A prejudiced, bigoted and hateful institution is one that will lose adherents and supporters. Their time is numbered.

8) By not supporting gay marriage, conservatives are suggesting cohabitation or forced celibacy is a desired goal. Indeed, "Unless conservatives also support enforced celibacy they are conceding that casual sex and cohabitation are acceptable."[1481] They <u>must</u> arrest and jail their teenaged children or forever be labeled the hypocrites they are.

Chapter Eight:
Merchants of Hate—The American Taliban

I love the First Amendment, all of it.

Congress shall make no law respecting an establishment of religion, or prohibiting the free exercise thereof; or abridging the freedom of speech, or of the press; or the right of the people peaceably to assemble, and to petition the Government for a redress of grievances.

Freedom of religion and freedom from religion. "Making no law respecting an establishment of religion," means that we are NOT a theocracy, that no church or no organization or no individual can be assisted in establishing a religion. The Congress must stay away from "respecting the establishment of a religion," it does not say a church; it says religion. That means doctrine, teaching, theology, beliefs, attitudes, ritual, or leadership pronouncements. No law respecting any of that. That is what the Constitution says.

The Constitution also says people will be free to exercise their religion, free from government interference. The readers of this book can address these issues from their own perspective, but we are a secular representative democracy, not a theocracy. We may very well have a majority, strong Christian culture. We shall not have a Christian government. We may have a government with many Christians in offices. They shall not impose their religion upon the citizens of the United States.

"Congress shall make no law…abridging the freedom of speech, or of the press…" "No law" means no law. I agree.

A man may say "Fire!" in an open field, in his auto, in his home. He may also commit a crime by shouting it in a crowded theater and cause injury and possibly death. The crime is not prosecutable under violating some rule of freedom of speech. However, to recklessly endanger the lives of other people is a specific crime.

Just as important is the intelligence and wisdom of knowing how, where and when to say what. Media people, politicians, and preachers are skilled with words, emotions, symbols, delivery; they know how to make people pray, purchase, vote, donate and act out.

It is abundantly evident many do not have the intelligence or wisdom to understand either the responsibility they have to protect the freedom of speech or the opportunities to do "good," to build common ground, to increase brotherhood and sisterhood and to aid in understanding.

As Adlai Stevenson II, wrote in 1953, " ... candidates claiming the people's confidence have even a higher mission; honestly to help man to know, as St. Thomas Aquinas said, what he ought to believe, to know what he ought to desire; to know what he ought to do."

The merchants of hate's lack of wisdom puts profit and power ahead of developing a cultural goodness. The people abusing these Constitutional protections are so interested in profit or power that they seem to care less about the damage they are doing to the very freedoms that protects them. They are unaware or don't care that there will be public reactions against their abuse.

They are the hate marketing televangelists, preachers, pseudo-religious organizations and their mouth-pieces. They are the Neo-con Republicans and their mouthpieces, and PACS. They are Skinheads with radio and television programs, and Skinheads without such programs.

It could be this hatred is not deeply held; it just could be that people use hatred to accomplish other goals, sick psychological needs to fulfill, money to be made, and votes to gain. It could be that simple; I think it often is.

Orwellians All?

In George Orwell's remarkable book, ***1984,*** Big Brother's henchman, O'Brien, asks Winston questions about the Party, "Now tell me *why* we cling to power. What is our motive, why should we want power?"

Winston answers, "You are ruling over us for our own good..." The electrical current was jolted upward and hit Winston's body....

"That was stupid, Winston, stupid!" O'Brien added, **"...Now I will tell you the answer to my question. It is this. The Party seeks power entirely for its own sake. We are not interested in the good of others; we are interested solely in power. Not wealth or luxury or long life or happiness; only power, pure power. ... Power is not a means; it is an end."**

The primary purpose and goal of active political people is to gain power to make decisions. The one who can make the most decisions has the most power. The biggest decision of all is who gets to make the decisions. That is what the fight is all about. To obtain that power the political professionals have learned how to divide American voters by fears, prejudices, hatreds, emotions, activities, incomes, living spaces and locations.

Loaded with survey, focus group, purchasing, lifestyle, and census data, the political professionals divide us into the smallest manageable and persuadable groups they can. Then using modern communication and persuasion techniques and delivery systems they play those emotions and the voters like puppets on a string. All for power.

Through the religious fears of those who listen to them, pastors of the Religious Right carefully select chapter and verse, then add their interpretation to increase their power over the purses, behaviors, and minds of their parishioners, listeners, readers and viewers. As this book will detail, these "religious" leaders and their fellow-travelers among the Republican Party and right-wing media are now gay-bashing for power and profit.

Communication experts, scholars of propaganda and persuasion, and psychologists can all attest to impact of language and charismatic leaders on individuals and masses. Some of these individuals have a screw loose and commit acts of violence and hatred, convinced by what they have heard. Masses of people learn to hate, act out, or at the least, "look the other way" while evil is done.

The estimated population of the United States in March of 2010 is 310 million people. The most scientifically based current studies estimate the lesbian and gay population to be eight per cent (8%), of the population. Who are these people who wish to deny 24,800,000 people constitutionally protected rights, immunities, privileges and opportunities?

It is vitally important that people read and think about what these people say and it is vitally important to truly "know" the folks they choose to follow, model themselves after, and listen to. Charismatic and well-spoken people can very well be very different when they are not on stage. These televangelists, politicians, television and radio personalities and right wing organizational leaders are often quite different when examined. In the following pages the reader will have an opportunity to examine The American Taliban. I go into great detail because I think it will be useful for the readers to discover and discuss with their friends and co-workers just how strange, obsessive, self-indulgent, and frightening most of these "people" are.

PART ONE: THE PREACHERS

The evangelicals are powerful with their TV shows, but it wasn't exactly clear how powerful until the early 1980s. A University of Pennsylvania survey conducted in 1984 estimated that 13.3 million people (or 6.2% of the national TV audience) regularly viewed fundamentalist/evangelical shows.[1482] *Time* reported, "That nearly equals the membership of the United Methodist, Presbyterian and Episcopal churches combined. A Nielsen survey last year, designed to add cable data to the broadcast ratings, showed that 21% of the nation's TV households tune in to Christian TV for at least six minutes in a week, and 40% for at least six minutes in a month. This adds up to 61 million Americans with at least minimal exposure. The survey counted viewers of only the ten biggest among 62 nationally syndicated shows. By this measure, [Pat] Robertson, whose CBN commissioned the survey, is at least briefly onscreen monthly in 16.3 million homes and reaches 27 million Americans."[1483] Evangelicals may have been the most powerful interest group of the 1980s.

Who were the televangelists?

The televangelists said the country was blessed, but in danger of sin: abortion, gays, AIDS, and "secular humanism."[1484] The world was a mess (as the 1970s and early 1980s seemed) and religion would save it.[1485] They were led by Jerry Falwell, Pat Roberston, Jimmy Swaggart, and Jim Bakker.

However, there were others who had huge bases of support, including Robert Schuller who *Time* described (1980s) as:

> "a bland-looking but calculatedly theatrical performer, [who] presides over the vast, glittery Crystal Cathedral in Garden Grove, Calif. Finished in 1980 at a cost of $18 million (paid largely by viewer donations), the structure serves as a dazzling stage set for Schuller's weekly Hour of Power. The show, seen in 169 cities, beats Swaggart in some audience listings. Schuller's TV budget is $37 million a year, and the 10,000-member cathedral spends an additional $5.7 million on non-TV operations. The author of several inspirational best sellers, Schuller shook 10,000 hands in a weeklong January tour promoting his latest volume, an upbeat rewrite of Jesus' Beatitudes titled The Be-Happy Attitudes. Schuller is affiliated with the mainline Reformed Church in America, as is his predecessor in hyperoptimism, Norman Vincent Peale."[1486]

Schuller's bank accounts and popularity took a real beating in 2008 due to the recession and his retirement.

Schuller does not approve of gay marriages but was never a gay-basher.

One would also have to look at Oral Roberts of Tulsa, who, according to *Time* in the late 1980s, was "the century's most famed faith healer...[with]... a TV flock that helped build the 4,600-student Oral Roberts University and the 294-bed City of Faith hospital and research center. The City of Faith is rumored to be in financial straits, but Roberts will divulge no details. The overall budget of his enterprises reportedly runs to $120 million. Roberts' Sunday half-hour still appears in 192 markets, but the 'Prairie Tornado' is showing his age."[1487]

A 1980s *Time* article asked, "What accounts for the surprising impact of the televangelists? In part, showbiz flair: outsize personalities, sermons carefully shaped around themes that pull audience response, dramatic personal stories of life-changing events, and toe-tapping music."[1488] The irony with Pray TV is that although the evangelists raise their funds to reach the "lost," they reinforce people already committed to evangelical religion.[1489] There is no saving. Televangelists preach to the choir, and the choir opened their wallets. Typically the televangelists had their own TV show, university, mailing list, law school, and mega church.

Donation Please

Televangelists had the common trait of abundant fundraising. *Time*'s Richard N. Ostling reported on televangelism in the wake of the Bakker and Swaggart scandals. Ostling illustrated (in August 1987) when it came to televangelism's funding, "In almost every instance, those holdings are dominated by a single dynamic individual who decides how the money will be spent and who strives, above all, to keep vital donations flowing from the faithful."[1490]

There was little oversight on these "non profit" organizations in the 1980s. Already in the 1970s, there was a foreshadowing of fiscally irresponsibility. According to NPR, in 1972, the SEC filed "charges of 'fraud and deceit' against [Jerry] Falwell's church for the issuance of $6.5 million in uninsured bonds."[1491] The organization won its case in 1973, but Liberty University filed for bankruptcy and reorganized, losing millions in church investors' money.[1492]

Time reported (August 1987), "Oral Roberts makes not even a token effort at financial openness. Only a handful of people know how donations to the cause are used. But according to an investigation by the daily *Tulsa Tribune*, revenues in Roberts' evangelical empire have been on a steady downward spiral: from $88 million in 1980 to $55 million in 1986."[1493]

The numbers were astonishing. Jim Bakker's PTL proceeds were $129 million in 1986. In 1987 the proceeds of these one-man led ministries included Jerry Falwell at $84 million (unrelated to the PTL he took over); Swaggart at $142 million; Oral Roberts at $120 million; Robert Schuller at $42 million annually.[1494]

The money stash of televangelists may have caused delusions of greatness. California Neopentecostalist Paul Crouch asked in the 1980s: "Do you realize what an awesome responsibility it is for me to stand here and encourage people to literally give all they have to God? I'm either the biggest fool and idiot and con man in the world or else I'm plugged into heaven." Crouch led the all-religion Trinity Broadcasting Network (nine stations, 6 million cable homes, and $35 million budget; and now was telling viewers that a widow donated her life savings of $7,000).[1495]

Whether it was Schuller, Roberts, Swaggart, or Bakker, *Time* noted, "none of these preachers can compare to [Pat] Robertson as a TV entrepreneur. Robertson pioneered the first religious TV station, the first religious network and the first Christian programming to use a talk-show format, as well as a number of now widely imitated viewer-response and fund-raising techniques. He was also the first Christian broadcaster to sign up commercial sponsors, a development that ...appears to be the trend of the 1980s."[1496] In the mid 1980s, Robertson's 24-hour CBN network reached 30 million subscribers; CBN was not only the largest Christian cable operation but the fifth largest of any kind (At the time, No. 1 was ESPN, with 36.9 million subscribers).[1497]

PAT ROBERTSON

Pat Robertson is a Baptist Minister and founder of the Christian Broadcasting Network as well as Regent University.[1498] CBN was founded in 1960 and was the first Christian television network established in the US.[1499] CBN's flagship program is *The 700 Club* hosted by Robertson.[1500] According to Robertson's website, "Located in Virginia Beach, Va., Regent University was founded in 1977 by Robertson, who serves as its president and chancellor.

Regent is a fully accredited graduate university that offers degrees in business, communication & the arts, divinity, education, government, law, organizational leadership and psychology & counseling."[1501] He is the son of Virginian U.S. Senator A. Willis Robertson.[1502]

Robertson for President: 1988

Robertson ran for president in the 1988 cycle. When he announced his campaign, many concluded it was a long shot bid against other GOP candidates, including Vice President George H.W. Bush.

Before he officially entered the campaign for the 1988 GOP nomination, *Time* described Robertson's chances: "Political pros are uncertain how big a factor he could be in the primaries, let alone the convention, but they are convinced that he could energize the Christian right and siphon votes from other candidates. True believers are tingling at the prospect. As ROBERTSON IN 1988 buttons blossomed, the amiable Virginian ...denounce[d] the evils of abortion, homosexuality and school violence, all to be overcome by a flood tide of moral regeneration."[1503]

Just the fact the Robertson was a presidential candidate who could make waves in the 1988 campaign was evidence at how far the televangelists had come. Before his presidential candidacy, CBN's annual income was $233 million; and annually his viewers of *The 700 Club* logged "4 million prayer calls to 4,500 volunteers manning telephone banks in 60 counseling centers."[1504]

Religious idiosyncrasies in a political campaign...

1) Robertson: I'm not an evangelist. *The New York Times* noted (Dec. 1987) the contradictions between presidential candidate and religious leader, "As a political candidate, he has increasingly distanced himself from such statements, and in some instances he has denied making them."[1505] The campaign strategy was to make Robertson a "Christian broadcaster" who had conservative values and deny he was ever a television evangelist.[1506] The fact Robertson distanced himself from televangelism was pathetic. *Time* reported on his successes in August of 1987, including from his TV ties: "His ministry's activities earn some $183 million annually."[1507] The man created the Christian Broadcasting Network, and now wanted to distance himself from Jim Bakker and Jimmy Swaggart; he couldn't.

2) Only Christians and Jews should serve in government. When he was a minister, Robertson stated he believed only devout Christians and Jews were qualified to govern.[1508] On *The 700 Club* in 1985, he was asked who should be able to serve in government. Robertson said, "Individual Christians are the only ones really - and Jewish people, those who trust the God of Abraham, Isaac and Jacob - are the only ones that are qualified to have the reign, because hopefully, they will be governed by God and submitted to him."[1509] Even more definitive, co-host Ben Kinchlow, interjected, "Obviously you're not saying that there are no other people qualified to be in government or whatever if they aren't Christians or

Jews."[1510] Robertson said, "Yeah, I'm saying that. I just said it...'I think anybody whose mind and heart is not controlled by God Almighty is not qualified in the ultimate sense to be the judge of someone else. . . . No one is fit to govern other people unless first of all something governs him. And there is only one governor I know of that is suitable to be judge of all the universe, that's God Almighty. Yes, I did say that. You can quote me. I believe it."[1511] In September 1987, Robertson completely denied making the statement, "I never said that in my life. . . . I never said only Christians and Jews. I never said that."[1512]

Mr. Robertson, as a presidential candidate said (Dec. 1987) that there was a difference between being an evangelical minister and a candidate for president: "As an evangelical minister I have had a very strong point of view, and as an evangelical Christian I still do...As President of the United States I would have to administer that office, in a very dispassionate sense, in relation to all people."[1513] This comment is astonishing because it negates the political activism of Robertson. The evangelists like Falwell and Robertson have infiltrated politics with anti-gay, anti-abortion, "pro-family" ideas wrapped around the bible; but when Robertson became a candidate he toned down his religious rhetoric.

3) Christians are more patriotic. In July 1986, Robertson said Christians feel more strongly about their country than others do: "I think patriotism, love of God, love of country, support of traditional family. They believe it would be good for our country if families were closer together. . . . I think they feel about them more strongly than others do."[1514] When Education Secretary William J. Bennett criticized the comment, Robertson denied saying it.[1515] By December 1987 Robertson acknowledged his comment.[1516]

4) Perfect government is controlled by God. In the 1980s, he wrote, "Perfect government comes from God and is controlled by God. Short of that, the next best government is a limited democracy in which the people acknowledge rights given by God but voluntarily grant government limited power to do those things the people cannot do individually."[1517]

5) As President, I will not destroy world. It's not a good situation for a campaign when the presidential candidate has to tell the *New York Times* he won't use the presidency to force the end of the world (Dec.1987): "When you get a humanist writer, he'll put his spin on it, play the Armageddon thing: Robertson will push the button. It's just a lot of bull. I have no intention of any such thing. I'd do everything in my power to avoid nuclear war."[1518]

The results of 1988

On March 8, 1988, Vice President Bush symbolically locked up the nomination when Republicans voted in 16 primaries, mostly in the south.[1519] Robertson won the Washington State caucus.[1520] In the delegate count, George H.W. Bush won the 1988 GOP nomination; Bob Dole finished second, and Robertson finished third ahead of Rep. Jack Kemp (NY).[1521]

After a southern-border state block of primaries, the *New York Times* reported (2.9.1988), Robertson "made a series of seemingly outlandish statements, saying that there were still Soviet nuclear missiles in Cuba, insisting that his Christian Broadcasting Network had once known the location of American hostages in Lebanon and implying that Mr. Bush had had something to do with disclosures of sexual misconduct by the Rev. Jimmy Swaggart, the television evangelist."[1522]

As Jerry Falwell once said, "Pat ran for president once and he's a very political person, and that is the way politicians talk. They all use intimidation and political strong-arming to hopefully pick up a vote or two."[1523]

The Irrational Ramblings of a Right Winger

In 1989, Robertson created the Christian Coalition as a conservative pressure group with influence on the GOP.[1524] In the meantime, he went back to *The 700 Club*. He has continued to erroneously predict severe events, just at he did before his presidential campaign.

There was a long staff prayer meeting in 1980 in which Mr. Robertson predicted the end of the world to occur in 1982.[1525] This revelation was brought up during his 1988 presidential campaign.[1526] Robertson has not denied those comments: "I'll tell you, in those days, under Jimmy Carter, I honest to goodness thought the end was near. I mean I really did. And I also thought that we were seeing forces coming together in the Middle East that looked like there would be some kind of confrontation over there."[1527]

Robertson was also convinced the Soviets were going to come after the United States. On New Years Day, 1980, Robertson made a prediction about the Soviet Union: "Now they are going to make the move, and that's what God is saying: we've got a couple of years. It's going to start, they are not going to let up from now on. I mean, from now on it's going to be bloodshed, war, revolution and trouble."[1528]

At least twice Robertson has claimed to have successfully prayed a hurricane to change direction, and in his book, *Beyond Reason*, he said he turned away Hurricane Betsy in the 1960's.[1529]

In January 2006, Robertson suggested God punished then-Israeli Prime Minister Ariel Sharon via stroke for ceding Israeli-controlled land to the Palestinians.[1530]

In May 2006, he predicted a big storm—maybe a tsunami—would hit the Pacific Northwest in 2006, noting "If I heard the Lord right about 2006, the coasts of America will be lashed by storms" and days later adding, "There well may be something as bad as a tsunami in the Pacific Northwest."[1531] In January 2007, Robertson acknowledged (even though a tsunami did not hit the U.S.) he generically cited the spring of 2006's heavy rains and flooding in New England as partially fulfilling the prediction.[1532]

In January 2007, he predicted a terrorist attack on the United States would result in "mass killing" later in the year.[1533] He stated on *The 700 Club*, "I'm not necessarily saying it's going to be nuclear...The Lord didn't say nuclear. But I do believe it will be something like that."[1534] In January 2008, noting the nuclear attack hadn't come to pass, Robertson said, "All I can think is that somehow the people of God prayed and God in his mercy spared us."[1535]

Perhaps, Pat Robertson is nuts; his crazy babbling spills over into gays, women and Democrats.

1) Hitler and Gays are alike. Robertson once said, "Many of those people involved in Adolf Hitler were Satanists, many were homosexuals - the two things seem to go together."[1536]

2) Another anti-Gay rant. Robertson asked, "How can there be peace when drunkards, drug dealers, communists, atheists, New Age worshipers of Satan, secular humanists, oppressive dictators, greedy money changers, revolutionary assassins, adulterers, and homosexuals are on top?"[1537]

3) Gays want to destroy Christians. Robertson said, "It is the Democratic Congress, the liberal-biased media and the homosexuals who want to destroy all Christians."[1538]

4) Feminism causes lesbians. Robertson said, "**Feminism is a socialist, anti-family, political movement that encourages women to leave their husbands, kill their children, practice witchcraft, destroy capitalism and become lesbians.**"[1539]

5) Gays are narcissistic. Robertson has said homosexuals are "self-absorbed narcissists who are willing to destroy any institution so long as they can have affirmation of their lifestyle."[1540]

"Thou shalt not kill," God. "Unless it is Chavez,"

In August 2005, Pat Robertson advocated breaking the Ten Commandments when he said the U.S. should assasinate Venezualan President Hugo Chavez. "If he thinks we're trying to assassinate him, I think that we really ought to go ahead and do it. It's a whole lot cheaper than starting a war."[1541] He made the recommendation on the 700 Club, which aired on ABC Family network three times daily.[1542]

Robertson blamed Haitan earthquake on a pact with the devil

In January 2010, Robertson said of the Haitians: "They were under the heel of the French ... and they got together and swore a pact to the devil. They said, 'We will serve you if you'll get us free from the French. True story. And so the devil said, 'OK, it's a deal.' They kicked the French out. The Haitians revolted and got themselves free. Ever since, they have been cursed by one thing after the other."

JERRY FALWELL

Jerry Falwell was a Baptist minister who used television to expand his message. He was the founder of the Moral Majority, which solidified the religious right.[1543] Falwell began broadcasting on radio and television shortly after opening his original Thomas Road Baptist Church in 1956.[1544] He founded Liberty University in 1971.[1545] Falwell began televising his sermons in 1968 and reaching millions during the mid-1970s with *The Old Time Gospel Hour*.'[1546]

Ironically, from the 1920s to the mid 1970s, evangelicals largely avoided the political debate; and Falwell, in fact, criticized Christian activism in the 1960s when the civil rights movement occurred and the Vietnam War peaked as a political issue.[1547] By the 1970s, Falwell changed his position in regard to politics and religion, as social issues came into public debate.[1548]

Falwell made his move into political activism in 1979, and was "armed with a solid computer bank of backers, financial and ideological."[1549] National Public Radio notes, "Falwell burst onto the national scene in 1979, when he launched an organization he presumptuously called the Moral Majority. Critics liked to say that it was neither. What is undisputed is that the Moral Majority became the vehicle that carried millions of born-again Christians out of their separatist tendencies and into the center of political activism."[1550] One of Falwell's goals was to overturn the Supreme Court's ban on school prayer and also reverse the country's direction on feminism, abortion and gay rights.[1551]

The Moral Majority organized Christians politically, and was partly responsible for Ronald Reagan's election in 1980.[1552] Falwell took credit for Reagan's 1980 victory.[1553] About 80 percent of the 45 million U.S. evangelical Christians voted Republican in the 1984 and 1988 presidential elections.[1554] In 1989 Falwell told the *Washington Times*, "You can't be elected today without the religious right."[1555] Moral Majority grew to over six million in membership,[1556] and then disbanded in 1989.[1557]

Falwell's roots are surprising. Falwell's father was one-time bootlegger who hated preachers, Falwell's grandfather was a staunch atheist.[1558]

Falwell was discovered without a pulse in May 2007 in his office at Liberty University in Lynchburg, Virginia.

Jerry Falwell: Rise And Fall

In the 1980s before the Jim Bakker and Jimmy Swaggart scandals, *Time* said Falwell:

> "presides at the 21,000-member Thomas Road Baptist Church in Lynchburg, Va., whose Sunday worship is seen in 172 markets. A Fundamentalist of genial manner and granite opinions, he used his TV clout to launch Moral Majority, the influential conservative political lobby. That group was subsumed last month under the new Liberty Federation, signaling Falwell's increased involvement in foreign affairs. He also runs Liberty University (7,000 students) in Lynchburg. The 1985 receipts of Falwell's ventures: $100 million. Last year he started a Sunday-night call-in show on Ted Turner's superstation, WTBS. Last month he purchased a cable hookup (rebaptized the Liberty

Broadcasting Network) that reaches 1.5 million homes. It will run a new daily Falwell talk show."[1559]

However, *Time* Magazine's (2005) list of the 25 most influential evangelicals in America did not include Falwell.[1560] And he had fiscal issues. In 1986 and 1987, the IRS found Falwell's *Old Time Gospel Hour* violated federal tax law, and revoked the show's tax-exempt status; Falwell paid $50,000 in back taxes.[1561] When he organized I Love America Committee PAC in 1983, it raised $485,000 in the first year but spent $413,000 to do it.[1562]

Falwell can't out do Robertson, but tries:

1) Don't vote Democrat. Falwell said (1996) Democrats "began to embrace all the radical extremist groups in the country -- the feminists, the homosexuals, abortionists, the left-wingers, you name it…At some point in time, Christians that take their faith seriously could find very little reason to give support to Democrats."[1563]

2) The Teletubbies' hidden agenda. BBC reported (2.15.1999), "The innocent world of the Teletubbies is under attack from America's religious right."[1564] Indeed, Jerry Falwell denounced the BBC TV children's show because he was convinced Tinky Winky of the Teletubbies was gay, and did so by announcing it in his *National Liberty Journal*.[1565] The article was titled, "Parents Alert: Tinky Winky Comes Out of the Closet."[1566]

Tinky Winky was the purple character with a triangular symbol on his head and carried a handbag, the only major attributes which separated him from his character friends: Laa-Laa, Dipsy and Po.[1567] Falwell said, "He is purple - the gay-pride color; and his antenna is shaped like a triangle - the gay-pride symbol."[1568] And there were intentional "subtle depictions" of gay sexuality: "As a Christian I feel that role modeling the gay lifestyle is damaging to the moral lives of children."[1569] The show was geared toward preschool children. The show's US licensing firm spokesman said, "The fact that he carries a magic bag doesn't make him gay…. [and] To out a Teletubby in a pre-school show is kind of sad on his part. I really find it absurd and kind of offensive."[1570]

3) AIDS is punishment. Falwell said, "AIDS is the wrath of a just God against homosexuals. To oppose it would be like an Israelite jumping in the Red Sea to save one of Pharaoh's charioteers ... AIDS is not just God's punishment for homosexuals; it is God's punishment for the society that tolerates homosexuals."[1571]

4) 9/11 was because of gays and pagans. He told (9.13.2001) *The 700 Club*, "I really believe that the pagans, and the abortionists, and the feminists, and the gays and the lesbians who are actively trying to make that an alternative lifestyle, the ACLU, People for an American Way, all of them who have tried to secularize America, I point the finger in their face and say 'you helped this happen.'" Falwell did apologize for his comments and told CNN he didn't mean to blame those groups and only the hijackers and terrorists were responsible for the attacks.[1572] Here is the entire portion of the transcript, and longer version:

> Two days after the terrorist attacks, Falwell told Pat Robertson, what "we saw on Tuesday, as terrible as it is, could be miniscule if, in fact -- if, in fact -- God continues to lift the curtain and allow the enemies of America to give us probably what we deserve."[1573] Robertson conceded: "Jerry, that's my feeling. I think we've just seen the antechamber to terror. We haven't even begun to see what they can do to the major population." Falwell added, "The ACLU's got to take a lot of blame for this."[1574] Robertson agreed. Then Falwell gave the most moronic comment after 9/11: "And, I know that I'll hear from them for this. But, throwing God out successfully with the help of the federal court system, throwing God out of the public square, out of the schools. The abortionists have got to bear some burden for this because God will not be mocked. And when we destroy 40 million little innocent babies, we make God mad. I really believe that the pagans, and the abortionists, and the feminists, and the gays and the lesbians who are actively trying to make that an alternative lifestyle, the ACLU, People For the American Way -- all of them who have tried to secularize America -- I point the finger in their face and say "you helped this happen."[1575] Robertson said, "Well, I totally concur, and the problem is we have adopted that agenda at the highest levels of our government. And so we're responsible as a free society for what the top people do. And, the top people, of course, is the court system."[1576]

5) Homosexuality is a perversion. Falwell told NPR in 1996: "I believe that homosexuality is moral perversion…I think it is a violation of the laws of nature, as well as the laws of God. I do not think that that gives me permission to be unkind or ungracious to a person who may be living a homosexual lifestyle."[1577] By the way, Jerry Falwell published his autobiography with the help of a gay ghostwriter.[1578]

6) Warning: Gays will destroy America with God's help… Falwell said, "Homosexuality is Satan's diabolical attack upon the family that will not only have a corrupting influence upon our next generation, but it will also bring down the wrath of God upon America."[1579]

7) Homosexuality isn't genetics. "I do not believe we can blame genetics for adultery, homosexuality, dishonesty and other character flaws"[1580]

More Falwell Quotes

1) Hillary Clinton and Lucifer. Falwell said at the Value Voter Summit: "Nothing will motivate conservative evangelical Christians to vote Republican in the 2008 presidential election more than a Democratic nominee named Hillary Rodham Clinton - not even a run by the devil himself ... I certainly hope that Hillary is the candidate. She has $300 million so far. But I hope she's the candidate. Because nothing will energize my [constituency] like Hillary Clinton. If Lucifer ran, he wouldn't."[1581]

2) Billy Graham is bad. Falwell once stated, "Billy Graham is the chief servant of Satan in America."[1582]

3) No public education a good thing. Falwell once stated, "I hope I live to see the day when, as in the early days of our country, we won't have any public

schools. The churches will have taken them over again and Christians will be running them. What a happy day that will be!"[1583]
4) Who is the antichrist? Falwell once told a gathering of ministers that the anti-Christ was a Jewish male who is alive in the world today."[1584]
5) American Civil Liberties Union is Nazi-like. Falwell said, "The ACLU is to Christians what the American Nazi party is to Jews."[1585]
6) Only Christians matter. Falwell said, "If you're not a born-again Christian, you're a failure as a human being."[1586]
7) Christians don't think. Falwell stated, "Christians, like slaves and soldiers, ask no questions."[1587]
8) Idea of 'Separation of Church and State' came from devil. Falwell also said, "The idea that religion and politics don't mix was invented by the Devil to keep Christians from running their own country."[1588]
9) Against global warming. "The whole (global warming) thing is created to destroy America's free enterprise system and our economic stability."[1589]

Jerry Falwell died May 15, 2007.

JIMMY SWAGGART

In 1988, Jimmy Swaggart was "America's leading television evangelist."[1590] At its height, *The Jimmy Swaggart Hour* was watched by 2 million families with donations topping $150 million annually.[1591] *People* said, "He had all the perquisites of that special priesthood—three spacious homes, a personal jet and the use of a luxurious ministry 'retreat' in California."[1592] Swaggart had his own 15,000 sq. ft. printing plant that printed 24 million items a year: books, pamphlets, posters, and album covers.[1593] As of 1988, he had sold over 150 million records.[1594] Swaggart told *Time*: "The Lord has been good to me."[1595]

Time reported (August 1987) of Swaggart, "The bayou spellbinder boasts the highest U.S. ratings for a televangelist, and his shows are broadcast by 3,200 stations in 145 countries."[1596]

Swaggart is a cousin to Mickey Gilley and Jerry Lee Lewis. *People* reported (1988), "So deep was the bond between them that after the success of Lewis' *Great Balls of Fire*, Jerry Lee bought Swaggart a new Oldsmobile to replace the jalopy that was providing him shaky transportation from one revival meeting to the next."[1597] Lewis was so overtaken by drugs in Ohio one night that Swaggart walked on stage and took him home.[1598]

An Intolerable Man

1) Roman Catholicism is a lie. Swaggart said Catholicism is "a false religion. It is not the Christian way."[1599]
2) Jews deserved their trials: "because of their rejection of Christ, they have known sorrow and heartache like no other people on the face of the Earth."[1600]

3) Evolution is satanic. "Evolution is a bankrupt speculative philosophy, not a scientific fact. Only a spiritually bankrupt society could ever believe it. Only atheists could accept this Satanic theory."[1601]
4) Anti-sex education. "Sex education classes in our public schools are promoting incest."[1602]
5) Media is the devil. "The Media is ruled by Satan. But yet I wonder if many Christians fully understand that."[1603]
6) U.S. Supreme Court is damned. In 1980s, Jimmy Swaggart said the Supreme Court is "an institution damned by God Almighty" for allowing abortions.[1604]
7) Muhammad is dead. *Time* quoted Swaggart's blazing speeches: "Muhammad is dead but Jesus is alive. He's alive. He's alive! GLORY!"[1605]

***Time* described Swaggart**

Before the Swaggart scandal of the 1980s, *Time* did an expose of televangelists. Swaggart was described as

> "a brash, rafter-ringing Pentecostal preacher and Gospel singer (his albums have sold 13 million copies) who preserves the old tent revival style at his striking 7,000-seat Family Worship Center outside Baton Rouge, La. In his weekly one-hour broadcasts, he prowls the stage, sometimes breaking into excited jig steps, as he revs up perorations assailing Communism, Catholicism and 'secular humanism,' the last of which he blames for abortion, pornography, AIDS and assorted social ills. He takes in $140 million a year. The money pays for his weekly show (aired in 197 markets), his daily Bible study, and in 1984 enabled him to launch the Jimmy Swaggart Bible College, which drew 18,000 applications for 400 openings."[1606]

Jimmy Swaggart and Family…

Swaggart was a self appointed king, especially when it came to his powers at Jimmy Swaggart Ministries: "The board does not run these organizations…Legally it has the final say. If it said, 'No, you can't build a Bible college,' I couldn't build one. But you know what I'd do? I'd fire the board, because I'm the spiritual head of this organization. It can't run without me."[1607] In addition, the board for Swaggart's ministry included himself, his wife Frances Swaggart, his son Donnie Swaggart, his daughter-in-Law Debbie, his Ministry Lawyer, and some clergy buddies.[1608] Jimmy Swaggart Ministries was a family business with 17 relatives on the payroll in 1987.[1609]

Jimmy Swaggart vs. Martin Gorman

Marvin Gorman had his own successful televangelist TV show in New Orleans.[1610] He was defrocked in 1986 after Swaggart accused him of "immoral dalliances."[1611]

Gorman was the pastor of the 5,000 member First Assembly of God Church in New Orleans.[1612] In July 1986, Swaggart summoned Gorman for a meeting and Gorman confessed to adultery. Swaggart then opened the bottle. Gorman admitted to one adulterous affair but claimed Swaggart lied about other affairs. Gorman unsuccessfully sued Swaggart for $90 million in 1986 for spreading rumors.[1613]

People noted (1988), "By the time Gorman's suit was dismissed last year (he is appealing the decision), the pastor had long since been banished from his denomination, deprived of his large church and TV ministry and had begun again, in an independent church located in a former warehouse on the outskirts of New Orleans. His promising career had been all but ruined, and meanwhile the ministry of his persecutor grew ever more glorious."[1614]

In September 1991, a "jury in New Orleans found that Swaggart and others had defamed Gorman with allegations of adulterous behavior and ordered the group to pay $10 million in damages."[1615]

Swaggart vs. Jim Bakker

BBC claimed Swaggart "unleashed fire and brimstone against rival TV evangelist Rev. Jim Bakker."[1616] *People* said (March 1988) it was Swaggart "who had wielded the avenger's sword, smiting Jim Bakker."[1617] He called Bakker "a cancer on the body of Christ."[1618] Swaggart engineered Bakker's downfall and damaged Bakker's PTL network (a rival to Swaggart) by telling religious leaders about Bakker's affair with his church secretary Jessica Hahn.[1619] *Time* reported Swaggart prodded his denomination, the Assemblies of God, into defrocking Bakker.[1620]

Swaggart goes down

For all of Swaggart's holy holies, there was a bit of hypocrisy in his vendettas against Gorman and Bakker. Indeed, it became apparent Mr. Swaggart had a taste for prostitutes.

The prostitute photographed with Swaggart, Debra Murphree, later told local media she was Swaggart's regular customer but said they had no sex.[1621] Murphree said Swaggart just liked to watch her undress.[1622] Another prostitute named Peggy appeared on a Baton Rouge TV station with her face obscured and implied Swaggart was cheap for offering $10 for a sex act: "I just laughed…because, you know, here is Jimmy Swaggart, and he has millions he could pay me, or at least thousands. I said, 'No,' and he said, 'Well, I guess you'd better get out of the car then.'"[1623]

How was Swaggart uncovered?

Marvin Gorman has been described as the "rival preacher" who circulated the Swaggart photos in New Orleans.[1624] Gorman began receiving anonymous telephone calls in 1987 informing him Jimmy Swaggart solicited prostitutes.[1625] A detective tracked Swaggart to the motel then told Gorman of the situation and the air was let out of one of Swaggart's tires to slow his getaway; Gorman found Swaggart fixing the flat.[1626] Gorman said Swaggart "was wearing a sweat suit…so that kind of does away with the theory that he was ministering to somebody."[1627]

Officials at the Assemblies of God Church were given photographs showing Swaggart taking a prostitute to a motel in Louisiana.[1628] Gorman handed the pictures in to the Assemblies of God Church.[1629] In a 10-hour session with church elders, Swaggart admitted that he paid the prostitute to perform pornographic acts and had a fascination with pornography since childhood.[1630]

The 1988 scandal forced Swaggart to quit his leadership post with the Assemblies of God, which at the time was "the nation's largest Pentecostal denomination, and nearly 200 television stations dropped his weekly program."[1631]

Warning Signs

There were warning signs of Swaggart's improprieties. Swaggart's Church was accused of preying on a wealthy California widow (Zoe Vance) so she would leave her estate to Swaggart ministries. Though she died in 1981, the settlement didn't finalize until 1984, when $10 million (70 percent of the estate) was given to Swaggart's ministries.[1632] In addition, John Camp, a reporter in Baton Rouge, found that money for children's aid was instead used for ministry buildings and furnishings.[1633]

The Confession

At his Family Worship Center in Baton Rouge, Louisiana, Swaggart confessed to "moral failure," begged for forgiveness, but did not give any details; there were 7,000 in attendance.[1634] Swaggart gave his speech on February 21, 1988.[1635] "I do not plan in any way to whitewash my sin or call it a mistake."[1636] He wept like a crocodile. *People* noted the "copious tears."[1637] Swaggart did not speak from a prepared script (add tears where you feel is appropriate):

> "Many times I have addressed the media in a very stern manner, and I have chastised them for what I thought and believed was error in their reporting or their investigation even. This time I do not. I commend them. I feel that the media, both in print and by television, radio, have been fair and objective and even compassionate. Ted Koppel on "Nightline," I feel, did everything within his power, in going the second, third, fourth, fifth, tenth mile to make doubly certain that what he reported was at least as fair and as honest as he, the spokesman for this world-famed news program, could make it. And I thank him for his objectivity, his kindness, and his fairness. And I also want to express appreciation to the entire media everywhere, but especially here in Baton Rouge -- Channels 9, 2, and 33, the newspapers, the radio stations. They've been hard, but they have been fair. They have been objective and at times, I believe, they have even been compassionate -- even my old nemesis, John Camp, that we have disagreed with very strongly. And I love you, John. And in spite of our differences, I think you are one of the finest investigative reporters in the world -- and I mean that."[1638]

Swaggart asked everyone for forgiveness, then vowed to preach on: "Many ask, as I close, this: will the ministry continue? Yes, the ministry will continue. Under the guidance, leadership and directives (as best we know how and can) of the Louisiana District of the Assemblies of God, we will continue to take this gospel of Jesus Christ all over the world. ..."[1639]

His audience interrupted him twice with standing ovations.[1640] *People* called the confession "the most tortured public display of contrition in recent memory."[1641] Cousin and country star Mickey Gilley said, "I admire him for confessing the way that he did in front of his church…It takes a lot to stand in front of a congregation and pull something out of your soul like that."[1642] It also takes a lot to stand in front of church and preach to God, then bash homosexuals, Jews, Muslims and Catholics.

Robertson-Swaggart '88

The evangelist scandals hurt Pat Robertson, whose 1988 presidential strategy was to get support from Bible Belt Southern states before Super Tuesday primaries on March 8, 1988.[1643] During the campaign, Robertson threatened to sue anyone who called him a TV evangelist, instead calling himself a businessman.[1644] The *New York Times* said Robertson implied Vice President George H.W. Bush had something to do with disclosures of sexual misconduct by the Rev. Jimmy Swaggart, the television evangelist."[1645] The BBC was more blunt, noting Robertson claimed the scandal was engineered by Bush to improve the vice president's White House bid; but Robertson retracted this accusation a week later, and flew to Louisiana for a public show of support for Swaggart.[1646]

He just couldn't help himself…

People reported in March, 1988, Swaggart was given a light sentence from the elders at the Assemblies of God (a three-month suspension from his U.S. pulpit, but he was free to honor preaching commitments elsewhere).[1647]

After the ordeal, Swaggart and his son Donnie continued to broadcast to over 30 countries but viewing numbers were once as high as 100 nations.[1648] Jimmy Swaggart didn't learn his lesson. In October 1991, he was faced with accusations for picking up a California prostitute for sex and said he would step down temporarily from his ministry.[1649] At the time, the ministry official administering Swaggart's school (the Family Christian Academy) said Donnie Swaggart would take over the ministry "until Brother Swaggart gets back on his feet," and co-pastor, Jim Rentz, would lead the church.[1650]

The prostitute, Rosemary Garcia, was a 31 year old from Indio, California, who was with Swaggart when he was pulled over for a traffic violation.[1651] *Time* reported the "latest foray prompted Swaggart to resign from his Baton Rouge-based ministry last Tuesday to seek 'professional counseling and medical care.' But the next day the preacher reversed the decision, explaining to his congregation that God told him to return to the pulpit."[1652]

Swaggart was less apologetic in 1991 than he was in 1988, and announced to supporters that "the Lord told me it's flat none of your business" and said he didn't have to apologize for his conduct.[1653] Not only was Swaggart found with his hand in the bag a second time, by the fall of 1991 he faced the $10 million court judgment against him for defaming Marvin Gorman.[1654]

Famous gay bashing quotes from Swaggart include…

1) Limp-wristed preachers are bad. He didn't like homosexuals, but particularly those who were ministers, noting, "We've got to get those limp-wristed preachers out of the pulpits."[1655]

2) Gay marriage is asinine. "I get amazed, I can't look at it but about 10 seconds, at these politicians dancing around this, dancing around this, I'm trying to find a correct name for it, this utter absolute, asinine, idiotic stupidity of men marrying men."[1656]

3) Jimmy Swaggart thanked President Bush. "I'm knocking our pitiful, pathetic lawmakers. And I thank God that President Bush has stated, we need a Constitutional amendment that states that marriage is between a man and a woman."[1657]

4) But Swaggart doesn't tease gays. "I'm not knocking the poor homosexual, I'm not. They need salvation just like anybody else."[1658]

5) I'll kill gays. Swaggart has also stated, "I've never seen a man in my life I wanted to marry. And I'm going to be blunt and plain: if one ever looks at me like that, I'm going to kill him and tell God he died."[1659]

Swaggart continues

Swaggart's website boasted (December 2008): "Jimmy Swaggart Ministries is doing its part through" TV (airing in 50 countries), radio (70 stations and a "potential" audience of millions, and his church in Baton Rouge (yes, Family Worship Center is still hanging around).[1660] The website also noted, "Jimmy Swaggart, in addition to being an Anointed Minister, is one of the best-selling Gospel Music Artists of all-time, with total sales in excess of 15,000,000 Recordings worldwide."[1661] He was one of the best-selling hypocrites.

JIM AND TAMMY FAYE BAKKER

The most popular of the TV preachers were Jerry Falwell, Pat Robertson, Jimmy Swaggart, and Jim Bakker.[1662] Jim Bakker's story is noteworthy because it includes all four. Robertson gave Bakker his start on *The 700 Club*; Swaggart unleashed the Hahn affair; and Falwell stepped in to take Bakker's spoils.[1663]

Bakker Beginnings

Tammy Faye LaValley was born in International Falls, Minnesota and graduated from North Central Bible College in Minneapolis, where they met.[1664] They married in 1961. [1665]

The Bakkers co-hosted *The 700 Club*, on the Christian Broadcasting Network from 1966 to 1973.[1666] CBN was founded by television evangelist and Christian Coalition founder, Rev. Pat Robertson.[1667] The Bakkers jointly hosted TV shows on Pat Robertson's Christian Broadcasting Network in Virginia before moving briefly to the Trinity Broadcasting Network in California; in 1974, they moved to Charlotte and started PTL.[1668] The Bakker's turned the PTL Club into a TV network.[1669]

Jim and Tammy Faye Bakker were one of the first religious programmers to use satellite transmission and cable television.[1670] Jim Bakker argued video technology was a way to fulfill Jesus' 2,000- year-old mission to reach out to spread the Gospel. He told *Time* if Jesus were on earth today, "he'd have to be on

TV. That would be the only way he could reach the people he loves."[1671] They had an estimated 12 million viewers and $10 million a month in revenue at its peak.[1672]

Time described Jim Bakker as "the boyish-faced Pentecostal proprietor of the PTL Network in Charlotte, N.C. The network ranks second to Robertson's CBN in Christian cable (13 million households, 24 hours, all religion). The featured offering is the daily *Jim and Tammy Show*, a variety-and-talk program with Bakker and his wife as hosts on an opulent, hacienda-style set with orchestra, singers and live audience."[1673]

Tammy's Trademark

Tammy Faye Bakker stood 4 feet 11 inches.[1674] She was famous for her heavy makeup and false eyelashes.[1675] CNN later reported (2007), "Before millions of viewers, she would often break into tears, prompting her trademark heavy mascara to run."[1676] Her lipliner, eyeliner and eyebrows were tattooed on.[1677] In her last public interview, she told Larry King she would most like to be remembered for "my eyelashes."[1678] She was once being photographed and the makeup artist asked her to take offer he fake eyelashes; she didn't because, "Without my eyelashes, I wouldn't be Tammy Faye."[1679]

Heritage USA

Their theme park opened in 1978 at the network's headquarters in Fort Mill, South Carolina.[1680] Its "Grand Hotel" came in 1984, and two years later a water park was added.[1681] In 1986, over 6 million people visited Heritage USA, ranking it the country's third most popular attraction after Walt Disney World and Disneyland.[1682] Heritage USA had shopping stores and a mini golf course.[1683] *Time* reported, "Unlike Walt Disney World and Disneyland, which rank ahead of it, Heritage USA charges no admission. The grandiose 2,300-acre project, which is years away from completion, includes Bakker's Assemblies of God church, a 500-room luxury hotel, a mock turn-of-the-century mall with 25 boutiques under an artificial sky, and an amphitheater for staging passion plays and living Nativity spectacles."[1684] Jim Bakker wanted to add a replica of the Crystal Palace to house a 30,000-seat auditorium and 5,000-seat TV studio.[1685] Heritage USA was valued at over $125 million.[1686]

Could we have some money?

Asking for money came naturally. When Jim Bakker was given a talk show, *The 700 Club*, he pleaded for viewers to donate $1,000 a month. [1687] Pat Roberston eventually took over the show.[1688]

Pentecostal preaching and appeals for viewer donations was commonplace, as Jim and Tammy Faye claimed God would reward donors with prosperity.[1689]

But already in 1979, PTL's finances were questioned. The *Charlotte Observer* claimed money supposedly raised for overseas work was diverted to expenses at home.[1690] Even before the big fraud scandal came out in the late 1980s, *Time* reported Jim Bakker "does live well, even as he pleads poverty on the air and lays off some 500 employees (as he did weeks ago). He tools around in a Mercedes, and he and Tammy have a $449,000 retreat in Palm Springs."[1691] Tammy Faye even had an air conditioned dog house.[1692] The Bakkers had matching Rolls-Royces.[1693]

Time had looked at the Bakkers' PTL and their fiscally irresponsibility in August 1987. The ministry once spent employee retirement funds to pay operating expenses.[1694] Indeed, "PTL had no reliable internal audits, no checks and balances for financial accountability and often no receipts or other devices for keeping track of incoming and outgoing cash. In the final months of the Bakker era, PTL was taking in $4.2 million a month and spending $7.2 million."[1695] There was constant turnover with executives, regular switching of legal advisors, and a time when PTL had 47 bank accounts and 17 vice presidents.[1696]

The IRS watched the Bakkers as early as 1981, and it was clear they felt by 1985 that PTL should have their tax-exempted status rejected because PTL personally benefited the Bakkers.[1697] The IRS concluded Jim Bakker's compensation for 1981 ($259,770.29), 1982 ($400,765.58) and 1983 ($638,112.27) was excessive.[1698]

The Affair

Jim resigned from PTL in March 1987.[1699] The affair with his secretary Jessica Hahn had occurred seven years earlier.[1700] Hahn received a one-time $115,000 payment to keep quiet, but she also received monthly interest payments from a $150,000 trust fund.[1701] In July 1987, Hahn's lawyer announced she would tell her story in *Playboy*.[1702]

The Crime

Weeks before Christmas 1988, the Federal Government gave Jim Bakker a 28-paged indictment of 24 counts of fraud and conspiracy.[1703] Tammy Faye got off easy. *Time* noted, "televangelism's dolled-up super-shopper, escaped by an eyelash, but three associates were also charged: PTL's former No. 2 administrator, Richard Dortch, and Bakker aides David and James Taggart."[1704]

Bakker and Dortch were charged with illegally taking around $4 million in bonuses out of the PTL funds.[1705] The Taggart brothers helped themselves to $1.1 million from PTL funds and evaded taxes.[1706] The Feds concluded the money was taken to satisfy their lifestyles. As of May 1987, Jim and Tammy Faye had been paid $4.6 million since 1984; Richard Dortch, who had succeeded Bakker as PTL leader, received $620,000 since early 1986; and David Taggart was paid $710,000 since January 1986.[1707] All this in a non-profit agency.

There was $3.4 million in bonuses for Jim and Tammy and $279,000 total to shut up Jessica Hahn.[1708] *Time* reported, "The grand jury spent 16 months investigating the scandal and detailed 42 misdeeds."[1709]

Their conviction in 1989 is generally blamed on the Heritage USA deal because Jim Bakker knowingly offered willing donators a deal he knew wasn't possible.[1710] In the spring of 1986, PTL needed cash desperately, so Bakker came up with a plan to sell on TV. For $1,000, Baker offered viewers a package of lodging at Heritage USA (worth $3,000). In less than two weeks, his followers contributed $16.6 million.[1711] There was no room for all the donators; otherwise known as fraud.[1712] The man of God oversold "lifetime memberships" to the church that included lodging at Heritage USA.[1713] A later court settlement granted each of the 165,000 lifetime partners a check for a $6.54.[1714]

Excuses

Tammy Faye made excuses on the wealth, noting "Jim and I didn't live that well…People said we had a mansion, but it was no mansion. It was just a little house on a lake. We did have drivers and decent cars and various people to help us, but we couldn't have survived without that kind of thing. We were so busy every day. And we didn't ever use the jet that much."[1715] When asked if she felt bad for the old ladies who sent in their savings, Tammy Faye said, "No. It was their money. Anybody I ever talked to who gave to the PTL said they never regretted a dime. We needed the money to keep our program going."[1716]

The Heritage USA theme park and hotel closed in 1989.[1717] When Jim was found guilty of fraud and conspiracy, she spoke at a news conference and, of course crying, sang, "On Christ the solid rock I stand/All other ground is sinking sand."[1718] It's hard to take the 1980s Tammy Faye seriously. The Bakkers said PTL also stood for "People that Love," skeptics dubbed it "Pass the Loot."[1719] In addition, it has been argued the Bakker saga was all a show. Their sincerity on TV between each other did not transcend backstage, where they were distant and apart.[1720]

Televangelist Backlash

Time noted (August 1987) whether it was Oral Roberts, Jerry Falwell, or Jimmy Swaggart: "All these entrepreneur-preachers have been hit hard, at least temporarily, by the PTL scandal."[1721]

Jim's Punishment

Jim Bakker was forced to give up his evangelical empire in 1987, and admitted he paid over $250,0000 to cover up the sexual relationship with his church secretary.[1722] He was indicted for fraud and conspiring to defraud churchgoers of $158 million; Tammy Faye Bakker was not named in this December 1988 indictment.[1723] Then in 1989, he was convicted of fraud and spent five years in federal prison.[1724] In 1989, Jim Bakker was convicted of 24 counts of fraud and conspiracy; he was sentenced to 45 years in prison.[1725] By 1994, Jim was paroled but Tammy Faye Bakker divorced him.[1726]

Tammy Faye's Punishment

In a 2007 interview with Larry King, Tammy Fay talked of the PTL Club: "I have gotten over that, thank God. That was a terrible, horribly bad experience."[1727] When she died, the *USA Today* concluded, "she emerged as a sympathetic figure in contrast to her disgraced first husband, Jim Bakker, who went to prison for fraud."[1728]

Tammy Faye Bakker never admitted fault, and claimed ignorance when it came to PTL's financial affairs.[1729] Critics argued Tammy Faye cashed in on her ditzy persona to look innocent. The only lock-up Tammy got was rehab. In 1987, she went to the Betty Ford Center for her prescription drug addiction.[1730]

Falwell's Gain: PTL

Televangelist Jerry Falwell of Lynchburg, Va. took control of the PTL after Jim Bakker's March 19, 1987 resignation, and within months told PTL viewers donations were substantially down since PTL formally filed for bankruptcy on June 12.[1731] The issue facing Falwell's PTL: if $1.75 million was not raised by July 31, 1987, PTL would likely be forced to stop broadcasting on their 160 plus stations.[1732]

There were unresolved issues for Falwell. There were the 120,000 PTL "Lifetime Partners" who each gave at least $1,000 to the organization in return for free lodging for three nights a year at the ministry's theme-park hotel.[1733] It wasn't even possible to fulfill the pledges, because number of donors surpassed available hotel rooms by a margin of 5 to 1.[1734] These types of issues made for certain that Falwell had nothing to gain (he wasn't going to turn PTL around); but perhaps Falwell would get access to PTL members mailing list. That may have been Falwell's true motive to take over PTL.

Bakker vs. Falwell

Once Bakker lost PTL to Falwell, Bakker denounced him.[1735] Bakker had loyalists, an issue heightened by the fact Falwell was a Fundamentalist.[1736] Fundamentalists reject faith healing and speaking in tongues that the PTL, which was Pentecostal-based, practiced.[1737] When Falwell's PTL had a fundraiser, Bakker PTLers sabotaged the phone lines with crank and obscene calls.[1738] Falwell then had to announce he would only accept checks by mail.[1739]

The stakes where high, because even in bankruptcy there was still the PTL daily TV show, its all-day religious cable service transmitted to 13 million homes, and the 2,300-acre Heritage USA theme park.[1740] In the name of God, fundamentalists were fighting over a vacation spot and a cable show. Once again, the televangelist crowd proved it was all about the money. But Falwell's backers denied he had taken PTL's 518,000 donor mailing list and that checks to PTL went to Falwell's Lynchburg ministry.[1741]

Jim Bakker asked, "Even if Jim and Tammy did everything we're accused of, does that give Jerry Falwell the right to steal my dream, my life, my home, my everything and my reputation from me?"[1742] Falwell was just another televangelist scavenging the remnants of another defrocked televangelist.

Falwell did bring some corporate responsibility to PTL. He ended sales of lifetime partnerships at the Heritage hotel, a ten-member board monitored the ministry finances, and a different accounting firm dug through PTL's finances (which was to prepare a comprehensive reorganization plan for presentation in federal bankruptcy court in late 1987).[1743]

Yet some of his arguments were typical political spin. Falwell argued (March 1988) the Bakker and Swaggart scandals strengthened broadcast evangelism and made Christianity stronger, more mature and more committed.[1744]

Jerry Falwell accused Jim Bakker of homosexuality and called him "the greatest scab and cancer on the face of Christianity in 2,000 years of Church history."[1745] Jim Bakker accused Falwell of running a manipulative smear campaign. [1746]

In May 1987, Bakker asserted "I've never been involved in wife swapping…I'm not a homosexual, and I've never been to a prostitute."[1747] This was the same time he callously said: "We have eight or nine million dollars in royalties we never received" from PTL.[1748] Bakker made those comments just days after Jerry Falwell made sure Bakker would never minister again in Fort Mill, S.C. [1749]

The situation got worse for Bakker. In a *Penthouse* article, John Wesley Fletcher, who had worked for Bakker, detailed homosexual encounters with Bakker and claimed he also procured other young men for Bakker.[1750]

The Public vs. Televangelists (1987)

The response against televangelists in 1987 was negative. In the political realm, the House Ways and Means oversight subcommittee launched an investigation into the tax-exempt status of the PTL and ten other major televangelist organizations.[1751]

Time reported (8.3.1987), "A Gallup poll survey this spring showed that since 1980 there has been a sharp decline in American public esteem for four of the country's most important TV preachers: Oklahoma-based Oral Roberts (whose approval rating dropped from 66% to 28%), Swaggart (76% to 44%), Virginia's Pat Robertson (65% to 50%) and California's Robert Schuller (78% to 61%)."[1752]

Tammy Remarried

Because of the debt and sex scandals of Jim, Tammy Faye divorced Jim then married Roe Messner in 1993.[1753] Jim and Tammy Faye were married over 30 years.[1754] Roe Messner's company built churches and developed the PTL resort, Heritage USA.[1755] He has been called a Christian constuction magnate; a former PTL contractor, and a friend of Jim Bakker.[1756] In 1995, Mr. Messner was sentenced to 27 months in federal prison for bankruptcy fraud.[1757]

In 2002, Tammy Faye said she and Jim had a good relationship: "It's wonderful. We're good friends. We'll always be good friends."[1758] Jim Bakker was kind when Tammy Faye died, stating, "She is now in Heaven with her mother and grandmother and Jesus Christ, the one who she loves and has served from childbirth…That is the comfort I can give to all who loved her."[1759]

Jim Bakker's Comeback

By 2007 Jim Bakker, was building a new television ministry in Branson, Mo.[1760] In 1998, Jim married his second wife Lori, and they started a new gig in Missouri in 2008.[1761] The site is called Morningside, and Jim and Lori have taped shows.[1762] Morningside includes hotels, and has similarities to Heritage USA.[1763]

Jim went out of his way to tell the *St. Louis Post-Dispatch*: "I don't own this [stage and show]."[1764] The *Post-Dispatch* reported (2.17.08), "Almost nothing is held in his name these days. He has no registered ownership interest in Morningside. Bakker's name is nowhere to be found on his church and TV show nonprofit registrations with the state. (They were registered by Lori Bakker's mother, Charlene Graham.) The Bakkers rent a house in Branson. Public records show the Bakkers own two vehicles: a 2006 Dodge Durango and a 2006 Chrysler 300."[1765] As of 2008, Jim Bakker still owed the IRS over $6 million.[1766]

Tammy Faye and the Gay Community

Her flamboyant appearance and open compassion made her a media star long after the collapse of her evangelical base.[1767] She believed homosexuality was a sin, but Tammy Faye Bakker was one of the few evangelicals to help AIDS victims; she even broadcasted a supportive program about an HIV-positive gay man on PTL.[1768] She once said, "I felt that Jesus would have gone to that person and put his arm round them."[1769] There is no doubt she had a huge following among gays appreciating her early displays of nonjudgmental compassion for those with AIDS.[1770] She was one of the few evangelical Chrisitians who was supported by the gay community.[1771] CNN has described her as "one of the first televangelists to reach out to those with AIDS when it was a little-known and much-feared disease."[1772] She commented it was the gays who got her back on her feet after the PTL scandel: "When I went -- when we lost everything, it was the gay people that came to my rescue, and I will always love them for that."[1773]

The Times in England reported, "Bakker became something of a camp icon, involved in events such as drag bingo AIDS benefits. With her oversized eyelashes, bright red hair, garish jewellery and make-up seemingly applied with a plasterer's trowel, the 4ft 11in Bakker was a popular model for drag queens."[1774] Tammy Faye once said drag queens "do me better than me."[1775] In 1996, she co-hosted the *Jim J. and Tammy Faye Show* with gay actor Jim J. Bullock.[1776]

She was asked if she was surprised by the acceptance she got from gays. She replied (2002), "I'm stunned. But you've got to remember that PTL was one of the very first [Christian television shows] to help the gays. And I was probably one of the first ever to have a gay man on my show. And so I think they remember that. They knew that we accepted them. Many of them watched PTL because they felt accepted by us and they *were* accepted by us. PTL loved everyone. We didn't turn anyone away. And I think the gays appreciated that. We accepted the gay community when most religious elements did not."[1777]

Her film, *The Eyes of Tammy Faye*, did well with the gay community. Tammy Faye commented in 2002: "It was popular with everybody -- not just the gays. It turned my life around, really. The gay guys have Tammy Faye parties all the time where they show the film. That just makes my heart melt right down to nothing. One young gay man came up to me and told me every time somebody comes to his house, they can't live without the film. And so he gives it to them and buys himself another one. He said, 'Tammy, I've bought twelve of them.' And that really touched my heart."[1778] She was asked why she thought it was so popular with gays. She said:

> "So many things have happened to the gay people -- they've been made fun of, they've been put down, they've been misunderstood. A couple of the gay guys told me, 'We put it on every time we get discouraged.' I've even heard people outside the gay community say that every time they get discouraged they put that movie on and they realize they can make it. I didn't know how that movie was going to turn out, I wasn't promised anything on that movie, but I'm just in disbelief of what has happened to my life [because of it]. I thought I was a Titanic and that I was going to sink and never come up again. But I guess I had the greatest captain in the world -- the lord Jesus Christ. He promises to get us safely to the other side and He certainly has."[1779]

Bold Comments From An Evangelical

What would you say to the parent who does not want to accept their child as gay? Tammy Faye Bakker was asked the question in 2002, and said if parents "don't accept it I would say shame on them. When you're a parent you accept your child as he or she is. But I understand that there are mothers and dads that just can't accept the fact that they have a gay child. I think a mother and dad should accept them, not fight with them, and just accept them because they *are* their children and they should love their children just the way they are. My boy has tattoos and piercings all over him and I love my boy more than I love my own life."[1780] She went on add that if the parent doesn't accept his or her gay child:

> "The parent loses. Because the most important relationship in the world is between mother and father and child, and I think when a parent refuses to accept any child the way they are -- I don't care if it's because they're gay or if they have a sickness or if they decide to do something different than what the parent wants -- I think the parent loses. They lose the most wonderful friendship they could ever have. I'm trying to educate parents and the Christian world and tell them, these are wonderful people, allow them to be in your church, love them. Don't be so judgmental. Christians are *so* judgmental and as a result of that they become very cruel. When I go and stand among those gay men and women, I tell them 'I am a preacher of the gospel that loves you. And I accept you just the way you are.' I cry when I say that but I mean that with all of my heart. Somebody's got to love them and accept them. And somebody who loves God has got to love them and accept them because so many of them really love God, too."[1781]

She was asked to comment on the many Christians who saw gay as evil or an abomination. Tammy Faye said, "I think being gay is just being a person who has a different thought on life. They're just people. I don't think that God categorizes people. I went to Disneyland one time, and it rained -- it's so awful when it rains at Disneyland -- and everyone disappeared inside. And when the rain stopped and everybody came out, every single person had yellow raincoats on. You couldn't tell the fat from the thin, the rich from the poor. You couldn't tell anyone from anyone else. And that day I looked up and I said, 'God, I think this is how you see us, all in yellow raincoats, and only you have the permission to look under those yellow raincoats.'"[1782]

Tammy Faye however, wouldn't comment on "political issues important to gays and lesbians, such as gay marriage or military service. And she says she doesn't like being where gay people flaunt their sexuality -- aside, of course, from drag-queen contests and sweaty dance parties."[1783]

She attended numerous pride gatherings, including Washington D.C.'s Capital Pride in 2002.[1784] Though she wasn't' a pride parade supporter, when in comes to pride gatherings, Tammy Faye said, "I do more hugging than probably any person alive because I feel that it is so important to reach out and touch someone. That's become a cliche, but I believe it. I believe that we all need hugs. We all need to know that someone loves us just the way we are and is willing to put their arms around us and hold us. I'm always right in the middle of everybody and everything because that's just me."[1785] But she also said (2002) she wouldn't be in gay pride parades: "... I don't think they need them…I believe in class -- I believe that people should have a bit of class about them."[1786]

Health & Death

She was diagnosed with colon cancer in 1996; which returned in 2004 by spreading to her lungs.[1787] The lung cancer was deemed inoperable.[1788]

She dropped to 65 pounds when doctors had stopped treating the cancer; in May 2007 she said she looked "like a scarecrow."[1789] She had a great relationship with Larry King of CNN, who was made aware of her death almost immediately.[1790] In her last interiview with Larry King, Tammy Faye said she was bedridden most of the time and had difficulty swallowing food.[1791]

Messner died at the age of 65 in July 2007.[1792] The family service was held in a private cemetery, where her ashes were interred[1793] in a remote part of Kansas at the Kansas-Oklahoma border.[1794]

Bakkers' Son also supportive of the gay community…

Tammy Faye and Jim had a son and a daughter. [1795] And the son now advocates for gays. According to CNN after Tammy Faye's death, "The Bakkers' 30-year-old son, Jay, is a pastor who co-founded the Revolution Church in Brooklyn, New York -- a church aimed at those who feel rejected by traditional approaches to Christianity, stating on the church's Web site that he wrestled with religion after seeing the "excommunicative" treatment his parents experienced from the church after the scandal."[1796]

In September 2008, the *Ashville Citizen-Times* reported, "The son of televangelists Jim and Tammy Faye Bakker is taking on one of his late mother's causes and fighting against religious and political discrimination against gays and lesbians."[1797]

Jay Bakker preaches God's love for gays and lesbians and is "fighting to end religious and political discrimination against gays and lesbians, and presenting a nonjudgmental, inclusive face to his Christian faith."[1798] He said (Oct.2008), "I ... talk about loving your neighbor as yourself, God's amazing grace and the dangers of apathy in our lives."[1799] His Revolution New York City church meets Sundays in a bar.[1800] He began his activism around 2005 when he saw his friends being mistreated because of their orientation.[1801]

Jay Baker thinks the passages against homosexuality refers to worship of a fertility god or male prostitution, but not intimate, respectful relationships between homosexuals.[1802] Jay Baker is not gay, but is separated from his wife.[1803] According to McClatchy Newspapers, "The celebrity preacher has paid a price among conservative and evangelical Christians for his convictions. Engagements to his widely sought-out church appearances were abruptly cancelled, and he stopped speaking publicly for a year. His journey was the subject of a documentary series broadcast on the Sundance Channel called *One Punk Under God.*"[1804]

The Bakkers are imperfect, but people could learn a lesson from Tammy Faye and Jay.

TED HAGGARD

Ted Haggard founded the New Life Church in the 1980s, and by the time of his sexual tryst had 14,000 members.[1805] *Time* (Jan.30,2005) said Haggard was one of the top 25 most influential evangelicals in America. A former evangelical preacher, "Pastor Ted" founded the New Life Church in Colorado Springs, Colorado. Built in the 1980s and sprawling over 55 acres, the New Life Church was the second-largest church in Colorado and the 60th largest in the U.S.[1806] In November 2004, New Life was finishing a new church building that could hold 8,000 in an oval formation.[1807] The New Life Church did not answer to a higher church organization.[1808]

Haggard was also the National Association of Evangelicals (NAE) President since 2003,[1809] and led it until 2006. The National Association of Evangelicals, which represented 30 million conservative Christians, "spread over 47,000 churches from 52 diverse denominations."[1810]

Evangelicals Held Political Power

In 2004, Haggard told the *Rocky Mountain News* Bill Clinton was receptive to evangelicals: "Bill Clinton's White House was the most responsive in recent history...He really wanted to please evangelical Christians. He's a Bible-believing Christian himself; his problem was, he was a sex addict."[1811] The next president was even more receptive.

Karl Rove, President George W. Bush's chief political adviser, said that the key to the 2004 was turning out four million evangelical Christians who did not vote in 2000.[1812] In 2004, Haggard said, "If evangelicals vote, Bush will win...If they don't, Kerry might."[1813] He also has stated, "If the evangelicals vote, they determine the election."[1814] The BBC reported (11.5.04), "the core of the president's support was Christian conservatives. Three-quarters of all white voters who described themselves as evangelical Christians voted for President Bush, according to national surveys of voters as they left the polls on Tuesday. And, this year, evangelicals made up one-in-five of all voters - a record."[1815]

Ted Haggard led his audiences to pray for President Bush to select an acceptable Supreme Court nominee.[1816] In 2004, the *Rocky Mountain News* reported he was "one of the nation's most influential evangelical Christians, whose overstuffed agenda includes a weekly conference call to the White House."[1817] The BBC noted (Nov.2004), "Pastor Ted has come a long way from his makeshift living room chapel. Twice over the last three years, he has been a guest of President Bush in the White House."[1818] *Time* quoted Haggard (Jan.2005): "We wanted him (Bush) to use the force of his office to campaign aggressively for a federal marriage amendment, which he did not do."[1819] In 2005, *Time* described Haggard as one of "two Evangelicals who join the White House's weekly Monday call with Christian leaders."[1820] The meetings were to plot strategy on gay marriage, abortion, and other social agendas.[1821] The associate pastor at New Life told a *New York Times* reporter (2004), "We're in regular contact with Karl Rove."[1822] The associate pastor told the *New York Times* "We are not going to hold hands and sing Kumbaya...We have issues [abortion, homosexuals]."[1823] In 2006, they also had issues with Haggard's orientation.

Evangelicals: Homosexuality Is NOT Inherited

The 2004 National Association of Evangelicals (NAE) resolution on homosexuality stated:

> "We believe that homosexuality is not an inherited condition in the same category as race, gender, or national origin, all of which are free from moral implication. We believe that homosexuality is a deviation from the Creator's plan for human sexuality. While homosexuals as individuals are entitled to civil rights, including equal protection of the law, the NAE opposes legislation which would extend special consideration to such individuals based on their "sexual orientation." Such legislation inevitably is perceived as legitimatizing the practice of homosexuality and elevates that practice to a level of an accepted moral standard."[1824]

Pastor Ted: Gay Basher

The easiest way to describe Haggard is that he was similar to the Baptists (see Anita Bryant, Pat Robertson). In 2003, Haggard said, "The Southern Baptist Convention and the NAE need to draw closer together. Both need the other. The

Southern Baptist Convention needs to connect with the rest of the evangelical body of believers, and the rest of the evangelical body of believers needs to be there with the Southern Baptist Convention."[1825] Like Baptists, Pastor Ted was critical of homosexuals.

ABC News described (11.3.2006) Haggard as "an outspoken opponent of gay marriage," and "a major figure in evangelicalism in the country, with a direct line to the White House."[1826]

Likewise, Haggard's followers believed homosexuals could change. The 2004 NAE resolution on homosexuality states, "We further call upon pastors and theologians, along with medical and sociological specialists with the Christian community to expand research on the factors which give rise to homosexuality and to develop therapy, pastoral care and congregational support leading to complete restoration."[1827]

Haggard was featured in the documentary of the summer camp *Jesus Camp*.[1828] In the documentary, a Pentecostal pastor is featured as a drill instructor to young evangelicals as children pray in tongues, cry and ask God to end abortion, and bless President George Bush.[1829] The "Kids on Fire" summer camp featured in the film had been run since 2002, but after the film came out, the drill instructor was accused of brainwashing the children, and the campground in North Dakota was vandalized.[1830] Haggard is included in *Jesus Camp*, and the directors visited New Life Church, where Haggard tells the audience: "We don't have to debate about what we should think about homosexual activity. It's written in the Bible."[1831] Of course the irony is Haggard looks into the camera and jokes: "I think I know what you did last night. If you send me a thousand dollars, I won't tell your wife."[1832]

Mike Jones

Mike Jones was from Denver, gay and a masseur; Jones said he engaged in gay sex with Pastor Ted and Haggard had probably purchased crystal meth.[1833] Jones later claimed Haggard said "he loved snorting meth before [he] has sex with his wife."[1834] In 2007, Jones claimed he never actually procured drugs for Haggard.[1835] As of November 8, 2006, just days after the scandal broke, Haggard acknowledged paying Jones for meth and massage, but said he didn't have sex or take the drug.[1836]

Jones said Haggard paid him for sex at regular intervals over a three-year period.[1837] Jones told KHOW-AM radio (Colorado): "He [Haggard] goes, 'A fantasy of mine is to have an orgy with about six young college guys ranging from 18 to 22 in age,' ...I will tell you it [the relationship between Haggard and Jones] was not emotional and just strictly physical."[1838] Jones said he only learned of Haggard's true identity watching TV a couple months before Jones broke the scandal.[1839]

Jones said he became upset upon discovering Haggard career and his opposition to same-sex marriage.[1840] The straw that supposedly broke the camel's back was Haggard's support for an anti-gay iniative on the ballot in Colorado.[1841] Jones said, "I wish him well. I wish his family well. My intent was never to destroy his family. My intent was to expose a hypocrite."[1842]

Jones claimed he was out of the sex business when seeing Haggard, though Jones said, Haggard "begged me to keep him on, and I did…I was doing personal training, I was modeling at different art schools around town, and I was also doing massage."[1843]

In 2008, Jones said of Haggard: "I spent three years with him…He was very nice. I don't hate Ted Haggard, but what he did was so wrong, and he put me in a very difficult position. When I'm outing Ted Haggard, I'm outing myself."[1844]

Haggard: I'm sexually immoral but not gay.

Haggard had to step down his leadership position for the New Life Church, and the NAE. Haggard's severance package from New Life Church made Haggard agree to leave Colorado Springs.[1845] The severance package paid Haggard through 2007 and made Haggard not publicly discuss the scandal.[1846] Haggard's annual salary was about $138,000, benefits excluded.[1847]

In the end, Haggard was vague on the details, but confessed "sexual immorality."[1848] Haggard did not address specific claims by the male escort.[1849] Intially Haggard was in denial. He said (11.3.2006) he bought meth but didn't use the drug or have sex: "I called him to buy some meth, but I threw it away. I bought it for myself but never used it…I was tempted, but I never used it."[1850] *ABCNews.com* reported (11.3.2006) Haggard got a massage from Jones "after receiving a recommendation from a Denver hotel, but said he never had sex with him."[1851]

A week after resigning as NEA president, Haggard gave a letter read to his megachurch (11.5.2006): "because of pride, I began deceiving those I love the most because I didn't want to hurt or disappoint them…The fact is I am guilty of sexual immorality. And I take responsibility for the entire problem. I am a deceiver and a liar. There's a part of my life that is so repulsive and dark that I have been warring against it for all of my adult life."[1852] Haggard wrote, "the accusations made against me are not all true but enough of them are that I was appropriately removed from this church leadership position."[1853] Haggard never admitted being gay; and neither did his church. The Overseer Board for his church released a statement, "Our investigation and Pastor Haggard's public statements have proven without a doubt that he has committed sexually immoral conduct."[1854]

Why a big deal?

The events occurred just before the 2006 midterms. *MSNBC.com* reported (Nov.5.2006), "The scandal has disappointed Christian conservatives, whom President Bush and other Republicans are courting heavily in the run-up to Tuesday's election. Many were already disheartened with the President and the Republican-controlled Congress over their failure to deliver big gains on social issues even before the congressional page scandal involving former Rep. Mark Foley."[1855]

More important were Haggard's close ties to the White House. Besides routine conference calls with the White House staffers, he lobbied Congress in 2005 on Supreme Court nominees. [1856] Lastly, the hypocrisy is an obvious—but sad—commentary on Evangelical gay-bashing.

Furthermore, another evangelist was tarnished. The *Dallas Morning News* reported (4.18.2007), "His former congregation has felt the sting of the scandal. Since Haggard's fall, attendance has fallen 20 percent and giving has dropped 10 percent, said Rob Brendle, an associate pastor. As a result of the decline, the church laid off 44 employees, or 12 percent of its work force."[1857]

Ted's "Reparative Therapy?"

Haggard's excuse for his behavior was blamed on pedophilia. Haggard claimed his behavior stemmed from when he was molested by someone who worked for his father, and this molestation haunted him when he rose to power later in life: "There I was, fifty years old, a conservative Republican. Loving the word of God, an Evangelical, Born-Again, spirit-filled, charismatic--all those things. But some of the things that were buried in the depths of the sea from when I was in the second grade started to rage in my mind and in my heart."[1858] It was the classic Evangelical answer. Rather than take the blame for getting masturbated by a gay prostitute, blame it on a pedophile. One can say the pathological liar was, maybe, telling the truth. But Haggard's excuse/recollection parallels the classic Evangelical response toward homosexuals: to blame them for pedophilia. Not surprisingly, little, if any, publicity was given to the man who supposedly "molested" Haggard.

Haggard took a "spiritual restoration" program in Phoenix in January 2007, and three weeks later proclaimed he was "completely heterosexual" due to his *Focus on the Family*-backed handlers.[1859] When Haggard went to Phoenix, it was the same church which helped failed televangelist Jim Bakker.[1860] Bakker stayed at the Phoenix church after being released from federal prison for stealing $158 million from supporters.[1861]

In Phoenix, Haggard still didn't publicly disclose what the sexual immorality was.[1862] The Rev. Mike Ware, a pastor who helped investigate the claims against Haggard, said (April 2007) Haggard was continuing to receive counseling, including exploration of his sexuality.[1863]

When Haggard completed the three weeks of ex-gay counseling, Mike Jones laughed: “Well, that's the quickest therapy I've ever heard of. It's hard for me to imagine someone who is performing oral sex and saying that he is 'straight.' That just doesn't jive." If you were to ask me 'Do I think is Ted Haggard gay?' I would have to say 'yes'."[1864] At the time of Haggard’s “successful” therapy, two others had accused Haggard of sexual encounters but wanted to remain anonymous.[1865]

One of Haggard’s counselors said Haggard’s activities were not a “constant thing.”[1866] Haggard was not gay, he just liked men helping him with sex. Sometimes.

Haggard sent an e-mail to his friend Kurt Serpe (October 2007), and wrote: "I was referred to Mike Jones from the concierge at a Marriott hotel when I asked for a masseur…It was during the massage that it started to become sensual, and that led to him masturbating me…That was and is our only sexual contact."[1867] It wasn’t until June 2008 this email got to the media, which was Haggard’s “first public revelation” of his gay contact with Jones.[1868] In regard to the drugs, Haggard wrote, "During the conversation with Mike during and after the time he masturbated me, he told me about some drugs that he could get for me that would enhance my masturbation experience."[1869]

Serpe said Haggard “craved sex” and “was a sexaholic," but Haggard’s forays had nothing to do with homosexuality, but more about masturbation and gratification: "This is something that he has been struggling with all of his life.”[1870] According to Serpe, Haggard claimed he knew Jones for three months not three years.[1871] Like any good friend, Serpe shared the email with Newschannel 13 in Colorado.[1872]

Where are they now?

In 2007, Mike Jones released his book *I Had To Say Something: The Art of Ted Haggard's Fall.*[1873] In 2008, he performed his one-man show, *Naked Before God: Exposing the Hypocrisy of Ted Haggard.*[1874] Jones was approached about creating the show by PoliMedia Entertainment from Palm Springs, Calif., and the company provided a writer to adapt the book to put together the 75-minute show.[1875] The one act play was income: “That's why I'm doing this play. I made a little bit on the book, not a whole lot. I'm barely making ends meet, to be honest with you."[1876] More noteworthy, Jones said he also had relations with Sen. Larry Craig (R-Idaho).[1877]

Two years after Jones went public, Haggard apologized for his sins: "I'm a stronger Christian than I've ever been in my life…I have a stronger marriage than I've ever had in my life….I really did sin and I'm very, very sorry that I sinned."[1878] Best yet, he is “not” gay. Haggard said the ordeal made him suicidal.[1879]

In January 2010, Haggard made more headlines for stating he was now "cured" of his homosexual tendencies. He and his wife went on *Larry King Live* to hype his wife's book, *Why I Stayed.* His website advertises his availibilty to go to various churches to deliver his message. We assume he is making money.

RICHARD ROBERTS

In the 1980s, Oral Roberts said he was reading a spy novel when God appeared to him and told him to raise $8 million for Roberts' university, or else he would be "called home."[1880] The university spouted bibilical principles, and was, of course, anti-gay. In 2001, gay alumni of ORU who kept their sexuality hidden as students planned a coming out at homecoming, but the university would not recognize the group ORU-OUT as an official organization.[1881]

Into the new century, the university was financially sucessful. Oral Roberts University reported nearly $76 million in revenue in 2005, according to the IRS.[1882] Oral Roberts, nearing 90, was living in California (2007).[1883] His son Robert took over the ORU. Richard Roberts headed the university since 1993,[1884] and in November 2007, Richard Roberts resigned.[1885]

In 2007, Richard Roberts was accused of using university money for his own personal uses.[1886] In fact, three former ORU professors sued Richard Roberts for being fired because they told administrators Richard Roberts and family misused ORU monies.[1887] The lawsuit by the three professors included, "allegations of a $39,000 shopping tab at one store for Roberts' wife, Lindsay; a $29,411 Bahamas senior trip on the university jet for one of Roberts' daughters; and the purchase of a stable of horses for the Roberts children."[1888] The Richard Roberts' home had been remodeled 11 times in the past 14 years.[1889] His wife was accussed of "sending scores of text messages on university-issued cellphones to people described in the lawsuit as underage males.'"[1890] In addition, it was alleged "A longtime maintenance employee was fired so that an underage male friend of Mrs. Roberts could have his position."[1891]

Roberts also made students in a government class work on a Republican Mayoral candidate's campaign in Tulsa, threatening the university's tax exempt status.[1892] Roberts, the Christian leader, denied any wronging despite receiving a "no confidence" vote from the tenured faculty.[1893] He did, however, resign. There has been no public comment on whether Mrs. Roberts stopped spending the night with 16 year old boys, as she had been charged by the University.

Like the other televangelists, the Roberts family was exposed. The televangelistic troubles were not just a 1980s-thing with Jimmy Swaggert and Jim Bakker. The hypocrits are just as alive and well today as they were in 1987.

FRED PHELPS

Raised in Mississippi, Fred Phelps and his wife Marge moved to Topeka in 1954. "Many of his 13 children bought homes in the same square block that since has been dubbed the Phelps Compound."[1894]

Phelps had difficulty earning a law degree because Kansas law required judges to vouch for his character, and Phelps had trouble finding judges to do so.[1895] He sued Sears for $50 million in 1974 over a failure to deliver a TV set on time; he settled for $126 and no TV.[1896] By 1989, Phelps turned over his law license for practicing at a federal level in return for his family members to continue practicing law.[1897] Phelps has had numerous failures in politics: governor of Kansas in 1990, U.S. Senate in 1992; Topeka Mayor in 1993; governor in 1994.[1898] Phelps ran in the primaries every time.[1899]

Westboro Baptist Church

The Westboro Baptist Church is based in Topeka Kansas.[1900] The WBC's first service was held in 1955.[1901] Phelps gained publicity for protesting Matthew Shepperd's funeral.[1902] The WBC equates America as a modern day Sodom and Gomorrah.[1903]

He caused his hometown Topeka economic damage. The *Oakland Tribune* reported (11.4.2002), "Burlington Northern and Santa Fe Railway planned to add 600 jobs in Topeka, but dropped the idea after Phelps wrote a letter to the company saying Topeka was 'well-known as Sodom City, U.S.A.'"[1904] In addition, Phelp's church is known nationally for picketing funerals of U.S. soldiers killed in combat since June 2005.[1905]

Phelps is a master at getting attention. In fact, critics question whether he should be given any attention at all, given that is what Phelps thrives on. In October 2008, Sony accused him of violating copyright laws after the release of a video parody of the song "Holding Out for a Hero" from the 1984 film *Footloose* to the WBC version of "There Are No Heroes."[1906] A year earlier they released a parody to "We are the World" to the new version of "God Hates the World."[1907]

The Church is incredibly vindictive. Even the *Topeka Capital-Journal* reports residents were reluctant to disclose their names for news stories about the church because they feared harassment.[1908]

Predestination

Phelps believes in predestination, the idea God has already selected those heaven-bound, with everyone else going to hell and there is nothing they can do about it.[1909] This point is important because it indicates their protests serve no purpose. Phelps once wrote a letter noting, "We don't strive to change your hearts or minds. Even if we wanted to, we couldn't make you believe the truth. Every person who is predestined for hell will remain in darkness."[1910]

WBC position on gays...

The WBC position is that soldiers are killed in war (both Iraq and Afghanistan) because God is punishing the U.S. for tolerating homosexuality.[1911] The WBC is less descriptive on why God punishes a military that does not allow open homosexuality. According to the AP (10.26.08), the WBC protests at soldier's funerals "have been the impetus for laws restricting funeral picketing by

37 states, including Kansas, and the federal government. But the church says its protesters always remain beyond the limits imposed by the law on how close they can get to a service."[1912]

There posters have included sayings such as: "Thank God for Dead Soldiers,"[1913] "Thank God for I.E.D.'s,"[1914] "You're Going to Hell." [1915] As of 2002, there was a 40-foot banner insulting gays on the Phelps compound.[1916]

Another Homophobic Statement From Fred Phelps:

WBC News Release in March 2004:

> "Gen. [Wesley] Clark opposed fags & dykes in the military—BUT—when he decided to run for President on the Democratic ticket he groveled like a mangy dog to the FagiNazis running the Democratic Party, and promised to lift the ban on gays in the military. His Christ-rejecting, God-hating Jew blood bubbled to the surface. Yes, like his boss [John] Kerry, Clark is a Jew....That these two turds are Jews would not matter—except when they ask for supreme political power & spit in the Face of God, pushing for same-sex marriage, threatening to bring down God's wrath on us as on Sodom—then some inquiries are in order. Beware! 'Jews killed the Lord Jesus, and their own prophets, and have persecuted us; and they please not God, and are contrary to all men; forbidding us to speak to the Gentiles that they might be saved, to fill up their sins always; for the wrath is come upon them to the uttermost." 1 Thess. 2:14.' Apostate fags & Jews certain to bring God's wrath."[1917]

Homosexuals Dominated Nazi Germany

In December 1996, the WBC gave a press release in which the WBC planned to picket the Holocaust Memorial Museum:

> American taxpayers are financing this unholy monument to Jewish mendacity and greed and to filthy fag lust...Homosexuals and Jews dominated Nazi Germany...just as they now dominate this doomed U.S.A....The Jews now wander the earth despised, smitten with moral and spiritual blindness by a divine judicial stroke...And god has smitten Jews with a certain unique madness, whereby they are an astonishment of heart, a proverb, and a byword (the butt of jokes and ridicule) among all peoples whither the Lord has driven and scattered them...Jews, thus perverted, out of all proportion to their numbers energize the militant sodomite agenda...The American Jews are the real Nazis (misusers and abusers of governmental power) who hate God and the rule of law.[1918]

Saddam Fan

Phelps political affiliations include Saddam Hussein. In 1997, Phelps wrote a letter to Saddam Hussein praising Iraq as "the only Muslim state that allows the Gospel of our Lord Jesus Christ to be freely and openly preached on the streets."[1919] A group of Phelps's WBC congregants traveled to Iraq to protest against the U.S.[1920] After the 2003 invasion of Iraq, Phelps consistently protested the war, including protests at U.S. soldier's funerals.[1921]

What kind of group?

The New York Times has described (April 2006) the WBC as "a tiny fundamentalist splinter group" and the WBC "is not affiliated with the mainstream Baptist church."[1922] The *New York Times* concluded, on average, six to twenty people are protesting soldiers funerals.[1923] The Church "consists almost entirely of 75 of Mr. Phelps's relatives."[1924] In other words, it is a cult. His church is small, family, and behaves like lunatics.

****

Pastors in Perspective

A note about adultery, hypocrisy and sin…

An article in a 1997 issue of *Newsweek* magazine noted that various surveys suggest that as many as 30 percent of male Protestant ministers have had sexual relationships with women other than their wives. *The Journal of Pastoral Care* in 1993 reported a survey of Southern Baptist pastors in which 14 percent acknowledged they had engaged in "sexual behavior inappropriate to a minister." It also reported that 70 percent had counseled at least one woman who had had intercourse with another minister. A 1988 survey of nearly 1000 Protestant clergy by *Leadership* magazine found that 12 percent admitted to sexual intercourse outside of marriage, and that 23 percent had done something sexually inappropriate with someone other than their spouse. The researchers also interviewed nearly 1000 subscribers to *Christianity Today* who were not pastors. They found the numbers were nearly double: 45 percent indicated having done something sexually inappropriate, and 23 percent having extramarital intercourse.

(See: Anderson, Kerby, 2003, *Adultery*, in Leadership U Series of Probe Ministries. August 5, 2003, www.leaderu.com/orgs/probe/docs/adultery.html.)

It is obvious from the above numbers 70 percent or more of America's pastors honor their profession. They are true servants of God. It is also obvious many stray.

Not all pastors are televangelists. The Web allows communication to the masses with out television. And there are many who communicate primarily through their pulpit, to their congregation, in their community. I studied, briefly to become a Pastor, and am a certified lay minister. I have served Methodist, American Baptist, Cumberland Presbyterian, and non-denominational community churches. I have preached, married and buried. I have past and present blood relatives who are pastors and a son-in-law who is a pastor. My criticism is only of those who preach hate and therefore foster hateful acts.

Such behavior is certainly not limited to infamous televangelists. I walked out of a Protestant Sunday School class, in 1960, because of a diatribe against Catholics. The Reverend Jeremiah Wright, of 2008 presidential campaign fame, is famous for his anti-white and anti-Jewish comments. The Reverend Baptist Pastor Steven L. Anderson of the Faithful Word Baptist Church says from his pulpit that he wants President Barack Obama to die and that he would not consider an assassin who killed the President a murderer. This man is a scary kind of whacko. If his congregants act out he should be legally culpable.

The Mullahs preaching hatred of Jews and Christians, the Rabbis preaching hatred of Muslims, Christian Pastors preaching hatred of Barack

Obama and homosexuals are all the same. They are Merchants of Hate. Nothing better.

They blaspheme Mohammed, God and Jesus Christ.

PART TWO: THE NEO CON REPUBLICANS

A little history...

The nation's historians ranked our Presidents in 2009. Republicans in the top ten are Abraham Lincoln (1), Theodore Roosevelt (4), Dwight Eisenhower (8), and Ronald Reagan (10). According to Rasmussen Polls in 2007, the American people put the same Republicans in the top ten, but not in exactly the same position.

In terms of the worst U.S. Presidents, Harding, Hoover and George W. Bush are Republicans in the bottom 10.

A political party is more than the reputation of its Presidents. Yet one cannot help but notice that Lincoln won the nomination, barely, and only after carefully orchestrating regional and personality differences among his opponents. However, they were all against slavery, putting them in direct opposition to the South.

Harding was President during the early 1920's. He had been having an affair with the wife of a friend. After winning the nomination, the Republican Party paid hush money and sent his girlfriend and her husband on a trip to Japan. The payments continued after that. His administration was riddled with corruption, including the Teapot Dome affair.

Hoover was President when the nation had entirely enough of the religious conservative driven Prohibition and failed to do enough to stop the downward spiral of the economy leading to the Great Depression. He is given credit as having been a very good Secretary of Commerce under Harding and Coolidge and a great humanitarian after his Presidency. Nevertheless, he is ranked among the bottom.

A broader look might phrase it this way: In the Roaring Twenties the Americans lived in exciting times; some of them anyway. The evangelical and fundamentalist churches and some women temperance groups gave us Prohibition. Prohibition brought organized crime, gangland killings, smuggling, moonshine and a mob that lasted for decades. It was so bad it had to be repealed. The era saw ugliness and violence against black Americans, Catholics, Jews, to name a few. It was an era of intolerance and hatred of minorities.

In the twenties, the top 5% of the American population earned 33% of the income. Real income for the rest barely moved. There was no fiscal policy. Wall Street, with Harding, Coolidge and Hoover's laissez faire capitalism run amok, lived in a world of speculation, "pooling" and shaky marginal trading. The stock market crashed from 381 to 41 in less than a year and 9000 banks failed.

In 1933, Democrat Franklin Roosevelt became President of the United States, a position he held until his death in 1945.

In 1948, the Democratic Party split at their National Convention and the Dixiecrats from the Old Confederacy left the Party to have their own and support Strom Thurmond, from South Carolina for U.S. President. Even with the southern split, President Truman ran against the Republican Congress as a platform, and was re-elected. The Dixiecrats left because of civil rights planks placed in the party platform. "States Rights" became a slogan to cover outright racism.

In 1952, conservative Robert Taft of Ohio, lost to General Eisenhower for the GOP nomination. Eisenhower became the first Republican President in 20 years and was opposed by Congressional Republicans and the conservatives within his own party.

Eisenhower defeated Governor Adlai Stevenson II of Illinois in the general election. Eisenhower won easily; yet, when the election was over, a survey by the University of Michigan Survey Center found that 47% of the American people considered themselves Democrats and only 27%, considered themselves Republican. Stevenson carried 81% of the Afro-American vote.

In 1960 Vice President Richard Nixon faced Massachusetts U.S. Senator John F. Kennedy for the Presidency. Kennedy was Catholic, rich, and from a liberal East Coast state. Both candidates faced the same political dilemma: The Southern white vote v. the Northern Afro-American vote.

Theodore H. White, in *The Making of the President, 1960,* stated succinctly: "The problems of civil rights in America—which is another way of speaking of the relations of Negro Americans with white Americans – poses, for political strategists, the sharpest choices in national planning. Since the northward migration of the Negro from the South, the Negro vote, in any close election, has become critical in carrying six of the most eight populous states of the Union. To ignore the Negro Vote and Negro insistence on civil rights must be either an act of absolute folly—or one of absolute calculation."

During the 1960 campaign, Martin Luther King was arrested in Atlanta, Georgia, and sentenced to four months hard labor. Many feared for his life. Nixon, although Vice-President of the United States, did nothing. The Kennedy family went to work on getting Dr. King released and John Kennedy called Coretta King. Bobby Kennedy prevailed with the sentencing Judge and got Dr. King released on bail.

Illinois was carried by Kennedy by 9,000 votes and over 250,000 Afro-Americans, Protestants almost all, voted for Kennedy. The same kind of results were found in Michigan and South Carolina. Lyndon Johnson worked the Southern white community through his colleagues in the Senate and the good old boys in the Court House. Henry Cabot Lodge, Nixon's running mate, told a meeting in New York's Harlem community that Nixon would appoint a Black to the Cabinet. Nixon, as White puts it, managed "in alienating Northern Negro and Southern Whites, losing both along with this election."

In 1964, following the assassination of President Kennedy and the elevation to the Presidency of Vice President Lyndon Johnson, the Republican Right came back to nominate U.S. Senator Barry Goldwater for President. Goldwater, a staunch conservative had voted against the Civil Rights Legislation of 1964. He carried only Arizona and the old Confederacy.

Remarkably, in 1966 and 1968, the Republicans bounced back. They did with two classes of social progressives and fiscal conservatives, Charles Percy of Illinois, George Romney of Michigan, Bob Ray of Iowa, John Love in Colorado, Dan Evans in Washington. Republican Everett Dirksen of Illinois and Democrat Mike Mansfield of Montana helped pass subsequent civil rights legislation. John Anderson of Illinois helped with open housing. Richard Nixon, more of a pragmatist than ideologue came back in to win the Presidency in 1968, helped by the above and the failed foreign and military policy of LBJ.

Race, Religion, Big Money, Credit Cards and the Changing Political Map

All of these historical events and election statistics were being constantly studied and analyzed, along with Census data and survey research. Ticket-splitters, typologies, cross-tabs, hard data, began to show the Republican insiders the paths to victory. In the North, Plains, West, Midwest, social progressives and fiscal conservatives rose to the top in state elections. In the South, where social and fiscal conservatism and patriotism and evangelical churches were most important, a new breed of Republicans ran.

The old Southern white had a memory and what goes around, comes around. In addition, survey research from across the South indicated a clear sense of alienation from American society by the evangelical churches. They did not think, at that time, that neither government or the political process, responded to their deep concerns for the souls of the American people, and their behavior. I personally sat in on briefings with political staffs from around the South and the Midwest concerning the coming programs and operations, amazing in their scientific statistical precision, to bring the evangelical community into the Republican fold. Southern whites were becoming Republicans because they were being told God would be better served. The Southern religious leaders, Falwell and crew, went to work.

In 1968, Nixon's Southern Strategy, would help win the Presidency over Vice President, Hubert Humphrey. Humphrey had authored the civil rights planks for the 1948 Democratic Convention.

The marriage...

The process started with the Southern Baptist Convention, then the Assembly of God, and then the Independents. The evangelicals took over the GOP and gave the GOP power in Congress and state houses and Governor's mansions it had not seen before. Abortion was identified as a connector to the Catholics.

In 1972, I attended a political strategy meeting in Chicago, where we shown census data, on clear thick plastic sheets, carefully analyzed and selected, laid over political voting precinct maps. We were told the maps showed trapped urban ethnics; they were Democrats but they were living right next to the Afro-American community and were feeling racial tensions. Democrats, we were told, became more liberal the further they lived from urban problems and racial tensions. We were to concentrate conservative messages about law and order issues in those closely adjacent areas and then turn out the voters in those areas.

I have seen politicians I knew personally practicing public prayers, and going to church when they had never done so. Praise the Lord, they were getting religion; I'd see these guys at the bars and clubs and after-hours underground joints at night and holding hands in prayer circles during the day. I would convince myself it was OK for me, they were paying me to be there. Now, I am disgusted with myself and the entire hypocritical process I saw unfold.

I lived in Alaska from 1974 to 1989. The evangelicals took over the Republican Party during that time. They literally organized in the church, practiced their roles, went to the conventions and caucuses en masse, and quietly voted the old Libertarian and small business Republicans out and themselves and their worldview in. Anti-Semite and racist Pat Buchannan wins an Alaskan presidential primary and Alaska's Sarah Palin becomes a phenomenon, of sorts. I personally worked with Terry Dolan, one of the nation's leading conservative organizers, working the religious right by day, a closet homosexual, according to many, who got a bad case of the crabs, while in Anchorage. He came to work suffering from his new "hitchhikers" and complaining about the stripper who had offloaded his new guests.

As Kevin Phillips describes it, the politics of theology, oil, big money, and power took over.

As time passed and generations changed, and language and culture changed, it became terribly incorrect to be a racist. Abortion became a major connector, then gay rights. It was still OK to hate gay people, or actually start hating them, in case you had not thought about it.

All of that brought the nation to the Defense of Marriage Amendment and Law, DOMA's in several states, and Don't Ask, Don't Tell. Homophobia replaced racism and hippies and war protestors as targets of political opportunity. The Lesbian and Gay community has the evangelicals, the neo-com Republicans, and their various groupies and mouthpieces demanding the LGBT community stay invisibile and be satisfied with their secondary citizenship status.

The Republican Party sold its soul.

Big Money…

There is another side to the Republican Party that needs to be considered also, an outright hatred of "Liberals". People will fight very hard to keep what they have, even if a consumer disposable. This side also helps explain the opposition to change and the tenacity with which Republicans will fight to maintain the status quo and even turn it back a bit.

At the end of World War II, the United States had immense manufacturing capacity, radio was now well understood and spread everywhere in the nation, television was not far behind. Folks had learned a great deal about mass communication, propaganda, and advertising. New techniques of survey research using the telephone and statistical sampling were evolving quickly. We, in effect, build anything and advertise it for sale in a most targeted manner. However, following the War and the Korean Conflict, there was little to no money for consumer products. So, the corporations, the banks, the people on Wall Street and California decided the consumers should have credit.

At the same time millions of Americans, who could afford it, went to our colleges and universities and became part of a superb educated workforce. Millions were left out. We passed civil rights legislation in 1964, 18 years after the end of WWII.

The post-war industrialization and growth in an international economy, oil based industries and automobiles, suburbia and commutes, television and cable television, the interstate highway system, air transportation and the computers the explosion of silicon and digital based economies and the creation of a consumer based economy instead of wealth based, created millions of new upper middle class families.

The new upper middle class and the nouveau riche had things their parents never dreamed of owning. The number one American value is not God and religion, it is not family, it is not country, it is not education or work, it is consumerism, buying stuff and storing it or throwing it in the land fill. It is disgusting.

But as consumption has grown, so too has the average size of the American house. The National Association of Homebuilders reports that the average American house went from 1,660 square feet in 1973 to 2,400 square feet in 2004. So, let's get this straight, houses got bigger, *average family sizes got smaller*, and yet we still need to tack on 2,2 billion-plus square feet to store our stuff? (T Vanderbilt, *Slate*)

To Paraphrase George Carlin: A house used to be a home; now it's merely cover for stuff.

And to pay for all of this… We have a plastic ticket to hell. $790 billion in credit card debt, $8000 per household, 43% of American households spend more than they make each year., 2 trillion dollars in consumer debt, does not include mortgages. It includes, credit cards, cars, trucks, boats, furniture, store accounts, and so on. The number is up more than 41% from the $1.3999 trillion consumers owed in 1998.

And as a result of not investing in wealth, More than 150,000 of the 600,000 bridges in the nation need significant repairs. One-third of our 4 million miles of highways are in substandard condition, over 1.4 million miles. 3,346 dams are listed as "could fail" and 1300 of those would endanger human lives. Every year old and inadequate sewer systems spill over 1.26 trillion gallons of sewage, costing over $50.6 billion to clean up. Over one-third of the city sewage systems in the nation are subjected to EPA enforcement actions every year.

America's electrical transmission lines are maxed out. There are not the lines to handle wind energy farms or new power plants. We've built no new refineries in 32 years. In many of our cities, the mass transportation systems are overloaded. The average age of America's public school buildings was reported to be 42 years old in, 1998; it is worse now. The cost just to repair old infrastructure: $1.6 TRILLION

The Republicans built a new constituency in the suburbs by promising "NO NEW TAXES", year after year after year. Americans could feed their Madison Avenue driven greed for things, and the Wall Street desire to extend credit, by not investing in their nation. The Cold War and more recently, the wars in Iraq and Afghanistan, and the interest on the debt, took what money was available.

When Medicare and Medicaid and and increasing numbers of Americans on Social Security came along to add to the need for public funds, the pressure on those making a living and paying taxes became even greater.

The perfect storm brews every day. Demand for funds from people who are overloaded in debt and driven by a standard of living based on consumer disposables, gives the Republicans the perfect strawman, i.e, Democrats and "Liberals "who want to raise taxes to pay for improvements in education, health care, the environment, energy, infrastructure.

The consuming Republican blames "Them", transferring the problem to "Liberals". The Republicans in the State Houses and Congress suck up the campaign money from big-medicine, big insurance, big oil, international conglomerates, and the beat goes on. Republicans and Conservative (Blue-Dog) Democrats campaign on an "anti-tax" platform in national campaigns, state-wide races for Governor, state senate and house races and locally. Consequently, the nation is falling apart.

Anyone who suggests actually solving a problem is a "hated Liberal." We scream at one another instead of civil political and public discourse seeking solutions to problems and opportunities for progress. This hatred of "Liberals" has led to murder.

2008

Fast forward to 2000 to 2008. Wall Street runs unchecked, the 'Fix" was in between the White House, the Congress and the big investment bankers. Fiscal policy was a joke with big expenditures "taken off the books". Savings by the population was almost non-existent, only the top two or three percent were doing really well, real earnings for the middle and lower class were spiraling down, The stock market crashed and banks began to fail. The economy tanked. Bush's military and foreign policy executions were disasters.

At the same time the evangelical and fundamentalist churches were in control of White House political and religious theory. The line between church and state was weakened, women, minorities were held back and this time, a new hatred rose since being anti-black wasn't acceptable anymore, so the gays and lesbians are the new targets.

In 2008 America swept out the Republicans, a black man, a Democrat, became President of the United States, the Democrats controlled both houses of Congress and the Grand Old Party won the old Confederacy and looked weak and foolish in the process.

And, there are still those who believe self-serving narcissists and hypocrites like Coulter, Limbaugh, Beck, Gingrich, the followers of that lunatic Pat Robertson, and neo-cons like Palin, Romney and Huckabee, are the leaders for the future of the Republican Party.

The history of the GOP states clearly that social progressives and fiscal conservatives win. They also can build the party. They are also more likely to solve some of the nation's problems. They certainly would diminish the hateful rhetoric.

MICHELE BACHMANN

Michele Bachmann presently represents the 6th Congressional District of Minnesota. She was reelected in 2008 by a slim margin. The Minnesota sixth district curves north from the Twin Cities and encompasses conservative St. Cloud.[1925]

Skating on the Edge: Michele Bachmann

She claimed her right to fame (or infamy) in October 2008, when Bachman was interviewed by MSNBC's Chris Matthews. She told him many of Barack Obama's associates and many of her colleagues in the Congress, could be characterized as anti-American.[1926] "The liberals that are Jeremiah Wright and that are Bill Ayers, they're over-the-top anti-American. And that's the question that Americans have. Remember, it was Michelle Obama who said she's only recently proud of her country. And so these are very anti-American views."[1927] And she later added, "What I would say -- what I would say is that the news media should do a penetrating expose and take a look. I wish they would. I wish the American media would take a great look at the views of the people in

Congress and find out, are they pro-America or anti-America? I think people would love to see an expose like that."[1928]

With just weeks until the election, the comment allowed her Democratic challenger, El Tinklenberg, to raise $2 million in donations.[1929] But early money is always better then late money. She defeated Tinklenberg 46 percent to 43 percent.[1930] Tinklenberg was former Gov. Jesse Ventura's transportation commissioner and earned praise for building a popular regional commuter line, but he struggled with name recognition.[1931] Independent candidate Bob Anderson got 10 pecent of the vote, and no doubt hurt Tinklenberg.[1932] Tinklenberg's spokesman said Anderson "got 5 percent more than we had hoped he would."[1933] Bachmann won reelection.

A Classic Arch-conservative

Bachmann is "pro-family," pro-life and critical of public education. She is the quintessential arch-conservative bible-thumping Republican.[1934] As one critic noted, "Bachmann's track record in the legislature reads like a parody of right-wing talk radio."[1935] Bachmann introduced bills to make English the official state language, to stop grants for clinics giving abortions, to prove citizenship at voting booths, to make stillbirths designated as births by the state, and to name Interstates 494 and 694 the Ronald Reagan Beltway.[1936] She also wanted Reagan's birthday officially recognized.[1937]

This type of political "leader"….

Bachmann: I'm not a scientist and am very flawed. In September 2003, she was quoted in the *Stillwater Gazette*: "I look at the Scripture and I read it and I take it for what it is. I give more credence in the Scripture as being kind of a timeless word of God to mankind, and I take it for what it is. And I don't think I give as much credence to my own mind, because I see myself as being very limited and very flawed, and lacking in knowledge, and wisdom and understanding. So, I just take the Bible for what it is, I guess, and recognize that I am not a scientist, not trained to be a scientist. I'm not a deep thinker on all of this. I wish I was. I wish I was more knowledgeable, but I'm not a scientist."[1938]

Theocratic. Bachmann stated (March.6.2004), "We're in a state of crisis where our nation is literally ripping apart at the seams right now, and lawlessness is occurring from one ocean to the other. And we're seeing the fulfillment of the Book of Judges here in our own time, where every man doing that which is right in his own eyes—in other words, anarchy."[1939]

God told Bachmann to run for Congress. In October 2006, she spoke at the Living Word Christian Center, a large suburban church in Brooklyn Park, Minnesota:

> God then called me to run for the United States Congress, and I thought "What in the world will that be for?" and my husband said "You need to do this," and I wasn't so sure, and we took 3 days and we fasted and we prayed and we said, "Lord. Is this what you want? Is this your will?" and after long about the afternoon of day two, he made that

calling sure. And its been now 22 months that I've been running for United States Congress. Who in their right mind would spend 2 years to run for a job that lasts 2 years? You'd have to be absolutely a fool to do that. You are now looking at a fool for Christ. This is a fool for Christ.[1940]

Old Time Religion. Bachmann does not separate her religious beliefs and politics. Her law degree was from Coburn School of Law in Tulsa, which is affiliated with Oral Roberts University.[1941] Before becoming a Minnesota state senator, Bachman ran for Stillwater School Board in 1999 as one of one of five conservatives running for seats; she lost.[1942] However, she set herself up with a network for social conservatives because she promoted a religious curriculum in an area charter school and said creationism should be taught in the school district.[1943]

Bachmann also has a relationship with Olive Tree Ministries, a Maple Grove-based organization believing the end of the world is near.[1944] Bachmann claimed to not know about Olive Tree and, in 2005, said she did not recall doing the interview with Jan Markell.[1945] In truth, she gave many comments bashing gays in her interview with Markell (included in the following pages). Olive Tree's two main themes is building up Israel and bashing gay marriage.[1946] Likewise, Bachman is one of the biggest homophobes in U.S. Congress.

Bachmann's View of Homosexuality

1) Cry to God to support gay marriage ban. In 2004, as a state senator, she supported a constitutional amendment to ban gay marriage. She said, "Listeners should rejoice right now, because there are believers all across your listening area that are praying now. And I would say that if you can't attend the rally, you can pray. And God calls us to fall on our faces and our knees and cry out to Him and confess our sins. And I would just ask your listeners to do that now. Cry out to a Holy God. He wants to hear us, He will hear us if we will confess our sins and cry out to Him. Our children are worth it and obedience to God demands it."[1947]

2) Gay marriage is the biggest issue facing the country in thirty years. In 2004 she said, "This is probably the biggest issue that will impact our state and our nation in the last, at least, thirty years. I am not understating that."[1948]

3) Public schools will teach homosexuality. Bachmann warned (3.6.2004) of the dangers if her same-sex marriage ban would fail to pass in 2004. "It isn't that some gay will get some rights. It's that everyone else in our state will lose rights. For instance, parents will lose the right to protect and direct the upbringing of their children. Because our K-12 public school system, of which ninety per cent of all youth are in the public school system, they will be required to learn that homosexuality is normal, equal and perhaps you should try it. And that will occur immediately, that all schools will begin teaching homosexuality."[1949]

She also said if the same-sex marriage ban amendment would not pass in 2004: "The sex curriculum will be essentially be taught by the local gay community."[1950]

4) Homosexuals are targeting our children. When discussing the gay community and same sex marriage, she said (3.20.2004), "This is a very serious matter, because it is our children who are the prize for this community, they are specifically targeting our children."[1951]

5) Homosexuality is not natural. Bachmann said Minnesotans needed to contact their state Senators to let voters decide on the gay-marriage ban, "Because otherwise, our children will be forced to learn that homosexuality is normal and natural and that perhaps they should try it, and that'll be very soon in our public schools all across the state, beginning in kindergarten."[1952]

6) **It's those activist judges.** Bachmann said (3.20.2004), "We are wide open and vulnerable and in all likelihood an activist judge will strike down our Defense of Marriage Act, our state law against gay marriage, this year. And in all likelihood, we will have gay marriage in 2004 in Minnesota, if we don't get this amendment on the ballot for November."[1953]

7) Bachman said religious organizations should actively confront Democrats in the state capital. Bachmann said (3.20.2004), "We only have until May 17 (2004) at the latest. But really, it is this next week that the DFL is going to try to kill this bill. It's within the Christian community's hands to get face to face, in front of these Democrats."[1954] Rather than some pastor telling parishioners to march to the state capital, Bachmann, as state senator, told Christian groups to get in the face of Democrats. Ironically, in the same interview, Bachmann wanted sympathy for gay supporters chastising her anti-gay bigotry.[1955]

8) Being gay is being enslaved. Bachmann said (11.6.2004), "If you're involved in the gay and lesbian lifestyle, it's bondage. It is personal bondage, personal despair and personal enslavement."[1956]

9) Gay bashing is love. She said to her supporters at the March 2004 rally against same sex marriage was "probably the most loving, warm-spirited, most beautiful rally that I have ever seen at the Capitol."[1957] She also noted (3.20.2004), "Two homosexuals that were holding up my picture this week at the Capitol and shouting that I want to hate people, I walked up to them and said: 'I don't hate you. I love you and the Savior who created you. He loves you, too, can I tell you why?' This is not about hating them, this is about loving them into the Kingdom."[1958] In March 2004 she said, "This is not about hating homosexuals. I don't. I love homosexuals."[1959] Then in 2005, When asked "do you hate homos?" Bachmann responded, "No, but ask my kids!" then laughed.[1960]

10) She bashed gay-friendly companies. Bachmann said (11.6.2004), "They aren't just kind of gay-friendly, they are gay advocates at Proctor and Gamble… Here's just a few other companies that support the pro-homosexual agenda. They include Levi-Strauss, American Airlines, Sarah Lee Bakery, Jaguar and LandRover."[1961]

11) Homosexual teachers equates to child abuse. Bachmann said, "You have a teacher talking about his gayness. (The elementary school student) goes home then and says 'Mom! What's gayness? We had a teacher talking about this today.' The mother says 'Well, that's when a man likes other men, and they don't like girls.' The boy's eight. He's thinking, 'Hmm. I don't like girls. I like boys. Maybe I'm gay.' And you think, 'Oh, that's, that's way out there. The kid isn't gonna think that.' Are you kidding? That happens all the time. You don't think that this is intentional, the message that's being given to these kids? That's child abuse."[1962]

12) A homosexual teen commits suicide. So what. Bachmann was asked about a leader of a teacher training workshop who said homophobic discrimination caused suicide among homosexual youth. Bachmann said the leader failed "to acknowledge other psychological factors that could contribute to homosexual youth committing suicide, like family problems or abuse or maybe the fact of what they're doing."[1963]

13) Don't acknowledge works done by homosexuals. Bachmann said (11.6.2004), "Normalization (of gayness) through desensitization. Very effective way to do this with a bunch of second graders, is take a picture of 'The Lion King' for instance, and a teacher might say, 'Do you know that the music for this movie was written by a gay man?' The message is: I'm better at what I do, because I'm gay."[1964]

14*)* **Homosexuality is a dysfunction.** Bachmann said (11.6.2004), "Don't misunderstand. I am not here bashing people who are homosexuals, who are lesbians, who are bisexual, who are transgender. We need to have profound compassion for people who are dealing with the very real issue of sexual dysfunction in their life and sexual identity disorders."[1965]

15) Fighting Pearl Harbor and fighting gay marriage: same thing. Bachmann once emailed supporters about the noble fighting of a local veteran at Pearl Harbor, an how it was similar to fighting gay marriage:

> On the morning of December 7, 1941, local St. Paulite Orville Ethier was aboard the USS Ward, a boat manned by 82 Navy reservists from St. Paul, when a small Japanese sub appeared near the entrance to Pearl Harbor. The Ward fired two shots, one of which struck and sank the sub, which constituted the first American shots of World War II. The commander of the Ward relayed a message about the incident back to military headquarters in Honolulu. The message stated "We have attacked, fired upon and dropped depth charges upon submarine operating in defensive sea area." The message, sent more than an hour before the 8 a.m. attack on Pearl Harbor, went unheeded. ...You are a type of Orville Ethier - a patriot looking to secure American freedoms. The question is, will the Senators of Minnesota act like the Honolulu military headquarters and ignore your message? Today we face perhaps the greatest attack on the family in our lifetime. Now is OUR time to stand up and send a message to avert an equally impending disaster. Please visit www.mnmarriage.com to read my recent column on the threat that legalized gay marriage poses to our civil and religious liberties and, to tax exempt organizations in particular.[1966]

Birds of a Feather?

Mitt Romney's political action committee (PAC) said (November 2008) Bachmann "is a passionate defender of the unborn and traditional values."[1967]

GARY BAUER & AMERICAN VALUES

Gary Bauer is a spokesman for social conservatives, and labels himself "pro-family."[1968] He was Ronald Reagan's Under Secretary of Education and Chief Domestic Policy Advisor.[1969] When he left the White House, he became the president of the Family Research Council in 1988, and served as a senior vice president of Focus on the Family.[1970]

According to the American Values website, "The Family Research Council is one of Washington's most respected centers for public policy. In ten years, Bauer led FRC from a three person, $1 million operation, to a 120 person, $14 million operation, housed in its own headquarters in downtown Washington."[1971]

Bauer also started a political action committee (Campaign for Working Families) to elect "pro family" candidates.[1972]

Who is Gary Bauer?

According to Dkospedia, the free political encyclopedia from the left-leaning *Daily Kos* website:

> Bauer, represents the nexus between the Christian right and the neoconservatives. A close friend of neocon bigwig William Kristol, Bauer's dossier of political activities dates back to the Reagan Administration, where he served in a number of posts under Education Secretary William Bennett. From this perch he lambasted "moral decay in public schools" and advocated controversial policies like school prayer. According to a 1986 *Washington Post* article, Bauer blamed "the public schools for what he called the decay in the nation's morals," criticized textbook publishers "as soft on the Soviet Union for saying that Russians enjoy some freedoms," and criticized teacher unions for promoting "leftist indoctrination aimed at turning today's students into tomorrow's campus radicals."[1973]

Why did Bauer consider running for president?

In June of 1998, Bauer had not yet decided on his run, but in Texas said it "may hinge partly on whether" Gov. George W. Bush was "conservative enough."[1974] Bauer said, "Gov. Bush refers to himself as a conservative. I certainly would take him at face value on that. But I know that there are a lot of issues that people are anxious for him to address."[1975] At the time, Bauer questioned whether Bush was "adamant enough against same-sex marriages and inclusion of homosexuals in the GOP."[1976] Bauer did not even think gays should be in the Republican Party.

2000 Presidential Candidate

Not surprisingly, he ran for president in the 2000 GOP cycle talking about "traditional marriage" and "sanctity of life" issues.[1977] His campaign was ill-timed. He announced his candidacy the day after the Columbine shootings.[1978] Also, Bauer ran his campaign on social conservative values. However, that social conservative niche was touted by other presidential candidates (Alan Keyes, George W. Bush, and Dan Quayle). Bauer finished last in the New Hampshire primary and dropped out of the race.[1979]

Savage v. Bauer

Working for *Salon*, Dan Savage, who was also (and still is) a nationally syndicated sex columnist, was asked to cover the Bauer campaign.[1980] Savage then wrote a story about the events which *Salon* published.[1981]

Days before the 2000 Iowa Caucus, Gary Bauer told MSNBC. "Our society will be destroyed if we say it's OK for a man to marry a man or a woman to marry a woman."[1982] In December 1999, when the Vermont Supreme Court came out for same-sex marriage, Bauer told the Associated Press, "I think what the Vermont Supreme Court did last week was in some ways worse than terrorism."[1983]

Savage wrote, "The amount of gay bashing that goes on during Republican campaigns is staggering, so pervasive that the mainstream media tunes it out like so much white noise."[1984]

Savage made calls for the Bauer campaign. One Bauer supporter in Des Moines was called, and told Savage: "Gary's the only one who can stop the homos…The Democrats are a bunch of goddam homo lovers, you know?…You know what we need to do? …We need to enforce God's law when it comes to homosexuals, that's what we need to do. God said that homosexuals have to die. We can shoot 'em, stone 'em, gas 'em or whatever. It's God's word."[1985]

Bauer's Campaign Dogged By Impropriety

His presidential campaign was hampered by Bauer's inability to disprove an alleged impropriety with a female campaign aide in October 1999.[1986] *Christianity Today* magazine (2.1.2000) surmised the incident: "several campaign aides charged Bauer with ill-advised private meetings with a 27-year old female campaign aide. In October, campaign manager Charles Jarvis and almost half of the campaign staff left Bauer over the charges of impropriety. Several FRC staffers say that they were deeply disturbed by Bauer's behavior, which was unlike what he practiced while at their organization. As a result of the controversy, Bauer replaced the solid wooden door to his office with one containing a glass window."[1987]

The *Washington Post* reported on the defections on September 30, 1999: "Charles Jarvis, the former Bauer campaign chairman who defected to the campaign of Steve Forbes, and Tim McDonald, former chief of advance operations, said Bauer spent hours behind closed doors with her and traveled alone with her, violating the strict rules they believe govern conservative Christian married men in their dealings with women."[1988] Bauer blamed the allegations on the Steve Forbes campaign.[1989]

Critics pointed that because Bauer represented the FRC and was closely tied to Focus on the Family, he should be held to a higher standard. Oddly, Bauer suggested he should not be held to such a standard, and was quoted in the *Washington Post*: "I am not a minister…I am not a pastor."[1990] However, there is an unspoken rule that Christian politicians and evangelical leaders don't meet or travel with women alone.[1991] Case in point, Rev. Billy Graham refused to be alone in a room with any woman except his wife since he married her in the 1940s.[1992]

Bauer dropped out before the South Carolina primary, but not before endorsing John McCain over George W. Bush.[1993]

After the 2000 campaign, Bauer founded American Values, a non-profit educational organization. He has used this organization to release op-ed pieces against gay marriage. Bauer was not allowed to come back to the FRC after his campaign, as the organization cited his partisan campaign as an obstacle for a non-profit organization, which had to remain nonpartisan.[1994]

American Values devoted a page to "Culture and Religion," which stated, "America today is in a virtue deficit where our standards of right and wrong have become increasingly hazy. Out of this haze have arisen great problems within our society including: hostility towards organized religion, sexual exploitation, the homosexual agenda, the demise of the family and the culture of death…These are disastrous trends for our country. If they aren't reversed, America – this great experiment in self-government – will be in jeopardy."[1995]

Gary Bauer thinks he is fighting a war on gays. This is no surprise. He once claimed the National Endowment for the Arts is run by "a small cadre of cultural revolutionaries, militant homosexuals, and anti-religious bigots who are intent on attacking the average American's most deeply held beliefs while sending them the bill."[1996]

SENATOR SAM BROWNBACK

Sam Brownback once was the Kansas state president of the Future Farmers of America, and at the age of 30 he became the state's youngest agriculture secretary.[1997] When he entered the House in the Republican Revolution of 1994, he said the departments of Commerce, Education, Energy, and Housing and Urban Development should be dismantled to downsize the federal government.[1998] He also previously presented the theory, according to the *Washington Post*, that abortion was a partial problem with Social Security because fewer children were growing up to become workers who could pay into the system."[1999]

Bob Dole announced he was leaving the U.S. Senate in the middle of 1996 to run for president, and Brownback ran for the open seat. Brownback won the special 1996 Republican primary with the help of William Bennett (former Reagan Education Secretary) and James Dobson (head of Focus on the Family).[2000] Pat Robertson helped Brownback get elected as well. These three leaders' support is symbolic of the support a Brownback presidential campaign expected, as he would attempt to lead the social conservatives for the 2008 GOP nomination. In the end, Brownback dropped out of contention before the first votes were cast.

McClatchy Newspapers reported how Thomas Monaghan, the founder of Dominos, was "putting his money and influence" to make Brownback the next president.[2001] Monaghan sold the pizza business for $1 billion in 1998, to which *McClatchy* said he had since built, "his own utopia on 5,000 acres in southwest Florida: Ave Maria, a planned community of 11,000 homes, built around a massive church and a doctrinaire Catholic university also called Ave Maria."[2002]

Brownback Claims Gays Hurt Marriage

In 2004, Congress tried to pass a constitutional amendment to ban gay marriage. Like in 2006, it would fail. But Sam Brownback did all he could to get his colleagues to support the ban in 2004.

In July 2004, Brownback wrote an op-ed to the *National Review* titled "Defining Marriage Down" as a constitutional ban on gay marriage was debated. "Social science on this matter is conclusive: Children need both a mom and a dad. Study after study has shown that children do best in a home with a married, biological mother and father…There is *no* reliable social-scientific data demonstrating that children raised by same-sex couples (or groups) do as well as children raised by married heterosexual parents."[2003] "Not least of the reasons heterosexual marriage is a positive social good is the fact that, in a married state, adults of both sexes are vastly healthier, happier, safer, and wealthier, and live longer lives."[2004]

Brownback says: Gay marriage all about money…

Brownback wrote (7.9.2004), "Proponents of same-sex unions have pointed to a recent study showing federal revenues increasing by upwards of $1 billion a year as a result of redefining marriage to include same-sex relationships. Ironically, most of the increased revenue would result from the still-existing marriage penalty in the tax code, which taxes married couples at higher rates than individuals. Pro-family groups have been trying to eliminate the marriage penalty for years."[2005]

He even suggested gays said the wedding industry would be helped if gay marriage occurred. Brownback said, "Some supporters of homosexual marriage have even cited a projected boon to the wedding industry as an argument for the economic benefits of mandating same-sex marriage."[2006] The momentum behind gay marriage wasn't equal constitutional rights, but rather David's Bridal Shoppe.

Having scolded the gays for trying to profit off of marriage, Brownback said straight marriages had given the country an economic boom (7.9.2004): "Traditional marriage is a boon to society in a variety of ways, and government has a vital interest in encouraging and providing the conditions to maintain as many traditional marriages as possible. Marriage has economic benefits not only for the spouses but for the economy at large. Even in advanced industrial societies such as ours, economists tell us that the uncounted but real value of home activities such as child care, senior care, home carpentry, and food preparation is still almost as large as the 'official' economy."[2007] Apparently Brownback had concluded homosexuals don't eat food, grow old or fix their houses.

Brownback says: Social Science Concludes Gay Marriage Hurts Children

Sam Brownback wrote (7.9.2004):

> "Marriage is at the center of the family, and the family is the basis of society itself. The government's interest in the marriage bond — and the reason it treats heterosexual unions in a manner unlike all other relationships — is closely related to the welfare of children. Government registers and endorses marriage between a man and a woman in order to ensure a stable environment for the raising and nurturing of children. Social science on this matter is conclusive: Children need both a mom and a dad. Study after study has shown that children do best in a home with a married, biological mother and father. And the government has a special responsibility to safeguard the needs of children; the social costs of *not* doing so are tremendous. As Child Trends, a mainstream child-welfare organization, has noted, "research clearly demonstrates that family structure matters for children, and the family structure that helps the most is a family headed by two biological parents in a low-conflict marriage. Children in single-parent families, children born to unmarried mothers, and children in stepfamilies or cohabiting relationships face higher risks of poor outcomes... There is thus value for children in promoting strong, stable marriages between biological parents."[2008]

Brownback went as far to suggest there was no evidence children do as well with gay parents as they do with straight parents: "Giving public sanction to homosexual 'marriage' would violate this government responsibility to safeguard the needs of children by placing individual adult desires above the best interests of children. There is *no* reliable social-scientific data demonstrating that children raised by same-sex couples (or groups) do as well as children raised by married, heterosexual parents. Redefining marriage is certain to harm children and the broader social good if that redefinition weakens government's legitimate goal of encouraging men and women who intend to have children to get married."[2009]

Brownback says: The strong institution of marriage is crumbling...

Brownback said, "It is possible to lose the institution of marriage in America. And that is precisely the hidden agenda of many in this cultural battle: To do away entirely with the traditional definition of the family. An influential organization of lawyers and judges, the American Law Institute, has already recommended sweeping changes in family law that would equalize marriage and cohabitation, extending rights and benefits now reserved for married couples to cohabiting domestic partners, both heterosexual and homosexual. Once the process of 'defining marriage down' begins, it is but a short step to the dissolution of marriage as a vital institution."

Brownback said marriage is such a bold institution, and then went out of his way to suggest it was weak and collapsing. Marriage disappearing is a strawman argument. It is nonsense. Still, Brownback wrote about how the last 40 years of *heterosexual* misconduct indicted *homosexual* marriage:

> "If the experience of the last 40 years tells us anything, it is that the consequences of weakening the institution of marriage are tragic for society at large. The movement away from traditional moral conventions left us with soaring divorce and out-of-wedlock birthrates, family breakdown on an unprecedented scale, and devastating consequences for children. Social science tells us that child poverty, child abuse, and child developmental problems increase with the decline of marriage. It also tells us that the children of intact, traditional marriages are much healthier in body, spirit, and mind, more successful in school and life, and much less likely to use illegal drugs, abuse alcohol, or engage in crime than are children from homes without a mother and a father. This is not to say that good children cannot be raised in other family settings. Many healthy children are raised in difficult circumstances and many single parents struggle heroically to raise good children. Still, the social science is clear. The best place for a child is with a mom and a dad. Both are needed. Traditional marriage is a social good because it dramatically reduces the social costs associated with dysfunctional behavior: Supporting and strengthening marriage significantly diminishes public expenditure on welfare, raises government revenues, and produces a more engaged, responsible citizenry."[2010]

Because 50% of heterosexuals can't handle marriage, penalize gays and heterosexual unmarried couples—it is an illogical leap of faith to blame another community.

Brownback says: Decline of Marriage = Decline in Fertility

Brownback wrote (7.9.2004), "The experience of Europe also shows that the decline of the institution of marriage goes hand in hand with a decline in married fertility, and a corresponding decline in population. Because of the birth rate in Europe, many countries find themselves faced with the prospect of aging (soon to be shrinking) populations and an impending collapse of their social-welfare systems because of a declining ratio of workers to retirees. Two proposed means of keeping the social and economic systems of these countries afloat — enormous tax hikes and importing vastly increased numbers of laborers — are widely viewed as infeasible. Whatever might be said in favor of mandating homosexual marriage, it certainly cannot be argued that it would increase the married fertility rate."[2011] Adolph Hitler and Benito Mussolini made similar arguments with their agendas and the need for fertile followers.

In addition, Brownback's argument is illogical. First, he argues against gay marriage because gays don't have kids. But if that was the case, then there would be no threat to marriage, because the amount of gays would be limited.

If homosexuals do not reproduce, why do they continue to survive and exist? It must be God's will.

Brownback Blocked Pro-Commitment Judge

In October 2006, Brownback put a hold on a Michigan Court of Appeals Judge Janet T. Neff's nomination for U.S. District Court in Michigan, despite that the Senate Judiciary Committee approved the nomination to go to the Senate.[2012]

Neff reportedly helped lead a commitment ceremony for a lesbian couple in 2002.[2013]

Like Bush: Brownback says, "Watch out for activist judges!"

Sam Brownback released a statement (6.7.06) citing his European example: "…if we allow activist judges to redefine marriage it will dramatically alter our society, as it has done in the European countries who are embracing same-sex marriage."[2014] Sadly, social conservatives never understand the judical branch of government. Supreme Courts are always a constitutional convention. Furthermore, the use of "activist" depends which side your on. If the Supreme Court decided in favor of gun rights, Brownback would be happy for the Court's action (i.e. activism). Brownback, like other GOP conservatives, too, warned of "judicially-mandated same-sex unions."[2015]

PAT BUCHANAN

Buchanan started out his prominance as a speechwriter and political adivisor to President Richard Nixon. He also worked for President Ronald Reagan. Since the 1980s, he has been a political advisor on cable shows, beginning with CNN. He ran for the GOP presidential nomination in 1992 and 1996, then ran as a Reform Party presidential candidate in 2000. Buchanan is partially credited for hurting the 1992 reelection campaign of President George H.W. Bush through divisive commentary on social issues. During the 2008 presidential campaign, he repeatedly commentated on MSNBC's *Hardball with Chris Matthews*.

Buchanan's Religious Views

Buchanan has called himself "a traditionalist Catholic."[2016] He has consistently taken his religious positions and molded them into his view for public policy. Already in 1984, he was quoted in the *San Diego Union*: "Should the United States be a pagan or a Christian country? …America was a Christian country. A quarter of a century ago, without prior consultation with a democratic people, without support in precedent or the Constitution, the Warren Court undertook the systematic de-Christianization of America, beginning, but not stopping, with the public schools...The school prayer crusade, then, is the first great counteroffensive of a badly routed Christian community to recapture their occupied public schools and re-establish *their* beliefs as the legitimate moral foundation of American society.'[2017]

Buchanan's on Afro-Americans

1) Buchanan has previously justified segregation. "There were no politics to polarize us then, to magnify every slight. The 'negroes' of Washington had their public schools, restaurants, bars, movie houses, playgrounds and churches; and we had ours."[2018]

2) Buchanan said Nixon should not talk to Mrs. King. In April of 1969, Buchanan told Richard Nixon not to visit Martin Luther King's widow because such a visit would "outrage many, many people who believe Dr. King was a fraud and a demagogue and perhaps worse.... Others consider him the Devil incarnate. Dr. King is one of the most divisive men in contemporary history."[2019]
3) Buchanan defended David Duke. Buchanan was a featured columnist for *The Spotlight*, "a patently anti-Semitic and anti-Black publication that championed David Duke."[2020] He also praised the "winning issues" of the ex-Ku Klux Klansman and politician.[2021] In 1989, Buchanan chastised the GOP for overreacting to Duke and his Nazi "costume": "Take a hard look at Duke's portfolio of winning issues and expropriate those not in conflict with GOP principles, [such as] reverse discrimination against white folks."[2022]

In December 1991, he was quoted in the Manchester (NH) *Union Leader*: "David Duke is busy stealing from me. I have a mind to go down there and sue that dude for intellectual property theft."[2023]
4) Multiculturalism is an assault. In a speech to the Christian Coalition (Sept.1993), Buchanan described multiculturalism as "an across-the-board assault on our Anglo-American heritage."[2024]

Buchanan on Jews

1) Washington is too Jewish. Buchanan has referred to Capital Hill (Oct.1990), as "Israeli-occupied territory."[2025]
2) Hitler was courageous. Buchanan wrote (1977) that despite Hitler's' anti-Semitism and support for genocide, Hitler was "an individual of great courage..."[2026]
3) Don't go after old Nazis. He criticized the U.S. Justice Department, and said they should stop prosecuting Nazi war criminals and was essentially "running down 70-year-old camp guards."[2027]

Buchanan also advocated restoring citizenship of Arthur Rudolph, an ex-Nazi rocket scientist (1985).[2028] He also lobbied (1987) to stop deportation of Karl Linnas, who was accused of Nazi atrocities in Estonia.[2029]
4) Buchanan's friends concede he is an anti-Semite. Even William Buckley, Buchanan's former mentor, wrote (1990) a 20,000 word essay on Buchanan which concluded: "I find it impossible to defend Pat Buchanan against the charge" of anti-Semitism.[2030]
5) Insensitive to the Jews and the Holocaust. Buchanan challenged the fact that thousands of Jews were gassed to death by diesel exhaust at Treblinka: "Diesel engines do not emit enough carbon monoxide to kill anybody."[2031]

In October 1990, Jacob Weisberg wrote an article titled "The Heresies of Pat Buchanan."[2032] Weisberg wrote:

> Buchanan stands by his bizarre claim about the diesel engines but refuses to discuss it on the record. Suffice it to say that he embraces a bolder debunking claim than he is yet willing to endorse in print...Where did he get the anecdote ("proving" his assertion about

the diesel)? 'Somebody sent it to me.'...Buchanan's source was almost certainly the July 1988 issue of a Newsletter of the German American Information and Education Association--a known Holocaust denial group which quotes extensively from a story of schoolchildren who emerged unharmed after being exposed to diesel fumes while trapped in a train tunnel."[2033]

In the *New York Post* (1990), he referred to what he called a "so called Holocaust survivors syndrome" involving "group fantasies of martyrdom and heroics."[2034]

6) Christianity is superior. In his September 1993 speech to the Christian Coalition, Buchanan said, "Our culture is superior. Our culture is superior because our religion is Christianity and that is the truth that makes men free."[2035]

Buchanan on Women

1) Women struggle in capitalism. In November 1983, Pat Buchanan wrote, "Rail as they will about 'discrimination,' women are simply not endowed by nature with the same measures of single-minded ambition and the will to succeed in the fiercely competitive world of Western capitalism."[2036]

2) Women were liberated by house appliances. He also wrote, "The real liberators of American women were not the feminist noise-makers, they were the automobile, the supermarket, the shopping center, the dishwasher, the washer-dryer, the freezer."[2037]

3) Women are too open to divorce and cling to their careers. And "If a woman has come to believe that divorce is the answer to every difficult marriage, that career comes before children ... no democratic government can impose another set of values upon her."[2038]

4) Women should be momma birds. In 1983, Buchanan said, "The momma bird builds the nest. So it was, so it ever shall be. Ronald Reagan is not responsible for this; God is."[2039]

5) Reproductive rights are a medical disaster and social catastrophe. He once said, "If the sexual revolution has been a medical disaster, socially it has been a catastrophe. Why do the media not report and explore the tragic results of the sexual revolution? Because many are collaborators."[2040]

6) Women and the military. Even during his 2000 presidential candidacy, Buchanan still believed women shouldn't serve in combat.[2041]

Buchanan on Gays

1) Buchanan regularly used anti-gay derogatory terms. In 1972, he told Nixon one of George McGovern's leading campaign contributors was a "screaming fairy."[2042] Into the 1990s, he repeatedly used the term "sodomites."[2043] Before the 1992 campaign he called gays "the pederast proletariat."[2044]

2) Gays are immoral, filthy, and not natural. In 1989, he wrote, "Homosexuality involves sexual acts most men consider not only immoral, but filthy. The reason public men rarely say aloud what most say privately is they are fearful of being branded 'bigots' by an intolerant liberal orthodoxy that holds, against all evidence and experience, that homosexuality is a normal, healthy lifestyle."[2045] Ironically, married straight folks are very often involved in the same acts. I do not think the men or women involved consider them immoral. Pat's logic is garbage.

3) Homosexuality is not a civil right, caused Germany to collapse. In 1977, he wrote gay groups should be thrashed: "Homosexuality is not a civil right. Its rise almost always is accompanied, as in the Weimar Republic, with a decay of society and a collapse of its basic cinder block, the family."[2046]

Buchannan would have to support the oversight involved to make sure homosexual acts would not occur, in anyone's bedroom. His opinion feeds into the notion of issue groups like Focus on the Family and the Family Research Council, who still support laws legislating what goes on in the bedroom. That's quite a remarkable statement from a self-described "conservative" who wants the government off our backs.

Buchanan's second sentence in the quote reinforces an oft read argument from the Right that Adolf Hitler rose to power because of homosexuals.

4) AIDS is retribution. In 1983, he said, "The poor homosexuals -- they have declared war upon nature, and now nature is extracting an awful retribution (AIDS)."[2047] This is not a comment Buchanan just said in his younger days. During his 1992 campaign, he said, "AIDS is nature's retribution for violating the laws of nature."[2048]

5) Gay advocates are responsible for AIDS spreading. Also in 1983, he said New York Gov. Mario Cuomo should cancel the Gay Pride Parade or else "be held personally responsible for the spread of the AIDS plague."[2049]

6) Gays promote anti-Judeo-Christian behavior. He wrote a *Wall Street Journal* column in 1993 stating, "Gay rights activists seek to substitute, for laws rooted in Judeo-Christian morality, laws rooted in the secular humanist belief that all consensual sexual acts are morally equal. That belief is anti-biblical and amoral; to codify it into law is to codify a lie."[2050]

7) Gays are Satanic. Buchanan wrote (1990), "With 80,000 dead of AIDS, our promiscuous homosexuals appear literally hell-bent on Satanism and suicide."[2051]

8) Proud to stand up to gay rights. On ABC's *Nightline*, March 11, 1992, Buchanan told anchorman, Chris Wallace: "I'm one of the few people in this city, Chris, who's had the guts to stand up to the agenda of the special interests, whether it's the civil rights lobbyist or the AIPAC lobby or the gay rights lobby, and say that their agenda is not in the interest of a good society and not in the interest of my country."[2052]

9) Gays benefit from the courts, just like criminals and atheists. Buchanan said, "Who are beneficiaries of the Court's protection? Members of various minorities including criminals, atheists, homosexuals, flag burners, illegal immigrants (including terrorists), convicts, and pornographers"[2053]

10) Buchanan made his stance on gay rights a major platforms of his presidential candidacies. At the 1992 convention, after losing the GOP primaries, Buchanan put George H.W. Bush in an awkward position and said, "Yes, we disagreed with President Bush. But we stand with him for freedom to choose religious schools. And we stand with him against the amoral idea that gay and lesbian couples should have the same standing in law as married men and women."[2054]

During his 2000 Reform Party candidacy, Buchanan said, "The homosexual lifestyle has always been associated with social decadence and national decline…And today it is associated as the prime means by which the AIDS virus, a terrible disease, is spread."[2055] In May 2000, he said, "I don't apologize for my views with regards to gay rights. I oppose the gay rights agenda in its entirety. …I did say that AIDS is in effect what happens to people as a consequence of unnatural and immoral sex. And, as you know, homosexual conduct is the primary--or was the primary way by which AIDS was spread. It was a truthful statement."[2056]

11) Homosexuality still not natural. In 2006, Buchanan defended his old position that homosexuality is not natural:

> As for homosexuality, where it has been prevalent – in the late Roman Empire, Weimar Germany, San Francisco – it has been regarded as a mark of and a metaphor for moral decadence and societal decline. But the bottom line is this: What is the truth? Is homosexuality moral or immoral, natural or unnatural, normal and healthy or deviant and destructive behavior? In 1983, when the AIDS epidemic first broke onto the national scene, this writer wrote in a column predicting scores of thousands could perish: "The poor homosexuals. They have declared war against nature, and nature is exacting an awful retribution." This sentence restated the Natural Law teaching of Thomas Aquinas. Homosexuality is against nature, *contra naturam*. It also said what was, by then, obvious to all. Acts that cannot be described in this publication were transmitting a dread and deadly disease that was killing homosexuals in the hundreds, and would soon kill them in the scores of thousands. Indeed, a subsequent clamor by homosexuals for a mass government education program on the use of condoms suggested they knew exactly how and why the disease was spreading. What does all of this tell us? Our society is being marinated in lies – the lie that homosexuality is a natural, normal and healthy lifestyle; the lie that those who think otherwise are all hateful bigots; the lie that the diseases that afflict the homosexual community are the fault of an uncaring society. [2057]

12) "All animals are created equal, some are just created more equal than others." Buchanan said (5.30.2000), "On your point about all Americans are equal, there's no doubt all of us have the same constitutional rights. I agree. However, I think a real problem America has is we've taken this idea of equality and extended it so beyond where it belongs. All lifestyles are not equal. All ideas are not equal. Some are wrong; some are right. And this is what America needs more than anything else; it needs truth. Now when it comes to myself and the leader of the gay rights movement nationally, [we] have identical constitutional rights. But I do not believe their ideas are equal to mine, or that lifestyle is equal to a traditional married lifestyle. And we've gotta stand up for truth even when it's unpopular and even when it's painful. Otherwise, your society breaks down."[2058]

13) After Vermont ruling, country could be on road to hell. On *Meet the Press* in October 2000, Buchanan said, "I think civil unions are absurd. They passed these up in Vermont where homosexual couples have been put on the same level as traditional marriage. And I'm delighted to say that five Republicans that voted for that were defeated and thrown out in the primary. If this country accepts the idea that homosexual liaisons are the same as traditional marriage, which is a God-ordained building block of society, this country is on the road to hell in a handbasket."[2059]

14) No to a homosexual president or cabinet member. When asked if he would be comfortable with a homosexual as president of the U.S., Buchanan said, "I would not be comfortable. Someone who is an out of the closet homosexual who supports the gay rights agenda, nope. I wouldn't vote for him, and I would oppose him with everything I had, and I would not be comfortable with him."[2060] And if some one was in the closet and president, "The truth is, I think you ought to have a president who sets clearly a moral example for the American people."[2061]

Buchanan said he would not put a gay or gay rights advocate in his cabinet (5.4.2000), "If someone is an out-of-the-closet homosexual and if someone advocates the homosexual rights agenda publicly they're not going to be in my Cabinet. I believe that homosexuality is a disorder. It's a wrong orientation."[2062]

15) Buchanan claims to be first person to tell government: take care of AIDS. He told NPR (5.30.2000), "[I wrote] a column in 1983, [when] 600 people had died of AIDS and 1,600 were infected. And I said, 'What is the matter with our government that it doesn't recognize this?' I said, 'This could kill thousands of people.' At the end of that column, I had that one throwaway line [that AIDS is a consequence of immoral sex], which I don't withdraw. But I was the first national columnist to demand why the government wasn't dealing with this national epidemic. I don't apologize for that or my views, sir."[2063]

LARRY CRAIG

Larry Craig was a legend in Idaho. The nonprofit Idaho Hall of Fame Association picked Craig to be inducted in March 2007, a few months before he pleaded guilty to a charge of disorderly conduct. In October 2007 the Hall of Fame decided to still induct Craig.[2064]

At the time of his incident, Craig was the senior senator from Idaho.[2065] Craig won five elections for House in the 1980s, and served there for a decade until being elected to the U.S. Senate in 1990.[2066] He was married with three grown children and nine grandchildren. Craig's seat was up for reelection in 2008. If Craig had won reelection in 2008 and finished the term, he would have been the longest-serving Idahoan ever in Congress.[2067]

Social Conservative

Because of his voting record, the American Family Association, Concerned Women for America, and the Family Research Council all gave Craig a high rating.[2068]

Craig's Senate record was thoroughly anti-gay. He supported a federal constitutional amendment banning same-sex marriage claiming it was "important for us to stand up now and protect traditional marriage, which is under attack by a few unelected judges and litigious activists."[2069] Craig voted for the Defense of Marriage Act in 1996.[2070] DOMA denies federal recognition to gay marriages and prevents states from being forced to recognize gay marriages legally performed in other states.[2071]

In May 2007, Craig said he supported unions between same-sex couples: "You can have a civil union, but you can't commandeer the institution of marriage. That's very special, religious, culturally, and you can't go there."[2072] But in 2006, Craig issued a statement saying he would vote for an amendment to the Idaho Constitution which banned both gay marriage and civil unions.[2073]

Craig voted against expanding federal hate crimes law to cover anti-gay offenses and voted against a bill outlawing employment discrimination based on sexual orientation, a vote that failed by one vote in the U.S. Senate.[2074] Craig opposed allowing gays or lesbians in the military.[2075]

Stalled in Minnesota

A Minnesota officer at the airport was on a mission. The police officer's search wasn't random, as he was dressed in plainclothes because of a complaint of sexual activity at that bathroom.[2076] Craig entered that stall and blocked the door with his rolling suitcase to block the front view of his stall.[2077]

The officer (Sgt. Dave Karsnia) who arrested him on June 11, 2007, said Craig peered through a crack in the bathroom stall for two minutes and gestured to the officer.[2078] In fact, Craig peered into the officer's stall several times through the crack in the door.[2079]

Karsnia wrote in the report: "Craig would look down at his hands, 'fidget' with his fingers, and then look through the crack into my stall again."[2080] Craig taped his right foot, which is the signal for those wanting to engage in such behavior, and Craig also ran his left hand several times underneath the partition dividing the stalls.[2081] The *New York Times* reported (8.29.07), "Mr. Craig also reportedly swiped his left hand under the stall three times before the officer held his police identification down by the floor so Mr. Craig could see it."[2082]

Craig's foot touched the side of the Sergeant's foot.[2083] Craig blamed the foot touching on a "wide stance when going to the bathroom."[2084] Craig said he reached down to pick up a piece of paper; the police officer said there was no paper to pick up.[2085]

Upon Karsnia's police interrogation, it's also possible Craig tried to bribe the officer, for Craig pulled out a U.S. Senate business card and asked the officer, "What do you think of that?"[2086]

The Penalty

Craig paid a $500 fine when he entered his guilty plea in Bloomington, Minnesota, and in the petition to enter a guilty plea, Craig acknowledged he "engaged in (physical) conduct which I knew or should have known tended to arouse alarm or resentment."[2087] Craig pleaded guilty to disorderly conduct on August 8.[2088] And a second charge of interference with privacy was dismissed.[2089] Craig was given a suspended 10-day jail sentence, fined more than $500, and placed on unsupervised probation for one year.[2090] In total, Craig paid $575 in fines and fees.[2091]

Craig's Delayed Response

Several weeks passed until the press learned about the disorderly conduct. The arrest was first publicly reported by *Roll Call.*[2092] Craig's wife didn't find out until August 27, when news of the disorderly conduct broke.[2093] Before analyzing Craig's reaction, the following is his statement released August 28, 2007:

> In June, I overreacted and made a poor decision. While I was not involved in any inappropriate conduct at the Minneapolis airport or anywhere else, I chose to plead guilty to a lesser charge in the hope of making it go away. I did not seek any counsel, either from an attorney, staff, friends, or family. That was a mistake, and I deeply regret it. Because of that, I have now retained counsel and I am asking my counsel to review this matter and to advise me on how to proceed.
>
> For a moment, I want to put my state of mind into context on June 11. For eight months leading up to June, my family and I had been relentlessly and viciously harassed by the Idaho Statesman. If you've seen today's paper, you know why. Let me be clear: I am not gay and never have been.
>
> Still, without a shred of truth or evidence to the contrary, the Statesman has engaged in this witch hunt. In pleading guilty, I overreacted in Minneapolis, because of the stress of the Idaho Statesman's investigation and the rumors it has fueled around Idaho. Again, that overreaction was a mistake, and I apologize for my misjudgment. Furthermore, I should not have kept this arrest to myself, and should have told my family and friends about it. I wasn't eager to share this failure, but I should have done so anyway.[2094]

What were Craig's lame arguments?

1) Pleading guilty would get rid of the issue. Craig pled guilty August 8th to a misdemeanor disorderly conduct.[2095] Craig claimed by pleading guilty to a "lesser charge," he hoped of making the situation go away and suggested he should have sought legal counsel.[2096] He said his deepest regret was pleading guilty to doing nothing wrong.[2097] The logic makes sense: a police officer accuses a U.S. Senator of making sexual advances in an airport stall, by pleading guilty, the public would never pick up on it. Right, Senator, you know the press hates sex scandals.

2) I'm the victim. Craig said (8.28.07) he was a victim of a "witch hunt" courtesy of the *Idaho Statesman*,[2098] and he and his family had been "relentlessly and viciously harassed" for months by the paper.[2099] Craig said (8.28.2007), "In pleading guilty, I overreacted in Minneapolis, because of the stress of the Idaho Statesman's investigation and the rumors it has fueled around Idaho....Again, that overreaction was a mistake, and I apologize for my misjudgment."[2100]

Craig claimed he was a victim of "profiling," telling Matt Lauer in an interview (aired Oct.16.2007), "I know what people feel like when they're profiled, when innocent people get caught up in what I was caught in as an innocent person."[2101] David Letterman had no sympathy: "Senator Craig from Idaho is blaming the media for his guilty plea, especially that cute guy from the Associated Press."[2102]

3) I am not gay. Craig made his first public statements on the issue on Tuesday, August 28.[2103] Craig claimed to have done nothing "inappropriate," and made sure to "be clear: I am not gay and never have been."[2104] Like Roy Cohn, Larry Craig was just another straight man who occasionally wanted to have sex with men.

4) Craig didn't hire an attorney. In addition, the Senator didn't have the clarity of thought to hire an attorney from the outset. At the very least, that was a dumb move.

5) Craig didn't tell his family. Remember that when he pled guilty, Craig had not consulted his family.[2105]

6) Craig didn't want to get in the details. In his initial statement (8.28.2007), he would not answer reporters' questions, and he offered no detailed explanation for the events at the airport. [2106]

Hypocrisy

CNN was apt to point out although Craig was claiming "never" to have been gay, this was the man "who has aligned himself with conservative groups who oppose gay rights."[2107] The satirical paper *The Onion* mocked the Repubilican's quandary with the headline: "Gay man admits being Republican Senator from Idaho." The Hypocrisy was obvious. The social conservative wanted to bash gay rights and gay marriage. But, as Jay Leno said, "Senator Craig defiantly vowed today to serve out his term. And when Larry Craig makes a vow, you know he means it. Okay, except for the marriage vow."[2108]

Romney Didn't Know This Guy Named Craig

It was an odd situation for Republicans. Senate Minority Leader Mitch McConnell (R-KY) informed Craig leaders in the GOP were calling for an ethics investigation.[2109] On August 27, Craig resigned as a Senate liaison for Mitt Romney's presidential campaign, and Romney's son Josh canceled a trip to Idaho (8.28.07).[2110]

***Idaho Statesman* Investigated Craig**

According to the *Statesman*, they interviewed Craig in May 2007 after a five month investigation starting in October 2006, after a blogger accused Craig of homosexual sex.[2111] Craig told the *Idaho Statesman* in May 2007 that he never engaged in homosexual acts.[2112] The arrest for a sexual advance at the Minnesota airport was just a month later.[2113]

The Idaho paper got interested in October 2006, when a gay activist blogger, Mike Rogers, published a claim that Craig had homosexual sex. Rogers believed he could raise the irony for the midterm elections, especially after the Rep. Mark Foley scandal.[2114] Buzz followed from numerous medias, such as *Wonkette*, and the *Washington Post*, *USA Today*, MSNBC, and four Idaho newspapers spread the story.[2115] The *Statesman* editor, Vicki Gowler, did not want to rely on Mike Roger's anonymous sources, so she had her paper investigate the widespread rumor dating back to 1982.[2116] [Roger's had issues with other sources he used, and didn't even know their last names.[2117]]

The *Statesman* interviewed 300 people, visited the ranch where Craig grew up, and made two trips to Washington, D.C.[2118] The *Statesman* interviewed Roger's "best source," a Washington-area man whose story remained consistent, beginning in an August 2004 e-mail to Mike Rogers: "I've hooked up with Craig ... why not out some actual members and not their staffers?"[2119] In the May 2007 interview with the Statesman, Craig said the man who talked to Rogers was an activist: "The gay movement, we know it for what it is. It's now aggressive and it's liberal and it's naming people to try to put them in compromising, difficult situations."[2120]

Idaho Statesman Was Critical, Thorough

The *Statesman* also reported (8.28.07): "Until Monday, the Statesman had declined to run a story about Craig's sex life, because the paper didn't have enough corroborating evidence and because of the senator's steadfast denial."[2121]

The *Statesman* did not put one or two gay sex stories together to tarnish Craig. For example, the *Statesman* reported (8.28.07), "The most serious finding by the *Statesman* was the report by a professional man with close ties to Republican officials. The 40-year-old man reported having oral sex with Craig at Washington's Union Station, probably in 2004. The *Statesman* also spoke with a man who said Craig made a sexual advance toward him at the University of Idaho in 1967 and a man who said Craig "cruised" him for sex in 1994 at the REI store in Boise. The *Statesman* also explored dozens of allegations that proved untrue, unclear or unverifiable."[2122]

Wife's Denial

Craig married in the 1980s and adopted the three children of his wife, Suzanne.[2123] Suzanne Craig was in denial, and perhaps always has been. When she heard the Roger's source, she cried then said (to the Statesman), "I'm incensed that you would even consider such a piece of trash as a credible source."[2124]

The *Idaho Statesman* asked (1990) Craig about an allegation that he was gay made by an opponent in his first Senate race; Craig said, "Why don't you ask my wife?"[2125]

Craig's History (Besides Minnesota)

1) College Days. His University of Idaho days had rumors too. He was a president of the Delta Chi fraternity, which had about 150 brothers of which the *Statesman* interviewed 41.[2126] Most agreed a homosexual wouldn't have been elected president of the fraternity, but three of the 41 said there were jokes about him being effeminate and, perhaps, gay.[2127] A women who dated him on and off for a year said, "I don't imagine that he ever held my hand. He was into the gotta-hold-the-door-for-the-woman sort of thing. But I always felt like I was an accessory. I might as well have been his briefcase."[2128]

2) National Guard. There is also the rumor Craig left the National Guard because he was gay. He was honorably discharged in 1972, but he had already served 20 months of a six year enlistment.[2129] Records show he was released because of a "physical disqualification," although nothing specific was written down; Craig says it was flat feet.[2130]

3) 1982 Page Scandal. In 1982, Craig denied he was under investigation by a federal probe over allegations that he had sexual relationships with congressional pages.[2131] The scandal broke in June of 1982, when over 13 million viewers of CBS News heard Leroy Williams, a page, allege he had sex with three House members when he was 17.[2132] The day after the story broke, Craig issued a statement saying reporters called him explaining they were going to publish his name in relation to the scandal, and Craig called the allegations "part of a concerted effort at character assassination."[2133] "I have done nothing that I need to be either publicly or privately ashamed of. I am guilty of no crime or impropriety, and I am convinced that this is an effort to damage my personal character and destroy my political career."[2134] Craig was the only member of the U.S. House of Representatives to issue such a statement.[2135]

At the time, Craig said he was "mad as hell" over the allegations.[2136] As the July 4th weekend came in 1982, Craig was followed by the national media, and said, "Persons who are unmarried as I am, by choice or by circumstance, have always been the subject of innuendos, gossip and false accusations. I think this is despicable."[2137]

Although Craig was not implicated in the 1982 investigation, two other congressmen were charged with ethic violations.[2138] In 2007, the *The Idaho Statesman* suggestively reported on Craig's "1982 pre-emptive denial that he had sex with underage congressional pages."[2139] Critics legitimately asked why would Craig be preemptive in his denials in the 1982 page ordeal. Indeed, the issue for Craig was his timing. For some reason he released a statement saying he had nothing to do with the page scandal, then he got engaged months after the ordeal, which some argue was to cover up his homosexuality.[2140] Craig married in 1983.[2141]

The crux of the argument from the senator's critics is the unnecessary comments on the page scandal. Apparently reporters from CBS and *The New York Post* said they were going to name Craig, which prompted his denial.[2142]

The irony is that Peter Fearon, who was with the *New York Post* in 1982, said he never was going to name Craig: "No, no — it wasn't 'are you under investigation?' It was simply an inquiry: 'Have you heard anything? Who have you heard about? Have you heard any names mentioned? What's your reaction to this news?' The next thing I know, Larry Craig has issued a press release: 'This isn't me.' Which I just thought was a bizarre and ultimately very foolish thing to do. He was the only person going on the record anywhere…And of course, when you do that, it's like raw meat. He's saying, 'Nobody's actually accusing, but it wasn't me!' It's no wonder it's dogged him. He denied something that no one had accused him of."[2143] Furthermore, Leroy Williams recanted a month later and said he'd made up the whole thing; and the House ethics committee probe exonerated those falsely accused.[2144]

4) Previous Cruising. Another man told the *Statesman* in November 1994, Craig "cruised" him in a REI store in Boise; Craig said, "Once again, I'm not gay, and I don't cruise, and I don't hit on men. I have no idea how he drew that conclusion. A smile? Here is one thing I do out in public: I make eye contact, I smile at people, they recognize me, they say, 'Oh, hi, Senator.' Or, 'Do I know you?' I've been in this business 27 years in the public eye here. I don't go around anywhere hitting on men, and by God, if I did, I wouldn't do it in Boise, Idaho! Jiminy!"[2145]

The Idaho Statesman reported (8.27.07) the Minnesota airport event "was similar to an incident in a men's room in a Washington, D.C., rail station described by a Washington-area man to the Idaho Statesman. In that case, the man said he and Craig had sexual contact."[2146]

5) Post-Minnesota Revelations: Mike Jones Again?

By December 2007, four other men publicly (and another anonymously) said they had homosexual encounters with Craig: David Phillips, Mike Jones, Greg Ruth, and Tom Russell. The most noteworthy of that list was Mike Jones, who also had sex with "Pastor Ted" Haggard.[2147] The *Statesman* could not disprove any of the five men's stories.[2148] However, that does not mean the Statesman proved them.

Jones contacted the *Statesman* in September 2007 after Craig signaled he might back away from his vow to resign Sept. 30; then when Craig said (10.4.2007) that he would complete his term in 2009 and appeared on NBC on Oct. 16, Jones went on the record with the *Idaho Statesman*.[2149] Jones had claimed he outed Haggard because Haggard was a hypocrite bashing gays. After the Minnesota story became public, Craig initially said he would resign from the

Senate then changed his mind and vowed to clear his name.[2150] That was apparently another reason for Jones to expose another hypocrite.

Unnecessary Stereotyping

Although Craig's actions and hypocrisy are inexcusable, the *Statesman* unfortunately portrayed stereotypes in their reporting. When the *Statesman* felt the need to discover Craig's homosexuality, they went all out to find who to interview: former staffers, acquaintances for Craig's college days, and fellow colleagues. But in some cases, the *Statesmen* relied on subtle stereotypes. For example, the *Statesmen* reported (8.28.07), "Craig also took piano lessons in high school and was in the high school choir."[2151]

The paper also brought up how Craig had a unique projection of his speeches that was different, implying Craig sounded gay.[2152] So the *Statesman* covered its bases by including a quote from a Jim McClure, whom Craig succeeded in the Senate: "Larry's speech patterns are very precise...They're not what you expect from a rancher from Midvale. His speech patterns say, 'Hey, here's a guy who's a little different.' And he is, he's a little different. But that doesn't mean he's homosexual for heaven's sakes! You have to jump from prejudice to suspicion to I don't know what to give the rumors any credibility."[2153]

Craig Admonished

Craig lost several GOP leadership positions in the wake of the scandal.[2154] The Senate Ethics Committee said (February 2008) they believed Craig was guilty, and Craig's attempt to withdraw his plea was merely an effort to avoid legal consequences of his actions.[2155] The Ethics Committee issued a "letter of admonition" to Craig, and stated his action discredited the U.S. Senate. The committee took issue with Craig using over $200,000 of his 2008 Senate reelection campaigns to pay legal fees for the case, and for flashing his U.S. Senate business card at the police officer who arrrested him.[2156] Craig said he was "disappointed" with the committee's conclusion, but was happy they acted in a "timely fashion," he added, "I will continue to serve the people of Idaho."[2157]

He did not seek reelection in 2008, though his seat remained in GOP hands as Idaho Lt. Gov. Jim Risch (R) won the seat.[2158]

One more failed appeal

In December 2008, Craig lost another attempt to withdraw his guilty plea when a three-judge panel of the Minnesota Court of Appeals rejected his bid to toss out his disorderly conduct conviction.[2159] When rejection occurred, Craig said he was still considering his options (perhaps the Minnesota Supreme Court).[2160] In a statement, Craig said, "I am extremely disappointed by the action of the Minnesota Court of Appeals...I disagree with their conclusion and remain steadfast in my belief that nothing criminal or improper occurred at the Minneapolis airport."[2161]

A Closer Look

Contrary to the general tone of this book, if I was serving on a jury asked to judge whether Larry Craig was a gay man, I would have to honestly say that being gay is not a crime. I make no apologies for his goofy erratic behaviors, but I must admit the arguments above, although strong and maybe proving a law broken in an airport, do not make "being" a gay man a crime. He may be gay. But, being gay is not a crime so what are we really judging? Our own prejudice is the most correct answer.

For Larry Craig and perhaps many of the others discussed in this chapter, a different upbringing, more supportive families and organizations, and assistance in realizing that neither being gay or recognizing gayness is something to hide. If these folks had grown up and lived in an accepting, nurturing society perhaps their behaviors and political behaviors and attitudes would have been entirely different. That difference could have moved this nation further along in its quest for equality for all its citizens.

BILL FRIST

With little experience in politics before, Dr. Bill Frist was elected to the U.S. Senate in 1994. Frist was the only Senate candidate to defeat a full-term incumbent that year, when he became the first practicing physician elected to the Senate since 1928.[2162] In 2000, he was named chairman of the National Republican Senatorial Committee with the goal (at which he was successful) to win back a Senate majority of Republicans in 2002; an effort that outspent the Democratic senatorial committee by $66 million.[2163]

Frist called the 2004 Senate victories a "monumental victory," and had a 'victory tour' of the South (Florida, Georgia, and the Carolinas) on the Wednesday after Election Day.[2164] But Frist restated he would not seek reelection in the Senate for 2006, and the Majority Leader became a lame duck during 2005 and 2006.[2165]

Dr. Frist

Bill Frist graduated from Princeton in 1974, and a decade later he came to Vanderbilt University Medical Center and founded its transplant center, where "he performed over 150 heart and lung transplant procedures, including the first successful combined heart-lung transplant in the Southeast."[2166] Frist had 100 writings and abstracts on medical research, including his co-authorship of *Grand Rounds in Transplantation*.[2167] Other books included *Transplant: A Heart Surgeon's Account of the Life-and-Death Dramas of the New Medicine* (1989), which focused on the myths of transplantation.[2168]

Frist Said *Lawrence v. Texas* Legalized Criminal Activity

In 2003, the Supreme Court ruled a Texas law prohibiting acts of sodomy between gays in a private home was unconstitutional. The conservative

Republican from Tennessee wanted more government interference, and was outraged by the decision.

Frist told ABC's *This Week* (June 2003), "I have this fear that this zone of privacy that we all want protected in our own homes is gradually — or I'm concerned about the potential for it gradually being encroached upon, where criminal activity within the home would in some way be condoned....And I'm thinking of — whether it's prostitution or illegal commercial drug activity in the home ... to have the courts come in, in this zone of privacy, and begin to define it gives me some concern."[2169]

Frist: Sodomy is a Local Decision

Frist told *This Week* the Supreme Court overstepped in their decision, but respected their decision.[2170] "Generally, I think matters such as sodomy should be addressed by the state legislature ...That's where those decisions — with the local norms, the local mores — are being able to have their input ... And that's where it should be decided, and not in the courts."[2171] Frist wanted the federal government away from such issues, and instead *Lawrence v. Texas* should have been a validation of a local decision—but not so local as a citizen's private house.

Frist said gay marriage should be a state issue *and* supported a federal amendment to ban it...

In this 2003 same interview, Frist said he supported a constitutional ban against gay marriage, (the AP article's headline referred to the ban, becoming one of the more early, pronounced formations of the ban's movement).[2172] "I very much feel that marriage is a sacrament, and that sacrament should extend and can extend to that legal entity of a union between — what is traditionally in our Western values has been defined — as between a man and a woman. So I would support the amendment."[2173]

A day before the Supreme Court ruled in *Lawrence v. Texas*, Rep. Marilyn Musgrave, R-Colo., sponsored a proposal offered to amend the Constitution and it was referred to the House Judiciary subcommittee on the Constitution.[2174] This reaction to *Lawrence v. Texas* was a major origin of the federal effort to ban gay marriage.

Frist on Gay Issues

Frist was a big supporter of the constitutional ban on same-sex marriage. In addition, he voted no on adding sexual orientation to the definition of hate crimes (2002), and voted against prohibiting job discrimination based on sexual orientation.[2175]

Already in February 2006, Frist scheduled a June 2006 vote on the constitutional amendment. CNN reported (2.13.2006) the scheduling move and potential vote was "likely to fail but sure to spark a fiery election-year debate."[2176] The timing of the vote showed how the marriage amendment was a red herring wedge issue designed to drive Bible belt state voters to the polls in November.

Frist and the GOP knew the marriage amendment was dead on arrival in the U.S. Senate but pushed it anyway, for purely partisan political reasons. Frist put party politics before reason and called it moral leadership.

The Bush Administration Sex Education Policy: Anti-Science

Frist once said, "Sound science must be a basis to governing our trade relations around the globe."[2177] However, sound science seldom entered his decision process on social issues.

The *Washington Post* lead (12.2.2004) was embarrassing for the Bush Administration: "Many American youngsters participating in federally funded abstinence-only programs have been taught over the past three years that abortion can lead to sterility and suicide, that half the gay male teenagers in the United States have tested positive for the AIDS virus, and that touching a person's genitals 'can result in pregnancy,' a congressional staff analysis has found."[2178]

According to Center for Health and Gender Equity, "In 2004 alone the Bush Administration's spent $170 million in the U.S. and $86 million in developing countries on 'abstinence only' prevention programs. Recent analysis by Rep. Henry Waxman (D-CA) has shown these programs teach inaccurate and misleading information.'"[2179]

The just-say-no-to-sex strategy for teenagers was not working, and spreading myths. Among the misconceptions cited by Waxman's investigators, were the following subjective information: that a 43-day-old fetus is a 'thinking person,' that HIV, the virus that causes AIDS, can be spread via sweat and tears; and that condoms failed to prevent HIV transmission as often as a third of the time in heterosexual intercourse.[2180]

In truth, the *Washington Post* pointed out "When used properly and consistently, condoms fail to prevent pregnancy and sexually transmitted diseases (STDs) less than 3 percent of the time, federal researchers say, and it is not known how many gay teenagers are HIV-positive. The assertion regarding gay teenagers may be a misinterpretation of data from the Centers for Disease Control and Prevention that found that 59 percent of HIV-infected males ages 13 to 19 contracted the virus through homosexual relations."[2181]

In Bush's first five years as President, the total abstinence funding was nearly $900 million.[2182] Federal tax dollars were being spent and purposely misleading children. Abstinence until marriage is a nice goal, but not always realistic. Still Bush defenders argued teaching young people about 'safer sex' invited them to have intercourse. Columbia University researchers found teenagers who take 'virginity pledges' will wait longer to initiate sexual activity, but "88 percent eventually have premarital sex."[2183]

This was the pseudo-science Dr. Bill Frist supported.

Frist On *This Week*

The following is a portion of the interview in regard to Bush myth-spreading sex education programs. It is important to note before the *Washington Post*'s article, Frist was unwilling to challenge the programs.[2184] Nor did he challenge them much after the information came out.

Frist defended Bush education on sex. George Stephanopoulos began, "Okay, let me switch to another subject. There was a bit of an uproar in Washington this week about this issue of these abstinence programs that are funded by the Federal government, the funding has doubled over the last four years but there was a report by the minority staff at the House Government Affairs Committee that showed that 11 of 13 of these programs are giving out false information. I want to show some of the claims they identified in the curricula. One of them was, one of the programs taught that 'The actual ability of condoms to prevent the transmission of HIV/AIDS, even if the product is intact, is not definitively known.' Another, 'The popular claim that condoms help prevent the spread of STDs is not supported by the data.' A third suggested that tears and sweat could transmit HIV and AIDS. Now, you're a doctor. Do you believe that tears and sweat can transmit HIV?" [2185]

Frist said, "I don't know. I can tell you ... I can tell you things like, like...."[2186] Surprised, Stephanopoulos interjected, "Well, wait, let me stop you, you don't know that, you believe that tears and sweat might be able to transmit AIDS?'[2187]

Dr. Frist said AIDS could spread through tears and sweat. Frist said, "Yeah, no, I can tell you that HIV is not very transmissible as an element like, compared to smallpox, compared to the flu…But about, about condoms, for example. We know there's about a 15 percent failure rate. You know, this is a deadly virus and you know it is directly transmissible with a relatively high degree of infectivity by, by sexual relations. If there's a 15 percent failure rate in, in condoms ..."[2188]

Stephanopoulos then pointed out, "But this was suggesting that they don't work even if the condom is intact."[2189] Frist said, "Oh, I know. But, but let me just say because the whole, the whole success, if you look in Africa today where as you know 28 million people are infected today … abstinence which is sort of the initial thrust itself which is the only way to prevent, only way to prevent."[2190]

When Stephanopoulos commented "Only surefire way," Frist said, "That's right. Only surefire. Very hard culturally in lots of approaches. Being faithful. Again, one partner and in certain cultures that is very hard and, then third, condoms. If you take out just condoms and say that is the answer with the 15 percent failure rate with a highly infective virus through sexual relations ..."[2191]

Frist was wrong on condom research. The Center for Health and Gender Equity noted (2004), "According to peer-reviewed studies, consistent and correct condom use is associated with a much smaller failure rate, about 2%. For people who use condoms inconsistently or incorrectly, failure rates can reach 13%."[2192]

Frist continued to defend Bush's sex-education programs. Stephanopoulos asked, "But do you think these abstinence programs should be reviewed and that they should be required to give out scientifically accurate information?"[2193] Frist said,"Oh, I think of course they should be reviewed, I mean, and that's in part our responsibility to make sure that all of these programs are reviewed but whether it's abstinence or whether it's condoms or whether it is better education on the infectivity of how washing hands in terms of the flu, all of these are public health challenges that we need in terms of better education, yes, the government has a role, especially if we're gonna be ..."[2194]

Frist still said AIDS could be spread by tears and sweat. Stephanopoulos went back to the AIDS topic: "Let me just, I wanted to move to another subject, let me just clear this up, though. Do you or do you not believe that tears and sweat can transmit HIV?"[2195] Frist said, "It would be very hard. It would be very hard for tears and sweat, I mean, you can get virus in tears and sweat but in terms of the degree of infecting somebody, it would be very hard."[2196]

Dr. Frist Lost Credibility

After the Stephanopoulos interview, a post on the liberal blog Wonkette sarcastically stated, "No wonder they let that compassionate conservatism thing slide! You can't even shed a tear for the gays without them giving you their wrath-of-God cooties. Actually, he does go on to admit that it would be 'very hard' to contract HIV via tears. Guess you can't kill all those cats in the name of science without learning *something*."[2197] (*The reader may, if interested, read what Google provides to the inquiry "Bill Frist and killing cats."*) The headline for that Wonkette article was "Bill Frist Says It Won't Happen If You Do It Standing Up."[2198] Frist hurt his doctor reputation over his Stephanopoulos interview; he completely abolished it with his handling the Terri Schiavo matter.

Terri Schiavo

By March 2005, Terry Schiavo had been in a persistent vegetative state for 15 years. Her biological family wanted her to live; her husband said it was time to take the tube out. Should the government intervene to reinstate her feeding tube? Republican staffers on Capital Hill circulated a memo hinting at political benefits for conservatives who took the issue up.[2199] *Fox News* reported one of the talking points was "this is an important moral issue and the pro-life base will be excited."[2200] Congress convened in a special weekend session to address the Schiavo issue.[2201] The legislation that developed, according to Frist, "would provide Mrs. Schiavo a clear and appropriate avenue for appeal in federal court, and most importantly, we are confident this compromise will restore nutrition and hydration to Mrs. Schiavo as long as that appeal endures."[2202]

Frist stated, "we in the Senate recognize that it is extraordinary that we as a body act."[2203] The public didn't think so. An ABC poll showed legislative action was "distinctly unpopular" and not only did 60 percent oppose congressional intervention; but 70 percent actually called it "inappropriate for Congress to get involved" as Congress did.[2204]

Quack Dr. Frist

Frist used his status as a doctor, claiming "there seems to be insufficient information to conclude that Terri Schiavo is in a persistent vegetative state…I don't see any justification in removing hydration and nutrition."[2205] With their leadership positions, Frist and House Majority Leader Tom DeLay got significant attention, though Sen. Rick Santorum (R-PA) entered the fray as well. Santorum thanked the Democratic leadership for cooperating on a hurried process to consider the legislation.[2206] The social conservatives of the Republican Party saw an opportunity to pander to the base and they overreached.

Frist spoke from the Senate floor: "based on a review of the video footage, which I spent an hour or so looking at last night in my office…that footage to me, depicts something very different than persistent vegetative state."[2207] His spokesman later went back and argued Frist did not make a diagnosis and had "carefully reviewed" medical records and court documents.[2208] "But it was the video Frist mentioned on the Senate floor," chided Tim Cuprisin of the *Milwaukee Journal Sentinel.*[2209]

Frist also implied from the Senate floor Mr. Schiavo was amoral: "Terri's husband will not divorce Terri and will not allow her parents to take care of her. Terri's husband, who I have not met, does have a girlfriend he lives with and they have children of their own."[2210] EJ Dionne of the *Washington Post* wrote, "No accusation here, just a brisk walk through innuendo city."[2211]

Even more convincing of Frist's incompetence was the release of Terri Schiavo's autopsy, which found Schiavo's brain had atrophied to about half its normal size and really had no hope of recovery.[2212] In defense of his remarks on the Senate floor in March 2005, Frist stated he had "never made a diagnosis."[2213] Frist stated in March: "when the neurologist [in the video of Terri Schiavo] said, 'Look up,' there is no question in the video that she actually looks up."[2214] The autopsy concluded Schiavo was blind.[2215] Some critics even went as far to say an autopsy of Bill Frist showed he himself had only half a brain.

Frist stated Schiavo "certainly seems to respond to visual stimuli."[2216] He was questioned on the *Today Show* (6.16.05) and declared, "I never said she responded" to stimulation.[2217] EJ Dionne wrote "We should not 'move on,' as Senate Majority Leader Bill Frist suggested. No, we cannot move on until those politicians who felt entitled to make up facts and toss around unwarranted conclusions about Schiavo's condition take responsibility for what they said—and apologize."[2218]

Critics were mad at Frist—they should have been irate at Santorum, who, according to *Newsweek*, had commented "he would consider impeachment proceedings against the federal judges in the Terri Schiavo case; that he favors term limits for federal judges, and that he would consider redrawing the boundaries of judicial districts to break up the liberal Ninth Circuit. Frist, aides say, does not support any such ideas."[2219] Frist led the government push in the Schiavo decision, but Santorum was right there prodding.

New York Mayor Michael Bloomberg later asked of the Schiavo fiasco: "Was there anything more inappropriate?"[2220]

Why didn't he run?

Bill Frist was a powerful politician in Washington. That's why he considered running for president.

Frist dropped out from his bid for the presidency and took what he called a "sabbatical" from politics in November 2006, and decided against running for president.[2221] His aides said, reported by the *New York Times*, Frist "decided that he simply did not have the fire to run."[2222] His announcement came in a released statement.[2223]

The *LA Times* reported (12.1.06) Frist was "assailed" for his diagnosis on Terri Shiavo, and that "Frist's associates said his decision…had nothing to do with an ongoing" Securities Exchange Commission's "investigation of insider-trading charges in connection with his sale of shares in HCA., the hospital chain his father helped found."[2224] A *Washington Post/AP* report rehashed the HCA controversy dogging the senator, and of course—Terri Schiavo: "an act," by Frist, "widely seen as a sop to religious conservatives."[2225] Joe Nichols wrote for *The Nation* (11.29.06):

> It is too bad that outgoing Senate Majority Leader Bill Frist… decided not to seek the Republican presidential nomination ... It would have been entertaining to watch this sorry excuse for a senator try and explain a political journey that deadended when the physician-turned-legislator diagnosed brain-damaged Terry Schiavo via videotape -- producing an assessment of her condition that completely contradicted that of doctors who had actually examined her. The storm that followed his intervention in the Schiavo case represented the only instance in which most Americans actually noticed that Frist was one of the nation's most powerful political leaders.[2226]

Mother Jones was another HCA critic:

> Some companies hire lobbyists to work Congress. Some have their executives lobby directly. But Tennessee's Frist family, the founders of Columbia/HCA Healthcare Corp., the nation's largest hospital conglomerate, has taken it a step further: They sent an heir to the Senate. And there, with disturbingly little controversy, Republican Sen. Bill Frist has co-sponsored bills that may allow his family's company to profit from the ongoing privatization of Medicare.[2227]

Frist was too mechanical. As Joe Klein wrote already in the spring of 2006, "Frist will leave the Senate at the end of the year and start his presidential campaign. Quote, 'He'll disappear,' said a Republican consultant. 'He's not built for heavy weather. He's just not an instinctive politician. And when you're a light candidate, every maneuver seems naked and tactical. With Frist, it's been college Republican sort of stuff.'"[2228]

Frist's Majority Leader position in the Senate caused difficulty in waging a presidential campaign. Former Majority Leader Trent Lott had previously said (5.10.06), "I think that the prospect of being a candidate is a distraction and makes his job more difficult … I say once again and it's been proven over and over again, majority leaders cannot be majority leader and run for president at the same time. It's an impossible job."[2229] Adding more injury to Frist's unsuccessful 2008 bid, Lott eventually became the GOP's Senate Leader after Frist left Congress.

Frist had little support from the social conservatives in his party—or at least not enough to run for president. In July 2005, he broke with the White House and supported the expansion of federal financing for embryonic stem cell research.[2230] So when the doctor finally made a decision based on leadership, he was punished by a loss of social conservative support. Dr. James Dobson of Focus on the Family was blunt at the time of Frist's switch: "The media have already begun speculating that Sen. Frist's announcement today is designed to improve his chances of winning the White House in 2008 ... If that is the case, he has gravely miscalculated."[2231]

What was the impact of Frist's departure?

The *LA Times* reported his decision "may boost support for other Republicans who have courted the party's social conservatives ...with his withdrawal, several potential candidates in the GOP race will have less competition wooing these voters."[2232]

Frist wasn't much of competition. It is hard to estimate who would have supported him. When Frist dropped out, the vice president of government affairs for the Family Research Council, Tom McClusky, praised Frist for the confirmation of Alito and Roberts, then added "But it is doubtful we would have supported him" because of the senator's stance on embryonic stem cell research.[2233] If any news developed the two-weeks after Frist's decision it was that he said he was open to running for governor of Tennessee in 2010. When Frist dropped out, he fell off a cliff and nobody asked about him. In early 2009, Frist said he would not run for governor.

TRENT LOTT

In June 1988, Senate Majority Leader Trent Lott (R-Miss.) equated homosexuality with alcoholism, sexual addiction and kleptomania.[2234] Was homosexuality a sin? Lott responded, "It is. My father had that problem, as I said, with alcoholism. Other people have sex addiction. Other people, you know, are kleptomaniacs. I mean, there are all kinds of problems and addictions and difficulties and experiences with things that you—that are wrong, but you should try to work with that person."[2235] Lott added: "You still love that person and you should not try to mistreat them or treat them as outcasts. You should try to show them a way to deal with that."[2236]

The GOP response to Lott varied.

There were a few Republicans who defended gays. Richard Tafel, executive director of Log Cabin Republicans, said "Senator Lott has insulted every gay person in the Republican Party…It was an insult to Congressman Jim Kolbe of Arizona, an Appropriations subcommittee chairman in the House, and to the dedicated and loyal gay and lesbian Republican activists across the country that helped the GOP win its majority." [2237]

Others worked the middle ground for the GOP. During this saga, John McCain said, "It's a very tough issue…We have a large party, a majority party. We have lots of facets to our party and lots of interests. The Log Cabin Republicans [a gay and lesbian organization] should be part of our party. The Christian Right should be part of our party."[2238]

Many Republican leaders hid behind their bibles. Assistant Majority Leader Don Nickles (R-Okla.) said Lott was "biblically correct" in describing gays; House Majority Leader Dick Armey (R-Texas) said, "My faith is based in the teachings of the Lord God Almighty, as found in the Holy Bible, and I do not quarrel with the Bible on this subject."[2239] Then there was former Seattle Seahawk wide receiver turned Congressmen Steve Largant (R-OK). In a then-recent fundrasing letter, Largent said, "As a father of four children, I am not about to allow liberal bureaucrats or irresponsible judges, who believe in everything from abortion to homosexuality to [hand] out condoms to 10-year-olds, to usurp my God-given rights." [2240]

As PBS noted, "Following Lott's comments, a coalition of conservative religious groups started a major lobbying and advertising campaign aimed at stopping Congress from passing what it considers gay rights legislation. The coalition spent $200,000 for ads in *The New York Times*, *The Washington Post*, and *USA Today*, focusing on Senator Lott's opinion that the lifestyle is a sin and that gays can be cured and become straight by having counseling."[2241] That brings this chapter back to reparative therapy and the ads, which included the Paulks.

Some have argued Trent Lott is gay, suggesting past experiences with gay escorts was the true reason he abruptly announced his resignation and/or retirement from the U.S. Senate in late 2007.[2242]

ALAN KEYES

Alan Keyes is a conservative author, activist, and candidate. Keyes worked for Ronald Reagan in international affairs, including his appointment to U.S. ambassador to the U.N. Economic and Social Council in 1983.[2243] Keyes also served as assistant secretary of state for international organizations (1985 to

1987).[2244] He has consistently represented hard-right conservative politics. (It's no surprise *The Weekly Standard*'s Bill Kristol was his former Harvard roommate.)[2245]

Keyes ran for president in 1996, 2000, and 2008. He ran for U.S. Senate in Maryland in 1988 and 1992; and in Illinois in 2004. Keyes had a conservative nationally syndicated radio talk-show from 1994 to 1999.[2246]

2000 Presidential Campaign

More recently, his 2000 presidential campaign focused on pro-life, family values. In the 2000 campaign for president, Keyes wanted to end the welfare system, ban gays in the military, prohibit abortion (except in the case of a mother's life), end the Department of Education, and ban sex education in public schools.[2247] He was known for his articulate speeches melting fire and brimstone tactics, such as calling homosexuality an "abomination."[2248] He finished 3rd in the Iowa Caucus in a crowded field. In one of the more awkward moments of the primaries, Keyes jumped into a mosh pit during the Iowa caucus as part of a segment on Michael Moore's TV series *The Awful Truth*.

The 2000 GOP nomination was crowded, but Keyes hung around long enough to appear as the third candidate after John McCain and George W. Bush. Keyes had his best finish in the Utah primary, which Bush won (63%), followed by Keyes (20%), then John McCain (15%).[2249]

Nobama

Late in the Illiniois Senate campaign, the GOP nominated Keyes to challenge Barack Obama. The innitial GOP nominee, Jack Ryan, dropped out after a sex scandel. Former Bears Coach Mike Ditka decided not to run, so the Republicans settled on Keyes. He never lived in Illinois, and carpetbagged. In 2004, Keyes accused Obama of taking "the wicked and evil position" on issues like abortion.[2250] The *Washington Post* editorialized that Keyes was a "carpetbagger," and noted "It's clear by now that Mr. Keyes loves the limelight and to hear himself speak, notwithstanding his rejection by voters in two U.S. Senate races in Maryland and two runs for the GOP presidential nomination. So it comes as no surprise that he would drop everything and hustle out to Illinois where he has never lived, to run for an office he can't win, and for a cause -- his own -- that deserves to lose."[2251] In 2000, Keyes said Hillary Clinton's Senate run in New York was a "destruction of federalism" which he deeply resented as she would "pretend to represent people there."[2252]

Cheney Broke With Bush on the Gay Marriage Amendment

This was the AP report from September 2004: "In the days before the Republican National Convention, Dick Cheney spoke at some length about the fact that Mary [Cheney, Dick's daughter] is a lesbian and his view of gay relationships. His tacit support for states' rights on the issue of same-sex marriage and less-than-ringing endorsement of President Bush's push for a constitutional amendment to ban gay unions drew criticism from several conservative groups."

Just before the 2004 GOP Convention, Cheney "said people ought to be free to enter into any kind of relationship they wanted. And he said individual states, and not Washington, should be allowed to rule on the issue of homosexual marriage."[2253] Genevieve Wood of the Family Research Council said Cheney's words were "disappointing. The fact is I think it sends a very mixed message to voters. Where does the administration stand on this issue?"[2254] Then Alan Keyes gave his opinion.

Alan Keyes And The GOP Convention

At the 2004 Republican Convention, Mike Signorile interviewed Alan Keyes. He asked about Cheney's separation from Bush on gay marriage: "What did you think of Vice President Cheney last week coming out and saying he doesn't agree with the President on the Federal Marriage Amendment? Seems to be a break with the party. Do you think he is sending a mixed signal?"[2255] Keyes said, "I don't know. I think he is entitled to his personal convictions, but I think that the party's position is the correct one. We have to stand in defense of the traditional marriage institution in order to preserve its basis in procreation and make sure that we retain an understanding of family life that is rooted in the tradition of procreation, of childbearing and childrearing. That is the essence of family life."[2256]

Keyes: Gays Can't Have Kids; Against Procreation

Signorile told Keyes, Cheney "seems very proud of his gay daughter. It seems like real family values and certainly seems like preserving the American family. Is his family un-American?" Keyes replied, "No, the point of the matter is that marriage, as an institution, involves procreation. It is in principle impossible for homosexuals to procreate. Therefore, they cannot marry. It is a simple logical syllogism, and one can wish all one might, but pigs don't fly and we can't change the course of nature." Signorile countered: "Well, one can wish that Bob and Liddy Dole would have a child, but that's just impossible. Pigs can't fly."[2257] Keyes argued the Doles, both senior citizens, could have children because, it's just "They *incidentally* face problems that prevent them from doing so. In principle..."[2258] Signorile asked, "Don't homosexuals incidentally face problems too?"[2259]

Keyes answered, "No, you don't understand the difference between incident and essence. Homosexuals are *essentially* incapable of procreation. They cannot mate. They are not made to do so. Therefore the idea of marriage for two such individuals is an absurdity."[2260] Signorile countered that one can procreate by donating sperm or a women can have babies. Keyes replied, "The definition and understanding of marriage is 'the two become one flesh.' In the child, the two transcend their persons and unite together to become a new individual. That can only be done through procreation and conception. It cannot be done by homosexuals."[2261]

What if a straight couple can't have kids?

Signorile said, "But what about a heterosexual couple who cannot bear children and then adopt? They are not becoming one as flesh, they are taking someone else's flesh."[2262] Keyes said, "And they are adopting the paradigm of family life. But the *essence* of that family life remains procreation. If we embrace homosexuality as a proper basis for marriage, we are saying that it is possible to have a marriage state that *in principle* excludes procreation and is based simply on the premise of selfish hedonism. This is unacceptable."[2263]

Mary Cheney: Hedonist

Signorile: "So Mary Cheney is a selfish hedonist, is that it?" Keyes was convinced, "Of course she is. That goes by definition. Of course she is."[2264] Signorile said, "I don't think Dick Cheney would like to hear that about his daughter."[2265] Keyes added, "He may or may not like to hear the truth, but it can be spoken. By definition, a homosexual engages in the exchange of mutual pleasure. I actually object to the notion that we call it sexual relations because it's nothing of the kind."[2266] Homosexual relations "is the mutual pursuit of pleasure through the stimulation of the organs intended for procreation, but it has nothing to do with sexuality because they are of the same sex. And with respect to them, the sexual difference does not exist. They are therefore not having sexual relations."[2267]

Signorile asked, "…how can you support President Bush then, because if something were to happen to him, the President would be Dick Cheney, who has a daughter who you say is a hedonist, and a selfish hedonist, and the President would be supporting that at that point?"[2268] Keyes was convinced the GOP ticket was "committed to the kinds of things that are necessary to defend this country, and we are all united in that support, in spite of what might be differences on issues here and there."[2269]

Mary Mostert at RenewAmerica.com defended Keyes: "A hedonist is a person whose highest goal in life is pleasure. Not all the selfish hedonists in our culture are homosexuals or lesbians, according to Keyes' clear definition. That definition would also fit heterosexuals who selfishly avoid procreation or whose selfishness leads to divorce. Keyes' sex education lesson to a confused homosexual ought to be required reading in every sex education class in the country. It might begin scaling back the flood of misery, disease, and early death that await those who choose to get involved in homosexual and lesbian life styles."[2270]

Keyes Is Gay

In September 2004, Maya Keyes's sexuality became public.[2271] Even after the "selfish hedonist" comment, Keyes told the *Chicago Tribune* he would even say the same thing to his own daughter, much less Dick Cheney's.[2272] "I have said that if you are actively engaging in homosexual relations, those relations are about selfish hedonism. …If my daughter were a lesbian, I'd look at her and say, 'That is a relationship that is based on selfish hedonism.' I would also tell my daughter that it's a sin, and she needs to pray to the Lord God to help her to deal with that sin."[2273] The *Washington Blade* noted the irony (10.15.2004), "If Maya is indeed a lesbian — and a blog that purports to be hers talks openly about being gay — she joins a growing list of gay children whose parents are Christian or conservative leaders."[2274]

The Keyes Lost A Family Member

The *Washington Post* reported (2.13.2005), "Now Maya Keyes -- liberal, lesbian and a little lost -- finds herself out on her own. She says her parents -- conservative commentator and perennial candidate Alan Keyes and his wife, Jocelyn -- threw her out of their house, refused to pay her college tuition and stopped speaking to her."[2275]

Maya Keyes went to an all-girls high school run by the Catholic Church's devout Opus Dei movement,[2276] which illustrates the difficulty of coming out for Maya. Alan Keyes knew Maya was a lesbian when he commented about Mary Cheney, because Maya had a *Washington Blade*, a gay weekly, in her bedroom while she was still in high school.[2277] Some rumblings of her sexuality was online during the 2004 Senate campaign in Illinois, but no corporate media picked it up.[2278]

Alan Keyes fired Maya from working at her political organization after she went to the "Counterinaugeral" for President Bush.[2279] When the *Washington Post* asked for a response on Maya, his secretary gave a prepared statement: "My daughter is an adult, and she is responsible for her own actions. What she chooses to do has nothing to do with my work or political activities."[2280] That was the entire statement.[2281]

CBS reported (2.13.2005) Maya Marcel-Keyes had "a Valentine" for her father when it was announced she would be making her first public appearance as a gay activist at a Maryland rally.[2282] It occurred only months after Alan made the comments about Mary Cheney.[2283] Maya told the *Washington Post*, of her dad's comments on Mary Cheney, "It was kind of strange that he said it like a hypothetical... It was really kind of unpleasant."[2284]

Because she is a lesbian, Maya said her parents threw her out of the house, stopped speaking to her, and refused to pay her college tuition.[2285] Maya said she still loved her parents.[2286] At the same time of Maya's disclosure, Alan Keyes' Web site said he was against "the homosexual rights agenda, including same-sex marriage."[2287]

Alan Keyes: A Political Fossil

Keyes announced his 2008 presidential candidacy on his website, RenewAmerica, in September 2007,[2288] a few months before the Iowa Caucus and it was hard to garner attention from the other dozen or so candidates who had already announced or dropped out. Garnering little attention as a Republican, he left the party to seek the Constitional Party's nomination in the spring of 2008.[2289]

But the Constitutionalists nominated the CP's 2004 VP candidate, Chuck Baldwin. Keyes started his own party, the America's Independent Party. Nothing could be more succint of an evaluation than this blogger commenting on Keyes results at the CP convention:

> Keyes? The wannabe who gets less votes every time he runs? The guy who got 0.1% of the GOP protest vote thinks he was railroaded out of the CP? Lets get the fact straight. The supreme optimist never joined the CP. He was not going to join unless he took all the marbles. Fact is - the man cannot win *any* election - even at the Constitution Party. Perhaps he needs to focus on being a better daddy to his daughter and win her heart before trying to win more than the two dozen votes from the fanatics at his site. His career is 100% over.[2290]

The day before the 2008 general election, Keyes website posted his opinion on John McCain and Obama: "Both major parties nominated individuals whose views discard the nation's founding principle of respect for the authority of the Creator God."[2291] That's an ironic statement coming from a man who is "concerned" about the nation's founding principles, but would walk over the Constitution's guarantee to separate church and state.

RICK SANTORUM

Rick Santorum was a two term U.S. Senator from Pennsylvania. He considered running for president for the 2008 cycle, but that proved to be a ridiculous goal after he was knocked out of the Senate because of his unsuccessful re-election bid in the 2006 elections.

Santorum on the Catholic Church Sex Scandel

Santorum bashes liberals and even claimed the Catholic Church sex abuse scandals occured because of liberals in Boston. Santorum wrote to *Catholic Online* in 2002: "while it is no excuse for this scandal, it is no surprise that Boston, a seat of academic, political, and cultural liberalism in America, lies at the center of the storm."[2292] In 2005, Santorum's quote was revived after the *Philadelphia News* columnist John Baer "raised them in print and prompted a political discourse in the blogosphere."[2293] Then the *Boston Globe* got involved. Mitt Romney came out against Santorum: "...I am going to suggest that he's wrong on the conclusion he's reached."[2294] Though Romney also said, "people are entitled to their own viewpoints."[2295] John McCain said Santorum, "...has probably written off Massachusetts."[2296]

Meanwhile, Ted Kennedy "upbraided" Santorum in an "unusually personal attack" on the Senate floor (7.13.05).[2297] John Kerry chimed in too.

Kerry spokesman David Wade stated Santorum owed an apology.[2298] Santorum then threw a bone to his base: "I don't think Ted Kennedy lecturing me on the teachings of the church and how the church should handle these problems is something I'm going to take particularly seriously."[2299]

On ABC's *This Week* (7.31.05), Santorum agreed he singled out Boston in 2002, noting that "In July of 2002, that was the epicenter."[2300] George Stephanopoulos interrupted (the *Globe* described it as cutting off) Santorum, "That simply is not true."[2301] The sex scandals were dispersed throughout the country, however, there was much national attention on Boston and Cardinal Bernard Law, who later resigned for his handling of previous abuses.

A grand jury (convened in April 2002) released a report in September 2005, alleging the Philadelphia archdiocese covered up the behavior of 63 abusive priests during the reign of two archbishops between 1961-2003, with church officials themselves saying 44 priests had been credibly accused of sexual assaults since the 1950s but only one had been indicted.[2302] By Santorum's standards there was "cultural liberalism" even in Pennsylvania.

Santorum's Infamous AP Interview

1) Giving in to gays will lead to rights toward incest, bigamy, adultery. In April 2003, Sen. Rick Santorum (R-PA) told the Associated Press, "If the Supreme Court says that you have the right to consensual (gay) sex within your home, then you have the right to bigamy, you have the right to polygamy, you have the right to incest, you have the right to adultery. You have the right to anything."[2303] Though Santorum said the AP's account was "misleading," unedited transcripts prove Santorum did not approve of "acts outside of traditional heterosexual relationships."[2304] Gay-bashers backed Santorum by suggesting the AP reporter, Lara Jakes Jordan, had Democratic Party ties.[2305] The transcript of Santorum's beliefs speak for itself.

2) Orientation is fine, acting on the orientation is evil. Santorum told Jakes-Jordan, "I have no problem with homosexuality. I have a problem with homosexual acts. As I would with acts of other, what I would consider to be, acts outside of traditional heterosexual relationships. And that includes a variety of different acts, not just homosexual. I have nothing, absolutely nothing against anyone who's homosexual. If that's their orientation, then I accept that. And I have no problem with someone who has other orientations. The question is, do you act upon those orientations? So it's not the person, it's the person's actions. And you have to separate the person from their actions."[2306]

3) Privacy doesn't matter. Days after the AP interview, a 23 year old gay confronted Santorum: "You attacked me for who I am .... How could you compare my sexuality and what I do in the privacy of my home to bigamy or incest." Santorum stood by his comments (even though he simultaneously said they were taken out of context) and said if states were not allowed to regulate homosexual activity in private homes, "you leave open the door for a variety of other sexual activities to occur within the home and not be regulated."[2307]

A Minor spilt within the GOP

Republicans rebuked Sen. Rick Santorum in 2003, when he made the controversial comments about homosexuality.

Sen. Susan Collins (R-Maine) said Santorum's choice of words was "regrettable" and his legal analysis "wrong."[2308] Sen. Olympia Snowe, (R-Maine) said, "Discrimination and bigotry have no place in our society, and I believe Senator Santorum's remarks undermine Republican principles of inclusion and opportunity."[2309] Sen. Lincoln Chafee (R-R.I) stated, "I thought his choice of comparisons was unfortunate and the premise that the right of privacy does not exist -- just plain wrong....Senator Santorum's views are not held by this Republican and many others in our party."[2310] Sen. Gordon Smith (R-Ore.) said, "America and the Republican Party" no longer equate "sexual orientation with sexual criminality."[2311] Sen. John McCain, said Santorum was "inartful" in the way that he described his position.[2312]

There are gay Republicans. Rep. Jim Kolbe (R-Ariz.), at the time of Santorum's flap, was the only openly gay Republican in Congress. He gave no comment on Santorum's position on homosexuality.[2313]

Santorum admits "homosexuals can be virtuous."

Santorum said (2005), "I would say that certainly people who are homosexuals can be virtuous and very often are. The problem is that when you talk about the institution of marriage as the foundation and building block of society which I say the family is, and the marriage is the glue that holds the family together. We need to do things to make sure that that institution stays stable for the benefit of children."[2314]

Santorum represses in his mind that fifty percent of "traditional" marriages end in divorce and there are millions of abused kids living in "traditional" families. If you want marriage to be a stable institution, make adultery a federal felony, abolish credit cards, and close all bars at 8 p.m.

Santorum's Homeland Security

Santorum has also said, "Isn't that the ultimate homeland security, standing up and defending marriage?"[2315]

Jon Stewart v. Rick Santorum

In an interview with Rick Santorum (R-PA), *Daily Show* host Jon Stewart aptly questioned the "traditionalness" of marriage. Stewart asked Santorum, "Isn't even the natural family evolving? All the way up until the 60's and 70's there were those head of household laws that a family could decide to move but it was basically the man who had final say, you know, and before that marriage was more a property arrangement. You know, love marriage only came in the 1700's and moved on from there. Is it possible that, through an examination or as we go along, or is this just a basic difference of opinion about what the nature of sexuality is and what the nature of virtue is?"[2316]

Santorum acted like the traditional marriage was part of nature. The anti-gay Senator was convinced nature validated his argument. "No I think it's the nature of what's best for society. From four thousand years of history we've decided and determined that marriage was so important, having a mother and father who had children who were together for the purpose of children. Remember, the reason societies elevate marriage to a special status is not because they want to affirm the relationship between two adults. That's important. A love relationship is important.[2317]

Santorum said, "...what's society's purpose in marriage? Society's purpose - the reasons civilizations have held up marriage is because they want to establish and support and secure the relationship that is in the best interest of the future of the society, which is, a man and a woman having children and providing the stability for those children to be raised in the future."[2318]

Jon Stewart told Santorum, "But wouldn't you say that society has an interest in understanding that the homosexual community also wants to form those same bonds and raise children and wouldn't a monogamous, good-hearted, virtuous homosexual couple be in society's best interest raising a child rather than a heterosexual couple with adultery, with alcohol issues, with other things, and by the way, I don't even need to make that sound as though a gay couple can only raise a child given failures in other couples."[2319]

Santorum can't grasp the fact that straight marriages often produce parents who harm their children... he is hung up on his belief that it is only a gay problem.

Rick Santorum said, "I think we should honor every person in America - that every person has worth and dignity. There's a difference though, when it comes to changing the laws of the country, that could harm children."[2320] He is singing Anita Bryant's song...

Santorum: There is No Right to Privacy

There is no right to privacy guaranteed in the constitution? Former Sen. Rick Santorum said (4.7.08), "this right to privacy that doesn't exist in my opinion in the United States Constitution, this right that was created, it was created in Griswold — Griswold was the contraceptive case — and abortion. And now we're just extending it out. And the further you extend it out, the more you — this freedom actually intervenes and affects the family. You say, well, it's my individual freedom. Yes, but it destroys the basic unit of our society because it condones behavior that's antithetical to strong healthy families."[2321] In the same interview, Santorum added, "The right to privacy is a right that was created in a law that set forth a (ban on) rights to limit individual passions. And I don't agree with that."[2322]

Acts outside of marriage are despicable?

Santorum said (2003) he had problems with "acts outside of traditional heterosexual relationships."[2323]

I suppose he would like to begin a mass movement and constitutional amendment to ban masturbation: off with their hands!

MIKE HUCKABEE

Former Arkansas Governor Mike Huckabee ran for president in 2008, and will likely seek the 2012 GOP presidential nomination.

Huckabee is tied closely to religion. In 1989, he became the president of the Arkansas Baptist Convention, whose membership neared half a million.[2324] He has been a Baptist minister for over a decade and his first book, *Character is the Issue*, talks of living a 'God-centered life.'[2325] As governor, Huckabee wrote to school superintendents reminding them students had a right to prayer.[2326] They seem to love him dearly at *Fox News*.

Huckabee Against Gay Foster Parents

In late June 2006, the Arkansas Supreme Court unanimously struck down a ban on gay foster parents, and upheld a lower court's 2004 decision that threw out the ban.[2327] The initial policy was put into effect in 1999, four people sued, and the Arkansas Child Welfare Board stopped the policy after the court defeat in 2004.[2328]

In Iowa, Huckabee was optimistic the Arkansas legislature would reinstate the ban on gay couples from being foster parents, and equally upbeat the court would uphold it.[2329] "Our attorney's read into that that if it was legislation it would likely stand, that we could in fact say that only married couples could be foster parents. We think that if we go back and codify that into law that probably takes care of it."[2330] Huckabee had legitimate hope in that the Court said officials went too far in imposing the ban, but,according to the AP, the court did not decide on the actual merit of such a ban.[2331] Still, the ruling said, "the driving force behind the adoption of the regulations was not to promote the health, safety and welfare of foster children but rather based upon the board's view of morality and its bias against homosexuals."[2332] Huckabee said it would not have been struck down if it had been state law and not just a regulation, and the legislature would make it a law next year.[2333]

Huckabee's justification: "What I feared was going on was that the plaintiffs in this case were not as interested in foster children as they were in making the political point of homosexual activism....That's troubling that we would use children as a political tool to enact something that has nothing to do with the best interest of a foster child."[2334] By that logic, if the plaintiffs were not making a political issue of the case, then Huckabee would have sided with the plaintiffs. Please.

Perhaps an equal argument would say Huckabee was using the children as a political tool. Huckabee would rather have a child be in an orphanage all his childhood (for the sake of pandering to the religious right) instead of them being allowed in a home of two caring adults.

An AP report quoted Huckabee in Iowa: "Marriage has historically never meant anything other than a man and a woman. It has never meant two men, two women, a man and his pet, or a man and a whole herd of pets," and activists "want to change rules that have been in place for thousands of years."[2335]

Huckabee v. Stewart; Stewart Wins

In a December 2008 interview on *The Daily Show*, Jon Stewart grilled Mike Huckabee. The following paragraph is a partial transcript of that exchange.

Stewart commented, "Segregation used to be the law until the courts intervened."[2336] Huckabee said, "There's a big difference between a person being black and a person practicing a lifestyle and engaging in a marital relationship."[2337] Stewart then commented, "Okay, actually this is helpful because it gets to the crux of it. … And I'll tell you this: religion is far more of a choice than homosexuality. And the protections that we have for religion — we protect religion. And talk about a lifestyle choice — that is absolutely a choice. Gay people don't choose to be gay. **At what age did you choose to not be gay?"**[2338] (Emphasis mine.) Huckabee concluded, "If the American people are not convinced that we should overturn the definition of marriage, then I would say that those who support the idea of same-sex marriage have a lot of work to do to convince the rest of us. And as I said, 60 percent of the American population has made the decision–…"[2339] Stewart interjected: "You know, you talk about the pro-life movement [abortion] being one of the great shames of our nation. I think if you want number two, I think it's that: It's a travesty that people have forced someone who is gay to have to make their case that they deserve the same basic rights as someone else."[2340]

NO SEX FOR YOU….

In December 2007, Huckabee went on *Meet the Press*, where host Tim Russert asked the former governor if he believed "people are born gay or choose to be gay?"[2341] Huckabee responded: "I don't know whether people are born that way but one thing I know, that the behavior one practices is a choice."[2342] Huckabee added, "people who are gay say that they're born that way," but then added that he himself believed "how we behave and how we carry out that behavior" is more important.[2343] Steve Benen of the *Washington Monthly* aptly commented: "I see. So, Huckabee doesn't actually care if someone is gay, he cares whether or not gays are celibate. And here I thought his years of bizarre criticism of the gay community were a sign of intolerance. I've clearly misjudged him."[2344]

NEWT GINGRICH

The Movable Moral Code

Newt Gingrich is woefully hypocritical on moral leadership. When he was considering running for president in 2008, Newt Gingrich was believed to have had the worst marriage past of all candidates.[2345]

Gingrich ran for Congress in 1978 on the slogan of "Let Our Family Represent Your Family," even though he very well may have been cheating on his wife simultaneously.[2346] His first marriage was to his former high school geometry teacher.[2347] On that marriage, Gingrich has said (March 2007), "I was married very young and had my first daughter when I was very young, in fact at the end of my freshman year in college."[2348] His first marriage lasted 18 years, and Gingrich remarried months after his divorce in 1981.[2349] Gingrich first wife had, according to the *Washington Monthly*, "helped put him through graduate school," and they hassled "over the terms [of the divorce] while in the hospital, as she recovered from uterine cancer surgery."[2350] Anne Manning, a supposed Gingrich mistress in the late 1970's told *Vanity Fair* (1995), "We had oral sex. He prefers that modus operandi because then he can say, 'I never slept with her.'"[2351]

Remarried, Gingrich then had another affair during the Clinton impeachment proceedings, but claimed he was not a hypocrite because the President was impeached for lying about an affair, not having it.[2352] Already in January 2005, the *LA Times* reported "Many Republicans were furious when it was disclosed, in the course of a divorce from his second wife in 1999, that Gingrich had been conducting an extramarital relationship with a congressional aide even as Republicans were impeaching Clinton for lying about an affair..."[2353] He divorced his second wife in 2000, and remarried to "a former congressional aide who was in her 20s when she and Gingrich began their affair."[2354]

Gingrich's dirty image is now clean. In December 2005, the *Church Report*'s editor-in-chief Jason Christy announced Newt Gingrich agreed to write a regular column for the magazine which was distributed to over 40,000 religious leaders nationwide.[2355] Christy said "For over 20 years Newt Gingrich has been on the cutting edge of conservative public policy and Christian issues in this nation."[2356] The *New York Times* reported (12.17.06) Gingrich set a goal of "what he calls the restoration of God to a central place in American government and culture."[2357] His ten-point Contract with America for the 21st Century included a call to "recenter America on the creator from whom all our liberties come" and judicial appointments for those understanding "the centrality of God in American history."[2358]

Mike Huckabee so aptly stated (April 2007), without naming names, particularly evangelical Christians, "talk as if, in this election cycle, Republican candidates aren't going to be held to a standard of personal accountability and responsibility for their personal lives. If that's true, there are going to be a lot of Republicans who will owe Bill Clinton a great big public apology."[2359]

It also appears, to this writer, that church related publications might run with some nasty people.

MITT ROMNEY: ALL FOR THE PRESIDENCY

Mitt Romney ran for U.S. Senate in 1994 in Massachusetts. He later saved the Salt Lake City Olympic Games in 2002 by getting its organization back on track. Later that year, he ran for governor of Massachusetts and won. He then ran for the Republican Presidential nomination in 2008. He has been for gay rights, he has been against gay rights.

Establishing Conservative Credentials; Forgetting the Past

In the December 2006 edition of the *National Review*, Romney insisted he was consistent on gay-marriage, and that the GOP should remain a pro-life party.[2360] On gay marriage he told the *National Review*, "Like the vast majority of Americans, I've opposed same-sex marriage, but I've also opposed unjust discrimination against anyone, for racial or religious reasons, or for sexual preference."[2361]

Simultaneously, the *Boston Globe* (Dec.2006) reported of "Romney's recently revived 1994 promise to 'provide more effective leadership' on gay rights than [Ted] Kennedy himself, his [Romney's] opponent in that year's Senate race."[2362] *Boston Globe* columnist Joan Vennochi wrote his position on abortion was a personality flaw, as Romney "ran for office twice in Massachusetts as a moderate, pro choice Republican."[2363] In 1994, Vennochi reminded, it was Romney who promised "to establish full equality for American gay and lesbian citizens" and even campaigned at a Gay Pride rally in 2002.[2364] Though as *OvalOffice2008.com* noted, "in fairness to Romney…there is polling evidence to suggest that most Americans distinguish between gay rights in general and gay marriage in particular."[2365]

Romney Problems On Homosexual Issues

The *National Group* concluded it was "an awful December" for Romney in 2006.[2366] A *Washington Post*/AP report talked (12.23.06) of the "apparent gulf" between the 1994 version and the presidential candidate: "Is he the self-described moderate who unsuccessfully challenged Kennedy in the year of the Republican landslide, the self-described conservative now ready to bid for the Republican nomination in 2008, or merely an ambitious and adaptable politician?"[2367] This report noted the governor declined an interview request on his evolution of thinking; aides said he did not have time for a telephone interview and Romney had answered questions on the topic numerous times.[2368] Indeed, reports suggested, "questions" about Romney's "conservative credentials" could provide an opening for Sam Brownback and Mike Huckabee's ambitions.[2369]

By Jan. 12, 2007, a longtime foe of Romney, Brain Camenker wrote a 28 page report which portrayed Romney as a gay rights sympathizer and it included five pages of footnotes.[2370] The AP article quoted Camenker: "...Romney is so clearly and blatantly faking this. He's a fraud."[2371] Camenker was a leader of MassResistance, which accused Romney as the "father of gay marriage."[2372]

As the *National Review* quoted Massachusetts Family Institute president Kris Mineau: "...In 2005, he ardently supported a citizen petition for an amendment to end same-sex marriage that ...[gathered]... a record number of 170,000 signatures. Throughout 2006 he lobbied the state legislature that was refusing to vote on the amendment. His intense involvement culminated with the filing of a suit in the State Supreme Judicial Court in December to mandate the legislature to hold the votes as required by the state constitution."[2373] The denial was the same on the abortion issue. Mineau said when people asked how Romney's switch on pro-life could be accepted, "I ask if they ever question Teddy Kennedy's or John Kerry's switches from pro-life to pro-choice."[2374] [Romney dug up a 1913 law in 2004 which said out-of-state couples could not marry if their marriage would be 'void' in their home state.[2375]] This NRO article (1.10.07) quoted U.S. Senator Jim DeMint who said Romney "fells passionately that the value of human life begins at conception."[2376]

Anti-gay Americans for Truth attacked Romney for criticizing Camenker. A *Christian Newswire* press release by the group quoted President Peter LaBarbera: "Few people have demonstrated the courage that Brian has in fighting the self-styled 'queer' movement,' as the release said "Romney uses liberal media stories to portray Camenker as an extremist troublemaker."[2377]

Romney's Log Cabin Letter

In a letter to Log Cabin Republicans, Romney complimented "Don't Ask, Don't Tell" as a "step in the right direction," and the first steps toward gays serving "openly" in the military.[2378] Other sources, such as EDGE Boston (12.19.06) also quoted Romney in that 1994 letter: "we must make equality for gays and lesbians a mainstream concern."[2379] The Log Cabin head in 1994, Rich Tafel, "told the *New York Times* that he was surprised by Romney's 180-degree turn on gay rights."[2380] The Log Cabin had new leadership in December 2006 right at the height of the Romney spiel, and Patrick Sammon came to the post saying Romney needed "to explain what" was "clearly a shift" from 1994.[2381] The *New York Times*/AP reported the letter "now looms as a serious complication to Romney's presidential hopes."[2382] The Family Research Council president Tony Perkins called the incident "quite disturbing" and Paul Weyrich said, "Unless he

[Romney] comes out with an abject repudiation of this, I think it make him out to be a hypocrite."[2383]

The Real Romney: Tacky

Just when Romney thought he had passed a hurdle, *You Tube* entered the fray, as a five-minute clip of an October 1994 debate with Ted Kennedy surfaced. By the end of the day on January 10, 2007, over 12,000 had seen it.[2384] Titled "The Real Romney," it showed Romney saying the Boy Scouts should allow participation "regardless of their sexual orientation," (while also supporting the organization's right to make its own decision).[2385] Yes, the old Romney opposed the Scouts policy that prohibited gays from being scoutmasters and did not allow the organization to publicly participate in the 2002 Olympics. [2386] This was the same debate he said "we should sustain and support" the *Roe v. Wade* decision.[2387] Ted Kennedy said Romney "was pro-choice, he's anti-choice, he's multiple choice."[2388] The 1994 version of Romney said, "You will not see me wavering on that matter, or be a multiple choice," and, as a cherry on top, said he "was an independent at the time of Reagan-Bush. I'm not trying to return to Reagan-Bush."[2389] The 2007 version of Romney went on the conservative internet broadcasts of *The Glenn and Helen Show* and called the footage "ancient,": '...If you want to know where I stand...you don't just have to listen to my words; you can go look at my record as governor."[2390] One should not have looked at his gubernatorial campaign: in both his senate and governor race; he was endorsed by the Log Cabin Republicans.[2391] He issued a 2003 proclamation declaring May 17 "Massachusetts Gay/Straight Youth Pride Day."[2392]

What was so comical was Romney thought he was better than John McCain. McCain said, "I believe in the sanctity and unique role of marriage between man and woman, but I certainly don't believe in discriminating against any American," and "I believe that gay marriage should not be legal."[2393]

Romney, "seeking to be seen as more conservative" than McCain, said "That's his position, and in my opinion, it's disingenuous."[2394] Romney also said, "Look, if somebody says they're in favor of gay marriage, I respect that view. If someone says, like I do, that I oppose same-sex marriage, I respect that view. But those who try and pretend to have it both ways, I find it to be disingenuous."[2395] The AP reported: "Never mind that Romney's own position on gay marriage has been questioned in recent weeks - after a 1994 letter surfaced from his unsuccessful Senate challenge to Sen. Edward M. Kennedy, D-Mass. In it, Romney pledged to be more effective in promoting the gay agenda than the liberal senator."[2396]

Mitt Romney's hypocrisy is ugly.

Romney also has some explaining to do.

TIME MAGAZINE's May 21, 2007 cover story asked what Mitt Romney believes. Then Time's story totally ignored the most important question of all.

Someone once asked if it was intolerant to be intolerant of intolerance. It may be.

People who believe and announce a belief that their position is the only correct view and the rest of us are infidels might be cause for concern.

Many people feel strongly about their religion. Some, as we have seen in the last five years, carry the religious fervor to the point of destructive fanaticism. Others believe, as do I, but have no problem if others believe differently. Some others, as do I, actually believe that a faith and particular way of expressing that faith may be correct but others may be correct also. It is even possible that others might be more correct.

I am very concerned when a presidential candidate proclaims, during his church's ritual, that his church is the only true church on the face of the earth. If the candidate sincerely and deeply believes that, does not that candidate in effect say there is no value in others' beliefs and those beliefs are therefore not worthy of discussion or study?

Further and even of more importance, does this fervent belief indicate a closed mind toward other issues? Does this indicate a refusal to even listen to positions that may be in conflict with those of the closed-minded candidate? A true believer does not have to convert the non-believer if that true believer merely shuts the door on the ideas of others. This is frightening if it is the prevalent mind set of a President of the United States.

The Church of Latter Day Saints of Jesus Christ, the Mormons, teaches and states in its' ritual known as the "Testimony": "Three great truths must be included in every valid testimony: 1. That Jesus Christ is the Son of God and the Savior of the world (D. & C. 46:13); 2. That Joseph Smith is the Prophet of God through whom the gospel was restored in this dispensation; and 3. That The Church of Jesus Christ of Latter-day Saints is "the only true and living church upon the face of the whole earth." (D. & C. 1:30.)

Make no mistake, there is no opposition from me to people who belong to the LDS Church. Although I am not a LDS member, I am married to a LDS member and helped raise four LDS step-daughters. I am very concerned, however, about the mindset of a man who wants to be President of the United States who professes such a belief, "the only true and living church upon the face of the whole earth." The Mormon Church also makes a statement about tolerance. It states, "We claim the privilege of worshipping Almighty God according to the dictates of our own conscience," says Article of Faith 11, "and allow all men the same privilege, let them worship, how, where or what they may.

That does not solve the intellectual problem I face. Yes, such tolerance allows others to exist. It infers, however, a position of superiority and does not open doors to dialogue, it does not allow that others just might have a better idea. The problem is not the Church; the problem is not an individual's belief, the problem is the belief that it is the only true one. And, that problem is minor compared to a person who wants to be President of the United States believing that his belief or idea or opinion is the only one that really counts.

Mitt Romney owes the people of the United Sates an explanation, not of his church, not of his religious beliefs, certainly not of the kind of underwear he wore at his wedding, but of his clinging to an idea that there is only one way.

Follow the Leaders....(?)

To quote Doc Holliday in *Tombstone*, "It appears my hypocrisy knows no bounds." The same must be said for the following people who have seeked public office and presented themselves as role models.

1802: Thomas Jefferson is rumored to be having an affair with his slave Sally Hemmings. DNA tests of their descendents confirm it in 1998.
1884: Grover Cleveland wins his election despite opponents making an issue of his illegitimate child with chants of "Ma, ma, where's my pa? Gone to the White House, ha, ha, ha."
1974: Police stop **Wilbur Mills**, an Arkansas Democrat and chairman of the House Ways and Means Committee, for speeding. His passenger, a stripper with the stage name "Fanne Fox, the Argentine firecracker," jumps out of the vehicle and walked into the capital's Tidal Basin.
1976: Rep. Wayne L. Hayes, an Ohio Democrat and chairman of the House Administration Committee, resigns after it was revealed he gave a pay raise to his secretary and mistress Elizabeth Ray.
1980: Rep. Robert Bauman, a leading Republican conservative from Maryland, pleads not guilty to soliciting sex from a 16-year-old boy. Charges are later dropped after Bauman agrees to be treated for alcoholism. He also wrote an autobiography, *The Gentleman from Maryland: The Conscience of a Gay Conservative,* which was published in 1986.
1983: The House reprimands **Illinois Republican Dan Crane** and Massachusetts **Democrat Gerry Studds** for having sexual affairs with congressional pages.
1986: Terry Dolan dies of AIDS. Dolan was a **Republican** activist, worked in the 1972 campaign of Richard Nixon and the 1974 U.S. Senate campaign of Clyde Lewis, a Republican John Birch Society activist. Terry Dolan was co-founder and chairman of the National Conservative Political Action Committee. A gay man, Dolan publicly campaigned against gay rights and frequented gay bars.
1987: Less than a month after Colorado **Sen. Gary Hart** announced his second Democratic presidential run in 1987, various news outlets report he was having an extramarital affair with 29-year-old model Donna Rice.

1988: Democratic Sen. Brock Adams of Washington decides not to run for re-election when women come forward with allegations of sexual misconduct.
1992: Gennifer Flowers details a long affair **with Arkansas Gov. Bill Clinton** to a tabloid newspaper shortly before the Democratic primaries.
1992: Republican Sen. Bob Packwood of Oregon is accused by 10 women of sexual harassment. Packwood later resigns after the Senate Ethics Committee found him guilty of sexual misconduct.
1994: Rep. Mel Reynolds, an Illinois Democrat, is indicted convicted for sexual assault of a 16-year-old campaign volunteer.
1996: Arthur Finkelstein, one of the United States' and **Republican's** smartest, successful, and cutting edge political consultants, is outed by *Boston Magazine*. In 2004 he marries his partner of over 40 years, in Massachusetts. They had/have two adopted children. He has made tons of money helping candidates who bash gays.
1998: President Bill Clinton admits to having an affair with former White House intern Monica Lewinsky, after denying it.
1998: Republican Bob Livingston. In the aftermath of the Lewinsky scandal, Livingston was chosen to replace Newt Gingrich as speaker. But he, instead, admitted an affair and stepped down.
1998: Republican Helen Chenoweth. The archconservative Idaho congresswoman, who blasted Bill Clinton's infidelity, admitted a six-year affair with a married rancher from her home state in the 1980s. "I've asked for God's forgiveness," she said in 1998, "and I've received it."
1998: Republican Dan Burton. Another conservative and outspoken critic of President Clinton, Burton admitted to 15 years earlier having an extramarital affair and fathering a child out of wedlock. He admitted it only after reporters said they were set to write about it.
1998: Republican Henry Hyde. When confronted by a reporter, the former House Judiciary Committee chairman became yet another Republican in the wake of the Lewinksy scandal to admit to having had an extramarital affair. His occured decades earlier.
2001: Democrat Gary Condit. The California congressman's affair with an intern became exposed after the girl, Chandra Levy, disappeared. It dominated national news before Sept. 11th. Levy was eventually found dead in a DC's Rock Creek Park and someone else was charged her murder.
2004: New Jersey Gov. Jim McGreevey steps down after disclosing he had an affair with another man.
2004: Republican Congressman Ed Schrock (VA) drops his re-election bid after reports of his solicitations for gay sex surface.
2005: Jim West, then mayor of Spokane, Wash., an important **Republican** politician in the Northwest with a strong reputation for opposing gay rights and

advocating the removal of gay teachers from schools and daycare centers. In 2005, the *Spokane Spokesman-Review* revealed West had been leading a double life, trolling for male sexual partners on the Internet and allegedly abusing two teenage boys who came under his care as a Boy Scout leader.

2006: Rep. Mark Foley, a **Florida Republican**, and congressional pages traded sexual e-mails and instant messages that began to surface just before the November midterm election.

2006: Republican Don Sherwood The then-65-year-old Pennsylvania congressman lost his House seat after it was revealed he'd had an extramarital affair with a 29-year-old woman who'd called 9-1-1 from a closet in Sherwood's DC apartment, charging he'd choked her.

2007: Bob Allen, a Republican member of the Florida House of Representatives and Chairman of John McCain's Presidential Campaign allegedly offered an undercover cop $20 to allow Allen to perform oral sex on him in a men's room in a public park.

2007: Sen. David Vitter, a Louisiana Republican, is reported to be on the phone records of a high-end Washington, D.C., prostitution ring.

2007: Sen. Larry Craig, an Idaho Republican, pleads guilty to disorderly conduct in a men's room. A police officer testified Craig was soliciting sex.

2007: Republican Newt Gingrich, as he was weighing a 2008 presidential run, the former speaker acknowledged, in an interview with the Christian conservative group Focus on the Family, having an extramarital affair during the 1990s. It is later reported he had more than one, cheating on more than one wife.

2007: Democrat Gavin Newsom. The married San Francisco mayor admitted to sleeping with the wife of a top aide.

2007: Democrat Antonio Villaraigosa. Weeks after separating from his wife, the Los Angeles Mayor admitting to having a secret affair with a TV reporter.

2008: New York Gov. Eliot Spitzer (D) admitted to having an affair with 22-year-old call girl Ashley Dupre.

2008: Republican Vito Fossella. The married former congressman from Staten Island, who had three children with his wife, admitted he'd had a secret affair with a retired Air Force lieutenant colonel, who'd birthed his love child in Virginia. After Fossella was arrested for drunken driving, Democrats took over his seat in 2008.

2008: Democrat Kwame Kilpatrick The Detroit mayor eventually ended up in jail after he was convicted of lying about a text message/sex scandal.

2008: Democrat Tim Mahoney. The man who replaced Foley was eventually derailed by his own sex scandal, and the seat went back to the GOP. Mahoney, it was widely reported, was paying hush money to a mistress.

2008: Former **North Carolina Sen. John Edwards** (D) admits he had an affair with former campaign videographer Rielle Hunter during his second presidential run. Edwards denied fathering Hunter's child for over a year.
2009: Sen. John Ensign, R-NV, confesses to having an extra-marital affair with another woman, later identified as 46-year-old Cindy Hampton, a former campaign aide. Ensign said the affair began in December 2007 and ended in August 2008.
2009: South Carolina Gov. Mark Sanford admitted to having an extramarital affair with a woman living in Buenos Aires, Argentina. Sanford was a right-winger's dream. He spoke out vigorously for the impeachment of Bill Clinton, he opposed abortion, marriage equality for gays, gays and lesbians adopting children, and stated homosexuality is a choice and a sin. He also cheated on his wife and did so at state expense.
2009: Republican State Senator Paul Stanley (TN), known for lectures about abstinence from sex and introducing legislation to prevent gay adoptions, resigned from the Tennessee Senate after details of his sexual affair with a 22 year old legislative female intern.

MUGWUMPS

Vice-President Dick Cheney

The former vice president has a gay daughter. He stated, on June 1, 2009, at the National Press Club in Washington DC: "I think, you know, freedom means freedom for everyone…I think people ought to be free to enter into any kind of union they wish, any kind of arrangement they wish….And I think that's the way it ought to be handled today, that is, on a state-by-state basis. Different states will make different decisions. But I don't have any problem with that. I think people ought to get a shot at that."

I don't get the doublespeak here; if people are "free to enter any kind of union they wish, any kind of arrangement they wish", and if freedom is for everyone how can different states make different decisions. I guess he means some people, if they live in the right state, can, others cannot. Cheney is not all bad on this issue, he is also not all that good. That makes him a fence-sitting mugwump.

President Barack Obama

"I do solemnly swear (or affirm) that I will faithfully execute the office of President of the United States, and will to the best of my ability, preserve, protect and defend the Constitution of the United States."

The oath also covers the 14th Amendment which states:

"Section. 1. All persons born or naturalized in the United States and subject to the jurisdiction thereof, are citizens of the United States and of the State wherein they reside. No State shall make or enforce any law which shall abridge the privileges or immunities of citizens of the United States; nor shall any State deprive any person of life, liberty, or property, without due process of law; nor deny to any person within its jurisdiction the equal protection of the laws."

Although Barack Obama has said he supports civil unions, he is against gay marriage. In an interview with the *Chicago Daily Tribune*, Obama said, "I'm a Christian. And so, although I try not to have my religious beliefs dominate or determine my political views on this issue, I do believe that tradition, and my religious beliefs say that marriage is something sanctified between a man and a woman." Barack Obama did vote against a Federal Marriage Amendment and opposed the Defense of Marriage Act in 1996.

He said he would support civil unions between gay and lesbian couples, as well as letting individual states determine if marriage between gay and lesbian couples should be legalized.

From the White House Web site:

President Obama supports full civil unions that give same-sex couples legal rights and privileges equal to those of married couples. Obama also believes we need to repeal the Defense of Marriage Act and enact legislation that would ensure that the 1,100+ federal legal rights and benefits currently provided on the basis of marital status are extended to same-sex couples in civil unions and other legally-recognized unions. These rights and benefits include the right to assist a loved one in times of emergency, the right to equal health insurance and other employment benefits, and property rights.

From the White House Website:

President Obama agrees with former Chairman of the Joint Chiefs of Staff John Shalikashvili and other military experts that we need to repeal the "don't ask, don't tell" policy. The key test for military service should be patriotism, a sense of duty, and a willingness to serve. Discrimination should be prohibited. The U.S. government has spent millions of dollars replacing troops kicked out of the military because of their sexual orientation. The President will work with military leaders to repeal the current policy and ensure it helps accomplish our national defense goals.

As Andrew Sullivan wrote in The Atlantic on May 13:

"Here we are, in the winter of 2009, with gay service members still being fired for the fact of their orientation. Here we are, with marriage rights spreading through the country and world and a president who cannot bring himself even to acknowledge these breakthroughs in civil rights, and having no plan in any distant future to do anything about it at a federal level. Here I am, facing a looming deadline to be forced to leave my American husband for good, and relocate abroad because the HIV travel and immigration ban remains in force and I have slowly run out of options (unlike most non-Americans with HIV who have no options at all).

And what is Obama doing about any of these things? What is he even *intending* at some point to do about these things? So far as I can read the administration, the answer is: nada. We're firing Arab linguists? So sorry. We won't recognize in any way a tiny minority of legally married couples in several states because they're, ugh, gay? We had no idea. There's a ban on HIV-positive tourists and immigrants? Really? Thanks for letting us know. Would you like to join Joe Solmonese and John Berry for cocktails? The inside of the White House is *fabulous* these days."

Although he has lifted the travel restrictions, as a University of Chicago law professor and a Harvard graduate he has to know what the Fourteenth

Amendment states. He also took an oath of office to support and defend the Constitution. To deny equal rights for lesbians and gays is a violation of his oath of office and he knows better. He is MUGWUMP-in-Chief.

I donated to and worked for the election of President Obama. I plan on doing so again. Although I am disappointed with his position and progress on equality, I am not a single issue activist.

Part Three: THE MEDIA AND OTHER MOUTHPIECES

ANITA BRYANT

Anita Bryant was born in Oklahoma in 1940. Eventually she was crowned Miss Oklahoma and was runner up in the Miss America pageant.[2397] She made hay on her second place finish. One of her biggest hits was *Paper Roses*.[2398]

In the 1970s, *Good Housekeeping* declared her the "Most Admired Woman in America" for three years running.[2399] She was hired to be the face of Florida Citrus, and sang *The Battle Hymn of the Republic* at President Lyndon Johnson's funeral.[2400] Bryant also plugged for Coca-Cola, Kraft Foods, Holiday Inn, and Tupperware.[2401] "A 1970 survey found that 75 percent of U.S. television viewers knew who she was and what she sold."[2402]

For all her fame, Bryant is probably most famous for what she started in 1977, when she led "Save our Children," a campaign to repeal a gay rights ordinance in Dade County.[2403]

The campaign was successful in Dade County, and her efforts then expanded to Florida legislators to ban gay adoptions.[2404] The County made an amendment to its human rights ordinance that made it illegal to discriminate in housing, employment, loans, and public accommodations based on "affectional or sexual preference."[2405] She pronounced: "I will lead such a crusade to stop it as this country has not seen before."[2406] The name of the group was based off Bryant's claim children would be molested or converted by so-called gay perverts: "As a mother, I know that homosexuals cannot biologically reproduce children; therefore, they must recruit our children."[2407] Through her efforts, it was once again legal to fire workers, deny housing, or refuse business based on how and with whom consenting adults have sex.[2408] In celebration, she promised to "seek help and change for homosexuals, whose sick and sad values belie the word 'gay' which they pathetically use to cover their unhappy lives."[2409]

In a *Playboy* article from 1978, Bryant commented on homosexuals:

> [Homosexuals] were asking for special privileges that violated the state [sodomy] law of Florida, not to mention God's law . . . Why do you think homosexuals are called fruits? It's because they eat the forbidden fruit of the tree of life . . . I was standing up for my rights as a mother to protect my children after I realized what the threat the homosexuals were posing meant . . . [The antidiscrimination ordinance] would have made it mandatory that flaunting homosexuals be hired in both the public and parochial schools . . . If

they're a legitimate minority group, then so are nail biters, dieters, fat people, short people and murderers . . . I have no respect for homosexuals who insist that their deviant lifestyle is normal. We pray for them, we try to lead them out of it . . . I love the sinner but I hate the sin.[2410]

Soon she was a national figure promoting the abolition of gay rights initiatives all across the country. In 1978, she supported the Briggs Initiative in California, which wanted to ban homosexuals and "gay lifestyle" advocates from public school teaching.[2411] The Briggs Initiative failed. After all her work, she still wrote in a fundraising letter, "I don't hate the homosexuals...But as a mother, I must protect my children from their evil influence."[2412]

A Fitting End

Her rise as a leading homophobe took her out of grace. At a news conference in Des Moines, Iowa, a gay activist posed as a reporter and hit Bryant in the face with a banana cream pie.[2413] The Des Moines incident was one of the first in which a political figure was pied.[2414] And *National Lampoon* published a parody ad for "Anita Bryant's Homo No Mo Macho-Building Course."[2415]

By 1980, her Florida Citrus contract was not renewed and she divorced her husband.[2416] In 1990, she remarried and moved to the Ozarks to revive her career; it didn't work.[2417] She racked up $116,000 in unpaid taxes during her spurt in Branson, Missouri.[2418] She filed Chapter 11 bankruptcy in Arkansas in 1997.[2419]

From 1998 to 2001, she attempted to open a new theater in Pigeon Forge, Tennessee, but she filed for Chapter 11 by December 2001.[2420] Bryant screwed over her employees at Pigeon Forge. The *St. Petersburg Times* (2002) quoted a once-devoted employee, who said of Bryant: "If I owed people like they owe people I would not be able to lay down at night and sleep."[2421] Workers were so poor and left unpaid that they stole popcorn and candy from the theater's concession stand so they could eat.[2422] In contrast, Bryant and her second husband were having no trouble paying their lease on a $350,000 home in the Smoky Mountains.[2423]

When the *Tulsa World* covered Bryant's concert appearance at her high school alma mater in 2007, one blogger noted, "How sad, the woman that was so full of hate so long ago is performing for free at a high school. I guess there really is a God and boy is he pissed at Anita Bryant."[2424] Another commented: "Good heavens, you old orange juice queen...you never did learn your lesson...not only morally bankrupt, but fiscally...and in three states!"[2425]

The *St. Petersburg Times* surmised her pathetic value: "Twenty-five years after her famous antigay crusade in Florida ended a high-flying career, Bryant, 62, is known in three other states for not paying bills. She has spent the past few years in small entertainment capitals across the Bible Belt, gamely attempting a comeback but leaving bankruptcy and ill will in her wake."[2426]

Bryant Doesn't Hate Gays

Her second husband said (2002), "It's not the gay people (she objects to), it's the sin" of homosexuality… She does not hate gay people."[2427] She told the *Tulsa World* (2007), "My stance has always been one out of love... The word of God has always been my guideline and I can't change that, nor would I want to."[2428]

Baptists Still Defend Her

Take this comment from Janet Folger at *World Daily Net* in March 2008: "Enter the real 'hate speech': pies in the face, kidnapping threats, death threats, threats to her children, acts of violence to her home. Like a scene out of Sodom, homosexual activists surrounded her home screaming at the top of their lungs. Her mother was afraid to open the front door. She lost her marriage. She lost her jobs and any means of supporting herself and her four children. She was a sacrificial lamb to wake a sleeping nation. She stood alone. And yet she stood….. This woman who sacrificed so much when she took a stand against normalization of homosexuality begs the Lord to have mercy on our country which has left his standards. When she performs the song on stage, she and the audience often have tears in their eyes."[2429]

Bryant's efforts in the gay bashing realm have been setback. On top of her personal wreck, her 1977 victory was overturned. Miami-Dade County reinstated human rights protections for homosexuals in 1998.[2430] And when the Christian Coalition backed a county-wide effort to repeal the law five years later, they lost and Bryant didn't even comment on the issue.[2431] One of her sons is reportedly gay.[2432]

RUSH LIMBAUGH

Rush Limbaugh is a nationally syndicated radio host and a darling to right-wing Republicans. He is arguably the most known conservative radio talk show host in the nation. He has been critical of gays. Perhaps the most telling incident occurred in 2004, when he implied high school students struggling with homosexality were infact militant homosexuals.

Militant Gays in School

In November 2004, a caller (a high school English teacher from South Carolina) talked about her concern for gay students and the trauma they endure at their age. Before the call was over, Limbaugh suggested the students were trumpeting their homosexuality and inviting dissent.[2433]

In the beginning, the caller pointed out, "I'm concerned about what their lives are going to be like, because whether they want to marry or not, they shouldn't, as little 16-, 17-, 18-year-old kids, face the vilification and the demeaning that -- that comes from primarily conservative sources. I don't hear love -- you know, 'Love the sinner, hate the sin?' They don't hear that…. And it's traumatizing. And I worry for them."[2434]

Limbaugh responded, "…what's important when you go to school…? Is it your sexual identity or learning? What's important when you go to school? Learning how to prepare yourself for the rest of your life or trumpeting your sexuality?..."[2435] The caller did not think the students were trumpeting their sexuality, Limbaugh interjected, "…how do we know it? I mean, there's -- there's -- how do we know who's gay and who's straight unless somebody's out there making a big case about it? I think …some people are inviting dissent."[2436]

Then in a discussion about high school gays, Limbaugh pivoted: "I think some of the militants in the gay community are actually asking for this fight, because … they want to be confrontational."[2437] The caller responded, "I'm in South Carolina. We don't have militant gays. I have students who have been hurt and have come to me to talk about it."[2438]

Rush's View On Women

1) Feminism was established to help ugly women. In August 2005, Limbaugh said, "feminism was established so as to allow unattractive women easier access to the mainstream of society. And even to this day, people pooh-poohed this and say it's insensitive: 'How can you possibly say something like that?' Well, because I mean it, because I believe there's something to it."[2439]

2) If the alleged criminal is a hot guy, women shouldn't be on the jury. He said: "Women should not be allowed on juries when the accused is a stud."[2440]

3) Limbaugh elevated the term feminazi. He has continued to defend his past use of "feminazi," claiming the term is "right" and "accurate."[2441] On the June 22, 2005 broadcast of *The Rush Limbaugh Show*, he said, "I haven't used that term on this program in years. But it still gets to 'em, doesn't it? And you know why? [chuckles] Because it's right. Because it's accurate. [laughs] And I'm not going to apologize, but I will apologize if it hurts your feelings. But you know what? I think if you're offended, it's your problem. It's not mine."[2442] Limbaugh was inaccurate; he had used the word numerous times in the spring of 2004.[2443]

JAMES DOBSON & FOCUS ON THE FAMILY

James Dobson is a child psychologist.[2444] Dobson mixes psychological and biblical "expertise."[2445] He founded the nonprofit organization Focus on the Family, which is located in Colorado Springs.[2446] Later, Dobson created the Family Research Council, which Gary Bauer eventually led (and Tony Perkins currently leads).[2447] Focus on the Family is a spiritual organization, and the FRC is Focus on the Family's public policy tool. Dobson stepped down as president in May 2003.[2448]

Dobson is generally credited with selling over 16 million books, and his radio broadcasts reaches 7 million weekly. His Focus on the Family newsletter went to 3 million donors, which paralleled the circulation of *Newsweek.*[2449] *Time* dubbed (2005) Dobson "The Culture Warrior."[2450]

His breakthrough book, *Dare to Discipline*, was released in 1970. It "encouraged parents to spank their children with belts or switches and to leave such items on the child's dresser to remind her of the consequences of challenging authority."[2451]

Dobson complains about continued funding for Planned Parenthood, safe-sex education, and the distribution of condoms.[2452] He demands loyalty from his network at Focus on the Family, comes off as a zealot, and customarily expects to get his way.[2453]

Dobson & Politics

In 1998, Dobson told Congressmen at a meeting in D.C., "Does the Republican Party want our votes—no strings attached—to court us every two years, and then to say, 'Don't call me. I'll call you,' and not to care for the moral law of the universe?...If it is, I'm gone, and if I go—I'm not going to threaten anybody because I don't influence the world—but if I go, I will do everything I can to take as many people with me as possible."[2454]

The *New York Times* said he was "one of the nation's most influential evangelical leaders, [who] has always sought to keep his public persona at a safe distance from the battlefield of partisan politics."[2455] Until 2004. He started backing candidates and even held a rally bringing in 20,000 supporters. The reason? "There are dangers, and that is why I have never done it before [entering politics so vocally]… But the attack and assault on marriage is so distressing that I just feel like I can't remain silent."[2456]In the 2000 campaign, Dobson didn't even endorse Gary Bauer's presidential campaign, perhaps because of the Bauer marital scandal that developed.[2457]

"Values" Victory In 2004

When asked if he thought "moral values … won it for George W. Bush," Dobson said there was "no question about it. My take on it is that people who are hard-working, middle American, mostly, who care about their families and care about moral values often go to church on Sunday, have been watching what's been going on in this country. They've seen the moral decline, they've seen what's happening in the schools, they've seen what's happening especially in Hollywood, and the entertainment industry, and then they saw what Massachusetts tried to do to the family. They were very alarmed by that. And we're not just talking about Evangelicals, they're Catholics, mainline Christians, people with no faith at all, but hold those views. And when they got an opportunity, they said enough is enough."[2458]

Dobson also stated, "I have no doubt whatsoever about the fact that the issue of marriage, of the effort to impose same-sex marriage on this country and on the family, especially by the courts, who are unelected and unaccountable and who are arrogant and determined to impose their views on us, that stuck in the hearts of the people, and when they got an opportunity, they expressed themselves at the polls."[2459]

Pro-life Occasionally

Dobson has said George W. Bush "is more actively pro-life and pro-family and pro-moral than any previous president."[2460] As Randall Balmer once aptly questioned: "Dobson has fashioned an entire career out of being 'pro-life' and 'pro-family.' But how does he (or Bush) reconcile that with support for capital punishment, torture, or the war in Iraq, which utterly fails to meet just war criteria?"[2461]

Fanaticism Is Always A Threat. What if it's Christian?

The irony of the 2004 election was that the war on terror, an issue helping Bush, was fought against Islamic extremists. Yet Bush's victory was made possible by Christian fundamentalists.

Sean Hannity stood up for Dobson in a *FOX News* interview: "Let me read a quote to you, if I can, and we don't have a lot of time here. And this is from [former *Washington Post* reporter] Carl Bernstein, he said, 'We have a minority religious group who want to impose their religious values on a secular country that has separation of church and state.' And he goes on, 'I think what is dangerous is we're fighting a war against fundamentalism that we must win, and if we become fundamentalists and try and establish values in our own country while trying to fight fundamentalist Muslim people who want to kill us, I think that's a terrible thing.' This is how some of these so-called journalists and pundits are seeing this. They can't be more wrong."[2462]

Dobson: Sen. Leahy Hates God's People

In November 2004, Dobson appeared on ABC's *This Week with George Stephanopoulos*, who quoted Dobson in the *Daily Oklahoman*. That paper reported Dobson's comment that, "Patrick Leahy is a God's people hater. I don't know if he hates God, but he hates God's people."[2463] Stephanopoulos told Dobson: "Now, Dr. Dobson, that doesn't sound like a particularly Christian thing to say. Do you think you owe Senator Leahy an apology?"[2464]

Dobson's response: "George, you think you ought to lecture me on what a Christian is all about? You know, I think -I think I'll stand by the things I have said. Patrick Leahy has been in opposition to most of the things that I believe. He is the one that took the reference to God out of the oath."[2465]

Stephanopoulos responded, "But Dr. Dobson, excuse me for a second. You use the word hate. You said that he's a 'God's people hater.' How do you back that up?"[2466] Dobson said, "Well, there's been an awful lot of hate expressed in this election. And most of it has been aimed at those who hold to conservative Christian views. He is certainly not the only one to take a position like that. But I think that that is -that's where he's coming from. He has certainly opposed most of the things that conservative Christians stand for."[2467] Dobson reaffirmed there would be no apology.[2468]

Dobson: Remove Specter From Senate Judiciary Committee

As a "private" individual, Dobson endorsed the campaign for conservative candidates like Representative Patrick J. Toomey's unsuccessful challenge to Senator Arlen Specter (then R-PA) in April 2004.[2469] After Bush's reelection, Specter said, "When you talk about judges who would change the right of a woman to choose, who'd overturn Roe versus Wade, I think that is unlikely…And I have said that bluntly during the course of the campaign, that Roe versus Wade was inviolate."[2470]

Dobson said (Nov.2004), "I'm very, very concerned about the possibility of Senator Specter being chairman of the Judiciary Committee because as such, he will have enormous power to stand in the roadway and block most of what — most of the social agenda that President Bush has promised to work for. Not only the judges, but he is — you know, rabidly pro-choice, he is against the federal marriage amendment."[2471] Weren't the Republicans selling themselves as a big-tent party? Dobson said (Nov.2004), "I don't want to be in the big tent. No.-- I think the party ought to stand for something."[2472]

A Classic Focus on the Family Response

The New Jersey Supreme Court ruled the Boy Scouts of America had to allow homosexual Scout leaders into their organization.[2473] This was the Focus on the Family's response, written by "ex-gay" Mike Haley, who was the Youth and Gender Specialist at Focus on the Family:

> The prize to the winner of this culture war is the children. I should know - I was once a gay teen. I was drawn into homosexuality through my first sexual experience with an adult male when I was only 12. Thus began a series of homosexual encounters that continued through my teen years. Simply put, I was starved for love. I was desperate for attention from adult males, in large part to make up for the attention I hadn't received from my father. In school, I remember feeling different from the other guys. I must be gay, I concluded. I became completely hopeless at the age of 16 after being told by my high school counselor that I was born homosexual and couldn't do anything about it. The message that I couldn't change - not intolerance by society - is what drove me to despair. Convinced that my sexual orientation was unchangeable, I began a 16-year journey steeped in homosexual sex and empty relationships. It led me to feeling dirty and worthless. In my experience, gay life was far from satisfying. It wasn't until years later - through the power of God - I began my walk away from homosexuality. I began to understand what real love is, and that my worth comes from my Creator, not from other men. I now have a new perspective on life and a freedom I never thought was possible when I was a teen-ager. I can at last look in the mirror without feeling overwhelmed by guilt and remorse. With my wife by my side, I am working to reach youth with the message of hope that I never had as a teen. [2474]

This author does not dispute Haley's argument that the BSA should not be forced to make gays scout leaders. Just as it is unconstitutional to tell what two private individuals should do in their private bedroom, it is unconstitutional to tell a private organization (BSA) what to do with their membership. However, sadly, Haley's comments on homosexuality are common responses from Focus on the Family.

The comments parley the position by right-wing "family" groups toward homosexuals. First, Haley says it's a "culture war." It's never about civil rights. Second, it's about the "children." Never mind that the children who grow up gay are outcast by their family and religion; or feel so unaccepted they cover it up and be "straight" (see Ted Haggard, Roy Cohn, and Larry Craig).

Next, the classic case of "I am gay because I was molested" comes up. This excuse has been used by the Mark Foleys and Ted Haggards of the world. When ever ex-gays or "not-so-straight straights" have to admit their gay behavior is wrong, they don't blame it on themselves, but rather convenient adults who touched them. No surprise Mike Haley used this excuse. Make all homosexuals molesters: that's the "pro-family way" at Focus on the Family. Haley is nothing but an "ex-gay" trashing openly gay people in the process.

As Haley's argument continues, he blames the public school educator, here it's the guidance counselor. "The public school teachers are making our kids gay by saying 'gay is okay'" argument. That argument neglects that fact that public school teachers must be accepting of all students, no matter their background. Teachers have to do this (and should) because it's public law.

Finally, Haley's whole argument is the Religious Right's assertion homosexuality can be changed, (and thereby second guesses the work of God).

Dobson: Homosexuality Comes From Identity Crisis

In his book, *Bringing Up Boys*, Dr. Dobson claimed, "At about three to five years of age…a lad gradually pulls away from his mom and sisters in an effort to formulate a masculine identity. …When fathers are absent at that time, or if they are inaccessible, distant, or abusive, their boys have only a vague notion of what it means to be male. … One of the primary objectives of parents is to help boys identify their gender assignments and understand what it means to be a man."[2475] Dobson has repeated this position elsewhere.

When asked if being gay is a choice, Dobson said (Nov.2006), "I never did believe that…Neither do I believe it's genetic. …I said that on your program one time and both of us got a lot of mail for it. I don't blame homosexuals for being angry when people say they've made a choice to be gay, because they don't. It usually comes out of very, very early childhood, and this is very controversial, but this is what I believe and many other people believe, that is has to do with an identity crisis that occurs too early to remember it, where a boy is born with an attachment to his mother and she is everything to him for about 18 months, and between 18 months and five years, he needs to detach from her and to reattach to his father. It's a very important developmental task, and if his dad is gone or abusive or disinterested or maybe there's just not a good fit there, what's he going to do? He remains bonded to his mother and ..." [2476]

Larry King interrupted: "Is that clinically true or is that theory?"[2477] Dobson said, "…it's clinically true, but it's controversial. What homosexual activists, especially, would like everybody to believe is that it is genetic, that they don't have any choice. If it were genetic, Larry—and before we went on this show, you and I were talking about twin studies—if it were genetic, identical twins would all have it. Identical twins, if you have a homosexuality in one twin, it would be there in the other…. So, it can't be simply genetic. I do believe that there are temperaments that individuals are born with that make them more vulnerable and maybe more likely to move in that direction, but it usually is related to a sexual identity crisis."[2478]

Vulnerable? Dobson thinks a person could be vulnerable to homosexuality as the influenza virus makes one vulnerable to the flu. Everyone might catch it.

Dobson's belief detachment from the father causes homosexuality is also supported by other social conservative groups. Jerry Leach, the director of Reality Resources, is a former transsexual and transvestite; he has said the "disconnect" with his father was part of his lifelong struggle with gender confusion.[2479] Leach claims to have worked with over 2,000 transgendered men, noting, "The connection with the male, or the failed connection with the male – the most significant male being that of a father – has been one of the most blame worthy causes of the condition."[2480]

Dobson on Gay Marriage

1) "The gospel of Jesus Christ will be severely curtailed." Dobson wrote:

> "The family has been God's primary vehicle for evangelism since the beginning. Its most important assignment has been the propagation of the human race and the handing down of the faith to our children. Malachi 2:15 reads, referring to husbands and wives, 'Has not the Lord made them one? In flesh and spirit they are His. And why one? Because He was seeking godly offspring. So guard yourself in your spirit, and do not break faith with the wife of your youth.' That responsibility to teach the next generation will never recover from the loss of committed, God-fearing families. The younger generation and those yet to come will be deprived of the Good News, as has already occurred in France, Germany, and other European countries. Instead of providing for a father and mother, the advent of homosexual marriage will create millions of motherless children and fatherless kids. Are we now going to join the Netherlands and Belgium to become the third country in the history of the world to "normalize" and legalize behavior that has been prohibited by God himself? Heaven help us if we do!"[2481]

2)The gay activists will stop at nothing. Dobson wrote:

> "…. marriage between homosexuals will destroy traditional marriage is that this is the ultimate goal of activists, and they will not stop until they achieve it. The history of the gay and lesbian movement has been that its adherents quickly move the goal line as soon as the previous one has been breached, revealing even more shocking and outrageous objectives. In the present instance, homosexual activists, heady with power and exhilaration, feel the political climate is right to tell us what they have wanted all along. This is the real deal: Most gays and lesbians do not want to marry each other. That would

entangle them in all sorts of legal constraints. Who needs a lifetime commitment to one person? The intention here is to create an entirely different legal structure. With marriage as we know it gone, everyone would enjoy all the legal benefits of marriage (custody rights, tax-free inheritance, joint ownership of property, health care and spousal citizenship, and much more) without limiting the number of partners or their gender. Nor would "couples" be bound to each other in the eyes of the law. This is clearly where the movement is headed. If you doubt that this is the motive, read what is in the literature today. Activists have created a new word to replace the outmoded terms infidelity, adultery, cheating and promiscuity."[2482]

3) **Gay marriage will destroy marriage.** Dobson wrote:

"We must all become soberly aware of a deeply disturbing reality: The homosexual agenda is not marriage for gays. It is marriage for no one. And despite what you read or see in the media, it is definitely not monogamous. What will happen sociologically if marriage becomes anything or everything or nothing? The short answer is that the State will lose its compelling interest in marital relationships altogether. After marriage has been redefined, divorces will be obtained instantly, will not involve a court, and will take on the status of a driver's license or a hunting permit. With the family out of the way, all rights and privileges of marriage will accrue to gay and lesbian partners without the legal entanglements and commitments heretofore associated with it."[2483]

4) Gays typically have 1000 partners in a lifetime. Dobson wrote:

"The implications for children in a world of decaying families are profound. Because homosexuals are rarely monogamous, often having as many as three hundred or more partners in a lifetime — some studies say it is typically more than one thousand — children in those polyamorous situations are caught in a perpetual coming and going. It is devastating to kids, who by their nature are enormously conservative creatures. They like things to stay just the way they are, and they hate change. Some have been known to eat the same brand of peanut butter throughout childhood."[2484]

5) Gay Marriage will ruin the economy, health care system. Dobson wrote:

"This could be the straw that breaks the back of the insurance industry in Western nations, as millions of new dependents become eligible for coverage. Every HIV-positive patient needs only to find a partner to receive the same coverage as offered to an employee. It is estimated by some analysts that an initial threefold increase in premiums can be anticipated; even with that, it may not be profitable for companies to stay in business. And how about the cost to American businesses? Will they be able to provide health benefits? If not, can physicians, nurses, and technicians be expected to work for nothing or to provide their services in exchange for a vague promise of payments from indigent patients? Try selling that to a neurosurgeon or an orthopedist who has to pay increased premiums for malpractice insurance. The entire health care system could implode. Is it possible? Yes. Will it happen? I don't know."[2485]

Dobson doesn't mention than many with AIDS may be single people already covered by health care. And of course he is implying AIDS is just a homosexual desease.

6) Dobson: Social Security will be severely stressed…With gay marriage, Dobson warned: "Again, with millions of new eligible dependents, what will happen to the Social Security system that is already facing bankruptcy? If it does collapse, what will that mean for elderly people who must rely totally on that meager support? Who is thinking through these draconian possibilities as we careen toward 'a brave new world'?"[2486] Apparently "Dr." Dobson doesn't think homosexuals presently received social security benefits.

7) Dobson: Other nations are watching our march toward homosexual marriage and will follow our lead. In truth, we are trailing the rest of civilized society. But Dobson warned if gay marriage was accepted in the U.S., it would spread worldwide. He wrote:

> "Marriage among homosexuals will spread throughout the world, just as pornography did after the Nixon Commission declared obscene material 'beneficial' to mankind. Almost instantly, the English-speaking countries liberalized their laws against smut. America continues to be the fountainhead of filth and immorality, and its influence is global. Dr. Darrell Reid, president of Focus on the Family Canada, told me recently that his country is carefully monitoring what is happening in the United States. If we take this step off a cliff, the family on every continent will splinter at an accelerated rate. Conversely, our Supreme Court has made it clear that it looks to European and Canadian law in the interpretation of our Constitution. What an outrage! That should have been grounds for impeachment, but the Congress, as usual, remained passive and silent."[2487]

Dobson: Haggard Can Be Restored

In late November 2006, Larry King asked Dobson about Ted Haggard: "...when you say 'restoration,' you mean restore him from being gay to not gay or what do you mean?"[2488] Dobson said, "Yeah, probably that, too. But in Galatians 6.1, there is a scripture that says when, 'Brothers, when one of you falls into sin, those who are spiritual should work to restore him gently.' That is the scripture behind the restoration process and that word, and three men, now will oversee discipline, punishment—if there is any, therapy, his behavior, his money, his future and will lead him if he is willing to cooperate, and apparently he is—through a restoration process. We don't want to just kick him out, I mean, he's lost his church, obviously, but there's still concern for him as an individual."[2489]

Dobson & SpongeBob

Dr. Dobson, a Ph.D., without even seeing the cartoon, blasted poor little SpongeBob for appearing in a message that supposedly promoted a homosexual lifestyle. As Keith Olbermann noted, the cartoon promoted tolerance of others but "contained no reference to sex, sexual lifestyle, sexual identity ...."

Dr. Dobson must have studied with Dr. Bill Frist, making scientific decisions without evidence. I am sure SpongeBob and the Teletubbies are laughing in their oatmeal.

TONY PERKINS & FAMILY RESEARCH COUNCIL

Tony Perkins is president of the Family Research Council, which is a conservative Christian think-tank and public policy foundation. James Dobson founded the Family Research Council as the Washington lobbying arm of his Focus on the Family.[2490]

The FRC's webpage states, "Since joining FRC in the fall of 2003 he has launched new initiatives to affirm and defend the Judeo-Christian values that this nation is founded upon. Tony Perkins and FRC have led the way in defending religious freedom in the public square, protecting the unborn and their mothers, defending and strengthening one man/one woman marriage and promoting pro-family public policy."[2491] Perkins hosts a regular national radio program, "Washington Watch Weekly," and broadcasts a daily commentary heard on over 300 stations nationwide.[2492] Perkins also sends daily email updates to tens of thousands of grassroots activists.[2493]

Perkins is also a veteran of the U.S. Marine Corps, and a former police officer and television news reporter.[2494] Perkins received his undergraduate degree from Liberty University, a Master's Degree in Public Administration from Louisiana State University, and an honorary doctorate in theology from Liberty University.[2495] FRC's website proudly notes, "Tony and Lawana, married in 1986, have five children."[2496]

He served two terms in the Louisiana legislature. There, he failed to get the Louisiana legislature to exclude lesbians and gays from protection from hate crimes; Perkins later said of the incident: "There was not a single person there working on behalf of families."[2497] Perkins implies gays don't care about families.

The FRC's webpage on Perkins bio stated, "Although he had no opposition for re-election, he kept his pledge to serve only two terms and left office at the completion of his term in 2004."[2498]

FRC & Focus on the Family

The FRC website explains the difference: "While FRC and Focus on the Family are both dedicated to promoting family values and uplifting the family, FRC is a public policy organization in Washington, D.C. that defends and promotes the pro-family agenda. Focus on the Family is a Christian ministry in Colorado that evangelizes and ministers to families."[2499] At its website, the FRC said it "was founded in 1983 as an organization dedicated to the promotion of marriage and family and the sanctity of human life in national policy. Through books, pamphlets, media appearances, public events, debates and testimony, FRC's team of experienced policy experts review data and analyze proposals that impact family law and policy in Congress and the executive branch."[2500]

History of FRC leadership

According to Bill Berkowitz, "The idea of the Family Research Council "originated at the 1980 White House Conference on Families ... [where] James Dobson stood out because of his rare combination of Christian social values and academic and professional credentials." Three years later, the FRC incorporated as a nonprofit educational institution in the District of Columbia; its founding board included Dobson and two noted psychiatrists, Armand Nicholoi, Jr. of Harvard University and George Rekers of the University of South Carolina."[2501]

In the early 1980s, the FRC was under the leadership of Jerry Regier, a former Reagan Administration official at the Department of Health and Human

Services.[2502] Gary Bauer, a domestic policy advisor to President Reagan, succeeded Regier in 1988.[2503] Some have argued, however, that Bauer was overshadowed by other works at the time by Ralph Reed.[2504] Bauer ran the FRC from 1988 to 1999, and then ran for president.[2505] Bauer was replaced by Ken Connor, and Bauer founded American Values.[2506] Connor was replaced by Perkins.[2507]

Woody Jenkins' Secretive Alliance

Woody Jenkins and Tony Perkins have a close relationship; and Perkins ran Jenkin's Republican campaign for U.S. Senate (1996).[2508]

According to *The Nation*, "For Tony Perkins, Justice Sunday was the fulfillment of a strategy devised more than two decades ago by his political mentor, Woody Jenkins. In May 1981, in the wake of Ronald Reagan's presidential victory, Jenkins and some fifty other conservative activists met at the Northern Virginia home of direct-mail pioneer Richard Viguerie to plot the growth of their movement. The Council for National Policy (CNP), an ultra-secretive, right-wing organization, was the outcome of that meeting. The CNP hooked up theocrats like R.J. Rushdoony, Pat Robertson and Jerry Falwell with wealthy movement funders like Amway founder Richard DeVos and beer baron Joseph Coors. As DeVos famously said, the CNP 'brings together the doers with the donors.'"[2509]

In 1999, Texas Gov. George Bush addressed the CNP, where he tried to prove he was a conservative.[2510] Bush did not release a public transcript his speech; in fact, he refused.[2511] Supposedly he promised he would appoint only anti-abortion judges if elected.[2512]

Perkins and David Duke

In 1996, Perkins paid former KKK Grand Wizard David Duke $82,500 for his mailing list when Perkins was the campaign manager for Woody Jenkins' U.S. Senate campaign in Louisiana.[2513]

According to *The Nation*, the Federal Election Commission fined the Perkins-run campaign $3,000 for trying to hide the money paid to Duke.[2514] The Duke list was learned about because Jenkins contested the election of his opponent Mary Landrieu, "But during the contest period, Perkins's surreptitious payment to Duke was exposed through an investigation conducted by the FEC, which fined the Jenkins campaign.'[2515]

The Family Research Council responded, "The assertions made by Mr. Blumenthal [at *The Nation*] are untrue and a distortion of the facts."[2516]

Perkins and the CCC

In 2001, Perkins spoke to the Lousiana chapter of the Council of Conservative Citizens (CCC). [2517] The CCC is a white supremist organization that succeded the White Citizens Councils that battled integration in the South.[2518] That information was reported in *The Nation*. Similar information on the CCC and David Duke has been reported in *The Vancouver Sun* and by the Southern Poverty Law Center.[2519]

The CCC's statement of principles says: "We also oppose all efforts to mix the races of mankind, to promote non-white races over the European-American people through so-called 'affirmative action' and similar measures, to destroy or denigrate the European-American heritage, including the heritage of the Southern people, and to force the integration of the races."[2520] Perkins acknowledged a CCC speech "but claimed he could not recall what he said."[2521] Perkins' told *The Vancouver Sun* (2006) he hadn't spoke to the CCC in 10 years ("Never spoke to them again. That was over a decade ago,").[2522] That meant he hadn't spoken with the CCC since 1996. The comment was false; *The Sun* found a CCC newsletter validating Perkins' 2001 appearance before the organization.[2523] At that point, the God-touting FRC did not deny the facts.[2524]

Media Matters surmises: "Despite extensive reporting on Perkins' connections to Duke and the CCC by *The Vancouver Sun*, *The Nation*, and the Southern Poverty Law Center, the U.S. media have generally failed to note Perkins' history. This omission occurred while Perkins emerged as a major national spokesman for the Christian right, using his platform as a regular pundit on CNN and Fox News, and in *The Washington Post* and *The New York Times* to attack opponents for their 'anti-Christian' attitudes." Since he became head of FRC, only a few national papers have reported on Perkins' Duke payment, and even less have reported on Perkins' CCC speech.[2525]

Revenge

When Mary Landrieu's Senate seat was up for election (2002), Perkins tried to avenge Woody Jenkin's 1996 defeat.[2526] However, Perkins was routinely asked questions about his involvement with David Duke.[2527] Perkins denied having anything to do with Duke, and denounced Duke.[2528] Still, Perkins's signature was on the document authorizing the purchase of Duke's list.[2529]

Perkins's meeting with the CCC before his campaign also showed the root of his associations.[2530] James Dobson backed Perkins; so did a bunch of CNP members, but Perkins wasn't even the leading Republican coming out of the primary.[2531] After his defeat, Dobson approved the promotion of Perkins, who moved to Washington to lead the Family Research Council.[2532]

Justice Sunday

Justice Sunday was a 2005 rally portraying Democrats as being "against people of faith."[2533] Speakers accused Democratic Senators of "filibustering people of faith."[2534] Many of the speakers at Justice Sunday said their plight as conservative Christians was like the civil rights movement.[2535] One of Justice Sunday's fliers read, "The filibuster was once abused to protect racial bias, and it is now being used against people of faith."[2536]

The event's main sponsor was Perkins, who emceed the event.[2537] At the event, Perkins gave phone numbers of senators wavering on President Bush's judicial nominees.[2538]

Sen. Bill Frist (R-TN) spoke at Justice Sunday.[2539] At Justice Sunday, Perkins introduced Frist as "a friend of the family."[2540] *The Nation* reported on the signifcance of the event: "With Justice Sunday, Perkins's ambition to become a national conservative leader was ratified; Bill Frist's presidential campaign for 2008 was advanced with the Christian right; and the faithful were imbued with the notion that they are being victimized by liberal Democratic evildoers."[2541] Eventually Bill Frist decided against running for president, but there is no doubt he tried to align himself with the Perkins crowd.

James Dobson told Justice Sunday, "The biggest Holocaust in world history came out of the Supreme Court" with the *Roe v. Wade* decision.[2542] Two weeks earlier on his radio show, Dobson compared "black robed men" on the Supreme Court to "men in white robes, the Ku Klux Klan."[2543]

Christian inconsistancy ruled Justice Sunday. For example, William Donohue, head of the Catholic League spoke at the event. So did Southern Baptist Theological Seminary president Dr. Albert Mohler.[2544] In a 2000 interview, Mohler said, "As an evangelical, I believe that the Roman Catholic Church is a false church…It teaches a false gospel. And the Pope himself holds a false and unbiblical office."[2545] But Donohue had no problem coming to an event held at Highview Baptist Church, in Louisville, Kentucky, which was Mohler's home church.[2546] Donohue said, "We're fed up and we're on the same side…And if the secular left is worried, they should be worried."[2547] Now that's true teamwork: a Catholic working with a Baptist, who believes Catholics are going to burn in hell.[2548] The year after Justice Sunday, Mohler wrote (9.16.2006) the power the Pope "holds is an unbiblical institution based in a monarchial ministry that is incompatible with the New Testament's vision of the church. Furthermore, he claims also to be a head of state –a situation that adds untold layers of additional confusion."[2549]

Other positions of Perkins

1) Terry Shiavo should live. In 2005, Perkins spent a great deal of time rallying support to keep Terry Shiavo alive. Shiavo was the Florida woman who died in March 2005 after being in a "persistent vegetative state" for more than 15 years.[2550] Americans United for Separation of Church and State executive director, Rev. Barry Lynn, surmised Perkins actions: "During the controversy Perkins repeatedly issued Schiavo commentaries that referred to her husband as 'estranged,' despite the fact that Michael Schiavo was caring for her, and [he] mention[ed] the 'questionable circumstances' surrounding her collapse, clearly implying foul play…I've worked in Washington a long time, but I've never seen anything as manipulative as what Perkins and the FRC did over Terri

Schiavo…They took a terminally ill woman and turned her into a political tool to gain leverage in Congress."[2551] In truth, Michael Schiavo became a nurse after Terri's injury so he could better care for her.[2552] Justice Sunday was held shortly after Schiavo's death.[2553]

2) AIDS victims should die. Perkins is against AIDS relief in Africa, "I applaud the actions of the African Anglican churches [in not giving money for AIDS relief]. No amount of silver is worth sacrificing your duty to your congregation and to God."[2554]

3) Liberals are unpatriotic. Just before the 2006 midterm elections, John Kerry made a botched joke about U.S. troops, Iraq, and President Bush. Tony Perkins said the joke by Kerry, a Vietnam veteran, "shows that many of the liberals just don't have an understanding of how there are people that have such commitment to this country that they would volunteer to defend the ways and the ideas of this nation."[2555]

4) Sex education is bad. According to it's website, "FRC maintains that contraceptive-based or comprehensive sex education is destructive, providing mixed risk messaging and an overly narrow focus on physical health alone."[2556] Perkins has advocated this position.

5) A radical minority threatens religion. Tony Perkins used his own radio show, *Washington Watch Weekly*, to level accusations of bigotry against Democrats (4.18.2005): "It's almost as if there's a radical minority in the U.S. Senate that's saying this [to Bush's judicial picks]: 'You have to choose between your faith and public service.'"[2557]

6) President Bush is critical of prayer. Perkins said (March 2006): "….on the issue of where Americans feel the country is moving, clearly there is a growing hostility toward Christianity. I mean, think back when FDR, … was president, and he led the nation in prayer from the White House. If President Bush were to do that today, before I could get back to my office I would be run over by ACLU attorneys on their way to file suit in federal court."[2558] The comments were to a straw man. President Bush had issued five annual national days of prayer (all in early May) in each of his first five years of his presidency.[2559]

7) Russ Feingold is a traitor. In 2006, when Sen. Russ Feingold proposed a censure of the President Bush for authorizing warrant-less domestic eavesdropping, Perkins said Feingold's proposal was "borderline treasonous behavior."[2560]

Family Research Council on Homosexuals

1) Sex should only occur within marriage. According to its website, "FRC believes the context for the full expression of human sexuality is within the bonds of marriage between one man and one woman. Upholding this standard of sexual behavior would help to reverse many of the destructive aspects of the sexual revolution, including sexually transmitted disease rates of epidemic proportion, high out-of-wedlock birth rates, adultery, and homosexuality."[2561]

2) FRC backs reparative therapy. The Family Research Council's website notes the "FRC does not consider homosexuality, bi-sexuality, and transgenderism as acceptable alternative lifestyles or sexual 'preferences'; they are unhealthy and destructive to individual persons, families, and society. Compassion compels us to support the healing of those who wish to change their destructive behavior."[2562]

3) Homosexuality is unnatural, but homosexuals need sympathy. According to it's website, the "Family Research Council believes that homosexual conduct is harmful to the persons who engage in it and to society at large, and can never be affirmed. It is by definition unnatural, and as such is associated with negative physical and psychological health effects. While the origins of same-sex attractions may be complex, there is no convincing evidence that a homosexual identity is ever something genetic or inborn. We oppose the vigorous efforts of homosexual activists to demand that homosexuality be accepted as equivalent to heterosexuality in law, in the media, and in schools. ...Sympathy must be extended to those who struggle with unwanted same-sex attractions, and every effort should be made to assist such persons to overcome those attractions, as many already have."[2563]

Perkins on Gay Marriage

1) Gay marriage compares to incest. Tony Perkins said, "No one has unrestrained liberties in this country to marry whomever they want. Someone can't marry a close blood relative or an underage person. There are restrictions upheld in almost every civilization for millennia."[2564]

2) Interracial marriage argument a "red herring." A week after Prop 8 passed, Dan Savage debated Tony Perkins on CNN. Savage is a gay activist and has written about his adopted son and marriage.[2565] Perkins argued the California Supreme Court was wrong for declaring homosexual couples had a right to marry.[2566] Savage argued the importance of 1967 U.S. Supreme Court case, *Loving v. Virginia*, which found interracial couples had a constitutional right to marry and struck down the bans that still existed in 16 states.[2567] Perkins told Savage, "You try to compare this to interracial marriage. It is not the same thing. There were extra provisions put that would prohibit people that were man and woman to marry. This is redefining marriage. It's a totally different issue."[2568]

3) Blinded with Science. Tony Perkins said when it came to gay marriage, "the social sciences show overwhelmingly that children do better with a mom and dad."[2569] Dan Savage interjected, "That is a lie. Those are studies that are funded by bigots; more bigots to justify bigotry. The studies you cite have all the validity of tobacco institute studies telling us in the 70's and 80's that smoking was safe."[2570]

4) Marriage is a 5,000 year old institution. Perkins told CNN (Nov.2008), "There's an attempt to redefine a 5,000-year-old institution called marriage and the people of California have twice now gone to the polls and defended it."[2571]
5) Gay's don't play by rules with gay marriage, riot. In Nov. 2008, Perkins told CNN, "The people [of California] have played by the rules. I mean, why will not the homosexual activists quit rioting and quit attacking Mormons and using religious bigotry."[2572] When confronted that anti-prop 8 protests weren't riots, Perkins said, "Well, I mean they've spray painted churches in California; they've been jumping on police cars…there were arrests the other night."[2573]
6) Gays shouldn't parent. Anderson Cooper asked (Nov.2008) about children being raised by gays, and that it would "actually help" the children if their parents were married. Perkins said, "You don't change public policy to accommodate a few. You shape public policy to what is beneficial to society as a whole."[2574]
7) VP Cheney's opinion only strengthens gay bashers. Perkins said Cheney's softer rhetoric on gays, including about his lesbian daughter, emboldened conservatives like Phyllis Schlafly to help draft the Republican Party platform (August 2004) to oppose not only gay marriage but other forms of legal recognition for gay couples, including civil unions and domestic partnerships.[2575]

Why doesn't the FRC go after divorce?

Here, the FRC gives excuses. They post the question on their websites: "With all of the divorces that are occurring in the United States, shouldn't FRC address this issue instead of same-sex marriage?"[2576] Their answer:

> Divorce causes tremendous devastation to families, children, and society. The issue of divorce reform has been an issue that FRC has dealt with since we began in 1983. We have consistently called for the repeal of no-fault divorce laws in all 50 states. We continue to promote the sanctity of marriage, and we will not relent in our insistence to reform divorce laws. Yet, the issue of divorce reform at the political level has struggled to receive much attention. Currently, FRC is faced with protecting marriage from being "redefined" so as not to include more than "just" one man and one woman, and this is what we must deal with at the present time. With our limited resources and staff number and considering the fact that our nation is seriously threatened by the legalization of same-sex "marriage," this is our current priority when it comes to public policy about marriage. We do, however, have a booklet that may be of interest to you, called "Deterring Divorce."[2577]

Why doesn't the FRC care about capital punishment?

The FRC claims to be a moral leader, but when it comes to less politically advantageous positions, they neglect an answer. For example, it's website comments on capital punishment: "Family Research Council, mindful of the strongly held and often conflicting views of many of our constituents on this important question, has never taken a definitive position for or against capital punishment. FRC's Board of Directors and staff wholly recognize and independently grapple with the central question pertaining to the death penalty: Can capital punishment be morally justified? Needless to say, a consensus within

FRC has never been reached regarding the moral permissibility of capital punishment."[2578] Capital punishment is too tough to take a position, but homosexuals are easier to judge.

Julaine K. Appling
Desperately Seeking A Personal Atonement

Juliane Appling is the CEO of the Wisconsin Family Council. She led the fight for faceless, nameless donors to ban gay marriages and civil unions in Wisconsin, via a 2006 Amendment to the Wisconsin Constitution.

The Wisconsin Family Council

The WFC is a state affiliate of Focus on the Family.[2579] According to the WFC, "The Wisconsin Family Council (WFC) was founded in 1986. Its mission is to forward Judeo-Christian principles and values in Wisconsin. WFC largely accomplishes this mission by informing Wisconsin citizens, churches and policymakers about the important pro-family legislative and cultural issues so that they will be inspired to be involved in preserving and strengthening marriage and family in Wisconsin."[2580] During the push for the constitutional amendment banning gay marriage in Wisconsin, the council was known as the Family Research Institute of Wisconsin.[2581]

Republicans Love WFC

For example, Representative Mark Gundrum, "Without The Wisconsin Family Council's public outreach, encouraging citizens to contact legislators and informing the like-minded, it is unlikely that we would have succeeded in getting the measure [Wisconsin's Defense of Marriage Constitutional Amendment resolution] through both houses for First Consideration this session [2003-2004]."[2582]

Juliane Appling: Head of WFC

Julaine K. Appling was born in Georgia.[2583] She has picked up numerous degrees, all from Bob Jones University.[2584] And she was the perfect person to lead the WFC. Her journey against gay marriage in Wisconsin was long. After the 2006 elections, *The Milwaukee Journal Sentinel* reported, "Nearly nine years after beginning her quest, and three-and-a-half years after starting the last lap of an intense lobbying and campaign battle, Appling was ebullient Wednesday as she reflected on the overwhelming passage of a state constitutional amendment on marriage."[2585] The *Capital Times* described (10.13.2006) Appling as the "main spokeswoman for a group supporting Wisconsin's proposed constitutional ban on gay marriage and civil unions."[2586]

In the majority of Wisconsin stories covering the gay marriage debate, she was included to give her opinion, pushing out all others in the movement.

She is blatantly theocratic. In April 2008 she said, "I want to openly and candidly admit that I am a social conservative—and beyond that, I am a Christian social conservative. Frankly, it's from a Christian worldview that that I make my decisions, view life, and weigh the messages I hear during political campaigns and legislative sessions."[2587]

Appling Testimony Before State Senate (March.1.2004)

The State Senate of Wisconsin believed in Julaine Appling. Here is some of the knowledge she enlightened senators with in March 2004.

1) It is positive amendment; not negative. Appling said (3.1.2004) "Marriage also establishes the 'gold standard' for the rearing of children, the future of our society. While this proposal is positive and does not target any particular subset of the population, the media and opponents in general have characterized it as 'anti-homosexual.' In truth, the resolution clearly and positively states what marriage is in Wisconsin, not what it is not."[2588]

2) Marriage is not a right. Appling said (3.1.2004), "Marriage is not a right—it is a privilege that is extended to people who meet the basic legal criteria—being the right age, not being close kin and choosing a spouse of the opposite sex. We all have the same right under this law."[2589]

3) Homosexuals are not a minority. Appling said, "Some claim the proposed resolution is discriminatory and therefore a 'civil rights' issue. It isn't. People involved in homosexuality meet none of the characteristics of minority groups. They are not suffering economically as a group. Statistics show homosexuals earn more per capita than the average American. They are not politically powerless. To the contrary, they are one of the most powerful and well-funded lobbying groups and political action groups in the country."[2590]

4) Homosexuals can change. Appling said (3.1.2004), homosexuals "do not have an immutable characteristic, such as race or ethnicity."[2591]

5) Homosexuals are the special interests. Appling told the Wisconsin State Senate, "This is not about equal or civil rights. It's about special rights for a special-interest group, and the government should not allow this small but vocal group to redefine, over the will of the majority, the essence of an institution that predates human government."[2592]

6) Gay marriage is anarchy. Appling said (3.1.2004), "The people of Wisconsin took note of what happened in Massachusetts and realized the necessity of protecting one-man/one-woman marriage in our state. I believe those numbers will continue to increase in the wake of the anarchy we've witnessed in San Francisco, New Mexico and New York."[2593]

7) Gay marriage could allow people to marry themselves. Appling said, "If we allow any combination other than one man and one woman to marry, we may as well allow anyone to marry whomever he or she chooses. Perhaps single people should be allowed to marry themselves, as a woman did last summer in one of the Scandinavian countries that also allows marriage to be between people of the same sex."[2594]

8) Gay marriage will spread AIDS. Appling testified in support of a constitutional ban on gay marriage by tying AIDS to gays. Appling told the State Senate (3.1.2004), "A minimum of 76 percent of the currently more than 5,000 AIDS cases in Wisconsin, according to the Winter 2003, Wisconsin AIDS/HIV Update, published by the Division of Public Health, Department of Health and Family Services, are related to homosexual activity. The government should not be in any way encouraging this deadly practice by giving it legal status and thereby spending even more of the taxpayers' money on this public health epidemic….If the government considers non-contagious diseases to be public health threats and takes action to prevent them, certainly it should not be giving any legal sanction to an activity that has been proven to create a contagious public health risk."[2595]

Other Appling Arguments on Gay Marriage

The amendment process lasted, legislatively and in campaigning, over three years. Appling made numerous comments after she appeared before the State Senate in 2004. Here are some more of her arguments.

1) The ban is good for business. According to the newstation NBC 15, "a spokesperson with the Family Research Institute [Appling's organization]...says an all–out ban could be better for business, because they say statistics show men who are married to women are better employees than single men."[2596] Appling echoed this bit of business expertise in other media interviews as well.

2) Gay marriage is about special rights. In February 2004, Julaine Appling said, "Allowing people of the same sex to legally marry in Wisconsin is not equality; it's an attempt of a small but vocal minority to have special rights, not equal rights."[2597]

3) Gay marriage isn't about gay bashing. After the election, Appling said she told Mike Tate of the pro-gay Fair Wisconsin that the debate was "about the amendment and the institution of marriage," and that she never viewed homosexuals as "the enemy…And we don't view you as the enemy today."[2598] Appling said (Nov.2006), "It wasn't about gay-bashing…It was standing up for the principles we held, that marriage is good and one-man, one-woman marriage needs protection."[2599] This was believable, given that she warned the State Senate AIDS would increase by giving "legal sanction" to gay behavior.

4) Banning gay marriage is the first step in improving marriage behavior. When the ban passed in 2006, Appling said the amendment was "just the first piece" of an effort to build a "culture of marriage in Wisconsin….We want to see marriage rates increase, cohabitation decrease, divorce rates decrease," then she added she was interested in "stopping the bleeding of no-fault divorce."[2600] How wonderful, Appling spent years fighting to increase marriages by preventing them. Then after spending four years on homosexuals, she wanted to finally go after no-fault divorce in heterosexual marriages.

5) Gays can still get insurance with the ban. In addition, after the ban passed, Julaine Appling said, "the government is free to give benefits to unmarried individuals on a basis that does not approximate marriage."[2601] In glaring inconsistancy, she told the State Senate (2004) it was inappropriate to give "legal sanction" to homosexual behavior, then supported giving gays health benefits.

6) Gay Marriage is linked to our nation's fiscal troubles

In April 2008, the Institute for American Values released a study, *The Taxpayer Costs of Divorce and Unwed Childbearing*, which according to Appling, "the estimated cost of family fragmentation to U.S. taxpayers is *at least $112 billion every year*. $737 million is our Wisconsin portion of that number."[2602] This cost included many government programs for dependent children who need help. Astonishingly, Appling linked the social programs with the fight against gay marriage:

> The breakdown of annual federal, state and local costs of family fragmentation speaks volumes. On the national level: $9.6 billion for food stamps, $9.2 billion for child welfare, $27.9 billion for Medicaid, $19.3 billion for the justice system—for juvenile delinquency. In Wisconsin: $284 million for the justice system alone, $198 million for Medicaid and $93 million for child welfare. Those are heartbreaking statistics! ....Friends, we are doing our children, the next generation, a huge disservice by promoting and encouraging nontraditional families when we flaunt promiscuity and tolerate teenage pregnancy, cohabitation, unilateral divorce and so-called homosexual marriage. The taxpayer costs in this study are daunting, but they are merely surface issues indicative of a much deeper, more pervasive and troubling problem—the breakdown of the family in America, in Wisconsin, in our communities, our churches and our homes.[2603]

7) Adam, Eve and Julaine. In April 2008, she said, "Our Creator defined family for us in the model He gave with the first male human, Adam, and the first female human, Eve, the two of whom He called 'husband' and 'wife,' and of whom His Son, Jesus Christ, said, 'What God has joined together, let not man separate.' Adam and Eve were commissioned with one primary task in the Garden of Eden: replenish the earth—and that's one thing they did right—and you and I are here tonight as proof that in this instance they did as they were told! The natural family then is a married mom and dad and any of their biological or adopted children. That is the gold standard, the ideal. Of course, we deal with reality—situations where the ideal has been fractured—through death or necessary divorce. These families need our compassion and our help and support. But the gold standard remains, and whenever we as a society or whenever government begins trying to create another gold standard for family, we all reap the whirlwind those attempts create."[2604] That gold standard had a 50 percent return rate of divorce.

Taking A Closer Look At Julaine Appling

The woman is shameless; she lives with her female partner of over thirty years wherever they choose, yet, speaking of gays and lesbians she says, "I think we've been extremely tolerant in allowing them to live wherever they choose." She opposes gay marriage, civil unions, breast feeding in public, hate crimes legislation, no fault divorce, freedom of choice for women, teaching evolution, birth control assistance for poor families, emergency contraception for sexual assault victims taken to private or religious hospitals by police, and even opposed a bill to remove statute of limitations on sexual abuse of children because she claimed it would be unfair to religious organizations. She also opposes anti - bullying legislation which would require school districts to adopt policies to minimize bullying in public schools. She must think homosexuals and minorities and slower learners deserve the verbal and physical abuse they receive. According to the Watertown newspaper, when serving on the Watertown School Board she slammed local Hispanics by saying "the best young Hispanic leaders are involved in street gang hierarchies." This is total nonsense. Appling knows nothing of the social strata and hierachies of young Hispanic males.

Appling attended Bob Jones University in the 1970s, receiving three degrees from there. The Christian fundamentalist school has threatened to arrest all gay graduates who return to campus. But the university then partially backed down, permitting gays to visit its art museum since a ban could affect the gallery's tax-exempt status. A 1998 letter from Bob Jones University stated alumni living as a homosexual would not be welcome on campus and would be arrested for trespassing if they did. That would have to apply to Juliane Appling and her long-term partner, Mary Diane Westphall.

Julaine Appling, CEO of the Wisconsin Family Council, not only claims civil unions and gay marriages and domestic benefits are all the same, and that people on the street or in a store should be allowed to stop a woman from breast feeding her baby if another considers it lewd, she now wants to eliminate no-fault divorces for couples with minor children.

Ms. Appling, who has never been married, has never raised a child, has lived with her partner, another woman, for nearly 30 years or more is now trying to force two people, one, at least, who wants a divorce, to live together.

First of all, try to prove that two warring parents are good for the children. Secondly, if one wants a divorce so bad that he or she has filed for one or would if they could, somebody is going to move out. It won't be long, if it hasn't happened already, extra-marital sexual activity, also known as "adultery" if that divorce has not been granted, will occur.

In Wisconsin, adultery is a class three felony, already. Julaine wants all who are getting divorced, if you have children, to be forced to label the other parent, in legal records as an adulterer, abuser or deserter. That will certainly be good for the kids.

But, here is the big surprise. Since adultery is a felony, and many will now have to fess up to it, they will lose their guns and their right to vote, and perhaps their professional license.

After equal rights for single people, breast feeding mothers and divorcing adults, these folks will, no doubt, push for the Attorney General and the law enforcement agencies of every town, city, county and the State to enforce the adultery law and take the guns, voting rights and professions from thousands, of both sexes. In spite of what that goofy Pat Robertson says, cheating spouses are with men or women, not ducks.

Being single and living with another woman, which is her choice and business, she has also chosen to not raise and nurture children, even though in Wisconsin she could have, nor has she been in a marriage, good or bad. But Julaine Appling will tell the rest of the world how to live and where they may feed their babies and certainly increase the number of bow-hunters in Wisconsin. She will continue to market hatred.

A Wisconsin Blogger writes:

> Julaine Appling is terrifying. No seriously. I first encountered her in an article about same-sex marriage that ran in The Isthmus, the local alternative weekly in Madison. … In the article, she actually said that she thought that we (obviously straight folk) have been extremely tolerant in letting them (homos) live wherever they want unlike blacks during segregation and before the Civil Rights Movement. I don't know why people don't quote her whole bit because from the moment I read it, I was so shocked I didn't know what to say. … Here is a straight woman saying gays don't have it that bad because we can share her drinking fountains. Because she has "let" us buy property instead of running us out of her neighborhood. …. It is all ok because the straights haven't burned down our homes or excluded us from their colleges. Everything is hunky f***ing dory because we don't have to cross to the other side of the road when we see her coming. What kind of f***ed up statement is that??? I'll tell you what it is, it is a warning. It is Julaine Appling's way of saying that if she wanted to, she could treat us a whole lot worse. She could destroy our homes, she could exclude us from the neighborhood and beat, intimidate, and terrorize us into submission. It is her way of saying "Give me a f***ing medal because I haven't annihilated you the way I would like to". She is saying "We straights deserve a big pat on the back for letting you exist". She is saying to the gay community that we only deserve what she is willing to give us. I say "f*** that". I say "f*** you Julaine". I get angry and I think she is batshit insane. …What if she doesn't want to "let" me have children? What if she doesn't want to "let" me be a public servant? What if she doesn't want to "let" me do my job or buy my sandwich or walk down the street unmolested? I'm terrified of the Julaine Appling's of the world because I fight for the right to live a life that she doesn't want to "let" me have, and I'm scared shitless that someday someone might take what little of that right I do have away. I'm terrified because her entire way of thinking can easily lend itself to something more sinister and I see nothing in her ideology that would hold her back from taking whatever action she thought necessary to not "let" us do whatever it is we could, would, or should be wanting to do. And that is why Julaine Appling scares the all mother living shit out me.

Another Wisconin blogger posted the following:

> Well, okay then, let me see if I understand this:

Fred Risser introduced a bill to ensure that women will not be legally prevented from breast feeding in public. A reporter from the Badger Herald asked Julaine Appling about her opinion on the bill, and printed a (and it looks reasonable to me) truncated quote from her...Now she is complaining that she was misquoted - because breast feeding is only lewd **sometimes** and you should only be fined if your breastfeeding somehow crosses the line and becomes lewd. How the hell do you determine that? How much breast shows? How pretty the woman in question is? How happy the baby seems? Is there a community standard for this? Are breasts more lewd in Poy Sippi than in Madison? My mind reels. I'm always amazed at how easy some folks think it is to determine what behavior should and shouldn't be regulated..The question that I **really** wonder about in this case is - is it more lewd to Julaine if the mother in question is gay? Or less? This all makes my head hurt. I must stop reading what Julaine Appling says.

-Posted March 3rd, 2007 by Steve Hanson in Civil Rights Gay Marriage Wisconsin

Why does she do what she does? It's a fair question.

One blogger writes (*Posted by: Gunner,* January 19, 2007):

Everyone in the gay community knows about Julaine Appling and her very bad case of the closet. It's hard to see a person like this, obviously deeply emotionally damaged, doing harm to others for no other reason than her own profound lack of comfort with her own life circumstance, but there you have it...By the way, her targets have now expanded to include, among others, breast-feeding mothers, people seeking divorce and victim of childhood sexual abuse at the hands of the Catholic Church.

Some Noteworthy Background

Appling owns a home in Watertown, Wisconsin, with a woman named Mary Diane Westphall. They attended Bob Jones University at the same time, in the late 60's and it is reported that they were college roommates. They both work for the Wisconsin Family Council, both were listed as daughters when Raymond Westphall, died, although Julianne's official bio states she was adopted by the Applings in Georgia, when she was 5 months old.

It is reported both have taught or teach at Watertown's Maranatha Baptist Bible College. A "*Mrs.*" Juliane Appling was listed to teach National Government in the Fall of 2009. Is this a typo? Diane Westphall was listed to teach Business Communication during the Spring of 2009. She was listed without a Miss or Mrs. or Dr., just Diane. Did Diane and Julaine sneak off and get married and not tell us? Renee Westphall, Diane's sister is listed as Dean of Students.

Maranatha Baptist Bible College reflects the policies of Bob Jones University and narrow limits placed upon student life. Passes and chaperones are required for dating and for many instances for leaving campus or driving and traveling in an automobile. Chaperones are even required for dating for older students living off campus. There are strict dress codes, music codes and a demerit system that follows every minute of the student's day. Falling asleep in church, in spite of the dullness of the message, may gain the student 10 to 25 demerits; ironing in the dorm room, 25 demerits; watching television a second time, 50 demerits and confiscation of equipment; an uncovered tattoo, 50; failure to check your guns with the Dean, 25 and confiscation; and horseplay or practical jokes, 15 to expulsion; What a fun place to be. Twenty-five demerits for not checking your gun at the door but fifty for showing your tattoo. Looney-land. Fits Julaine, perfectly.

Maranatha's Board of Directors consists of seventeen white men, of which seven are pastors. A disagreement between the Board and the President led to the departure of Dr. Chuck Phelps, a Bob Jones University Graduate. With twelve of the seventeen being from states other Wisconsin, it is probably safe to assume the reason for his dispute was not his wearing of a Patriot sweatshirt in his own home.

Although, given the dress code, maybe.

Raymond Westphall's obituary in the *Watertown Daily Times* did list Julaine, as well as Diane, as a daughter, "Survivors include his daughters, Diane Westphall, Renée Westphall, Janet (Ben) Peterson, and Julaine Appling, all of Watertown ..." As one blogger put it: "It is fairly common to include such "children by affection" in obituaries, in Wisconsin as elsewhere, without regard to blood or legal relationship."

Threads of the same blanket they seem, close friends, co-workers, partners, residence, all the same, for many years. I frankly do not want to know about their sex life. It is absolutely none of my business. Conversely, other's sex life is none of their business. What a hypocrite and fraud.

When the 2009 General Assembly passed and the Governor signed a Domestic Registry Bill giving gay couples some 48 benefits out of the 200 that married couples receive in Wisconsin, Appling and her group flied suit against it, declaring it unconstitutional. She had testified and campaigned for the Constitutional Amendment of 2006, banning gay marriage and any thing similar. During that time she swore that the Amendment would not stop domestic benefits. In 2009, she files suit against a minor domestic benefits law.

Julaine Appling is not only a fraud and a hypocrite, she is a liar.

MICHAEL SAVAGE

Savage: A.K.A. Michael Weiner

Michael Savage is a right-wing columnist syndicated nationwide.[2605] He was born Michael Weiner and was a "perpetual student in the 1960s and 1970s, when he picked up four degrees. His own sexual orientation is a matter of dispute. Early in his life, he had writings in which the protagonist wrestled with homosexual tendencies.[2606] He was once a friend of beat poet Allen Ginsberg, who was openly gay.[2607] A 1970 letter to Ginsberg from "someone signed Michael Weiner" describes a homoerotic encounter with a Fiji man, Weiner claimed not to write the letter, which had a return address from Honolulu, where Weiner resided at the time.[2608] Weiner attended the University of Hawaii.[2609]

But the man formerly known as Weiner gave praise when he found out Ginsberg died and claimed he praised God, "One of the blights of the human race" was gone.[2610] By the mid 1990s he was hired as "Michael Savage" to work in San Francisco.[2611] By June of 2007, *The Savage Nation* reached 8 million listeners, which ranked it the third most popular radio talk show, only trailing behind Rush Limbaugh and Sean Hannity.[2612]

He routinely says outrageous remarks. During the December 15, 2008, broadcast of *The Savage Nation*, Savage suggested John F. Kennedy Jr. was killed so Hillary Clinton could eventually become president. Savage said, "... And to this day, people wonder why he died in a plane crash, and then suddenly, enter from the -- from stage left, the carpetbagger Hillary Clinton, who moved to Chappaquiddick (sic: Chappaqua), and next you know, she's running for the presidency. That's a whole story that only a novelist could write. I can't write it. But now, you see, she's suddenly secretary of state and now they want to fill it with a shoo-in. Why shouldn't it go to a Puerto Rican or a black person rather than Caroline Kennedy? Huh?"[2613]

Savage's turn to the far right coincided with the rise of gay activism, as he linked homosexuality to the spread of not only AIDS, but the general spread of disease. Savage frequently associates homosexuality with pedophilia.[2614]

MSNBC Incident

Savage's meteoric rise to getting a TV show died as quick as it rose, nonetheless, he retained his syndication to over 350 stations nationwide.[2615]

Savage's show on MSNBC lasted only four months.[2616] In June 2003, MSNBC fired Savage and ended his televised version of The Savage Nation, which began in March of 2003.[2617] His radio show "didn't translate into a television hit" and, according to MSNBC, the ratings increased only marginally.[2618]

Savage told a caller, "So you're one of those sodomists. Are you a sodomite?" When the caller affirmed, Savage added, "Oh, you're one of the sodomites. You should only get AIDS and die, you pig. How's that? Why don't you see if you can sue me, you pig. You got nothing better than to put me down, you piece of garbage. You have got nothing to do today, go eat a sausage and choke on it."[2619] Savage then asked for another phone caller who "didn't have a nice night in the bathhouse who's angry at me today" and concluded these bums "mean nothing to me."[2620] Savage's callous words were only reaffirmed in his continuous criticisms of gays.

Savage claims homosexual parents equates with child abuse

In June 2007, on *The Savage Nation*, Savage called gay parenting "child abuse."[2621] The issue occurred over a Mitt Romney campaign incident. According to a AP article (which Savage discussed) a New Hampshire woman came up to Romney and said, "I am a gay woman and I have children. Your comment that you just made, it sort of invalidates my family... I wish you could explain to me more, why if we are sending our troops over to fight for liberty and justice for all throughout this country, why not for me? Why not for my family?"[2622] Romney praised her: "Wonderful…I'm delighted that you have a family and you're happy with your family. That's the American way. ... People can live their lives as they choose and children can be a great source of joy, as you know. And I welcome that…There are other ways to raise kids that's fine: single moms, grandparents raising kids, gay couples raising kids. That's the American way, to have people have their freedom of choice."[2623] Savage concluded the proper answer would be to tell the mother such parenting is child abuse: "I need a conservative candidate all the way who would say to a gay woman: 'You know what? I'm very sorry for your children. I think it's child abuse for you to raise children.' [and…] Marriage is a fragile institution and I think you're making a mockery of it in this manner by doing this."[2624]

Savage Gay Bashes

Savage referred to *Brokeback Mountain* to Bareback Mounting, "making him as original as the guy who comes up with puns for pornographic movie titles."[2625]

Savage claimed he is worried about "degenerates on the left who want to sell Americans on the idea that homosexuality, bisexuality, transsexuality, even sex with animals is normal."[2626]

The San Francisco Human Rights Commission condemned the San Francisco Police Officers association for promoting tickets to an event featuring Savage, so Savage responded by equating gay rights activists with neo-fascists, communists and Nazis.[2627] Savage also tied gays to rape: "Now I'm extremely popular, but the San Francisco Human Rights Commission thinks that their Nazi background gives them an opportunity to say that I'm a hateful person because they don't like what I say about homosexuals. ... When you hear 'human rights,' think gays. When you hear 'human rights,' think only one thing: someone who wants to rape your son. And you'll get it just right. OK, you got it, right? When you hear 'human rights,' think only someone who wants to molest your son, and send you to jail if you defend him. Write that down, make a note of it. So anyway, let's get back to the serious stuff here."[2628]

As one critic noted, "It's curious that a man with such an intense hatred of homosexuals has spent most of his adult life in Northern California, never moving to a less tolerant place where he could be more comfortable."[2629]

PHYLLIS SCHLAFLY

In the early 1970s, Phyllis Schlafly was one of the most important conservatives in America as she fought the Equal Rights Amendment.[2630] In the 1970s, she led the fight to killing the ERA, in part by claiming it would pave the way for gay weddings.[2631] She is pro-life, and against gay marriage. In fact, that's what her whole career revolves around.

Feminist Betty Friedan said she wanted Schlafly burnt at the stake.[2632] Schlafly created the Eagle Forum as an organization to promote her conservative agenda. Schlafly called for women to be banned from being firefighters, soldiers and construction workers.[2633] She argued a woman cannot be raped by her husband: "By getting married, the woman has consented to sex, and I don't think you can call it rape."[2634]

Schlafly: Gay Agenda Goes After Free Speech

In an op-ed that appeared on Human Events online, Schlafly wrote (2006), "Same-sex marriage is not the only goal of the gay rights movement. It's becoming clear that another goal is the suppression of Americans' First Amendment right to criticize the gay agenda. The gay lobby tried a broadside attempt to censor criticism by passing a national 'hate crimes' law. Fortunately, Congress didn't pass that law, but gay activists are obviously trying to achieve much the same effect through political pressure and intimidation."[2635] It is appalling that so many "Christian" activists and pastors oppose hate crime legislation.

Schlafly: Public Schools Censor Criticism Of Gays

Schlafly wrote (2006):

> "Public schools are a major battleground in the gays' efforts to censor any criticism of their goals or lifestyle. Every year, the National Education Association passes resolutions not only demanding that schools not discriminate against sexual orientation, but also insisting that classroom language be monitored to punish "homophobia" and to "promote 'acceptance' and/or 'respect' instead of 'tolerance'" of the gay lifestyle. Taking their demands for censorship into the courts, gays have been winning. After Poway High School near San Diego endorsed the gay project called "Day of Silence," the 9th U.S. Circuit Court of Appeals upheld the school in forbidding student Tyler Harper to wear a T-shirt with the words "Homosexuality is shameful, Romans 1:27." The dissenting judge pointed out the intolerance of those who claim they want tolerance for minority views. But Judge Stephen Reinhardt, who sided with the school, wrote that Tyler's defenders "still don't get the message." I am getting the message: For Reinhardt, gay rights means intolerance for free speech. Clinton apologists once defended his scandalous conduct by saying it was "only about sex." It's increasingly clear that the gay ideology is about far more than sex; it assaults our fundamental right to free speech."[2636]

The teachers union is too gay-friendly.

In June 2005, Schlafly wrote about a Southern Baptist Convention potentially proposing a resolution critical of public school teachers. Schlafly wrote the "resolution correctly identifies the National Education Association as an ally of the campaign to use the public schools to promote acceptance of the homosexual lifestyle. Every year for at least a decade, the annual NEA convention has passed about a dozen resolutions urging implementation of the gay rights agenda in curriculum, extra-curricular activities, and employment regulations. NEA convention resolutions repeatedly demand that the schools be permitted to determine (without parental approval) what is taught in sex-ed programs. The NEA resolutions demand that school programs include information on 'diversity of sexual orientation and/or gender identification.'"[2637]

Her son is gay.

The *Boston Globe* reported on Schlafly at the 2004 GOP Convention. She fielded reporter's questions, mostly on homosexuality: "Which brings Schlafly to another thing she wishes: that people would stop asking her about her gay son."[2638] The oldest of her children, John, acknowledged his homosexuality in 1992.[2639] So, as the *Globe* described it, "Since then, Phyllis Schlafly -- who believes homosexuality is wrong, because all sex outside marriage is wrong -- has had to publicly square her vehement opposition to gay rights with her son's sexuality."[2640]

Schlafly said, "It's not a problem for anybody but the press…He is very supportive of everything I do. He's a good lawyer and very helpful. He is not a proponent of same-sex marriage."[2641] Indeed her son, who traveled to the 2004 GOP Convention, was still working for the Eagle Forum.[2642]

John Schlafly was outed by a homosexual magazine.[2643] John was outed by *Queer World*, also known as *QW*, which at the time was a New York based publication.[2644] Phyllis Schlafly said, "Nobody had anything against my son. It was a deliberate strike at me. It just shows how hateful those people are."[2645] Those people.

Schlafly had a point, her son shouldn't be outed. But she isn't the victim when it comes to gay issues.

When John Schlafly came-out, the *Washington Post* reported (9.19.1992), "he came out swinging at gay leaders rather than at the GOP, which has been accused of vilifying homosexuals."[2646] John said, "I think there has been a hysterical overreaction in the gay community" to the Republican platform… "We have a band of screechy gay activists and Washington-based pressure groups who get all the attention. The truth is: Family values people, of which my mother is a part, are not out to bash gay people."[2647] His comments were oxymoronic: we are "not out to bash gay people," and then he turned around and called them "screechy activists."

In 2004, Phyllis Schlafly was also asked her opinion on a U.S. representative deciding not to seek reelection after an activist for same-sex rights posted rumors online that he is gay. Schlafly said, "That just shows how vicious the gays are. They're very mean."[2648] *They're mean.*

For the record, the *QW* story may not have been that caustic. True, the editor of *QW* published the story to showcase Schlafly's hypocrisy.[2649] But John Schlafly was cordial throughout his hour long telephone interview with *QW*, and even asked if a picture was needed.[2650] Nor was John as closeted: he went to gay film festivals and seen at gay Republican meetings.[2651]

Pro-choicers And Gay Rights Advocates: Two Peas In A Pod

Phyllis's attacks are strategic. For example, she claimed the *QW* story was retaliation for her anti-abortion lobbying, and the outing story just "shows the political alliance between the pro-choice movement and gays."[2652] The only thing pro-choice activists and gay-activists have in common is that social conservatives like Schlafly hate them both. Gay rights is a separate issue, but not if your Phyllis Schlafly, who needs to motivate her pro-life supporters to hating gays.

When John Is Brought Up, Gay Rights Not Part of Phyllis' Politics

At the time of John's outing, the National Gay and Lesbian Task Force claimed she was "one of the top five most powerful anti-gay forces in the country."[2653]

Phyllis Schlafly has tried to play the victim. After a *Meet the Press* Interview with Tim Russert (early 1990s), she claimed the interview was "obnoxious!"[2654] "It didn't have anything to do with the subject. We were going to talk about the Republican convention and the future of the Republican Party, and Tim Russert just threw that in.... The only reason people bring it up is to embarrass me."[2655] But as a *Knight-Ridder* article aptly pointed out, Russert brought it up in the context of the GOP Convention.

If Phyllis Schlafly is talking about politics, her specialty is social issues (i.e. abortion or gay marriage). At the 1992 convention, Pat Robertson said, "If it were not for this lady we would have had homosexual rights written into the Constitution."[2656] (For the record, even John Schlafly refused to condemn Pat Robertson for mocking gays.[2657]) It was perfectly germane for Tim Russert to ask Phyllis Schlafly about her son.

So is homosexuality a choice?

Schlafly said she knew her son was gay "a long time ago," it wasn't that he told her, but moreso that she "just knew."[2658] She said she never discussed the issue with her son until after the *QW* story broke.[2659] Schlafly said. "He thinks he's always been [gay]. But about this thing of being born gay, he doesn't know that. I don't know if anybody knows that."[2660] In a *Meet the Press* interview after John's admission, Phyllis said her attitude toward non-traditional lifestyles like homosexuality was unchanged.[2661] She noted gays were entitled to equal rights, but not "preferential rights."[2662]

Phyllis: Irritated By Cheney's Response

Schlafly actually criticized Dick Cheney for coming out against a federal amendment to ban gay marriage: "I thought [Cheney] was out of line. But what he said is not the view of the Republican Party. So I just think that's a blip that's going to pass in the night."[2663] God forbid Dick Cheney support his daughter over his political party. Such behavior is despised by Phyllis Schlafly; or maybe she is just jealous that Dick Cheney shows respect for his daughter.

ERA

Schlafly rose to prominence during the Equal Rights Amendment of the 1970s. The ERA said: "S*ection 1.* Equality of rights under the law shall not be denied or abridged by the United States or by any state on account of sex. *Section 2.* The Congress shall have the power to enforce, by appropriate legislation, the provisions of this article. *Section 3.* This amendment shall take effect two years after the date of ratification."[2664]

The contrast in the ERA's beginning and its end is remarkable. The ERA sailed through Congress in 1972.[2665] In the first year, the ERA had 22 of the necessary 38 state ratifications; but the rate quickly slowed: only eight ratifications in 1973, three in 1974, one in 1975, and none in 1976.[2666] In 1977, Indiana became the 35th (and so far the last state to ratify the ERA.[2667] In 1980, the Republican Party removed ERA support from its platform.[2668]

In a 2007 National Right to Life Committee letter to members of the US House of Representatives, the NRLC gave "ADDITIONAL INFORMATION ON THE 1972 ERA." It serves as a good summation of the timeline of the ERA:

> The 1972 ERA was ratified by 35 legislatures before the seven-year ratification deadline expired. (Of these, 26 explicitly referred to the deadline in their resolutions of ratification.) However, five of these 35 states withdrew their ratifications before the deadline arrived. The only federal court to consider the issue ruled that these rescissions were valid. In 1978, Congress passed a controversial bill, by majority vote, that purported to extend the ratification deadline for 39 months. During this disputed "extension," no new states ratified or rescinded. In 1981 a federal court ruled that the rescissions were valid, and also ruled that the purported deadline extension was unconstitutional. In 1982, the Supreme Court declined to review this case, holding that the issue was moot because the ERA had failed ratification with or without the rescissions and with or without the purported extension...In 1983, the House majority (Democratic) leadership also recognized that the 1972 ERA was dead. They brought to the House floor, under suspension of the rules, a new resolution containing the same proposed constitutional amendment, again with a seven-year deadline -- an effort that, if successful, would have begun the entire ratification process anew. However, the resolution was defeated on the floor of the House (278-147, November 15, 1983). Among those voting "no" were 14 co-sponsors, most of whom were among the majority who wanted to add the abortion-neutral amendment. Neither house of Congress has voted on an ERA since that day.[2669]

Basic criticisms of the ERA

ERA opponents feared there would be no traditional distinctions between the sexes. Women would have to register for the draft and fight in combat like men. They also argued laws or company policy that protect women would be removed (ex: existing laws where women didn't have to lift above a certain amount or could avoid dealing with heavy industrial equipment). By the 1980s, abortion was a major concern surrounding ERA. Some critics have argued the judiciary would rule the ERA mandates same-sex marriage. Even today, ERA opponents say the amendment would also ban single-sex schools, sports teams and restrooms.

Schlafly's version of ERA

Phyliss Schlafly and her Eagle Forum played one of the biggest roles in halting ratification of the ERA. She is routinely validated as a conservative icon. In April 2007, the *AP* reported, "The matriarch of the conservative movement is showing no signs of slowing down. At 82, Phyllis Schlafly is still speaking out against abortion and illegal immigration, still fighting the Equal Rights Amendment, still a thorn in the side of not only Democrats but of Republicans she sees as leaning too far to the left."[2670] The following is some of the reasons she has argued against the ERA.

1) Her recollection is skewed. Schlafly uses vitrolic language to tell her skewed version of history. For example, "A radical feminist organization called the National Organization for Women stormed the halls of Congress and forced a vote on the Equal Rights Amendment. Only 24 members in the House, and eight in the Senate, voted against it. On March 22, 1972, Congress sent the amendment to the states, which had seven years to ratify it."[2671] It's amazing how NOW "stormed" Congress, given that support for ERA was bipartisan. It included Ted Kennedy, George Wallace; Presidents Nixon, Ford, and Carter.[2672] Schflaly wrote an *LA Times* op-ed (2007), "The Equal Rights Amendment was actively supported by most of the pushy women's organizations, a consortium of 33 women's magazines, numerous Hollywood celebrities and virtually all the media."[2673]

2) She inflates her efforts. Schlafly describes her efforts heroically: "The opposition was totally outmanned. We had no Rush Limbaughs, no Fox News, no "no-spin zone" to challenge the need for the amendment. We had no Internet, no e-mail, no fax machines to help rally an opposition."[2674] ERA supporters didn't have internet, email, or fax machines either.

3) ERA folks had no argument. In the 1970s, Schlafly testified at 41 state hearings.[2675] She has even stated, "the pro-amendment crowd could not show how the ERA would confer any benefit on women, not even in employment, because employment laws were already gender-neutral."[2676] Women still don't make the equavalent of men in the same working positions.

4) Feminist got what they wanted. Schlafly said "feminists appealed to Carter and Congress for a time extension and won. The ratification deadline was extended to June 30, 1982."[2677] After the extension, five states worked to undo their support.[2678]

5) Feminist got tangled with homosexuals. In an op-ed to the *LA Times* in 2007, Schlafly wrote:

> In 1977, ERA advocates realized that they were approaching the seven-year time limit three states short of the 38 needed for ratification, so they persuaded Congress to give them $5 million to stage a conference, called International Women's Year, in Houston. The conference featured virtually every known feminist leader and received massive

media coverage. But it backfired. When conference delegates voted for taxpayer funding of abortions and the entire gay rights agenda, Americans discovered the ERA's hidden agenda. A couple of months later, a reporter asked the governor of Missouri if he was for the ERA. "Do you mean the old ERA or the new ERA?" he replied. "I was for equal pay for equal work, but after those women went down to Houston and got tangled up with the abortionists and the lesbians, I can tell you ERA will never pass in the Show-Me State."[2679]

6) Gays would get more rights. She also said the "ERA would allow the courts to legalize same-sex marriages."[2680] Eleanor Smeal, president of the Feminist Majority Foundation, said ERA opponents are motivated by homophobia: "They want to bring bias, bigotry into this discussion…It's just more gay-bashing; that's all it is."[2681]

7) More prostitution, co-ed prisons. Schlafly also argues an ERA would legalize prostitution and the co-ed of federal prisons: "It's opening up a Pandora's box for the judges."[2682]

8) Women would be drafted. Schlafly argued (Feb. 2008) the "ERA would require young women to register for military service (even though we don't have a draft), and if they fail to register, they would immediately lose their federal college grants and loans, and they would never be able to get a federal job."[2683]

Schlafly's role for women

Clearly Schlafly is against reproductive rights for women. She said the ERA would require "taxpayer funding of Medicaid abortions."[2684] This is an argument used by much of the anti-ERA crowd. A National Right to Life Committee letter sent to the U.S. House members in March 2007 said, "Leading pro-abortion groups – including NARAL, the ACLU, and Planned Parenthood -- have strongly urged state courts to construe state ERAs to require tax-funded abortion on demand, and state ERAs have been so construed in New Mexico and Connecticut."[2685] In 1998, the New Mexico Supreme Court ruled that the 1973 amendment allowed for state-funded abortions through Medicaid.[2686]

Schlafly sees women's place as the home. When the Illinois legislature considered ratification of the amendment, Schlafly brought lawmakers homemade apple pies as symbols of traditional housewives.[2687]

She still argued (Feb.2008) the "ERA would deprive wives and widows of their 'dependent wife' benefits in Social Security."[2688] She added "Ruth Bader Ginsburg...says the 'equality principle' of ERA requires us to get rid of 'archaic' notions such as the dependency of a homemaker on her husband's financial support. Beware! A vote for ERA is a vote to take away Social Security checks received by most mothers and grandmothers."[2689]

The Homophobe's Role for Women

It is no surprise those who despise homosexual rights also want to take away the rights of women.

May 2008, Tony Perkins made comments in regard to the possibility John McCain would change the Republican Party platform to include exceptions for rape, incest, and health of the mother. Perkins said, "If he [McCain] were to change the party platform…I think that would be political suicide…I think he would be aborting his own campaign because that is such a critical issue to so many Republican voters and the Republican brand is already in trouble."[2690] Tony Perkins thinks a raped woman should be forced to retain her pregnancy.

Jerry Falwell made comments devaluing women. For example, he said, "*Grown men should not be having sex with prostitutes unless they are married to them.*"[2691]

Falwell also stated, "*It appears that America's anti-Biblical feminist movement is at last dying, thank God, and is possibly being replaced by a Christ-centered men's movement which may become the foundation for a desperately needed national spiritual awakening.*"[2692] In 1989, Falwell said, *"I listen to feminists and all these radical gals... These women just need a man in the house. That's all they need. Most of the feminists need a man to tell them what time of day it is and to lead them home. And they blew it and they're mad at all men. Feminists hate men. They're sexist. They hate men; that's their problem.*"[2693]

Meanwhile, Pat Robertson said, *"Feminism is a socialist, anti-family, political movement that encourages women to leave their husbands, kill their children, practice witchcraft, destroy capitalism and become lesbians.*"[2694]

The Family Research Institute warns (Oct.2008), "The West has produced the richest and most vital civilization ever to grace the planet, but our civilization is dying by slow degrees. Western nations are producing too few children to maintain their population. Most of our demographic decline is due to a mix of a self-centered reluctance to have children, birth control, wholesale abortion, and women in the workplace. The rise of militant homosexuality has also been a significant factor. It is both a symptom and a cause of our decline."[2695]

The homophobic leaders tie women rights to gay rights. The Schlaflys, Robertsons, and Dobsons hurt women and gays. Women will be the next target for the American Taliban.

Anti-gay Marriage is Sexist

As Dan Savage told Tony Perkins, "You know who redefined marriage? Straight people … Marriage used to be one man acquiring the property of another man, a daughter that became a wife. Straight people redefined marriage to be two individuals who commit to each other because of a bond of love. There can be children or no children, it could be a monogamous sexual relationship or not a monogamous sexual relationship. There can be a sexual relationship or not a sexual relationship. That's what marriage means now in our culture and they [anti-Prop 8 and social conservatives against gay marriage] want to define it back to the patriarchal sexist institution it was."[2696]

Chapter Nine:
Constitutions and Constitutional Arguments

I am not a lawyer. As such I take a certain degree of license with legal reasoning. Nevertheless, I stand by my reasoning and my conclusions.

Abraham Lincoln once posed the following, "If you call a dog's tail a leg, how many legs has a dog? Five you say; no, calling it a leg does not make it so."

The U.S. Constitution says what it says, in plain and simple language. It does cover subjects unknown to man at the time of its writing or adoption. But in it's meaning it is wise.

The U.S. Supreme Court is a constitutional convention in continuous session. However, unlike the work of a convention, the decisions are not required to be formally ratified. They become the law of the land until reversed or the law is changed. The Court can be wrong, as in Dred Scott. Calling a man a piece of property doesn't make him one. The law of the land is what the court says it is, but the law can be wrong. A "ball" is a "strike" if the umpire says so; such is the Supreme Court and the law of the land, until the next pitch or case.

Martin Luther King posited the ultimate legal question when he stated that it is just as bad to obey a bad law as it is to break a good one.

The Constitution says three very specific things that impact the issues of hatred and restrictions upon the freedoms and liberty of groups of people.

Article IV, Section 1: *Full faith and credit shall be given in each state to the public acts, records, and judicial proceedings of every other state. And the Congress may by general laws prescribe the manner in which such acts, records, and proceedings shall be proved, and the effect thereof.*

The First Amendment: *Congress shall make no law respecting an establishment of religion, or prohibiting the free exercise thereof; or abridging the freedom of speech, or of the press; or the right of the people peaceably to assemble, and to petition the Government for a redress of grievances.*

The Fourteenth Amendment: *Section 1. All persons born or naturalized in the United States, and subject to the jurisdiction thereof, are citizens of the United States and of the State wherein they reside. No State shall make or enforce any law which shall abridge the privileges or immunities of citizens of the United States; nor shall any State deprive any person of life, liberty, or property, without due process of law; nor deny to any person within its jurisdiction the equal protection of the laws.*

Relevant Cases

Meyer v. Nebraska 262 U.S. 390 (1923)
The State of Nebraska had a law that prohibited the teaching of a foreign language to grade school children. It read:

"Section 1. No person, individually or as a teacher, shall, in any private, denominational, parochial or public school, teach any subject to any person in any language other than the English language...Section 2. Languages, other than the English language, may be taught as languages only after a pupil shall have attained and successfully passed the eighth grade as evidenced by a certificate of graduation issued by the county superintendent of the county in which the child resides."

Meyer, a teacher in a Lutheran school was teaching German and was arrested for doing so. In *Meyer v. Nebraska* the U.S. Supreme Court specifically addressed the liberty protected by the due process clause:

"*While this court has not attempted to define with exactness the liberty thus guaranteed, the term has received much consideration and some of the included things have been definitely stated. Without doubt, it denotes not merely freedom from bodily restraint but also the right of the individual to contract, to engage in any of the common occupations of life, to acquire useful knowledge, to marry, establish a home and bring up children,* [emphasis mine] *to worship God according to the dictates of his own conscience, and generally to enjoy those privileges long recognized at common law as essential to the orderly pursuit of happiness by free men.*"

Loving v. Virginia 388 U.S. 1 (1967)

In *Loving V. Virginia* (1967), an interracial couple married in Washington D.C. (1958), then moved back to Virginia and was indicted for their marriage. In 1959, the Lovings pleaded guilty and were sentenced to a year in jail, but the trial judge suspended the sentence for a quarter century on the condition that the couple leave Virginia and not return for 25 years.[2697] The Virginia judge stated: "Almighty God created the races white, black, yellow, malay and red, and he placed them on separate continents. And but for the interference with his arrangement there would be no cause for such marriages. The fact that he separated the races shows that he did not intend for the races to mix."[2698] "I think marrying who you want is a right no man should have anything to do with. It's a God-given right," said Mildred Loving to ABC News (1967).[2699]

In an unanimous decision (9-0), the Court ruled against Virginia's laws prohibiting interracial marriages. Chief Justice Warren wrote the opinion of the Court:

"The freedom to marry has long been recognized as one of the vital personal rights essential to the orderly pursuit of happiness by free men. Marriage is one of the "basic civil rights of man," fundamental to our very existence and survival. To deny this fundamental freedom on so unsupportable a basis as the racial classifications embodied in these statutes, classifications so directly subversive of the principle of equality at the heart of the Fourteenth Amendment, is surely to deprive all the State's citizens of liberty without due process of law. The Fourteenth Amendment requires that the freedom of choice to marry not be restricted by invidious racial discriminations. Under our Constitution, the freedom to marry, or not marry, a person of another race resides with the individual and cannot be infringed by the State."

The Historic Decision

According to ABC News, "The Loving decision struck down anti-miscegenation laws in Virginia and 15 other states. In doing so, it put an end to the last piece of state-sanctioned segregation in the country. Yet for decades after the decision, many states left the unenforceable laws on the books. South Carolina did not remove its prohibitive clause until 1998, and Alabama held on to its ban until 2000. Clearly, even today, a gap remains between what is officially permitted and what is universally accepted. Unsurprisingly, some interracial couples say despite social progress, they still get looks, comments and even hostile threats."[2700]

Romer v. Evans 517 U.S. 620 (1996)

The following description of this case comes from the U.S. Supreme Court decision:

> *"The enactment challenged in this case is an amendment to the Constitution of the State of Colorado, adopted in a 1992 statewide referendum. The parties and the state courts refer to it as "Amendment 2," its designation when submitted to the voters. The impetus for the amendment and the contentious campaign that preceded its adoption came in large part from ordinances that had been passed in various Colorado municipalities. For example, the cities of Aspen and Boulder and the City and County of Denver each had enacted ordinances which banned discrimination in many transactions and activities, including housing, employment, education, public accommodations, and health and welfare services. ... What gave rise to the statewide controversy was the protection the ordinances afforded to persons discriminated against by reason of their sexual orientation... Amendment 2 repeals these ordinances to the extent they prohibit discrimination on the basis of 'homosexual, lesbian or bisexual orientation, conduct, practices or relationships.'...Yet Amendment 2, in explicit terms, does more than repeal or rescind these provisions. It prohibits all legislative, executive or judicial action at any level of state or local government designed to protect the named class, a class we shall refer to as homosexual persons or gays and lesbians."*

The Court's Decision Stated:

> *"Amendment 2 bars homosexuals from securing protection against the injuries that these public accommodations laws address. That in itself is a severe consequence, but there is more. Amendment 2, in addition, nullifies specific legal protections for this targeted class in all transactions in housing, sale of real estate, insurance, health and welfare services, private education, and employment...*
>
> *"Not confined to the private sphere, Amendment 2 also operates to repeal and forbid all laws or policies providing specific protection for gays or lesbians from discrimination by every level of Colorado government...Amendment 2's reach may not be limited to specific laws passed for the benefit of gays and lesbians. It is a fair, if not necessary, inference from the broad language of the amendment that it deprives gays and lesbians even of the protection of general laws and policies that prohibit arbitrary discrimination in governmental and private settings...*
>
> *"Homosexuals are forbidden the safeguards that others enjoy or may seek without constraint. They can obtain specific protection against discrimination only by enlisting the citizenry of Colorado to amend the state constitution or perhaps, on the State's view, by trying to pass helpful laws of general applicability. This is so no matter how local or discrete the harm, no matter how public and widespread the injury. We find nothing special in the protections Amendment 2 withholds. These are protections taken for granted by most people either because they already have them or do not need them; these are protections against exclusion from an almost limitless number of transactions and endeavors that*

constitute ordinary civic life in a free society... The 'ultimate effect' [emphasis mine] *of Amendment 2 is to prohibit any governmental entity from adopting similar, or more protective statutes, regulations, ordinances, or policies in the future unless the state constitution is first amended to permit such measures."*

" It is not within our constitutional tradition to enact laws of this sort. Central both to the idea of the rule of law and to our own Constitution's guarantee of equal protection is the principle that government and each of its parts remain open on impartial terms to all who seek its assistance

"If the constitutional conception of 'equal protection of the laws' means anything, it must at the very least mean that a bare desire to harm a politically unpopular group cannot constitute a legitimate governmental interest." [emphasis mine]

An interesting side bar...

When Judge John G. Roberts was nominated for the Supreme Court in August 2005, it was learned he advised gay rights advocates and helped them win a landmark 1996 ruling protecting homosexuals from state-sanctioned discrimination.[2701] According to the *New York Times*, although he did not argue the case or write the legal briefs as an appellate lawyer, Roberts provided "invaluable strategic guidance working pro bono to formulate legal theories and coach them in moot court sessions" for *Romer v. Evans*.[2702] This participation was affirmed in different papers, including the *LA Times*, which first reported the connection.[2703]

The White House had to immediately reassure social conservatives already backing Roberts; including Richard Land of the Southern Baptist Convention.[2704] Land wasn't as worried as James C. Dobson, head of Focus on the Family, who said Roberts work in *Romer v. Evans* was "not welcome news to those of us who advocate for traditional values."[2705] Rush Limbaugh commented: "There's no question this is going to upset people on the right...There's no question the people on the right are going to say: 'Wait a minute. Wait a minute! The guy is doing pro bono work and helping gay activists?'"[2706]

Roberts only gave six hours of advice in the *Romer v. Evans* case, which included Roberts suggesting to win the middle ideology on the Supreme Court and convince the high court that *Bowers v. Hardwick* did not have to be addressed to rule in favor of gays in *Romer*.[2707] At the time of Roberts' confirmation, the justices Roberts was being compared to were Justices Rehnquist, Scalia, and Thomas, who all issued a harsh dissent in *Romer v. Evans*.[2708] According to the *New York Times* (8.5.2005), "Judge Roberts did not mention the *Romer* case in the response he filed to a questionnaire from the Senate Judiciary Committee, which asked about pro bono work. Committee Democrats said they were not troubled by the omission, because it did not appear that Judge Roberts had spent a significant amount of time on the case."[2709]

One person who worked at the law firm in 1996 observed this about Roberts: "Every good lawyer knows that if there is something in his client's cause that so personally offends you, morally, religiously, if it so offends you that you think it would undermine your ability to do your duty as a lawyer, then you shouldn't take it on, and John wouldn't have...So at a minimum he had no concerns that would rise to that level."[2710] I sincerely hope Justice Roberts advocates the constitutionally protected rights of all American citizens when the lesbian and gay community is before his Court.

Lawrence v. Texas 539 U.S. 558 (2003)

In *Lawrence v. Texas* the Supreme Court (6-3) declared unconstitutional a Texas law prohibiting sexual acts between same-sex couples.[2711]

Was it legal for Texas and other states to prosecute sexual relations between homosexuals but not straight couples?[2712] That was a fundamental question in *Lawrence v. Texas*. After the decision, making lover was no longer a crime for gay Americans.[2713]

The Lawrence Case

John Lawrence and Tyron Garner were arrested in Lawrence's apartment in 1998.[2714] The couple was fined $200 when police, after notified of a disturbance, entered the apartment and caught two gay men having sex.[2715] The Texas law prohibited "deviate" sexual activity.[2716]

Lawrence's side had an equal protection claim because Texas law was just one of four state laws remaining that criminalized homosexuals—but not heterosexuals—for sodomy.[2717] *The Nation* commented on how time was on Lawrence's side: "by 2003 only thirteen states still had laws against consensual sodomy on the books. Almost all Americans aged 15-44 engaged in oral sex; half of that cohort had also engaged in anal sex. The United States stood virtually alone among Western nations in maintaining sodomy prohibitions. Moreover, even conservatives were barely defending sodomy laws anymore. While twenty-nine religious groups filed briefs supporting the reversal of Bowers, no denomination wrote a brief in support of Texas. Remarkably, the Bush Administration did not file in the case. Neither did the Texas attorney general."[2718]

Furthermore the social tradition in the case wasn't so much sodomy, but rather the deeply rooted principle that police patrolling your bedroom was unacceptable.

Was the issue in *Lawrence* the 14th Amendment's guarantee of "equal protection of the laws"? The *LA Times* suggested that if the Court considered the 14th Amendment, "such discrimination" would be forbidden, and the decision "could affect state laws on adoptions, foster care, marriage and employment."[2719] The justices did hear an "equal protection" challenge to the Texas law.[2720]

The Court's Ruling

In short, states can no longer prohibit private homosexual activity between consenting adults. In this case, too, the right to privacy was part of the majority opinion, written by Justice Anthony Kennedy.[2721] *Bowers v. Hardwick* (1986) had come to the opposite conclusion and, thru the *Lawrence v. Texas* decision, was overturned.[2722] Sandra Day O'Connor sided with Kennedy, but for a different reason. O'Connor concluded the Texas law was unconstitutional in regard to equal protection: sexual acts between gays were prohibited, but the same acts were allowed with straight couples.[2723] O'Connor, a Reagan appointee, had a unique position given her support for the *Bower* decision.[2724] Antonin Scalia, William Rehnquist (Chief Justice), and Clarence Thomas dissented, in an opinion that argued states had the right to make moral judgment against homosexual conduct and use law enforcement to do so.[2725]

Justice Kennedy wrote for the Court:

> *"The Court began its substantive discussion in Bowers as follows: 'The issue presented is whether the Federal Constitution confers a fundamental right upon homosexuals to engage in sodomy and hence invalidates the laws of the many States that still make such conduct illegal and have done so for a very long time.' That statement, we now conclude, discloses the Court's own failure to appreciate the extent of the liberty at stake. To say that the issue in Bowers was simply the right to engage in certain sexual conduct demeans the claim the individual put forward, just as it would demean a married couple were it to be said marriage is simply about the right to have sexual intercourse." He further stated: "When sexuality finds overt expression in intimate conduct with another person, the conduct can be but one element in a personal bond that is more enduring. The liberty protected by the Constitution allows homosexual persons the right to make this choice."*

Justice Kennedy also called *Bowers* "demeaning" and claimed the decision was wrong the moment it was decided (something the Court almost never says).[2726]

Justice Thomas, dissenting:

> *"I join Justice Scalia's dissenting opinion. I write separately to note that the law before the Court today "is ... uncommonly silly." Griswold v. Connecticut, 381 U.S. 479, 527 (1965) (Stewart, J., dissenting). If I were a member of the Texas Legislature, I would vote to repeal it. Punishing someone for expressing his sexual preference through noncommercial consensual conduct with another adult does not appear to be a worthy way to expend valuable law enforcement resources.* [emphasis mine] *Notwithstanding this, I recognize that as a member of this Court I am not empowered to help petitioners and others similarly situated. My duty, rather, is to "decide cases 'agreeably to the Constitution and laws of the United States... And, just like Justice Stewart, I can find neither in the Bill of Rights nor any other part of the Constitution a general right of privacy..."*

Other Courts

Federal Appeals Court (Tenth Circuit) in Finstuen v. Crutcher (2007)

The Court upheld a lower district court decision that an Oklahoma law barring the recognition of same-sex couple adoptions of minor children, approved by the state of the adoption, was unconstitutional, violating the full faith and credit clause of the U.S. Constitution. The Court stated, *"Because the Oklahoma statute at issue categorically rejects a class of out- of-state adoption decrees, it violates the Full Faith and Credit Clause."*

Iowa Supreme Court: Varnum et al v. Brien (2009)

In August of 2007, the Iowa District Court for Polk County ruled in favor of six same-sex couples who sued to obtain the marriage licenses that had been denied them by the County. The County appealed to the State Supreme Court. The decision of the Iowa Supreme Court declared the Iowa statute banning gay marriage unconstitutional. In an incredibly logical and well written unanimous decision, the Court dismantled all the arguments presented by the County. The Court stated:

> *"The primary constitutional principle at the heart of this case is the doctrine of equal protection. The concept of equal protection is deeply rooted in our national and state history, but that history reveals this concept is often expressed far more easily than it is practiced...*
>
> *"For sure, our nation has struggled to achieve a broad national consensus on equal protection of the laws when it has been forced to apply that principle to some of the institutions, traditions, and norms woven into the fabric of our society...*
>
> *"So, today, this court again faces an important issue that hinges on our definition of equal protection. This issue comes to us with the same importance as our landmark cases of the past. The same-sex-marriage debate waged in this case is part of a strong national dialogue centered on a fundamental, deep-seated, traditional institution that has excluded, by state action, a particular class of Iowans. This class of people asks a simple and direct question: How can a state premised on the constitutional principle of equal protection justify exclusion of a class of Iowans from civil marriage?*
>
> *"It is true the marriage statute does not expressly prohibit gay and lesbian persons from marrying; it does, however, require that if they marry, it must be to someone of the opposite sex. Viewed in the complete context of marriage, including intimacy, civil marriage with a person of the opposite sex is as unappealing to a gay or lesbian person as civil marriage with a person of the same sex is to a heterosexual. Thus, the right of a gay or lesbian person under the marriage statute to enter into a civil marriage only with a person of the opposite sex is no right at all. Under such a law, gay or lesbian individuals cannot simultaneously fulfill their deeply felt need for a committed personal relationship, as influenced by their sexual orientation, and gain the civil status and attendant benefits granted by the statute. Instead, a gay or lesbian person can only gain the same rights under the statute as a heterosexual person by negating the very trait that defines gay and lesbian people as a class—their sexual orientation. In re Marriage Cases, 183 P.3d at 441. The benefit denied by the marriage statute—the status of civil marriage for same-sex couples—is so "closely correlated with being homosexual" as to make it apparent the law is targeted at gay and lesbian people as a class...*
>
> *"Classifications based on factors like race, alienage, national origin, sex, or illegitimacy are so seldom relevant to achievement of any legitimate state interest that laws grounded in such considerations are deemed to reflect prejudice and antipathy."*

The Court carefully examined same sex marriage and other government objectives.

On maintaining traditional marriage:

> *"First, the County argues the same-sex marriage ban promotes the "integrity of traditional marriage" by "maintaining the historical and traditional marriage norm ([as] one between a man and a woman)." This argument is straightforward and has superficial appeal. A*

specific tradition sought to be maintained cannot be an important governmental objective for equal protection purposes, however, when the tradition is nothing more than the historical classification currently expressed in the statute being challenged.
This approach is, of course, an empty analysis. It permits a classification to be maintained "'for its own sake. Moreover, it can allow discrimination to become acceptable as tradition and helps to explain how discrimination can exist for such a long time. If a simple showing that discrimination is traditional satisfies equal protection, previous successful equal protection challenges of invidious racial and gender classifications would have failed.

On the promotion of an optimal environment to raise children:

Another governmental objective proffered by the County is the promotion of "child rearing by a father and a mother in a marital relationship which social scientists say with confidence is the optimal milieu for child rearing." Plaintiffs presented an abundance of evidence and research, confirmed by our independent research, supporting the proposition that the interests of children are served equally by same-sex parents and opposite-sex parents.

On the other hand, we acknowledge the existence of reasoned opinions that dual-gender parenting is the optimal environment for children. These opinions, while thoughtful and sincere, were largely unsupported by reliable scientific studies. [emphasis mine] *The civil marriage statute is under-inclusive because it does not exclude from marriage other groups of parents—such as child abusers, sexual predators, parents neglecting to provide child support, and violent felons—that are undeniably less than optimal parents. Such under-inclusion tends to demonstrate that the sexual-orientation-based classification is grounded in prejudice or "overbroad generalizations about the different talents, capacities, or preferences" of gay and lesbian people, rather than having a substantial relationship to some important objective. If the marriage statute was truly focused on optimal parenting, many classifications of people would be excluded, not merely gay and lesbian people.*

On the promotion of procreation:

The County also proposes that government endorsement of traditional civil marriage will result in more procreation... While heterosexual marriage does lead to procreation, the argument by the County fails to address the real issue in our required analysis of the objective: whether exclusion of gay and lesbian individuals from the institution of civil marriage will result in more procreation? If procreation is the true objective, then the proffered classification must work to achieve that objective.

Conceptually, the promotion of procreation as an objective of marriage is compatible with the inclusion of gays and lesbians within the definition of marriage. Gay and lesbian persons are capable of procreation. Thus, the sole conceivable avenue by which exclusion of gay and lesbian people from civil marriage could promote more procreation is if the unavailability of civil marriage for same-sex partners caused homosexual individuals to "become" heterosexual in order to procreate within the present traditional institution of civil marriage.

On promoting stability in opposite-sex relationships:

A fourth suggested rationale supporting the marriage statute is "promoting stability in opposite sex relationships. While the institution of civil marriage likely encourages stability in opposite-sex relationships, we must evaluate whether excluding gay and lesbian people from civil marriage encourages stability in opposite- sex relationships. The County offers no reasons that it does, and we can find none. The stability of opposite-sex relationships is an important governmental interest, but the exclusion of same-sex couples from marriage is not substantially related to that objective.

On Constitutional Infirmity:

> *We are firmly convinced the exclusion of gay and lesbian people from the institution of civil marriage does not substantially further any important governmental objective. The legislature has excluded a historically disfavored class of persons from a supremely important civil institution without a constitutionally sufficient justification. There is no material fact, genuinely in dispute, that can affect this determination.*

Sometimes we have to go to Court. It is our right. It is the place we go after the legislature or even the voters violate our Constitutional freedoms.

In the November, 2006, election, over 1.2 million people in Wisconsin voted for a constitutional amendment that defined marriage as a union between a man and a woman and banned any legal status 'substantially similar' to marriage, such as civil unions.[2727] The amendment passed 59-41 percent.

Among voters who turned out for the midterm elections, it seems the first reason they turned out was to vote on the amendment. The only Wisconsin official to outpoll the amendment was U.S. Senator Herb Kohl, who received 1.44 million votes to win re-election.[2728] Kohl is a well-established senator who had minimal competition.

There were only a handful of counties that voted to kill the amendment, or came close to it. The ban lost in Dane (67-33) and La Crosse (by 16 votes), and it barely won in Eau Claire (52-48) and Iowa (51-49).[2729]

The GOP Quest Helped Democrats

Although the measure was intended to increase GOP turnout, the *Milwaukee Journal Sentinel* reported (11.9.06), "…the measure clearly had an unintended consequence by sparking a larger-than-expected turnout, especially among left-leaning college students, who flooded their campus polling places. The result: Dems scored some unexpected gains in the Statehouse."[2730]

The state Republicans lost over a half dozen seats in the Assembly, and five of the new Democratic legislators were elected in districts including a UW campus.[2731] The Repubilcans said (before the election) their data concluded gubernatorial candidate Rep. Mark Green needed 940,000 votes to unseat Gov. Doyle; Green passed the goal by 36,000 votes but was seven percentage points short of victory.[2732] Although Fair Wisconsin's Mike Tate said Gov. Doyle would have won without Fair Wisconsin, Tate did say he felt his organization helped Democrats in legislative races.[2733]

Conservative Democrats came to the polls, as about 275,000 people cast ballots for the ban on same-sex marriages but did not vote for Mark Green.[2734] U.S. Rep. Jim Sensenbrenner, a Republican, said the GOP strategy gave opponents 1 ½ years to organize and raise money, and "was a lose-lose situation….You had Reagan Democrats and socially conservative union members who wanted to vote yes and yes (on the referendums [including one on capital punishment]) and then voted for Doyle. And then you had liberals who voted no on both, then voted for Democrats."[2735]

The purpose of the amendment was to ensure Republican victories. The amendment's supporters, in the following court case, ignored this basic truth. These merchants of hate used the lives of real people for crass political gamesmanship. And they failed. The Democrats won.

McConkey vs. Van Hollen: Filed in July 2007

The specific language in the following suit filed against the State of Wisconsin explains my reasoning and my attack on the fallacies of logic of the gay-marriage and anti-civil union opponents. The proponents of this Amendment could have cared less about the "rights of man", or Constitutional protections.

Please note that this case was filed *Pro Per*. I did not have a lawyer. I did not have the money to hire one. I looked at other cases filed on the same subject, in the nation, others cases filed in Wisconsin district courts, and followed their format. In addition, I represented myself, in the oral arguments before the Circuit Court. Only after I won the right to proceed on the "single subject "requirement for Constitutional Amendments, was I approached about the assistance of an attorney. The exact wording of the document follows. Please, you are free to use this document to copy and to aid in lawsuits against government restrictions on individual liberties and rights. Exact formats will change from court to court, however the case below will give any plaintiff a good start. This will perhaps sound self-serving, but I think one can learn a lot about the issues by reading the Iowa decision and the following. I attempted to take the issue apart, piece by piece.

IN THE CIRCUIT COURT FOR DANE COUNTY
IN THE FIFTH JUDICIAL DISTRICT
OF THE STATE OF WISCONSIN

WILLIAM C. MCCONKEY, pro per *(Plaintiff)* *v.*

JAMES DOYLE, IN HIS ROLE AS GOVERNOR OF WISCONSIN AND J.B. VAN HOLLEN, IN HIS ROLE AS ATTORNEY GENERAL OF WISCONSIN

PETITION FOR INJUNCTION AND DECLARATION OF UNCONSTITUTIONALITY

Now comes William C. McConkey, plaintiff, and hereafter returned to as the plaintiff, and petitions this court to issue an injunction precluding the named defendants from promulgating or enforcing any laws, regulations, policies or procedures enforcing in any way the Constitutional amendment passed in November 2006, as question seven that stated "Shall section 13 of article XIII of the constitution be created to provide that only a marriage between one man and one woman shall be valid or recognized as a marriage in this state and that a legal status identical or substantially similar to that of marriage for unmarried individuals shall not be valid or recognized in this state?"

The passed Amendment hereafter referred to as the Amendment states the following, "Only a marriage between one man and one woman shall be valid or recognized as a marriage in this state. A legal status identical or substantially similar to that of marriage for unmarried individuals shall not be valid or recognized in this state."

Further the plaintiff asks the Court to issue the injunction until the Constitutional questions contained herein are decided and the plaintiff asks the Court to declare the Amendment unconstitutional and null and void for the reasons described by any or all of the arguments presented below and to set the Amendment aside.

Further the plaintiff asks the Court to recognize that the plaintiff is filing pro per and is not and never has been an attorney and that the plaintiff be allowed certain technical, wording or procedural errors that might occur and that the matters contained herein be considered upon their merits.

I.

STANDING

The plaintiff, William C. McConkey, is a bona fide resident of Wisconsin, … Further, the plaintiff, William C. McConkey, is a registered voter in the town of … Further, the plaintiff, William C. McConkey, does business in Wisconsin, headquartered… Further the plaintiff is employed in Wisconsin and pays taxes in Wisconsin. As such above, the plaintiff, William C. McConkey, has standing to request this injunction.

II.

PRIOR PROCEEDINGS

The Wisconsin legislature per Section 1 of Article XII of the Wisconsin Constitution agreed to the amendment written and presented above and according to Section 1 of Article XII and presented such amendment to the people for a vote. Please note that nothing in the above sentence infers the Constitutionality of the proposed Amendment or the adherence to the Constitution of Wisconsin or the United States in the process of writing or pushing the Amendment through the legislature. The voters approved the Amendment in the general election in November, 2006.

III.

ARGUMENTS

A. The legislature erred and the voters erred when they approved an amendment that is, as it is written and passed, outlaws all Constitutional and legal protections, rights and privileges for unmarried individuals in direct violation of the 14th Amendment to the U.S. Constitution. The Amendment states, “Only a marriage between one man and one woman shall be valid or recognized as a marriage in this state and a legal status identical or similar to that of marriage for unmarried individuals shall not be valid or recognized in this state.”

“Identical or substantially similar to that of marriage” is, by the first part of the amendment, between one man and one woman. The construction of the amendment defines marriage as between one man and one woman and then says anything identical or similar to that (one man and woman) for unmarried individuals shall not be valid.

The logical and technical construction of this amendment makes legal and binding arrangements concerning unmarried men and women by their employers null and void. This certainly violates the equal protections of the 14th Amendment to the U.S. Constitution.

At the same time, a profile of Wisconsin households, released by the United States Census Bureau, shows a significant decline in the percent of households containing married couples, with a corresponding increase in unmarried households, including those with unmarried couples. The profile is the first data released from the 2005 Census on the various types of households in Wisconsin.

Married couples now live in 50.8 percent of the state's households compared with 57.5 percent in 1990. Households occupied by unmarried adults increased from 42.5 percent in 1990 to 49.1 percent in 2000. If this trend continues, most Wisconsin households will be unmarried by the time the next full Census is taken in 2010.

Wisconsin households containing unmarried adults who identified as "unmarried partners" increased significantly from 69,311 in 1990 to 144,272 in 2000 -- a numeric jump of 108 percent. The Census Bureau refers to "unmarried partners" as two unmarried adults who live together in an intimate relationship. They can be two adults of the same sex or of the opposite sex.

A profile of the nation's households, which was released in August 2006, Census Bureau, showed over half of America's households are now unmarried.

Only 49.8 percent of the nation's households containing a “couple” contain a married couple in 2005., down from 55 percent in 1990. 60.8 percent in 1980, and 70.5 percent in 1970. Unmarried couples make up 50.2% of the couples and 33.1% of all adults.

There are 30 million living alone.

This amendment will create havoc in interstate commerce and contracts. Obligations between unmarried men and women from all over the United States will be null and void in Wisconsin. There were 144,272 households or 288,544 Wisconsin citizens in August 2005, who will lose Constitutional contracting protections and civil rights and liberty protections under the Defense of Marriage

Amendment. This sentence is a nightmare for unmarried people living together, regardless of gender. This sentence creates a Constitutional bias against unmarried adults sharing households and children. This sentence was too vague to be on the ballot. Its implications are horrendous.

There are those who will argue Legislative intent was to deny these Constitutional and legal protections, rights and privileges to couples of the same gender. If that was the intent, the Amendment fails to match intent. And, indeed, that intent violates the "equal protection of the laws" clause of the Fourteenth Amendment to the U.S. Constitution.

INDEED, *Lawrence v. Texas*, 539 U.S. 558 (2003), and *Romer v. Evans*, 517 U.S. 620 (1996), both explicitly state that the States may not inhibit or limit the rights and protections of a targeted group of people that other people get to enjoy. This amendment does exactly that; it directly, willfully and purposefully limits the rights of unmarried couples of the same genders and it limits the rights of homosexuals to enjoy the benefits of either marriage or civil unions, just because of who they are. The amendment does not even pass a rational-basis scrutiny for it does nothing to protect a legitimate government interest. It will be argued by some that the amendment protects traditional marriage. It does nothing of the kind. It may protect the image of traditional marriage in the mind of some, but it protects no actual marriage. No one is married until they have said their vows, signed the papers that legally marries them. Only then is there a marriage to protect. The amendment does nothing to protect that marriage from being harmed by adultery, abuse, financial mismanagement, sexual incompatibility, alcoholism, desertion, drug abuse, or any other cause of divorce. The term "traditional marriage" must include broken marriages since at least fifty percent of them are broken. There is no way the rational-basis scrutiny test is met. If it is constitutional to ban behaviors such as marriage to "protect marriage," banning divorce seems to make much more sense.

B. The legislature erred when it approved the proposed amendment based upon a false premise and presented it to the citizens on a false premise. The premise posited by the legislature is that this amendment "defends marriage." The amendment does nothing to defend marriage. The history of divorce, broken marriages and spousal abuse during the last 50 years is one of steady, dramatic and tragic increase. Claiming to defend marriage by outlawing civil unions is patently absurd and an infringement on the rights of many people without benefit to any person.

C. The legislature erred and the voters erred when they approved the amendment which discriminates against a class of people in favor of another class. The proposed amendment is in direct conflict with the 14th Amendment to the U.S. Constitution. Animus against a class of people is not a legitimate goal of government. If the "equal protection of the law" Clause means anything it has to mean that harming a politically unpopular group cannot be a legitimate government interest or activity. The proposed amendment harms a group simply unpopular with others. Further, in *Romer v. Evans*, Supp. 12, the U.S. Supreme Court struck down a state constitutional amendment which both overturned local ordinances prohibiting discrimination against homosexuals and prohibited any state or local governmental action to either remedy discrimination or to grant preferences based on sexual orientation.

In *Romer*, the Court stated, "In order to reconcile the Fourteenth Amendment's promise that no person shall be denied equal protection with the practical reality that most legislation classifies for one purpose or another, the Court has stated that it will uphold a law that neither burdens a fundamental right nor targets a suspect class so long as the legislative classification bears a rational relation to some independent and legitimate legislative end."

The Wisconsin Amendment defies, even this conventional inquiry. First, the amendment is at once too narrow and too broad, identifying persons by a single trait (unmarried or gay/lesbian) and then denying them the possibility of protection across the board. This disqualification of a class of persons from the right to obtain specific protection from the law is unprecedented and is itself a denial of equal protection in the most literal sense.

Second, the sheer breadth of Amendment which creates a general cause that gays and lesbians and unmarried persons shall not have any particular protections from the law, is so far removed from the reasons offered for it .

The Amendment raises the inevitable inference that it is born of animosity toward the class that it affects. It may be argued that the Amendment is not aimed at all single persons but has at its aim the prohibition of marriage between gays and lesbians, man to man, woman to woman, targeting only homosexuals. Then, the Wisconsin Amendment is a status based classification of persons undertaken for its animus against a class of people, homosexuals., something the Equal Protection Clause, clearly does not permit. (*Romer v. Evans*, ibid.)

D. The legislature and the voters erred when they approved a proposed amendment which creates distinctions between people because of their ancestry. *Hirabayashi v. United States*, 329 U.S. 81, 100 (1943) states that "distinctions between citizens solely because of their ancestry" as being "odious to a free people whose institution we founded upon the doctrine of equality.

This amendment also targets homosexuals, people of the same sex who wish to marry. Homosexuality may be genetically caused, caused by *in utero* events and changes, or by one's environment, or all three. All of these possibilities are recognized scientifically as causes of one's ancestry and who one is. If any homosexual is of that sexual preference because of genetics, *in utero* Impacts, environment or ancestry, that person cannot be discriminated against and the cause of the discrimination be consistent with the U.S. Constitution's 14th Amendment.

E. The legislature and the voters erred when they approved a proposed amendment which is in direct opposition to and in conflict with the First Amendment of the U.S. Constitution's protection of free speech. The freedom of speech has long been held by the Court to include acts of expression of thought, conscience and emotion. The definition of speech has included dance and art and acts of protest and even pornography. Freedom of expression also includes expression of love and trust and commitment. Marriage, civil unions, common law agreements, mutual benefits are all expressions of a deeper conscious emotion and thought which have must have an avenue of expression and communication. If public displays of the most graphic of sexual acts are protected expression, those same protections must certainly shelter expressions of trust, commitment and love. To ban these avenues, to ban the protection of the freedom of speech clause to two groups of people while allowing only for married heterosexuals is, as does this Wisconsin amendment, is a direct violation of the First Amendment of the U.S. Constitution.

F. The legislature erred in its failure to divide the proposed amendment into more than one amendment as clearly stated in the Wisconsin Constitution in Article XII, Section 1, to wit, "...provided that if more than one amendment be submitted, they should be submitted in such a manner that the people may vote for or against such amendments separately."

Any reasonable person knows that in the public discussions of the wide area of marriage between people of the same sex and the issue commonly referred to as "civil unions," the two are separate issues and separate topics. The way this proposed amendment is drafted, the legal status of unmarried people of different genders is a third major issue. "A legal status identical or substantially similar to that of marriage for unmarried individuals shall not be valid or recognized in this state." Marriage between people of the same sex is one issue. The ability of people of the same sex to enter civil unions, to adopt and raise children, share real and personal property and money through contracts and wills and spousal benefits, enter into the medical decision agreements, use sick or bereavement leave to take care of a partner or partner's child, to receive pension or Social Security benefits, or to receive benefits from an employer, is another distinct subject. A third issue is the ability of unmarried people, of different genders, to enter into any contract, trust, debt, or agreement concerning children, to name but a few.

Indeed, legislative debates have identified these subjects as separate subjects during discussion in hearings and on the floor. The media has discussed the issues as separate subjects. Public polling has shown a wide disparity between the issues in public sentiment. There is no question that this amendment as written, is three separate amendments, and as written should not have been allowed on the ballot.

G. The legislature erred when it wrote and passed a proposed constitutional amendment and the voters erred when they approved said amendment because it is in direct conflict with other sections of the Wisconsin Constitution. These conflicts will do much public harm. These direct and clear conflicts follow:

Conflict 1:

Article I, Section 1 of the Wisconsin Constitution states: "All people are born equally free and independent and have certain inherent rights; among these are life, liberty and the pursuit of happiness…"

The Amendment creates different classes of adults and allows certain rights for some people while prohibiting these rights to others with that prohibition based solely on gender, with no crime committed as prior public harm demanding punishment. The second sentence, "A legal status identical or substantially similar to that of marriage for unmarried individuals shall not be valid or recognized in this state," also creates two distinct classes of people, married and unmarried, regardless of gender, and states that legal status available to one shall not be available to the other. That could very include trusts, contracts, living wills, joint ownership, parental rights, and protection from abuse harm, residential responsibilities and debts. The proposed amendment is clearly in direct conflict with Article I, Section 1.

Conflict 2:

Article I, Section 9, of the Wisconsin Constitution states: "Every person is entitled to a certain remedy in the laws for all injuries, or wrongs which he may receive in his person, property or character; he ought to obtain justice freely…"

The amendment is clearly in direct conflict with Article I, Section 9, where this section states "every person." It does not say every person except gay people, or single people. "Every person" means every person.

The amendment certainly keeps large numbers of people from obtaining justice freely." There is no rational way the proposed amendment can be in concert with this "justice" clause.

Conflict 3:

Article I, Section 11, of the Wisconsin Constitution states, "The right of people to be secure in their persons, houses, papers and effects shall not be violated." The amendment places clear ownership of homes, houses, papers and effects in jeopardy for people of the same gender and unmarried people of any gender living in arrangements similar to marriage and may cause a lost of property and effects from employers and organizations.

Conflict 4:

Article I, Section 12, of the Wisconsin Constitution states, "No bill of attainder, ex post facto law, or any law impairing the obligation of contracts, shall ever be passed..."

The amendment would impair the obligation of contracts between employers and employees concerning benefits for domestic partners, agreements concerning adopted children, and property. There is a clear conflict between the proposed amendment and Article I, Section 12.

Conflict 5:

Article I, Section 18, of the Wisconsin Constitution states "...nor shall any control of, or interference with, the rights of conscience be permitted..."

Conscience without expression is meaningless. Except for treason, or expression that is harmful to individual or public safety, is expression constitutionally or statutorily restricted. Love and/or trust are expressions of conscience. That expression is certainly controlled or interfered with by the proposed amendment.

Conflict 6:

Article I, Section 27, of the Wisconsin Constitution states "The blessings of a free government can only be maintained by a firm adherence to justice..."

The proposed amendment, as written, is certainly not "just" for those who wish to marry or enter into a civil union or domestic partnership. The proposed amendment is in direct conflict with the concept of justice.

IV.

PRAYER FOR RELIEF

Wherefore, the plaintiff, William C. McConkey, a citizen of Wisconsin, prays that this Court issue an temporary injunction enjoining the named defendants from promulgating or enforcing any regulations, policies or procedures enforcing in any way the Constitutional amendment passed in November 2006, as question seven that stated "Shall section 13 of article XIII of the constitution be created to provide that only a marriage between one man and one woman shall be valid or recognized as a marriage in this state and that a legal status identical or substantially similar to that of marriage for unmarried individuals shall not be valid or recognized in this state?" Further the plaintiff, William C. McConkey asks this court to declare the amendment which states, "Only a marriage between one man and one woman shall be valid or recognized as a marriage in this state. A legal status identical or substantially similar to that of marriage for unmarried individuals shall not be valid or recognized in this state." as unconstitutional, for all or any combination, or any single one of the above reasons.

...

Respectfully submitted,
William C. McConkey...pro per

Circuit Court Ruling

Judge Niess of the Dane County Circuit Court ruled (Sept.2007) I had not been individually and directly "harmed" by the amendment; but the court did not dismiss the entirety of the lawsuit and invited briefs by both sides.[2736] I originally claimed the amendment violated the equal protection clause of the U.S. Constitution but Niess ruled I did not have standing to sue on that issue. However Niess allowed me to proceed on the single-amendment requirement. [2737]

Banning Civil Unions is NOT Banning Gay Marriage

In March 2005, State Representative Mark Gundrum, R-New Berlin said, "It is a constitutional amendment that would put into our Constitution that marriage in this state should only be between a man and a woman…The amendment would also make sure gay marriages termed by something else, like civil union or civil covenant, also are precluded from being legalized by an activist court in this state in the future."[2738] A civil union is not gay marriage. That's why it is called a *civil union.* Yet Gundrum said he wanted both banned, and the constitutional amendment did that.

The *Milwaukee Journal Sentinel* also reported (11.8.2006), "In practical terms, the amendment appears to ban the possibility of civil unions."[2739] "Civil unions" was not specifically word for word in the amendment passed.

Fair Wisconsin publically sided with my argument, noting that polling data from April 2006 showed a huge disparity between the 65% of people who supported banning gay marriage and the 37% who supported a ban on civil unions.[2740] Likewise, a 2004 Badger Poll showed, "Support for an amendment rose when language excluding civil unions was dropped. In that case, 66 percent of Wisconsin residents said they would support the amendment, while 28 percent said they would not. When asked whether they would favor an amendment banning civil unions, support for the proposal by Wisconsin residents dropped by 11 percentage points to 53 percent."[2741]

These polls thwart Julaine Appling's logic. Appling said the will of Wisconsin was vindicated in November 2006. In truth, the amendment banned civil unions which Wisconsinites had considerably more favorability too. Though a ban on civil unions may too have passed, clearly banning civil unions and banning gay marriage are two different items. Judge Niess argued both sections of the amendment served a single purpose. It's illogical to put two provisions in an amendment if they both serve a single purpose. If they were both *flip sides of one coin,* then only one for the provisions would have been needed in the amendment. There was no need to have the second sentence in amendment unless it was a different subject, which it was!

Arguing The Single Subject Rule

The State's Attorney General, a right wing self-promoting Republican, and one of the defendants in my suit, filed an appeal of the District's court ruling. At this point attorney Lester Pines, a well respected attorney in Madison, Wisconsin, volunteered to assist. I was and am eternally grateful for his patience and assistance, and for that of his associate Tamara Packard and for that of Edward Marion, also of Madison.

I know a "little bit of knowledge" can be dangerous and my impatience and frustration over what I considered legal minutia and legalese was impertinent. I just wanted to win this case so badly to correct what was a monstrous attack on human liberty that I couldn't let go of it. I do apologize, here, publicly, if I offended them or their profession, with my barrage of emails and pseudo-legal interpretations.

The Wisconsin Constitution says if more than one amendment is submitted, voters must be able to vote for or against the amendments separately.[2742]

Pines and Packard argued in a May 19, 2009, brief that the first proposition in the referendum question "stated who may marry, and the second proposition limited unmarried individuals from accessing the same or a substantially similar set of rights and obligations to those provided to married people. That is a far different purpose than the first: defining what is and is not a valid marriage in Wisconsin."[2743] With two distinct purposes, their argument was that "the ballot question violated the single general purpose prong of the single-amendment requirement."[2744]

There was precedent. The Wisconsin Supreme Court had ruled three times in the past 125 years on whether a constitutional amendment was improperly put to voters, but only once did the court find a referendum question (on redistricting in 1953) did not pass the single amendment requirement.[2745]

My Alternative Opinion

Regardless of the wording or the precedents, during the preparations for court hearings I personally made the following arguments to my attorneys:

The Department claims McConkey has suffered no injury due to the passage of the amendment that states "only a marriage between one man and one woman shall be valid in this state, and a legal status identical or substantially similar to that of marriage for unmarried individual shall not be valid or recognized."

Quite the contrary to the Department's claim McConkey has no family who has suffered from the ban on same sex marriage or "marriage-like" status, McConkey has a daughter who lives in Wisconsin who is homosexual and lives with her female partner. His daughter is forbidden by the Amendment to marry her partner and enter into a civil union that will provide marriage like benefits. The Department apparently relied on inaccurate press reporting for its conjecture.

...McConkey also is directly impacted as a parent. McConkey tries to assist his daughter to understand and cope with the violation of her First and Fourteenth Amendment protections and the ability of the State to single out a group of people and eliminate their U.S. Constitutional rights and protections, just because of who they are. U.S. Supreme Court decisions have overturned such attempts. *Lawrence v. Texas (2003); Romer v. Evans (1996); Hirabayashi v. United States (1943); Meyer v. State of Nebraska (1923).*

Finally, since this Amendment fosters such discrimination and prejudice, McConkey fears for such a social climate that would be and is harmful to his daughter. This causes McConkey stress. Such social climate leads to events such as the attack upon and killing of Matt Shepard, a gay young man. Any parent of a homosexual child can testify to the fear of social harm and/or ridicule to their children. The Amendment adds to that fear, directly. The Department completely fails to recognize the impact of such pressures on a family. The Department either failed to even think about such fears or has chosen to ignore them. Both are unacceptable and inhumane.

The State claims McConkey has no standing to claim any First Amendment violations. As the parent of a gay child, that claim is certainly false. The U.S. Supreme Court has long stated non-verbal, as well as verbal expression, is protected. McConkey, by the Amendment, is prohibited the expression, either verbal or non-verbal that goes with the pride and joy in the wedding, marriage and life together of his daughter and her choice of partner as a married couple. He cannot celebrate with this child as he does with his other daughters.

The State cannot believe its own words when it writes the Amendment "does not purport to proscribe speech and expressive conduct because it disapproves of the ideas expressed." The whole purpose of the Amendment was and is to keep people from expressing their love and trust and commitment to one another because they are gay and believe they should be married. The very idea of gay marriage is what drove this issue in the voters' minds. The State's argument in this instance is void of reasonable support. When the State claims marriage is "simply a civil contract that creates a legal status," the State admits it prohibits contracts to a class a people that others can obtain and the State admits that it doesn't know much about marriage and the view of marriage this Amendment purports. Indeed, the argument that the Amendment is necessary to protect marriage is absurd on its face in light of the State's argument that it is "simply a civil contract".

As the parent of a gay child, McConkey is forbidden to enter a contract with her and her married partner as a married couple. That contract could also be an expression of love and commitment.

McConkey is a voter in Wisconsin. The State claims being a voter does not give standing. McConkey argues it certainly does because the Amendment was placed upon the ballot in conflict with Wisconsin's own Constitution.

A. The legislature erred in its failure to divide the proposed amendment into more than one amendment as clearly stated in the Wisconsin Constitution in Article XII, Section 1, to wit, "...provided that if more than one amendment be submitted, they should be submitted in such a manner that the people may vote for or against such amendments separately."

Any reasonable person knows that in the public discussions of the wide area of marriage between people of the same sex and the issue commonly referred to as "civil unions", the two are separate issues and separate topics. The way this proposed amendment is drafted, the legal status of unmarried people of different genders is a third major issue. "<u>A legal status identical or substantially similar to that of marriage for unmarried individuals shall not be valid or recognized in this state</u>." Marriage between people of the same sex is one issue. The ability of people of the same sex to enter civil unions, to adopt and raise children, to share real and personal property and money through contracts and wills and spousal benefits, to enter into medical decision agreements, to use sick or bereavement leave to take care of a partner or partner's child, to receive pension or Social Security benefits, or to receive benefits form an employer, are distinctly different subjects. A third issue is the ability of unmarried people, <u>of different genders</u>, to enter into any contract, trust, debt, or agreement concerning children, to name but a few.

Indeed, legislative debates have identified these subjects as separate subjects during discussion in hearings and on the floor. The media has discussed the issues as separate subjects. Public polling has shown a wide disparity between the issues in public sentiment. There is no question this amendment as written, is three separate amendments, and as written, should not have been allowed on the ballot.

Indeed, the State treats the issue of marriage and domestic benefits as two separate issues in the Motion to Dismiss.

The extreme irony is the state claims a plaintiff lacks standing thereby claiming the amendment has direct impact upon only those who are homosexual and wish to be married but the amendment was placed on the ballot to be voted upon by millions who, by the definition of the state, were not impacted and therefore had no standing. Had the ballot been limited to homosexuals, only those who were directly impacted using the definition of the state, the results would have been quite different. <u>The state should not be allowed to have it both ways.</u> When the political process abuses the citizen, the citizen must go to the court. When the political process gives millions of citizens the standing to abuse a small minority, other members of the millions must also be given standing by the judicial process, to challenge the majority decision or mob rule prevails.

This is no different than saying the German people had no standing or responsibility to protect the retarded and the Roma (Gypsies) and the Jews during the reign of the Nazis.

The Plaintiff recognizes standing is an issue of judicial review. In this instance standing is a question of constitutional importance far beyond causes and damages. Although the Plaintiff has standing under causes and damages and has shown so above, the equally important issues are of major importance to the conduct of State government in a constitutional system and precedent and logic that states the State has violated the equal protections, immunities, rights and privileges of United States citizens residing in Wisconsin.

When the discussion moves to merits it will be further shown that the State can defend no claim of compelling interest of the state as connected to the Amendment. See *Meyer v. Nebraska*. In *Meyer* the Court stated:

> "While this court has not attempted to define with exactness the liberty thus guaranteed, the term has received much consideration and some of the included things have been definitely stated. Without doubt, it denotes not merely freedom from bodily restraint but also the right of the individual to contract, to engage in any of the common occupations of life, to acquire useful knowledge, to marry, establish a home and bring up children, to worship God according to the dictates of his own conscience, and generally to enjoy those privileges long recognized at common law as essential to the orderly pursuit of happiness by free men."

The proponents of amendments to limit civil unions and gay marriage claim the amendments are necessary to protect "traditional marriage" and they prohibit such arrangements by making a gender based decision, i.e, men or women. In Wisconsin the language structurally outlaws civil unions between a man and a woman and no one else. They claim it will support traditional marriage. There is absolutely no proof this is true.

The Supreme Court ruled against such gender based suits and laws without a proven compelling interest and a direct connection with the law. In *Craig. v. Boren* (1976) Brennan wrote for the Court, Blackmun, Powell, Stevens, and Stewart concurring; Burger and Rehnquist in dissent. The Court announced for the first time that sex-based classifications were subjected to stricter scrutiny under the Equal Protection Clause of the Fourteenth Amendment than was provided by the rational basis or "ordinary scrutiny" test. As stated by Justice Brennan, the constitutional standard that would have to be met for a statute classifying by gender is that it "must serve important governmental objectives and must be substantially related to those objectives."

If the goal is to preserve and protect traditional marriage there is no direct connection or any statistical evidence that these amendments concerning gay marriage or civil unions will assist in anyway.

If the goal is to keep gay men and lesbians from enjoying the same Constitutional protections as the rest of the population, it is in direct animus with a class of people and strictly prohibited by the Fourteenth Amendment.

Simply put, there may be cultural or religious reasons for some people to want to void and/or prohibit the gay marriages and/or civil unions of others, but there are none that are constitutional.

There is nothing in the amendment to "preserve" or "protect" "the unique and historical status of traditional marriage." Divorce Court, adultery, bigamy, alcohol and drug abuse, financial stress, child-raising difficulties, career conflicts, and domestic violence are not covered by the amendment.

I can find no record of any divorce requested, in Wisconsin or any other state, because that state did not have a ban on gay marriage or civil unions. No where, ever.

Unique? Millions of Americans live together, have sexual intercourse, comingle funds, raise children and grandchildren, squabble and laugh, love and die, they do all the things that married people do, without being married. Even oaths of fidelity and love before God are often taken before witnesses, without marriage. This "unique" word was and is a semantic creation of purpose by the judge, Judge Niess. This situation describes the relationship of many older Americans who cannot marry because the law would strip them of Social Security, their major source of income, and this amendment now keeps them from caring for one another the way married couples can.

So what is unique about marriage in Wisconsin? "Unique" is the paper work, a civil contract, a license. In addition, in Wisconsin, marriages are unique from other relationships because a marriage causes the partners to be susceptible to felony charges that no other person may be charged with, namely, adultery and bigamy. To be susceptible to those charges is the only way a relationship could be identical or substantially similar to marriage. No other arrangement would cause this situation.

"...historical status of traditional marriage"

Traditional means what? First marriage, second, third? With clergy or without? At what age? With or without parental consent? To whom? Partners based on race, religion? Jewish, Hmong, Korean, Japanese, Somali, Sicilian, Catholic, Protestant, Amish, Mormon, Hindu, Muslim, Buddhist, rural, all have different traditions. Which applies to Wisconsin, a state with all nationalities and religions within our population?

Maybe traditional means the "Old Testament" tradition of plural wives and concubines and sisters of deceased brothers. Which historical status and which traditional marriage?

The Amendment bases all of this on gender…

The Wisconsin Supreme Court has ruled, "*A gender-based rule must serve important governmental objectives and the means employed must be substantially related to the achievement of those objectives." (Marshfield Clinic v. Discher, 105 Wis. 2d 506, 314 N.W.2d 326 (1982).*

What is the government objective, or objectives and what was the purpose of these objectives?

One: The Circuit Court Judge said, **"…the preservation and protection of the unique and historical status of traditional marriage."**

Will there be fewer divorces, less spousal abuse, less child abuse and neglect, less adultery, fewer financial difficulties, less personal incompatibility, homicides? Will fewer people get married if this amendment did not exist? It did not exist from 1848 until 2006, for 158 years. Its absence had no impact on marriages beginning or ending.

The means employed are not substantially related to the achievement of the objective.

Two: It appears, another objective is to prohibit the legislature or any local government or public institution from issuing or honoring domestic benefits and civil unions, for unmarried couples, regardless of gender. What are the specific objectives? Again, Judge Neiss said, **"…the preservation and protection of the unique and historical status of traditional marriage."**

Again, will there be fewer divorces, less spousal abuse, less child abuse and/or neglect, less adultery, fewer financial difficulties, less personal incompatibility, or homicides? Will fewer people get married because if this amendment did not exist? It did not exist from 1848 until 2006, for 158 years. Its absence had no impact on marriages beginning or ending.

The Appeals Court, on April 09, 2009, certified the case to go directly to the Supreme Court, and The Supreme Court of the State of Wisconsin agreed to hear my case.

I hoped for a broad and deep argument on all the issues and thought the Court, indeed, would accept that. My reasoning came from the words *"…the entire appeal, which includes all issues, not merely the issues certified or the issue for which the court accepts the certification. Further, the court has jurisdiction over issues not certified because the court may review an issue directly on its own motion."*

The briefs and counter briefs went right back to narrow definitions and interpretations about what the legislature could or could not do. The State also appealed the lower court's ruling on my standing.

Probably to their dismay I started to send my opinions to Lester, Tamara, and Ed Marion. They were the same as my earlier work. What follows is what I thought would make the best approach for our oral arguments.

My thoughts for oral arguments
9/16/09
To: Lester, Tamara, Edward
From: Bill McConkey

The issues of standing and whether the amendment one amendment or two, or one amendment with one purpose or more than one purpose, or one subject or more than one subject, are before the Court.

The plaintiff, William McConkey, a voter in Wisconsin in 2006, and still a registered voter in Wisconsin, like all Wisconsin voters in 2006, was given a single amendment on the ballot that included, in its wording and in it implications and effects, to him, the voter, all the following questions:

1. Shall the voters of the State, by a simple majority of one vote, of those voters actually voting on the question, have the power to remove United States and Wisconsin Constitutional protections, rights, privileges and immunities from selected groups of people?
2. Shall marriage, under a State License, be limited to one man and one woman?
3. Shall legal arrangements identical or substantially similar to marriage be allowed for opposite gender adults in Wisconsin?
4. Shall legal arrangements identical or substantially similar to marriage be allowed for same-sex adults in Wisconsin?
5. Shall legal marriages and civil union and other legal arrangements between same-sex couples from other States and nations be recognized in Wisconsin or shall Wisconsin violate the full faith and credit clause of the U.S. Constitution?
6. Shall the Legislature be allowed to, or prohibited from, establishing some OR ANY certain legal protections and benefits for non-married single adults that are held and enjoyed by married people in Wisconsin?
7. Shall Article I, Section 1, be stricken from the Wisconsin Constitution? Article I, Section 1 of the Wisconsin Constitution states: "All people are born equally free and independent and have certain inherent rights; among these are life, liberty and the pursuit of happiness…"?
8. Shall "Freedom of Conscience," Article I, Section 18, be stricken from the Wisconsin Constitution? It reads, in part, "…nor shall any control of, or interference with, the rights of conscience be permitted…"?

9. Since married people are vulnerable to felony charges for adultery and bigamy and are the only group of people so vulnerable, would not substantially similar have to require the same vulnerability?
10. What would be the interference with the rights of religious organizations and churches to marry or not marry individuals within their churches, according to their religious beliefs and decisions?
11. The Defendant claims that since McConkey said he would have voted "No" on both sections of the single Amendment had the amendment been broken into the two parts, he has no standing to bring this case to Court. The Defendant absolutely refuses to look at the following facts:

A. A "no" vote, is not necessarily in opposition to the proposition, but also is the means of saying I do not have enough information to approve it. It is the same as the court finding a defendant not guilty, instead of innocent. The jury or the court has not been convinced by the State that the defendant is guilty; so "not guilty" is the decision. Innocence is not proven.
B. There is no clear definition of what "substantially similar" to marriage means and because of the overwhelming "log rolling" effect of banning gay marriage, there was no ability of the voter to determine such meaning before the election.
C. Because of the "log rolling" impact of gay marriage, there was no fair and reasonable information provided …and an informed decision was impossible:

As a voter, facing all the above points, questions, issues, subjects, purposes, in one amendment that he strongly felt was several, and who, because of the log rolling effect of the first section, he certainly has standing to bring this issue to the court system of Wisconsin, as the district court stated….

The defendant claims the Legislature has the right to propose amendments. The plaintiff agrees. But the Legislature does not have the right to do it wrong. Doing it wrong means violating the protection of the voters and people of Wisconsin, provided in the Constitution, by the requirement that when there are more than two <u>amendments</u>, they shall be presented separately.

The Defendant and the District Court brings the argument that both sections had but one purpose, to preserve and protect traditional marriage... a man and a woman. It is traditional because the rest were banned and not allowed. Gays were persecuted for years in this nation. Discrimination against gays continued and still continues in employment, bullying in schools, rentals, health care, and marriage. And, tradition allowed common law marriages.

Again, I am sure there are arguments, outside of these, that you all feel must be made, and they will trump mine, if we make cannot mine also. Thank you, again.

****

Oral arguments were heard by Wisconsin's seven Supreme Court Justices on November 3, 2009. Lester Pines did an excellent job representing me before the Court. He argued that the Legislature itself had said the purpose of the Amendment was to define marriage as between a man and a woman and that the first section of the amendment did that. The second section went far beyond that definition and prohibited the legislature from passing benefits to any single person or persons. Therefore, the Amendment, as presented, contained two different purposes. As of the publication of this book, no decision had been handed down.

When the political process abuses the citizen, the citizen must go to the court. When the political process gives millions of citizens the standing to abuse a small minority, other members of the millions must also be given standing by the judicial process, to challenge the majority decision or mob rule prevails.

Shall the voters of the State, by a simple majority of one vote, of those voters actually voting on the question, have the power to remove United States and State Constitutional protections, rights, privileges and immunities from selected groups of people they just don't happen to like?

And let us not forget, the real purpose of this amendment was to increase the voter turnout of conservatives in the 2006 gubernatorial election, to help defeat Wisconsin's Democratic Governor, Jim Doyle. It did not work, as pointed out in the beginning of this chapter. It was a ploy by the Republicans. They wanted to use a Constitutional Amendment, robbing people of their rights and privileges, for political campaign purposes.

The amendment does nothing to protect "traditional" marriage, whatever that is. **If this process of the majority unraveling minority protections is allowed to continue, this nation, as a nation of free people, will cease to exist.**

A POSTSCRIPT ON PRECEDENT:

THE 14TH AMENDMENT...STATES... *No State shall make or enforce any law which shall abridge the privileges or immunities of citizens of the United States; nor shall any State deprive any person of life*, liberty*, or property, without due process of law.*

THE UNITED STATES SUPREME COURT HAS RULED:

MEYERS V NEBRASKA (1923) LIBERTY MEANS "*Without doubt, it denotes not merely freedom from bodily restraint but also the right of the individual to contract, to engage in any of the common occupations of life, to acquire useful knowledge, to marry, establish a home and bring up children, to worship God according to the dictates of his own conscience.*" ***MEYER HAS NEVER BEEN OVERTURNED***.

LOVING V VIRGINIA (1967) *"The freedom to marry has long been recognized as one of the vital personal rights essential to the orderly pursuit of happiness by free men. Marriage is one of the "basic civil rights of man," ."* ***LOVING HAS NEVER BEEN OVERTURNED.***

ROMER V EVANS (1996) THE EFFECT "]f the constitutional conception of `equal protection of the laws' means anything, it must at the very least mean that a bare desire to harm a politically unpopular group cannot constitute a legitimate governmental interest." ***ROMER HAS NEVER BEEN OVERTURNED.***

LAWRENCE V TEXAS (2003) *"When sexuality finds overt expression in intimate conduct with another person, the conduct can be but one element in a personal bond that is more enduring. The liberty protected by the Constitution allows homosexual persons the right to make this choice." ."* ***LAWRENCE HAS NOT BEEN OVERTURNED.***

OTHER COURTS

1. Federal Appeals court in an Oklahoma case (2007)... gay adoption in one state good in another... the full faith and credit clause... ***HAS NOT BEEN OVERTURNED***
2. STATE SUPREME COURT IOWA CASE (2009) BAN ON GAY MARRIAGE UNCONSTITUTIONAL**... A UNANIMOUS 7-0 DECISION.** ***HAS NOT BEEN OVERTURNED***

Equality: 6- inequality: 0

However...

STARE DECISIS

Lat. "to stand by what has been decided," Is a principle that the precedent decisions are to be followed by the courts.

However, Chief Justice Roberts wrote in the United Citizens (*588 U.S. ____(2010) pp.70-71)...*

"departures from precedent are inappropriate in the absence of a 'special justification,'" He added, however, that

"*Stare decisis* is the preferred course because it promotes the evenhanded, predictable, and consistent development oflegal principles, fosters reliance on judicial decisions, and contributes to the actual and perceived integrity of the judicial process." Payne v. Tennessee, 501 U. S. 808, 827 (1991). For these reasons, we have long recognized that departures from precedent are inappropriate in the absence of a "special justification." Arizona v. Rumsey, 467U. S. 203, 212 (1984).

At the same time, stare decisis is neither an "inexorable command,"

Lawrence v. Texas, 539 U. S. 558, 577 (2003), nor "a mechanical formula of adherence to the latest decision," Helvering v. Hallock, 309 U. S. 106, 119 (1940), especially in constitutional cases, see United States v. Scott, 437 U. S. 82, 101 (1978). If it were, segregation would be legal, minimum wage laws would be unconstitutional, and the Government could wiretap ordinary criminal suspects without first obtaining warrants.

Stare decisis is instead a "principle of policy." Helvering, supra, at 119. When considering whether to reexamine a prior erroneous holding, we must balance the importance of having constitutional questions decided against the importance of having them decided right. As Justice Jackson explained, this requires a "sober appraisal of the disadvantages of the innovation as well as those of the questioned case, a weighing of practical effects of one against the other." Jackson, Decisional Law and Stare Decisis, 30 A. B. A. J. 334 (1944).

In conducting this balancing, we must keep in mind that *stare decisis* is not an end in itself. It is instead "the means by which we ensure that the law will not merely change erratically, but will develop in a principled and intelligible fashion." Vasquez v. Hillery, 474 U. S. 254, 265(1986). Its greatest purpose is to serve a constitutional ideal—the rule of law. It follows that in the unusual circumstance when fidelity to any particular precedent does more to damage this constitutional ideal than to advance it, we must be more willing to depart from that precedent."

Do the words of Chief Justice portend ill or good for equality? Would the Supreme Court of John Roberts gut the 14th Amendment and overturn six previous decisions, four of the Supreme Court, one of an U.S. Appellate Court, and one of a State Supreme Court? Would the Supreme Court of John Roberts turn a blind eye to the unconstitutional discrimination against 24 million Americans and their families?

If the Roberts Court does such a thing, then the Roberts philosophy about *stare decisis* is even more of a reason why the LGBT community must use the Courts and continue using the Courts to fight for equality. It is even more of a reason the LGBT community MUST become more effective political warriers. Twenty-four million American families are an immense political potential.

Chapter Ten: My Bible vs. Their Bible

When I started this book I planned on writing a chapter on the Bible, Jesus, Christianity and homosexuality. I have decided that effort would be folly. "True Believing" theo-dominionists and right wing crazies go after Bible verses to support their cause like a blind hog goes after slop. Trying to reason with them would be useless. Instead, here is what I know and what I believe:

The "One-Man, One Woman, Save Our Marriage" banner, is false advertising. The most serious issues were and still are the teaching of hatred by some and the ambivalent ignoring of those teachings by others.

One of my daughters is a lesbian. I have known, since she was in her twenties that my eldest daughter was so-inclined. I have never asked *why*. I have studied and prayed and thought for years. I am not a dummy. I know how to study and think. I think I know how to pray.

First of all, there is a genetic code, a DNA list, call it what you wish, a gift from God, that determines what kind of person that you "naturally" become. There are also altering events for some.

Secondly, I believe God works in some mysterious ways. I have not been given the wisdom to understand all that happens. I can choose to accept or reject the work of God. I choose to accept. Who am I to question the work of God? Who the hell are these people who do?

My daughter is a child of God. She is also my child. I love her deeply and always will. This essay could end here. But, there needs to be more.

I have done a lot of self-talk; thinking it is called, rare I believe, by many. I have read, studied, listened and prayed. In my review of my life's experiences, in a small town, in a Methodist Church, including Sunday School and Church services. My brother and I went every Sunday morning, Sunday evening and occasionally on Wednesdays, from 1942 to 1960. No one ever preached to us about homosexuality.

As a kid growing up in a very small Midwestern town of less than 500 people, "us kids" were very much aware of a couple of our peers who were "queer." We knew it, yet were in the band, went to church, and attended class and social functions with them.

I do know that no one hated them or, as far as I know, worried about their souls. Perhaps the adults talked about it, but I doubt it. We were farm kids; we pulled calves, helped animals breed, and had large families in close quarters and our mothers nursed us. I cannot imagine much being left out. We were more concerned about villagers who were mentally off-kilt or "crazy", than we were our classmates who were "queer". The man who murdered my father was straight, white, Midwestern, rural.

Just in case you are wondering, my friends and I could not have been more macho, testosterone motivated, girl loving, country boys. No angst, no guilt, no problems and almost no conscience. May God forgive us.

So, who are the people who started teaching all this hate, and still teach it? You know, the hate that led two young men to cruelly torture and murder young Matt Shepard, just because he was gay and the hate that caused three idiots to murder James Byrd Jr., just because he was an Afro-American? Are you pastors, believers, Christians or disciples of Satan?

Teaching, you ask. Absolutely! You must be taught to hate. Life and dependency creates a need for others in every infant. The human infant is dependent on others for life and care far longer than any other mammal on earth. Yet that young person, some time in his or her life is taught to hate. To change that dependency to hate as a young adult requires teaching. That teaching is *THE* horrible sin.

I do not understand where all the hatred has come from. I really do not. Why are their so many people trying to convince Americans to hate one another over sexual preference issues? They claim they are not spreading hate. But spreading distrust and causing division is a precursor to hate. To some, with less than full deck, that teaching, preaching and waving of hateful signs may be enough to trigger violence. You teachers of hatred have blood on your hands.

Your slurs, comments, your preaching and teaching, your interpretation of God's intent, should cause you great spiritual pause and concern about *your* hereafter.

Now, about us who remained and still remain silent.

In May, 2000, in a Midwestern hospital, I had spinal fusion surgery, with apparatus left in. Lots of blood, lots of time, several hands, clamps, bolts and screws left in there. It was not a "piece of cake". Neither was recovery. Immediate post-op brought my eldest daughter and spouse to visit. I muttered something, wanted more morphine, I think. They left for dinner.

The next day my spouse came back and informed me that my daughter and her partner wanted to have a commitment ceremony. "Oh? Really? I'll roast a hog. We'll have a party." Those were almost the first words ever spoken in our family about our eldest's homosexuality. The only other time was when my spouse said we needed to talk about our gay daughter and I said, "No we don't." That was in 1997 and here was it was 2000 and not another word had been said.

She is my daughter, I love her like a father loves his daughter. In addition, I don't talk about the love life of my other six daughters and I didn't think there was any need to talk about her's unless she was having troubles.

My daughter is who she is. She is a professional who works and pays taxes and obeys the laws of the land. She and her partner are over 45 years of age. They have been together for years.

But through my approach, I avoided not only talking, I avoided supporting. She went to my spouse, her stepmother, to discuss a commitment ceremony. She did not know how I would react. Why didn't my daughter come to me with the request for the ceremony in our home? She didn't know how I would react. Now, that is sad. Her sexual oreintation is nothing compared to that. Where had I been throughout the years? Why hadn't I been there to tell her that the crazy people are not right, and that she is a child of God, and I am always by her side, also. May God forgive me. My daughter has.

And, that silence is almost as bad as teaching hatred. We may not know what to say, but we must reach out and embrace our children, as they are.

To those of you with deeply held religious views, love your children. "Judge not, lest ye be judged." But for your own sanity and emotional well-being, do not hate your children, support them, listen to them, talk with them, let them know you are there for them. Beware of false prophets who teach hatred.

Matthew 22: 36-4

> *"Master, which is the great commandment in the law?" Jesus said unto him, "Thou shalt love the Lord thy God with all thy heart, and with all thy soul, and with all thy mind. This is the first and great commandment. And the second is like unto it, Thou shalt love thy neighbor as thyself. On these two commandments hang all the law and the prophets."*

Please listen to me, do not hate or shun your children if they are gay. Actively support them. God may ultimately forgive you if you shun them, even your children might. You won't, however. <u>It will haunt you to your grave</u>.

We were told that on the above two commandments hangs all the law. But look what the merchants of hate use to justify themselves.

According to one source, 667 different sins against God in the Bible. <u>One</u> of them is sex between adults of the same gender. There are 23,145 verses in the Old Testament and 7,957 verses in the New Testament, for a total of 31,102 verses. The number of verses specifically about homosexuality: six. In *And Say Hi To Joyce*, Deb Price describes the following incident:

> An engineering professor is treating her husband, a loan officer, to dinner for finally giving in to her pleas to shave off the scraggly beard he grew on vacation. His favorite restaurant is a casual place where they both feel comfortable in slacks and cotton/polyester-blend golf shirts. But, as always, she wears the gold and pearl pendant he gave her the day her divorce decree was final. They're laughing over their menus because they know he always ends up diving into a giant plate of ribs but she won't be talked into anything more fattening than shrimp.
> Quiz: How many biblical prohibitions are they violating? Well, wives are supposed to be 'submissive' to their husbands (I Peter 3:1). And all women are forbidden to teach men (I Timothy 2:12), wear gold or pearls (I Timothy 2:9) or dress in clothing that 'pertains to a man' (Deuteronomy 22:5). Shellfish and pork are definitely out (Leviticus 11:7, 10) as are usury (Deuteronomy 23:19), shaving (Leviticus 19:27) and clothes of more than one fabric (Leviticus 19:19). And since the Bible rarely recognizes divorce,

they're committing adultery, which carries the rather harsh penalty of death by stoning (Deuteronomy 22:22).

So why are they having such a good time? Probably because they wouldn't think of worrying about rules that seem absurd, anachronistic or - at best - unrealistic. Yet this same modern-day couple could easily be among the millions of Americans who never hesitate to lean on the Bible to justify their own anti-gay attitudes.[2746]

As I have asked previously, what is it about some of the folks that cause them to act like lunatics about what consenting adults do with their genitals. Did their boyfriends run off with their brothers? Were they weaned too soon? And, opposing breast-feeding? Are they nuts?

As humorist Lynn Lavner has succinctly stated, "The Bible contains six admonishments to homosexuals and 362 admonishments to heterosexuals. That doesn't mean that God doesn't love heterosexuals. It's just that they need more supervision."[2747]

"Love the sinner, hate the sin," so I was told by an Appleton, Wisconsin insurance executive. Is being a child of God the way God made them a sin? Or is the sin expressing their love to one another? That is it… they can love but they must remain celibate. I have news. Jesus ran the money-changers out of the temple, not the lesbians and gays.

Of all the sins, adultery, murder, theft, physical violence, blasphemy, dishonoring your parents, defiling the Sabbath, and so on, why is homosexual intimacy the one that so many care so much about? Would some one please explain why it is so high on the priority list when compared to all the evil in the world.

Tutu on South Africa, Homosexuals & Anglican Church

Desmond Tutu has fought against homophobia. He was the Former Archbishop of Cape Town, and former head of the Anglican Church in South Africa; he has also won a Nobel Peace Prize.[2748] He has been a stout leader for gays on a continent that has made them an outcast.

When it comes to gay violence and gay loathing, Archbishop Tutu notes such "destructive forces" of "hatred and prejudice" are an evil: "A parent who brings up a child to be a racist damages that child, damages the community in which they live, damages our hopes for a better world. A parent who teaches a child that there is only one sexual orientation and that anything else is evil denies our humanity and their own too."[2749]

Consider Deuternomy 22: 22

If a man is found sleeping with another man's wife, both the man who slept with her and the woman must die.

There you have it. Preach on that one. That will get rid of millions of hypocrites, from legislatures, organizations, right wing hate groups, neo-con Republicans, actually all political parties, and even the clergy. Peace might then prevail.

Another important issue is simply that the United States is not a theocracy. We do not have a State church. Indeed, attempting such an argument is foolish. Our churches do not speak with one voice. The evangelicals may take one position, the Lutherans may split, the Methodists who have pastors doing things counter to the denomination's rules, the Congregationalists and Episcopalians might marry and accept the LGBT community and the Independents go which ever way they choose.

As the Apostle Paul describes love in 1 Corinthians 13:4-7: *"Love is patient and kind. Love is not jealous or boastful or proud or rude. It does not demand its own way. It is not irritable, and it keeps no record of being wronged. It does not rejoice about injustice but rejoices whenever the truth wins out. Love never gives up, never loses faith, is always hopeful, and endures through every circumstance."*[2750]

As I tell those who send me hate mail, "Just try living without hate for 90 days, it will forever change your life."

CHAPTER ELEVEN: ARE YOU ON THEIR LIST?

Between 1882 and 1968, in the United States, over 3,400 Afro-Americans were lynched and thousands were leased into convict labor, another name for slavery, and died there. Throughout the United States, Afro-American men, women and children suffered under Jim Crow laws in the South and equally venomous segregation and discrimination in the North. Poll taxes, examinations, and out right physical intimidation eliminated voting in the South. Police brutality, inequality on juries, no firearm ownership, housing discrimination, segregated cities, segregated schools, poor education, poor medical care, housing discrimination, making 70% less in the labor force, almost no credit opportunities, were all facts of life for Afro-Americans, in both the north and the south.

All of this was true into the 1960's. I remember the civil rights movement, the riots, the legislative struggles of the 1960's. I also remember the rhetoric of the Right in those days. I am amazed at how little the rhetoric has changed, even though aimed at different people. And, the subtle ways of injuring those folks remain eerily similar.

Between1848-1829, some 529 Mexicans were lynched in the southwestern United States, a rate of lynchings per 100,000 population much higher than that suffered by Afro-Americans. Now, in an anti-immigrant fervor and in disgusting acts of hatred, Mexicans are killed, beaten, robbed and raped. (See William Carrigan's, *The lynching of persons of Mexican origin or descent in the United States,1848 to 1028*, in the Journal of Social History, Winter 2003.)

Meanwhile, hate marches on. It isn't just about the gays. It is every group with which the American Taliban disagrees, every minority group with which the right wing has heartburn, every group with minimal political clout who the neo-con Republican can use for political benefit, every sinner who can help suck money out of wallets for the Religious Right; everyone who is targeted by the millionaire, media mouthpieces for these organizations; every body who is different than the non-thinking, cliché-driven hate filled individual looking for someone to blame. Everyone who is targeted is subject to political denial of basic rights, freedoms, and opportunities, vandalism, beatings and even death.

No one is safe from these crazies; sooner or later, most Americans will be on a list. Just examine the political-social climate, in this nation, since we fought World War II.

Neither is this hatred just about political action, although the mistakes made in the political arena impact millions, it is also about fomenting and stirring up individual acts of hatred against people, just because of who they are. It is also about living in communities gated by insensitivity and both wanted and unwanted ignorance of what happens to others. It is hatred, some in your face, some subtle, some horrifically in your face.

In June of 1998, James Byrd Jr., a 49 year-old Afro-American man was beaten unconscious and then dragged behind a pick up truck until decapitated. His murder, just outside the town of Jasper, Texas, was carried out by three white men, two of whom were linked to white supremacy groups.

In October, 1998, Matt Shepard was beaten and left to die on a fence outside Laramie, Wyoming. Shepard, who had been pistol-whipped,[2751] was struck 18 times in the head with a .357-caliber Magnum handgun.[2752] Not only did Shepard have a severe skull fracture, he was burned in the attack.[2753] He finally reached a hospital, but struggled five days before dying.[2754]

He was small. He was gay. Local residents Aaron McKinney and Russell Henderson, (both 21 at the time) were charged with and convicted of Shepard's murder.[2755] Their girlfriends were charged with assisting in the attempted cover-up. The two men had gone into a bar, well known as a bar for gays.

The Family Research Council, trying to show their compassion and sensitivity, immediately issued (10.9.1998) a press release stating they were still opposed to hate crimes legislation, despite Matthew Shepherd's beating, burning and death.[2756]

In October, 2009, in New York City , a gay man and in a separate incident, a Mexican immigrant were beaten, in what police called obvious hate crimes. Both men were hospitalized in serious condition.

The Southern Poverty Law Center counted 926 **active** hate groups in the United States in 2008. That included 10 in Wisconsin, 38 in Tennessee (including 20 active chapters of the Klu Klux Klan and 7 White Nationalist chapters.), 2 in Wyoming, 66 in Texas, and 23 in Illinois. Check out their web site, www.splccenter.org. They reported a 50% increase in the number of active hate the groups since 2000.

Popular White Supremacists

Membership to white supremacist groups in the U.S. are estimated at about 50,000 or less.[2757] A 2008 report by *USA Today* said, "From 2006 to 2007, the number of such groups rose by 5% to 888, says the Southern Poverty Law Center (SPLC), which tracks them through news reports and other sources. The number is up 48% since 2000."[2758]

The nation's largest white-power website is Stormfront, which includes a social networking page.[2759] Stormfront had over 40,000 visitors in one day (October 2008).[2760] The Stormfront website has 144,000 registered members.[2761]

Marketing Hatred

Neo-Nazis are changing their marketing. The country's largest neo-Nazi group got rid of their brown Nazi uniform (swastika armband), and now wear black fatigues.[2762] Keystone State Skinheads in Pennsylvania changed its name to Keystone United to attract followers.[2763]

As 2008 came to a close, white supremacists were continuing to market their ideas to the middle class. Two issues helping them were illegal immigration, and the struggling economy.[2764]

Jeff Schoep, head of the National Socialist Movement, told the *USA Today*, "Historically, when times get tough in our nation, that's how movements like ours gain a foothold...When the economy suffers, people are looking for answers. ... We are the answer for white people. And now this immigrant thing in the past couple of years has been the biggest boon to us...The immigration issue is the biggest problem we're facing because it's changing the face of our country. We see stuff in English and Spanish. ... They are turning our country into a Third World ghetto."[2765] The National Socialist Movement is the biggest United States neo-Nazi group (according to the Anti-Defamation League, and the Southern Poverty Law Center).[2766]

A Proud Aryan Family

In December 2008, a Pennsylvania couple demanded a local grocer put "Adolph Hitler" on a birthday cake for their child, Adolf Hitler Campbell.[2767] Their living room was decorated with war books, German combat knives and swastikas.[2768] Swastikas also decorated walls, jackets, a pillow and the freezer.[2769]

The ShopRite store had previously refused to make the cake for the couple's daughter, JoyceLynn Aryan Nation Campbell.[2770] Their youngest child is Honszlynn Hinler Jeannie Campbell, a girl named for Schutzstaffel head Heinrich Himmler.[2771] After the ShopRite incident, the Campbells decided to go to Wal-Mart for the cakes, because they made them for Adolf's first two birthdays.[2772] According to a local report, the parents "say they aren't racists but believe races shouldn't mix."[2773]

Obama Plot

In October 2008, two neo-Nazis (one from Tennessee and one from Arkansas[2774]) appeared in court accused of plotting to kill Barack Obama. The two met on the internet.[2775] According to the BBC, "Paul Schlesselman and Daniel Cowart planned a murder spree targeting dozens of black people and culminating in Mr. Obama's murder, officials said. ...An ATF official said agents had seized a rifle, a sawn-off shotgun and three pistols during the arrests. They were charged with making threats against a presidential candidate, illegal possession of a sawed-off shotgun and conspiracy to rob a gun dealer. The pair allegedly planned to rob a gun store and then carry out a killing spree at an unnamed predominantly African-American high school..."[2776] U.S. authorities clearly believed that the two had the means and intent to carry out an attack on black students.[2777] The day they were arrested, they had shot at a glass window at Beech Grove Church of Christ, a congregation of about 60 black members in Brownsville, Tenn.[2778]

Daniel Cowart's My Space page showed him holding a weapon, which paralleled the pictures of gun-touting Islamic fundamentalist terrorists.[2779] The two men planned to shoot 88 Afro Americans and decapitate another 14 because the numbers 88 and 14 are symbolic in the white supremacist community.[2780] According to a CBS affiliate, "The numbers 14 and 88 are symbols in skinhead culture, referring to a 14-word phrase attributed to an imprisoned white supremacist: 'We must secure the existence of our people and a future for white children' and to the eighth letter of the alphabet, H. Two '8's or 'H's stand for 'Heil Hitler.'"[2781]

According to legal documents, Cowart and Schlesselman "planned to drive their vehicle as fast as they could toward Obama shooting at him from the windows."[2782]

Anti-Semitism Today

Jews were scapegoats for many problems people suffered. They were blamed for causing the "Black Death" in Europe during the Middle Ages. In addition, "In Spain in the 1400s, Jews were forced to convert to Christianity, leave the country, or be executed. In Russia and Poland in the late 1800s the government organized or did not prevent violent attacks on Jewish neighborhoods, called *pogroms*, in which mobs murdered Jews and looted their homes and stores."[2783]

Furthermore, anti-Semitism didn't end with Hitler's Holocaust. Anti-Semitism is rampant worldwide—not just in the Middle East, where Iran's president has denied the Holocaust. Jews face hatred in South America. In Rio de Janeiro, Brazil (Jan. 2008), an anti-Jewish group wanted their float for the carnival parade to include dead mannequins depicting naked bodies of Holocaust victims with an Adolf Hitler dancer for the float.[2784]

Some of the United State's most notorious anti-Semites come from Don Black's Stormfront and Matt Hale's World Church of the Creator.[2785] When Joe Lieberman (D-Conn) was chosen as Al Gore's running mate in 2000, Hale said, "While undoubtedly some will be surprised by this, I am very happy that the Jew Joseph Lieberman has been chosen by Al Gore to be his running mate, for it brings the pervasive Jewish influence of the federal government out in the open so that people can see what we anti-Semites are talking about."[2786]

Anti-Semitic incidents increased in 2000. According to the ADL, "acts of vandalism, harassment and other expressions of hatred against Jews increased 4 percent nationwide, according to the ADL's annual Audit of Anti-Semitic Incidents. The 2000 ADL *Audit* recorded 1,606 anti-Semitic incidents in 44 states and the District of Columbia, representing a slight increase over the 1,547 incidents reported in 1999."[2787]

A 2002 nationwide survey released by the Anti-Defamation League concluded 17% of Americans hold strongly anti-Semitic beliefs, a percentage that doubled among Hispanics and African Americans.[2788] Only 3 percent of U.S. college and university students were considered strongly anti-Semitic.[2789]

These groups commit few crimes as groups. Instead they provide their members the hateful nourishment needed to feed their desires for active violence against someone else.

The United States Department of Justice reported 9,335 reported hate crimes in 2007. Race was the cause of 4,956 of those crimes, 3,434 were "Anti-Black" and 908 were "Anti-White". "Anti-Jewish" accounted for 1,127; 142 were "Anti-Islamic." There were 1,512 hate crimes committed against homosexuals.

According to FBI statistics, 2008 saw 1148 hate crimes committed based on the "perceived ethnicity or national origin of the victim." Sixty-four percent of those were against people of Hispanic backgrounds.

Hispanics, although not subjected to the nation-wide difficulties of Afro-Americans, suffered involuntary repatriation to Mexico after the Mexican war, a period of lynchings from 1848-1829, with one report of some 529 such events. In the southwestern part of the nation Mexican-Americans have suffered from segregation in housing, employment, education, has have Afro-Americans, nation-wide. Unlawful immigration, national security and a severe economic recession creates an underlying tension that could increase such crimes and practices.

Crimes against people because of who they are, indeed, because of how God created them or because of their religious choices, are blasphemy. The preachers and their neo-con mouthpieces opposing hate crime legislation should have some explaining to do at the Pearly Gates. One hundred thirty one Republican Congressmen voted against the Hate Crimes Bill. They are in bed with, shudder the metaphor, the Family Research Council. FRC's vice-president, Tom McClusky contends that hate crime legislation is just part of a "homosexual agenda." In 2007, five homosexuals were murdered and 690 were assaulted, just because they were gay. No other group suffered as many homicides.

In 2009, James Von Brunn, an 88-year-old anti-Semite and white supremacist opened fire at the U.S. Holocaust Museum and killed Steven Johns, a black security guard. In 2009, a grand jury indicted four men for planning to blow up two synagogues in the Riverdale, New York. There were 830 acts of vandalism against American Jews, in 2007. As I write this page, September 15, 2009, reports of swastikas, hateful comments, and even purposefully set fires are being reported by a United Jewish Community Center in Newport News, Virginia. In 2009, two killings in Brockton, Massachusetts, the killing of three Pittsburgh police officers, and the shooting of American soldiers in Arkansas, were all connected by Anti-Semitism.

We are a violent nation, with over 1,382,000 violent crimes a year, 89,000 of them known forcible rapes and 16,000 murders. That is a lot of hatred, over 243 known forcible rapes per day, ten an hour, and 44 murders every single day.

The most commonly used statistics in the press and in government and NGO reports indicate 30% of the women in America will be subject to domestic abuse and 18% will subjected to a completed or attempted rape sometime during their lives. Those are mind-boggling numbers; here we are in the 21st century and we still are abusing and raping women, here in the United States. According to the Women's Institute for Freedom of the Press, The National Census of Domestic Violence Services collected a national, unduplicated count of adults and children who received life-saving services from domestic violence programs on November 2, 2006. During this single 24-hour survey period 47,864, almost 50,000 women and kids, came in for help from the effects of domestic violence. And, some of Hollywood's elite want Roman Polanski to be let off the hook for raping a 13 year old girl.

And then come the merchants of this hateful violence. The present murder, rape, violence without any of the "whole story" that you see on TV is a complete fraud. As the son of a man who was murdered when I was just eight years old, I can tell you first hand the price that is exacted from widows and children is very long, very painful. The tragedy for a rape victim, whether by a stranger, a relative or a spouse can be played over an entire lifetime and impact many lives. Most murders involve alcohol or drugs, are not committed by Caucasians and do not have Caucasian victims, and are not committed by strangers. Television shows just the opposite, downplays the involvement of drugs and alcohol, downplays the crime that devastates our minority communities, and downplays violence within families. You do not see the truth on television. You know why; it's the money. It is merchandising violence for profit.

Another subtle and continuing attack on women, is the marketplace that pays them 77 cents on the dollar compared to men. In the Right Wing churches you can still hear sermons on "women submit to your husbands" and they mean it. And, of course, there Shalt Not Be Reproductive Rights or Free-Choice for women. In Wisconsin they are even taking on women's right to breastfeed their infants. These crazies on the Right have no limit to their madness. Their efforts against women will not subside. Try an Equal Rights Amendment again and see what they do.

And then, there are the attacks on the Right's favorite target, the liberals. One may certainly visit the Patriot Shop and buy a "Liberal Hunting License" ticket for $2.75. It says, "Liberal Hunting License, 2009-2013, No Bag Limit-Tagging Not Required."

In July 2008, Jim David Atkinson, from Powell, Tennessee, walked into a the Tennessee Valley Unitarian-Universalist Church in Knoxville and killed two people and wounded seven before being tackled by men in the Church. He targeted the church because its "liberal teachings and... he hated the liberal movement in general and gays." Notes in home stated that he wanted to kill every Democrat in the House and Senate. He said, "Liberals are a pest like termites... The only way we can rid ourselves of this evil is kill them in the streets. Kill them where they gather."[2790]

Ann Coulter, famous for her idiotic comments stated, "When contemplating college liberals, you really regret once again that John Walker [a convicted spy for the Soviet Union] is not getting the death penalty. We need to execute people like John Walker in order to physically intimidate liberals, by making them realize that they can be killed, too. Otherwise, they will turn out to be outright traitors."[2791]

Poor Ann Coulter, she can't remember the assassinations of President Jack Kennedy, Martin Luther King, Jr., or U.S. Senator Robert Kennedy. She just has got to have a ghost writer, she doesn't seem smart enough to do it herself. But then, she is quoted as saying, unbelievably, "My only regret with Timothy McVeigh is he did not go to the New York Times Building."[2792] Her only regret about McVeigh??? What about the 168 children, women and men who died in Oklahoma City?

That is sick, she must be terribly sick.

The neglect of America's young people of color, be it Hispanic or Afro-American, cannot be ignored. It is a subtle but deadly hatred.

The wealth and the votes moved to the suburbs and the exurbs. They left behind cities in economic difficulty. No federal programs, no urban renewal programs and no HUD could for see or forestall the problems that have engulfed most of our cities. These problems have maimed generations of young people. We have urban drug gangs and murders without limit of our young. More than 30 high school students in Chicago were murdered in 2008-2009.

In the 16 months prior to March 209, **508** Chicago public school students had been shot. **Five hundred and eight kids in 16 months.** Drug gangs and related criminal activities threaten the children in most of America's largest cities. Many political people do not want to even talk about it. After all, they don't live there anymore.

In Milwaukee, a city of about 600,000 people, there were 56 murders in 2008, and 56 murders in the first nine months of 2009, in 2008, there were 155 reported sexual assaults, and 159 in the first nine months of 2009.

With city budgets feeling terrible pains across the nation, counter terrorism money and the President Obama's stimulus money will help. When the wars in Iraq and Afghanistan end, hundreds, if not thousands, of policemen in the reserves and military can come home and resume patrols. That might help.

The Religious Right and their fellow travelers will write these crimes off as a problem of the cities and moral decay without a whimper about what to do about it. In an attempt to just bring it up for discussion, in October of 2009, with a national political right wing group, I was told in no uncertain terms that they were not only uninterested, they were outright opposed to it being part of a political discussion.

The one thing our governments, at all levels, demand on doing themselves and even restrict private efforts, is keeping our people safe from criminal harm. Well guess what, all of our governments, all three branches, stink at the job they are performing. Whether the elderly from cyber crime and phony publishing house deals, whether consumers from being ripped off by the billions per year, whether women from rape and assault, whether all of us from credit card companies and banks and Wall Street ripping us off, or whether the poor young people who are mere targets for the murdering thugs on our streets. Government has failed to keep us safe and is continuing to fail.

And, Government is a reflection of the people who control it. That has been, for sometime, in ever increasing numbers, the suburbs and the exurbs, the Right. What is with the mentality that defines terrorism as fear for our safety in our own communities and we refuse to recognize that our nation is full of terrorists, by that definition? Our financial resources and our warriors and our equipment should be used to defeat the enemy among us.

And, we must also come to terms with the fact that there innumerable numbers of radical, militant Muslims who wish to do us harm, within our boundaries. They are here. Whether in New York, Florida, California, or Fort Hood. They are among us. They hate us. It is not prejudice, bias, or religious bigotry to want them identified, and one way or another, prevented from killing, maiming, wounding ourselves, our families, our neighbors. It is the government's job to keep us safe. They need to get on with the task and stop apologizing for it.

I am deeply concerned for the future of our elderly. You, the reader, may wonder what this topic has to do with this book. As I said earlier, people who are not afraid to fight, have a moral obligation to fight for those who are afraid, or cannot fight for themselves for other reasons.

The nation's unwillingness to fund the commons and dislike of helping those who need it does not bode well for those of advanced age. In 2010 we will have over 37 million Americans 65 years of age or older. One in eight persons 65 and over have Alzheimer's and nearly half of persons over age 85 have Alzheimer's disease."[2793] According to the Alzheimer's Association, "The direct and indirect costs of Alzheimer's and other dementias amount to more than $148 billion annually."[2794] Medicare spends nearly three times as much for people with Alzheimer's and other dementias as for a beneficiary without dementia. In 2000, this disparity was $13,000 versus $4,450.[2795] For nursing home residents with

Alzheimer's and other dementias, half relied on Medicaid to help pay for nursing home care in 2000.[2796] Nursing home residents who qualify for Medicaid have to spend all of their Social Security check and any other monthly income (exception for a small personal needs allowance) to pay nursing homes… "Medicaid only makes up the difference if the resident cannot pay the full cost of care."[2797] Whatever the case, Alzheimer's drains personal finances and the federal budget. The future costs are even worse.

"When baby boomers with severe disabilities or disease like Alzheimer's disease begin to reach the median age for admission to a nursing home in 2025, Medicaid long-term care spending will skyrocket. Medicaid costs for nursing home care alone will climb from $21 billion in 2005 to $38 billion in 2025."[2798] In 2005, Medicare spent $91 billion on beneficiaries with Alzheimer's/other dementias; a total which is expected to increase to $160 billion by 2010 and $189 billion by 2015.[2799]

About 47 percent of nursing home residents have an Alzheimer's/other dementia diagnosis.[2800] "The average daily cost for a private room in a nursing home was $206 in 2006, or $75,190 a year."[2801] Assisted Living, though cheaper, is still expensive. The average monthly cost for a private, one-bedroom unit in an assisted living facility was $2,968, or $35,616 a year in 2006. Assisted living facilities that provide specialized dementia care often charge additional fees ranging from $750 to $2,200 monthly.[2802]

Do we care enough for our grandparents to care for them? What will happen to the poor elderly with poor children?

Finally, and by that I mean no disregard toward Muslims, American Indians, the elderly poor, the immigrants, the developmentally disabled, all who have and who will again fill the sting from the far right. By finally, I mean simply the last entry for this chapter. "Left Behind in America: The Nation's Dropout Crisis," using census data from American Community surveys, it was discovered that in 2007, 21 percent of Afro-Americans between 16 and 24 dropped out of high school, with 27.5 percent of Latinos and 12.2 percent of white students doing the same. Nearly 19 percent of all young men quit school before they finished. Economic disadvantage certainly follows.

This nation, if it has the will, certainly can afford the research and the development of schools and educational systems our young people will be anxious to attend, regardless of color, language difficulties, problems or poverty at home. The fact we are not developing such educational opportunities is indicative of shortsighted economics and a frightening inhumanity. There is just no other way to state it. To fail to build and operate an educational system that holds and enriches all our young people is just another form of class hatred, I don't care what the teachers' say, they have the kids 8 hours a day. I don't care what the parent or parents say, you had these children, raise them. I don't care what the taxpayers say, it is better for you and better for our nation if we are all educated to the highest degree we are capable of handling and desire. And, we ought to make it so everybody wants some and everybody wants more.

CHAPTER TWELVE: HOW YOU CAN MAKE OUR WORLD A BETTER PLACE

During my Court Case against Wisconsin's anti-freedom, anti-liberty and anti-equality constitutional amendment, I have received emails, comments through Blogs, hand written letters and phone calls. For every enemy, I have made a dozen friends. I will admit that some fringe lunatic enemy might seek to do me harm, but it is worth the exchange.

Another thing that I have noticed over my years of political and social activism is that hatred produces such unhappy people. Our position produces much happier people, even in the face of disappointment. Disappointment today is an opportunity for tomorrow.

One of the things I teach in my classes at the University is critical thinking. The first step is questioning the basic assumption. Thinking is rare. Intra-personal communication is almost as important as talking with God. Thinking, a talk with one's self, is necessary for change and improvement in human attitudes, intentions and behavior.

I have no doubts that, with the exception of the true psychotic, hard thinking, systems thinking and critical thinking can diminish individual hatreds of groups by people. Courage to stand up to group talk, mob mentality, and misguided friends may also be required. People can choose their friends and choose to belong to groups of people that are not hateful, bigoted, and destructive.

Think about any hatred toward groups that you may harbor. What is the factual basis or the need or the personal good gained by this hatred? Does it really make you feel better? Hatred, like jealousy, consumes the one who holds it. It becomes self-inflicted emotional suicide and if acted upon, can break up families, destroy marriages, destroy business and land you behind bars.

I have seen and heard young macho, chest thumping, men repeating the hateful bigoted mantras of their group. When isolated one on one, they cannot explain or [2803]defend their hatred. If they are so tough, they would change the group, or change groups. I am well aware of my stupid homophobic statements when I was not thinking and just spouting off to hear myself talk. I am eternally grateful that I have been spared being a racist.

The other tragedy of my earlier homophobic ramblings is that no one stopped to correct me. Paraphrasing Dag Hammarskjold, "The madman shouted in the marketplace and since know one stopped to correct him the children grew up believing him."

We must all think about what we are thinking. You become what you think As stated in *St. Paul's Letter to the Philippians*, "Finally brothers and sisters, whatever is true, all that deserves respect, all that is honest, pure, decent, admirable, virtuous or worthy of praise…think on these things…" Similarily from *The Teaching of Buddha*, "As surely as the cart follows the ox, a man shall become what he thinks."

If we think positive things and if we think about "how can I make things better and what can I do," and really search for answers then that is the person we will become. If we think about evil we will end up doing evil. It begins with thinking.

Then we must control and direct our communication, our words, body language, actions that speak. We do not use the "N" word. Why then, the use of "faggot" or "queer" or "homo"?

If one really thinks, there is no reason to hate the homosexual. Their existence is of absolutely no threat to your existence. A gay marriage in no way threatens yours. If it does, your marriage is hanging on by a thread. Your belief that a philosophical, religious and cultural technical question concerning whom other people may marry hurts your marriage means you should do your spouse a big favor and call it off. The existence of homosexuals since the beginning of recorded time should help the homophobe realize homosexuals are part of every society and have been forever and are no threat. They exist. They will not steal your children. They will not attempt to seduce you. They will not try to convert you.

Homophobia created this world of fear and a horrible world it must be. Fear is a real thing and to be afraid to be true to one's self must be horrific. I have met and know people who are afraid to "come out" or even to speak up. I know of professionals who live in that world, hidden. I cannot counsel or give advice except go the nearest Outreach Office or PFLAG group or a professional counselor for help in the transition or for help in staying hidden.

The other big issue is equally important: do not become a public, hateful, homophobe in an effort to hide your identity. First, become at peace with yourself, and others, whether gay or straight. Second, gain and keep the courage to stop hateful speech, regardless whether racism, nativism, homophobia, sexism, ageism or anti-Semitism.

A word about our families…

Obviously and known to most, children will grow up to be their parents. You are an alcoholic, you will raise one. You are a hateful bigot, you will raise one. You are a coward, you will raise one. If you allow your child to be a self-serving bully, don't be surprised when he ends up in jail or dead.

Our father was shot killed in the line of duty as an Illinois State Policeman. My brother was six; I was eight years old. Our mother turned very tough. She had two very large, headstrong, small town - country boys to raise. She picked friends for my brother and me; if she didn't approve, no way. Same with dates. Until we were seventeen, we were in church every Sunday morning, every Sunday evening and until 15, on Wednesday nights, unless ballgames or track meets interfered.

We were not allowed to use the word hate. We were not allowed to tell our host, at the table, I don't like beets. It would be, instead, "No thank you, I don't care for any, at this time." Swear? Are you kidding, you swear, you get your face slapped. Sass my mom, my uncle beats my hind end. Table manners, chores, part time and summer jobs, discipline and self-discipline, religion and respect, no smoking, no beer or booze, good grades, help others, work hard, give thanks, visit your grand-parents. Yes Ma'am. Yes Sir. Please and Thank you.

God bless her. I miss her.

Have the courage to raise your kids. Adults who have children but do not take the time or have the courage to raise them, should have had a vasectomy and their tubes tied.I repeated to my children and my grandchildren, old enough to listen, the following mantra:

> *"I am your father or grandfather. My number one job is to protect you and keep you safe, even from yourself. My number two job is to provide you with food, shelter, warmth, water, and clothes. My number three job is to prepare you for life after parental care. My number four job is to develop your understanding of learning, culture, interpersonal relationships, survival in the tribe in which you exist and respect for the Almighty, the environment, and for those who have gone before. Then, I will do my best to enjoy you and have you enjoy me. I am your father, I really love you. None of your friends will do these things for you, therefore, I am not your friend. I am your father."*

You will decide what kind of person you want your child to be. Caring, giving, smart, accomplished, honest, respectful. Or hateful, uneducated, lazy and selfish. It is really up to you.

The dangerous ground in parenthood has many minefields. They are, chronologically, the following: (a) Minding, respecting, sharing; (b) Respect and grades and honesty; (c) Social groups and friends, the best group possible, your choice, not theirs; (d) no beer, no booze, no drugs, none; (e) Relationships and attitudes with the romantic partners, sex, deep respect and care, absolutely no violence, never, ever; (f) Higher education and career goals; (g) Helping without harming the marriage; (not the expensive, wasteful wedding). Be tough, be strong, be wise, get professional help, if necessary.

Neither allow nor accept hate or hateful speech in your home. None.

On a more proactive basis, discuss every news story or other input, and its impact upon human relations, with your children. Build an understanding of other cultures, nations, races and lifestyles and people through proactive discussions, not lectures, but discussions. Start it early.

Be active in groups opposing hatred and supporting the common threads of humanity. Involve your children in those activities, with you. Recruit them into those activities. Start youth groups with the same purposes.

If you and your spouse do not agree upon issues of bigotry, hatred and prejudice, you will be in for a mentally painful marriage. This very situation was one of the major reasons for the divorce of one of my daughters. If you are not in fear of physical harm, argue your case, do not accept it. Educate and teach your children the way of understanding and thinking and brother/sisterhood. Teach them to have courage to stand up to wrong. If they ask why their parents have different opinions, be truthful and state you do not know why your spouse has the views he/she have, but you sure can tell people why their position is wrong and will lead others the wrong direction.

ISSUES FOR PARENTS

Can't understand why your son or daughter is a homosexual? The following are suggestions for parents in the situation. Here are some thoughts worth reflection.

Youth Are the Most Vulnerable

The American Psychological Association points out, "The younger a person is when she or he acknowledges a non-heterosexual identity, the fewer internal and external resources she or he is likely to have. Therefore, youths who come out early are particularly in need of support from parents and others."[2804]

Who do I blame?

If you are upset your child is gay, blame no one. Homosexuality is genetic. It's a sad commentary that you're trying to blame someone for your child's homosexuality. You are not accepting your child if you are trying to blame someone.

Are you bargaining?

Many kids say they feel relieved after coming out to their parents because they're glad they don't have to carry the baggage by themselves any longer. But parents tend to enter a period similar to grieving, feeling anger, denial, guilt, and shame. They may even bargain with themselves, thinking that if their child doesn't have a gay partner, then the child isn't gay.

How many homosexuals have you offended, even accidently?

Bruce Bawer wrote in *The Advocate* (4.28.1998), "Straight Americans need... an education of the heart and soul. They must understand - to begin with - how it can feel to spend years denying your own deepest truths, to sit silently through classes, meals, and church services while people you love toss off remarks that brutalize your soul."[2805]

Are you aware of your heterosexual bias?

Heterosexism is assuming a heterosexual viewpoint. One should use gender-neutral language, words and phrases that avoid assumptions based on gender identity and sexual orientation.[2806] "Do you have a boyfriend?" is a question with heterosexist implications (discriminatory, based on a straight viewpoint).[2807] Instead parents should ask, "Are you seeing anyone?" or "Is there anyone that you like?"[2808] Perhaps the daughter says, "What do you mean 'anyone,' I like boys." She catches on and is surprised by the parents gender neutral comments. Good. The parents can confirm their neutrality in judging orientation and say, "I'd welcome who ever you would like."

What if you found out accidentally?

It's not about you. If you were snooping around, you shouldn't let them know you are aware of their sexuality. Coming out isn't about you, its about your child. Your gay son should be the one to tell you he is gay when he is ready. It's not about your saying, "Hey, I found some gay comments in your diary." Your son may be hiding his feelings to begin with; the last thing he needs to know is you are snooping around. It's very likely he is insecure about his public safety and comfort (especially if everyone at school knew he was gay), his bedroom is his safety net. Parents have a right to snoop. They own the house. But they also have an obligation as a parent to let their kids feel safe.

What if you want your child to come out to you?

You have a strong feeling your child is gay (perhaps because of issues like the previous question). Don't expect you son to say "I'm GAAAAYYY!" Instead, use teachable moments. The best way to foster relationship is using moments as they arise when you child grows up. Maybe at the age of 8 they ask, "What does it mean to be gay?" That's an opportunity for the parent to say something short that models understanding. Kids don't want to tell their parents they are gay because they have perceived notions on what their parents think. That's why you should not laugh at a gay joke in front of your kids. If your daughter grows up to be a lesbian, she, for years, has internalized your opinion of gays. If your child laughed at your gay joke, they may have laughed because they were acting, not because they were straight and thought it was funny. If you want your kid to come out to you, (or you want to make sure they will come out should they someday be gay) you need to model accepting attitudes when the child is growing up.

Are you educated on the topic?

Parents need to be armed with arguments defending your child. Read. The only way you can be a better advocate for you child is if you know how to defend him. Parents often clam up with their gay child because they don't have the knowledge base and feel embarrassed and lack confidence in answering questions.

How will you cope?

In many cases, the parents are upset when they find out their child is gay.[2809] If you feel depressed and isolated, there's plenty of websites to help you. Never underestimate a counselor, and don't forget the best counselor might be you child. Find the closest PFLAG (Parents and Friends of Lesbians And Gays), a support based organization run by parents of gays and lesbians.

Who do I tell?

The parents often need someone to talk to. But don't tell Uncle Ivan, who might tell Grandma Marge, who will tell half the county. Never out your child, or force him or her to attend a support group.[2810] If you want to lose trust with your child immediately, tell someone else your child is gay. This isn't the parents' secret, it's the child's. You child's sexual orientation is not your right to discuss with someone else. You may need guidance, but if you're talking with some outside the medical field or reverend (that insures privacy) you better okay it with your child.

How do I balance my former goals and my child's sexuality?

Separate your dreams from your child's dream. The future will likely be different than what you hoped for. There likely won't be a wedding and grandchildren. As Kathy Belge wrote, "Letting go of that dream for your child can be hard. Remember though, that was your dream. Your child may still choose to spend their life with one partner and have children. Gay marriage may even become legal in his lifetime. Even though your child did not choose to be gay, they may make some life choices you do not agree with. Although this may be hard for you, remember, it's their life and they have the right to live it as their own."[2811]

How prevalent is homophobia?

Relax. Times are changing. Homophobia is popular. But it is not as popular as it was in the 1950s. And it will be less prevalent by 2050. It was once written, "Those who once inhabited the suburbs of human contempt find that without changing their address they eventually live in the metropolis."[2812]

PARENTAL ADVICE

There are numerous concerns for parents. Some questions are protective, some are stereotypical, and some are unable to be answered. What is the risk for my child getting HIV? What if my child becomes a target for gay bashers? What to I do when my husband is crying because his son is gay?

You might judge yourself harshly and wonder: Did I do something to make him gay? Whether it's you're fault doesn't immediately matter. You still have a task at hand: to raise your child. The following is a list of tips to help parents raise and advise their gay children. But first, always remind them that you love them.

The following is a various list of points, behaviors, and issues that affect homosexuality and the family. Some are points to consider when raising children who are too young to even think about sexuality, others span to when the parents are already aware of the child's homosexuality.

Parents are Models

In the film *Mississippi Burning*, Mrs. Pell comments on racism: "It's ugly. This whole thing is so ugly. Have you any idea what it's like to live with all this? People look at us and only see bigots and racists. Hatred isn't something you're born with. It gets taught. At school, they said segregation what's said in the Bible... Genesis 9, Verse 27. At 7 years of age, you get told it enough times, you believe it. You believe the hatred. You live it... you breathe it. You marry it."[2813] Homophobia is no different, especially when it comes to the religious sectors who praise God and bash homosexuals in the same sentence.

Parental support for gay children is so important, because the family's other children might already be homophobic (primarily because of their parents' modeling in earlier years). This fact is not a point for parents to feel bad, but for parents to understand why it is important to support their gay child to prevent rejection by siblings. Parents make their children dislike gays. Perhaps it was subtle. For example, "That's gay" is used to say "That's stupid." Therefore something being "gay" is not a compliment, thereby being negative.

Children internalize what their parents say. Parents not only should accept the fact their child is gay, but also figure out how to change the homophobia they caused in their remaining straight children. The easiest way to do this is to preempt homophobia by being tolerant of all people when your child is young.

Parents are Educators

The American Social Health Association strongly believes sex education begins at home and that a parent is a child's most important sexuality educator. Although this advice was orientation neutral, the American Social Health Association states it well, "Consider what might happen if you do not talk with your child. If a child doesn't learn about sexuality issues from a parent, the child will learn about sexuality elsewhere-from friends, magazines, television and other sources. This information can be incorrect, confusing, and may not agree with the parent's beliefs. Research shows that uninformed children are at greater risk for early sexual activity, sexually transmitted diseases or infections (including AIDS), pregnancy, sexual exploitation, and abuse."[2814]

Become an Approachable Parent

Does your child feel it's OK to talk with you about sexuality? If not, have you thought about who will answer your child's questions? Do you have good communication skills for talking about sexuality? If you want to be asked questions by your child and be confided in, admit you don't have all the answers. Don't laugh when a child asks a question, even if you are reacting to you child's cute questions. Be careful of insulting them. And listen. Allow your child to vent.

According to the American Social Health Association, good "askable parents" don't "expect to be perfect, and knows that admitting mistakes is a valuable lesson for the child."[2815] Sometimes discussing sexuality (straight or gay) is embarrassing. Openly acknowledge the discomfort to your child.

Teachable Moments

The American Social Health Association notes, when your child asks a question that raises a teachable moment, make sure you know what the child is asking (Ask your child, "Do you mean...?" or "Do you want to know about...?").[2816] Why is your child asking the question? Perhaps it is to fact check or explore his beliefs.[2817] Don't leave a moment unanswered. If time is short, give a short answer and come back to it later after brainstorming ideas. And don't leave out humor. Break the ice, humor and a smile will neutralize tension. Take advantage of the ripe opportunity. If something about LGBT issues comes up in the news, parents should discuss it with their child, to show that you can talk comfortably about being gay.[2818]

Don't let regular quality time change.

"Take this opportunity to connect as you did before you knew she was gay. Was there a meal you liked to cook together, a favorite TV show you watched? Make sure you continue to do the things you did as a family."[2819] Changing routines suggest you have changed your opinion toward your child.

Remind you your child your glass is not half full. It's fuller.

Even if the parent is open-minded, its traumatic to find out there's a part of their child's personality that they never knew about. That's what is great about the coming out process: relationships grow stronger. Look at on the bright side: you know more about your kid. Think of all the years you didn't know this about your child's sexuality. You now know your child more in-depth. Don't be disappointed that you didn't know sooner.

Show an Interest in Your Gay Child's Life.

As time goes by, ask you child about their personal life. (Do they need help finding someone). Ask questions about your child's gay life. If your son was straight, would you ask which girls he liked in his class? You should ask the parallel questions to your gay son. If not, he will notice the difference. Here is a real life example among brothers:

> I particularly fell this with my brother Arthur. He knows I'm gay, but had never had side conversation about it with me. His wife, on the other hand, has offered to help me with dating websites like Match.com. She wants me to find someone. He has said he would like my future partner to be part of the family, but he has not said much else. Arthur is hardcore straight, it's awkward for him to talk to me about my homosexuality. I need to not take so much offense to it, but at the same time, I'm led to believe he doesn't like to think about my sexual preference any more than he has to.

Remind the child there is a place in the family.

Family may be the only place they won't feel isolated, you have a moral obligation to make you child feel safe and loved.

Ask your child for leeway.

Parents should communicate to their child they may foul up. But it is not on purpose.[2820] Remind your child you are imperfect, and don't have the same perspective.

Create a positive environment. Now.

Foster an environment that is comfortable for kids to any sexuality, that way it doesn't matter if your child is a homosexual. Don't wait to create a comfortable environment for your gay child until they come-out. Some kids may realize they are gay as young as four or five, and most LGBT adults acknowledge felling different as children and not understanding much beyond that.[2821]

Watch for Teasing

"According to a 2005 national study released by GLSEN, 93 percent of school children in New York State said that they had heard homophobic remarks at school, including words like 'faggot' and 'dyke' and phrases like 'You're so gay.' In addition, one in five students heard teachers or school staff make homophobic comments, and 61 percent of LGBT students said that they felt unsafe in schools because of sexual orientation."[2822] Children who are gay or even perceived as gay are more likely to be harassed.[2823]

Kids at school can be mean. Many gay teens are too embarrassed, afraid, or confused to share their concerns, so they have anxiety or depression.[2824] Rejection by friends and family can be devastating. Children closeted may overcompensate in acting heterosexual.[2825]

Bullying Doesn't Have to Continue

Parents should go to school and advocate for their child. A child should respond to a bully by saying "Stop It." And tell an adult. So much bullying continues because teachers and staff don't find out. No responsible teacher is going to let a student continually get harassed. Kids should seek out "allies," who are family, friends, and teachers that are gay-friendly.[2826] A parent can sit down with their child and map out who they can trust, this might be a good communication tool between the gay child and the parent.[2827]

Guilt by Omission

When adults are silent about gay and lesbian people being teased, students learn from this omission that it is acceptable to use anti-gay put-downs.

Watch for Health Signs

In some cases gay kids are under more stress than their straight counterparts, so they may be at a higher risk for depression, alcoholism, promiscuity, drug addiction, or even suicide. One sign that there is an issue is if the child is anti-social or sleeping all the time.[2828] When a person feels bad about themselves, they are less likely to protect themselves.[2829] It's the "What is the big deal if I drink a little?" <u>Study and know the signs of possible suicide.</u> These issues for gay males can not be overemphasized.

Laugh

The hateful comments from the homophobes is painful. Sometimes, the best remedy is humor. Take this story.

> I remember coming out to my friend Sherm. At the time, no one besides my cousin Linda knew I was gay. I was 23, Sherm was 43. In hindsight, I should have known Sherm would be accepting because he has a lesbian daughter. But I was so nervous. When I told him I was gay, I basically broke down crying. Sherm really wanted to help me out, so he told me how much fun he has going bar hopping with his lesbian daughter and the fact that they often hit on the same women. I knew he was joking and it helped break the ice.

Use PFLAG

Straight people may be accused of being gay if they are too defensive for gay rights. That's why it is so important for straight folks to develop strategies that help their cause. PFLAG is a great organization for Parent and Friends of Lesbians And Gays to come together in support of acceptance, to work in teams and find courage, as well as support.

A nonprofit organization, PFLAG was founded in 1973, and has about 250,000 members in more than 500 chapters.[2830] It evolved from one mother, Jeanne Manford, who in 1972 marched with her gay son Morty in a New York pride parade.[2831] PFLAG helps give straight people who oppose discrimination against LGBT people tools and information that will help them be good allies.[2832] However, the majority of the chapters are volunteer driven.[2833] Volunteer.

Don'ts for parents

1) Don't rush the process of trying to understand your loved one's sexuality or gender identity.[2834]
2) Don't assume your loved one should see a professional counselor or encourage them to participate in "reparative therapy."[2835]
3) Don't try to force your loved one to conform to your ideas of proper sexual behavior.[2836]
4) Don't insist that your morality is the only right one.[2837]

The extended family

Uncles and aunts, cousins, brothers and sisters, grandparents certainly may not share your view on these issues. I have a dear cousin, I love him. I also put him on my spam list because of the intolerant extreme religious-right messages I kept getting about gay issues, stem cell research and abortion. He literally would not stop in spite of my requests for him to do so and the same requests from our eldest uncle, the head of the McConkey family, went unheeded. I just did not want to fight with someone I love, so I blocked him from my system. When his daughter died suddenly, I wrote a long personal, handwritten letter, about our long history, my love and my sorrow, nothing on the issues that divide.

We met in the summer or 2009 and have agreed to forget the anger and move forward loving each other but not agreeing or badgering.

At the same time I have expanded my fight against hatred and the desire of many for the United States to become a theocratic state. I tell my children simply that others disagree and I think they are wrong. And, I tell the truth. I discuss my battles with other members of my extended family. Some of my family are encouraging, others are quietly thankful, yet others quietly disagree.

Heterosexuals have the power to change homophobia.

The American Psychological Association notes:

> "Heterosexual people who wish to help reduce prejudice and discrimination can examine their own response to antigay stereotypes and prejudice. They can make a point of coming to know lesbian, gay, and bisexual people, and they can work with lesbian, gay, and bisexual individuals and communities to combat prejudice and discrimination. Heterosexual individuals are often in a good position to ask other heterosexual people to consider the prejudicial or discriminatory nature of their beliefs and actions. Heterosexual allies can encourage nondiscrimination policies that include sexual orientation. They can work to make coming out safe. ..Studies of prejudice, including prejudice against gay people, consistently show that prejudice declines when members of the majority group interact with members of a minority group. In keeping with this general pattern, one of the most powerful influences on heterosexuals' acceptance of gay people is having personal contact with an openly gay person. Antigay attitudes are far less common among members of the population who have a close friend or family member who is lesbian or gay, especially if the gay person has directly come out to the heterosexual person."[2838]

In the workplace...

Working in fear is a terrible thing. People are often afraid to speak up, even at the "water cooler, in the break room, or after hours." Jobs are precious things and people are often afraid to speak up because they do not want to jeopardize their employment or possible promotion. All of that is sad, and I have not ever been that afraid. Neither have I ever been fired for speaking my mind on matters of conscience.

My wife thinks that her defense of "gay at birth" in a lunchroom with a group of male counterparts was one of the reasons for her difficulties with one employer. It probably was; but she stood her ground and I am proud of her. I have had very strong exchanges, some of them including words of only four letters or less, with male co-workers, over homophobia, race, and gender issues. Have the courage to do so. Furthermore, have the courage to report inappropriate actions and language to the appropriate people. Do not fear being a "whistle-blower." Be truthful and be brave. I "wrote up" a direct supervisor of mine. Could have cost me my job. But my statement was truthful, her behavior and language was wrong, and I did it.

At the same time, seek others who agree and organize socially in the workplace with them. If you speak of good things your numbers will grow. If you organize activities, speakers, discussions, your numbers will grow. If you politely and with great logic and facts, destroy the arguments of your opponents, you will make new friends.

At work, spread the word, fight the hate, organize people and activities, blow a whistle on the evil. Have the courage to fight. No fear!

In the community and in our public/private schools…

It is perhaps harder, you may think, to find allies and no one likes to fight alone. Quite the contrary, there are allies and friends if you persevere, communicate clearly and represent a rational defensible position. If you are nearly a certifiable crackpot in the eyes of the community, you may fight alone. But, you can still fight.

Hatred, as an approved way of life and as the basis for civic action, will not be a subject in public schools. Yet many policies and standard ways of speaking within our schools continue the subtle and not so subtle attacks on gays, Muslims, Afro-Americans, immigrants, the poor, girls and women. The brutality of the physical, verbal, cultural, sexual, sociological and psychological violence against young women and girls in our public middle and high schools, right under the noses of many administrators and teachers, is a national shame. It is hardly better toward gays and the poor, the developmentally disabled, or the very bright.

Disrespect toward one group is only a symptom of a different, deeper problem. The symptom and the disease need to be addressed. Active concerned caring people within the community should work to address this deeper cultural issue. A policy on bullying is far to shallow, a necessary step, but far to shallow.

A continuing discussion is necessary. Deep, rigorous, well taught courses on the causes, impacts, causes, preventions and mitigations of hatred should be required and taught, in addition to, not instead of other social science courses.

Do not buy the "we don't have time to teach more subjects or material arguments." Computers, fewer study halls, longer days, longer school years, are all available. With the amount of knowledge doubling about every four years why do we expect to learn it all in less time anyway? Lack of time is an excuse for staying ignorant of far to many things. This curriculum on fighting hatred may very well save lives, help stop wars, decrease crime, and decrease violence in America. Good deal.

Get in the face of school board, community boards and commissions and demand such curriculum and hate prevention/brotherhood/sisterhood promotion programs in the schools. Demand the expulsion of student bullies and sexual predators. Reward students whose activities in the school and community illustrate hate prevention, understanding and diversity. Make the rewards meaningful.

"No Place For Hate and Totally Safe Schools", must be a priority in every community. I cannot understate the damage that is done to academic records, esteem, even causing suicide that hateful harassment causes in our public schools. Be proactive in getting schools to be hate-free places. Indeed, every school must proactively promote and practice understanding, care, compassion and diversity.

Be active in the Gay, Lesbian and Straight Education Network (GLSEN) and Gay Straight Advocates for Education (GSAFE). If there are no chapters in your community, start them. We must do all we can in our families, community and schools to make doing good and doing well the cool things to do.

Sunshine, preachers, politicians, and public spokespeople.

Sunshine can be effective everywhere. It must start in the local community. Hatred, bigotry, homophobia, bullying, unfair discrimination, prejudice: all must be exposed to the full light of day at every level. They must not go unanswered. On the web, in the newspaper, on the radio, on protestor's placards, they must be exposed. Use their quotes, their records, and their own activities against them.

Effective sunshine requires courage, a desire to help, research and more research, persistence, more courage and a media outlet. It is easy with a computer. Do the research, track every word, do detailed opposition research about your protagonists. Make public the results of your work. If someone refuses to improve the situation, that is also news to be shared.

In my lifetime I have helped discover fake educational claims, degrees that didn't exist, fake military records, unpaid taxes, unpaid child support, DWI's, adultery, travel abuse, investments in South Africa during Apartheid, lack of legal residence, bad political donations, tax shelters using pseudo-churches, embarrassing statements, inappropriate memberships and friendships, bad votes, absenteeism, civil suits, and horrific laziness. Almost no one is without fault that we would not want to be made public.

If a potential public disclosure is not about an innocent bystander, such as spouse or child, or the uninvolved, it is fair game, in the battle between public people. Make sure it is true, to the very best of your ability, quote others, be not afraid.

Expose the words, the methods and means, the activities, the pasts and the current activities. It is fair to question the motives; it is not wise to claim to know the motivations of others.

Sunshine should shine on the lives and records of every public official, media spokesperson, pastor, fundraiser, organizational mouthpiece and organization that promotes or attempts to promote hatred. Attack every mistake they make, every vote, every speech. Keep them on the defensive and wear them down. Use whatever means you can to get the lists of people who sign petitions contrary to equality and freedom, people who contribute to the organizations that oppose equality and freedom, the board members and directors and employees of such organizations.

Donate money, time, effort and talent to the campaigns of your friends, as much as you can. Reward your supporters. Donate to them, buy from them, speak kindly of them wherever you go.

Churches, as you have read herein, and as the news reminds us, are very often merchants of hatred. It is a sinful tragedy, but true. Research, make copies of materials, tape sermons, get the proof and go public. Pastors are human beings, they are not God, and as such will sin. Document same, expose the same. Make life difficult for those who preach and merchandise hatred.

The media

People of all political stripes complain of their treatment by the media. Conservatives tell me that *National Public Radio* and all the states' public radio stations are bastions of liberals. *Fox News* is rightwing; *MSNBC*, except for Pat Buchanan and Joe Scarborough is primarily left wing; *HLN* is about the same as *Entertainment Tonight*; the worldwide web, *CNN* and the *BBC*, the *New York Times*, the *Washington Post*, the *Chicago Tribune*, the *Milwaukee Journal Sentinel* and the *Capital Times* in Madison is where I go for my news.

Many progressives complain to me that there is no effective media opposition to the *Fox News Network*. I think they are correct. However, there are things that can be done and must be done to counter the right-wing perspective constantly doled out on *Fox* and by its radio fellow travelers.

Boycotts work. They may or may not cost someone their job, but they cost the companies money and shine real sunshine upon the activities of the network or media outlet. They will not like the bad press, neither will the advertisers. It is time all LGBT and PFLAG groups organize on the web as well as did *colorofchange.org*, with its 600,000 plus members.

Media personalities and local reporters and editors and columnists are all potential targets for investigation and sunshine as well.

Organize

Sometimes we go it alone. I recommend it, only if necessary. Going with allies is much more effective and enjoyable. Build strong coalitions. Be willing to help others and to give on a point or two in policies, but build coalitions. There are many groups of people who have, for years, been marginalized or ignored by the mainstream. The internet gives us the ability to reach out and join with others who share our values.

We must remember that sometimes values conflict. For example, we value family, education and work. Many of my students are married with kids, a job, and are trying to get a university education. Something has to give, there is not enough time for everything. From time to time one value has priority over another. Such is cooperation among coalitions.

The values of equality, freedom and the right to pursue happiness, protecting our young people, are common to all. We can build on those with many people, some sooner and easier than others. Join with all who are opposed by the neo-con Republicans and the theological dominionists. The gay community and other anti-hatred groups will find many more friends among Democrats at all levels, on and off campus, than Republicans. These friends include professional women's groups, feminist groups, environmental groups, organized labor, Unitarians, Congregationalists, ACLU members, Obama's coalition, Libertarians, Hillary's supporters, most educators, newspaper reporters.

Contact representatives of these groups and attempt to reach an accommodation on matters of mutual interest. Build a working coalition. Build a specific calendar of goals, a list of objectives and the dated milestones to accomplish those objectives. Reach out to national and regional groups. There is strength in numbers. Work with and support the efforts of The Gill Foundation.

Projects for hate free schools, domestic benefits for all couples, equality and the freedom to be happy, repeal of Defense of Marriage Amendments, are all good places to start.

Buy from merchants who advertise in your magazines and support your causes. Encourage others to do the same.

A note on the words equality and pursuit of happiness: In Wisconsin the primary gay rights group is named *Fair Wisconsin*. Fair may not be equal. In terms of the treatment of people I prefer words that are not open to debate, such as equality and the pursuit of happiness, both of which are constitutionally guaranteed.

Political Season

During political season, by all means, organize, recruit and assist pro-equality candidates and vigorously oppose the others. Have the opposition research done and be ready to disseminate the information, raise and donate money, put out dozens of yard signs and monitor their health. Go to public meetings to support your candidates and to ask very hard questions of your opponents. Get in their face, <u>but politely</u>. Always back your arguments with research. Work hard for your local and state candidates. Work equally hard against the homophobes, racists, and other hateful people.

Incumbent politicians are vulnerable to two types of errors: errors of omission and errors of commission. There will always be things they have not done, errors of omission. They may cover many items of import to your state, district, or community. Each one of those omitted or poorly preformed areas is a good place to attack.

Study campaign research, management and communication. Work in campaigns. Become a professional level campaign consultant and work to help as many candidates as you have time for. <u>Conduct and publish opposition research.</u>

Research, write and publish on public policy.

Become a respected spokesman and community leader. Write and write and write. But, do not harm your cause by being a crackpot. Satire, yes occasionally, but remember, some folks don't get it. Stay serious, factual, and use careful and defensible logic. Sign with others who assisted. Write on subjects that are important and in a way that increases your reputation and, if possible, diminishes those of your opponents.

Testify about all legislation that impacts equality and freedom and the separation of Church and State.

Blog, email blast, and include other bloggers and the traditional media on your list.

After research, draft resolutions, ordinances, bills, and initiatives and organize around those documents. Find someone to introduce them, attend public meetings and ask that they be introduced, get press about them, and start a public debate and discussion about them. Keep the pressure on!

File a law suit.

I did. Go to court, threaten to go to Court, use the legal system and the media that accompanies it. It is way to educate and debate and draw the public to view the issue. You do not have to have an attorney. You may represent your self and file the case, *pro per.* Chapter Nine of this book illustrates my case and the way I filed it. I researched other cases in my home state, studied Wisconsin's court site on the web, looked at other case filed on a similar subject across the country and, thanks to Google, was able to study more than a dozen cases from around the nation.

You will be challenged if you do not have standing. Standing is entirely up to the court, it is decision of the Judge(s) or Justice(s). Basically there must be some direct connection or damage specific to you to bring the case. If there is not, find someone who is hurt by a situation and get them to agree to a law suit that will cost only filing fees and reproductions of documents.

I am extremely grateful to Lester Pines, Tamara Packard and Edward Marion, for taking my case, pro bono. The appeals process and the Supreme Court would have been quite daunting without their help. I would have attempted it per se, but am more pleased than I can express, that I received their help, and that of Fair Wisconsin, Lamda Legal and the ACLU of Wisconsin.

Thou Shalt Not:

In my opinion, PDA, (public displays of affection) is inappropriate whether straight or gay. Why? Most Americans don't like it. It will not help you make friends. It may cost you some.

In my opinion, the LGBT community will gain more support, quicker, by ending ALL bare ass, bare-chested, and other nude or seminude displays of the human body and graphics of same. It hurts the cause, it really does. Gay pride parades without those elements of "acting out" are a chance to build solidarity with other marginalized groups and mainstream supporters. Don't do it.

Have a little bit of patience… The young support gay rights. Pew Research concludes: "People under age 30 favor gay marriage by 52% to 40%;

they support civil unions by 58% to 37%."[2839] On days were homophobia smacks you in the face, go to bed knowing there will be better tomorrows.

A Cultural Thing...

Americans commit over **11,400,000** crimes a year: murder, rape, robbery, assault, burglary, larceny, auto-theft. **1,400,000 are violent.** Terrorism is fear of violent harm at home, in our communities. We do not have to travel to other nations to find terrorists, they live among us. 6,600,000 crimes are larceny and theft, plus another 1 million stolen autos. Consumer fraud and ID theft are add-ons to that. We are a nation and culture of crime, costing us over $1 trillion per year

Why do people break the law in such ways? They are not stealing bread to eat. Why do they steal? Why do they assault? Why do they rape? Why do the murder? WHY? If they are not psychopaths in the technical/medical sense of the word, WHY?

All of these crimes are horrid evidence of our lack of concern for others and our emphasis on self- gratification, at any cost, even at the cost of human suffering.

IT IS A CULTURAL THING... we are taught, even before birth to have our every want satisfied, no hunger no pain,, and nothing for anyone else.... Nothing for the commons.. we must have.. self gratification, competition, IT IS A CULTURAL THING.

People are taught, from birth on, to care only for themselves at horrible expense to others and to the entire nation. The next step in that process is hatred. We must completely reverse that cultural determinant.

We must do it all. "If not us, who? If not now, when?"

APPENDIX

A very brief comment on religious opposition to equality.

I am deeply saddened and bothered by the hierarchies and clergy of Christian churches who preach and practice hatred. The Mormons, of all people, wanted to practice polygamy and actually went to war with the United States in 1857-1858 over the issue. The Mormons were forced to changer their religion, and now attack people who wish to marry in a civil ceremony.

I am pleased that *Affirmation*, the support organization for Gay and Lesbian Mormons, stands up to the Church hierarchy on the issues of equality. Since the Church claims to support the rights of civil unions, but not marriage equality, I am even more convinced that the LDS Church's activities across the nation is a front end move of Romney for President,

For Afro-American clergy to deny this most basic civil right to loving couples is an absurd hypocrisy of the worst kind.

The next time you read or hear of the Catholic Church working against equality, just remember, this is the same Vatican who brought you the Inquisition, turned it's back on Jews during the Third Reich, refuses to support the use of condoms to attack AIDS, and through it's benign indifference allowed the damage of pedophilia to happen to thousands of innocent children around the world.

The Roman Catholic Church, through out its long history, has been no stranger to inequality, oppression and ill treatment of people other than themselves. As colonizers of the much of the world, the Church was very often in partnership with Kings and Queens, tyrannical despots, and greedy merchants. Their hypocrisy, as servants of God and believers in the teachings of Jesus, historically has known almost no bounds. Of course, much of this has been true of all colonizers and conquerors.

It is strange however, even to me, a jaded and well read student of history, that the Church and it's Bishops would claim any moral authority now, as they are doing. According to the *John Jay Report*, of 2002, there were over 11,000 allegations of sexual abuse of minors concerning 4,392 priests between 1950 and 2002, in the USA, alone. Instead of defrocking these pedophiles and having them arrested the Bishops covered up the transgressions and moved the priests to a different parish, where their crimes against children often continued. Consequently, the Church has paid hundreds of millions of dollars and several dioceses have filed for bankruptcy.

These sad events have, as of March 2010, were reported to have been a problem of the church in Germany when present-Pope Benedict XVI was an archibishop. As the Vancouver Sun reported (March 2010).[2840] The BBC reported on March 20, 2010, of a hideous situation in Ireland. Four bishops resigned, the entire Irish Catholic hierarchy was summoned to Rome to explain themselves to the Pope and the nation was traumatized by the size of the scandal, the number of children involved and the cover-up by senior Catholic officials.

As stated above, I am deeply saddened by the misinterpretation of God's love for his people and their mistreatment by clergy.

As anyone might suppose, I have received dozens of emails and postal letters concerning my fight for equality. The vast majority have warm, personal and supportive and often talk struggles and mistreatment of the writer and/or their children.

I quote from one: "Again, thank you for taking this stand for what is a human dignity issue, as well as a justice issue. In my opinion, you have formed your conscience well; your moral compass is right on! God Bless you and your family..."

The writer of that letter, a kind Catholic mother of a gay son, was too kind, but was deeply and sincerely appreciated.

Then there is this one... from a man in Beloit, WI: "I am assuming that you have never taken the time to do some research on this issue as I find it hard to believe that an educated college professor would excuse such an unhealthy perversion unless a victim of that addiction himself... God's Word teaches that the sins of the father may be manifest in the lives of the children to the third and fourth generation. Your rebellion against God's Word can anger God to the point that he withdraws the hand of protection from your whole family."

Believe it or not, I also appreciate this man's letter. He reminds me that the world is a dangerous place, that scary whacko people abound, and that the message of love, kindness, and joy that the Bible also brings is being missed by those who do not want to listen or hear.

He should try not hating for 60 days; it will make his life so much better.

McConkey: a one-man battle against state's gay marriage ban

Judith Davidoff — 7/15/2009

The Capitol Times, Madison, WI.

Bill McConkey's street cred as a straight man, as he finds himself reminding people these days, is ironclad.

"I've been married three times," he says, with just a touch of swagger. "If this one slips away, the next one will be a woman."

The topic keeps coming up because McConkey, a father of seven and grandfather of eight, is the man behind the pending challenge to Wisconsin's constitutional ban on gay marriage that will be heard this fall by the Wisconsin Supreme Court.

Adding to the incongruity of his challenge is McConkey's deep Christian faith, conservative leanings and, until recently, long association with the Republican Party.

McConkey filed his lawsuit in Dane County Circuit Court in July 2007, eight months after Wisconsin voters passed a statewide referendum amending the Wisconsin Constitution to ban gay marriage and civil unions. He was told at the time that his suit didn't have a chance, but he didn't listen.

"I'm not impressed by people," he says. "I'm too old. I've been on Air Force One. I've worked in the White House."

McConkey, who turned 67 on July 4, is a political science and communications professor at UW-Oshkosh. He's also a constitutional scholar, mediator, motivational speaker, author of a book on voting behavior and a "semi-trashy, supernatural murder mystery," and, as of this year, owner of a livestock fencing and watering systems business in Tennessee. Conspicuously absent from his long and varied resume is a law degree. But as he recently told a roomful of lawyers in Milwaukee gathered for a symposium on "Marriage Equality in the Heartland," his lack of legal credentials has some advantages.

"That gives me a great deal of license in interpreting what the law means," he said to laughter.

So when faced with what he saw as an egregious, unconstitutional assault on the fundamental rights of Wisconsin's gay citizens -- and a personal attack on his own lesbian daughter -- McConkey filed a lawsuit seeking to overturn the ban: "I was outraged as a scholar and a professor but I was energized because it was my daughter."

At the time, local and national gay rights groups declined to sign on to the lawsuit. Legal observers say caution is always advised in these matters since a court could, if provoked, hand down a broad ruling that would actually set back the fight for marriage equality. But McConkey was undeterred. The legal issues now before the Supreme Court are much more narrow than were originally proposed but, if successful, the effect will be the same: an overturning of Wisconsin's constitutional ban on gay marriage.

McConkey continues to have skeptics and there are those who consider him an oddball. But Milwaukee attorney Christian Thomas Eichenlaub is grateful that

McConkey, once an amateur boxer, threw himself into the ring despite a lack of institutional support.

"You can't fail if you don't try," says Eichenlaub, who worked as a volunteer with Fair Wisconsin, the statewide group that organized opposition to the amendment.

As it turns out, McConkey's timing is looking a little better these days. Though much opposition still remains, public support for gay marriage has grown considerably in the last few years, with supporters racking up several victories, most recently in Vermont and Iowa. Gay marriage is now legal in six states:Massachusetts, Connecticut, Iowa, Vermont, Maine and New Hampshire.

Howard Schweber, a professor of law and political science at the University of Wisconsin-Madison, says courts in general are leery of doing something "totally at odds with public opinion." And politics can play an even greater role when the law under review is unclear. "This is one of those cases," Schweber says. "Since the law on its face is not clear, it's not helpful to simply say 'refer to the law.' You have to have some interpretive method for resolving the ambiguity."

Settled into a table at the Perkins Restaurant on Madison's east side one sunny June morning, McConkey is remarkably fresh the day after a 12-hour drive from Tennessee, where he and his wife have a second house. The couple live year-round in Baileys Harbor, though McConkey also has a place in Oshkosh, where he teaches during the school year.

McConkey is making a brief stop in Madison to visit one of his daughters before proceeding to Milwaukee to participate in a panel discussion on the legal prohibitions on same-sex marriage, organized by the local chapter of the American Constitutional Society, a progressive legal group.

Though he's already polished off a slice of berry pie, his ears perk up when he hears the waitress tick off a list of muffin flavors. "Did you say lemon poppy?" he says with a grin before ordering one.

McConkey loves to eat and cook and, in general, live large. While at Illinois State University on a track scholarship, he lettered in the sport all four years while taking a full load of courses and working 40 hours a week. He was also married at the time. After college he went straight to graduate school for a master's degree in social science and he and his first wife had their first child, a girl born on Nov. 3, 1964. It was the same day, he recalls, that Democratic President Lyndon B. Johnson won re-election over Republican Sen. Barry Goldwater.

"I have a Midwest work ethic," he says, explaining his drive. Though he fell in love with the study of constitutional law as an undergraduate, going to law school was out of the question at the time. He was poor and already had a family to support. He didn't go back for his PhD for decades, eventually receiving a doctorate in mass communication from Florida State University in 1994.

Over the years he's worn many hats. Among them: professor; owner of an advertising company; analyst in the National Security Division of the Office of Management and Budget under former Presidents Johnson and Richard M. Nixon; director of the Division of Energy and Power Development for the state of Alaska; legislative analyst for the Florida Senate Committee on Higher Education; lay Methodist preacher; judge for the World Boxing Association; club boxer; and Illinois field director for Nixon's re-election campaign in 1972.

Because of his time in Alaska, McConkey was familiar with Sarah Palin, though he didn't know her personally. But he knew enough, he says, to consider her unqualified to be president. And so when former presidential candidate John McCain chose Palin as his running mate, it was the final straw for McConkey, who at that point severed his long ties with the Republican Party.

"I lost it," he says. "That just showed a disregard for the American people." It was not a decision he made lightly. The McConkey family's allegiance to the Republican Party dates to the Civil War, when his relatives fought on the side of the Union. "They were Lincoln Republicans," he says. "That's how far back it goes for our family."

The McConkey family's roots in the country go back to at least the Revolutionary War. Ancestors running McConkey's Tavern rented boats to George Washington for his famous 1776 crossing of the Delaware River.

Originally from Scotland and Ireland, the family had emigrated to New York, with one branch staying on the East Coast and another heading south and eventually to Illinois.

McConkey grew up in Champaign, Ill. He says it was conservative in the old mold: the help-your-neighbor, work hard and mind-your-own-business, way. Not, he adds, "this new neo-con theocratic nonsense that permeates the Republican Party." His father, an Illinois state trooper, was killed at 32 while on duty. It was 1950 and McConkey was just 8. Despite the family's great loss, his mother never let her children harbor bitterness about anything.

"We were taught not to hate," McConkey says. "We were not even allowed to say we don't like beets. We'd have to say, 'No thank you. I don't care for any at this time.'"

He was raised Christian and to this day is a man of deep faith. He recalls a great uncle of his, a preacher, asking him a couple of years after his dad's death whether he still believed in God. "Yes, I believe in God but more importantly he believes in me," he told his uncle. "If you live your life so God approves of what you're doing, you won't have any problems."

McConkey was recently asked to speak about his lawsuit at UW-Oshkosh. As the discussion moved forward, he sensed fear in the room among the young gay men, many of whom were not out to their parents. It bothered him. "These are 20-year-old men who should be at the top of their life and instead they're intimidated," he says.

McConkey says he understands their fear and feels compelled to act in their stead. "I believe to my very core that people who are not afraid should fight for those who are. And what I hope I've done with this case, whether I win or lose, is give more people the courage to fight things when they're wrong."

The daughter who inspired McConkey's lawsuit declined to be interviewed for this article. McConkey says she's a private person and was not interested in filing her own legal challenge. "It's just not her personality," he says. But McConkey says she is supportive of his lawsuit.

McConkey first started thinking of filing a lawsuit even before the measure made it to the ballot. But when he informed Mike Tate, then executive director of Fair Wisconsin, of his intentions, Tate visited him in Door County to talk him out of it, believing it was not the right strategic move. He thinks Tate, now chairman of the Wisconsin Democratic Party, had ulterior motives.

"He was interested in the re-election of Gov. Doyle and he didn't want to chance this getting kicked off the ballot," asserts McConkey. "He was not interested in the plight of gays and lesbians in this state at all." The referendum is believed to have motivated liberals to go to the polls -- helping to seal victories for Doyle and other Democratic lawmakers -- as much as or more than the evangelical voters at whom it was aimed.

"Did he really say that?" Tate says incredulously, when asked about McConkey's charges. "Nobody wanted the amendment on the ballot, myself included," he says. "I know Fair Wisconsin looked at all available possibilities and they settled on putting their energy toward defeating the referendum because the possibility of success in the courts was not very high." "We were in the thick of the campaign at the time," Tate adds. "All that a lawsuit would have done at the time is distract time, energy and money away from the sole goal, which was defeating the amendment."

McConkey held off on the lawsuit, something he still regrets. But after the referendum passed in November 2006, he started thinking again about legal action. He once again asked Fair Wisconsin to join him and also put a call in to Lambda Legal, the national gay rights organization that most recently brought the case that legalized same-sex marriage in Iowa. Neither group wanted in.

"I didn't care," McConkey says. "I was fighting for my daughter." Christopher Clark, an attorney in the Chicago office of Lambda Legal, says he cannot comment on confidential conversations his group has had with people seeking legal advice. Katie Belanger, who recently became executive director of Fair Wisconsin, says her group was regrouping after its expensive and ultimately unsuccessful campaign to defeat the amendment and decided to focus its attention on seeking domestic partner protections for same-sex couples. As she points out, even if the constitutional amendment is overturned, there's still a state law on the books that prohibits same-sex marriage.

Both Fair Wisconsin and Lambda are reviewing the case now, however, to determine whether they will seek to submit briefs to the state Supreme Court in support of McConkey.

"We definitely are supportive of the suit," says Belanger. "The amendment is something Fair Wisconsin fought very hard against and something we think was a wrong step for Wisconsin."

While it's true that groups like Fair Wisconsin and Lambda Legal and just about everybody else underestimated the potential of McConkey's challenge, there were reasons for a bit of skepticism, starting with the over-the-top news release he sent to media the day he filed his lawsuit in Madison. "If I fail to make it to the court in time it will be because of an act of catastrophic proportions," he wrote. "I plan to file this in Dane County Circuit Court before noon, approximately 10:30 a.m."

In his July 27, 2007, complaint, McConkey challenged the amendment on substance and procedure, claiming it violated the so-called "single subject rule" pertaining to referendums. He said the referendum illegally asked two questions in one -- whether to ban same-sex marriage and whether to ban civil unions. Attorney General J.B. Van Hollen and Gov. Jim Doyle were listed as defendants, though Doyle was later dismissed as a party to the suit.

The circuit court ruled in September 2007 that McConkey, because he was not gay, did not have standing to challenge the substance of the amendment, but allowed him to proceed with his challenge to the procedure. At this point, prominent Madison attorney Lester Pines contacted McConkey and offered to represent him pro bono. In November 2007, the court rejected a motion by Van Hollen to dismiss the procedural challenge.

(The issue of standing, which has again been raised by the defense and will next be decided by the Supreme Court, continues to mystify McConkey: "If I have no standing, how is it that straight married people got to vote on the amendment?")

Pines says he offered his help to make it a fair fight. "When confronted with really sophisticated legal issues it becomes almost impossible for a lay person to adequately make a case legally," says Pines. "The train had left the station," he adds.

"Either we were going to be on the train or watch it go down the tracks."
Both parties briefed the circuit court on the single subject rule challenge and on May 30, 2008, the court ruled against McConkey on his procedural challenge. Pines appealed the decision and Van Hollen cross-appealed on McConkey's standing to bring the challenge. On April 9, 2009, the Court of Appeals referred the case to the Wisconsin Supreme Court, saying it presents "several novel issues" and was a matter of "significant public interest with statewide implications." The Supreme Court subsequently agreed to hear the case.

When the Court of Appeals issued its ruling, Julaine Appling of the Wisconsin Family Council, which led the campaign to pass the gay marriage ban, intimated in a news release that the justices were swayed by gay marriage victories in other states.

"Two days after a state Supreme Court election and not even a week after Vermont's legislature and Iowa's Supreme Court legalized 'same-sex marriage' in those states, a Wisconsin Court of Appeals referred the case challenging Wisconsin's Marriage Protection Amendment to the state Supreme Court. Coincidence? We may never know, but we cannot ignore the events of the last week and their potential impact on this decision."

In a January web posting on McConkey's lawsuit, Appling assured her followers that her group would not rest as long as "Satan and his minions" are around. "The good fight is a daily battle to glorify Christ on earth through our Christian witness, by being salt and light in a dark and dying world. Supporting God's design for the institution of marriage is simply one of the battles we're fighting right now."

The Satan reference, given his own Christian faith, amuses McConkey, who said he thinks a lot these days about those he calls "matrons of hatred." They're the politicians who use hate to get votes and preachers who use it to raise money. It's the subject, in fact, of his next book, whose working title is, "Why I Fight: The Battle Against Hatred In America."

McConkey says the most hateful e-mails he has received about his lawsuit have come from individuals who use the Bible to justify their disapproval of homosexuality. He sees the same irony in conservative Christian church opposition to national hate crime legislation.

"If Jesus is coming back he'd better hurry," says McConkey. "These people are ruining his name."

One additional note from the author.

In the mid-1950's I saw the movie version of Rogers and Hammerstein's *South Pacific*. The following lyrics have never left my subconscious thought. And, although I have often failed to be able to recite them accurately, the first seven words have never left my abilities to remember, even when I unfortunately failed to live up to their message.

"You've got to be taught
To hate and fear,
You've got to be taught
From year to year,
It's got to be drummed
In your dear little ear
You've got to be carefully taught.

You've got to be taught to be afraid
Of people whose eyes are oddly made,
And people whose skin is a diff'rent shade,
You've got to be carefully taught.

You've got to be taught before it's too late,
Before you are six or seven or eight,
To hate all the people your relatives hate,
You've got to be carefully taught!"**

** www.stlyrics.com/lyrics/southpacific/youvegottobecarefullytaught.htm

William C. McConkey, Ph.D.

Bill McConkey is a social activist, fighting for equality for those who are marginalized by those who hate.

Dr. Bill McConkey teaches Leadership and Organizational Studies and Political Science courses at the University of Wisconsin in Oshkosh. Dr. McConkey received his BS and MS degrees in the Social Sciences from Illinois State University in 1964 and 1965. He received his Ph.D. from Florida Sate University in 1994, at the age of 52.

He has worked for several government agencies, including the Executive Office of the President of the United States, the Florida Senate's Committee on Higher Education, and for the Governors of Illinois and Alaska.

He has owned and operated his own communication research and consulting firm for over 30 years. He also has managed or consulted to over 150 political campaigns, with well over a 90% success rate. He is a powerful, inspirational public speaker and humorist.

Bill McConkey is married and has 7 daughters and stepdaughters and 8 grandchildren. He and his wife share their home with their Schipperkes. They also own a farm in Tennessee. His favorite things to do are cooking, public speaking, hunting, fishing, gardening, raising livestock, reading and writing.

His email signature states, "Fear is real, and I believe, to my very core, that those who are not afraid have a moral obligation to fight for those who are."

He may be contacted through:

Doingwhatsrightwmc@Gmail.com

Endnotes

---

[1] See http://thinkexist.com/quotes/joseph_goebbels/.
[2] See http://www.wiredstrategies.com/robertson.html.
[3] See http://www.quotelucy.com/quotes/pat-robertson-quotes.html.
[4] See http://www.imdb.com/title/tt0149408/quotes.
[5] See http://www.imdb.com/title/tt0149408/quotes.
[6] See http://www.imdb.com/title/tt0149408/quotes.
[7] See http://www.imdb.com/title/tt0149408/quotes.
[8] See http://www.theocracywatch.org.
[9] See http://labradorite.wordpress.com/2006/10/11/julaine-appling-scares-the-shit-out-of-me/.
[10] See http://www.brainyquote.com/quotes/authors/j/jimmy_swaggart.html.
[11] See http://mediamatters.org/mmtv/200508160001.
[12] See http://www.baptiststandard.com/2000/4_3/pages/mohler.html.
[13] See http://www.adl.org/learn/ext_us/WBC/WBC-on-Jews.asp?LEARN_Cat=Extremism&LEARN_SubCat=Extremism_in_America&xpicked=3&item=WBC.
[14] See http://www.religioustolerance.org/quot_intol1.htm.
[15] See (Mormon Doctrine, p.670).
[16] See http://message.snopes.com/showthread.php?p=176730.
[17] See http://womenshistory.about.com/od/quotes/a/antifeminism_quotes.htm
[18] See www.truenews.org/**Homosexual**ity/same_sex_marriage_talking_points.html.
[19] See http://www.rightwingwatch.org/category/groups/faithful-word-baptist-church.
[20] Gay marriage ruling galvanizes both sidesBy Alexandra Marks| Staff writer of The Christian Science Monitorhttp://www.csmonitor.com/2005/0316/p02s01-ussc.html
[21] Voters backing same-sex marriage ban. John Wildermuth, Chronicle Staff Writer, Wednesday, November 5, 2008. *http://sfgate.com/cgi-bin/article.cgi?f=/c/a/2008/11/05/MNCC13QR90.DTL. This article appeared on page A - 3 of the San Francisco Chronicle.*
[22] Voters backing same-sex marriage ban. John Wildermuth, Chronicle Staff Writer, Wednesday, November 5, 2008. *http://sfgate.com/cgi-bin/article.cgi?f=/c/a/2008/11/05/MNCC13QR90.DTL. This article appeared on page A - 3 of the San Francisco Chronicle*
[23] Gay marriage ruling galvanizes both sidesBy Alexandra Marks| Staff writer of The Christian Science Monitorhttp://www.csmonitor.com/2005/0316/p02s01-ussc.html
[24] Voters backing same-sex marriage ban. John Wildermuth, Chronicle Staff Writer, Wednesday, November 5, 2008. *http://sfgate.com/cgi-bin/article.cgi?f=/c/a/2008/11/05/MNCC13QR90.DTL. This article appeared on page A - 3 of the San Francisco Chronicle*
[25] Prop 8: California gay marriage fight divides LDS faithful. The church's effort against gay marriage is its most vigorous since 1970s. By Peggy Fletcher Stack. The Salt Lake Tribune. Updated: 10/26/2008.
[26] Jerry Brown's wording may trip up Prop. 8. Phillip Matier,Andrew Ross. Sunday, October 26, 2008. *http://sfgate.com/cgi-bin/article.cgi?f=/c/a/2008/10/26/BADT13NUOH.DTL. See also* http://www.sfgate.com/cgi-bin/article.cgi?f=/c/a/2008/10/26/BADT13NUOH.DTL&type=printable.
[27] California Supreme Court Overturns Gay Marriage Ban
By **ADAM LIPTAK**. may 16, 2008 http://www.nytimes.com/2008/05/16/us/16marriage.html?_r=1&ref=us&pagewanted=print&oref=slogin
[28] Today Marks a Milestone in Gay Marriage. The first couple will marry as California's new law takes effect at 5:01 p.m. *By Justin Ewers.* Posted June 16, 2008. http://www.usnews.com/articles/news/national/2008/06/16/today-marks-a-milestone-in-gay-marriage_print.htm
[29] Same-Sex-Marriage Battle Appears Over in California. *By Justin Ewers* Posted November 5, 2008. http://www.usnews.com/articles/news/politics/2008/11/05/same-sex-marriage-battle-appears-over-in-california.html
[30] Gay Marriage in Peril in California. OCTOBER 22, 2008, By JIM CARLTON. http://online.wsj.com/article/SB122463078466356397.html?mod=googlenews_wsj#.
[31] Gay Marriage in Peril in California. OCTOBER 22, 2008, By JIM CARLTON. http://online.wsj.com/article/SB122463078466356397.html?mod=googlenews_wsj#.
[32] Today Marks a Milestone in Gay Marriage. The first couple will marry as California's new law takes effect at 5:01 p.m. *By Justin Ewers.* Posted June 16, 2008. http://www.usnews.com/articles/news/national/2008/06/16/today-marks-a-milestone-in-gay-marriage_print.htm
[33] Newsom was central to same-sex marriage saga. Erin Allday, Chronicle Staff Writer. Thursday, November 6, 2008. ***http://sfgate.com/cgi-bin/article.cgi?f=/c/a/2008/11/06/MN1B13S3D3.DTL.*** *This article appeared on page A - 1 of the San Francisco Chronicle*
[34] Newsom was central to same-sex marriage saga. Erin Allday, Chronicle Staff Writer. Thursday, November 6, 2008. ***http://sfgate.com/cgi-bin/article.cgi?f=/c/a/2008/11/06/MN1B13S3D3.DTL.*** *This article appeared on page A - 1 of the San Francisco Chronicle*
[35] Newsom was central to same-sex marriage saga. Erin Allday, Chronicle Staff Writer. Thursday, November 6, 2008. ***http://sfgate.com/cgi-bin/article.cgi?f=/c/a/2008/11/06/MN1B13S3D3.DTL.*** *This article appeared on page A - 1 of the San Francisco Chronicle*
[36] Newsom was central to same-sex marriage saga. Erin Allday, Chronicle Staff Writer. Thursday, November 6, 2008. ***http://sfgate.com/cgi-bin/article.cgi?f=/c/a/2008/11/06/MN1B13S3D3.DTL.*** *This article appeared on page A - 1 of the San Francisco Chronicle*
[37] Gay rights backers file 3 lawsuits challenging Prop. 8. By Maura Dolan and Tami Abdollah. November 6, 2008. http://www.latimes.com/news/printedition/california/la-me-gaylegal6-2008nov06,0,5471913.story
[38] Voters backing same-sex marriage ban. John Wildermuth, Chronicle Staff Writer, Wednesday, November 5, 2008. *http://sfgate.com/cgi-bin/article.cgi?f=/c/a/2008/11/05/MNCC13QR90.DTL. This article appeared on page A - 3 of the San Francisco Chronicle*
[39] Today Marks a Milestone in Gay Marriage. The first couple will marry as California's new law takes effect at 5:01 p.m. *By Justin Ewers.* Posted June 16, 2008. http://www.usnews.com/articles/news/national/2008/06/16/today-marks-a-milestone-in-gay-marriage_print.htm
[40] Today Marks a Milestone in Gay Marriage. The first couple will marry as California's new law takes effect at 5:01 p.m. *By Justin Ewers.* Posted June 16, 2008. http://www.usnews.com/articles/news/national/2008/06/16/today-marks-a-milestone-in-gay-marriage_print.htm
[41] Today Marks a Milestone in Gay Marriage. The first couple will marry as California's new law takes effect at 5:01 p.m. *By Justin Ewers.* Posted June 16, 2008. http://www.usnews.com/articles/news/national/2008/06/16/today-marks-a-milestone-in-gay-marriage_print.htm
[42] Today Marks a Milestone in Gay Marriage. The first couple will marry as California's new law takes effect at 5:01 p.m. *By Justin Ewers.* Posted June 16, 2008. http://www.usnews.com/articles/news/national/2008/06/16/today-marks-a-milestone-in-gay-marriage_print.htm
[43] Taken from protectmarriage.com in October 2008.
[44] Same-Sex-Marriage Battle Appears Over in California. *By Justin Ewers* Posted November 5, 2008. http://www.usnews.com/articles/news/politics/2008/11/05/same-sex-marriage-battle-appears-over-in-california.html
[45] Health Buzz: California Ruling Protects Gays and Other Health News. Posted August 19, 2008. http://health.usnews.com/articles/health/2008/08/19/health-buzz-california-ruling-protects-gays-and-other-health-news.html.
[46] **Calif. Court Puts Gays' Care Over Doctors' Faith.** By Ashley Surdin. Washington Post Staff Writer. Tuesday, August 19, 2008; A03 http://www.washingtonpost.com/wp-dyn/content/article/2008/08/18/AR2008081802080_pf.html.
[47] **Calif. Court Puts Gays' Care Over Doctors' Faith.** By Ashley Surdin. Washington Post Staff Writer. Tuesday, August 19, 2008; A03 http://www.washingtonpost.com/wp-dyn/content/article/2008/08/18/AR2008081802080_pf.html
[48] **Calif. Court Puts Gays' Care Over Doctors' Faith.** By Ashley Surdin. Washington Post Staff Writer. Tuesday, August 19, 2008; A03 http://www.washingtonpost.com/wp-dyn/content/article/2008/08/18/AR2008081802080_pf.html
[49] **Calif. Court Puts Gays' Care Over Doctors' Faith.** By Ashley Surdin. Washington Post Staff Writer. Tuesday, August 19, 2008; A03 http://www.washingtonpost.com/wp-dyn/content/article/2008/08/18/AR2008081802080_pf.html
[50] A Line in the Sand for Same-Sex Marriage Foes. By **LAURIE GOODSTEIN**. October 27, 2008. From http://www.nytimes.com/2008/10/27/us/27right.html?_r=1&oref=slogin&partner=rssnyt&emc=rss&pagewanted=print.
[51] A Line in the Sand for Same-Sex Marriage Foes. By **LAURIE GOODSTEIN**. October 27, 2008. From http://www.nytimes.com/2008/10/27/us/27right.html?_r=1&oref=slogin&partner=rssnyt&emc=rss&pagewanted=print.
[52] A Line in the Sand for Same-Sex Marriage Foes. By **LAURIE GOODSTEIN**. October 27, 2008. From http://www.nytimes.com/2008/10/27/us/27right.html?_r=1&oref=slogin&partner=rssnyt&emc=rss&pagewanted=print.
[53] A Line in the Sand for Same-Sex Marriage Foes. By **LAURIE GOODSTEIN**. October 27, 2008. From http://www.nytimes.com/2008/10/27/us/27right.html?_r=1&oref=slogin&partner=rssnyt&emc=rss&pagewanted=print.
[54] A Line in the Sand for Same-Sex Marriage Foes. By **LAURIE GOODSTEIN**. October 27, 2008. From http://www.nytimes.com/2008/10/27/us/27right.html?_r=1&oref=slogin&partner=rssnyt&emc=rss&pagewanted=print.
[55] Six Consequences the Coalition Has Identified If Proposition 8 Fails. September 14, 2008 by Guy Murray. http://protectingmarriage.wordpress.com/2008/09/14/six-consequences-the-coalition-has-identified-if-proposition-8-fails/.
[56] California Supreme Court Overturns Gay Marriage Ban
By **ADAM LIPTAK**. may 16, 2008 http://www.nytimes.com/2008/05/16/us/16marriage.html?_r=1&ref=us&pagewanted=print&oref=slogin
[57] California Supreme Court Overturns Gay Marriage Ban
By **ADAM LIPTAK**. may 16, 2008 http://www.nytimes.com/2008/05/16/us/16marriage.html?_r=1&ref=us&pagewanted=print&oref=slogin
[58] Six Consequences the Coalition Has Identified If Proposition 8 Fails. September 14, 2008 by Guy Murray. http://protectingmarriage.wordpress.com/2008/09/14/six-consequences-the-coalition-has-identified-if-proposition-8-fails/.

[59] Gay Marriage in Peril in California. OCTOBER 22, 2008, By J I M C A R L T O N . http://online.wsj.com/article/SB122463078466356397.html?mod=googlenews_wsj#.
[60] A Line in the Sand for Same-Sex Marriage Foes. By **LAURIE GOODSTEIN**. October 27, 2008. From http://www.nytimes.com/2008/10/27/us/27right.html?_r=1&oref=slogin&partner=rssnyt&emc=rss&pagewanted=print.
[61] Parents outraged after kids shown in Prop 8 ad. Sunday, October 26, 2008 | 6:36 PM By Tomas Roman .
[62] Parents outraged after kids shown in Prop 8 ad. Sunday, October 26, 2008 | 6:36 PM By Tomas Roman .
[63] Parents outraged after kids shown in Prop 8 ad. Sunday, October 26, 2008 | 6:36 PM By Tomas Roman .
[64] Six Consequences the Coalition Has Identified If Proposition 8 Fails. September 14, 2008 by Guy Murray. http://protectingmarriage.wordpress.com/2008/09/14/six-consequences-the-coalition-has-identified-if-proposition-8-fails/.
[65] A Line in the Sand for Same-Sex Marriage Foes. By **LAURIE GOODSTEIN**. October 27, 2008. From http://www.nytimes.com/2008/10/27/us/27right.html?_r=1&oref=slogin&partner=rssnyt&emc=rss&pagewanted=print.
[66] Six Consequences the Coalition Has Identified If Proposition 8 Fails. September 14, 2008 by Guy Murray. http://protectingmarriage.wordpress.com/2008/09/14/six-consequences-the-coalition-has-identified-if-proposition-8-fails/.
[67] An Economic Boost From Gay Marriage. Same-sex marriage is expected to add millions to California coffers. *By Justin Ewers.*Posted June 11, 2008 http://www.usnews.com/articles/news/national/2008/06/11/an-economic-boost-from-gay-marriage.html.
[68] An Economic Boost From Gay Marriage. Same-sex marriage is expected to add millions to California coffers. *By Justin Ewers.*Posted June 11, 2008 http://www.usnews.com/articles/news/national/2008/06/11/an-economic-boost-from-gay-marriage.html.
[69] An Economic Boost From Gay Marriage. Same-sex marriage is expected to add millions to California coffers. *By Justin Ewers.*Posted June 11, 2008 http://www.usnews.com/articles/news/national/2008/06/11/an-economic-boost-from-gay-marriage.html.
[70] Gay Marriage in Peril in California. OCTOBER 22, 2008, By J I M C A R L T O N . http://online.wsj.com/article/SB122463078466356397.html?mod=googlenews_wsj#.
[71] Gay Marriage in Peril in California. OCTOBER 22, 2008, By J I M C A R L T O N . http://online.wsj.com/article/SB122463078466356397.html?mod=googlenews_wsj#.
[72] Gay Marriage in Peril in California. OCTOBER 22, 2008, By J I M C A R L T O N . http://online.wsj.com/article/SB122463078466356397.html?mod=googlenews_wsj#.
[73] Gay Marriage in Peril in California. OCTOBER 22, 2008, By J I M C A R L T O N . http://online.wsj.com/article/SB122463078466356397.html?mod=googlenews_wsj#.
[74] A Line in the Sand for Same-Sex Marriage Foes. By **LAURIE GOODSTEIN**. October 27, 2008. From http://www.nytimes.com/2008/10/27/us/27right.html?_r=1&oref=slogin&partner=rssnyt&emc=rss&pagewanted=print.
[75] Prop. 8 foes concede defeat, vow to fight on. Bob Egelko,John Wildermuth, Chronicle Staff Writers. Thursday, November 6, 2008. San Francisco Chronicle. *http://sfgate.com/cgi-bin/article.cgi?f=/c/a/2008/11/06/BA1313VJQH.DTL.*
[76] Prop. 8 foes concede defeat, vow to fight on. Bob Egelko,John Wildermuth, Chronicle Staff Writers. Thursday, November 6, 2008. San Francisco Chronicle. *http://sfgate.com/cgi-bin/article.cgi?f=/c/a/2008/11/06/BA1313VJQH.DTL.*
[77] Prop. 8 foes concede defeat, vow to fight on. Bob Egelko,John Wildermuth, Chronicle Staff Writers. Thursday, November 6, 2008. San Francisco Chronicle. *http://sfgate.com/cgi-bin/article.cgi?f=/c/a/2008/11/06/BA1313VJQH.DTL.*
[78] California Same-Sex Marriage Initiative Campaigns Shatter Spending Records *By Justin Ewers* Posted October 29, 2008. http://www.usnews.com/articles/news/national/2008/10/29/california-same-sex-marriage-initiative-campaigns-shatter-spending-records.html
[79] California Same-Sex Marriage Initiative Campaigns Shatter Spending Records *By Justin Ewers* Posted October 29, 2008. http://www.usnews.com/articles/news/national/2008/10/29/california-same-sex-marriage-initiative-campaigns-shatter-spending-records.html
[80] LA Times quoted in *Spielberg Adds $100K to the No on 8 Campaign*. September 24, 2008 from http://www.advocate.com/print_article_ektid62142.asp
[81] Donations From California Teachers, HRC Lead to $2.25 Million for No on 8. October 16, 2008. http://www.advocate.com/news_detail_ektid63808.asp
[82] A Line in the Sand for Same-Sex Marriage Foes. By **LAURIE GOODSTEIN**. October 27, 2008. From http://www.nytimes.com/2008/10/27/us/27right.html?_r=1&oref=slogin&partner=rssnyt&emc=rss&pagewanted=print.
[83] Donations From California Teachers, HRC Lead to $2.25 Million for No on 8. October 16, 2008. http://www.advocate.com/news_detail_ektid63808.asp
[84] California Same-Sex Marriage Initiative Campaigns Shatter Spending Records *By Justin Ewers* Posted October 29, 2008. http://www.usnews.com/articles/news/national/2008/10/29/california-same-sex-marriage-initiative-campaigns-shatter-spending-records.html
[85] California Same-Sex Marriage Initiative Campaigns Shatter Spending Records *By Justin Ewers* Posted October 29, 2008. http://www.usnews.com/articles/news/national/2008/10/29/california-same-sex-marriage-initiative-campaigns-shatter-spending-records.html
[86] California Same-Sex Marriage Initiative Campaigns Shatter Spending Records *By Justin Ewers* Posted October 29, 2008. http://www.usnews.com/articles/news/national/2008/10/29/california-same-sex-marriage-initiative-campaigns-shatter-spending-records.html
[87] California Same-Sex Marriage Initiative Campaigns Shatter Spending Records *By Justin Ewers* Posted October 29, 2008. http://www.usnews.com/articles/news/national/2008/10/29/california-same-sex-marriage-initiative-campaigns-shatter-spending-records.html
[88] Spielberg Adds $100K to the No on 8 Campaign. September 24, 2008 from http://www.advocate.com/print_article_ektid62142.asp
[89] California Same-Sex Marriage Initiative Campaigns Shatter Spending Records *By Justin Ewers* Posted October 29, 2008. http://www.usnews.com/articles/news/national/2008/10/29/california-same-sex-marriage-initiative-campaigns-shatter-spending-records.html
[90] Schwarzenegger Won't Waver on Prop. 8, Aide Says. October 15, 2008 http://www.advocate.com/news_detail_ektid63716.asp.
[91] **Democratic National Committee gave $25,000 to defeat Calif. marriage amendment. August 18, 2008 · 2 Commentshttp://thestateofamericasfamily.wordpress.com/2008/08/18/democratic-national-committee-gave-25000-to-defeat-calif-marriage-amendment/**
[92] Jerry Brown's wording may trip up Prop. 8. Phillip Matier,Andrew Ross. Sunday, October 26, 2008. *http://sfgate.com/cgi-bin/article.cgi?f=/c/a/2008/10/26/BADT13NUOH.DTL, See also* http://www.sfgate.com/cgi-bin/article.cgi?f=/c/a/2008/10/26/BADT13NUOH.DTL&type=printable.
[93] Jerry Brown's wording may trip up Prop. 8. Phillip Matier,Andrew Ross. Sunday, October 26, 2008. *http://sfgate.com/cgi-bin/article.cgi?f=/c/a/2008/10/26/BADT13NUOH.DTL, See also* http://www.sfgate.com/cgi-bin/article.cgi?f=/c/a/2008/10/26/BADT13NUOH.DTL&type=printable.
[94] Jerry Brown's wording may trip up Prop. 8. Phillip Matier,Andrew Ross. Sunday, October 26, 2008. *http://sfgate.com/cgi-bin/article.cgi?f=/c/a/2008/10/26/BADT13NUOH.DTL, See also* http://www.sfgate.com/cgi-bin/article.cgi?f=/c/a/2008/10/26/BADT13NUOH.DTL&type=printable.
[95] Jerry Brown's wording may trip up Prop. 8. Phillip Matier,Andrew Ross. Sunday, October 26, 2008. *http://sfgate.com/cgi-bin/article.cgi?f=/c/a/2008/10/26/BADT13NUOH.DTL, See also* http://www.sfgate.com/cgi-bin/article.cgi?f=/c/a/2008/10/26/BADT13NUOH.DTL&type=printable.
[96] Jerry Brown's wording may trip up Prop. 8. Phillip Matier,Andrew Ross. Sunday, October 26, 2008. *http://sfgate.com/cgi-bin/article.cgi?f=/c/a/2008/10/26/BADT13NUOH.DTL, See also* http://www.sfgate.com/cgi-bin/article.cgi?f=/c/a/2008/10/26/BADT13NUOH.DTL&type=printable.
[97] Jerry Brown's wording may trip up Prop. 8. Phillip Matier,Andrew Ross. Sunday, October 26, 2008. *http://sfgate.com/cgi-bin/article.cgi?f=/c/a/2008/10/26/BADT13NUOH.DTL, See also* http://www.sfgate.com/cgi-bin/article.cgi?f=/c/a/2008/10/26/BADT13NUOH.DTL&type=printable.
[98] Jerry Brown's wording may trip up Prop. 8. Phillip Matier,Andrew Ross. Sunday, October 26, 2008. *http://sfgate.com/cgi-bin/article.cgi?f=/c/a/2008/10/26/BADT13NUOH.DTL, See also* http://www.sfgate.com/cgi-bin/article.cgi?f=/c/a/2008/10/26/BADT13NUOH.DTL&type=printable.
[99] This seems a limited number if visiting website on October 26, 2008. Retrieved from http://www.protectmarriage.com/endorsements/officials.
[100] Schwarzenegger Won't Waver on Prop. 8, Aide Says. October 15, 2008 http://www.advocate.com/news_detail_ektid63716.asp.
[101] Schwarzenegger Won't Waver on Prop. 8, Aide Says. October 15, 2008 http://www.advocate.com/news_detail_ektid63716.asp.
[102] Ellen Buys $100K in Airtime for No on 8 PSA. 10/18/08-10/20/08 http://www.advocate.com/news_detail_ektid63964.asp
[103] Spielberg Adds $100K to the No on 8 Campaign. September 24, 2008 from http://www.advocate.com/print_article_ektid62142.asp
[104] Entrepreneur Vows to Match $500K Worth of No on 8 Contributions. October 01, 2008http://www.advocate.com/news_detail_ektid62696.asp
[105] Donations From California Teachers, HRC Lead to $2.25 Million for No on 8. October 16, 2008. http://www.advocate.com/news_detail_ektid63808.asp
[106] Donations From California Teachers, HRC Lead to $2.25 Million for No on 8. October 16, 2008. http://www.advocate.com/news_detail_ektid63808.asp
[107] Donations From California Teachers, HRC Lead to $2.25 Million for No on 8. October 16, 2008. http://www.advocate.com/news_detail_ektid63808.asp
[108] Levi Strauss Pairs With PG&E to Fight Proposition 8 09/27/08-09/29/08 http://www.advocate.com/news_detail_ektid62426.asp.
[109] Levi Strauss Pairs With PG&E to Fight Proposition 8 09/27/08-09/29/08 http://www.advocate.com/news_detail_ektid62426.asp.
[110] Levi Strauss Pairs With PG&E to Fight Proposition 8 09/27/08-09/29/08 http://www.advocate.com/news_detail_ektid62426.asp.
[111] Levi Strauss Pairs With PG&E to Fight Proposition 8 09/27/08-09/29/08 http://www.advocate.com/news_detail_ektid62426.asp.
[112] Nationally Acclaimed Pastor Rick Warren Announces Support for Proposition 8. October 24, 2008. Contact: Meg Waters, 949-461-9700. See http://saddlebackfamily.com/blogs/newsandviews/index.html?contentid=1502. See also http://www.protectmarriage.com/article/nationally-acclaimed-pastor-rick-warren-announces-support-for-proposition-8.
[113] TIME Names the 25 Most Influential EVANGELICALS in America. Sunday, Jan. 30, 2005 http://www.time.com/time/printout/0,8816,1022576,00.html
[114] California Same-Sex Marriage Initiative Campaigns Shatter Spending Records *By Justin Ewers* Posted October 29, 2008. http://www.usnews.com/articles/news/national/2008/10/29/california-same-sex-marriage-initiative-campaigns-shatter-spending-records.html
[115] Nationally Acclaimed Pastor Rick Warren Announces Support for Proposition 8. October 24, 2008. Contact: Meg Waters, 949-461-9700. See http://saddlebackfamily.com/blogs/newsandviews/index.html?contentid=1502. See also http://www.protectmarriage.com/article/nationally-acclaimed-pastor-rick-warren-announces-support-for-proposition-8.
[116] **Gay leaders furious with Obama,** By: Ben Smith and Nia-Malika Henderson. December 18, 2008 11:53 AM EST Politico. http://dyn.politico.com/printstory.cfm?uuid=472FEFF0-18FE-70B2-A8BF144E41102509
[117] **Gay leaders furious with Obama,** By: Ben Smith and Nia-Malika Henderson. December 18, 2008 11:53 AM EST Politico. http://dyn.politico.com/printstory.cfm?uuid=472FEFF0-18FE-70B2-A8BF144E41102509
[118] Gay Marriage in Peril in California. OCTOBER 22, 2008, By J I M C A R L T O N . http://online.wsj.com/article/SB122463078466356397.html?mod=googlenews_wsj#.
[119] California Same-Sex Marriage Initiative Campaigns Shatter Spending Records *By Justin Ewers* Posted October 29, 2008. http://www.usnews.com/articles/news/national/2008/10/29/california-same-sex-marriage-initiative-campaigns-shatter-spending-records.html

[120] A Line in the Sand for Same-Sex Marriage Foes. By **LAURIE GOODSTEIN**. October 27, 2008. From http://www.nytimes.com/2008/10/27/us/27right.html?_r=1&oref=slogin&partner=rssnyt&emc=rss&pagewanted=print.
[121] California Same-Sex Marriage Initiative Campaigns Shatter Spending Records
By Justin Ewers Posted October 29, 2008. http://www.usnews.com/articles/news/national/2008/10/29/california-same-sex-marriage-initiative-campaigns-shatter-spending-records.html
[122] A Line in the Sand for Same-Sex Marriage Foes. By **LAURIE GOODSTEIN**. October 27, 2008. From http://www.nytimes.com/2008/10/27/us/27right.html?_r=1&oref=slogin&partner=rssnyt&emc=rss&pagewanted=print.
[123] A Line in the Sand for Same-Sex Marriage Foes. By **LAURIE GOODSTEIN**. October 27, 2008. From http://www.nytimes.com/2008/10/27/us/27right.html?_r=1&oref=slogin&partner=rssnyt&emc=rss&pagewanted=print.
[124] A Line in the Sand for Same-Sex Marriage Foes. By **LAURIE GOODSTEIN**. October 27, 2008. From http://www.nytimes.com/2008/10/27/us/27right.html?_r=1&oref=slogin&partner=rssnyt&emc=rss&pagewanted=print.
[125] Prop 8: California gay marriage fight divides LDS faithful. The church's effort against gay marriage is its most vigorous since 1970s. By Peggy Fletcher Stack. The Salt Lake Tribune. Updated: 10/26/2008.
[126] California Same-Sex Marriage Initiative Campaigns Shatter Spending Records
By Justin Ewers Posted October 29, 2008. http://www.usnews.com/articles/news/national/2008/10/29/california-same-sex-marriage-initiative-campaigns-shatter-spending-records.html
[127] Gay activists protest Mormon church. **By Ben Arnoldy** | Staff writer of The Christian Science Monitor. From the November 13, 2008 edition. http://www.csmonitor.com/2008/1113/p03s07-uspo.html.
[128] Catholics, Mormons allied to pass Prop. 8. Matthai Kuruvila, Chronicle Religion Writer. Monday, November 10, 2008 E-mail Matthai Kuruvila at mkuruvila@sfchronicle.com. *http://sfgate.com/cgi-bin/article.cgi?f=/c/a/2008/11/10/MNU1140AQQ.DTL*. This article appeared on page ***A - 1*** of the San Francisco Chronicle.
[129] Mormons Bankroll Anti–Gay Marriage Amendments in California, Arizona. October 22, 2008. http://www.advocate.com/news_detail_ektid64163.asp
[130] Gay Marriage in Peril in California. OCTOBER 22, 2008, By JIM CARLTON. http://online.wsj.com/article/SB122463078466356397.html?mod=googlenews_wsj#.
[131] Mormons Bankroll Anti–Gay Marriage Amendments in California, Arizona. October 22, 2008. http://www.advocate.com/news_detail_ektid64163.asp.
[132] Mormons Bankroll Anti–Gay Marriage Amendments in California, Arizona. October 22, 2008. http://www.advocate.com/news_detail_ektid64163.asp
[133] Mormons Bankroll Anti–Gay Marriage Amendments in California, Arizona. October 22, 2008. http://www.advocate.com/news_detail_ektid64163.asp
[134] A Line in the Sand for Same-Sex Marriage Foes. By **LAURIE GOODSTEIN**. October 27, 2008. From http://www.nytimes.com/2008/10/27/us/27right.html?_r=1&oref=slogin&partner=rssnyt&emc=rss&pagewanted=print.
[135] Prop 8: California gay marriage fight divides LDS faithful. The church's effort against gay marriage is its most vigorous since 1970s. By Peggy Fletcher Stack. The Salt Lake Tribune. Updated: 10/26/2008.
[136] Prop 8: California gay marriage fight divides LDS faithful. The church's effort against gay marriage is its most vigorous since 1970s. By Peggy Fletcher Stack. The Salt Lake Tribune. Updated: 10/26/2008.
[137] Prop 8: California gay marriage fight divides LDS faithful. The church's effort against gay marriage is its most vigorous since 1970s. By Peggy Fletcher Stack. The Salt Lake Tribune. Updated: 10/26/2008.
[138] Mormons Targeted for Role Supporting Prop 8. Critics Question Church's Role in Lobbying; Accuse Mormons of Bigotry. By DAN HARRIS. Nov. 12, 2008— http://www.abcnews.go.com/print?id=6238226.
[139] Mormons Targeted for Role Supporting Prop 8. Critics Question Church's Role in Lobbying; Accuse Mormons of Bigotry. By DAN HARRIS. Nov. 12, 2008— http://www.abcnews.go.com/print?id=6238226.
[140] Mormons Targeted for Role Supporting Prop 8. Critics Question Church's Role in Lobbying; Accuse Mormons of Bigotry. By DAN HARRIS. Nov. 12, 2008— http://www.abcnews.go.com/print?id=6238226.
[141] Mormons Targeted for Role Supporting Prop 8. Critics Question Church's Role in Lobbying; Accuse Mormons of Bigotry. By DAN HARRIS. Nov. 12, 2008— http://www.abcnews.go.com/print?id=6238226.
[142] Mormons Targeted for Role Supporting Prop 8. Critics Question Church's Role in Lobbying; Accuse Mormons of Bigotry. By DAN HARRIS. Nov. 12, 2008— http://www.abcnews.go.com/print?id=6238226.
[143] Gay activists protest Mormon church. **By Ben Arnoldy** | Staff writer of The Christian Science Monitor. From the November 13, 2008 edition. http://www.csmonitor.com/2008/1113/p03s07-uspo.html.
[144] Gay activists protest Mormon church. **By Ben Arnoldy** | Staff writer of The Christian Science Monitor. From the November 13, 2008 edition. http://www.csmonitor.com/2008/1113/p03s07-uspo.html.
[145] Mormons Targeted for Role Supporting Prop 8. Critics Question Church's Role in Lobbying; Accuse Mormons of Bigotry. By DAN HARRIS. Nov. 12, 2008— http://www.abcnews.go.com/print?id=6238226.
[146] Gay activists protest Mormon church. **By Ben Arnoldy** | Staff writer of The Christian Science Monitor. From the November 13, 2008 edition. http://www.csmonitor.com/2008/1113/p03s07-uspo.html.
[147] Gay activists protest Mormon church. **By Ben Arnoldy** | Staff writer of The Christian Science Monitor. From the November 13, 2008 edition. http://www.csmonitor.com/2008/1113/p03s07-uspo.html.
[148] Gay activists protest Mormon church. **By Ben Arnoldy** | Staff writer of The Christian Science Monitor. From the November 13, 2008 edition. http://www.csmonitor.com/2008/1113/p03s07-uspo.html.
[149] Catholics, Mormons allied to pass Prop. 8. Matthai Kuruvila, Chronicle Religion Writer. Monday, November 10, 2008 E-mail Matthai Kuruvila at mkuruvila@sfchronicle.com. *http://sfgate.com/cgi-bin/article.cgi?f=/c/a/2008/11/10/MNU1140AQQ.DTL*. This article appeared on page ***A - 1*** of the San Francisco Chronicle.
[150] Catholics, Mormons allied to pass Prop. 8. Matthai Kuruvila, Chronicle Religion Writer. Monday, November 10, 2008 E-mail Matthai Kuruvila at mkuruvila@sfchronicle.com. *http://sfgate.com/cgi-bin/article.cgi?f=/c/a/2008/11/10/MNU1140AQQ.DTL*. This article appeared on page ***A - 1*** of the San Francisco Chronicle.
[151] Catholics, Mormons allied to pass Prop. 8. Matthai Kuruvila, Chronicle Religion Writer. Monday, November 10, 2008 E-mail Matthai Kuruvila at mkuruvila@sfchronicle.com. *http://sfgate.com/cgi-bin/article.cgi?f=/c/a/2008/11/10/MNU1140AQQ.DTL*. This article appeared on page ***A - 1*** of the San Francisco Chronicle.
[152] Catholics, Mormons allied to pass Prop. 8. Matthai Kuruvila, Chronicle Religion Writer. Monday, November 10, 2008 E-mail Matthai Kuruvila at mkuruvila@sfchronicle.com. *http://sfgate.com/cgi-bin/article.cgi?f=/c/a/2008/11/10/MNU1140AQQ.DTL*. This article appeared on page ***A - 1*** of the San Francisco Chronicle.
[153] Mormons Bankroll Anti–Gay Marriage Amendments in California, Arizona. October 22, 2008. http://www.advocate.com/news_detail_ektid64163.asp
[154] Nov 2008 08:29 am. The Mormons Spin Away From Prop 8. Quoting the San Francisco Chronicle. http://www.typepad.com/t/trackback/2224950/35590754
Listed below are links to weblogs that reference 'The Mormons Spin Away From Prop 8'. See also http://www.dailykos.com/storyonly/2008/11/3/15369/3779. http://andrewsullivan.theatlantic.com/the_daily_dish/2008/11/the-mormon-cath.html
[155] Nov 2008 08:29 am. The Mormons Spin Away From Prop 8. Quoting the San Francisco Chronicle. http://www.typepad.com/t/trackback/2224950/35590754
Listed below are links to weblogs that reference 'The Mormons Spin Away From Prop 8'
http://andrewsullivan.theatlantic.com/the_daily_dish/2008/11/the-mormon-cath.html
[156] AC360: Dan Savage Takes On Tony Perkins Over Prop 8. By Heather Thursday Nov 13, 2008 2:00pm http://videocafe.crooksandliars.com/heather/ac360-dan-savage-takes-tony-perkins-over-p
[157] Voters backing same-sex marriage ban. John Wildermuth, Chronicle Staff Writer, Wednesday, November 5, 2008. *http://sfgate.com/cgi-bin/article.cgi?f=/c/a/2008/11/05/MNCC13QR90.DTL. This article appeared on page A - 3 of the San Francisco Chronicle.*
[158] Same-Sex-Marriage Battle Appears Over in California. *By Justin Ewers* Posted November 5, 2008. http://www.usnews.com/articles/news/politics/2008/11/05/same-sex-marriage-battle-appears-over-in-california.html
[159] California Same-Sex Marriage Initiative Campaigns Shatter Spending Records
By Justin Ewers Posted October 29, 2008. http://www.usnews.com/articles/news/national/2008/10/29/california-same-sex-marriage-initiative-campaigns-shatter-spending-records.html
[160] Survey: Asian-Americans overwhelmingly against outlawing gay marriage. By Ken McLaughlin. Mercury News. Article Launched: 10/15/2008 09:18:46 AM PDThttp://www.mercurynews.com/ci_10726071.
[161] Survey: Asian-Americans overwhelmingly against outlawing gay marriage. By Ken McLaughlin. Mercury News. Article Launched: 10/15/2008 09:18:46 AM PDThttp://www.mercurynews.com/ci_10726071.
[162] Survey: Asian-Americans overwhelmingly against outlawing gay marriage. By Ken McLaughlin. Mercury News. Article Launched: 10/15/2008 09:18:46 AM PDThttp://www.mercurynews.com/ci_10726071.
[163] Survey: Asian-Americans overwhelmingly against outlawing gay marriage. By Ken McLaughlin. Mercury News. Article Launched: 10/15/2008 09:18:46 AM PDThttp://www.mercurynews.com/ci_10726071.
[164] Survey: Asian-Americans overwhelmingly against outlawing gay marriage. By Ken McLaughlin. Mercury News. Article Launched: 10/15/2008 09:18:46 AM PDThttp://www.mercurynews.com/ci_10726071.
[165] Survey: Asian-Americans overwhelmingly against outlawing gay marriage. By Ken McLaughlin. Mercury News. Article Launched: 10/15/2008 09:18:46 AM PDThttp://www.mercurynews.com/ci_10726071.
[166] The fight over Prop. 8 goes to the courts. Thursday, November 6, 2008. *http://sfgate.com/cgi-bin/article.cgi?f=/c/a/2008/11/06/EDAH13URJS.DTL*. This article appeared on page ***B - 8*** of the San Francisco Chronicle
[167] Latin and Black Voters Instrumental to the Success of Proposition 8 By Eric Blair
16:11, November 6th 2008.http://www.efluxmedia.com/news_Latin_and_Black_Voters_Instrumental_to_the_Success_of_Proposition_8_28299.html
[168] Gay Marriage in Peril in California. OCTOBER 22, 2008, By JIM CARLTON. http://online.wsj.com/article/SB122463078466356397.html?mod=googlenews_wsj#.
[169] Gay Marriage in Peril in California. OCTOBER 22, 2008, By JIM CARLTON. http://online.wsj.com/article/SB122463078466356397.html?mod=googlenews_wsj#.
[170] Same-Sex-Marriage Battle Appears Over in California. *By Justin Ewers* Posted November 5, 2008. http://www.usnews.com/articles/news/politics/2008/11/05/same-sex-marriage-battle-appears-over-in-california.html
[171] Gay Marriage Is Back On The Radar For Republicans, Evangelicals. But Overall Opposition to Gay Marriage is Less Than in 2004. June 12, 2008. PEW RESEARCH CENTER FOR THE PEOPLE & THE PRES. http://pewresearch.org/pubs/868/gay-marriage.

[172] Report: African-Americans more likely to oppose gay marriage. **By Bob Roehr - Contributing Writer. May 29, 2008, http://www.dallasvoice.com/artman/publish/article_9008.php.**
[173] Report: African-Americans more likely to oppose gay marriage. **By Bob Roehr - Contributing Writer. May 29, 2008, http://www.dallasvoice.com/artman/publish/article_9008.php.**
[174] Report: African-Americans more likely to oppose gay marriage. **By Bob Roehr - Contributing Writer. May 29, 2008, http://www.dallasvoice.com/artman/publish/article_9008.php.**
[175] Report: African-Americans more likely to oppose gay marriage. **By Bob Roehr - Contributing Writer. May 29, 2008, http://www.dallasvoice.com/artman/publish/article_9008.php.**
[176] Report: African-Americans more likely to oppose gay marriage. **By Bob Roehr - Contributing Writer. May 29, 2008, http://www.dallasvoice.com/artman/publish/article_9008.php.**
[177] Report: African-Americans more likely to oppose gay marriage. **By Bob Roehr - Contributing Writer. May 29, 2008, http://www.dallasvoice.com/artman/publish/article_9008.php.**
[178] Over-Generalizing? October 2, 2008. http://andrewsullivan.theatlantic.com/the_daily_dish/2008/10/over-generalizi.html. From Andrew Sullivan.
[179] California Schools Are Pulled Into a Debate on Same-Sex Marriage
November 03, 2008.Eddy Ramírez http://www.usnews.com/blogs/on-education/2008/11/3/california-schools-are-pulled-into-a-debate-on-same-sex-marriage.html.
[180] California Schools Are Pulled Into a Debate on Same-Sex Marriage
November 03, 2008.Eddy Ramírez http://www.usnews.com/blogs/on-education/2008/11/3/california-schools-are-pulled-into-a-debate-on-same-sex-marriage.html.
[181] California Schools Are Pulled Into a Debate on Same-Sex Marriage
November 03, 2008.Eddy Ramírez http://www.usnews.com/blogs/on-education/2008/11/3/california-schools-are-pulled-into-a-debate-on-same-sex-marriage.html.
[182] California Schools Are Pulled Into a Debate on Same-Sex Marriage
November 03, 2008.Eddy Ramírez http://www.usnews.com/blogs/on-education/2008/11/3/california-schools-are-pulled-into-a-debate-on-same-sex-marriage.html.
[183] Catholics, Mormons allied to pass Prop. 8. Matthai Kuruvila, Chronicle Religion Writer. Monday, November 10, 2008 E-mail Matthai Kuruvila at mkuruvila@sfchronicle.com.
http://sfgate.com/cgi-bin/article.cgi?f=/c/a/2008/11/10/MNU1140AQQ.DTL. This article appeared on page ***A - 1*** of the San Francisco Chronicle.
[184] Catholics, Mormons allied to pass Prop. 8. Matthai Kuruvila, Chronicle Religion Writer. Monday, November 10, 2008 E-mail Matthai Kuruvila at mkuruvila@sfchronicle.com.
http://sfgate.com/cgi-bin/article.cgi?f=/c/a/2008/11/10/MNU1140AQQ.DTL. This article appeared on page ***A - 1*** of the San Francisco Chronicle.
[185] A Line in the Sand for Same-Sex Marriage Foes. By **LAURIE GOODSTEIN**. October 27, 2008. From
http://www.nytimes.com/2008/10/27/us/27right.html?_r=1&oref=slogin&partner=rssnyt&emc=rss&pagewanted=print.
[186] Same-sex marriage issue back to state top court. Bob Egelko, Chronicle Staff Writer. Thursday, November 6, 2008. ***http://sfgate.com/cgi-bin/article.cgi?f=/c/a/2008/11/06/MN3B13UM63.DTL***.
*This article appeared on page **A - 19** of the San Francisco Chronicle.*
[187] Same-sex marriage issue back to state top court. Bob Egelko, Chronicle Staff Writer. Thursday, November 6, 2008. ***http://sfgate.com/cgi-bin/article.cgi?f=/c/a/2008/11/06/MN3B13UM63.DTL***.
*This article appeared on page **A - 19** of the San Francisco Chronicle.*
[188] Gay rights backers file 3 lawsuits challenging Prop. 8. By Maura Dolan and Tami Abdollah. November 6, 2008. http://www.latimes.com/news/printedition/california/la-me-gaylegal6-2008nov06,0,5471913.story
[189] Same-sex marriage issue back to state top court. Bob Egelko, Chronicle Staff Writer. Thursday, November 6, 2008. ***http://sfgate.com/cgi-bin/article.cgi?f=/c/a/2008/11/06/MN3B13UM63.DTL***.
*This article appeared on page **A - 19** of the San Francisco Chronicle.*
[190] Race and Sexual Orientation: Commonalities, Comparisons, and Contrasts Relevant to Military Policyhttp://psychology.ucdavis.edu/rainbow/HTML/military_race_comparison.html.
[191] Race and Sexual Orientation: Commonalities, Comparisons, and Contrasts Relevant to Military Policyhttp://psychology.ucdavis.edu/rainbow/HTML/military_race_comparison.html. See also, Ambrose, S.E. (1972). Blacks in the army in two world wars. In S.E. Ambrose & J.A. Barber, Jr. (Eds.), *The military and American society* (pp. 177-191). New York: Free Press.
[192] Race and Sexual Orientation: Commonalities, Comparisons, and Contrasts Relevant to Military Policyhttp://psychology.ucdavis.edu/rainbow/HTML/military_race_comparison.html
[193]Race and Sexual Orientation: Commonalities, Comparisons, and Contrasts Relevant to Military Policyhttp://psychology.ucdavis.edu/rainbow/HTML/military_race_comparison.html. See also Binkin, M., Eitelberg, M.J., Schexnider, A. J., & Smith, M. M. (1982). *Blacks and the military*. Washington, DC: The Brookings Institution.
[194] Race and Sexual Orientation: Commonalities, Comparisons, and Contrasts Relevant to Military Policyhttp://psychology.ucdavis.edu/rainbow/HTML/military_race_comparison.html.
[195] Lesbians and Gay Men in the U.S. Military: Historical Background. Dr. Herek. http://psychology.ucdavis.edu/rainbow/HTML/military_history.html.
[196] Lesbians and Gay Men in the U.S. Military: Historical Background. Dr. Herek. http://psychology.ucdavis.edu/rainbow/HTML/military_history.html.
[197] Lesbians and Gay Men in the U.S. Military: Historical Background. Dr. Herek. http://psychology.ucdavis.edu/rainbow/HTML/military_history.html.
[198] Lesbians and Gay Men in the U.S. Military: Historical Background. Dr. Herek. http://psychology.ucdavis.edu/rainbow/HTML/military_history.html.
[199] Lesbians and Gay Men in the U.S. Military: Historical Background. Dr. Herek. http://psychology.ucdavis.edu/rainbow/HTML/military_history.html.
[200] Reexamining "Don't Ask, Don't Tell"; **Tuesday, Mar. 13, 2007. By Mark Thompson/Washington**http://www.time.com/time/printout/0,8816,1598653,00.html.
[201] 'Don't ask, don't tell' is reexamined. Thursday, July 24, 2008. By Vimal Patel *print edition A-8*. http://articles.latimes.com/2008/jul/24/nation/na-dontask24.
[202] Reexamining "Don't Ask, Don't Tell"; **Tuesday, Mar. 13, 2007. By Mark Thompson/Washington**http://www.time.com/time/printout/0,8816,1598653,00.html.
[203] Reexamining "Don't Ask, Don't Tell"; **Tuesday, Mar. 13, 2007. By Mark Thompson/Washington**http://www.time.com/time/printout/0,8816,1598653,00.html.
[204] Reexamining "Don't Ask, Don't Tell"; **Tuesday, Mar. 13, 2007. By Mark Thompson/Washington**http://www.time.com/time/printout/0,8816,1598653,00.html.
[205] Conservative leader Schlafly says 'outing' of son was 'strike at me'. By Mary Voboril. Knight-Ridder Newspapers http://www.qrd.org/qrd/misc/text/schlafly.outing.reaction-KNIGHT.RIDDER
[206] Psychologist Testifies Against Military's Anti-Gay Ban. Researcher Cites Scientific Evidence That Nondiscriminatory Military Policy Can Be Implemented. Retrieved October 2008 from http://psychology.ucdavis.edu/rainbow/HTML/miltest1.html.
[207] Psychologist Testifies Against Military's Anti-Gay Ban. Researcher Cites Scientific Evidence That Nondiscriminatory Military Policy Can Be Implemented. Retrieved October 2008 from http://psychology.ucdavis.edu/rainbow/HTML/miltest1.html.
[208] Lesbians and Gay Men in the U.S. Military: Historical Background. Dr. Herek. http://psychology.ucdavis.edu/rainbow/HTML/military_history.html.
[209] Lesbians and Gay Men in the U.S. Military: Historical Background. Dr. Herek. http://psychology.ucdavis.edu/rainbow/HTML/military_history.html.
[210] Don't Ask, Don't Tell Revisited. Dr. Herek. Retrieved October 2008 from http://psychology.ucdavis.edu/rainbow/HTML/military.html.
[211] Don't Ask, Don't Tell Revisited. Dr. Herek. Retrieved October 2008 from http://psychology.ucdavis.edu/rainbow/HTML/military.html
[212] Don't Ask, Don't Tell Revisited. Dr. Herek. Retrieved October 2008 from http://psychology.ucdavis.edu/rainbow/HTML/military.html
[213] Don't Ask, Don't Tell Revisited. Dr. Herek. Retrieved October 2008 from http://psychology.ucdavis.edu/rainbow/HTML/military.html
[214] Reexamining "Don't Ask, Don't Tell"; **Tuesday, Mar. 13, 2007. By Mark Thompson/Washington**http://www.time.com/time/printout/0,8816,1598653,00.html.
[215] ("Hardball," CNBC, 6/15). Call Senator Trent Lott and Register Your Opinion on His Recent Comments About Gays. June 16, 1998 Copyright © 2008, Georgia Log Cabin Republicans, Inc. http://www.lcrga.com/news/Trent+Lott+Gary+Bauer/98061602.shtml
[216] Newsday Staff Writer. Facts and Figures on the "Don't Ask, Don't Tell" Statute. Copyright 2006, retrieved August 11, 2006 from
http://www.newsday.com/features/printedition/longislandlife/ny-lfcov0806-side,0,2018198,print.story?coll=ny-lilife-print.
[217] Reexamining "Don't Ask, Don't Tell"; **Tuesday, Mar. 13, 2007. By Mark Thompson/Washington**http://www.time.com/time/printout/0,8816,1598653,00.html.
[218] Newsday Staff Writer. Facts and Figures on the "Don't Ask, Don't Tell" Statute. Copyright 2006, retrieved August 11, 2006 from
http://www.newsday.com/features/printedition/longislandlife/ny-lfcov0806-side,0,2018198,print.story?coll=ny-lilife-print.
[219] Newsday Staff Writer. Facts and Figures on the "Don't Ask, Don't Tell" Statute. Copyright 2006, retrieved August 11, 2006 from
http://www.newsday.com/features/printedition/longislandlife/ny-lfcov0806-side,0,2018198,print.story?coll=ny-lilife-print.
[220] Newsday Staff Writer. Facts and Figures on the "Don't Ask, Don't Tell" Statute. Copyright 2006, retrieved August 11, 2006 from
http://www.newsday.com/features/printedition/longislandlife/ny-lfcov0806-side,0,2018198,print.story?coll=ny-lilife-print,
[221] Newsday Staff Writer. Facts and Figures on the "Don't Ask, Don't Tell" Statute. Copyright 2006, retrieved August 11, 2006 from
http://www.newsday.com/features/printedition/longislandlife/ny-lfcov0806-side,0,2018198,print.story?coll=ny-lilife-print.
[222] 'Don't Ask, Don't Tell' Hits Women Much More . New York Times. June 23, 2008. Thomas Shanker. Retrieved October 30, 2008 @
http://www.nytimes.com/2008/06/23/washington/23pentagon.html.
[223] Newsday Staff Writer. Facts and Figures on the "Don't Ask, Don't Tell" Statute. Copyright 2006, retrieved August 11, 2006 from
http://www.newsday.com/features/printedition/longislandlife/ny-lfcov0806-side,0,2018198,print.story?coll=ny-lilife-print.
[224] MSNBC.com. Army dismisses gay Arabic linguist. AP. Retrieved 8.14.07 and posted 7.27.06 from http://www.msnbc.msn.com/id/14052513/print/1/dsiplaymode/1098/
[225] Newsday Staff Writer. Facts and Figures on the "Don't Ask, Don't Tell" Statute. Copyright 2006, retrieved August 11, 2006 from
http://www.newsday.com/features/printedition/longislandlife/ny-lfcov0806-side,0,2018198,print.story?coll=ny-lilife-print
[226] Jake Tapper and Scott McCartney. Arabic Speaker Discharged for Being Gay. August 6, 2006 and retrieved August 11, 2006 from http://abcnews.go.comGMA/print?id=2274124.
[227] MSNBC.com. Army dismisses gay Arabic linguist. AP. Retrieved 8.14.07 and posted 7.27.06 from http://www.msnbc.msn.com/id/14052513/print/1/dsiplaymode/1098/.
[228] MSNBC.com. Army dismisses gay Arabic linguist. AP. Retrieved 8.14.07 and posted 7.27.06 from http://www.msnbc.msn.com/id/14052513/print/1/dsiplaymode/1098/.
[229] MSNBC.com. Army dismisses gay Arabic linguist. AP. Retrieved 8.14.07 and posted 7.27.06 from http://www.msnbc.msn.com/id/14052513/print/1/dsiplaymode/1098/
[230] Jake Tapper and Scott McCartney. Arabic Speaker Discharged for Being Gay. August 6, 2006 and retrieved August 11, 2006 from http://abcnews.go.comGMA/print?id=2274124.
[231] Jake Tapper and Scott McCartney. Arabic Speaker Discharged for Being Gay. August 6, 2006 and retrieved August 11, 2006 from http://abcnews.go.comGMA/print?id=2274124.
[232] Jake Tapper and Scott McCartney. Arabic Speaker Discharged for Being Gay. August 6, 2006 and retrieved August 11, 2006 from http://abcnews.go.comGMA/print?id=2274124.
[233] PinkNews.com.uk. US Army dismisses gay translator. Posted July 27 and retrieved August 11, 2006 from http://www.pinknews.co.uk/news/articles/2005-2077.html.
[234] Jake Tapper and Scott McCartney. Arabic Speaker Discharged for Being Gay. August 6, 2006 and retrieved August 11, 2006 from http://abcnews.go.comGMA/print?id=2274124.
[235] MSNBC.com. Army dismisses gay Arabic linguist. AP. Retrieved 8.14.07 and posted 7.27.06 from http://www.msnbc.msn.com/id/14052513/print/1/dsiplaymode/1098/
[236] MSNBC.com. Army dismisses gay Arabic linguist. AP. Retrieved 8.14.07 and posted 7.27.06 from http://www.msnbc.msn.com/id/14052513/print/1/dsiplaymode/1098/
[237] Jake Tapper and Scott McCartney. Arabic Speaker Discharged for Being Gay. August 6, 2006 and retrieved August 11, 2006 from http://abcnews.go.comGMA/print?id=2274124.
[238] Jim Boulet Jr. The Peril of Perfidious Translators. October 8, 2003 in the National Review Online. Retrieved August 11, 2006 from
http://www.nationalreview.com/comment/boulet200310080856.asp.
[239] Jim Boulet Jr. The Peril of Perfidious Translators. October 8, 2003 in the National Review Online. Retrieved August 11, 2006 from
http://www.nationalreview.com/comment/boulet200310080856.asp.
[240] PinkNews.com.uk. US Army dismisses gay translator. Posted July 27 and retrieved August 11, 2006 from http://www.pinknews.co.uk/news/articles/2005-2077.html.
[241] MSNBC.com. Army dismisses gay Arabic linguist. AP. Retrieved 8.14.07 and posted 7.27.06 from http://www.msnbc.msn.com/id/14052513/print/1/dsiplaymode/1098/
[242] NBC News. Meet the Press. Transcript for December 7. MSNBC.com. Dec. 7, 2003 and retrieved Sept.25, 2006 from http://www.msnbc.msn.com/id/3660558/print/1/displaymode/1098/.

[243] CNN.com. CNN's Late Edition with Wolf Blitzer—aired December 19, 2004. CNN. Retrieved November 17, 2005 from http://transcripts.cnn.com/TRANSCRIPTS/0412/19/le.00.html.
[244] NBC News. Meet the Press. MTP Transcript for Dec.10. Retrieved 12.14.06 from http://www.msnbc.msnc.com/id/16095251/print/1/displaymode/1098/.
[245] NBC NEWS. Meet the Press. December 17, 2006. MSNBC.com. Retrieved 12.22.06 from http://www.msnbc.msn.com/id/16153676/.
[246] English, other languages are compatible in a free country. Richard Doehring. 6.14.07 and retrieved 7.11.07 from http://www.thetimesherald.com/apps/pbcs.dll/articles?AID=20070614/OPINION03/706140314/1014/OPINION.
[247] Executive Order 13166. HUD. Retrieved 7.11.07 from http://www.hud.gov/offices/fheo/FHLaws/EXO13166.cfm.
[248] Nathan Burchfiel. CNSNews.com. Conservatives Rally Around General Pace. March 15, 2007, Retrieved 3.28.07 from http://www.cnsnews.com/ViewNation.asp?Page=/Nation/archive/200703/NAT20070315e.html.
[249] William Neikirk and Karoun Demirjian. Pace takes fire on gays remark. Published 3.14.07 and retrieved 3.28.07 from http://www.chicagotribune.com/news/nationworld/chi-0703140183mar14,1,5001378.story?coll=chi-newsnationworld-hed.
[250] Nathan Burchfiel. CNSNews.com. Conservatives Rally Around General Pace. March 15, 2007, Retrieved 3.28.07 from http://www.cnsnews.com/ViewNation.asp?Page=/Nation/archive/200703/NAT20070315e.html
[251] Examiner.com. Pauline Jelinek. AP. Pace Won't Apologize for Gay Remark. 3.13.07 and retrieved 3.28.07 from http://www.examiner.com/a-616307~Pace-Won_t_Apologize_for_Gay_Remark.html
[252] Reexamining "Don't Ask, Don't Tell"; **Tuesday, Mar. 13, 2007**. **By Mark Thompson/Washington**http://www.time.com/time/printout/0,8816,1598653,00.html.
[253] Joshua Lynsen. White House hopefuls fumble Pace response. March 23, 2007. Retrieved 3.28.07 from http://www.sovo.com/2007/3/23/news/national/6687.cfm.
[254] Nathan Burchfiel. CNSNews.com. Conservatives Rally Around General Pace. March 15, 2007, Retrieved 3.28.07 from http://www.cnsnews.com/ViewNation.asp?Page=/Nation/archive/200703/NAT20070315e.html
[255] Steve Shives. Reactions to General Pace Prove Cowardice Abounds in Both Parties. March 17, 2007. 3.28.07 from http://www.americanchronicle.com/articles/viewArticle.asp?articleID=22278.
[256] Nathan Burchfiel. CNSNews.com. Conservatives Rally Around General Pace. March 15, 2007, Retrieved 3.28.07 from http://www.cnsnews.com/ViewNation.asp?Page=/Nation/archive/200703/NAT20070315e.html
[257] NewsMax.com. Hillary Clinton, Barack Obama: Homosexuality Not 'Immoral". Posted 3.16.07 and retrieved [illegible] from [illegible]
[258] Joshua Lynsen. White House hopefuls fumble Pace response. March 23, 2007. Retrieved 3.28.07 from http://www.sovo.com/2007/3/23/news/national/6687.cfm.
[259] Steve Shives. Reactions to General Pace Prove Cowardice Abounds in Both Parties. March 17, 2007. 3.28.07 from http://www.americanchronicle.com/articles/viewArticle.asp?articleID=22278
[260] NewsMax.com. Hillary Clinton, Barack Obama: Homosexuality Not 'Immoral". Posted 3.16.07 and retrieved 3.28.07 from http://www.newsmax.com/archives/ic/20073/16/114325.shtml?s=ic
[261] NewsMax.com. Hillary Clinton, Barack Obama: Homosexuality Not 'Immoral". Posted 3.16.07 and retrieved 3.28.07 from http://www.newsmax.com/archives/ic/20073/16/114325.shtml?s=ic
[262] Sam Hananel. Brownback supports Pace's remark on gays. Yahoo! News. 3.15.07 and retrieved 3.28.07 from http://news.yahoo.com/s/ap/20070316/ap_on_el_pr/brownback_gays&printer=1;_ylt=AuJhNmZJF5CObA2NMEcwxSRh24cA
[263] Joshua Lynsen. White House hopefuls fumble Pace response. March 23, 2007. Retrieved 3.28.07 from http://www.sovo.com/2007/3/23/news/national/6687.cfm.
[264] Joshua Lynsen. White House hopefuls fumble Pace response. March 23, 2007. Retrieved 3.28.07 from http://www.sovo.com/2007/3/23/news/national/6687.cfm.
[265] Sam Hananel. Brownback supports Pace's remark on gays. Yahoo! News. 3.15.07 and retrieved 3.28.07 from http://news.yahoo.com/s/ap/20070316/ap_on_el_pr/brownback_gays&printer=1;_ylt=AuJhNmZJF5CObA2NMEcwxSRh24cA
[266] AP. Gates declines comment on Pace's gay remarks. MSNBC.com. Posted 3.19.06 and retrieved 3.28.07 from http://www.msnbc.msn.com/id/17686685/print/1/displaymode/1098/.
[267] Sam Hananel. Brownback supports Pace's remark on gays. Yahoo! News. 3.15.07 and retrieved 3.28.07 from http://news.yahoo.com/s/ap/20070316/ap_on_el_pr/brownback_gays&printer=1;_ylt=AuJhNmZJF5CObA2NMEcwxSRh24cA
[268] Joshua Lynsen. White House hopefuls fumble Pace response. March 23, 2007. Retrieved 3.28.07 from http://www.sovo.com/2007/3/23/news/national/6687.cfm.
[269] Nathan Burchfiel. CNSNews.com. Conservatives Rally Around General Pace. March 15, 2007, Retrieved 3.28.07 from http://www.cnsnews.com/ViewNation.asp?Page=/Nation/archive/200703/NAT20070315e.html
[270] Nathan Burchfiel. CNSNews.com. Conservatives Rally Around General Pace. March 15, 2007, Retrieved 3.28.07 from http://www.cnsnews.com/ViewNation.asp?Page=/Nation/archive/200703/NAT20070315e.html
[271] Sam Hananel. Brownback supports Pace's remark on gays. Yahoo! News. 3.15.07 and retrieved 3.28.07 from http://news.yahoo.com/s/ap/20070316/ap_on_el_pr/brownback_gays&printer=1;_ylt=AuJhNmZJF5CObA2NMEcwxSRh24cA
[272] Nathan Burchfiel. CNSNews.com. Conservatives Rally Around General Pace. March 15, 2007, Retrieved 3.28.07 from http://www.cnsnews.com/ViewNation.asp?Page=/Nation/archive/200703/NAT20070315e.html
[273] Newsmax.com. Sen. Brownback 'Applauds" Pace Remark on Gays. Posted 3.15.07 and retrieved 3.28.07 from http://www.newsmax.com/archives/ic/2007/3/15/145629.shtml.
[274] Sam Hananel. Brownback supports Pace's remark on gays. Yahoo! News. 3.15.07 and retrieved 3.28.07 from http://news.yahoo.com/s/ap/20070316/ap_on_el_pr/brownback_gays&printer=1;_ylt=AuJhNmZJF5CObA2NMEcwxSRh24cA
[275] Reuters. Columnist under fire for gay slur. MSNBC.com. March 5, 2007. retrieved 3.28.07 from http://www.msnbc.msn.com/id/17458248/print/1/diplaymode/1098/.
[276] Adam Nagourney. G.O.P. Candidates Criticize Slur by Conservative Author. March 4, 2007. 3.28.07 and retrieved 3.28.07 from http://www.nytimes.com/2007/03/04/us/politics/04coulter.html?ei=5090&en=a9da398f95d639ef&ex=1330664400.
[277] Adam Nagourney. G.O.P. Candidates Criticize Slur by Conservative Author. March 4, 2007. 3.28.07 and retrieved 3.28.07 from http://www.nytimes.com/2007/03/04/us/politics/04coulter.html?ei=5090&en=a9da398f95d639ef&ex=1330664400.
[278] John Aravosis. Romney and McCain campaigns attack Coulter for calling John Edwards a 'faggot." Retrieved 3.28.07 from http://americablog.blogspot.com/2007/03/romney-and-mccain-campaigns-attack.html.
[279] Adam Nagourney. G.O.P. Candidates Criticize Slur by Conservative Author. March 4, 2007. 3.28.07 and retrieved 3.28.07 from http://www.nytimes.com/2007/03/04/us/politics/04coulter.html?ei=5090&en=a9da398f95d639ef&ex=1330664400
[280] Adam Nagourney. G.O.P. Candidates Criticize Slur by Conservative Author. March 4, 2007. 3.28.07 and retrieved 3.28.07 from http://www.nytimes.com/2007/03/04/us/politics/04coulter.html?ei=5090&en=a9da398f95d639ef&ex=1330664400
[281] Adam Nagourney. G.O.P. Candidates Criticize Slur by Conservative Author. March 4, 2007. 3.28.07 and retrieved 3.28.07 from http://www.nytimes.com/2007/03/04/us/politics/04coulter.html?ei=5090&en=a9da398f95d639ef&ex=1330664400
[282] Reuters. Columnist under fire for gay slur. MSNBC.com. March 5, 2007. retrieved 3.28.07 from http://www.msnbc.msn.com/id/17458248/print/1/diplaymode/1098/.
[283] The Flying Fascist. 3.4.07. Retrieved 3.28.07 from http://samhensel.wordpress.com/2007/03/04/romney-giuliani-and-mccain-all-denounce-coulter-elizabeth-edwards-also-comments/.
[284] William Neikirk and Karoun Demirjian. Pace takes fire on gays remark. Published 3.14.07 and retrieved 3.28.07 from http://www.chicagotribune.com/news/nationworld/chi-0703140183mar14,1,5001378.story?coll=chi-newsnationworld-hed.
[285] AP. Gates declines comment on Pace's gay remarks. MSNBC.com. Posted 3.19.07 and retrieved 3.28.07 from http://www.msnbc.msn.com/id/17686685/print/1/displaymode/1098/.
[286] Sam Hananel. Brownback supports Pace's remark on gays. Yahoo! News. 3.15.07 and retrieved 3.28.07 from http://news.yahoo.com/s/ap/20070316/ap_on_el_pr/brownback_gays&printer=1;_ylt=AuJhNmZJF5CObA2NMEcwxSRh24cA
[287] William Neikirk and Karoun Demirjian. Pace takes fire on gays remark. Published 3.14.07 and retrieved 3.28.07 from http://www.chicagotribune.com/news/nationworld/chi-0703140183mar14,1,5001378.story?coll=chi-newsnationworld-hed.
[288] William Neikirk and Karoun Demirjian. Pace takes fire on gays remark. Published 3.14.07 and retrieved 3.28.07 from http://www.chicagotribune.com/news/nationworld/chi-0703140183mar14,1,5001378.story?coll=chi-newsnationworld-hed. See also http://www.mahalo.com/General_Peter_Pace.
[289] William Neikirk and Karoun Demirjian. Pace takes fire on gays remark. Published 3.14.07 and retrieved 3.28.07 from http://www.chicagotribune.com/news/nationworld/chi-0703140183mar14,1,5001378.story?coll=chi-newsnationworld-hed.
[290] The New York Times. Third G.O.P. Debate. June 5, 2007. CNN/WMUR-TV Debate. Retrieved 6.18.07 from http://www.nytimes.com/2007/06/05/us/politics/05cnd-transcript.html?ei=5070&en=f0c775eaec7ab19a&ex=1182312000&pagewanted=print. 30/63.
[291] The New York Times. Third G.O.P. Debate. June 5, 2007. CNN/WMUR-TV Debate. Retrieved 6.18.07 from http://www.nytimes.com/2007/06/05/us/politics/05cnd-transcript.html?ei=5070&en=f0c775eaec7ab19a&ex=1182312000&pagewanted=print. 30/63.
[292] The New York Times. Third G.O.P. Debate. June 5, 2007. CNN/WMUR-TV Debate. Retrieved 6.18.07 from http://www.nytimes.com/2007/06/05/us/politics/05cnd-transcript.html?ei=5070&en=f0c775eaec7ab19a&ex=1182312000&pagewanted=print. 30/63.
[293] Selwyn Duke. American Chronicle. Mitt Romney: A Massachusetts Liberal for President. Posted 1.11 and retrieved 1.13 from http://www.americanchronicle.com/articles/viewArticle.asp?articleID=189980.
[294] The New York Times. Third G.O.P. Debate. June 5, 2007. CNN/WMUR-TV Debate. Retrieved 6.18.07 from http://www.nytimes.com/2007/06/05/us/politics/05cnd-transcript.html?ei=5070&en=f0c775eaec7ab19a&ex=1182312000&pagewanted=print. 31/63
[295] The New York Times. Third G.O.P. Debate. June 5, 2007. CNN/WMUR-TV Debate. Retrieved 6.18.07 from http://www.nytimes.com/2007/06/05/us/politics/05cnd-transcript.html?ei=5070&en=f0c775eaec7ab19a&ex=1182312000&pagewanted=print. 31/63
[296] The New York Times. Third G.O.P. Debate. June 5, 2007. CNN/WMUR-TV Debate. Retrieved 6.18.07 from http://www.nytimes.com/2007/06/05/us/politics/05cnd-transcript.html?ei=5070&en=f0c775eaec7ab19a&ex=1182312000&pagewanted=print. 31/63
[297] Daily Show, June 2007, after the 3rd GOP debate.
[298] Gay Iraq war hero takes on General Pace. John Aravosis. Posted 3.16.07 and retrieved 3.28.07 from http://americablog.blogspot.com/2007/03/gay-iraq-war-hero-takes-on-general-pace.html.
[299] Joshua Lynsen. White House hopefuls fumble Pace response. March 23, 2007. Retrieved 3.28.07 from http://www.sovo.com/2007/3/23/news/national/6687.cfm.
[300] The New York Times. Third G.O.P. Debate. June 5, 2007. CNN/WMUR-TV Debate. Retrieved 6.18.07 from http://www.nytimes.com/2007/06/05/us/politics/05cnd-transcript.html?ei=5070&en=f0c775eaec7ab19a&ex=1182312000&pagewanted=print. 30/63.
[301] The New York Times. Third G.O.P. Debate. June 5, 2007. CNN/WMUR-TV Debate. Retrieved 6.18.07 from http://www.nytimes.com/2007/06/05/us/politics/05cnd-transcript.html?ei=5070&en=f0c775eaec7ab19a&ex=1182312000&pagewanted=print. 31/63
[302] Hardball's College Tour with John McCain. MSNBC.com. Oct. 18, retrieved 10.31.2006 from http://www.msnbc.msn.com/id/15330717/page/2/print/1/displaymode/1098/.
[303] The New York Times. Third G.O.P. Debate. June 5, 2007. CNN/WMUR-TV Debate. Retrieved 6.18.07 from http://www.nytimes.com/2007/06/05/us/politics/05cnd-transcript.html?ei=5070&en=f0c775eaec7ab19a&ex=1182312000&pagewanted=print.29/63.

[304] William Neikirk and Karoun Demirjian. Pace takes fire on gays remark. Published 3.14.07 and retrieved 3.28.07 from http://www.chicagotribune.com/news/nationworld/chi-0703140183mar14,1,5001378.story?coll=chi-newsnationworld-hed.
[305] William Neikirk and Karoun Demirjian. Pace takes fire on gays remark. Published 3.14.07 and retrieved 3.28.07 from http://www.chicagotribune.com/news/nationworld/chi-0703140183mar14,1,5001378.story?coll=chi-newsnationworld-hed
[306] Examiner.com. Pauline Jelinek. Pace Won't Apologize for Gay Remark. 3.13.07 and retrieved 3.28.07 from http://www.examiner.com/a-616307~Pace-Won_t_Apologize_for_Gay_Remark.html.
[307] Examiner.com. Pauline Jelinek. Pace Won't Apologize for Gay Remark. 3.13.07 and retrieved 3.28.07 from http://www.examiner.com/a-616307~Pace-Won_t_Apologize_for_Gay_Remark.html
[308] Mike Calls For End of "Don't Ask, Don't Tell" Gravel 2008. Dec. 10, 2006 and retrieved 12.14.06 from http://www.gravel2008.us/?q=node/267.
[309] Think Progress. Conservative Candidates All Support Banning Gays From The Military. Retrieved 6.15.07 from http://thinkprogress.org/2007/06/05/debate-dadt/.
[310] Exclusive: Gravel on The Gays/Queerty. June 8th, 2007. Retrieved 6.15.07 from http://www.queerty.com/news/exclusive-gravel-on-the-gays-20070608/.
[311] Reexamining "Don't Ask, Don't Tell"; **Tuesday, Mar. 13, 2007. By Mark Thompson/Washington**http://www.time.com/time/printout/0,8816,1598653,00.html.
[312] CNN.com. Transcripts. Situation Room Gays in the Military?... Aired March 13, 2007. Retrieved 3.28.07 from http://transcripts.cnn.com/TRANSCRIPTS/0703/13/sitroom.02.html. 2/11
[313] CNN.com. Transcripts. Situation Room Gays in the Military?... Aired March 13, 2007. Retrieved 3.28.07 from http://transcripts.cnn.com/TRANSCRIPTS/0703/13/sitroom.02.html. 2/11
[314] CNN.com. Transcripts. Situation Room Gays in the Military?... Aired March 13, 2007. Retrieved 3.28.07 from http://transcripts.cnn.com/TRANSCRIPTS/0703/13/sitroom.02.html. 2/11
[315] CNN.com. Transcripts. Situation Room Gays in the Military?... Aired March 13, 2007. Retrieved 3.28.07 from http://transcripts.cnn.com/TRANSCRIPTS/0703/13/sitroom.02.html. Newsday Staff Writer. Facts and Figures on the "Don't Ask, Don't Tell" Statute. Copyright 2006, retrieved August 11, 2006 from http://www.newsday.com/features/printedition/longislandlife/ny-lfcov0806-side,0,2018198,print.story?coll=ny-lilife-print
[316] CNN.com. Transcripts. Situation Room Gays in the Military?... Aired March 13, 2007. Retrieved 3.28.07 from http://transcripts.cnn.com/TRANSCRIPTS/0703/13/sitroom.02.html. 2/11
[317] Newsday Staff Writer. Facts and Figures on the "Don't Ask, Don't Tell" Statute. Copyright 2006, retrieved August 11, 2006 from http://www.newsday.com/features/printedition/longislandlife/ny-lfcov0806-side,0,2018198,print.story?coll=ny-lilife-print
[318] Study: Congress Should Repeal 'Don't Ask, Don't Tell'
Monday, July 07, 2008 AP. http://www.foxnews.com/story/0,2933,377585,00.html.
[319] Study: Congress Should Repeal 'Don't Ask, Don't Tell'
Monday, July 07, 2008 AP. http://www.foxnews.com/story/0,2933,377585,00.html.
[320] Study: Congress Should Repeal 'Don't Ask, Don't Tell'
Monday, July 07, 2008 AP. http://www.foxnews.com/story/0,2933,377585,00.html.
[321] Study: Congress Should Repeal 'Don't Ask, Don't Tell'
Monday, July 07, 2008 AP. http://www.foxnews.com/story/0,2933,377585,00.html.
[322] Study: Congress Should Repeal 'Don't Ask, Don't Tell'
Monday, July 07, 2008 AP. http://www.foxnews.com/story/0,2933,377585,00.html.
[323] Study: Congress Should Repeal 'Don't Ask, Don't Tell'
Monday, July 07, 2008 AP. http://www.foxnews.com/story/0,2933,377585,00.html.
[324] 'Don't Ask, Don't Tell' Hits Women Much More . New York Times. June 23, 2008. Thomas Shanker. Retrieved October 30, 2008 @ http://www.nytimes.com/2008/06/23/washington/23pentagon.html.
[325] 'Don't ask, don't tell' is reexamined. Thursday, July 24, 2008. By Vimal Patel *print edition A-8.* http://articles.latimes.com/2008/jul/24/nation/na-dontask24.
[326] Lesbians and Gay Men in the U.S. Military: Historical Background. Dr. Herek. http://psychology.ucdavis.edu/rainbow/HTML/military_history.html.
[327] By **Andrea Stone**, USA TODAY. [illegible]http://www.usatoday.com/news/military/2008-01-07-gay-troops_N.htm Updated 1/20/2008.
[328] Court to Weigh Texas' Ban on Gay Sodomy. By David G. Savage
December 03, 2002 *in print edition A-21* http://articles.latimes.com/2002/dec/03/nation/na-gays3
[329] 'Don't Ask, Don't Tell' Hits Women Much More . New York Times. June 23, 2008. Thomas Shanker. Retrieved October 30, 2008 @ http://www.nytimes.com/2008/06/23/washington/23pentagon.html.
[330] 'Don't Ask, Don't Tell' Hits Women Much More . New York Times. June 23, 2008. Thomas Shanker. Retrieved October 30, 2008 @ http://www.nytimes.com/2008/06/23/washington/23pentagon.html.
[331] Barack Obama's Military Adviser Says to Stick With Gay Ban
October 31, 2008. Paul Bedard. http://www.usnews.com/blogs/washington-whispers/2008/10/31/barack-obamas-military-adviser-says-to-stick-with-gay-ban.html.
[332] Barack Obama's Military Adviser Says to Stick With Gay Ban
October 31, 2008. Paul Bedard. http://www.usnews.com/blogs/washington-whispers/2008/10/31/barack-obamas-military-adviser-says-to-stick-with-gay-ban.html.
[333] **Admirals**, generals call for repeal of Don't Ask, Don't Tell. By The Associated Press, 11.18.2008. http://www.365gay.com/news/**admirals**-generals-call-for-repeal-of-dont-ask-dont-tell/
[334] **Admirals**, generals call for repeal of Don't Ask, Don't Tell. By The Associated Press, 11.18.2008. http://www.365gay.com/news/**admirals**-generals-call-for-repeal-of-dont-ask-dont-tell/
[335] **Admirals**, generals call for repeal of Don't Ask, Don't Tell. By The Associated Press, 11.18.2008. http://www.365gay.com/news/**admirals**-generals-call-for-repeal-of-dont-ask-dont-tell/
[336] **Admirals**, generals call for repeal of Don't Ask, Don't Tell. By The Associated Press, 11.18.2008. http://www.365gay.com/news/**admirals**-generals-call-for-repeal-of-dont-ask-dont-tell/
[337] Why Do People Have To Push Me Like That?" By Mark Thompson/Fort Campbell Sunday, Dec. 05, 1999 http://www.time.com/time/printout/0,8816,35513,00.html
[338] Why Do People Have To Push Me Like That?" By Mark Thompson/Fort Campbell Sunday, Dec. 05, 1999 http://www.time.com/time/printout/0,8816,35513,00.html
[339] Why Do People Have To Push Me Like That?" By Mark Thompson/Fort Campbell Sunday, Dec. 05, 1999 http://www.time.com/time/printout/0,8816,35513,00.html
[340] Why Do People Have To Push Me Like That?" By Mark Thompson/Fort Campbell Sunday, Dec. 05, 1999 http://www.time.com/time/printout/0,8816,35513,00.html.
[341] Why Do People Have To Push Me Like That?" By Mark Thompson/Fort Campbell Sunday, Dec. 05, 1999 http://www.time.com/time/printout/0,8816,35513,00.html
[342] Why Do People Have To Push Me Like That?" By Mark Thompson/Fort Campbell Sunday, Dec. 05, 1999 http://www.time.com/time/printout/0,8816,35513,00.html
[343] Why Do People Have To Push Me Like That?" By Mark Thompson/Fort Campbell Sunday, Dec. 05, 1999 http://www.time.com/time/printout/0,8816,35513,00.html
[344] Why Do People Have To Push Me Like That?" By Mark Thompson/Fort Campbell Sunday, Dec. 05, 1999 http://www.time.com/time/printout/0,8816,35513,00.html
[345] Why Do People Have To Push Me Like That?" By Mark Thompson/Fort Campbell Sunday, Dec. 05, 1999 http://www.time.com/time/printout/0,8816,35513,00.html
[346] Why Do People Have To Push Me Like That?" By Mark Thompson/Fort Campbell Sunday, Dec. 05, 1999 http://www.time.com/time/printout/0,8816,35513,00.html
[347] Why Do People Have To Push Me Like That?" By Mark Thompson/Fort Campbell Sunday, Dec. 05, 1999 http://www.time.com/time/printout/0,8816,35513,00.html
[348] Why Do People Have To Push Me Like That?" By Mark Thompson/Fort Campbell Sunday, Dec. 05, 1999 http://www.time.com/time/printout/0,8816,35513,00.html
[349] Why Do People Have To Push Me Like That?" By Mark Thompson/Fort Campbell Sunday, Dec. 05, 1999 http://www.time.com/time/printout/0,8816,35513,00.html
[350] Why Do People Have To Push Me Like That?" By Mark Thompson/Fort Campbell Sunday, Dec. 05, 1999 http://www.time.com/time/printout/0,8816,35513,00.html
[351] Why Do People Have To Push Me Like That?" By Mark Thompson/Fort Campbell Sunday, Dec. 05, 1999 http://www.time.com/time/printout/0,8816,35513,00.html
[352] Why Do People Have To Push Me Like That?" By Mark Thompson/Fort Campbell Sunday, Dec. 05, 1999 http://www.time.com/time/printout/0,8816,35513,00.html
[353] Why Do People Have To Push Me Like That?" By Mark Thompson/Fort Campbell Sunday, Dec. 05, 1999 http://www.time.com/time/printout/0,8816,35513,00.html
[354] Slain Gay Soldier's Case Slows a General's Rise. New York Times. **May 18, 2003**
http://query.nytimes.com/gst/fullpage.html?res=940DEEDD123EF93BA25756C0A9659C8B63&sec=&spon=&pagewanted=print.
[355] Lesbians and Gay Men in the U.S. Military: Historical Background. Dr. Herek. http://psychology.ucdavis.edu/rainbow/HTML/military_history.html.
[356] Pentagon Orders Punishment for Any Harassment of Gays. **By ELAINE SCIOLINO. July 22, 2000**
http://query.nytimes.com/gst/fullpage.html?res=990CE3D6143AF931A15754C0A9669C8B63&sec=&spon=&pagewanted=print
[357] Pentagon Orders Punishment for Any Harassment of Gays. **By ELAINE SCIOLINO. July 22, 2000**
http://query.nytimes.com/gst/fullpage.html?res=990CE3D6143AF931A15754C0A9669C8B63&sec=&spon=&pagewanted=print
[358] Lesbians and Gay Men in the U.S. Military: Historical Background. Dr. Herek. http://psychology.ucdavis.edu/rainbow/HTML/military_history.html.
[359] Lesbians and Gay Men in the U.S. Military: Historical Background. Dr. Herek. http://psychology.ucdavis.edu/rainbow/HTML/military_history.html.
[360] Hearing on Promotion for Commander of Slain Gay G.I. Is Closed. Published: October 12, 2002 http://query.nytimes.com/gst/fullpage.html?res=9905E7DC123AF931A25753C1A9649C8B63.
[361] Hearing on Promotion for Commander of Slain Gay G.I. Is Closed. Published: October 12, 2002 http://query.nytimes.com/gst/fullpage.html?res=9905E7DC123AF931A25753C1A9649C8B63.
[362] Why Do People Have To Push Me Like That?" By Mark Thompson/Fort Campbell Sunday, Dec. 05, 1999 http://www.time.com/time/printout/0,8816,35513,00.html
[363] Why Do People Have To Push Me Like That?" By Mark Thompson/Fort Campbell Sunday, Dec. 05, 1999 http://www.time.com/time/printout/0,8816,35513,00.html
[364] Why Do People Have To Push Me Like That?" By Mark Thompson/Fort Campbell Sunday, Dec. 05, 1999 http://www.time.com/time/printout/0,8816,35513,00.html
[365] Why Do People Have To Push Me Like That?" By Mark Thompson/Fort Campbell Sunday, Dec. 05, 1999 http://www.time.com/time/printout/0,8816,35513,00.html
[366] Why Do People Have To Push Me Like That?" By Mark Thompson/Fort Campbell Sunday, Dec. 05, 1999 http://www.time.com/time/printout/0,8816,35513,00.html
[367] Why Do People Have To Push Me Like That?" By Mark Thompson/Fort Campbell Sunday, Dec. 05, 1999 http://www.time.com/time/printout/0,8816,35513,00.html
[368] Why Do People Have To Push Me Like That?" By Mark Thompson/Fort Campbell Sunday, Dec. 05, 1999 http://www.time.com/time/printout/0,8816,35513,00.html
[369] Why Do People Have To Push Me Like That?" By Mark Thompson/Fort Campbell Sunday, Dec. 05, 1999 http://www.time.com/time/printout/0,8816,35513,00.html
[370] Why Do People Have To Push Me Like That?" By Mark Thompson/Fort Campbell Sunday, Dec. 05, 1999 http://www.time.com/time/printout/0,8816,35513,00.html
[371] Why Do People Have To Push Me Like That?" By Mark Thompson/Fort Campbell Sunday, Dec. 05, 1999 http://www.time.com/time/printout/0,8816,35513,00.html
[372] Why Do People Have To Push Me Like That?" By Mark Thompson/Fort Campbell Sunday, Dec. 05, 1999 http://www.time.com/time/printout/0,8816,35513,00.html
[373] Military's Gay Policy On Trial. Slain Soldier's Gay Colleague Opens Up. FORT CAMPBELL, Kentucky, 1999, CBS Worldwide Inc., http://www.cbsnews.com/stories/1999/12/09/national/main73973.shtml
[374] Pentagon Orders Punishment for Any Harassment of Gays. **By ELAINE SCIOLINO. July 22, 2000**
http://query.nytimes.com/gst/fullpage.html?res=990CE3D6143AF931A15754C0A9669C8B63&sec=&spon=&pagewanted=print
[375] Pentagon Orders Punishment for Any Harassment of Gays. **By ELAINE SCIOLINO. July 22, 2000**
http://query.nytimes.com/gst/fullpage.html?res=990CE3D6143AF931A15754C0A9669C8B63&sec=&spon=&pagewanted=print
[376] Pentagon Orders Punishment for Any Harassment of Gays. **By ELAINE SCIOLINO. July 22, 2000**
http://query.nytimes.com/gst/fullpage.html?res=990CE3D6143AF931A15754C0A9669C8B63&sec=&spon=&pagewanted=print

[377] Pentagon Orders Punishment for Any Harassment of Gays. **By ELAINE SCIOLINO. July 22, 2000**
http://query.nytimes.com/gst/fullpage.html?res=990CE3D6143AF931A15754C0A9669C8B63&sec=&spon=&pagewanted=print

[378] Why Do People Have To Push Me Like That?" By Mark Thompson/Fort Campbell Sunday, Dec. 05, 1999 http://www.time.com/time/printout/0,8816,35513,00.html

[379] Why Do People Have To Push Me Like That?" By Mark Thompson/Fort Campbell Sunday, Dec. 05, 1999 http://www.time.com/time/printout/0,8816,35513,00.html

[380] Slain Gay Soldier's Case Slows a General's Rise. New York Times. **May 18, 2003**
http://query.nytimes.com/gst/fullpage.html?res=940DEEDD123EF93BA25756C0A9659C8B63&sec=&spon=&pagewanted=print.

[381] Pentagon Orders Punishment for Any Harassment of Gays. **By ELAINE SCIOLINO. July 22, 2000**
http://query.nytimes.com/gst/fullpage.html?res=990CE3D6143AF931A15754C0A9669C8B63&sec=&spon=&pagewanted=print

[382] Slain Gay Soldier's Case Slows a General's Rise. New York Times. **May 18, 2003**
http://query.nytimes.com/gst/fullpage.html?res=940DEEDD123EF93BA25756C0A9659C8B63&sec=&spon=&pagewanted=print.

[383] Hearing on Promotion for Commander of Slain Gay G.I. Is Closed. Published: October 12, 2002 http://query.nytimes.com/gst/fullpage.html?res=9905E7DC123AF931A25753C1A9649C8B63.

[384] Slain Gay Soldier's Case Slows a General's Rise. New York Times. **May 18, 2003**
http://query.nytimes.com/gst/fullpage.html?res=940DEEDD123EF93BA25756C0A9659C8B63&sec=&spon=&pagewanted=print.

[385] Slain Gay Soldier's Case Slows a General's Rise. New York Times. **May 18, 2003**
http://query.nytimes.com/gst/fullpage.html?res=940DEEDD123EF93BA25756C0A9659C8B63&sec=&spon=&pagewanted=print.

[386] Hearing on Promotion for Commander of Slain Gay G.I. Is Closed. Published: October 12, 2002 http://query.nytimes.com/gst/fullpage.html?res=9905E7DC123AF931A25753C1A9649C8B63.

[387] Slain Gay Soldier's Case Slows a General's Rise. New York Times. **May 18, 2003**
http://query.nytimes.com/gst/fullpage.html?res=940DEEDD123EF93BA25756C0A9659C8B63&sec=&spon=&pagewanted=print.

[388] Slain Gay Soldier's Case Slows a General's Rise. New York Times. **May 18, 2003**
http://query.nytimes.com/gst/fullpage.html?res=940DEEDD123EF93BA25756C0A9659C8B63&sec=&spon=&pagewanted=print.

[389] Slain Gay Soldier's Case Slows a General's Rise. New York Times. **May 18, 2003**
http://query.nytimes.com/gst/fullpage.html?res=940DEEDD123EF93BA25756C0A9659C8B63&sec=&spon=&pagewanted=print.

[390] Pentagon Orders Punishment for Any Harassment of Gays. **By ELAINE SCIOLINO. July 22, 2000**
http://query.nytimes.com/gst/fullpage.html?res=990CE3D6143AF931A15754C0A9669C8B63&sec=&spon=&pagewanted=print.

[391] Pentagon Orders Punishment for Any Harassment of Gays. **By ELAINE SCIOLINO. July 22, 2000**
http://query.nytimes.com/gst/fullpage.html?res=990CE3D6143AF931A15754C0A9669C8B63&sec=&spon=&pagewanted=print

[392] Military's Gay Policy On Trial. Slain Soldier's Gay Colleague Opens Up. FORT CAMPBELL, Kentucky, 1999, CBS Worldwide Inc.,
http://www.cbsnews.com/stories/1999/12/09/national/main73973.shtml.

[393] Military's Gay Policy On Trial. Slain Soldier's Gay Colleague Opens Up. FORT CAMPBELL, Kentucky, 1999, CBS Worldwide Inc.,
http://www.cbsnews.com/stories/1999/12/09/national/main73973.shtml.

[394] Military's Gay Policy On Trial. Slain Soldier's Gay Colleague Opens Up. FORT CAMPBELL, Kentucky, 1999, CBS Worldwide Inc.,
http://www.cbsnews.com/stories/1999/12/09/national/main73973.shtml.

[395] Hearing on Promotion for Commander of Slain Gay G.I. Is Closed. Published: October 12, 2002 http://query.nytimes.com/gst/fullpage.html?res=9905E7DC123AF931A25753C1A9649C8B63.

[396] Nazis in the military: 'I'm so proud of my kills' By David Neiwert Sunday Dec 14, 2008 12:00pm http://crooksandliars.com/david-neiwert/nazis-military-im-so-proud-my-skills

[397] Nazis in the military: 'I'm so proud of my kills' By David Neiwert Sunday Dec 14, 2008 12:00pm http://crooksandliars.com/david-neiwert/nazis-military-im-so-proud-my-skills

[398] Nazis in the military: 'I'm so proud of my kills' By David Neiwert Sunday Dec 14, 2008 12:00pm http://crooksandliars.com/david-neiwert/nazis-military-im-so-proud-my-skills

[399] Mens News Daily. US Congress Rejects Proposal to Ban Gay Marriage. Posted June 6, 2006 and retrieved June 16, 2006 from http://mensdaily.com/2006/06/06/us-congress-rejects-proposal-to-ban-gay-marriage/.

[400] Craig Gilbert. Gay marriage amendment fails in Senate. Milwaukee Journal Sentinel, June 8, 2006, 3A. SB Green 40.

[401] MSNBC.com. NBC News. Meet the Press. MTP Transcript for June 4. Retrieved June 16, 2006 from http://www.msnbc.msn.com/id/13085904/print/1/displaymode/1098/. Page 15 of 17.

[402] Law and Civil Rights. Gallup Poll. May8-11, 2006. MoE +/-3. Retrieved June 30, 2006 from http://www.pollingreport.com/civil.htm.

[403] Scott Keeter. Politics and the "Dot Net" Generation" Posted May 30 and retrieved July 28, 2006 from http://pewresearch.org/?ObDeckID=27.

[404] Scott Keeter. Politics and the "Dot Net" Generation" Posted May 30 and retrieved July 28, 2006 from http://pewresearch.org/?ObDeckID=27.

[405] Scott Keeter. Politics and the "Dot Net" Generation" Posted May 30 and retrieved July 28, 2006 from http://pewresearch.org/?ObDeckID=27.

[406] Senator Sam Brownback. Brownback Comments on Senate Marriage Vote. Posted June 7, 2006 and retrieved June 16, 2006 from http://brownback.senate.gov/pressapp/record.cfm?id=256597.

[407] Michael Foust. SUMMARY: What senators said during debate Tuesday. Baptist press June 6, 2006 and retrieved June 16, 2006 from http://www.sbcbaptistpress.org/bpnews.asp?ID=23411.

[408] TV Squad. The Daily Show: June 6, 2006. Posted June 7, 2006 and retrieved June 16, 2006 from http://www.tvsquad.com/2006/06/07/the-daily-show-june-6-2006/.

[409] Brownback: Gay marriage ban 'imperative,' 'not bigotry'. Posted June 6. Lawrence Journal World. Retrieved June 16, 2006 from
http://www2.ljworld.com/blogs/kansas_congress/2006/june/06/gay/.

[410] David Waters. Marriage is under attack, but not by 'them'. Scripps Howard News Service. May 31, 2006. Retrieved June 16, 2006 from
http://www.shns.com/shns/g_index2.cfm?action=detail&pk=FAITH-FAITH-05-31-06.

[411] Craig Gilbert. Gay marriage amendment fails in Senate. Milwaukee Journal Sentinel, June 8, 2006, 3A. SB Green 40.

[412] Brownback: Gay marriage ban 'imperative,' 'not bigotry'. Posted June 6. Lawrence Journal World. Retrieved June 16, 2006 from
http://www2.ljworld.com/blogs/kansas_congress/2006/june/06/gay/.

[413] Mike Huckabee on Gay marriage. Posted July 10, 2006 and retrieved July 14, 2006 from http://www.mikehuckabeepresident2008.blogspot.com/.

[414] Craig Gilbert. Marriage ban won't go down without a fight. Milwaukee Journal Sentinel, June 7, 2006, 4A.

[415] Lou Chibbaro Jr. Senate rejects gay marriage amendment amid heated debate. Washington Blade Online. Posted June 8, 2006 and retrieved June 30, 2006 from
http://www.washblade.com/2006/6-8/news/national/battle.cfm. page 3 of 5.

[416] Lou Chibbaro Jr. Senate rejects gay marriage amendment amid heated debate. Washington Blade Online. Posted June 8, 2006 and retrieved June 30, 2006 from
http://www.washblade.com/2006/6-8/news/national/battle.cfm. page 3 of 5

[417] Michael Foust. SUMMARY: What senators said during debate Tuesday. Baptist press June 6, 2006 and retrieved June 16, 2006 from http://www.sbcbaptistpress.org/bpnews.asp?ID=23411.

[418] Craig Gilbert. Marriage ban won't go down without a fight. Milwaukee Journal Sentinel, June 7, 2006, 4A.

[419] Inhofe 'Very Proud' There's Never Been a Homosexual Relationship in the 'Recorded History of Our Family. 6.6.2006. Think Progress. http://thinkprogress.org/2006/06/06/inhofe-gay-marriage/

[420] Washington Monthly. June 7, 2006. Guest: Steve Benen.

[421] Washington Monthly. June 7, 2006. Guest: Steve Benen.

[422] Washington Monthly. June 7, 2006. Guest: Steve Benen.

[423] AP. Gay marriage ban defeated in Senate vote. MSNBC.com. Posted June 7, 2006 and retrieved June 16, 2006 from http://www.msnbc.msn.com/id/13181735/print/1/displaymode/1098/.

[424] AP. Gay marriage ban defeated in Senate vote. MSNBC.com. Posted June 7, 2006 and retrieved June 16, 2006 from http://www.msnbc.msn.com/id/13181735/print/1/displaymode/1098/.

[425] ILW.COM. Immigration News: President Bush Speaks On Comprehensive Immigration. http://www.ilw.com/immigdaily/news/2006,0608-bush.shtm.

[426] Lou Chibbaro Jr. Senate rejects gay marriage amendment amid heated debate. Washington Blade Online. Posted June 8, 2006 and retrieved June 30, 2006 from
http://www.washblade.com/2006/6-8/news/national/battle.cfm. page 2 of 5

[427] AP. Gay marriage ban defeated in Senate vote. MSNBC.com. Posted June 7, 2006 and retrieved June 16, 2006 from http://www.msnbc.msn.com/id/13181735/print/1/displaymode/1098/. Page 3 of 3.

[428] U.S. Senate: Legislation & Records Home. ON the Cloture Motion. Voted June 7, 2006 and retrieved June 16, 2006 from
http://www.senate.gov/legislative/LIS/roll_call_lists/roll_call_vote_cfm.cfm?congress=109&session=2&vote=00163.

[429] Meir Rinde. Skipping the Vote. Hartford Advocate. Posted June 15, 2006 and retrieved next day from http://hartfordadvocatecom/gbase/News/content?oid=oid:158632.

[430] Meir Rinde. Skipping the Vote. Hartford Advocate. Posted June 15, 2006 and retrieved next day from http://hartfordadvocatecom/gbase/News/content?oid=oid:158632

[431] Lou Chibbaro Jr. Senate rejects gay marriage amendment amid heated debate. Washington Blade Online. Posted June 8, 2006 and retrieved June 30, 2006 from
http://www.washblade.com/2006/6-8/news/national/battle.cfm. page 2 of 5

[432] Lou Chibbaro Jr. Senate rejects gay marriage amendment amid heated debate. Washington Blade Online. Posted June 8, 2006 and retrieved June 30, 2006 from
http://www.washblade.com/2006/6-8/news/national/battle.cfm. page 2 of 5

[433] AP. Gay marriage ban defeated in Senate vote. MSNBC.com. Posted June 7, 2006 and retrieved June 16, 2006 from http://www.msnbc.msn.com/id/13181735/print/1/displaymode/1098/.

[434] CNN. Senate blocks same-sex marriage ban. CNN.com.

[435] CNN Late Edition. Aired June 4, 2006. CNN.com. Retrieved June 16, 2006 from http://transcripts.cnn.com/TRANSCRIPTS/0606/04/le.01.html page 8,9 of 17.

[436] CNN Late Edition. Aired June 4, 2006. CNN.com. Retrieved June 16, 2006 from http://transcripts.cnn.com/TRANSCRIPTS/0606/04/le.01.html page 9 of 17.

[437] Samantha Donisi. Gay marriage again written on Bush's hot button. The Northern Iowa News. Retrieved June 30, 2006 from http://fp.uni.edu/northia/article2.asp?ID=4851&SECTION=1.

[438] AP. Gay marriage ban defeated in Senate vote. MSNBC.com. Posted June 7, 2006 and retrieved June 16, 2006 from http://www.msnbc.msn.com/id/13181735/print/1/displaymode/1098/.

[439] Maria Newman. Bush Backs Gay Marriage Ban as Senate Debates. Connecting*the*dots. Retrieved June 16, 2006 from http://www.seancoon.org/index.php?tag=sam_brownback.

[440] Amy Goldstein. Courts in 2 states reject gay marriage. Washington Post. July 7, 2006 and retrieved July 14, 2006 from
http://www.boston.com/news/nation/articles/2006/07/07/courts_in_2_states_reject_gay_marriage/.

[441] Amy Goldstein. Courts in 2 states reject gay marriage. Washington Post. July 7, 2006 and retrieved July 14, 2006 from
http://www.boston.com/news/nation/articles/2006/07/07/courts_in_2_states_reject_gay_marriage/

[442] Joan Biskupic. USA Today. Same-sex marriage fails at N.Y. court. Posted July 7, 2006 and retrieved July 14, 2006 from http://www.usatoday.com/news/nation/2006-07-06-ny-gay-marriage_x.htm.

[443] Danny Hakim. Spitzer Says He Would Do What Pataki and Courts Have Not. Published July 7, 2006 in the NY Times and retrieved July 14, 2006 from
http://www.nytimes.com/2006/07/07/nyregion/07albany.html.

[444] Danny Hakim. Spitzer Says He Would Do What Pataki and Courts Have Not. Published July 7, 2006 in the NY Times and retrieved July 14, 2006 from http://www.nytimes.com/2006/07/07/nyregion/07albany.html
[445] Danny Hakim. Spitzer Says He Would Do What Pataki and Courts Have Not. Published July 7, 2006 in the NY Times and retrieved July 14, 2006 from http://www.nytimes.com/2006/07/07/nyregion/07albany.html
[446] Danny Hakim. Spitzer Says He Would Do What Pataki and Courts Have Not. Published July 7, 2006 in the NY Times and retrieved July 14, 2006 from http://www.nytimes.com/2006/07/07/nyregion/07albany.html
[447] Gay-marriage opponents win in 2 states. Kevin O'Hanlon. AP. MSJ. July 15, 2006. sb 7 pg 9.
[448] Libby Copeland. Faith Based Initiative. Washington Post. Published June 7, 2006, C01. Retrieved June 16, 2006 from http://www.washingtonpost.com/wp-dyn/content/article/2006/06/06/AR2006060601616.html.
[449] Libby Copeland. Faith Based Initiative. Washington Post. Published June 7, 2006, C01. Retrieved June 16, 2006 from http://www.washingtonpost.com/wp-dyn/content/article/2006/06/06/AR2006060601616.html. page 1 of 5.
[450] Libby Copeland. Faith Based Initiative. Washington Post. Published June 7, 2006, C01. Retrieved June 16, 2006 from http://www.washingtonpost.com/wp-dyn/content/article/2006/06/06/AR2006060601616.html. page 1 of 5.
[451] Libby Copeland. Faith Based Initiative. Washington Post. Published June 7, 2006, C01. Retrieved June 16, 2006 from http://www.washingtonpost.com/wp-dyn/content/article/2006/06/06/AR2006060601616.html. pages....three different,
[452] Libby Copeland. Faith Based Initiative. Washington Post. Published June 7, 2006, C01. Retrieved June 16, 2006 from http://www.washingtonpost.com/wp-dyn/content/article/2006/06/06/AR2006060601616.html. page 2 of 5.
[453] Libby Copeland. Faith Based Initiative. Washington Post. Published June 7, 2006, C01. Retrieved June 16, 2006 from http://www.washingtonpost.com/wp-dyn/content/article/2006/06/06/AR2006060601616.html. page 2 of 5.
[454] Libby Copeland. Faith Based Initiative. Washington Post. Published June 7, 2006, C01. Retrieved June 16, 2006 from http://www.washingtonpost.com/wp-dyn/content/article/2006/06/06/AR2006060601616.html. page 2 of 5.
[455] Libby Copeland. Faith Based Initiative. Washington Post. Published June 7, 2006, C01. Retrieved June 16, 2006 from http://www.washingtonpost.com/wp-dyn/content/article/2006/06/06/AR2006060601616.html. page 2 of 5.
[456] Libby Copeland. Faith Based Initiative. Washington Post. Published June 7, 2006, C01. Retrieved June 16, 2006 from http://www.washingtonpost.com/wp-dyn/content/article/2006/06/06/AR2006060601616.html. page 2 of 5.
[457] Libby Copeland. Faith Based Initiative. Washington Post. Published June 7, 2006, C01. Retrieved June 16, 2006 from http://www.washingtonpost.com/wp-dyn/content/article/2006/06/06/AR2006060601616.html. page 2 of 5.
[458] Libby Copeland. Faith Based Initiative. Washington Post. Published June 7, 2006, C01. Retrieved June 16, 2006 from http://www.washingtonpost.com/wp-dyn/content/article/2006/06/06/AR2006060601616.html. page 2 of 5.
[459] Craig Gilbert. Amendment falls one vote short in Senate. Milwaukee Journal Sentinel. 1 A. June 28, 2006. SB Green 47.
[460] Pew Research Center for the People & the Press. Little Consensus on Global Warming. Released July 12, 2006, Retrieved July 28, 2006 from http://people-press.org/reports/print.php3?PageID=1062. page 3 of 4.
[461] Pew Research Center for the People & the Press. Little Consensus on Global Warming. Released July 12, 2006, Retrieved July 28, 2006 from http://people-press.org/reports/print.php3?PageID=1062. page 3 of 4.
[462] CNN.com. CNN Late Edition for May 14. Retrieved May 22, 2006 from http://transcripts.cnn.com/TRANSCRIPTS/0605/14/le.01.html
[463] FOXNews.com. Transcript: Senate Majority Leader Frist on 'FNS'. FOX News Sunday. Aired May 28 and retrieved May 31, 2006 from http://www.foxnews.com/story/0,2933,197309,00.html
[464] FOXNews.com. Transcript: Senate Majority Leader Frist on 'FNS'. FOX News Sunday. Aired May 28 and retrieved May 31, 2006 from http://www.foxnews.com/story/0,2933,197309,00.html
[465] Speeches. Bill Frist, M.D. Frist highlights Importance of Protecting Traditional Marriage. Posted May 26, 2006 and retrieved May 31, 2006 from http://frist.senate.gov/index.cfm?FuseAction=Speeches.Detail&Speech_id=404&Month=5&Year=2006. good web.
[466] Newsbusters. Matt Lauer Presses Bill Frist: Aren't You Just Pandering to Conservatives? Tim Graham. May 24, 2006 and retrieved May 31, 2006 from http://newsbusters.org/node/5517.
[467] Gay marriage around the globe. BBC. from: http://news.bbc.co.uk/2/hi/americas/4081999.stm.
[468] NZ recognises same-sex unions. 2004. BBC from: http://news.bbc.co.uk/2/hi/technology/default.stm.
[469] NZ recognises same-sex unions. 2004. BBC from: http://news.bbc.co.uk/2/hi/technology/default.stm.
[470] **The Gay Year in Review: The Top 10 News Stories**
by Steve Weinstein EDGE Editor-In-Chief Wednesday Dec 31, 2008http://www.edgeboston.com/index.php?ch=news&sc=&sc2=&sc3=&id=85182
[471] Gay marriage around the globe. BBC. from: http://news.bbc.co.uk/2/hi/americas/4081999.stm.
[472] Gay marriage around the globe. BBC. from: http://news.bbc.co.uk/2/hi/americas/4081999.stm.
[473] The Conservative Case for Gay Marriage. Time. **By Andrew Sullivan**. http://www.time.com/time/printout/0,8816,460232,00.html. **Sunday, Jun. 22, 2003**
[474] Gay marriage around the globe. BBC. from: http://news.bbc.co.uk/2/hi/americas/4081999.stm.
[475] Gay marriage around the globe. BBC. from: http://news.bbc.co.uk/2/hi/americas/4081999.stm.
[476] Gay marriage around the globe. BBC. from: http://news.bbc.co.uk/2/hi/americas/4081999.stm.
[477] Gay marriage around the globe. BBC. from: http://news.bbc.co.uk/2/hi/americas/4081999.stm.
[478] Gay marriage around the globe. BBC. from: http://news.bbc.co.uk/2/hi/americas/4081999.stm.
[479] Gay marriage around the globe. BBC. from: http://news.bbc.co.uk/2/hi/americas/4081999.stm.
[480] Gay marriage around the globe. BBC. from: http://news.bbc.co.uk/2/hi/americas/4081999.stm.
[481] Gay marriage around the globe. BBC. from: http://news.bbc.co.uk/2/hi/americas/4081999.stm.
[482] Gay marriage around the globe. BBC. from: http://news.bbc.co.uk/2/hi/americas/4081999.stm.
[483] Gay marriage around the globe. BBC. from: http://news.bbc.co.uk/2/hi/americas/4081999.stm.
[484] Greeks protest government crackdown on gay marriage. Reuters. Mon 29 Sep 2008, 15:58 http://africa.reuters.com/wire/news/usnLT695789.html.
[485] Greeks protest government crackdown on gay marriage. Reuters. Mon 29 Sep 2008, 15:58 http://africa.reuters.com/wire/news/usnLT695789.html.
[486] Greeks protest government crackdown on gay marriage. Reuters. Mon 29 Sep 2008, 15:58 http://africa.reuters.com/wire/news/usnLT695789.html. And Gay marriage around the globe. BBC. from: http://news.bbc.co.uk/2/hi/americas/4081999.stm
[487] Gay marriage around the globe. BBC. from: http://news.bbc.co.uk/2/hi/americas/4081999.stm.
[488] Gay marriage around the globe. BBC. from: http://news.bbc.co.uk/2/hi/americas/4081999.stm.
[489] Gay marriage around the globe. BBC. from: http://news.bbc.co.uk/2/hi/americas/4081999.stm.
[490] A ruling 'may allow gay unions' from the BBC @ http://news.bbc.co.uk/2/hi/africa/4055549.stm.
[491] Desmond Tutu: ***By staff writer*** "Homophobia equals apartheid" **afrol News**, 7 July.
[492] Desmond Tutu: ***By staff writer*** "Homophobia equals apartheid" **afrol News**, 7 July.
[493] Desmond Tutu: ***By staff writer*** "Homophobia equals apartheid" **afrol News**, 7 July.
[494] Desmond Tutu: ***By staff writer*** "Homophobia equals apartheid" **afrol News**, 7 July.
[495] Desmond Tutu: ***By staff writer*** "Homophobia equals apartheid" **afrol News**, 7 July.
[496] The Most Homophobic Place on Earth? By **TIM PADGETT/KINGSTON** Wednesday, Apr. 12, 2006 **http://www.time.com/time/world/article/0,8599,1182991,00.html**
[497] The Most Homophobic Place on Earth? By **TIM PADGETT/KINGSTON** Wednesday, Apr. 12, 2006 **http://www.time.com/time/world/article/0,8599,1182991,00.html**
[498] The Most Homophobic Place on Earth? By **TIM PADGETT/KINGSTON** Wednesday, Apr. 12, 2006 **http://www.time.com/time/world/article/0,8599,1182991,00.html**
[499] The Most Homophobic Place on Earth? By **TIM PADGETT/KINGSTON** Wednesday, Apr. 12, 2006 **http://www.time.com/time/world/article/0,8599,1182991,00.html**
[500] The Most Homophobic Place on Earth? By **TIM PADGETT/KINGSTON** Wednesday, Apr. 12, 2006 **http://www.time.com/time/world/article/0,8599,1182991,00.html**
[501] The Most Homophobic Place on Earth? By **TIM PADGETT/KINGSTON** Wednesday, Apr. 12, 2006 **http://www.time.com/time/world/article/0,8599,1182991,00.html**
[502] The Most Homophobic Place on Earth? By **TIM PADGETT/KINGSTON** Wednesday, Apr. 12, 2006 **http://www.time.com/time/world/article/0,8599,1182991,00.html**
[503] The Most Homophobic Place on Earth? By **TIM PADGETT/KINGSTON** Wednesday, Apr. 12, 2006 **http://www.time.com/time/world/article/0,8599,1182991,00.html**
[504] The Most Homophobic Place on Earth? By **TIM PADGETT/KINGSTON** Wednesday, Apr. 12, 2006 **http://www.time.com/time/world/article/0,8599,1182991,00.html**
[505] The Most Homophobic Place on Earth? By **TIM PADGETT/KINGSTON** Wednesday, Apr. 12, 2006 **http://www.time.com/time/world/article/0,8599,1182991,00.html**
[506] The Most Homophobic Place on Earth? By **TIM PADGETT/KINGSTON** Wednesday, Apr. 12, 2006 **http://www.time.com/time/world/article/0,8599,1182991,00.html**
[507] The Most Homophobic Place on Earth? By **TIM PADGETT/KINGSTON** Wednesday, Apr. 12, 2006 **http://www.time.com/time/world/article/0,8599,1182991,00.html**
[508] 'Milk' star Sean Penn: Pal of anti-gay dictators? Dec 11 2008 http://latimesblogs.latimes.com/the_big_picture/2008/12/milk-star-sean.html
[509] 'Milk' star Sean Penn: Pal of anti-gay dictators? Dec 11 2008 http://latimesblogs.latimes.com/the_big_picture/2008/12/milk-star-sean.html
[510] Gay Rights and Wrongs in Cuba, by Peter Tatchell *Gay and Lesbian Humanist*. Spring 2002 http://www.pinktriangle.org.uk/glh/213/cuba.html
[511] Gay Rights and Wrongs in Cuba, by Peter Tatchell *Gay and Lesbian Humanist*. Spring 2002 http://www.pinktriangle.org.uk/glh/213/cuba.html
[512] Gay Rights and Wrongs in Cuba, by Peter Tatchell *Gay and Lesbian Humanist*. Spring 2002 http://www.pinktriangle.org.uk/glh/213/cuba.html
[513] Gay Rights and Wrongs in Cuba, by Peter Tatchell *Gay and Lesbian Humanist*. Spring 2002 http://www.pinktriangle.org.uk/glh/213/cuba.html
[514] Gay Rights and Wrongs in Cuba, by Peter Tatchell *Gay and Lesbian Humanist*. Spring 2002 http://www.pinktriangle.org.uk/glh/213/cuba.html
[515] Gay Rights and Wrongs in Cuba, by Peter Tatchell *Gay and Lesbian Humanist*. Spring 2002 http://www.pinktriangle.org.uk/glh/213/cuba.html
[516] Gay Rights and Wrongs in Cuba, by Peter Tatchell *Gay and Lesbian Humanist*. Spring 2002 http://www.pinktriangle.org.uk/glh/213/cuba.html
[517] Gay Rights and Wrongs in Cuba, by Peter Tatchell *Gay and Lesbian Humanist*. Spring 2002 http://www.pinktriangle.org.uk/glh/213/cuba.html
[518] 'Milk' star Sean Penn: Pal of anti-gay dictators? Dec 11 2008 http://latimesblogs.latimes.com/the_big_picture/2008/12/milk-star-sean.html
[519] Clare Nullis. South Africa passes gay marriage bill. AP. MJS, Nov.15, 2006. 3a. SB 8 p 52.

[520] Gay marriage around the globe. BBC. from: http://news.bbc.co.uk/2/hi/americas/4081999.stm.
[521] Desmond Tutu: ***By staff writer*** "Homophobia equals apartheid" **afrol News**, 7 July.
[522] Desmond Tutu: ***By staff writer*** "Homophobia equals apartheid" **afrol News**, 7 July.
[523] **The Gay Year in Review: The Top 10 News Stories**
by Steve Weinstein EDGE Editor-In-Chief Wednesday Dec 31, 2008http://www.edgeboston.com/index.php?ch=news&sc=&sc2=&sc3=&id=85182
[524] **Activists Express Concern Over Sentencing of Gay Men in Senegal.** By Fid Thompson. Dakar. *15 January 2009*http://www.voanews.com/english/2009-01-15-voa45.cfm
[525] **Activists Express Concern Over Sentencing of Gay Men in Senegal.** By Fid Thompson. Dakar. *15 January 2009*http://www.voanews.com/english/2009-01-15-voa45.cfm
[526] **Activists Express Concern Over Sentencing of Gay Men in Senegal.** By Fid Thompson. Dakar. *15 January 2009*http://www.voanews.com/english/2009-01-15-voa45.cfm
[527] **Activists Express Concern Over Sentencing of Gay Men in Senegal.** By Fid Thompson. Dakar. *15 January 2009*http://www.voanews.com/english/2009-01-15-voa45.cfm
[528] **Activists Express Concern Over Sentencing of Gay Men in Senegal.** By Fid Thompson. Dakar. *15 January 2009*http://www.voanews.com/english/2009-01-15-voa45.cfm
[529] Struggle for gay rights in the Middle East, By CNN's Hala Gorani. Friday, June 2, 2006. http://www.cnn.com/2006/WORLD/meast/06/02/ime.gorani/
[530] Struggle for gay rights in the Middle East, By CNN's Hala Gorani. Friday, June 2, 2006. http://www.cnn.com/2006/WORLD/meast/06/02/ime.gorani/
[531] Struggle for gay rights in the Middle East, By CNN's Hala Gorani. Friday, June 2, 2006. http://www.cnn.com/2006/WORLD/meast/06/02/ime.gorani/
[532] Struggle for gay rights in the Middle East, By CNN's Hala Gorani. Friday, June 2, 2006. http://www.cnn.com/2006/WORLD/meast/06/02/ime.gorani/
[533] Struggle for gay rights in the Middle East, By CNN's Hala Gorani. Friday, June 2, 2006. http://www.cnn.com/2006/WORLD/meast/06/02/ime.gorani/
[534] Struggle for gay rights in the Middle East, By CNN's Hala Gorani. Friday, June 2, 2006. http://www.cnn.com/2006/WORLD/meast/06/02/ime.gorani/
[535] Don't Ask, Don't Tell, Do Kill. Nobody wants to talk about gays in Iraq, much less who is killing them. **Lennox Samuels. NEWSWEEK WEB EXCLUSIVE.** Aug 26, 2008 | http://www.newsweek.com/id/155656/output/print.
[536] Don't Ask, Don't Tell, Do Kill. Nobody wants to talk about gays in Iraq, much less who is killing them. **Lennox Samuels. NEWSWEEK WEB EXCLUSIVE.** Aug 26, 2008 | http://www.newsweek.com/id/155656/output/print.
[537] Don't Ask, Don't Tell, Do Kill. Nobody wants to talk about gays in Iraq, much less who is killing them. **Lennox Samuels. NEWSWEEK WEB EXCLUSIVE.** Aug 26, 2008 | http://www.newsweek.com/id/155656/output/print.
[538] Don't Ask, Don't Tell, Do Kill. Nobody wants to talk about gays in Iraq, much less who is killing them. **Lennox Samuels. NEWSWEEK WEB EXCLUSIVE.** Aug 26, 2008 | http://www.newsweek.com/id/155656/output/print.
[539] Ahmadinejad speaks; outrage and controversy follow Mon September 24, 2007. (CNN) www.cnn.com/2007/US/09/24/us.iran/.
[540] Ahmadinejad had said in U.S. speech that his country had no gay people. http://www.msnbc.msn.com/id/20999705/
[541] Ahmadinejad had said in U.S. speech that his country had no gay people. http://www.msnbc.msn.com/id/20999705/
[542] Ahmadinejad had said in U.S. speech that his country had no gay people. http://www.msnbc.msn.com/id/20999705/
[543] Ahmadinejad had said in U.S. speech that his country had no gay people. http://www.msnbc.msn.com/id/20999705/
[544] **Iran Executes Two Gay Teens In Public Hanging**21 July 2005. http://www.ukgaynews.org.uk/Archive/2005july/2101.htm
[545] **Iran Executes Two Gay Teens In Public Hanging**21 July 2005. http://www.ukgaynews.org.uk/Archive/2005july/2101.htm
[546] **Iran Executes Two Gay Teens In Public Hanging**21 July 2005. http://www.ukgaynews.org.uk/Archive/2005july/2101.htm
[547] **Iran Executes Two Gay Teens In Public Hanging**21 July 2005. http://www.ukgaynews.org.uk/Archive/2005july/2101.htm
[548] **Iran Executes Two Gay Teens In Public Hanging**21 July 2005. http://www.ukgaynews.org.uk/Archive/2005july/2101.htm
[549] Struggle for gay rights in the Middle East, By CNN's Hala Gorani. Friday, June 2, 2006. http://www.cnn.com/2006/WORLD/meast/06/02/ime.gorani/
[550] Struggle for gay rights in the Middle East, By CNN's Hala Gorani. Friday, June 2, 2006. http://www.cnn.com/2006/WORLD/meast/06/02/ime.gorani/
[551] Struggle for gay rights in the Middle East, By CNN's Hala Gorani. Friday, June 2, 2006. http://www.cnn.com/2006/WORLD/meast/06/02/ime.gorani/
[552] Struggle for gay rights in the Middle East, By CNN's Hala Gorani. Friday, June 2, 2006. http://www.cnn.com/2006/WORLD/meast/06/02/ime.gorani/
[553] Struggle for gay rights in the Middle East, By CNN's Hala Gorani. Friday, June 2, 2006. http://www.cnn.com/2006/WORLD/meast/06/02/ime.gorani/
[554] **Egyptian rights group 'cannot protect gays'** Monday, 11 February, 2002 http://news.bbc.co.uk/2/hi/middle_east/1811327.stm
[555] Egypt jails men in gay sex trial Wednesday, 14 November, 2001, 22:53 GMT By Heba Salah in Cairo http://news.bbc.co.uk/2/hi/middle_east/1655961.stm
[556] **Egyptian rights group 'cannot protect gays'** Monday, 11 February, 2002 http://news.bbc.co.uk/2/hi/middle_east/1811327.stm
[557] Egypt jails men in gay sex trial Wednesday, 14 November, 2001, 22:53 GMT By Heba Salah in Cairo http://news.bbc.co.uk/2/hi/middle_east/1655961.stm
[558] Anger over Egypt gay trial Wednesday, 15 August, 2001 By Caroline Hawley in Cairo http://news.bbc.co.uk/2/hi/middle_east/1493041.stm
[559] **Egyptian rights group 'cannot protect gays'** Monday, 11 February, 2002 http://news.bbc.co.uk/2/hi/middle_east/1811327.stm
[560] Egypt jails men in gay sex trial Wednesday, 14 November, 2001, 22:53 GMT By Heba Salah in Cairo http://news.bbc.co.uk/2/hi/middle_east/1655961.stm
[561] Anger over Egypt gay trial Wednesday, 15 August, 2001 By Caroline Hawley in Cairo http://news.bbc.co.uk/2/hi/middle_east/1493041.stm
[562] Anger over Egypt gay trial Wednesday, 15 August, 2001 By Caroline Hawley in Cairo http://news.bbc.co.uk/2/hi/middle_east/1493041.stm
[563] Anger over Egypt gay trial Wednesday, 15 August, 2001 By Caroline Hawley in Cairo http://news.bbc.co.uk/2/hi/middle_east/1493041.stm
[564] **Egyptian rights group 'cannot protect gays'** Monday, 11 February, 2002 http://news.bbc.co.uk/2/hi/middle_east/1811327.stm
[565] **Egyptian rights group 'cannot protect gays'** Monday, 11 February, 2002 http://news.bbc.co.uk/2/hi/middle_east/1811327.stm
[566] **Egyptian rights group 'cannot protect gays'** Monday, 11 February, 2002 http://news.bbc.co.uk/2/hi/middle_east/1811327.stm
[567] **Egyptian rights group 'cannot protect gays'** Monday, 11 February, 2002 http://news.bbc.co.uk/2/hi/middle_east/1811327.stm
[568] Anger over Egypt gay trial Wednesday, 15 August, 2001 By Caroline Hawley in Cairo http://news.bbc.co.uk/2/hi/middle_east/1493041.stm
[569] **Egyptian rights group 'cannot protect gays'** Monday, 11 February, 2002 http://news.bbc.co.uk/2/hi/middle_east/1811327.stm
[570] **Egyptian rights group 'cannot protect gays'** Monday, 11 February, 2002 http://news.bbc.co.uk/2/hi/middle_east/1811327.stm
[571] **Egyptian rights group 'cannot protect gays'** Monday, 11 February, 2002 http://news.bbc.co.uk/2/hi/middle_east/1811327.stm
[572] Struggle for gay rights in the Middle East, By CNN's Hala Gorani. Friday, June 2, 2006. http://www.cnn.com/2006/WORLD/meast/06/02/ime.gorani/
[573] Dubai closes club after gay night Sunday, 1 April, 2001, By Middle East correspondent Frank Gardner http://news.bbc.co.uk/2/hi/middle_east/1254897.stm
[574] Dubai closes club after gay night Sunday, 1 April, 2001, By Middle East correspondent Frank Gardner http://news.bbc.co.uk/2/hi/middle_east/1254897.stm
[575] Dubai closes club after gay night Sunday, 1 April, 2001, By Middle East correspondent Frank Gardner http://news.bbc.co.uk/2/hi/middle_east/1254897.stm
[576] Dubai closes club after gay night Sunday, 1 April, 2001, By Middle East correspondent Frank Gardner http://news.bbc.co.uk/2/hi/middle_east/1254897.stm
[577] Greeks protest government crackdown on gay marriage. Reuters. Mon 29 Sep 2008, 15:58
http://africa.reuters.com/wire/news/usnLT695789.html.
[578] Greeks protest government crackdown on gay marriage. Reuters. Mon 29 Sep 2008, 15:58
http://africa.reuters.com/wire/news/usnLT695789.html.
[579] Greeks protest government crackdown on gay marriage. Reuters. Mon 29 Sep 2008, 15:58
http://africa.reuters.com/wire/news/usnLT695789.html.
[580] **The Gay Year in Review: The Top 10 News Stories**
by Steve Weinstein EDGE Editor-In-Chief Wednesday Dec 31, 2008http://www.edgeboston.com/index.php?ch=news&sc=&sc2=&sc3=&id=85182
[581] Culture & Lifestyle | **06.01.2004**. When Turkish Men Love Men Cem http://www.dw-world.de/dw/article/0,2144,1079381,00.html. Rifat Sey.
[582] Culture & Lifestyle | **06.01.2004**. When Turkish Men Love Men Cem http://www.dw-world.de/dw/article/0,2144,1079381,00.html. Rifat Sey.
[583] Why should homosexuality be a crime? Time of India. 18 Sep 2003, http://timesofindia.indiatimes.com/cms.dll/html/uncomp/articleshow?msid=187403
[584] Why should homosexuality be a crime? Time of India. 18 Sep 2003, http://timesofindia.indiatimes.com/cms.dll/html/uncomp/articleshow?msid=187403
[585] Last Updated: Tuesday, 17 May 2005, **Fear and loathing in gay India** http://news.bbc.co.uk/2/hi/south_asia/4304081.stm
[586] Why should homosexuality be a crime? Time of India. 18 Sep 2003, http://timesofindia.indiatimes.com/cms.dll/html/uncomp/articleshow?msid=187403
[587] Why should homosexuality be a crime? Time of India. 18 Sep 2003, http://timesofindia.indiatimes.com/cms.dll/html/uncomp/articleshow?msid=187403
[588] Last Updated: Tuesday, 17 May 2005, **Fear and loathing in gay India** http://news.bbc.co.uk/2/hi/south_asia/4304081.stm
[589] Last Updated: Tuesday, 17 May 2005, **Fear and loathing in gay India** http://news.bbc.co.uk/2/hi/south_asia/4304081.stm
[590] Last Updated: Tuesday, 17 May 2005, **Fear and loathing in gay India** http://news.bbc.co.uk/2/hi/south_asia/4304081.stm
[591] Last Updated: Tuesday, 17 May 2005, **Fear and loathing in gay India** http://news.bbc.co.uk/2/hi/south_asia/4304081.stm
[592] UN body slams India on rights of gays. 24 Apr 2008, http://timesofindia.indiatimes.com/India/UN_body_slams_India_on_rights_of_gays/articleshow/2977196.cms, Dhananjay Mahapatra.
[593] **The Gay Year in Review: The Top 10 News Stories**
by Steve Weinstein EDGE Editor-In-Chief Wednesday Dec 31, 2008http://www.edgeboston.com/index.php?ch=news&sc=&sc2=&sc3=&id=85182
[594] Hostile society keeps China's gay community cowed. by Tiffany Bown Beijing, Dec 12 (AFP) - "http://www.fordham.edu/halsall/pwh/china-mod.html
[595] Hostile society keeps China's gay community cowed. by Tiffany Bown Beijing, Dec 12 (AFP) - "http://www.fordham.edu/halsall/pwh/china-mod.html
[596] China Daily. **Lesbians, gays gaining acceptance on mainland www.chinaview.cn 2005-10-10**http://news.xinhuanet.com/english/2005-10/10/content_3599661.htm
[597] **The Gay Year in Review: The Top 10 News Stories**
by Steve Weinstein EDGE Editor-In-Chief Wednesday Dec 31, 2008http://www.edgeboston.com/index.php?ch=news&sc=&sc2=&sc3=&id=85182
[598] **A Gay-Pride Revolution in Hong Kong.**By **DEENA GUZDER AND ANN BINLOT / HONG KONG** Sunday, Dec. 14, 2008http://www.time.com/time/world/article/0,8599,1866308,00.html
[599] **A Gay-Pride Revolution in Hong Kong.**By **DEENA GUZDER AND ANN BINLOT / HONG KONG** Sunday, Dec. 14, 2008http://www.time.com/time/world/article/0,8599,1866308,00.html
[600] **A Gay-Pride Revolution in Hong Kong.**By **DEENA GUZDER AND ANN BINLOT / HONG KONG** Sunday, Dec. 14, 2008http://www.time.com/time/world/article/0,8599,1866308,00.html
[601] **A Gay-Pride Revolution in Hong Kong.**By **DEENA GUZDER AND ANN BINLOT / HONG KONG** Sunday, Dec. 14, 2008http://www.time.com/time/world/article/0,8599,1866308,00.html
[602] **A Gay-Pride Revolution in Hong Kong.**By **DEENA GUZDER AND ANN BINLOT / HONG KONG** Sunday, Dec. 14, 2008http://www.time.com/time/world/article/0,8599,1866308,00.html
[603] **A Gay-Pride Revolution in Hong Kong.**By **DEENA GUZDER AND ANN BINLOT / HONG KONG** Sunday, Dec. 14, 2008http://www.time.com/time/world/article/0,8599,1866308,00.html
[604] **A Gay-Pride Revolution in Hong Kong.**By **DEENA GUZDER AND ANN BINLOT / HONG KONG** Sunday, Dec. 14, 2008http://www.time.com/time/world/article/0,8599,1866308,00.html
[605] **A Gay-Pride Revolution in Hong Kong.**By **DEENA GUZDER AND ANN BINLOT / HONG KONG** Sunday, Dec. 14, 2008http://www.time.com/time/world/article/0,8599,1866308,00.html

[606] Lies My Teacher Told Me. James W. Loewen. Chapter 2. The True Importance of Christopher Columbus. A Touchstone Book published by Simon & Schuster. 1995.
[607] Lies My Teacher Told Me. James W. Loewen. Chapter 2. The True Importance of Christopher Columbus. A Touchstone Book published by Simon & Schuster. 1995.
[608] Lies My Teacher Told Me. James W. Loewen. Chapter 2. The True Importance of Christopher Columbus. A Touchstone Book published by Simon & Schuster. 1995.
[609] Lies My Teacher Told Me. James W. Loewen. Chapter 2. The True Importance of Christopher Columbus. A Touchstone Book published by Simon & Schuster. 1995.
[610] Lies My Teacher Told Me. James W. Loewen. Chapter 2. The True Importance of Christopher Columbus. A Touchstone Book published by Simon & Schuster. 1995.
[611] Lies My Teacher Told Me. James W. Loewen. Chapter 2. The True Importance of Christopher Columbus. A Touchstone Book published by Simon & Schuster. 1995.
[612] Lies My Teacher Told Me. James W. Loewen. Chapter 2. The True Importance of Christopher Columbus. A Touchstone Book published by Simon & Schuster. 1995.
[613] Lies My Teacher Told Me. James W. Loewen. Chapter 2. The True Importance of Christopher Columbus. A Touchstone Book published by Simon & Schuster. 1995.
[614] Lies My Teacher Told Me. James W. Loewen. Chapter 2. The True Importance of Christopher Columbus. A Touchstone Book published by Simon & Schuster. 1995.
[615] Lies My Teacher Told Me. James W. Loewen. Chapter 2. The True Importance of Christopher Columbus. A Touchstone Book published by Simon & Schuster. 1995.
[616] Lies My Teacher Told Me. James W. Loewen. Chapter 2. The True Importance of Christopher Columbus. A Touchstone Book published by Simon & Schuster. 1995.
[617] Lies My Teacher Told Me. James W. Loewen. Chapter 2. The True Importance of Christopher Columbus. A Touchstone Book published by Simon & Schuster. 1995.
[618] Lies My Teacher Told Me. James W. Loewen. Chapter 2. The True Importance of Christopher Columbus. A Touchstone Book published by Simon & Schuster. 1995.
[619] Lies My Teacher Told Me. James W. Loewen. Chapter 2. The True Importance of Christopher Columbus. A Touchstone Book published by Simon & Schuster. 1995.
[620] Lies My Teacher Told Me. James W. Loewen. Chapter 2. The True Importance of Christopher Columbus. A Touchstone Book published by Simon & Schuster. 1995.
[621] Lies My Teacher Told Me. James W. Loewen. Chapter 2. The True Importance of Christopher Columbus. A Touchstone Book published by Simon & Schuster. 1995.
[622] Section 2. New England. Chapter 3 Colonial America 1578-1776. History of a Free Nation. Henry W. Bragdon, Samuel P. McClutchen, and Donald Ritchie. 1998. Glencoe McGraw-Hill. Page 66-67.
[623] Section 2. New England. Chapter 3 Colonial America 1578-1776. History of a Free Nation. Henry W. Bragdon, Samuel P. McClutchen, and Donald Ritchie. 1998. Glencoe McGraw-Hill. Page 66-67.
[624] Section 2. New England. Chapter 3 Colonial America 1578-1776. History of a Free Nation. Henry W. Bragdon, Samuel P. McClutchen, and Donald Ritchie. 1998. Glencoe McGraw-Hill. Page 66-67.
[625] Section 2. New England. Chapter 3 Colonial America 1578-1776. History of a Free Nation. Henry W. Bragdon, Samuel P. McClutchen, and Donald Ritchie. 1998. Glencoe McGraw-Hill. Page 66-67.
[626] Section 2. New England. Chapter 3 Colonial America 1578-1776. History of a Free Nation. Henry W. Bragdon, Samuel P. McClutchen, and Donald Ritchie. 1998. Glencoe McGraw-Hill. Page 66-67.
[627] Section 2. New England. Chapter 3 Colonial America 1578-1776. History of a Free Nation. Henry W. Bragdon, Samuel P. McClutchen, and Donald Ritchie. 1998. Glencoe McGraw-Hill. Page 66-67.
[628] Section 2. New England. Chapter 3 Colonial America 1578-1776. History of a Free Nation. Henry W. Bragdon, Samuel P. McClutchen, and Donald Ritchie. 1998. Glencoe McGraw-Hill. Page 66-67.
[629] Anne Hutchinson. Colonial America, 1591-1643. Travel & History. Retrieved May 20, 2009 @ http://www.u-s-history.com/pages/h577.html.
[630] Anne Hutchinson. Colonial America, 1591-1643. Travel & History. Retrieved May 20, 2009 @ http://www.u-s-history.com/pages/h577.html.
[631] Encyclopedia. HUTCHINSON, Anne, An article from *Funk & Wagnalls® New Encyclopedia*. © 2006 World Almanac Education Group. Retrieved May 20, 2009 @ http://www.history.com/reference/encyclopedia/viewArticle?id=212390.
[632] Encyclopedia. HUTCHINSON, Anne, An article from *Funk & Wagnalls® New Encyclopedia*. © 2006 World Almanac Education Group. Retrieved May 20, 2009 @ http://www.history.com/reference/encyclopedia/viewArticle?id=212390.
[633] Anne Hutchinson. Colonial America, 1591-1643. Travel & History. Retrieved May 20, 2009 @ http://www.u-s-history.com/pages/h577.html.
[634] Anne Hutchinson. Colonial America, 1591-1643. Travel & History. Retrieved May 20, 2009 @ http://www.u-s-history.com/pages/h577.html.
[635] Encyclopedia. HUTCHINSON, Anne, An article from *Funk & Wagnalls® New Encyclopedia*. © 2006 World Almanac Education Group. Retrieved May 20, 2009 @ http://www.history.com/reference/encyclopedia/viewArticle?id=212390.
[636] Anne Hutchinson. Colonial America, 1591-1643. Travel & History. Retrieved May 20, 2009 @ http://www.u-s-history.com/pages/h577.html.
[637] Section 2. New England. Chapter 3 Colonial America 1578-1776. History of a Free Nation. Henry W. Bragdon, Samuel P. McClutchen, and Donald Ritchie. 1998. Glencoe McGraw-Hill. Page 66-67.
[638] Encyclopedia. HUTCHINSON, Anne, An article from *Funk & Wagnalls® New Encyclopedia*. © 2006 World Almanac Education Group. Retrieved May 20, 2009 @ http://www.history.com/reference/encyclopedia/viewArticle?id=212390.
[639] The Encyclopedia of American History. Edited by Richard B. Morris. Harper & Row Publishers, New York. 1965. Page 805.
[640] Anne Hutchinson. Colonial America, 1591-1643. Travel & History. Retrieved May 20, 2009 @ http://www.u-s-history.com/pages/h577.html.
[641] Anne Hutchinson. Colonial America, 1591-1643. Travel & History. Retrieved May 20, 2009 @ http://www.u-s-history.com/pages/h577.html.
[642] Encyclopedia. HUTCHINSON, Anne, An article from *Funk & Wagnalls ® New Encyclopedia*. © 2006 World Almanac Education Group. Retrieved May 20, 2009 @ http://www.history.com/reference/encyclopedia/viewArticle?id=212390.
[643] Encyclopedia. HUTCHINSON, Anne, An article from *Funk & Wagnalls ® New Encyclopedia*. © 2006 World Almanac Education Group. Retrieved May 20, 2009 @ http://www.history.com/reference/encyclopedia/viewArticle?id=212390.
[644] Anne Hutchinson. Colonial America, 1591-1643. Travel & History. Retrieved May 20, 2009 @ http://www.u-s-history.com/pages/h577.html.
[645] Anne Hutchinson. Colonial America, 1591-1643. Travel & History. Retrieved May 20, 2009 @ http://www.u-s-history.com/pages/h577.html.
[646] Anne Hutchinson. Colonial America, 1591-1643. Travel & History. Retrieved May 20, 2009 @ http://www.u-s-history.com/pages/h577.html.
[647] Anne Hutchinson. Colonial America, 1591-1643. Travel & History. Retrieved May 20, 2009 @ http://www.u-s-history.com/pages/h577.html.
[648] Anne Hutchinson. Colonial America, 1591-1643. Travel & History. Retrieved May 20, 2009 @ http://www.u-s-history.com/pages/h577.html.
[649] Anne Hutchinson. Colonial America, 1591-1643. Travel & History. Retrieved May 20, 2009 @ http://www.u-s-history.com/pages/h577.html.
[650] The Encyclopedia of American History. Edited by Richard B. Morris. Harper & Row Publishers, New York. 1965. Page 805.
[651] Encyclopedia. HUTCHINSON, Anne, An article from *Funk & Wagnalls® New Encyclopedia*. © 2006 World Almanac Education Group. Retrieved May 20, 2009 @ http://www.history.com/reference/encyclopedia/viewArticle?id=212390.
[652] Encyclopedia. HUTCHINSON, Anne, An article from *Funk & Wagnalls® New Encyclopedia*. © 2006 World Almanac Education Group. Retrieved May 20, 2009 @ http://www.history.com/reference/encyclopedia/viewArticle?id=212390.
[653] Encyclopedia. HUTCHINSON, Anne, An article from *Funk & Wagnalls® New Encyclopedia*. © 2006 World Almanac Education Group. Retrieved May 20, 2009 @ http://www.history.com/reference/encyclopedia/viewArticle?id=212390. See also Anne Hutchinson. Colonial America, 1591-1643. Travel & History. Retrieved May 20, 2009 @ http://www.u-s-history.com/pages/h577.html.
[654] Section 2. New England. Chapter 3 Colonial America 1578-1776. History of a Free Nation. Henry W. Bragdon, Samuel P. McClutchen, and Donald Ritchie. 1998. Glencoe McGraw-Hill. Page 66-67.
[655] Anne Hutchinson. Colonial America, 1591-1643. Travel & History. Retrieved May 20, 2009 @ http://www.u-s-history.com/pages/h577.html.
[656] A Brief History of the Salem Witch Trials. One town's strange journey from paranoia to pardon. By Jess Blumberg. Smithsonian.com, October 24, 2007 ***http://www.smithsonianmag.com/history-archaeology/brief-salem.html.***
[657] The Salem Witch Trials @ the History Channel. In Search of History. DVD Release Date: April 1, 2005. Retrieved May 20, 2009 @ http://shop.history.com/detail.php?a=71941.
[658] The Salem Witch Trials @ the History Channel. In Search of History. DVD Release Date: April 1, 2005. Retrieved May 20, 2009 @ http://shop.history.com/detail.php?a=71941.
[659] The Salem Witch Trials @ the History Channel. In Search of History. DVD Release Date: April 1, 2005. Retrieved May 20, 2009 @ http://shop.history.com/detail.php?a=71941.
[660] A Brief History of the Salem Witch Trials. One town's strange journey from paranoia to pardon. By Jess Blumberg. Smithsonian.com, October 24, 2007 ***http://www.smithsonianmag.com/history-archaeology/brief-salem.html.***
[661] A Brief History of the Salem Witch Trials. One town's strange journey from paranoia to pardon. By Jess Blumberg. Smithsonian.com, October 24, 2007 ***http://www.smithsonianmag.com/history-archaeology/brief-salem.html.***
[662] A Brief History of the Salem Witch Trials. One town's strange journey from paranoia to pardon. By Jess Blumberg. Smithsonian.com, October 24, 2007 ***http://www.smithsonianmag.com/history-archaeology/brief-salem.html.***
[663] A Brief History of the Salem Witch Trials. One town's strange journey from paranoia to pardon. By Jess Blumberg. Smithsonian.com, October 24, 2007 ***http://www.smithsonianmag.com/history-archaeology/brief-salem.html.***
[664] A Brief History of the Salem Witch Trials. One town's strange journey from paranoia to pardon. By Jess Blumberg. Smithsonian.com, October 24, 2007 ***http://www.smithsonianmag.com/history-archaeology/brief-salem.html.***
[665] A Brief History of the Salem Witch Trials. One town's strange journey from paranoia to pardon. By Jess Blumberg. Smithsonian.com, October 24, 2007 ***http://www.smithsonianmag.com/history-archaeology/brief-salem.html.***
[666] A Brief History of the Salem Witch Trials. One town's strange journey from paranoia to pardon. By Jess Blumberg. Smithsonian.com, October 24, 2007 ***http://www.smithsonianmag.com/history-archaeology/brief-salem.html.***
[667] A Brief History of the Salem Witch Trials. One town's strange journey from paranoia to pardon. By Jess Blumberg. Smithsonian.com, October 24, 2007 ***http://www.smithsonianmag.com/history-archaeology/brief-salem.html.***
[668] A Brief History of the Salem Witch Trials. One town's strange journey from paranoia to pardon. By Jess Blumberg. Smithsonian.com, October 24, 2007 ***http://www.smithsonianmag.com/history-archaeology/brief-salem.html.***
[669] A Brief History of the Salem Witch Trials. One town's strange journey from paranoia to pardon. By Jess Blumberg. Smithsonian.com, October 24, 2007 ***http://www.smithsonianmag.com/history-archaeology/brief-salem.html.***
[670] A Brief History of the Salem Witch Trials. One town's strange journey from paranoia to pardon. By Jess Blumberg. Smithsonian.com, October 24, 2007 ***http://www.smithsonianmag.com/history-archaeology/brief-salem.html.***
[671] The Salem Witch Trials @ the History Channel. In Search of History. DVD Release Date: April 1, 2005. Retrieved May 20, 2009 @ http://shop.history.com/detail.php?a=71941.
[672] The Salem Witch Trials @ the History Channel. In Search of History. DVD Release Date: April 1, 2005. Retrieved May 20, 2009 @ http://shop.history.com/detail.php?a=71941.
[673] The Salem Witch Trials @ the History Channel. In Search of History. DVD Release Date: April 1, 2005. Retrieved May 20, 2009 @ http://shop.history.com/detail.php?a=71941.
[674] A Brief History of the Salem Witch Trials. One town's strange journey from paranoia to pardon. By Jess Blumberg. Smithsonian.com, October 24, 2007 ***http://www.smithsonianmag.com/history-archaeology/brief-salem.html.***
[675] A Brief History of the Salem Witch Trials. One town's strange journey from paranoia to pardon. By Jess Blumberg. Smithsonian.com, October 24, 2007 ***http://www.smithsonianmag.com/history-archaeology/brief-salem.html.***
[676] Chapter 18: A Violent Decade. Splintering Parties. The American Republic. Volume One to 1865. Prentice-Hall. Richard Hofstadter, William Miller, and Daniel Aaron. 1960. Page 573 &574.
[677] Chapter 18: A Violent Decade. Splintering Parties. The American Republic. Volume One to 1865. Prentice-Hall. Richard Hofstadter, William Miller, and Daniel Aaron. 1960. Page 573 &574.
[678] Chapter 18: A Violent Decade. Splintering Parties. The American Republic. Volume One to 1865. Prentice-Hall. Richard Hofstadter, William Miller, and Daniel Aaron. 1960. Page 573 &574.

[679] Chapter 18: A Violent Decade. Splintering Parties. The American Republic. Volume One to 1865. Prentice-Hall. Richard Hofstadter, William Miller, and Daniel Aaron. 1960. Page 573 &574.
[680] Chapter 18: A Violent Decade. Splintering Parties. The American Republic. Volume One to 1865. Prentice-Hall. Richard Hofstadter, William Miller, and Daniel Aaron. 1960. Page 573 &574.
[681] Chapter 18: A Violent Decade. Splintering Parties. The American Republic. Volume One to 1865. Prentice-Hall. Richard Hofstadter, William Miller, and Daniel Aaron. 1960. Page 573 &574.
[682] The American Republic. Volume One to 1865. Prentice-Hall. Richard Hofstadter, William Miller, and Daniel Aaron. 1960. Page 695, Presidential Elections, 1789-1864.
[683] America's Worst Immigration War. *By Jon Grinspan Retrieved April 20, 2008* @ http://www.americanheritage.com/events/articles/web/20061104-know-nothing-nativism-american-party-immigration-catholicism.shtml.
[684] America's Worst Immigration War. *By Jon Grinspan Retrieved April 20, 2008* @ http://www.americanheritage.com/events/articles/web/20061104-know-nothing-nativism-american-party-immigration-catholicism.shtml.
[685] America's Worst Immigration War. *By Jon Grinspan Retrieved April 20, 2008* @ http://www.americanheritage.com/events/articles/web/20061104-know-nothing-nativism-american-party-immigration-catholicism.shtml.
[686] Chapter 18: A Violent Decade. Splintering Parties. The American Republic. Volume One to 1865. Prentice-Hall. Richard Hofstadter, William Miller, and Daniel Aaron. 1960. Page 573 &574.
[687] Chapter 18: A Violent Decade. Splintering Parties. The American Republic. Volume One to 1865. Prentice-Hall. Richard Hofstadter, William Miller, and Daniel Aaron. 1960. Page 573 &574.
[688] Chapter 18: A Violent Decade. Splintering Parties. The American Republic. Volume One to 1865. Prentice-Hall. Richard Hofstadter, William Miller, and Daniel Aaron. 1960. Page 573 &574.
[689] Chapter 18: A Violent Decade. Splintering Parties. The American Republic. Volume One to 1865. Prentice-Hall. Richard Hofstadter, William Miller, and Daniel Aaron. 1960. Page 573 &574.
[690] America's Worst Immigration War. *By Jon Grinspan Retrieved April 20, 2008* @ http://www.americanheritage.com/events/articles/web/20061104-know-nothing-nativism-american-party-immigration-catholicism.shtml.
[691] America's Worst Immigration War. *By Jon Grinspan Retrieved April 20, 2008* @ http://www.americanheritage.com/events/articles/web/20061104-know-nothing-nativism-american-party-immigration-catholicism.shtml.
[692] America's Worst Immigration War. *By Jon Grinspan Retrieved April 20, 2008* @ http://www.americanheritage.com/events/articles/web/20061104-know-nothing-nativism-american-party-immigration-catholicism.shtml.
[693] America's Worst Immigration War. *By Jon Grinspan Retrieved April 20, 2008* @ http://www.americanheritage.com/events/articles/web/20061104-know-nothing-nativism-american-party-immigration-catholicism.shtml.
[694] America's Worst Immigration War. *By Jon Grinspan Retrieved April 20, 2008* @ http://www.americanheritage.com/events/articles/web/20061104-know-nothing-nativism-american-party-immigration-catholicism.shtml.
[695] America's Worst Immigration War. *By Jon Grinspan Retrieved April 20, 2008* @ http://www.americanheritage.com/events/articles/web/20061104-know-nothing-nativism-american-party-immigration-catholicism.shtml.
[696] America's Worst Immigration War. *By Jon Grinspan Retrieved April 20, 2008* @ http://www.americanheritage.com/events/articles/web/20061104-know-nothing-nativism-american-party-immigration-catholicism.shtml.
[697] America's Worst Immigration War. *By Jon Grinspan Retrieved April 20, 2008* @ http://www.americanheritage.com/events/articles/web/20061104-know-nothing-nativism-american-party-immigration-catholicism.shtml.
[698] Chapter 18: A Violent Decade. Splintering Parties. The American Republic. Volume One to 1865. Prentice-Hall. Richard Hofstadter, William Miller, and Daniel Aaron. 1960. Page 573 &574.
[699] America's Worst Immigration War. *By Jon Grinspan Retrieved April 20, 2008* @ http://www.americanheritage.com/events/articles/web/20061104-know-nothing-nativism-american-party-immigration-catholicism.shtml.
[700] America's Worst Immigration War. *By Jon Grinspan Retrieved April 20, 2008* @ http://www.americanheritage.com/events/articles/web/20061104-know-nothing-nativism-american-party-immigration-catholicism.shtml.
[701] Chapter 18: A Violent Decade. Splintering Parties. The American Republic. Volume One to 1865. Prentice-Hall. Richard Hofstadter, William Miller, and Daniel Aaron. 1960. Page 573 &574.
[702] America's Worst Immigration War. *By Jon Grinspan Retrieved April 20, 2008* @ http://www.americanheritage.com/events/articles/web/20061104-know-nothing-nativism-american-party-immigration-catholicism.shtml.
[703] America's Worst Immigration War. *By Jon Grinspan Retrieved April 20, 2008* @ http://www.americanheritage.com/events/articles/web/20061104-know-nothing-nativism-american-party-immigration-catholicism.shtml.
[704] Declaration of Independence. [Adopted in Congress 4 July 1776] The Unanimous Declaration of the Thirteen United States of America. Retrieved @ http://www.constitution.org/usdeclar.htm.
[705] Declaration of Independence. [Adopted in Congress 4 July 1776] The Unanimous Declaration of the Thirteen United States of America. Retrieved @ http://www.constitution.org/usdeclar.htm.
[706] Stephen Ambrose. To America—Personal Reflections of an Historian. Simon & Schuster, 2002. Chapter 2, The Battle of New Orleans. Page 18 and 19.
[707] Stephen Ambrose. To America—Personal Reflections of an Historian. Simon & Schuster, 2002. Chapter 2, The Battle of New Orleans. Page 18 and 19.
[708] Stephen Ambrose. To America—Personal Reflections of an Historian. Simon & Schuster, 2002. Chapter 2, The Battle of New Orleans. Page 18 and 19.
[709] Section 2. Jacksonian Democracy. Chapter 11 Age of Jackson 1828-1842. History of a Free Nation. Henry W. Bragdon, Samuel P. McClutchen, and Donald Ritchie. 1998. Glencoe McGraw-Hill. Page 317-318.
[710] Section 2. Jacksonian Democracy. Chapter 11 Age of Jackson 1828-1842. History of a Free Nation. Henry W. Bragdon, Samuel P. McClutchen, and Donald Ritchie. 1998. Glencoe McGraw-Hill. Page 317-318.
[711] Section 2. Jacksonian Democracy. Chapter 11 Age of Jackson 1828-1842. History of a Free Nation. Henry W. Bragdon, Samuel P. McClutchen, and Donald Ritchie. 1998. Glencoe McGraw-Hill. Page 317-318.
[712] **Cherokee Constitution of 1827 Andrew Jackson: Good, Evil & The Presidency. Glossary. Retrieved May 20, 2009 @** http://www.pbs.org/kcet/andrewjackson/glossary/#cherokeeconstitution.
[713] **Cherokee Constitution of 1827 Andrew Jackson: Good, Evil & The Presidency. Glossary. Retrieved May 20, 2009 @** http://www.pbs.org/kcet/andrewjackson/glossary/#cherokeeconstitution.
[714] **Cherokee Constitution of 1827 Andrew Jackson: Good, Evil & The Presidency. Glossary. Retrieved May 20, 2009 @** http://www.pbs.org/kcet/andrewjackson/glossary/#cherokeeconstitution.
[715] **Cherokee Constitution of 1827 Andrew Jackson: Good, Evil & The Presidency. Glossary. Retrieved May 20, 2009 @** http://www.pbs.org/kcet/andrewjackson/glossary/#cherokeeconstitution.
[716] Section 2. Jacksonian Democracy. Chapter 11 Age of Jackson 1828-1842. History of a Free Nation. Henry W. Bragdon, Samuel P. McClutchen, and Donald Ritchie. 1998. Glencoe McGraw-Hill. Page 317-318.
[717] Section 2. Jacksonian Democracy. Chapter 11 Age of Jackson 1828-1842. History of a Free Nation. Henry W. Bragdon, Samuel P. McClutchen, and Donald Ritchie. 1998. Glencoe McGraw-Hill. Page 317-318.
[718] Section 2. Jacksonian Democracy. Chapter 11 Age of Jackson 1828-1842. History of a Free Nation. Henry W. Bragdon, Samuel P. McClutchen, and Donald Ritchie. 1998. Glencoe McGraw-Hill. Page 317-318.
[719] Section 2. Jacksonian Democracy. Chapter 11 Age of Jackson 1828-1842. History of a Free Nation. Henry W. Bragdon, Samuel P. McClutchen, and Donald Ritchie. 1998. Glencoe McGraw-Hill. Page 317-318.
[720] **The "Trail of Tears" Andrew Jackson: Good, Evil & The Presidency. Glossary. Retrieved May 20, 2009 @** http://www.pbs.org/kcet/andrewjackson/glossary/#cherokeeconstitution.
[721] **The "Trail of Tears" Andrew Jackson: Good, Evil & The Presidency. Glossary. Retrieved May 20, 2009 @** http://www.pbs.org/kcet/andrewjackson/glossary/#cherokeeconstitution.
[722] Section 2. Jacksonian Democracy. Chapter 11 Age of Jackson 1828-1842. History of a Free Nation. Henry W. Bragdon, Samuel P. McClutchen, and Donald Ritchie. 1998. Glencoe McGraw-Hill. Page 317-318.
[723] Section 2. Jacksonian Democracy. Chapter 11 Age of Jackson 1828-1842. History of a Free Nation. Henry W. Bragdon, Samuel P. McClutchen, and Donald Ritchie. 1998. Glencoe McGraw-Hill. Page 317-318.
[724] Section 2. Jacksonian Democracy. Chapter 11 Age of Jackson 1828-1842. History of a Free Nation. Henry W. Bragdon, Samuel P. McClutchen, and Donald Ritchie. 1998. Glencoe McGraw-Hill. Page 317-318.
[725] **Source:** Henry Clay, Address to the Colonization Society of Kentucky, [Washington, DC] *National Intelligencer*, January 12, 1830.
PDF "Henry Clay on Native Americans" Retrieved May 20, 2009 @ http://www.pbs.org/kcet/andrewjackson/edu/ps_doc_clay_nativeam.pdf. See also ANDREW JACKSON: GOOD, EVIL AND THE PRESIDENCY www.pbs.org/andrewjackson.
[726] **Source:** Henry Clay, Address to the Colonization Society of Kentucky, [Washington, DC] *National Intelligencer*, January 12, 1830.
PDF "Henry Clay on Native Americans" Retrieved May 20, 2009 @ http://www.pbs.org/kcet/andrewjackson/edu/ps_doc_clay_nativeam.pdf. See also ANDREW JACKSON: GOOD, EVIL AND THE PRESIDENCY www.pbs.org/andrewjackson.
[727] **Source:** Henry Clay, Address to the Colonization Society of Kentucky, [Washington, DC] *National Intelligencer*, January 12, 1830.
PDF "Henry Clay on Native Americans" Retrieved May 20, 2009 @ http://www.pbs.org/kcet/andrewjackson/edu/ps_doc_clay_nativeam.pdf. See also ANDREW JACKSON: GOOD, EVIL AND THE PRESIDENCY www.pbs.org/andrewjackson.
[728] **Source:** Henry Clay, Address to the Colonization Society of Kentucky, [Washington, DC] *National Intelligencer*, January 12, 1830.
PDF "Henry Clay on Native Americans" Retrieved May 20, 2009 @ http://www.pbs.org/kcet/andrewjackson/edu/ps_doc_clay_nativeam.pdf. See also ANDREW JACKSON: GOOD, EVIL AND THE PRESIDENCY www.pbs.org/andrewjackson.
[729] **Source:** Henry Clay, Address to the Colonization Society of Kentucky, [Washington, DC] *National Intelligencer*, January 12, 1830.
PDF "Henry Clay on Native Americans" Retrieved May 20, 2009 @ http://www.pbs.org/kcet/andrewjackson/edu/ps_doc_clay_nativeam.pdf. See also ANDREW JACKSON: GOOD, EVIL AND THE PRESIDENCY www.pbs.org/andrewjackson.
[730] **Source:** Henry Clay, Address to the Colonization Society of Kentucky, [Washington, DC] *National Intelligencer*, January 12, 1830.
PDF "Henry Clay on Native Americans" Retrieved May 20, 2009 @ http://www.pbs.org/kcet/andrewjackson/edu/ps_doc_clay_nativeam.pdf. See also ANDREW JACKSON: GOOD, EVIL AND THE PRESIDENCY www.pbs.org/andrewjackson.
[731] **Source:** Henry Clay, Address to the Colonization Society of Kentucky, [Washington, DC] *National Intelligencer*, January 12, 1830.
PDF "Henry Clay on Native Americans" Retrieved May 20, 2009 @ http://www.pbs.org/kcet/andrewjackson/edu/ps_doc_clay_nativeam.pdf. See also ANDREW JACKSON: GOOD, EVIL AND THE PRESIDENCY www.pbs.org/andrewjackson.
[732] United States History. Holt Social Studies. William Deverell and Deborah Gray White. 2009 Religion and Government in New England. Page 82.
[733] United States History. Holt Social Studies. William Deverell and Deborah Gray White. 2009 Religion and Government in New England. Penn's Colony, page 87.
[734] SHORT OVERVIEW OF CALIFORNIA INDIAN HISTORY. Castillo, Edward D. (1998)., California Native American Heritage Commission. Retrieved June 10, 2009 @ http://www.ceres.ca.gov/nahc/califindian.html.

[735] SHORT OVERVIEW OF CALIFORNIA INDIAN HISTORY. Castillo, Edward D. (1998)., California Native American Heritage Commission. Retrieved June 10, 2009 @ http://www.ceres.ca.gov/nahc/califindian.html.
[736] SHORT OVERVIEW OF CALIFORNIA INDIAN HISTORY. Castillo, Edward D. (1998)., California Native American Heritage Commission. Retrieved June 10, 2009 @ http://www.ceres.ca.gov/nahc/califindian.html.
[737] SHORT OVERVIEW OF CALIFORNIA INDIAN HISTORY. Castillo, Edward D. (1998)., California Native American Heritage Commission. Retrieved June 10, 2009 @ http://www.ceres.ca.gov/nahc/califindian.html.
[738] World Book Encyclopedia. California. (History, page 60). Volume 3, C-Ch. 1989. World Book Inc.
[739] SHORT OVERVIEW OF CALIFORNIA INDIAN HISTORY. Castillo, Edward D. (1998)., California Native American Heritage Commission. Retrieved June 10, 2009 @ http://www.ceres.ca.gov/nahc/califindian.html.
[740] SHORT OVERVIEW OF CALIFORNIA INDIAN HISTORY. Castillo, Edward D. (1998)., California Native American Heritage Commission. Retrieved June 10, 2009 @ http://www.ceres.ca.gov/nahc/califindian.html.
[741] SHORT OVERVIEW OF CALIFORNIA INDIAN HISTORY. Castillo, Edward D. (1998)., California Native American Heritage Commission. Retrieved June 10, 2009 @ http://www.ceres.ca.gov/nahc/califindian.html.
[742] SHORT OVERVIEW OF CALIFORNIA INDIAN HISTORY. Castillo, Edward D. (1998)., California Native American Heritage Commission. Retrieved June 10, 2009 @ http://www.ceres.ca.gov/nahc/califindian.html.
[743] SHORT OVERVIEW OF CALIFORNIA INDIAN HISTORY. Castillo, Edward D. (1998)., California Native American Heritage Commission. Retrieved June 10, 2009 @ http://www.ceres.ca.gov/nahc/califindian.html.
[744] Section 1. People of the Plains. Chapter 17 Into the West 1860-1900. History of a Free Nation. Henry W. Bragdon, Samuel P. McClutchen, and Donald Ritchie. 1998. Glencoe McGraw-Hill. Page 474-475.
[745] Section 1. People of the Plains. Chapter 17 Into the West 1860-1900. History of a Free Nation. Henry W. Bragdon, Samuel P. McClutchen, and Donald Ritchie. 1998. Glencoe McGraw-Hill. Page 474-475.
[746] Section 1. People of the Plains. Chapter 17 Into the West 1860-1900. History of a Free Nation. Henry W. Bragdon, Samuel P. McClutchen, and Donald Ritchie. 1998. Glencoe McGraw-Hill. Page 474-475.
[747] Section 1. People of the Plains. Chapter 17 Into the West 1860-1900. History of a Free Nation. Henry W. Bragdon, Samuel P. McClutchen, and Donald Ritchie. 1998. Glencoe McGraw-Hill. Page 474-475.
[748] Section 1. People of the Plains. Chapter 17 Into the West 1860-1900. History of a Free Nation. Henry W. Bragdon, Samuel P. McClutchen, and Donald Ritchie. 1998. Glencoe McGraw-Hill. Page 474-475.
[749] Section 1. People of the Plains. Chapter 17 Into the West 1860-1900. History of a Free Nation. Henry W. Bragdon, Samuel P. McClutchen, and Donald Ritchie. 1998. Glencoe McGraw-Hill. Page 474-475.
[750] Section 1. People of the Plains. Chapter 17 Into the West 1860-1900. History of a Free Nation. Henry W. Bragdon, Samuel P. McClutchen, and Donald Ritchie. 1998. Glencoe McGraw-Hill. Page 474-475.
[751] Waller Hastings from Northern State University. L. Frank Baum's Editorials on the Sioux Nation. Retrieved May 20, 2009 @ http://web.archive.org/web/20071209193251/http://www.northern.edu/hastingw/baumedts.htm.
[752] Waller Hastings from Northern State University. L. Frank Baum's Editorials on the Sioux Nation. Retrieved May 20, 2009 @ http://web.archive.org/web/20071209193251/http://www.northern.edu/hastingw/baumedts.htm.
[753] 'Oz' Family Apologizes for Racist Editorials. By Charles Ray of South Dakota Public Radio. *Morning Edition*, August 17, 2006. Retrieved May 20, 2009 @ http://www.npr.org/templates/story/story.php?storyId=5662524.
[754] Waller Hastings from Northern State University. L. Frank Baum's Editorials on the Sioux Nation. Retrieved May 20, 2009 @ http://web.archive.org/web/20071209193251/http://www.northern.edu/hastingw/baumedts.htm.
[755] Waller Hastings from Northern State University. L. Frank Baum's Editorials on the Sioux Nation. Retrieved May 20, 2009 @ http://web.archive.org/web/20071209193251/http://www.northern.edu/hastingw/baumedts.htm.
[756] Waller Hastings from Northern State University. L. Frank Baum's Editorials on the Sioux Nation. Retrieved May 20, 2009 @ http://web.archive.org/web/20071209193251/http://www.northern.edu/hastingw/baumedts.htm.
[757] Waller Hastings from Northern State University. L. Frank Baum's Editorials on the Sioux Nation. Includes the The Sitting Bull editorial (*Aberdeen Saturday Pioneer*, December 20, 1890). Retrieved May 20, 2009 @ http://web.archive.org/web/20071209193251/http://www.northern.edu/hastingw/baumedts.htm.
[758] Waller Hastings from Northern State University. L. Frank Baum's Editorials on the Sioux Nation. Includes the The Sitting Bull editorial (*Aberdeen Saturday Pioneer*, December 20, 1890). Retrieved May 20, 2009 @ http://web.archive.org/web/20071209193251/http://www.northern.edu/hastingw/baumedts.htm.
[759] Waller Hastings from Northern State University. L. Frank Baum's Editorials on the Sioux Nation. Retrieved May 20, 2009 @ http://web.archive.org/web/20071209193251/http://www.northern.edu/hastingw/baumedts.htm.
[760] Waller Hastings from Northern State University. L. Frank Baum's Editorials on the Sioux Nation. Retrieved May 20, 2009 @ http://web.archive.org/web/20071209193251/http://www.northern.edu/hastingw/baumedts.htm.
[761] Waller Hastings from Northern State University. L. Frank Baum's Editorials on the Sioux Nation. Retrieved May 20, 2009 @ http://web.archive.org/web/20071209193251/http://www.northern.edu/hastingw/baumedts.htm.
[762] Waller Hastings from Northern State University. L. Frank Baum's Editorials on the Sioux Nation. Includes the The Wounded Knee editorial (*Aberdeen Saturday Pioneer*, January 3, 1891) Retrieved May 20, 2009 @ http://web.archive.org/web/20071209193251/http://www.northern.edu/hastingw/baumedts.htm
[763] Waller Hastings from Northern State University. L. Frank Baum's Editorials on the Sioux Nation. Includes the The Wounded Knee editorial (*Aberdeen Saturday Pioneer*, January 3, 1891) Retrieved May 20, 2009 @ http://web.archive.org/web/20071209193251/http://www.northern.edu/hastingw/baumedts.htm
[764] Waller Hastings from Northern State University. L. Frank Baum's Editorials on the Sioux Nation. Includes the The Wounded Knee editorial (*Aberdeen Saturday Pioneer*, January 3, 1891) Retrieved May 20, 2009 @ http://web.archive.org/web/20071209193251/http://www.northern.edu/hastingw/baumedts.htm
[765] 'Oz' Family Apologizes for Racist Editorials. By Charles Ray of South Dakota Public Radio. *Morning Edition*, August 17, 2006. Retrieved May 20, 2009 @ http://www.npr.org/templates/story/story.php?storyId=5662524.
[766] **Teddy Roosevelt and *The Winning of the West.* (9/5/04)** Featuring selected quotes from Roosevelt's *The Winning of the West, Volume Three: The Founding of the Trans-Alleghany Commonwealths, 1784-1790*: 2007 by Robert Schmidt. http://www.bluecorncomics.com/roosvelt.htm.
[767] **Teddy Roosevelt and *The Winning of the West.* (9/5/04)** Featuring selected quotes from Roosevelt's *The Winning of the West, Volume Three: The Founding of the Trans-Alleghany Commonwealths, 1784-1790*: 2007 by Robert Schmidt. http://www.bluecorncomics.com/roosvelt.htm.
[768] **Teddy Roosevelt and *The Winning of the West.* (9/5/04)** Featuring selected quotes from Roosevelt's *The Winning of the West, Volume Three: The Founding of the Trans-Alleghany Commonwealths, 1784-1790*: 2007 by Robert Schmidt. http://www.bluecorncomics.com/roosvelt.htm.
[769] Section 3. Patterns of Immigration. Chapter 19 An Urban Society. History of a Free Nation. Henry W. Bragdon, Samuel P. McClutchen, and Donald Ritchie. 1998. Glencoe McGraw-Hill. Page 532.
[770] Section 3. Patterns of Immigration. Chapter 19 An Urban Society. History of a Free Nation. Henry W. Bragdon, Samuel P. McClutchen, and Donald Ritchie. 1998. Glencoe McGraw-Hill. Page 532.
[771] Section 3. Patterns of Immigration. Chapter 19 An Urban Society. History of a Free Nation. Henry W. Bragdon, Samuel P. McClutchen, and Donald Ritchie. 1998. Glencoe McGraw-Hill. Page 532.
[772] People v. Hall 4 Cal. 399 (California Supreme Court 1854). Retrieved June 10, 2009 @ http://www.uchastings.edu/racism-race/people-hall.html.
[773] Source: Dennis Kearney, President, and H. L. Knight, Secretary, "Appeal from California. The Chinese Invasion. Workingmen's Address," Indianapolis *Times*, 28 February 1878. Retrieved June 10, 2009 @http://historymatters.gmu.edu/d/5046/%7C.
[774] Source: Dennis Kearney, President, and H. L. Knight, Secretary, "Appeal from California. The Chinese Invasion. Workingmen's Address," Indianapolis *Times*, 28 February 1878. Retrieved June 10, 2009 @http://historymatters.gmu.edu/d/5046/%7C.
[775] Source: Dennis Kearney, President, and H. L. Knight, Secretary, "Appeal from California. The Chinese Invasion. Workingmen's Address," Indianapolis *Times*, 28 February 1878. Retrieved June 10, 2009 @http://historymatters.gmu.edu/d/5046/%7C.
[776] Source: Dennis Kearney, President, and H. L. Knight, Secretary, "Appeal from California. The Chinese Invasion. Workingmen's Address," Indianapolis *Times*, 28 February 1878. Retrieved June 10, 2009 @http://historymatters.gmu.edu/d/5046/%7C.
[777] Section 3. Patterns of Immigration. Chapter 19 An Urban Society. History of a Free Nation. Henry W. Bragdon, Samuel P. McClutchen, and Donald Ritchie. 1998. Glencoe McGraw-Hill. Page 532.
[778] The Chinese Exclusion Act page was retrieved June 12, 2009 @ http://www.usnews.com/usnews/documents/docpages/document_page47.htm. See also In formation excerpted from *Teaching With Documents: Using Primary Sources From the National Archives*. [Washington, DC: National Archives and Records Administration, 1989.] pp. 82-85.
[779] The Chinese Exclusion Act page was retrieved June 12, 2009 @ http://www.usnews.com/usnews/documents/docpages/document_page47.htm. See also In formation excerpted from *Teaching With Documents: Using Primary Sources From the National Archives*. [Washington, DC: National Archives and Records Administration, 1989.] pp. 82-85.
[780] From the WSJ Opinion Archives. **FROM THE RECORD.** Whitewash. *The racist history the Democratic Party wants you to forget.* by BRUCE BARTLETT. *Monday, December 24, 2007.* Mr. Bartlett is author of "Wrong on Race: The Democratic Party's Buried Past," to be published next month by Palgrave Macmillan. Retreived May 20, 2009 @ http://www.opinionjournal.com/extra/?id=110011033.
[781] From the WSJ Opinion Archives. **FROM THE RECORD.** Whitewash. *The racist history the Democratic Party wants you to forget.* by BRUCE BARTLETT. *Monday, December 24, 2007.* Mr. Bartlett is author of "Wrong on Race: The Democratic Party's Buried Past," to be published next month by Palgrave Macmillan. Retreived May 20, 2009 @ http://www.opinionjournal.com/extra/?id=110011033.
[782] From the WSJ Opinion Archives. **FROM THE RECORD.** Whitewash. *The racist history the Democratic Party wants you to forget.* by BRUCE BARTLETT. *Monday, December 24, 2007.* Mr. Bartlett is author of "Wrong on Race: The Democratic Party's Buried Past," to be published next month by Palgrave Macmillan. Retreived May 20, 2009 @ http://www.opinionjournal.com/extra/?id=110011033.
[783] From the WSJ Opinion Archives. **FROM THE RECORD.** Whitewash. *The racist history the Democratic Party wants you to forget.* by BRUCE BARTLETT. *Monday, December 24, 2007.* Mr. Bartlett is author of "Wrong on Race: The Democratic Party's Buried Past," to be published next month by Palgrave Macmillan. Retreived May 20, 2009 @ http://www.opinionjournal.com/extra/?id=110011033.
[784] From the WSJ Opinion Archives. **FROM THE RECORD.** Whitewash. *The racist history the Democratic Party wants you to forget.* by BRUCE BARTLETT. *Monday, December 24, 2007.* Mr. Bartlett is author of "Wrong on Race: The Democratic Party's Buried Past," to be published next month by Palgrave Macmillan. Retreived May 20, 2009 @ http://www.opinionjournal.com/extra/?id=110011033.
[785] Harold Evans. The American Century. Commentary: Accidental Empire. Page 52. Manifest Destiny, 1867 to 1900. New York: Alfred A. Knopf.
[786] Harold Evans. The American Century. Commentary: Accidental Empire. Page 53. Manifest Destiny, 1867 to 1900. New York: Alfred A. Knopf.
[787] Section 3. Becoming a World Power. Chapter 22 Imperialism 1867-1908. History of a Free Nation. Henry W. Bragdon, Samuel P. McClutchen, and Donald Ritchie. 1998. Glencoe McGraw-Hill.
[788] Harold Evans. The American Century. Commentary: Accidental Empire. Page 52. Manifest Destiny, 1867 to 1900. New York: Alfred A. Knopf.
[789] Harold Evans. The American Century. Commentary: Accidental Empire. Page 51. Manifest Destiny, 1867 to 1900. New York: Alfred A. Knopf.
[790] Harold Evans. The American Century. Commentary: Accidental Empire. Page 51. Manifest Destiny, 1867 to 1900. New York: Alfred A. Knopf.

[791] Harold Evans. The American Century. Commentary: Accidental Empire. Page 54. Manifest Destiny, 1867 to 1900. New York: Alfred A. Knopf.
[792] Harold Evans. The American Century. Commentary: Accidental Empire. Page 55. Manifest Destiny, 1867 to 1900. New York: Alfred A. Knopf.
[793] Harold Evans. The American Century. Commentary: Accidental Empire. Page 55. Manifest Destiny, 1867 to 1900. New York: Alfred A. Knopf.
[794] Harold Evans. The American Century. Commentary: Accidental Empire. Page 55. Manifest Destiny, 1867 to 1900. New York: Alfred A. Knopf.
[795] Harold Evans. The American Century. Commentary: Accidental Empire. Page 55. Manifest Destiny, 1867 to 1900. New York: Alfred A. Knopf.
[796] Section 3. Becoming a World Power. Chapter 22 Imperialism 1867-1908. History of a Free Nation. Henry W. Bragdon, Samuel P. McClutchen, and Donald Ritchie. 1998. Glencoe McGraw-Hill.
[797] Harold Evans. The American Century. Commentary: Accidental Empire. Page 55. Manifest Destiny, 1867 to 1900. New York: Alfred A. Knopf.
[798] Harold Evans. The American Century. Commentary: Accidental Empire. Page 55. Manifest Destiny, 1867 to 1900. New York: Alfred A. Knopf.
[799] Section 3. Becoming a World Power. Chapter 22 Imperialism 1867-1908. History of a Free Nation. Henry W. Bragdon, Samuel P. McClutchen, and Donald Ritchie. 1998. Glencoe McGraw-Hill.
[800] Harold Evans. The American Century. Commentary: Accidental Empire. Page 50. Manifest Destiny, 1867 to 1900. New York: Alfred A. Knopf.
[801] Section 3. Becoming a World Power. Chapter 22 Imperialism 1867-1908. History of a Free Nation. Henry W. Bragdon, Samuel P. McClutchen, and Donald Ritchie. 1998. Glencoe McGraw-Hill.
[802] Section 3. Becoming a World Power. Chapter 22 Imperialism 1867-1908. History of a Free Nation. Henry W. Bragdon, Samuel P. McClutchen, and Donald Ritchie. 1998. Glencoe McGraw-Hill.
[803] Section 3. Becoming a World Power. Chapter 22 Imperialism 1867-1908. History of a Free Nation. Henry W. Bragdon, Samuel P. McClutchen, and Donald Ritchie. 1998. Glencoe McGraw-Hill.
[804] Section 3. Becoming a World Power. Chapter 22 Imperialism 1867-1908. History of a Free Nation. Henry W. Bragdon, Samuel P. McClutchen, and Donald Ritchie. 1998. Glencoe McGraw-Hill.
[805] Stephen Ambrose. To America. Chapter Six. Theodore Roosevelt and the Beginning of the American Century. Simon & Schuster. 2002. Page 75 to 92.
[806] Section 3. Becoming a World Power. Chapter 22 Imperialism 1867-1908. History of a Free Nation. Henry W. Bragdon, Samuel P. McClutchen, and Donald Ritchie. 1998. Glencoe McGraw-Hill.
[807] Section 3. Becoming a World Power. Chapter 22 Imperialism 1867-1908. History of a Free Nation. Henry W. Bragdon, Samuel P. McClutchen, and Donald Ritchie. 1998. Glencoe McGraw-Hill.
[808] Harold Evans. The American Century. Commentary: Accidental Empire. Page 55. Manifest Destiny, 1867 to 1900. New York: Alfred A. Knopf.
[809] Harold Evans. The American Century. Commentary: Accidental Empire. Page 56. Manifest Destiny, 1867 to 1900. New York: Alfred A. Knopf.
[810] Section 3. Becoming a World Power. Chapter 22 Imperialism 1867-1908. History of a Free Nation. Henry W. Bragdon, Samuel P. McClutchen, and Donald Ritchie. 1998. Glencoe McGraw-Hill.
[811] Section 3. Becoming a World Power. Chapter 22 Imperialism 1867-1908. History of a Free Nation. Henry W. Bragdon, Samuel P. McClutchen, and Donald Ritchie. 1998. Glencoe McGraw-Hill.
[812] Section 3. Becoming a World Power. Chapter 22 Imperialism 1867-1908. History of a Free Nation. Henry W. Bragdon, Samuel P. McClutchen, and Donald Ritchie. 1998. Glencoe McGraw-Hill.
[813] Section 3. Becoming a World Power. Chapter 22 Imperialism 1867-1908. History of a Free Nation. Henry W. Bragdon, Samuel P. McClutchen, and Donald Ritchie. 1998. Glencoe McGraw-Hill.
[814] General Grant's Infamy. Sources: American Jewish Historical Society and Karp, Abraham, *From the Ends of the Earth: Judaic Treasures of the Library of Congress*. DC: Library of Congress, 1991. Retrieved June 10, 2009 @ http://www.jewishvirtuallibrary.org/jsource/anti-semitism/grant.html.
[815] General Grant's Infamy. Sources: American Jewish Historical Society and Karp, Abraham, *From the Ends of the Earth: Judaic Treasures of the Library of Congress*. DC: Library of Congress, 1991. Retrieved June 10, 2009 @ http://www.jewishvirtuallibrary.org/jsource/anti-semitism/grant.html.
[816] General Grant's Infamy. Sources: American Jewish Historical Society and Karp, Abraham, *From the Ends of the Earth: Judaic Treasures of the Library of Congress*. DC: Library of Congress, 1991. Retrieved June 10, 2009 @ http://www.jewishvirtuallibrary.org/jsource/anti-semitism/grant.html.
[817] General Grant's Infamy. Sources: American Jewish Historical Society and Karp, Abraham, *From the Ends of the Earth: Judaic Treasures of the Library of Congress*. DC: Library of Congress, 1991. Retrieved June 10, 2009 @ http://www.jewishvirtuallibrary.org/jsource/anti-semitism/grant.html.
[818] General Grant's Infamy. Sources: American Jewish Historical Society and Karp, Abraham, *From the Ends of the Earth: Judaic Treasures of the Library of Congress*. DC: Library of Congress, 1991. Retrieved June 10, 2009 @ http://www.jewishvirtuallibrary.org/jsource/anti-semitism/grant.html.
[819] General Grant's Infamy. Sources: American Jewish Historical Society and Karp, Abraham, *From the Ends of the Earth: Judaic Treasures of the Library of Congress*. DC: Library of Congress, 1991. Retrieved June 10, 2009 @ http://www.jewishvirtuallibrary.org/jsource/anti-semitism/grant.html.
[820] Wilson nominates Brandeis to the Supreme Court. January 28, 1916. The History Channel. Retrieved May 20, 2009 @ http://www.history.com/this-day-in-history.do?action=Article&id=132.
[821] Judicial Injustice: The Attacks on Louis Brandeis. From The Archivist. posted by Jeff Kisseloff on 05/08/2009. Retreived May 20, 2009 @ http://www.thenation.com/blogs/from_the_archive/434009/judicial_injustice_the_attacks_on_louis_brandeis.
[822] Judicial Injustice: The Attacks on Louis Brandeis. From The Archivist. posted by Jeff Kisseloff on 05/08/2009. Retreived May 20, 2009 @ http://www.thenation.com/blogs/from_the_archive/434009/judicial_injustice_the_attacks_on_louis_brandeis.
[823] Judicial Injustice: The Attacks on Louis Brandeis. From The Archivist. posted by Jeff Kisseloff on 05/08/2009. Retreived May 20, 2009 @ http://www.thenation.com/blogs/from_the_archive/434009/judicial_injustice_the_attacks_on_louis_brandeis.
[824] Judicial Injustice: The Attacks on Louis Brandeis. From The Archivist. posted by Jeff Kisseloff on 05/08/2009. Retreived May 20, 2009 @ http://www.thenation.com/blogs/from_the_archive/434009/judicial_injustice_the_attacks_on_louis_brandeis.
[825] Jewish Virtual Library. Louis D. Brandeis. (1856-1941) Retrieved May 20, 2009 @ http://www.jewishvirtuallibrary.org/jsource/biography/Brandeis.html.
[826] Judicial Injustice: The Attacks on Louis Brandeis. From The Archivist. posted by Jeff Kisseloff on 05/08/2009. Retreived May 20, 2009 @ http://www.thenation.com/blogs/from_the_archive/434009/judicial_injustice_the_attacks_on_louis_brandeis.
[827] Wilson picks Brandeis, Jan. 28, 1916. By ANDREW GLASS | 1/28/09. Source: "Louis Brandeis," by Jacob Marcus (1997).http://www.politico.com/news/stories/0109/18069.html.
[828] Louis D. Brandeis, 1916-1939. Retrieved May 20, 2009 @ http://www.supremecourthistory.org/history/supremecourthistory_history_assoc_057brandeis.htm.
[829] Wilson nominates Brandeis to the Supreme Court. January 28, 1916. The History Channel. Retrieved May 20, 2009 @ http://www.history.com/this-day-in-history.do?action=Article&id=132.
[830] Wilson nominates Brandeis to the Supreme Court. January 28, 1916. The History Channel. Retrieved May 20, 2009 @ http://www.history.com/this-day-in-history.do?action=Article&id=132.
[831] Louis D. Brandeis, 1916-1939. Retrieved May 20, 2009 @ http://www.supremecourthistory.org/history/supremecourthistory_history_assoc_057brandeis.htm.
[832] Louis D. Brandeis, 1916-1939. Retrieved May 20, 2009 @ http://www.supremecourthistory.org/history/supremecourthistory_history_assoc_057brandeis.htm.
[833] Wilson nominates Brandeis to the Supreme Court. January 28, 1916. The History Channel. Retrieved May 20, 2009 @ http://www.history.com/this-day-in-history.do?action=Article&id=132.
[834] Jewish Virtual Library. Louis D. Brandeis. (1856-1941) Retrieved May 20, 2009 @ http://www.jewishvirtuallibrary.org/jsource/biography/Brandeis.html.
[835] Wilson nominates Brandeis to the Supreme Court. January 28, 1916. The History Channel. Retrieved May 20, 2009 @ http://www.history.com/this-day-in-history.do?action=Article&id=132.
[836] Wilson nominates Brandeis to the Supreme Court. January 28, 1916. The History Channel. Retrieved May 20, 2009 @ http://www.history.com/this-day-in-history.do?action=Article&id=132.
[837] Wilson nominates Brandeis to the Supreme Court. January 28, 1916. The History Channel. Retrieved May 20, 2009 @ http://www.history.com/this-day-in-history.do?action=Article&id=132.
[838] Judicial Injustice: The Attacks on Louis Brandeis. From The Archivist. posted by Jeff Kisseloff on 05/08/2009. Retreived May 20, 2009 @ http://www.thenation.com/blogs/from_the_archive/434009/judicial_injustice_the_attacks_on_louis_brandeis.
[839] Judicial Injustice: The Attacks on Louis Brandeis. From The Archivist. posted by Jeff Kisseloff on 05/08/2009. Retreived May 20, 2009 @ http://www.thenation.com/blogs/from_the_archive/434009/judicial_injustice_the_attacks_on_louis_brandeis.
[840] Judicial Injustice: The Attacks on Louis Brandeis. From The Archivist. posted by Jeff Kisseloff on 05/08/2009. Retreived May 20, 2009 @ http://www.thenation.com/blogs/from_the_archive/434009/judicial_injustice_the_attacks_on_louis_brandeis.
[841] Judicial Injustice: The Attacks on Louis Brandeis. From The Archivist. posted by Jeff Kisseloff on 05/08/2009. Retreived May 20, 2009 @ http://www.thenation.com/blogs/from_the_archive/434009/judicial_injustice_the_attacks_on_louis_brandeis.
[842] Judicial Injustice: The Attacks on Louis Brandeis. From The Archivist. posted by Jeff Kisseloff on 05/08/2009. Retreived May 20, 2009 @ http://www.thenation.com/blogs/from_the_archive/434009/judicial_injustice_the_attacks_on_louis_brandeis.
[843] Judicial Injustice: The Attacks on Louis Brandeis. From The Archivist. posted by Jeff Kisseloff on 05/08/2009. Retreived May 20, 2009 @ http://www.thenation.com/blogs/from_the_archive/434009/judicial_injustice_the_attacks_on_louis_brandeis.
[844] Judicial Injustice: The Attacks on Louis Brandeis. From The Archivist. posted by Jeff Kisseloff on 05/08/2009. Retreived May 20, 2009 @ http://www.thenation.com/blogs/from_the_archive/434009/judicial_injustice_the_attacks_on_louis_brandeis.
[845] Judicial Injustice: The Attacks on Louis Brandeis. From The Archivist. posted by Jeff Kisseloff on 05/08/2009. Retreived May 20, 2009 @ http://www.thenation.com/blogs/from_the_archive/434009/judicial_injustice_the_attacks_on_louis_brandeis.
[846] The Jewish Problem: How To Solve It by Louis D. Brandeis. Speech to the Conference of Eastern Council of Reform Rabbis, April 25, 1915. Louis D. Brandeis School of Law Brandeis, Louis. Retrieved May 20, 2009 @ http://www.law.louisville.edu/library/collections/brandeis/node/234.
[847] The Jewish Problem: How To Solve It by Louis D. Brandeis. Speech to the Conference of Eastern Council of Reform Rabbis, April 25, 1915. Louis D. Brandeis School of Law Brandeis, Louis. Retrieved May 20, 2009 @ http://www.law.louisville.edu/library/collections/brandeis/node/234.
[848] Jewish Virtual Library. Louis D. Brandeis. (1856-1941) Retrieved May 20, 2009 @ http://www.jewishvirtuallibrary.org/jsource/biography/Brandeis.html.
[849] Jewish Virtual Library. Louis D. Brandeis. (1856-1941) Retrieved May 20, 2009 @ http://www.jewishvirtuallibrary.org/jsource/biography/Brandeis.html.
[850] CONFIRM BRANDEIS BY VOTE OF 47 TO 22; Long Fight in Senate Over His Nomination Ends in Victory for Administration. ONE DEMOCRAT OPPOSED Newlands Later Explains His Vote ;- Three Republicans for Him ;- May Take Oath June 12. CONFIRM BRANDEIS BY VOTE OF 47 TO 22. Special to The New York Times.. June 2, 1916, Friday. Page 1, 1707 words. Retrieved May 20, 2009 @ http://query.nytimes.com/gst/abstract.html?res=980CE7D7163BE633A25751C0A9609C946796D6CF. Wilson picks Brandeis, Jan. 28, 1916. By ANDREW GLASS | 1/28/09. Source: "Louis Brandeis," by Jacob Marcus (1997).http://www.politico.com/news/stories/0109/18069.html.
[851] Wilson picks Brandeis, Jan. 28, 1916. By ANDREW GLASS | 1/28/09. Source: "Louis Brandeis," by Jacob Marcus (1997).http://www.politico.com/news/stories/0109/18069.html.
[852] Jewish Virtual Library. Louis D. Brandeis. (1856-1941) Retrieved May 20, 2009 @ http://www.jewishvirtuallibrary.org/jsource/biography/Brandeis.html.
[853] Henry Ford Invents a Jewish Conspiracy. Sources: American Jewish Historical Society; Library of Congress. Posted in Jewish Virtual Library. Retrieved June 10, 2009 @ http://www.jewishvirtuallibrary.org/jsource/anti-semitism/ford1.html.
[854] Henry Ford Invents a Jewish Conspiracy. Sources: American Jewish Historical Society; Library of Congress. Posted in Jewish Virtual Library. Retrieved June 10, 2009 @ http://www.jewishvirtuallibrary.org/jsource/anti-semitism/ford1.html.
[855] Henry Ford Invents a Jewish Conspiracy. Sources: American Jewish Historical Society; Library of Congress. Posted in Jewish Virtual Library. Retrieved June 10, 2009 @ http://www.jewishvirtuallibrary.org/jsource/anti-semitism/ford1.html.
[856] Henry Ford Invents a Jewish Conspiracy. Sources: American Jewish Historical Society; Library of Congress. Posted in Jewish Virtual Library. Retrieved June 10, 2009 @ http://www.jewishvirtuallibrary.org/jsource/anti-semitism/ford1.html.
[857] Henry Ford Invents a Jewish Conspiracy. Sources: American Jewish Historical Society; Library of Congress. Posted in Jewish Virtual Library. Retrieved June 10, 2009 @ http://www.jewishvirtuallibrary.org/jsource/anti-semitism/ford1.html.

[858] Henry Ford Invents a Jewish Conspiracy. Sources: American Jewish Historical Society; Library of Congress. Posted in Jewish Virtual Library. Retrieved June 10, 2009 @ http://www.jewishvirtuallibrary.org/jsource/anti-semitism/ford1.html.
[859] From the WSJ Opinion Archives. **FROM THE RECORD.** Whitewash. *The racist history the Democratic Party wants you to forget.* by BRUCE BARTLETT. *Monday, December 24, 2007.* Mr. Bartlett is author of "Wrong on Race: The Democratic Party's Buried Past," to be published next month by Palgrave Macmillan. Retreived May 20, 2009 @ http://www.opinionjournal.com/extra/?id=110011033.
[860] Stephen E. Ambrose. To America—Personal Reflections of an Historian. Simon & Schuster, 2002. Chapter 1, The Founding Fathers. Page 4.
[861] Stephen E. Ambrose. To America—Personal Reflections of an Historian. Simon & Schuster, 2002. Chapter 1, The Founding Fathers. Page 4.
[862] Stephen E. Ambrose. To America—Personal Reflections of an Historian. Simon & Schuster, 2002. Chapter 1, The Founding Fathers. Page 4.
[863] Stephen E. Ambrose. To America—Personal Reflections of an Historian. Simon & Schuster, 2002. Chapter 1, The Founding Fathers. Page 11.
[864] Stephen E. Ambrose. To America—Personal Reflections of an Historian. Simon & Schuster, 2002. Chapter 1, The Founding Fathers. Page 11.
[865] World Book Encyclopedia. Volume 1, A. 1989. World Book, Inc. John Quincy Adams. Page 43.
[866] World Book Encyclopedia. Volume 1, A. 1989. World Book, Inc. John Quincy Adams. Page 43.
[867]World Book Encyclopedia. Volume 1, A. 1989. World Book, Inc. John Quincy Adams. Page 43.
[868]World Book Encyclopedia. Volume 1, A. 1989. World Book, Inc. John Quincy Adams. Page 43.
[869] The Complete Book of U.S. Presidents. William A. DeGregorio. 5th Edition, 2002. John Tyler Chapter, page 159.
[870] World Book Encyclopedia. Volume 20, UV. 1989. World Book, Inc. Martin Van Buren. Page 289.
[871] The Complete Book of U.S. Presidents. William A. DeGregorio. 5th Edition, 2002. Page 132 and 181.
[872] From the WSJ Opinion Archives. **FROM THE RECORD.** Whitewash. *The racist history the Democratic Party wants you to forget.* by BRUCE BARTLETT. *Monday, December 24, 2007.* Mr. Bartlett is author of "Wrong on Race: The Democratic Party's Buried Past," to be published next month by Palgrave Macmillan. Retreived May 20, 2009 @ http://www.opinionjournal.com/extra/?id=110011033.
[873] From the WSJ Opinion Archives. **FROM THE RECORD.** Whitewash. *The racist history the Democratic Party wants you to forget.* by BRUCE BARTLETT. *Monday, December 24, 2007.* Mr. Bartlett is author of "Wrong on Race: The Democratic Party's Buried Past," to be published next month by Palgrave Macmillan. Retreived May 20, 2009 @ http://www.opinionjournal.com/extra/?id=110011033.
[874] From the WSJ Opinion Archives. **FROM THE RECORD.** Whitewash. *The racist history the Democratic Party wants you to forget.* by BRUCE BARTLETT. *Monday, December 24, 2007.* Mr. Bartlett is author of "Wrong on Race: The Democratic Party's Buried Past," to be published next month by Palgrave Macmillan. Retreived May 20, 2009 @ http://www.opinionjournal.com/extra/?id=110011033.
[875] From the WSJ Opinion Archives. **FROM THE RECORD.** Whitewash. *The racist history the Democratic Party wants you to forget.* by BRUCE BARTLETT. *Monday, December 24, 2007.* Mr. Bartlett is author of "Wrong on Race: The Democratic Party's Buried Past," to be published next month by Palgrave Macmillan. Retreived May 20, 2009 @ http://www.opinionjournal.com/extra/?id=110011033.
[876] Volume One of The American Republic, Chapter Fourteen. Page 462 to 464. Prentice Hall, 1959.
[877] Volume One of The American Republic, Chapter Fourteen. Page 462 to 464. Prentice Hall, 1959.
[878] Volume One of The American Republic, Chapter Fourteen. Page 462 to 464. Prentice Hall, 1959.
[879] Volume One of The American Republic, Chapter Fourteen. Page 462 to 464. Prentice Hall, 1959.
[880] From the WSJ Opinion Archives. **FROM THE RECORD.** Whitewash. *The racist history the Democratic Party wants you to forget.* by BRUCE BARTLETT. *Monday, December 24, 2007.* Mr. Bartlett is author of "Wrong on Race: The Democratic Party's Buried Past," to be published next month by Palgrave Macmillan. Retreived May 20, 2009 @ http://www.opinionjournal.com/extra/?id=110011033.
[881] From the WSJ Opinion Archives. **FROM THE RECORD.** Whitewash. *The racist history the Democratic Party wants you to forget.* by BRUCE BARTLETT. *Monday, December 24, 2007.* Mr. Bartlett is author of "Wrong on Race: The Democratic Party's Buried Past," to be published next month by Palgrave Macmillan. Retreived May 20, 2009 @ http://www.opinionjournal.com/extra/?id=110011033.
[882] From the WSJ Opinion Archives. **FROM THE RECORD.** Whitewash. *The racist history the Democratic Party wants you to forget.* by BRUCE BARTLETT. *Monday, December 24, 2007.* Mr. Bartlett is author of "Wrong on Race: The Democratic Party's Buried Past," to be published next month by Palgrave Macmillan. Retreived May 20, 2009 @ http://www.opinionjournal.com/extra/?id=110011033.
[883] From the WSJ Opinion Archives. **FROM THE RECORD.** Whitewash. *The racist history the Democratic Party wants you to forget.* by BRUCE BARTLETT. *Monday, December 24, 2007.* Mr. Bartlett is author of "Wrong on Race: The Democratic Party's Buried Past," to be published next month by Palgrave Macmillan. Retreived May 20, 2009 @ http://www.opinionjournal.com/extra/?id=110011033.
[884] From the WSJ Opinion Archives. **FROM THE RECORD.** Whitewash. *The racist history the Democratic Party wants you to forget.* by BRUCE BARTLETT. *Monday, December 24, 2007.* Mr. Bartlett is author of "Wrong on Race: The Democratic Party's Buried Past," to be published next month by Palgrave Macmillan. Retreived May 20, 2009 @ http://www.opinionjournal.com/extra/?id=110011033.
[885] From the WSJ Opinion Archives. **FROM THE RECORD.** Whitewash. *The racist history the Democratic Party wants you to forget.* by BRUCE BARTLETT. *Monday, December 24, 2007.* Mr. Bartlett is author of "Wrong on Race: The Democratic Party's Buried Past," to be published next month by Palgrave Macmillan. Retreived May 20, 2009 @ http://www.opinionjournal.com/extra/?id=110011033.
[886] From the WSJ Opinion Archives. **FROM THE RECORD.** Whitewash. *The racist history the Democratic Party wants you to forget.* by BRUCE BARTLETT. *Monday, December 24, 2007.* Mr. Bartlett is author of "Wrong on Race: The Democratic Party's Buried Past," to be published next month by Palgrave Macmillan. Retreived May 20, 2009 @ http://www.opinionjournal.com/extra/?id=110011033.
[887] From the WSJ Opinion Archives. **FROM THE RECORD.** Whitewash. *The racist history the Democratic Party wants you to forget.* by BRUCE BARTLETT. *Monday, December 24, 2007.* Mr. Bartlett is author of "Wrong on Race: The Democratic Party's Buried Past," to be published next month by Palgrave Macmillan. Retreived May 20, 2009 @ http://www.opinionjournal.com/extra/?id=110011033.
[888] From the WSJ Opinion Archives. **FROM THE RECORD.** Whitewash. *The racist history the Democratic Party wants you to forget.* by BRUCE BARTLETT. *Monday, December 24, 2007.* Mr. Bartlett is author of "Wrong on Race: The Democratic Party's Buried Past," to be published next month by Palgrave Macmillan. Retreived May 20, 2009 @ http://www.opinionjournal.com/extra/?id=110011033.
[889] Editorial, "The Political Future of the South," New York Times, May 10, 1900). From the WSJ Opinion Archives. **FROM THE RECORD.** Whitewash. *The racist history the Democratic Party wants you to forget.* by BRUCE BARTLETT. *Monday, December 24, 2007.* Mr. Bartlett is author of "Wrong on Race: The Democratic Party's Buried Past," to be published next month by Palgrave Macmillan. Retreived May 20, 2009 @ http://www.opinionjournal.com/extra/?id=110011033.
[890] ***Inaugural Addresses of the Presidents of the United States. 1989. William Howard Taft. Inaugural Address. Thursday, March 4, 1909 @ http://www.bartleby.com/124/pres43.html.***
[891] ***Inaugural Addresses of the Presidents of the United States. 1989. William Howard Taft. Inaugural Address. Thursday, March 4, 1909 @ http://www.bartleby.com/124/pres43.html.***
[892] Lies My Teacher Told Me. James W. Loewen.. Chapter 1. Handicapped by History—The Process of Hero-Making. A Touchstone Book published by Simon & Schuster. 1995.
[893] Lies My Teacher Told Me. James W. Loewen.. Chapter 1. Handicapped by History—The Process of Hero-Making. A Touchstone Book published by Simon & Schuster. 1995.
[894] Lies My Teacher Told Me. James W. Loewen.. Chapter 1. Handicapped by History—The Process of Hero-Making. A Touchstone Book published by Simon & Schuster. 1995.
[895] A MAN FOR THE TIMES. From the National Park Service. Booker T. Washington. An appreciation of the Man and his Times. Last Updated: 20-Feb-2009. Retrieved May 20, 2009.
[896] A MAN FOR THE TIMES. From the National Park Service. Booker T. Washington. An appreciation of the Man and his Times. Last Updated: 20-Feb-2009. Retrieved May 20, 2009.
[897] A MAN FOR THE TIMES. From the National Park Service. Booker T. Washington. An appreciation of the Man and his Times. Last Updated: 20-Feb-2009. Retrieved May 20, 2009.
[898] A MAN FOR THE TIMES. From the National Park Service. Booker T. Washington. An appreciation of the Man and his Times. Last Updated: 20-Feb-2009. Retrieved May 20, 2009.
[899] Dixiecrats Triumphant The menacing Mr. Wilson. *Charles Paul Freund* | December 18, 2002. Retrieved May 20, 2009 @ http://www.reason.com/news/show/33906.html.
[900] Dixiecrats Triumphant The menacing Mr. Wilson. *Charles Paul Freund* | December 18, 2002. Retrieved May 20, 2009 @ http://www.reason.com/news/show/33906.html.
[901] Dixiecrats Triumphant The menacing Mr. Wilson. *Charles Paul Freund* | December 18, 2002. Retrieved May 20, 2009 @ http://www.reason.com/news/show/33906.html.
[902] Lies My Teacher Told Me. James W. Loewen.. Chapter 1. Handicapped by History—The Process of Hero-Making. A Touchstone Book published by Simon & Schuster. 1995.
[903] Dixiecrats Triumphant The menacing Mr. Wilson. *Charles Paul Freund* | December 18, 2002. Retrieved May 20, 2009 @ http://www.reason.com/news/show/33906.html.
[904] Quote from Victoria Bissell Brown. Wilson-A Portrait. Afircan American. From PBS.com Retrieved May 20, 2009 @ http://www.pbs.org/wgbh/amex/wilson/portrait/wp_african.html.
[905] Dixiecrats Triumphant The menacing Mr. Wilson. *Charles Paul Freund* | December 18, 2002. Retrieved May 20, 2009 @ http://www.reason.com/news/show/33906.html.
[906] Lies My Teacher Told Me. James W. Loewen.. Chapter 1. Handicapped by History—The Process of Hero-Making. A Touchstone Book published by Simon & Schuster. 1995.
[907] Wilson-A Portrait. African American. From PBS.com Retrieved May 20, 2009 @ http://www.pbs.org/wgbh/amex/wilson/portrait/wp_african.html.
[908] Lies My Teacher Told Me. James W. Loewen.. Chapter 1. Handicapped by History—The Process of Hero-Making. A Touchstone Book published by Simon & Schuster. 1995.
[909] Dixiecrats Triumphant The menacing Mr. Wilson. *Charles Paul Freund* | December 18, 2002. Retrieved May 20, 2009 @ http://www.reason.com/news/show/33906.html.
[910] The Progressive Era and Race: Reform and Reaction, 1900–1917, by David W. Southern, Wheeling, W.V.: Harlan Davidson, 240 pages. Review by Damon W. Root | May 2006: When Bigots Become Reformers The Progressive Era's shameful record on race. Retrieved @ http://www.reason.com/news/show/36650.html.
[911] Wilson-A Portrait. African American. From PBS.com Retrieved May 20, 2009 @ http://www.pbs.org/wgbh/amex/wilson/portrait/wp_african.html.
[912] Dixiecrats Triumphant The menacing Mr. Wilson. *Charles Paul Freund* | December 18, 2002. Retrieved May 20, 2009 @ http://www.reason.com/news/show/33906.html.
[913] Wilson-A Portrait. African American. From PBS.com Retrieved May 20, 2009 @ http://www.pbs.org/wgbh/amex/wilson/portrait/wp_african.html.
[914] Dixiecrats Triumphant The menacing Mr. Wilson. *Charles Paul Freund* | December 18, 2002. Retrieved May 20, 2009 @ http://www.reason.com/news/show/33906.html.
[915] From the WSJ Opinion Archives. **FROM THE RECORD.** Whitewash. *The racist history the Democratic Party wants you to forget.* by BRUCE BARTLETT. *Monday, December 24, 2007.* Mr. Bartlett is author of "Wrong on Race: The Democratic Party's Buried Past," to be published next month by Palgrave Macmillan. Retreived May 20, 2009 @ http://www.opinionjournal.com/extra/?id=110011033.
[916] From the WSJ Opinion Archives. **FROM THE RECORD.** Whitewash. *The racist history the Democratic Party wants you to forget.* by BRUCE BARTLETT. *Monday, December 24, 2007.* Mr. Bartlett is author of "Wrong on Race: The Democratic Party's Buried Past," to be published next month by Palgrave Macmillan. Retreived May 20, 2009 @ http://www.opinionjournal.com/extra/?id=110011033.

[917] From the WSJ Opinion Archives. **FROM THE RECORD.** Whitewash. *The racist history the Democratic Party wants you to forget.* by BRUCE BARTLETT. *Monday, December 24, 2007.* Mr. Bartlett is author of "Wrong on Race: The Democratic Party's Buried Past," to be published next month by Palgrave Macmillan. Retreived May 20, 2009 @ http://www.opinionjournal.com/extra/?id=110011033.

[918] From the WSJ Opinion Archives. **FROM THE RECORD.** Whitewash. *The racist history the Democratic Party wants you to forget.* by BRUCE BARTLETT. *Monday, December 24, 2007.* Mr. Bartlett is author of "Wrong on Race: The Democratic Party's Buried Past," to be published next month by Palgrave Macmillan. Retreived May 20, 2009 @ http://www.opinionjournal.com/extra/?id=110011033.

[919] The Birth Of A Nation (1915). Review by Tim Dirks. Retrieved May 20, 2009 @ http://www.filmsite.org/birt.html.

[920] The Birth Of A Nation (1915). Review by Tim Dirks. Retrieved May 20, 2009 @ http://www.filmsite.org/birt.html.

[921] Birth of a Nation. D.W. Griffith. Retrieved May 2009 @ http://www.sparknotes.com/film/birthofanation/context.html.

[922] The Birth Of A Nation (1915). Review by Tim Dirks. Retrieved May 20, 2009 @ http://www.filmsite.org/birt.html.

[923] The Birth Of A Nation (1915). Review by Tim Dirks. Retrieved May 20, 2009 @ http://www.filmsite.org/birt.html.

[924] The Birth of a Nation (1915). Roger Ebert / March 30, 2003. Retrieved May 20, 2009 @ http://rogerebert.suntimes.com/apps/pbcs.dll/article?AID=/20030330/REVIEWS08/303300301/1023.

[925] The Birth of a Nation (1915). Roger Ebert / March 30, 2003. Retrieved May 20, 2009 @ http://rogerebert.suntimes.com/apps/pbcs.dll/article?AID=/20030330/REVIEWS08/303300301/1023.

[926] The Birth of a Nation (1915). Roger Ebert / March 30, 2003. Retrieved May 20, 2009 @ http://rogerebert.suntimes.com/apps/pbcs.dll/article?AID=/20030330/REVIEWS08/303300301/1023.

[927] "Art [and History] by Lightning Flash": *The Birth of a Nation* and Black Protest. Retrieved May 20, 2009 @ http://chnm.gmu.edu/features/episodes/birthofanation.html.

[928] "Art [and History] by Lightning Flash": *The Birth of a Nation* and Black Protest. Retrieved May 20, 2009 @ http://chnm.gmu.edu/features/episodes/birthofanation.html.

[929] **The Birth of a Nation (1915)** Author: Preston Mark Stone from New York, NY. Retrieved May 20, 2009 @ http://www.imdb.com/title/tt0004972/.

[930] D.W. Griffith, *The Birth of a Nation* (1915). Retreved May 2009 @ http://www.library.csi.cuny.edu/dept/history/lavender/birth.html.

[931] The Birth Of A Nation (1915). Review by Tim Dirks. Retrieved May 20, 2009 @ http://www.filmsite.org/birt.html.

[932] The Birth Of A Nation (1915). Review by Tim Dirks. Retrieved May 20, 2009 @ http://www.filmsite.org/birt.html.

[933] Birth of a Nation. D.W. Griffith. Retrieved May 2009 @ http://www.sparknotes.com/film/birthofanation/context.html.

[934] Dixiecrats Triumphant The menacing Mr. Wilson. *Charles Paul Freund* | December 18, 2002. Retrieved May 20, 2009 @ http://www.reason.com/news/show/33906.html.

[935] "Art [and History] by Lightning Flash": *The Birth of a Nation* and Black Protest. Retrieved May 20, 2009 @ http://chnm.gmu.edu/features/episodes/birthofanation.html.

[936] Birth of a Nation. D.W. Griffith. Retrieved May 2009 @ http://www.sparknotes.com/film/birthofanation/context.html.

[937] Birth of a Nation. D.W. Griffith. Retrieved May 2009 @ http://www.sparknotes.com/film/birthofanation/context.html.

[938] Dixiecrats Triumphant The menacing Mr. Wilson. *Charles Paul Freund* | December 18, 2002. Retrieved May 20, 2009 @ http://www.reason.com/news/show/33906.html.

[939] The Birth Of A Nation (1915). Review by Tim Dirks. Retrieved May 20, 2009 @ http://www.filmsite.org/birt.html.

[940] The Birth Of A Nation (1915). Review by Tim Dirks. Retrieved May 20, 2009 @ http://www.filmsite.org/birt.html.

[941] The Birth of a Nation (1915). Roger Ebert / March 30, 2003. Retrieved May 20, 2009 @ http://rogerebert.suntimes.com/apps/pbcs.dll/article?AID=/20030330/REVIEWS08/303300301/1023.

[942] The Birth of a Nation (1915). Roger Ebert / March 30, 2003. Retrieved May 20, 2009 @ http://rogerebert.suntimes.com/apps/pbcs.dll/article?AID=/20030330/REVIEWS08/303300301/1023.

[943] The Birth Of A Nation (1915). Review by Tim Dirks. Retrieved May 20, 2009 @ http://www.filmsite.org/birt.html.

[944] D.W. Griffith, *The Birth of a Nation* (1915). Retreved May 2009 @ http://www.library.csi.cuny.edu/dept/history/lavender/birth.html.

[945] Birth of a Nation. D.W. Griffith. Retrieved May 2009 @ http://www.sparknotes.com/film/birthofanation/context.html.

[946] D.W. Griffith, *The Birth of a Nation* (1915). Retreved May 2009 @ http://www.library.csi.cuny.edu/dept/history/lavender/birth.html.

[947] Birth of a Nation. D.W. Griffith. Retrieved May 2009 @ http://www.sparknotes.com/film/birthofanation/context.html.

[948] Wilson-A Portrait. African American. From PBS.com Retrieved May 20, 2009 @ http://www.pbs.org/wgbh/amex/wilson/portrait/wp_african.html.

[949] Wilson-A Portrait. African American. From PBS.com Retrieved May 20, 2009 @ http://www.pbs.org/wgbh/amex/wilson/portrait/wp_african.html.

[950] Wilson-A Portrait. African American. From PBS.com Retrieved May 20, 2009 @ http://www.pbs.org/wgbh/amex/wilson/portrait/wp_african.html.

[951] A MAN FOR THE TIMES. From the National Park Service. Booker T. Washington. An appreciation of the Man and his Times. Last Updated: 20-Feb-2009. Retrieved May 20, 2009.

[952] A MAN FOR THE TIMES. From the National Park Service. Booker T. Washington. An appreciation of the Man and his Times. Last Updated: 20-Feb-2009. Retrieved May 20, 2009.

[953] A MAN FOR THE TIMES. From the National Park Service. Booker T. Washington. An appreciation of the Man and his Times. Last Updated: 20-Feb-2009. Retrieved May 20, 2009.

[954] Wilson-A Portrait. African American. From PBS.com Retrieved May 20, 2009 @ http://www.pbs.org/wgbh/amex/wilson/portrait/wp_african.html.

[955] Wilson-A Portrait. African American. From PBS.com Retrieved May 20, 2009 @ http://www.pbs.org/wgbh/amex/wilson/portrait/wp_african.html.

[956] Wilson-A Portrait. African American. From PBS.com Retrieved May 20, 2009 @ http://www.pbs.org/wgbh/amex/wilson/portrait/wp_african.html.

[957] Wilson-A Portrait. African American. From PBS.com Retrieved May 20, 2009 @ http://www.pbs.org/wgbh/amex/wilson/portrait/wp_african.html.

[958] Wilson-A Portrait. African American. From PBS.com Retrieved May 20, 2009 @ http://www.pbs.org/wgbh/amex/wilson/portrait/wp_african.html.

[959] Wilson-A Portrait. African American. From PBS.com Retrieved May 20, 2009 @ http://www.pbs.org/wgbh/amex/wilson/portrait/wp_african.html.

[960] Wilson-A Portrait. African American. From PBS.com Retrieved May 20, 2009 @ http://www.pbs.org/wgbh/amex/wilson/portrait/wp_african.html.

[961] Wilson-A Portrait. African American. From PBS.com Retrieved May 20, 2009 @ http://www.pbs.org/wgbh/amex/wilson/portrait/wp_african.html.

[962] Wilson-A Portrait. African American. From PBS.com Retrieved May 20, 2009 @ http://www.pbs.org/wgbh/amex/wilson/portrait/wp_african.html.

[963] The Progressive Era and Race: Reform and Reaction, 1900–1917, by David W. Southern, Wheeling, W.V.: Harlan Davidson, 240 pages. Review by Damon W. Root | May 2006: When Bigots Become Reformers The Progressive Era's shameful record on race. Retrieved @ http://www.reason.com/news/show/36650.html.

[964] Lies My Teacher Told Me. James W. Loewen.. Chapter 1. Handicapped by History—The Process of Hero-Making. A Touchstone Book published by Simon & Schuster. 1995.

[965] Lies My Teacher Told Me. James W. Loewen.. Chapter 1. Handicapped by History—The Process of Hero-Making. A Touchstone Book published by Simon & Schuster. 1995.

[966] D.W. Griffith, *The Birth of a Nation* (1915). Retreved May 2009 @ http://www.library.csi.cuny.edu/dept/history/lavender/birth.html.

[967] Birth of a Nation. D.W. Griffith. Retrieved May 2009 @ http://www.sparknotes.com/film/birthofanation/context.html.

[968] Lies My Teacher Told Me. James W. Loewen.. Chapter 1. Handicapped by History—The Process of Hero-Making. A Touchstone Book published by Simon & Schuster. 1995.

[969] Dixiecrats Triumphant The menacing Mr. Wilson. *Charles Paul Freund* | December 18, 2002. Retrieved May 20, 2009 @ http://www.reason.com/news/show/33906.html.

[970] Dixiecrats Triumphant The menacing Mr. Wilson. *Charles Paul Freund* | December 18, 2002. Retrieved May 20, 2009 @ http://www.reason.com/news/show/33906.html.

[971] **Eugenic Laws Against Race Mixing.** Paul Lombardo, University of Virginia http://www.eugenicsarchive.org/html/eugenics/essay7text.html.

[972] **Eugenic Laws Against Race Mixing.** Paul Lombardo, University of Virginia http://www.eugenicsarchive.org/html/eugenics/essay7text.html.

[973] **Eugenic Laws Against Race Mixing.** Paul Lombardo, University of Virginia http://www.eugenicsarchive.org/html/eugenics/essay7text.html.

[974] **Eugenic Laws Against Race Mixing.** Paul Lombardo, University of Virginia http://www.eugenicsarchive.org/html/eugenics/essay7text.html.

[975] **Eugenic Laws Against Race Mixing.** Paul Lombardo, University of Virginia http://www.eugenicsarchive.org/html/eugenics/essay7text.html.

[976] **Eugenic Laws Against Race Mixing.** Paul Lombardo, University of Virginia http://www.eugenicsarchive.org/html/eugenics/essay7text.html.

[977] **Eugenic Laws Against Race Mixing.** Paul Lombardo, University of Virginia http://www.eugenicsarchive.org/html/eugenics/essay7text.html.

[978] **Eugenic Laws Against Race Mixing.** Paul Lombardo, University of Virginia http://www.eugenicsarchive.org/html/eugenics/essay7text.html.

[979] **Eugenic Laws Against Race Mixing.** Paul Lombardo, University of Virginia http://www.eugenicsarchive.org/html/eugenics/essay7text.html.

[980] **Eugenic Laws Against Race Mixing.** Paul Lombardo, University of Virginia http://www.eugenicsarchive.org/html/eugenics/essay7text.html.

[981] **Eugenic Laws Against Race Mixing.** Paul Lombardo, University of Virginia http://www.eugenicsarchive.org/html/eugenics/essay7text.html.

[982] 1921-1940. **April 26, 1932. Cotton Tom's Last Blast.** Retrieved May 20, 2009 @ http://www.senate.gov/artandhistory/history/minute/Cotton_Toms_Last_Blast.htm.

[983] 1921-1940. **April 26, 1932. Cotton Tom's Last Blast.** Retrieved May 20, 2009 @ http://www.senate.gov/artandhistory/history/minute/Cotton_Toms_Last_Blast.htm.

[984] 1921-1940. **April 26, 1932. Cotton Tom's Last Blast.** Retrieved May 20, 2009 @ http://www.senate.gov/artandhistory/history/minute/Cotton_Toms_Last_Blast.htm.

[985] National Affairs: Again, Heflin. Monday, Feb. 17, 1930. Retrieved May 20, 2009 from http://www.time.com/time/magazine/article/0,9171,738655,00.html.

[986] National Affairs: Again, Heflin. Monday, Feb. 17, 1930. Retrieved May 20, 2009 from http://www.time.com/time/magazine/article/0,9171,738655,00.html.

[987] National Affairs: Again, Heflin. Monday, Feb. 17, 1930. Retrieved May 20, 2009 from http://www.time.com/time/magazine/article/0,9171,738655,00.html.

[988] National Affairs: Again, Heflin. Monday, Feb. 17, 1930. Retrieved May 20, 2009 from http://www.time.com/time/magazine/article/0,9171,738655,00.html.

[989] 1921-1940. **April 26, 1932. Cotton Tom's Last Blast.** Retrieved May 20, 2009 @ http://www.senate.gov/artandhistory/history/minute/Cotton_Toms_Last_Blast.htm.

[990] 1921-1940. **April 26, 1932. Cotton Tom's Last Blast.** Retrieved May 20, 2009 @ http://www.senate.gov/artandhistory/history/minute/Cotton_Toms_Last_Blast.htm.

[991] 1921-1940. **April 26, 1932. Cotton Tom's Last Blast.** Retrieved May 20, 2009 @ http://www.senate.gov/artandhistory/history/minute/Cotton_Toms_Last_Blast.htm.

[992] 1921-1940. **April 26, 1932. Cotton Tom's Last Blast.** Retrieved May 20, 2009 @ http://www.senate.gov/artandhistory/history/minute/Cotton_Toms_Last_Blast.htm.

[993] 1921-1940. **April 26, 1932. Cotton Tom's Last Blast.** Retrieved May 20, 2009 @ http://www.senate.gov/artandhistory/history/minute/Cotton_Toms_Last_Blast.htm.

[994] 1921-1940. **April 26, 1932. Cotton Tom's Last Blast.** Retrieved May 20, 2009 @ http://www.senate.gov/artandhistory/history/minute/Cotton_Toms_Last_Blast.htm.

[995] 1921-1940. **April 26, 1932. Cotton Tom's Last Blast.** Retrieved May 20, 2009 @ http://www.senate.gov/artandhistory/history/minute/Cotton_Toms_Last_Blast.htm.

[996] 1921-1940. **April 26, 1932. Cotton Tom's Last Blast.** Retrieved May 20, 2009 @ http://www.senate.gov/artandhistory/history/minute/Cotton_Toms_Last_Blast.htm.

[997] 1921-1940. **April 26, 1932. Cotton Tom's Last Blast.** Retrieved May 20, 2009 @ http://www.senate.gov/artandhistory/history/minute/Cotton_Toms_Last_Blast.htm.

[998] 1921-1940. **April 26, 1932. Cotton Tom's Last Blast.** Retrieved May 20, 2009 @ http://www.senate.gov/artandhistory/history/minute/Cotton_Toms_Last_Blast.htm.

[999] From the WSJ Opinion Archives. **FROM THE RECORD.** Whitewash. *The racist history the Democratic Party wants you to forget.* by BRUCE BARTLETT. *Monday, December 24, 2007.* Mr. Bartlett is author of "Wrong on Race: The Democratic Party's Buried Past," to be published next month by Palgrave Macmillan. Retreived May 20, 2009 @ http://www.opinionjournal.com/extra/?id=110011033.

[1000] The Progressive Era and Race: Reform and Reaction, 1900–1917, by David W. Southern, Wheeling, W.V.: Harlan Davidson, 240 pages. Review by Damon W. Root | May 2006: When Bigots Become Reformers The Progressive Era's shameful record on race. Retrieved @ http://www.reason.com/news/show/36650.html.

[1001] From the WSJ Opinion Archives. **FROM THE RECORD.** Whitewash. *The racist history the Democratic Party wants you to forget.* by BRUCE BARTLETT. *Monday, December 24, 2007.* Mr. Bartlett is author of "Wrong on Race: The Democratic Party's Buried Past," to be published next month by Palgrave Macmillan. Retreived May 20, 2009 @ http://www.opinionjournal.com/extra/?id=110011033.

[1002] The Progressive Era and Race: Reform and Reaction, 1900–1917, by David W. Southern, Wheeling, W.V.: Harlan Davidson, 240 pages. Review by Damon W. Root | May 2006: When Bigots Become Reformers The Progressive Era's shameful record on race. Retrieved @ http://www.reason.com/news/show/36650.html.

[1003] The Progressive Era and Race: Reform and Reaction, 1900–1917, by David W. Southern, Wheeling, W.V.: Harlan Davidson, 240 pages. Review by Damon W. Root | May 2006: When Bigots Become Reformers The Progressive Era's shameful record on race. Retrieved @ http://www.reason.com/news/show/36650.html.

[1004] The Progressive Era and Race: Reform and Reaction, 1900–1917, by David W. Southern, Wheeling, W.V.: Harlan Davidson, 240 pages. Review by Damon W. Root | May 2006: When Bigots Become Reformers The Progressive Era's shameful record on race. Retrieved @ http://www.reason.com/news/show/36650.html.

[1005] From the WSJ Opinion Archives. **FROM THE RECORD.** Whitewash. *The racist history the Democratic Party wants you to forget.* by BRUCE BARTLETT. *Monday, December 24, 2007.* Mr. Bartlett is author of "Wrong on Race: The Democratic Party's Buried Past," to be published next month by Palgrave Macmillan. Retreived May 20, 2009 @ http://www.opinionjournal.com/extra/?id=110011033.

[1006] From the WSJ Opinion Archives. **FROM THE RECORD.** Whitewash. *The racist history the Democratic Party wants you to forget.* by BRUCE BARTLETT. *Monday, December 24, 2007.* Mr. Bartlett is author of "Wrong on Race: The Democratic Party's Buried Past," to be published next month by Palgrave Macmillan. Retreived May 20, 2009 @ http://www.opinionjournal.com/extra/?id=110011033.

[1007] Grover Cleveland. The Complete Book of U.S. Presidents. William A. DeGregorio. Revised and Updated Through 2002. Fifth Edition. Gramercy Books. Pag 348.

[1008] From the WSJ Opinion Archives. **FROM THE RECORD.** Whitewash. *The racist history the Democratic Party wants you to forget.* by BRUCE BARTLETT. *Monday, December 24, 2007.* Mr. Bartlett is author of "Wrong on Race: The Democratic Party's Buried Past," to be published next month by Palgrave Macmillan. Retreived May 20, 2009 @ http://www.opinionjournal.com/extra/?id=110011033.

[1009] From the WSJ Opinion Archives. **FROM THE RECORD.** Whitewash. *The racist history the Democratic Party wants you to forget.* by BRUCE BARTLETT. *Monday, December 24, 2007.* Mr. Bartlett is author of "Wrong on Race: The Democratic Party's Buried Past," to be published next month by Palgrave Macmillan. Retreived May 20, 2009 @ http://www.opinionjournal.com/extra/?id=110011033.

[1010] From the WSJ Opinion Archives. **FROM THE RECORD.** Whitewash. *The racist history the Democratic Party wants you to forget.* by BRUCE BARTLETT. *Monday, December 24, 2007.* Mr. Bartlett is author of "Wrong on Race: The Democratic Party's Buried Past," to be published next month by Palgrave Macmillan. Retreived May 20, 2009 @ http://www.opinionjournal.com/extra/?id=110011033.

[1011] The Progressive Era and Race: Reform and Reaction, 1900–1917, by David W. Southern, Wheeling, W.V.: Harlan Davidson, 240 pages. Review by Damon W. Root | May 2006: When Bigots Become Reformers The Progressive Era's shameful record on race. Retrieved @ http://www.reason.com/news/show/36650.html.

[1012] The Progressive Era and Race: Reform and Reaction, 1900–1917, by David W. Southern, Wheeling, W.V.: Harlan Davidson, 240 pages. Review by Damon W. Root | May 2006: When Bigots Become Reformers The Progressive Era's shameful record on race. Retrieved @ http://www.reason.com/news/show/36650.html.

[1013] The Progressive Era and Race: Reform and Reaction, 1900–1917, by David W. Southern, Wheeling, W.V.: Harlan Davidson, 240 pages. Review by Damon W. Root | May 2006: When Bigots Become Reformers The Progressive Era's shameful record on race. Retrieved @ http://www.reason.com/news/show/36650.html.

[1014] The Progressive Era and Race: Reform and Reaction, 1900–1917, by David W. Southern, Wheeling, W.V.: Harlan Davidson, 240 pages. Review by Damon W. Root | May 2006: When Bigots Become Reformers The Progressive Era's shameful record on race. Retrieved @ http://www.reason.com/news/show/36650.html.

[1015] The Progressive Era and Race: Reform and Reaction, 1900–1917, by David W. Southern, Wheeling, W.V.: Harlan Davidson, 240 pages. Review by Damon W. Root | May 2006: When Bigots Become Reformers The Progressive Era's shameful record on race. Retrieved @ http://www.reason.com/news/show/36650.html.

[1016] The Progressive Era and Race: Reform and Reaction, 1900–1917, by David W. Southern, Wheeling, W.V.: Harlan Davidson, 240 pages. Review by Damon W. Root | May 2006: When Bigots Become Reformers The Progressive Era's shameful record on race. Retrieved @ http://www.reason.com/news/show/36650.html.

[1017] The Progressive Era and Race: Reform and Reaction, 1900–1917, by David W. Southern, Wheeling, W.V.: Harlan Davidson, 240 pages. Review by Damon W. Root | May 2006: When Bigots Become Reformers The Progressive Era's shameful record on race. Retrieved @ http://www.reason.com/news/show/36650.html.

[1018] The Progressive Era and Race: Reform and Reaction, 1900–1917, by David W. Southern, Wheeling, W.V.: Harlan Davidson, 240 pages. Review by Damon W. Root | May 2006: When Bigots Become Reformers The Progressive Era's shameful record on race. Retrieved @ http://www.reason.com/news/show/36650.html.

[1019] February 26, 1939 - Eleanor Roosevelt Resigns from the Daughters of the American Revolution. Retrieved June 20, 2009 @ from http://www.fdrlibrary.marist.edu/tmirhfee.html.

[1020] February 26, 1939 - Eleanor Roosevelt Resigns from the Daughters of the American Revolution. Retrieved June 20, 2009 @ from http://www.fdrlibrary.marist.edu/tmirhfee.html.

[1021] February 26, 1939 - Eleanor Roosevelt Resigns from the Daughters of the American Revolution. Retrieved June 20, 2009 @ from http://www.fdrlibrary.marist.edu/tmirhfee.html.

[1022] February 26, 1939 - Eleanor Roosevelt Resigns from the Daughters of the American Revolution. Retrieved June 20, 2009 @ from http://www.fdrlibrary.marist.edu/tmirhfee.html.

[1023] February 26, 1939 - Eleanor Roosevelt Resigns from the Daughters of the American Revolution. Retrieved June 20, 2009 @ from http://www.fdrlibrary.marist.edu/tmirhfee.html.

[1024] Eleanor Roosevelt's letter of resignation and "My Day" column: FEBRUARY 27, 1939. MY DAY. Eleanor Roosevelt. Taken from February 26, 1939 - Eleanor Roosevelt Resigns from the Daughters of the American Revolution. Retrieved June 20, 2009 @ from http://www.fdrlibrary.marist.edu/tmirhfee.html.

[1025] From the WSJ Opinion Archives. **FROM THE RECORD.** Whitewash. *The racist history the Democratic Party wants you to forget.* by BRUCE BARTLETT. *Monday, December 24, 2007.* Mr. Bartlett is author of "Wrong on Race: The Democratic Party's Buried Past," to be published next month by Palgrave Macmillan. Retreived May 20, 2009 @ http://www.opinionjournal.com/extra/?id=110011033.

[1026] From the WSJ Opinion Archives. **FROM THE RECORD.** Whitewash. *The racist history the Democratic Party wants you to forget.* by BRUCE BARTLETT. *Monday, December 24, 2007.* Mr. Bartlett is author of "Wrong on Race: The Democratic Party's Buried Past," to be published next month by Palgrave Macmillan. Retreived May 20, 2009 @ http://www.opinionjournal.com/extra/?id=110011033.

[1027] By Randall Kennedy, Pantheon. Nigger: The Strange Career of a Troublesome Word Friday, January 11, 2001, Chapter One The Protean N-Word. Retrieved June 10, 2009 @ http://www.washingtonpost.com/wp-srv/style/longterm/books/chap1/nigger.htm.

[1028] By Randall Kennedy, Pantheon. Nigger: The Strange Career of a Troublesome Word Friday, January 11, 2001, Chapter One The Protean N-Word. Retrieved June 10, 2009 @ http://www.washingtonpost.com/wp-srv/style/longterm/books/chap1/nigger.htm.

[1029] By Randall Kennedy, Pantheon. Nigger: The Strange Career of a Troublesome Word Friday, January 11, 2001, Chapter One The Protean N-Word. Retrieved June 10, 2009 @ http://www.washingtonpost.com/wp-srv/style/longterm/books/chap1/nigger.htm.

[1030] By Randall Kennedy, Pantheon. Nigger: The Strange Career of a Troublesome Word Friday, January 11, 2001, Chapter One The Protean N-Word. Retrieved June 10, 2009 @ http://www.washingtonpost.com/wp-srv/style/longterm/books/chap1/nigger.htm.

[1031] From the WSJ Opinion Archives. **FROM THE RECORD.** Whitewash. *The racist history the Democratic Party wants you to forget.* by BRUCE BARTLETT. *Monday, December 24, 2007.* Mr. Bartlett is author of "Wrong on Race: The Democratic Party's Buried Past," to be published next month by Palgrave Macmillan. Retreived May 20, 2009 @ http://www.opinionjournal.com/extra/?id=110011033.

[1032] **Educator Kenneth Clark and His Fight for Integration.** by Margot Adler. *All Things Considered,* May 2, 2005http://www.npr.org/templates/story/story.php?storyId=4627755.

[1033] Section 1. A New Beginning. Chapter 32: The Civil Rights Era 1954-1975. History of a Free Nation. Henry W. Bragdon, Samuel P. McClutchen, and Donald Ritchie. 1998. Glencoe McGraw-Hill. Page 899.

[1034] Section 2. Sucesses and Setbacks. Chapter 32: The Civil Rights Era 1954-1975. History of a Free Nation. Henry W. Bragdon, Samuel P. McClutchen, and Donald Ritchie. 1998. Glencoe McGraw-Hill. Page 908.

[1035] By Randall Kennedy, Pantheon. Nigger: The Strange Career of a Troublesome Word Friday, January 11, 2001, Chapter One The Protean N-Word. Retrieved June 10, 2009 @ http://www.washingtonpost.com/wp-srv/style/longterm/books/chap1/nigger.htm.

[1036] From the WSJ Opinion Archives. **FROM THE RECORD.** Whitewash. *The racist history the Democratic Party wants you to forget.* by BRUCE BARTLETT. *Monday, December 24, 2007.* Mr. Bartlett is author of "Wrong on Race: The Democratic Party's Buried Past," to be published next month by Palgrave Macmillan. Retreived May 20, 2009 @ http://www.opinionjournal.com/extra/?id=110011033.

[1037] From the WSJ Opinion Archives. **FROM THE RECORD.** Whitewash. *The racist history the Democratic Party wants you to forget.* by BRUCE BARTLETT. *Monday, December 24, 2007.* Mr. Bartlett is author of "Wrong on Race: The Democratic Party's Buried Past," to be published next month by Palgrave Macmillan. Retreived May 20, 2009 @ http://www.opinionjournal.com/extra/?id=110011033.

[1038] From the WSJ Opinion Archives. **FROM THE RECORD.** Whitewash. *The racist history the Democratic Party wants you to forget.* by BRUCE BARTLETT. *Monday, December 24, 2007.* Mr. Bartlett is author of "Wrong on Race: The Democratic Party's Buried Past," to be published next month by Palgrave Macmillan. Retreived May 20, 2009 @ http://www.opinionjournal.com/extra/?id=110011033.

[1039] From the WSJ Opinion Archives. **FROM THE RECORD.** Whitewash. *The racist history the Democratic Party wants you to forget.* by BRUCE BARTLETT. *Monday, December 24, 2007.* Mr. Bartlett is author of "Wrong on Race: The Democratic Party's Buried Past," to be published next month by Palgrave Macmillan. Retreived May 20, 2009 @ http://www.opinionjournal.com/extra/?id=110011033.

[1040] From the WSJ Opinion Archives. **FROM THE RECORD.** Whitewash. *The racist history the Democratic Party wants you to forget.* by BRUCE BARTLETT. *Monday, December 24, 2007.* Mr. Bartlett is author of "Wrong on Race: The Democratic Party's Buried Past," to be published next month by Palgrave Macmillan. Retreived May 20, 2009 @ http://www.opinionjournal.com/extra/?id=110011033.

[1041] Section 3. War on the Homefront. Chapter 25, World War 1 Era, 1914-1920. History of a Free Nation. Henry W. Bragdon, Samuel P. McClutchen, and Donald Ritchie. 1998. Glencoe McGraw-Hill. Page 699.

[1042] Section 3. War on the Homefront. Chapter 25, World War 1 Era, 1914-1920. History of a Free Nation. Henry W. Bragdon, Samuel P. McClutchen, and Donald Ritchie. 1998. Glencoe McGraw-Hill. Page 699.

[1043] Section 3. War on the Homefront. Chapter 25, World War 1 Era, 1914-1920. History of a Free Nation. Henry W. Bragdon, Samuel P. McClutchen, and Donald Ritchie. 1998. Glencoe McGraw-Hill. Page 699.

[1044] Section 3. War on the Homefront. Chapter 25, World War 1 Era, 1914-1920. History of a Free Nation. Henry W. Bragdon, Samuel P. McClutchen, and Donald Ritchie. 1998. Glencoe McGraw-Hill. Page 699.

[1045] Section 3. War on the Homefront. Chapter 25, World War 1 Era, 1914-1920. History of a Free Nation. Henry W. Bragdon, Samuel P. McClutchen, and Donald Ritchie. 1998. Glencoe McGraw-Hill. Page 699.

[1046] Lies My Teacher Told Me. James W. Loewen.. Chapter 1. Handicapped by History—The Process of Hero-Making. A Touchstone Book published by Simon & Schuster. 1995.

[1047] Section 3. War on the Homefront. Chapter 25, World War 1 Era, 1914-1920. History of a Free Nation. Henry W. Bragdon, Samuel P. McClutchen, and Donald Ritchie. 1998. Glencoe McGraw-Hill. Page 699.

[1048] Lies My Teacher Told Me. James W. Loewen.. Chapter 1. Handicapped by History—The Process of Hero-Making. A Touchstone Book published by Simon & Schuster. 1995.

[1049] Lies My Teacher Told Me. James W. Loewen.. Chapter 1. Handicapped by History—The Process of Hero-Making. A Touchstone Book published by Simon & Schuster. 1995.

[1050] Section 3. War on the Homefront. Chapter 25, World War 1 Era, 1914-1920. History of a Free Nation. Henry W. Bragdon, Samuel P. McClutchen, and Donald Ritchie. 1998. Glencoe McGraw-Hill. Page 699.

[1051] Lies My Teacher Told Me. James W. Loewen.. Chapter 1. Handicapped by History—The Process of Hero-Making. A Touchstone Book published by Simon & Schuster. 1995.

[1052] ***E. V. Debs. Statement to the Court. Upon Being Convicted of Violating the Sedition Act.*** Delivered: September 18, 1918. First Published: 1918. Source: *Court Stenographer.* Retrieved April 29, 2009 @ http://www.marxists.org/archive/debs/works/1918/court.htm.

[1053] ***E. V. Debs. Statement to the Court. Upon Being Convicted of Violating the Sedition Act.*** Delivered: September 18, 1918. First Published: 1918. Source: *Court Stenographer.* Retrieved April 29, 2009 @ http://www.marxists.org/archive/debs/works/1918/court.htm.

[1054] Lies My Teacher Told Me. James W. Loewen.. Chapter 1. Handicapped by History—The Process of Hero-Making. A Touchstone Book published by Simon & Schuster. 1995.

[1055] Lies My Teacher Told Me. James W. Loewen.. Chapter 1. Handicapped by History—The Process of Hero-Making. A Touchstone Book published by Simon & Schuster. 1995.
[1056] EUGENE V. DEBS DIES AFTER LONG ILLNESS; Socialist Leader Succumbs to Heart Ailments After Month in Illinois Sanitarium. ONCE LEADER OF RAIL UNION He Led Pullman Strike In 1895 -- Served Nearly Three Years In Prison for Opposing War. Special to The New York Times. October 21, 1926, Thursday. Section: AMUSEMENTS, Page 25, 1942 words http://select.nytimes.com/gst/abstract.html?res=F40812F7345E1B7A93C3AB178BD95F428285F9/.
[1057] Lies My Teacher Told Me. James W. Loewen.. Chapter 1. Handicapped by History—The Process of Hero-Making. A Touchstone Book published by Simon & Schuster. 1995.
[1058] Lies My Teacher Told Me. James W. Loewen.. Chapter 1. Handicapped by History—The Process of Hero-Making. A Touchstone Book published by Simon & Schuster. 1995.
[1059] Lies My Teacher Told Me. James W. Loewen.. Chapter 1. Handicapped by History—The Process of Hero-Making. A Touchstone Book published by Simon & Schuster. 1995.
[1060] Lies My Teacher Told Me. James W. Loewen.. Chapter 1. Handicapped by History—The Process of Hero-Making. A Touchstone Book published by Simon & Schuster. 1995.
[1061] Lies My Teacher Told Me. James W. Loewen.. Chapter 1. Handicapped by History—The Process of Hero-Making. A Touchstone Book published by Simon & Schuster. 1995.
[1062] From the WSJ Opinion Archives. **FROM THE RECORD.** Whitewash. *The racist history the Democratic Party wants you to forget.* by BRUCE BARTLETT. *Monday, December 24, 2007.* Mr. Bartlett is author of "Wrong on Race: The Democratic Party's Buried Past," to be published next month by Palgrave Macmillan. Retreived May 20, 2009 @ http://www.opinionjournal.com/extra/?id=110011033.
[1063] From the WSJ Opinion Archives. **FROM THE RECORD.** Whitewash. *The racist history the Democratic Party wants you to forget.* by BRUCE BARTLETT. *Monday, December 24, 2007.* Mr. Bartlett is author of "Wrong on Race: The Democratic Party's Buried Past," to be published next month by Palgrave Macmillan. Retreived May 20, 2009 @ http://www.opinionjournal.com/extra/?id=110011033.
[1064] From the WSJ Opinion Archives. **FROM THE RECORD.** Whitewash. *The racist history the Democratic Party wants you to forget.* by BRUCE BARTLETT. *Monday, December 24, 2007.* Mr. Bartlett is author of "Wrong on Race: The Democratic Party's Buried Past," to be published next month by Palgrave Macmillan. Retreived May 20, 2009 @ http://www.opinionjournal.com/extra/?id=110011033.
[1065] From the WSJ Opinion Archives. **FROM THE RECORD.** Whitewash. *The racist history the Democratic Party wants you to forget.* by BRUCE BARTLETT. *Monday, December 24, 2007.* Mr. Bartlett is author of "Wrong on Race: The Democratic Party's Buried Past," to be published next month by Palgrave Macmillan. Retreived May 20, 2009 @ http://www.opinionjournal.com/extra/?id=110011033.
[1066] 1921-1940. **April 26, 1932**. **Cotton Tom's Last Blast**. Retrieved May 20, 2009 @ http://www.senate.gov/artandhistory/history/minute/Cotton_Toms_Last_Blast.htm.
[1067] 1921-1940. **April 26, 1932**. **Cotton Tom's Last Blast**. Retrieved May 20, 2009 @ http://www.senate.gov/artandhistory/history/minute/Cotton_Toms_Last_Blast.htm.
[1068] National Affairs: Again, Heflin. Monday, Feb. 17, 1930. Retrieved May 20, 2009 from http://www.time.com/time/magazine/article/0,9171,738655,00.html.
[1069] 1921-1940. **April 26, 1932**. **Cotton Tom's Last Blast**. Retrieved May 20, 2009 @ http://www.senate.gov/artandhistory/history/minute/Cotton_Toms_Last_Blast.htm.
[1070] 1921-1940. **April 26, 1932**. **Cotton Tom's Last Blast**. Retrieved May 20, 2009 @ http://www.senate.gov/artandhistory/history/minute/Cotton_Toms_Last_Blast.htm.
[1071] 1921-1940. **April 26, 1932**. **Cotton Tom's Last Blast**. Retrieved May 20, 2009 @ http://www.senate.gov/artandhistory/history/minute/Cotton_Toms_Last_Blast.htm.
[1072] Warning Against the "Roman Catholic Party": Catholicism and the 1928 Election. Source: *Congressional Record* (January 28, 1928), 1st Session, 70th Congress, vol. 69, pt. 2, 1654–55, 1658. Retrieved @ http://historymatters.gmu.edu/d/5073/. Speech delivered by Thomas J. Heflin.
[1073] Warning Against the "Roman Catholic Party": Catholicism and the 1928 Election. Source: *Congressional Record* (January 28, 1928), 1st Session, 70th Congress, vol. 69, pt. 2, 1654–55, 1658. Retrieved @ http://historymatters.gmu.edu/d/5073/. Speech delivered by Thomas J. Heflin.
[1074] Warning Against the "Roman Catholic Party": Catholicism and the 1928 Election. Source: *Congressional Record* (January 28, 1928), 1st Session, 70th Congress, vol. 69, pt. 2, 1654–55, 1658. Retrieved @ http://historymatters.gmu.edu/d/5073/. Speech delivered by Thomas J. Heflin.
[1075] Warning Against the "Roman Catholic Party": Catholicism and the 1928 Election. Source: *Congressional Record* (January 28, 1928), 1st Session, 70th Congress, vol. 69, pt. 2, 1654–55, 1658. Retrieved @ http://historymatters.gmu.edu/d/5073/. Speech delivered by Thomas J. Heflin.
[1076] Warning Against the "Roman Catholic Party": Catholicism and the 1928 Election. Source: *Congressional Record* (January 28, 1928), 1st Session, 70th Congress, vol. 69, pt. 2, 1654–55, 1658. Retrieved @ http://historymatters.gmu.edu/d/5073/. Speech delivered by Thomas J. Heflin.
[1077] Warning Against the "Roman Catholic Party": Catholicism and the 1928 Election. Source: *Congressional Record* (January 28, 1928), 1st Session, 70th Congress, vol. 69, pt. 2, 1654–55, 1658. Retrieved @ http://historymatters.gmu.edu/d/5073/. Speech delivered by Thomas J. Heflin.
[1078] Warning Against the "Roman Catholic Party": Catholicism and the 1928 Election. Source: *Congressional Record* (January 28, 1928), 1st Session, 70th Congress, vol. 69, pt. 2, 1654–55, 1658. Retrieved @ http://historymatters.gmu.edu/d/5073/. Speech delivered by Thomas J. Heflin.
[1079] Warning Against the "Roman Catholic Party": Catholicism and the 1928 Election. Source: *Congressional Record* (January 28, 1928), 1st Session, 70th Congress, vol. 69, pt. 2, 1654–55, 1658. Retrieved @ http://historymatters.gmu.edu/d/5073/. Speech delivered by Thomas J. Heflin.
[1080] National Affairs: Again, Heflin. Monday, Feb. 17, 1930. Retrieved May 20, 2009 from http://www.time.com/time/magazine/article/0,9171,738655,00.html.
[1081] Warning Against the "Roman Catholic Party": Catholicism and the 1928 Election. Source: *Congressional Record* (January 28, 1928), 1st Session, 70th Congress, vol. 69, pt. 2, 1654–55, 1658. Retrieved @ http://historymatters.gmu.edu/d/5073/. Speech delivered by Thomas J. Heflin.
[1082] "I Will Not Be Influenced in Appointments": Al Smith Accepts the Nomination for President. Source: Courtesy of the Michigan State University, G. Robert Vincent Voice Library. Retrieved @ http://historymatters.gmu.edu/d/5075.
[1083] "I Will Not Be Influenced in Appointments": Al Smith Accepts the Nomination for President. Source: Courtesy of the Michigan State University, G. Robert Vincent Voice Library. Retrieved @ http://historymatters.gmu.edu/d/5075.
[1084] O'Connor, Vaughan, Cuomo, Al Smith, J.F.K. By Arthur Schlesinger Jr.; Arthur Schlesinger Jr. is professor in the humanities at the City University of New York. Published: Friday, February 2, 1990 A version of this op-ed appeared in print on Friday, February 2, 1990, on section A page 31 of the New York edition. See .http://www.nytimes.com/1990/02/02/opinion/o-connor-vaughan-cuomo-al-smith-jfk.html.
[1085] O'Connor, Vaughan, Cuomo, Al Smith, J.F.K. By Arthur Schlesinger Jr.; Arthur Schlesinger Jr. is professor in the humanities at the City University of New York. Published: Friday, February 2, 1990 A version of this op-ed appeared in print on Friday, February 2, 1990, on section A page 31 of the New York edition. See .http://www.nytimes.com/1990/02/02/opinion/o-connor-vaughan-cuomo-al-smith-jfk.html.
[1086] O'Connor, Vaughan, Cuomo, Al Smith, J.F.K. By Arthur Schlesinger Jr.; Arthur Schlesinger Jr. is professor in the humanities at the City University of New York. Published: Friday, February 2, 1990 A version of this op-ed appeared in print on Friday, February 2, 1990, on section A page 31 of the New York edition. See .http://www.nytimes.com/1990/02/02/opinion/o-connor-vaughan-cuomo-al-smith-jfk.html.
[1087] Origins of Eugenics. University of Virginia Health System, Claude Moore Health Sciences Library @ http://www.hsl.virginia.edu/historical/eugenics/2-origins.cfm.
[1088] Origins of Eugenics. University of Virginia Health System, Claude Moore Health Sciences Library @ http://www.hsl.virginia.edu/historical/eugenics/2-origins.cfm.
[1089] Origins of Eugenics. University of Virginia Health System, Claude Moore Health Sciences Library @ http://www.hsl.virginia.edu/historical/eugenics/2-origins.cfm.
[1090] Origins of Eugenics. University of Virginia Health System, Claude Moore Health Sciences Library @ http://www.hsl.virginia.edu/historical/eugenics/2-origins.cfm.
[1091] Origins of Eugenics. University of Virginia Health System, Claude Moore Health Sciences Library @ http://www.hsl.virginia.edu/historical/eugenics/2-origins.cfm.
[1092] **Eugenics in Virginia.** University of Virginia Health System, Claude Moore Health Sciences Library @ http://www.hsl.virginia.edu/historical/eugenics/4-influence.cfm.
[1093] Origins of Eugenics. University of Virginia Health System, Claude Moore Health Sciences Library @ http://www.hsl.virginia.edu/historical/eugenics/2-origins.cfm.
[1094] Origins of Eugenics. University of Virginia Health System, Claude Moore Health Sciences Library @ http://www.hsl.virginia.edu/historical/eugenics/2-origins.cfm.
[1095] Origins of Eugenics. University of Virginia Health System, Claude Moore Health Sciences Library @ http://www.hsl.virginia.edu/historical/eugenics/2-origins.cfm.
[1096] Harry H. Laughlin. For information contact: speccoll@truman.edu Retrieved April 28, 2009 @ http://library.truman.edu/manuscripts/laughlinbio.htm.
[1097] Harry Laughlin's "Model Eugenical Sterilization Law." Retrieved April 28, 2009 @ http://www.people.fas.harvard.edu/~wellerst/laughlin/.
[1098] Harry Laughlin's "Model Eugenical Sterilization Law." Retrieved April 28, 2009 @ http://www.people.fas.harvard.edu/~wellerst/laughlin/.
[1099] Harry H. Laughlin. For information contact: speccoll@truman.edu Retrieved April 28, 2009 @ http://library.truman.edu/manuscripts/laughlinbio.htm.
[1100] Harry Laughlin's "Model Eugenical Sterilization Law." Retrieved April 28, 2009 @ http://www.people.fas.harvard.edu/~wellerst/laughlin/.
[1101] Harry Laughlin's "Model Eugenical Sterilization Law." Retrieved April 28, 2009 @ http://www.people.fas.harvard.edu/~wellerst/laughlin/.
[1102] Harry Laughlin's "Model Eugenical Sterilization Law." Retrieved April 28, 2009 @ http://www.people.fas.harvard.edu/~wellerst/laughlin/.
[1103] Harry Laughlin's "Model Eugenical Sterilization Law." Retrieved April 28, 2009 @ http://www.people.fas.harvard.edu/~wellerst/laughlin/.
[1104] Harry Laughlin's "Model Eugenical Sterilization Law." Retrieved April 28, 2009 @ http://www.people.fas.harvard.edu/~wellerst/laughlin/.
[1105] Harry Laughlin's "Model Eugenical Sterilization Law." Retrieved April 28, 2009 @ http://www.people.fas.harvard.edu/~wellerst/laughlin/.
[1106] Harry Laughlin's "Model Eugenical Sterilization Law." Retrieved April 28, 2009 @ http://www.people.fas.harvard.edu/~wellerst/laughlin/.
[1107] Eugenical Sterilization in the United States. By HARRY HAMILTON LAUGHLIN. Published by the PSYCHOPATHIC LABORATORY OF THE MUNICIPAL COURT OF CHICAGO DECEMBER, 1922http://www.people.fas.harvard.edu/~wellerst/laughlin/.
[1108] Eugenical Sterilization in the United States. By HARRY HAMILTON LAUGHLIN. Published by the PSYCHOPATHIC LABORATORY OF THE MUNICIPAL COURT OF CHICAGO DECEMBER, 1922http://www.people.fas.harvard.edu/~wellerst/laughlin/.
[1109] Eugenical Sterilization in the United States. By HARRY HAMILTON LAUGHLIN. Published by the PSYCHOPATHIC LABORATORY OF THE MUNICIPAL COURT OF CHICAGO DECEMBER, 1922http://www.people.fas.harvard.edu/~wellerst/laughlin/.
[1110] Eugenical Sterilization in the United States. By HARRY HAMILTON LAUGHLIN. Published by the PSYCHOPATHIC LABORATORY OF THE MUNICIPAL COURT OF CHICAGO DECEMBER, 1922http://www.people.fas.harvard.edu/~wellerst/laughlin/.
[1111] Harry Laughlin's "Model Eugenical Sterilization Law." Retrieved April 28, 2009 @ http://www.people.fas.harvard.edu/~wellerst/laughlin/.
[1112] Harry H. Laughlin. For information contact: speccoll@truman.edu Retrieved April 28, 2009 @ http://library.truman.edu/manuscripts/laughlinbio.htm.
[1113] Harry H. Laughlin. For information contact: speccoll@truman.edu Retrieved April 28, 2009 @ http://library.truman.edu/manuscripts/laughlinbio.htm.
[1114] Eugenical Sterilization in the United States. By HARRY HAMILTON LAUGHLIN. Published by the PSYCHOPATHIC LABORATORY OF THE MUNICIPAL COURT OF CHICAGO DECEMBER, 1922http://www.people.fas.harvard.edu/~wellerst/laughlin/.

[1115] Eugenical Sterilization in the United States. By HARRY HAMILTON LAUGHLIN. Published by the PSYCHOPATHIC LABORATORY OF THE MUNICIPAL COURT OF CHICAGO DECEMBER, 1922http://www.people.fas.harvard.edu/~wellerst/laughlin/.
[1116] Eugenical Sterilization in the United States. By HARRY HAMILTON LAUGHLIN. Published by the PSYCHOPATHIC LABORATORY OF THE MUNICIPAL COURT OF CHICAGO DECEMBER, 1922http://www.people.fas.harvard.edu/~wellerst/laughlin/.
[1117] Eugenical Sterilization in the United States. By HARRY HAMILTON LAUGHLIN. Published by the PSYCHOPATHIC LABORATORY OF THE MUNICIPAL COURT OF CHICAGO DECEMBER, 1922http://www.people.fas.harvard.edu/~wellerst/laughlin/.
[1118] Eugenical Sterilization in the United States. By HARRY HAMILTON LAUGHLIN. Published by the PSYCHOPATHIC LABORATORY OF THE MUNICIPAL COURT OF CHICAGO DECEMBER, 1922http://www.people.fas.harvard.edu/~wellerst/laughlin/.
[1119] Was Nazi eugenics created in the US? Garland E. Allen A review of Edwin Black's *War Against the Weak*. http://www.nature.com/embor/journal/v5/n5/full/7400158.html.
[1120] The Horrifying American Roots of Nazi Eugenics.By Edwin Black. Orignially published in the *San Francisco Chronicle*. Retrieved @ http://hnn.us/articles/1796.html.
[1121] The Horrifying American Roots of Nazi Eugenics.By Edwin Black. Orignially published in the *San Francisco Chronicle*. Retrieved @ http://hnn.us/articles/1796.html.
[1122] The Horrifying American Roots of Nazi Eugenics.By Edwin Black. Orignially published in the *San Francisco Chronicle*. Retrieved @ http://hnn.us/articles/1796.html.
[1123] The Horrifying American Roots of Nazi Eugenics.By Edwin Black. Orignially published in the *San Francisco Chronicle*. Retrieved @ http://hnn.us/articles/1796.html.
[1124] The Horrifying American Roots of Nazi Eugenics.By Edwin Black. Orignially published in the *San Francisco Chronicle*. Retrieved @ http://hnn.us/articles/1796.html.
[1125] The Horrifying American Roots of Nazi Eugenics.By Edwin Black. Orignially published in the *San Francisco Chronicle*. Retrieved @ http://hnn.us/articles/1796.html.
[1126] Symposium and Exhibit Recognize 100 Year Anniversary of Indiana Eugenics Legislation: Hoosier State Led World In Enactment of Involuntary Sterilization Laws. February 28, 2007 http://www.medicine.indiana.edu/news_releases/viewRelease.php4?art=646&print=true.
[1127] INDIANA'S STERILIZATION STATUTE. Passed 1907, FULL TEXT. Passed 59-22 in the House, 28-16 in the Senate @ http://library.truman.edu/manuscripts/laughlinbio.htm.
[1128] Symposium and Exhibit Recognize 100 Year Anniversary of Indiana Eugenics Legislation: Hoosier State Led World In Enactment of Involuntary Sterilization Laws. February 28, 2007 http://www.medicine.indiana.edu/news_releases/viewRelease.php4?art=646&print=true.
[1129] Symposium and Exhibit Recognize 100 Year Anniversary of Indiana Eugenics Legislation: Hoosier State Led World In Enactment of Involuntary Sterilization Laws. February 28, 2007 http://www.medicine.indiana.edu/news_releases/viewRelease.php4?art=646&print=true.
[1130] Symposium and Exhibit Recognize 100 Year Anniversary of Indiana Eugenics Legislation: Hoosier State Led World In Enactment of Involuntary Sterilization Laws. February 28, 2007 http://www.medicine.indiana.edu/news_releases/viewRelease.php4?art=646&print=true.
[1131] **Carrie Buck, Virginia's Test Case** University of Virginia Health System, Claude Moore Health Sciences Library @ http://www.hsl.virginia.edu/historical/eugenics/3-buckvbell.cfm.
[1132] **Carrie Buck, Virginia's Test Case** University of Virginia Health System, Claude Moore Health Sciences Library @ http://www.hsl.virginia.edu/historical/eugenics/3-buckvbell.cfm.
[1133] **Carrie Buck, Virginia's Test Case** University of Virginia Health System, Claude Moore Health Sciences Library @ http://www.hsl.virginia.edu/historical/eugenics/3-buckvbell.cfm.
[1134] **Carrie Buck, Virginia's Test Case** University of Virginia Health System, Claude Moore Health Sciences Library @ http://www.hsl.virginia.edu/historical/eugenics/3-buckvbell.cfm.
[1135] **Carrie Buck, Virginia's Test Case** University of Virginia Health System, Claude Moore Health Sciences Library @ http://www.hsl.virginia.edu/historical/eugenics/3-buckvbell.cfm.
[1136] **Carrie Buck, Virginia's Test Case** University of Virginia Health System, Claude Moore Health Sciences Library @ http://www.hsl.virginia.edu/historical/eugenics/3-buckvbell.cfm.
[1137] **Carrie Buck, Virginia's Test Case** University of Virginia Health System, Claude Moore Health Sciences Library @ http://www.hsl.virginia.edu/historical/eugenics/3-buckvbell.cfm.
[1138] **Carrie Buck, Virginia's Test Case** University of Virginia Health System, Claude Moore Health Sciences Library @ http://www.hsl.virginia.edu/historical/eugenics/3-buckvbell.cfm.
[1139] **Carrie Buck, Virginia's Test Case** University of Virginia Health System, Claude Moore Health Sciences Library @ http://www.hsl.virginia.edu/historical/eugenics/3-buckvbell.cfm.
[1140] **Carrie Buck, Virginia's Test Case** University of Virginia Health System, Claude Moore Health Sciences Library @ http://www.hsl.virginia.edu/historical/eugenics/3-buckvbell.cfm.
[1141] **Carrie Buck, Virginia's Test Case** University of Virginia Health System, Claude Moore Health Sciences Library @ http://www.hsl.virginia.edu/historical/eugenics/3-buckvbell.cfm.
[1142] Image Archive on the American Eugenics Movement. Dolan DNA Learning Center, Cold Spring Harbor Laboratory. **Eugenic Sterilization Laws.** Paul Lombardo, University of Virginia @ http://www.eugenicsarchive.org/html/eugenics/essay8text.html.
[1143] Eugenics: Three Generations, No Imbeciles: Virginia, Eugenics & Buck v. Bell. University of Virginia Health System, Claude Moore Health Sciences Library. Retrieved @ http://www.hsl.virginia.edu/historical/eugenics/.
[1144] **Carrie Buck, Virginia's Test Case** University of Virginia Health System, Claude Moore Health Sciences Library @ http://www.hsl.virginia.edu/historical/eugenics/3-buckvbell.cfm.
[1145] **Carrie Buck, Virginia's Test Case** University of Virginia Health System, Claude Moore Health Sciences Library @ http://www.hsl.virginia.edu/historical/eugenics/3-buckvbell.cfm.
[1146] Eugenics: Three Generations, No Imbeciles: Virginia, Eugenics & Buck v. Bell. University of Virginia Health System, Claude Moore Health Sciences Library. Retrieved @ http://www.hsl.virginia.edu/historical/eugenics/.
[1147] Eugenics: Three Generations, No Imbeciles: Virginia, Eugenics & Buck v. Bell. University of Virginia Health System, Claude Moore Health Sciences Library. Retrieved @ http://www.hsl.virginia.edu/historical/eugenics/.
[1148] Image Archive on the American Eugenics Movement. Dolan DNA Learning Center, Cold Spring Harbor Laboratory. **Eugenic Sterilization Laws.** Paul Lombardo, University of Virginia @ http://www.eugenicsarchive.org/html/eugenics/essay8text.html.
[1149] **Carrie Buck, Virginia's Test Case** University of Virginia Health System, Claude Moore Health Sciences Library @ http://www.hsl.virginia.edu/historical/eugenics/3-buckvbell.cfm.
[1150] **Carrie Buck, Virginia's Test Case** University of Virginia Health System, Claude Moore Health Sciences Library @ http://www.hsl.virginia.edu/historical/eugenics/3-buckvbell.cfm.
[1151] Oliver Wendell Holmes, Jr., 1902-1932 Retrieved @ http://www.supremecourthistory.org/history/supremecourthistory_history_assoc_049holmes.htm.
[1152] Oliver Wendell Holmes, Jr., 1902-1932 Retrieved @ http://www.supremecourthistory.org/history/supremecourthistory_history_assoc_049holmes.htm.
[1153] Oliver Wendell Holmes, Jr., 1902-1932 Retrieved @ http://www.supremecourthistory.org/history/supremecourthistory_history_assoc_049holmes.htm.
[1154] Oliver Wendell Holmes, Jr., 1902-1932 Retrieved @ http://www.supremecourthistory.org/history/supremecourthistory_history_assoc_049holmes.htm.
[1155] Eugenics: Three Generations, No Imbeciles: Virginia, Eugenics & Buck v. Bell. University of Virginia Health System, Claude Moore Health Sciences Library. Retrieved @ http://www.hsl.virginia.edu/historical/eugenics/3-buckvbell.cfm.
[1156] Eugenics: Three Generations, No Imbeciles: Virginia, Eugenics & Buck v. Bell. University of Virginia Health System, Claude Moore Health Sciences Library. Retrieved @ http://www.hsl.virginia.edu/historical/eugenics/.
[1157] Eugenics: Three Generations, No Imbeciles: Virginia, Eugenics & Buck v. Bell. University of Virginia Health System, Claude Moore Health Sciences Library. Retrieved @ http://www.hsl.virginia.edu/historical/eugenics/3-buckvbell.cfm.
[1158] Image Archive on the American Eugenics Movement. Dolan DNA Learning Center, Cold Spring Harbor Laboratory. **Eugenic Sterilization Laws.** Paul Lombardo, University of Virginia @ http://www.eugenicsarchive.org/html/eugenics/essay8text.html.
[1159] Eugenics: Three Generations, No Imbeciles: Virginia, Eugenics & Buck v. Bell. University of Virginia Health System, Claude Moore Health Sciences Library. Retrieved @ http://www.hsl.virginia.edu/historical/eugenics/3-buckvbell.cfm.
[1160] Image Archive on the American Eugenics Movement. Dolan DNA Learning Center, Cold Spring Harbor Laboratory. **Eugenic Sterilization Laws.** Paul Lombardo, University of Virginia @ http://www.eugenicsarchive.org/html/eugenics/essay8text.html.
[1161] Eugenics: Three Generations, No Imbeciles: Virginia, Eugenics & Buck v. Bell. University of Virginia Health System, Claude Moore Health Sciences Library. Retrieved @ http://www.hsl.virginia.edu/historical/eugenics/3-buckvbell.cfm.
[1162] Image Archive on the American Eugenics Movement. Dolan DNA Learning Center, Cold Spring Harbor Laboratory. **Eugenic Sterilization Laws.** Paul Lombardo, University of Virginia @ http://www.eugenicsarchive.org/html/eugenics/essay8text.html.
[1163] Image Archive on the American Eugenics Movement. Dolan DNA Learning Center, Cold Spring Harbor Laboratory. **Eugenic Sterilization Laws.** Paul Lombardo, University of Virginia @ http://www.eugenicsarchive.org/html/eugenics/essay8text.html.
[1164] Eugenics: Three Generations, No Imbeciles: Virginia, Eugenics & Buck v. Bell. University of Virginia Health System, Claude Moore Health Sciences Library. Retrieved @ http://www.hsl.virginia.edu/historical/eugenics/.
[1165] **Carrie Buck, Virginia's Test Case** University of Virginia Health System, Claude Moore Health Sciences Library @ http://www.hsl.virginia.edu/historical/eugenics/3-buckvbell.cfm.
[1166] **Carrie Buck, Virginia's Test Case** University of Virginia Health System, Claude Moore Health Sciences Library @ http://www.hsl.virginia.edu/historical/eugenics/3-buckvbell.cfm.
[1167] **Carrie Buck, Virginia's Test Case** University of Virginia Health System, Claude Moore Health Sciences Library @ http://www.hsl.virginia.edu/historical/eugenics/3-buckvbell.cfm.
[1168] Image Archive on the American Eugenics Movement. Dolan DNA Learning Center, Cold Spring Harbor Laboratory. **Eugenic Sterilization Laws.** Paul Lombardo, University of Virginia @ http://www.eugenicsarchive.org/html/eugenics/essay8text.html.
[1169] Eugenics: Three Generations, No Imbeciles: Virginia, Eugenics & Buck v. Bell. University of Virginia Health System, Claude Moore Health Sciences Library. Retrieved @ http://www.hsl.virginia.edu/historical/eugenics/.
[1170] Harry Laughlin's "Model Eugenical Sterilization Law." Retrieved April 28, 2009 @ http://www.people.fas.harvard.edu/~wellerst/laughlin/.
[1171] Harry Laughlin's "Model Eugenical Sterilization Law." Retrieved April 28, 2009 @ http://www.people.fas.harvard.edu/~wellerst/laughlin/.
[1172] Image Archive on the American Eugenics Movement. Dolan DNA Learning Center, Cold Spring Harbor Laboratory. **Eugenic Sterilization Laws.** Paul Lombardo, University of Virginia @ http://www.eugenicsarchive.org/html/eugenics/essay8text.html.
[1173] Image Archive on the American Eugenics Movement. Dolan DNA Learning Center, Cold Spring Harbor Laboratory. **Eugenic Sterilization Laws.** Paul Lombardo, University of Virginia @ http://www.eugenicsarchive.org/html/eugenics/essay8text.html.
[1174] Image Archive on the American Eugenics Movement. Dolan DNA Learning Center, Cold Spring Harbor Laboratory. **Eugenic Sterilization Laws.** Paul Lombardo, University of Virginia @ http://www.eugenicsarchive.org/html/eugenics/essay8text.html.
[1175] Image Archive on the American Eugenics Movement. Dolan DNA Learning Center, Cold Spring Harbor Laboratory. **Eugenic Sterilization Laws.** Paul Lombardo, University of Virginia @ http://www.eugenicsarchive.org/html/eugenics/essay8text.html.
[1176] Image Archive on the American Eugenics Movement. Dolan DNA Learning Center, Cold Spring Harbor Laboratory. **Eugenic Sterilization Laws.** Paul Lombardo, University of Virginia @ http://www.eugenicsarchive.org/html/eugenics/essay8text.html.
[1177] Origins of Eugenics. University of Virginia Health System, Claude Moore Health Sciences Library @ http://www.hsl.virginia.edu/historical/eugenics/2-origins.cfm.
[1178] **Eugenics in Virginia**. University of Virginia Health System, Claude Moore Health Sciences Library @ http://www.hsl.virginia.edu/historical/eugenics/4-influence.cfm.
[1179] **Eugenics in Virginia**. University of Virginia Health System, Claude Moore Health Sciences Library @ http://www.hsl.virginia.edu/historical/eugenics/4-influence.cfm.
[1180] **Eugenics in Virginia**. University of Virginia Health System, Claude Moore Health Sciences Library @ http://www.hsl.virginia.edu/historical/eugenics/4-influence.cfm.
[1181] **Eugenics in Virginia**. University of Virginia Health System, Claude Moore Health Sciences Library @ http://www.hsl.virginia.edu/historical/eugenics/4-influence.cfm.

[1182] Psychology. Stephen F. Davis & Joseph J. Palladino. Fourth Edition. Pearson Prentice Hall. 2003. Page 348.
[1183] The Horrifying American Roots of Nazi Eugenics.By Edwin Black. Orignially published in the *San Francisco Chronicle*. Retrieved @ http://hnn.us/articles/1796.html.
[1184] The Horrifying American Roots of Nazi Eugenics.By Edwin Black. Orignially published in the *San Francisco Chronicle*. Retrieved @ http://hnn.us/articles/1796.html.
[1185] The History of Eugenics in North Carolina. Provided by Daniel Smith at the Health
Sciences Library at UNC-Chapel Hill. April 2009. @ http://carolinacurator.blogspot.com/2009/04/eugenics-in-north-carolina.html.
[1186] The History of Eugenics in North Carolina. Provided by Daniel Smith at the Health
Sciences Library at UNC-Chapel Hill. April 2009. @ http://carolinacurator.blogspot.com/2009/04/eugenics-in-north-carolina.html.
[1187] The Horrifying American Roots of Nazi Eugenics.By Edwin Black. Orignially published in the *San Francisco Chronicle*. Retrieved @ http://hnn.us/articles/1796.html.
[1188] **Eugenics in Virginia**. University of Virginia Health System, Claude Moore Health Sciences Library @ http://www.hsl.virginia.edu/historical/eugenics/4-influence.cfm.
[1189] **Eugenics in Virginia**. University of Virginia Health System, Claude Moore Health Sciences Library @ http://www.hsl.virginia.edu/historical/eugenics/4-influence.cfm.
[1190] Harry Laughlin's "Model Eugenical Sterilization Law." Retrieved April 28, 2009 @ http://www.people.fas.harvard.edu/~wellerst/laughlin/.
[1191] **Eugenics in Virginia**. University of Virginia Health System, Claude Moore Health Sciences Library @ http://www.hsl.virginia.edu/historical/eugenics/4-influence.cfm.
[1192] Quoted in the Richmond Times Dispatch. The Horrifying American Roots of Nazi Eugenics.By Edwin Black. Orignially published in the *San Francisco Chronicle*. Retrieved @ http://hnn.us/articles/1796.html.
[1193] **Eugenics in Virginia**. University of Virginia Health System, Claude Moore Health Sciences Library @ http://www.hsl.virginia.edu/historical/eugenics/4-influence.cfm.
[1194] **Was Nazi eugenics created in the US?** Garland E. Allen A review of Edwin Black's *War Against the Weak*. http://www.nature.com/embor/journal/v5/n5/full/7400158.html.
[1195] The Horrifying American Roots of Nazi Eugenics.By Edwin Black. Orignially published in the *San Francisco Chronicle*. Retrieved @ http://hnn.us/articles/1796.html.
[1196] The Horrifying American Roots of Nazi Eugenics.By Edwin Black. Orignially published in the *San Francisco Chronicle*. Retrieved @ http://hnn.us/articles/1796.html.
[1197] The Horrifying American Roots of Nazi Eugenics.By Edwin Black. Orignially published in the *San Francisco Chronicle*. Retrieved @ http://hnn.us/articles/1796.html.
[1198] The Horrifying American Roots of Nazi Eugenics.By Edwin Black. Orignially published in the *San Francisco Chronicle*. Retrieved @ http://hnn.us/articles/1796.html.
[1199] The Horrifying American Roots of Nazi Eugenics.By Edwin Black. Orignially published in the *San Francisco Chronicle*. Retrieved @ http://hnn.us/articles/1796.html.
[1200] The Horrifying American Roots of Nazi Eugenics.By Edwin Black. Orignially published in the *San Francisco Chronicle*. Retrieved @ http://hnn.us/articles/1796.html.
[1201] Section 3. Patterns of Immigration. Chapter 19 An Urban Society. History of a Free Nation. Henry W. Bragdon, Samuel P. McClutchen, and Donald Ritchie. 1998. Glencoe McGraw-Hill. Page 531.
[1202] Section 3. Patterns of Immigration. Chapter 19 An Urban Society. History of a Free Nation. Henry W. Bragdon, Samuel P. McClutchen, and Donald Ritchie. 1998. Glencoe McGraw-Hill. Page 531.
[1203] Section 3. Patterns of Immigration. Chapter 19 An Urban Society. History of a Free Nation. Henry W. Bragdon, Samuel P. McClutchen, and Donald Ritchie. 1998. Glencoe McGraw-Hill. Page 531.
[1204] Origins of Eugenics. University of Virginia Health System, Claude Moore Health Sciences Library @ http://www.hsl.virginia.edu/historical/eugenics/2-origins.cfm.
[1205] Harry H. Laughlin. For information contact: speccoll@truman.edu Retrieved April 28, 2009 @
http://library.truman.edu/manuscripts/laughlinbio.htm.
[1206] Harry H. Laughlin. For information contact: speccoll@truman.edu Retrieved April 28, 2009 @ http://library.truman.edu/manuscripts/laughlinbio.htm.
[1207] Harry H. Laughlin. For information contact: speccoll@truman.edu Retrieved April 28, 2009 @
http://library.truman.edu/manuscripts/laughlinbio.htm.
[1208] Harry H. Laughlin. For information contact: speccoll@truman.edu Retrieved April 28, 2009 @
http://library.truman.edu/manuscripts/laughlinbio.htm.
[1209] Origins of Eugenics. University of Virginia Health System, Claude Moore Health Sciences Library @ http://www.hsl.virginia.edu/historical/eugenics/2-origins.cfm.
[1210] **Eugenics in Virginia**. University of Virginia Health System, Claude Moore Health Sciences Library @ http://www.hsl.virginia.edu/historical/eugenics/4-influence.cfm.
[1211] Section 1. The Harding Years. Chapter 26 The Decade of Normalcy. 1920-1928. History of a Free Nation. Henry W. Bragdon, Samuel P. McClutchen, and Donald Ritchie. 1998. Glencoe McGraw-Hill. Page 717.
[1212] Section 1. The Harding Years. Chapter 26 The Decade of Normalcy. 1920-1928. History of a Free Nation. Henry W. Bragdon, Samuel P. McClutchen, and Donald Ritchie. 1998. Glencoe McGraw-Hill. Page 717.
[1213] From the WSJ Opinion Archives. **FROM THE RECORD.** Whitewash. *The racist history the Democratic Party wants you to forget.* by BRUCE BARTLETT. *Monday, December 24, 2007.* Mr. Bartlett is author of "Wrong on Race: The Democratic Party's Buried Past," to be published next month by Palgrave Macmillan. Retreived May 20, 2009 @ http://www.opinionjournal.com/extra/?id=110011033.
[1214] Religion: Priest in Politics. Monday, Dec. 11, 1933. Retrieved June 20, 2009 @ http://www.time.com/time/magazine/article/0,9171,746503,00.html.
[1215] Father Charles E. Coughlin, The Radio Priest. July 23, 1995. The Detroit News. Retrieved June 2009 @ http://apps.detnews.com/apps/history/index.php?id=43.
[1216] CHARLES E. COUGHLIN. United States Holocaust Memorial Museum Retrieved June 2009 @ http://www.ushmm.org/wlc/article.php?lang=en&ModuleId=10005516.
[1217] Father Charles E. Coughlin, The Radio Priest. July 23, 1995. The Detroit News. Retrieved June 2009 @ http://apps.detnews.com/apps/history/index.php?id=43.
[1218] Religion: Priest in Politics. Monday, Dec. 11, 1933. Retrieved June 20, 2009 @ http://www.time.com/time/magazine/article/0,9171,746503,00.html.
[1219] Religion: Priest in Politics. Monday, Dec. 11, 1933. Retrieved June 20, 2009 @ http://www.time.com/time/magazine/article/0,9171,746503,00.html.
[1220] Religion: Priest in Politics. Monday, Dec. 11, 1933. Retrieved June 20, 2009 @ http://www.time.com/time/magazine/article/0,9171,746503,00.html.
[1221] Religion: Priest in Politics. Monday, Dec. 11, 1933. Retrieved June 20, 2009 @ http://www.time.com/time/magazine/article/0,9171,746503,00.html.
[1222] Father Charles E. Coughlin, The Radio Priest. July 23, 1995. The Detroit News. Retrieved June 2009 @ http://apps.detnews.com/apps/history/index.php?id=43.
[1223] Religion: Priest in Politics. Monday, Dec. 11, 1933. Retrieved June 20, 2009 @ http://www.time.com/time/magazine/article/0,9171,746503,00.html.
[1224] Father Charles E. Coughlin, The Radio Priest. July 23, 1995. The Detroit News. Retrieved June 2009 @ http://apps.detnews.com/apps/history/index.php?id=43.
[1225] **Father Charles Edward Coughlin (1891-1971).** Richard Sanders, Editor, *Press for Conversion!***Source:** *Press for Conversion!* magazine, Issue # 53, "Facing the Corporate Roots of American Fascism," March 2004. Published by the Coalition to Oppose the Arms Trade. Retrieved June 10, 2009 @ http://coat.ncf.ca/our_magazine/links/53/coughlin.html.
[1226] **Father Charles Edward Coughlin (1891-1971).** Richard Sanders, Editor, *Press for Conversion!***Source:** *Press for Conversion!* magazine, Issue # 53, "Facing the Corporate Roots of American Fascism," March 2004. Published by the Coalition to Oppose the Arms Trade. Retrieved June 10, 2009 @ http://coat.ncf.ca/our_magazine/links/53/coughlin.html.
[1227] **Father Charles Edward Coughlin (1891-1971).** Richard Sanders, Editor, *Press for Conversion!***Source:** *Press for Conversion!* magazine, Issue # 53, "Facing the Corporate Roots of American Fascism," March 2004. Published by the Coalition to Oppose the Arms Trade. Retrieved June 10, 2009 @ http://coat.ncf.ca/our_magazine/links/53/coughlin.html.
[1228] Father Charles E. Coughlin, The Radio Priest. July 23, 1995. The Detroit News. Retrieved June 2009 @ http://apps.detnews.com/apps/history/index.php?id=43.
[1229] **Father Charles Edward Coughlin (1891-1971).** Richard Sanders, Editor, *Press for Conversion!***Source:** *Press for Conversion!* magazine, Issue # 53, "Facing the Corporate Roots of American Fascism," March 2004. Published by the Coalition to Oppose the Arms Trade. Retrieved June 10, 2009 @ http://coat.ncf.ca/our_magazine/links/53/coughlin.html.
[1230] **Catholic Social Reform and the New Deal: The Papers of Monsignor John A. Ryan and Bishop Francis J. Haas.** Vol. 30:1 ISSN 0160-8460 March 2002. By Joseph M. Turrini. Retrieved June 10, 2009 @ http://www.archives.gov/nhprc/annotation/march-2002/catholic-social-reform.html.
[1231] **Catholic Social Reform and the New Deal: The Papers of Monsignor John A. Ryan and Bishop Francis J. Haas.** Vol. 30:1 ISSN 0160-8460 March 2002. By Joseph M. Turrini. Retrieved June 10, 2009 @ http://www.archives.gov/nhprc/annotation/march-2002/catholic-social-reform.html.
[1232] Father Charles E. Coughlin, The Radio Priest. July 23, 1995. The Detroit News. Retrieved June 2009 @ http://apps.detnews.com/apps/history/index.php?id=43.
[1233] CHARLES E. COUGHLIN. United States Holocaust Memorial Museum Retrieved June 2009 @ http://www.ushmm.org/wlc/article.php?lang=en&ModuleId=10005516.
[1234] CHARLES E. COUGHLIN. United States Holocaust Memorial Museum Retrieved June 2009 @ http://www.ushmm.org/wlc/article.php?lang=en&ModuleId=10005516.
[1235] **Father Charles Edward Coughlin (1891-1971).** Richard Sanders, Editor, *Press for Conversion!***Source:** *Press for Conversion!* magazine, Issue # 53, "Facing the Corporate Roots of American Fascism," March 2004. Published by the Coalition to Oppose the Arms Trade. Retrieved June 10, 2009 @ http://coat.ncf.ca/our_magazine/links/53/coughlin.html.
[1236] **Father Charles Edward Coughlin (1891-1971).** Richard Sanders, Editor, *Press for Conversion!***Source:** *Press for Conversion!* magazine, Issue # 53, "Facing the Corporate Roots of American Fascism," March 2004. Published by the Coalition to Oppose the Arms Trade. Retrieved June 10, 2009 @ http://coat.ncf.ca/our_magazine/links/53/coughlin.html.
[1237] **Father Charles Edward Coughlin (1891-1971).** Richard Sanders, Editor, *Press for Conversion!***Source:** *Press for Conversion!* magazine, Issue # 53, "Facing the Corporate Roots of American Fascism," March 2004. Published by the Coalition to Oppose the Arms Trade. Retrieved June 10, 2009 @ http://coat.ncf.ca/our_magazine/links/53/coughlin.html.
[1238] Father Charles E. Coughlin, The Radio Priest. July 23, 1995. The Detroit News. Retrieved June 2009 @ http://apps.detnews.com/apps/history/index.php?id=43.
[1239] CHARLES E. COUGHLIN. United States Holocaust Memorial Museum Retrieved June 2009 @ http://www.ushmm.org/wlc/article.php?lang=en&ModuleId=10005516.
[1240] Father Charles E. Coughlin, The Radio Priest. July 23, 1995. The Detroit News. Retrieved June 2009 @ http://apps.detnews.com/apps/history/index.php?id=43.
[1241] CHARLES E. COUGHLIN. United States Holocaust Memorial Museum Retrieved June 2009 @ http://www.ushmm.org/wlc/article.php?lang=en&ModuleId=10005516.
[1242] CHARLES E. COUGHLIN. United States Holocaust Memorial Museum Retrieved June 2009 @ http://www.ushmm.org/wlc/article.php?lang=en&ModuleId=10005516.
[1243] CHARLES E. COUGHLIN. United States Holocaust Memorial Museum Retrieved June 2009 @ http://www.ushmm.org/wlc/article.php?lang=en&ModuleId=10005516.
[1244] CHARLES E. COUGHLIN. United States Holocaust Memorial Museum Retrieved June 2009 @ http://www.ushmm.org/wlc/article.php?lang=en&ModuleId=10005516.
[1245] Father Charles E. Coughlin, The Radio Priest. July 23, 1995. The Detroit News. Retrieved June 2009 @ http://apps.detnews.com/apps/history/index.php?id=43.
[1246] Father Charles E. Coughlin, The Radio Priest. July 23, 1995. The Detroit News. Retrieved June 2009 @ http://apps.detnews.com/apps/history/index.php?id=43.
[1247] Section 4. War on the Home Front. Chapter 29 World War II 1933-1945. History of a Free Nation. Henry W. Bragdon, Samuel P. McClutchen, and Donald Ritchie. 1998. Glencoe McGraw-Hill. Page 831.
[1248] Americans Sent to Internment Camps. The American Century. Harold Evans. 2000. Panic after Pearl Harbor. Pages 350-351. New York: Alfred A. Knopf.
[1249] Americans Sent to Internment Camps. The American Century. Harold Evans. 2000. Panic after Pearl Harbor. Pages 350-351. New York: Alfred A. Knopf.
[1250] Americans Sent to Internment Camps. The American Century. Harold Evans. 2000. Panic after Pearl Harbor. Pages 350-351. New York: Alfred A. Knopf.
[1251] Americans Sent to Internment Camps. The American Century. Harold Evans. 2000. Panic after Pearl Harbor. Pages 350-351. New York: Alfred A. Knopf.
[1252] The American Dream compiled by Marvin Miller. Japanese Internment, page 311 to 313. 1976, Classic Publications.
[1253] Americans Sent to Internment Camps. The American Century. Harold Evans. 2000. Panic after Pearl Harbor. Pages 350-351. New York: Alfred A. Knopf.
[1254] Americans Sent to Internment Camps. The American Century. Harold Evans. 2000. Panic after Pearl Harbor. Pages 350-351. New York: Alfred A. Knopf.
[1255] The American Dream compiled by Marvin Miller. Japanese Internment, page 311 to 313. 1976, Classic Publications.
[1256] Americans Sent to Internment Camps. The American Century. Harold Evans. 2000. Panic after Pearl Harbor. Pages 350-351. New York: Alfred A. Knopf.
[1257] Americans Sent to Internment Camps. The American Century. Harold Evans. 2000. Panic after Pearl Harbor. Pages 350-351. New York: Alfred A. Knopf.
[1258] The American Dream compiled by Marvin Miller. Japanese Internment, page 311 to 313. 1976, Classic Publications.

[1259] Section 4. War on the Home Front. Chapter 29 World War II 1933-1945. History of a Free Nation. Henry W. Bragdon, Samuel P. McClutchen, and Donald Ritchie. 1998. Glencoe McGraw-Hill. Page 831.
[1260] Americans Sent to Internment Camps. The American Century. Harold Evans. 2000. Panic after Pearl Harbor. Pages 350-351. New York: Alfred A. Knopf.
[1261] Section 4. War on the Home Front. Chapter 29 World War II 1933-1945. History of a Free Nation. Henry W. Bragdon, Samuel P. McClutchen, and Donald Ritchie. 1998. Glencoe McGraw-Hill. Page 831.
[1262] Section 4. War on the Home Front. Chapter 29 World War II 1933-1945. History of a Free Nation. Henry W. Bragdon, Samuel P. McClutchen, and Donald Ritchie. 1998. Glencoe McGraw-Hill. Page 832.
[1263] Americans Sent to Internment Camps. The American Century. Harold Evans. 2000. Panic after Pearl Harbor. Pages 350-351. New York: Alfred A. Knopf.
[1264] Americans Sent to Internment Camps. The American Century. Harold Evans. 2000. Panic after Pearl Harbor. Pages 350-351. New York: Alfred A. Knopf.
[1265] Americans Sent to Internment Camps. The American Century. Harold Evans. 2000. Panic after Pearl Harbor. Pages 350-351. New York: Alfred A. Knopf.
[1266] Americans Sent to Internment Camps. The American Century. Harold Evans. 2000. Panic after Pearl Harbor. Pages 350-351. New York: Alfred A. Knopf.
[1267] Section 4. War on the Home Front. Chapter 29 World War II 1933-1945. History of a Free Nation. Henry W. Bragdon, Samuel P. McClutchen, and Donald Ritchie. 1998. Glencoe McGraw-Hill. Page 831.
[1268] Section 4. War on the Home Front. Chapter 29 World War II 1933-1945. History of a Free Nation. Henry W. Bragdon, Samuel P. McClutchen, and Donald Ritchie. 1998. Glencoe McGraw-Hill. Page 832.
[1269] Americans Sent to Internment Camps. The American Century. Harold Evans. 2000. Panic after Pearl Harbor. Pages 350-351. New York: Alfred A. Knopf.
[1270] Section 4. War on the Home Front. Chapter 29 World War II 1933-1945. History of a Free Nation. Henry W. Bragdon, Samuel P. McClutchen, and Donald Ritchie. 1998. Glencoe McGraw-Hill. Page 832.
[1271] Americans Sent to Internment Camps. The American Century. Harold Evans. 2000. Panic after Pearl Harbor. Pages 350-351. New York: Alfred A. Knopf.
[1272] Americans Sent to Internment Camps. The American Century. Harold Evans. 2000. Panic after Pearl Harbor. Pages 350-351. New York: Alfred A. Knopf.
[1273] Americans Sent to Internment Camps. The American Century. Harold Evans. 2000. Panic after Pearl Harbor. Pages 350-351. New York: Alfred A. Knopf.
[1274] Americans Sent to Internment Camps. The American Century. Harold Evans. 2000. Panic after Pearl Harbor. Pages 350-351. New York: Alfred A. Knopf.
[1275] Americans Sent to Internment Camps. The American Century. Harold Evans. 2000. Panic after Pearl Harbor. Pages 350-351. New York: Alfred A. Knopf.
[1276] Americans Sent to Internment Camps. The American Century. Harold Evans. 2000. Panic after Pearl Harbor. Pages 350-351. New York: Alfred A. Knopf.
[1277] The American Century. Harold Evans. Women Reach the White House. 2000. New York: Alfred A. Knopf.
[1278] The American Century. Harold Evans. Women Reach the White House. 2000. New York: Alfred A. Knopf.
[1279] The American Century. Harold Evans. Women Reach the White House. 2000. New York: Alfred A. Knopf.
[1280] The American Century. Harold Evans. Women Reach the White House. 2000. New York: Alfred A. Knopf.
[1281] The American Century. Harold Evans. Women Reach the White House. 2000. New York: Alfred A. Knopf.
[1282] The American Century. Harold Evans. Women Reach the White House. 2000. New York: Alfred A. Knopf.
[1283] Helen Gahagan Douglas Redux. October 2, 2008 by Frank Gannon. Filed Under Richard Nixon, U.S. History.
Retrieved May 20, 2008 @ http://thenewnixon.org/2008/10/02/helen-gahagan-douglas-redux/.
[1284] Helen Gahagan Douglas Redux. October 2, 2008 by Frank Gannon. Filed Under Richard Nixon, U.S. History.
Retrieved May 20, 2008 @ http://thenewnixon.org/2008/10/02/helen-gahagan-douglas-redux/.
[1285] Helen Gahagan Douglas Redux. October 2, 2008 by Frank Gannon. Filed Under Richard Nixon, U.S. History.
Retrieved May 20, 2008 @ http://thenewnixon.org/2008/10/02/helen-gahagan-douglas-redux/.
[1286] Helen Gahagan Douglas Redux. October 2, 2008 by Frank Gannon. Filed Under Richard Nixon, U.S. History.
Retrieved May 20, 2008 @ http://thenewnixon.org/2008/10/02/helen-gahagan-douglas-redux/.
[1287] Helen Gahagan Douglas Redux. October 2, 2008 by Frank Gannon. Filed Under Richard Nixon, U.S. History.
Retrieved May 20, 2008 @ http://thenewnixon.org/2008/10/02/helen-gahagan-douglas-redux/.
[1288] Lies My Teacher Told Me. James W. Loewen. Chapter 5. "Gone with the Wind." A Touchstone Book published by Simon & Schuster. 1995. Page 154.
[1289] See *(www.quotegarden.com/)*
[1290] Family Research Institute. Sourcewatch. http://www.sourcewatch.org/index.php?title=Family_Research_Institute
[1291] Huckabee called homosexuality 'sinful' By: Mike Allen
Dec 8, 2007. **Updated: December 9, 2007** http://www.politico.com/news/stories/1207/7270.html.
[1292] http://www.quotegarden.com/homosexuality.html
[1293] http://www.quotegarden.com/homosexuality.html
[1294] http://www.quotegarden.com/homosexuality.html
[1295] http://www.quotegarden.com/homosexuality.html
[1296] See http://www.quotegarden.com/homosexuality.html
[1297] See http://www.quotegarden.com/homosexuality.html
[1298] http://www.quotegarden.com/homosexuality.html
[1299] **Dr.** Gregory **Herek** Facts About Homosexuality and Child Molestation. Courtesy of UC Davis @ http://psychology.ucdavis.edu/rainbow/HTML/facts_molestation.html
[1300] Answers to Your Questions; For a Better Understanding of Sexual Orientation & Homosexuality http://www.apa.org/topics/sorientation.html;
[1301] Answers to Your Questions; For a Better Understanding of Sexual Orientation & Homosexuality http://www.apa.org/topics/sorientation.html;
[1302] Answers to Your Questions; For a Better Understanding of Sexual Orientation & Homosexuality http://www.apa.org/topics/sorientation.html;
[1303] Census finds more same-sex households. Increase attributed to greater openness, better counting procedures. By NAHAL TOOSIof the Journal Sentinel staff/ *Last Updated: Aug. 21, 2001*
Appeared in the Milwaukee Journal Sentinel on Aug. 22, 2001. http://www2.jsonline.com/news/metro/aug01/samesex22082101a.asp
[1304] Census finds more same-sex households. Increase attributed to greater openness, better counting procedures. By NAHAL TOOSIof the Journal Sentinel staff/ *Last Updated: Aug. 21, 2001*
Appeared in the Milwaukee Journal Sentinel on Aug. 22, 2001. http://www2.jsonline.com/news/metro/aug01/samesex22082101a.asp
[1305] Census finds more same-sex households. Increase attributed to greater openness, better counting procedures. By NAHAL TOOSIof the Journal Sentinel staff/ *Last Updated: Aug. 21, 2001*
Appeared in the Milwaukee Journal Sentinel on Aug. 22, 2001. http://www2.jsonline.com/news/metro/aug01/samesex22082101a.asp
[1306] Census finds more same-sex households. Increase attributed to greater openness, better counting procedures. By NAHAL TOOSIof the Journal Sentinel staff/ *Last Updated: Aug. 21, 2001*
Appeared in the Milwaukee Journal Sentinel on Aug. 22, 2001. http://www2.jsonline.com/news/metro/aug01/samesex22082101a.asp
[1307] Census finds more same-sex households. Increase attributed to greater openness, better counting procedures. By NAHAL TOOSIof the Journal Sentinel staff/ *Last Updated: Aug. 21, 2001*
Appeared in the Milwaukee Journal Sentinel on Aug. 22, 2001. http://www2.jsonline.com/news/metro/aug01/samesex22082101a.asp
[1308] Census finds more same-sex households. Increase attributed to greater openness, better counting procedures. By NAHAL TOOSIof the Journal Sentinel staff/ *Last Updated: Aug. 21, 2001*
Appeared in the Milwaukee Journal Sentinel on Aug. 22, 2001. http://www2.jsonline.com/news/metro/aug01/samesex22082101a.asp
[1309] *Graphic/Mike Johnson* Same Sex Households. http://www2.jsonline.com/news/metro/aug01/samesex22082101a.asp
[1310] Census finds more same-sex households. Increase attributed to greater openness, better counting procedures. By NAHAL TOOSIof the Journal Sentinel staff/ *Last Updated: Aug. 21, 2001*
Appeared in the Milwaukee Journal Sentinel on Aug. 22, 2001. http://www2.jsonline.com/news/metro/aug01/samesex22082101a.asp
[1311] Daley Backs Marriage for Gays in Chicago **February 20, 2004**http://query.nytimes.com/gst/fullpage.html?res=9C00E7D6103DF933A15751C0A9629C8B63&sec=&spon=&pagewanted=print
[1312] Daley Backs Marriage for Gays in Chicago **February 20, 2004**http://query.nytimes.com/gst/fullpage.html?res=9C00E7D6103DF933A15751C0A9629C8B63&sec=&spon=&pagewanted=print
[1313] Blogs posted on Washington Monthly. June 7, 2006. Guest: Steve Benen.
[1314] See (Please see www.infoplease.com/ipa/A0923080.html.)
[1315] USA Today. Posted 4/23/2003. Excerpt from Santorum interview. The Associated Press. Unedited. Taped April 7, 2003. http://www.usatoday.com/news/washington/2003-04-23-santorum-excerpt_x.htm.
[1316] Gay Marriage Is Back On The Radar For Republicans, Evangelicals. But Overall Opposition to Gay Marriage is Less Than in 2004. June 12, 2008. P E W R E S E A R C H C E N T E R F O R T H E P E O P L E & T H E P R E S . http://pewresearch.org/pubs/868/gay-marriage.
[1317] Gay Marriage Is Back On The Radar For Republicans, Evangelicals. But Overall Opposition to Gay Marriage is Less Than in 2004. June 12, 2008. P E W R E S E A R C H C E N T E R F O R T H E P E O P L E & T H E P R E S . http://pewresearch.org/pubs/868/gay-marriage.
[1318] Gay Marriage Is Back On The Radar For Republicans, Evangelicals. But Overall Opposition to Gay Marriage is Less Than in 2004. June 12, 2008. P E W R E S E A R C H C E N T E R F O R T H E P E O P L E & T H E P R E S . http://pewresearch.org/pubs/868/gay-marriage.
[1319] Gay Marriage Is Back On The Radar For Republicans, Evangelicals. But Overall Opposition to Gay Marriage is Less Than in 2004. June 12, 2008. P E W R E S E A R C H C E N T E R F O R T H E P E O P L E & T H E P R E S . http://pewresearch.org/pubs/868/gay-marriage.
[1320] Gay Marriage Is Back On The Radar For Republicans, Evangelicals. But Overall Opposition to Gay Marriage is Less Than in 2004. June 12, 2008. P E W R E S E A R C H C E N T E R F O R T H E P E O P L E & T H E P R E S . http://pewresearch.org/pubs/868/gay-marriage.
[1321] Gay Marriage Is Back On The Radar For Republicans, Evangelicals. But Overall Opposition to Gay Marriage is Less Than in 2004. June 12, 2008. P E W R E S E A R C H C E N T E R F O R T H E P E O P L E & T H E P R E S . http://pewresearch.org/pubs/868/gay-marriage.
[1322] Gay Marriage Is Back On The Radar For Republicans, Evangelicals. But Overall Opposition to Gay Marriage is Less Than in 2004. June 12, 2008. P E W R E S E A R C H C E N T E R F O R T H E P E O P L E & T H E P R E S . http://pewresearch.org/pubs/868/gay-marriage.
[1323] Gay Marriage Is Back On The Radar For Republicans, Evangelicals. But Overall Opposition to Gay Marriage is Less Than in 2004. June 12, 2008. P E W R E S E A R C H C E N T E R F O R T H E P E O P L E & T H E P R E S . http://pewresearch.org/pubs/868/gay-marriage.
[1324] See http://www.washingtonpost.com/wp-srv/politics/polls/postpoll_021010.html.
[1325] See http://www.quotegarden.com/homosexuality.html
[1326] Gays not bashed enough? Posted by Barbara Wilcox on November 19, 2008http://hottopics.gay.com/2008/11/huckabee-gays-n.html.
[1327] Arkansas to vote on gay adoption ban. By 365gay Newscenter Staff. 08.25.2008 http://www.365gay.com/news/082508-arkansas-adoption-ban/.

[1328] Arkansas high court unanimously rejects gay adoption ban. RAW STORY. Published: Thursday June 29, 2006. http://www.rawstory.com/news/2006/Arkansas_high_court_unanimously_rejects_gay_0629.html
[1329] Arkansas to vote on gay adoption ban. By 365gay Newscenter Staff. 08.25.2008 http://www.365gay.com/news/082508-arkansas-adoption-ban/.
[1330] Arkansas high court unanimously rejects gay adoption ban. RAW STORY. Published: Thursday June 29, 2006. http://www.rawstory.com/news/2006/Arkansas_high_court_unanimously_rejects_gay_0629.html
[1331] Arkansas high court unanimously rejects gay adoption ban. RAW STORY. Published: Thursday June 29, 2006. http://www.rawstory.com/news/2006/Arkansas_high_court_unanimously_rejects_gay_0629.html
[1332] Arkansas to vote on gay adoption ban. By 365gay Newscenter Staff. 08.25.2008 http://www.365gay.com/news/082508-arkansas-adoption-ban/.
[1333] Arkansas to vote on gay adoption ban. By 365gay Newscenter Staff. 08.25.2008 http://www.365gay.com/news/082508-arkansas-adoption-ban/.
[1334] Arkansas to vote on gay adoption ban. By 365gay Newscenter Staff. 08.25.2008 http://www.365gay.com/news/082508-arkansas-adoption-ban/.
[1335] Arkansas to vote on gay adoption ban. By 365gay Newscenter Staff. 08.25.2008 http://www.365gay.com/news/082508-arkansas-adoption-ban/.
[1336] Ban on umarried adoptions passes in Arkansas. 07:52 AM CST on Thursday, November 6, 2008. **The Associated Press** http://www.dallasnews.com/sharedcontent/dws/news/texassouthwest/stories/110608dntexadoptions.4a25097.html.
[1337] Ban on umarried adoptions passes in Arkansas. 07:52 AM CST on Thursday, November 6, 2008. **The Associated Press** http://www.dallasnews.com/sharedcontent/dws/news/texassouthwest/stories/110608dntexadoptions.4a25097.html.
[1338] Ban on umarried adoptions passes in Arkansas. 07:52 AM CST on Thursday, November 6, 2008. **The Associated Press** http://www.dallasnews.com/sharedcontent/dws/news/texassouthwest/stories/110608dntexadoptions.4a25097.html.
[1339] Ban on unmarried adoptions passes in Arkansas. 07:52 AM CST on Thursday, November 6, 2008. **The Associated Press** http://www.dallasnews.com/sharedcontent/dws/news/texassouthwest/stories/110608dntexadoptions.4a25097.html.
[1340] Ban on unmarried adoptions passes in Arkansas. 07:52 AM CST on Thursday, November 6, 2008. **The Associated Press** http://www.dallasnews.com/sharedcontent/dws/news/texassouthwest/stories/110608dntexadoptions.4a25097.html.
[1341] Ban on unmarried adoptions passes in Arkansas. 07:52 AM CST on Thursday, November 6, 2008. **The Associated Press** http://www.dallasnews.com/sharedcontent/dws/news/texassouthwest/stories/110608dntexadoptions.4a25097.html.
[1342] Ban on unmarried adoptions passes in Arkansas. 07:52 AM CST on Thursday, November 6, 2008. **The Associated Press** http://www.dallasnews.com/sharedcontent/dws/news/texassouthwest/stories/110608dntexadoptions.4a25097.html.
[1343] Emerging Gay Adoption Fight Shares Battle Lines of Same-Sex Marriage Debate *By Amanda Ruggeri*. Posted October 31, 2008. http://www.usnews.com/articles/news/national/2008/10/31/emerging-gay-adoption-fight-shares-battle-lines-of-same-sex-marriage-debate.html.
[1344] Emerging Gay Adoption Fight Shares Battle Lines of Same-Sex Marriage Debate *By Amanda Ruggeri*. Posted October 31, 2008. http://www.usnews.com/articles/news/national/2008/10/31/emerging-gay-adoption-fight-shares-battle-lines-of-same-sex-marriage-debate.html.
[1345] Emerging Gay Adoption Fight Shares Battle Lines of Same-Sex Marriage Debate *By Amanda Ruggeri*. Posted October 31, 2008. http://www.usnews.com/articles/news/national/2008/10/31/emerging-gay-adoption-fight-shares-battle-lines-of-same-sex-marriage-debate.html.
[1346] Ban on unmarried adoptions passes in Arkansas. 07:52 AM CST on Thursday, November 6, 2008. **The Associated Press** http://www.dallasnews.com/sharedcontent/dws/news/texassouthwest/stories/110608dntexadoptions.4a25097.html.
[1347] Emerging Gay Adoption Fight Shares Battle Lines of Same-Sex Marriage Debate *By Amanda Ruggeri*. Posted October 31, 2008. http://www.usnews.com/articles/news/national/2008/10/31/emerging-gay-adoption-fight-shares-battle-lines-of-same-sex-marriage-debate.html.
[1348] Ban on unmarried adoptions passes in Arkansas. 07:52 AM CST on Thursday, November 6, 2008. **The Associated Press** http://www.dallasnews.com/sharedcontent/dws/news/texassouthwest/stories/110608dntexadoptions.4a25097.html. See also
[1349] Ban on unmarried adoptions passes in Arkansas. 07:52 AM CST on Thursday, November 6, 2008. **The Associated Press** See also Emerging Gay Adoption Fight Shares Battle Lines of Same-Sex Marriage Debate *By Amanda Ruggeri*. Posted October 31, 2008. http://www.usnews.com/articles/news/national/2008/10/31/emerging-gay-adoption-fight-shares-battle-lines-of-same-sex-marriage-debate.html.http://www.dallasnews.com/sharedcontent/dws/news/texassouthwest/stories/110608dntexadoptions.4a25097.html. See also Emerging Gay Adoption Fight Shares Battle Lines of Same-Sex Marriage Debate *By Amanda Ruggeri*. Posted October 31, 2008. http://www.usnews.com/articles/news/national/2008/10/31/emerging-gay-adoption-fight-shares-battle-lines-of-same-sex-marriage-debate.html.
[1350] Emerging Gay Adoption Fight Shares Battle Lines of Same-Sex Marriage Debate *By Amanda Ruggeri*. Posted October 31, 2008. http://www.usnews.com/articles/news/national/2008/10/31/emerging-gay-adoption-fight-shares-battle-lines-of-same-sex-marriage-debate.html.
[1351] Emerging Gay Adoption Fight Shares Battle Lines of Same-Sex Marriage Debate *By Amanda Ruggeri*. Posted October 31, 2008. http://www.usnews.com/articles/news/national/2008/10/31/emerging-gay-adoption-fight-shares-battle-lines-of-same-sex-marriage-debate.html.
[1352] Emerging Gay Adoption Fight Shares Battle Lines of Same-Sex Marriage Debate *By Amanda Ruggeri*. Posted October 31, 2008. http://www.usnews.com/articles/news/national/2008/10/31/emerging-gay-adoption-fight-shares-battle-lines-of-same-sex-marriage-debate.html.
[1353] Emerging Gay Adoption Fight Shares Battle Lines of Same-Sex Marriage Debate *By Amanda Ruggeri*. Posted October 31, 2008. http://www.usnews.com/articles/news/national/2008/10/31/emerging-gay-adoption-fight-shares-battle-lines-of-same-sex-marriage-debate.html.
[1354] Emerging Gay Adoption Fight Shares Battle Lines of Same-Sex Marriage Debate *By Amanda Ruggeri*. Posted October 31, 2008. http://www.usnews.com/articles/news/national/2008/10/31/emerging-gay-adoption-fight-shares-battle-lines-of-same-sex-marriage-debate.html.
[1355] Emerging Gay Adoption Fight Shares Battle Lines of Same-Sex Marriage Debate *By Amanda Ruggeri*. Posted October 31, 2008. http://www.usnews.com/articles/news/national/2008/10/31/emerging-gay-adoption-fight-shares-battle-lines-of-same-sex-marriage-debate.html.
[1356] Emerging Gay Adoption Fight Shares Battle Lines of Same-Sex Marriage Debate *By Amanda Ruggeri*. Posted October 31, 2008. http://www.usnews.com/articles/news/national/2008/10/31/emerging-gay-adoption-fight-shares-battle-lines-of-same-sex-marriage-debate.html.
[1357] Emerging Gay Adoption Fight Shares Battle Lines of Same-Sex Marriage Debate *By Amanda Ruggeri*. Posted October 31, 2008. http://www.usnews.com/articles/news/national/2008/10/31/emerging-gay-adoption-fight-shares-battle-lines-of-same-sex-marriage-debate.html.
[1358] Answers to Your Questions; For a Better Understanding of Sexual Orientation & Homosexuality http://www.apa.org/topics/sorientation.html;
[1359] Answers to Your Questions; For a Better Understanding of Sexual Orientation & Homosexuality http://www.apa.org/topics/sorientation.html;
[1360] Answers to Your Questions; For a Better Understanding of Sexual Orientation & Homosexuality http://www.apa.org/topics/sorientation.html;
[1361] Answers to Your Questions; For a Better Understanding of Sexual Orientation & Homosexuality http://www.apa.org/topics/sorientation.html;
[1362] Answers to Your Questions; For a Better Understanding of Sexual Orientation & Homosexuality http://www.apa.org/topics/sorientation.html;
[1363] Answers to Your Questions; For a Better Understanding of Sexual Orientation & Homosexuality http://www.apa.org/topics/sorientation.html;
[1364] What Makes People Gay? By Neil Swidey | August 14, 2005/ The Boston Globe. http://www.boston.com/news/globe/magazine/articles/2005/08/14/what_makes_people_gay/.
[1365] What Makes People Gay? By Neil Swidey | August 14, 2005/ The Boston Globe. http://www.boston.com/news/globe/magazine/articles/2005/08/14/what_makes_people_gay/.
[1366] What Makes People Gay? By Neil Swidey | August 14, 2005/ The Boston Globe. http://www.boston.com/news/globe/magazine/articles/2005/08/14/what_makes_people_gay/.
[1367] Michael Bailey and Richard Pillard. 12/17/91) New York Times. Are some people born gay? Michael Bailey is assistant professor of psychology at Northwestern University. Richard Pillard is associate professor of psychiatry at Boston University School of Medicine. http://www.cs.cmu.edu/afs/cs.cmu.edu/user/scotts/bulgarians/nature-nurture/bailey-pillard.html
[1368] Michael Bailey and Richard Pillard. 12/17/91) New York Times. Are some people born gay? Michael Bailey is assistant professor of psychology at Northwestern University. Richard Pillard is associate professor of psychiatry at Boston University School of Medicine. http://www.cs.cmu.edu/afs/cs.cmu.edu/user/scotts/bulgarians/nature-nurture/bailey-pillard.html.
[1369] Randolph E. Schmid. Men with older brothers more likely to be gay, study finds. Milwaukee Journal Sentinel, AP, June 27, 2006 11A.
[1370] What Makes People Gay? By Neil Swidey | August 14, 2005/ The Boston Globe. http://www.boston.com/news/globe/magazine/articles/2005/08/14/what_makes_people_gay/.
[1371] What Makes People Gay? By Neil Swidey | August 14, 2005/ The Boston Globe. http://www.boston.com/news/globe/magazine/articles/2005/08/14/what_makes_people_gay/.
[1372] What Makes People Gay? By Neil Swidey | August 14, 2005/ The Boston Globe. http://www.boston.com/news/globe/magazine/articles/2005/08/14/what_makes_people_gay/.
[1373] What Makes People Gay? By Neil Swidey | August 14, 2005/ The Boston Globe. http://www.boston.com/news/globe/magazine/articles/2005/08/14/what_makes_people_gay/.
[1374] What Makes People Gay? By Neil Swidey | August 14, 2005/ The Boston Globe. http://www.boston.com/news/globe/magazine/articles/2005/08/14/what_makes_people_gay/.
[1375] Michael Bailey and Richard Pillard. 12/17/91) New York Times. Are some people born gay? Michael Bailey is assistant professor of psychology at Northwestern University. Richard Pillard is associate professor of psychiatry at Boston University School of Medicine. http://www.cs.cmu.edu/afs/cs.cmu.edu/user/scotts/bulgarians/nature-nurture/bailey-pillard.html.
[1376] What Makes People Gay? By Neil Swidey | August 14, 2005/ The Boston Globe. http://www.boston.com/news/globe/magazine/articles/2005/08/14/what_makes_people_gay/.
[1377] What Makes People Gay? By Neil Swidey | August 14, 2005/ The Boston Globe. http://www.boston.com/news/globe/magazine/articles/2005/08/14/what_makes_people_gay/.
[1378] What Makes People Gay? By Neil Swidey | August 14, 2005/ The Boston Globe. http://www.boston.com/news/globe/magazine/articles/2005/08/14/what_makes_people_gay/.
[1379] Michael Bailey and Richard Pillard. 12/17/91) New York Times. Are some people born gay? Michael Bailey is assistant professor of psychology at Northwestern University. Richard Pillard is associate professor of psychiatry at Boston University School of Medicine. http://www.cs.cmu.edu/afs/cs.cmu.edu/user/scotts/bulgarians/nature-nurture/bailey-pillard.html.
[1380] What Makes People Gay? By Neil Swidey | August 14, 2005/ The Boston Globe. http://www.boston.com/news/globe/magazine/articles/2005/08/14/what_makes_people_gay/.
[1381] What Makes People Gay? By Neil Swidey | August 14, 2005/ The Boston Globe. http://www.boston.com/news/globe/magazine/articles/2005/08/14/what_makes_people_gay/.
[1382] What Makes People Gay? By Neil Swidey | August 14, 2005/ The Boston Globe. http://www.boston.com/news/globe/magazine/articles/2005/08/14/what_makes_people_gay/.
[1383] What Makes People Gay? By Neil Swidey | August 14, 2005/ The Boston Globe. http://www.boston.com/news/globe/magazine/articles/2005/08/14/what_makes_people_gay/.
[1384] What Makes People Gay? By Neil Swidey | August 14, 2005/ The Boston Globe. http://www.boston.com/news/globe/magazine/articles/2005/08/14/what_makes_people_gay/.
[1385] Laurie Goodstein. Catholics forming new guidelines on ministering to gays. MJS. October 29, 2006. 8A. SB 8 p 30.
[1386] Rachel Zoll. Guidelines approved on ministry for gay Catholics. AP. Milwaukee Journal Sentinel, Nov. 15, 2006.8A. SB 8 p 52.
[1387] What Makes People Gay? By Neil Swidey | August 14, 2005/ The Boston Globe. http://www.boston.com/news/globe/magazine/articles/2005/08/14/what_makes_people_gay/.
[1388] What Makes People Gay? By Neil Swidey | August 14, 2005/ The Boston Globe. http://www.boston.com/news/globe/magazine/articles/2005/08/14/what_makes_people_gay/.
[1389] What Makes People Gay? By Neil Swidey | August 14, 2005/ The Boston Globe. http://www.boston.com/news/globe/magazine/articles/2005/08/14/what_makes_people_gay/.
[1390] What Makes People Gay? By Neil Swidey | August 14, 2005/ The Boston Globe. http://www.boston.com/news/globe/magazine/articles/2005/08/14/what_makes_people_gay/.
[1391] What Makes People Gay? By Neil Swidey | August 14, 2005/ The Boston Globe. http://www.boston.com/news/globe/magazine/articles/2005/08/14/what_makes_people_gay/.

[1392] What Makes People Gay? By Neil Swidey | August 14, 2005/ The Boston Globe. http://www.boston.com/news/globe/magazine/articles/2005/08/14/what_makes_people_gay/.
[1393] What Makes People Gay? By Neil Swidey | August 14, 2005/ The Boston Globe. http://www.boston.com/news/globe/magazine/articles/2005/08/14/what_makes_people_gay/.
[1394] Jody's Family Affair. PFLAG head, Huckaby, talks about allies, outings and his "biological clock" by Will O'Bryan. Published on *May 1, 2008* in Metro Weekly. http://www.metroweekly.com/gauge/?ak=3412
[1395] From the issue dated March 31, 2008. Personal Experience Guides Leader of Group for Families of Gay People. By Peter Panepento. The Chronicle of Philanthropy Managing. http://philanthropy.com/free/articles/v17/i12/12005001.htm
[1396] Jody's Family Affair. PFLAG head, Huckaby, talks about allies, outings and his "biological clock" by Will O'Bryan. Published on *May 1, 2008* in Metro Weekly. http://www.metroweekly.com/gauge/?ak=3412
[1397] From the issue dated March 31, 2008. Personal Experience Guides Leader of Group for Families of Gay People. By Peter Panepento. The Chronicle of Philanthropy Managing. http://philanthropy.com/free/articles/v17/i12/12005001.htm
[1398] Documentary Tests Gay Theories BY CARLOS SANTOSCOY . PUBLISHED: JULY 18, 2008. http://www.ontopmag.com/article.aspx?id=2042&MediaType=1&Category=26
[1399] Jody's Family Affair. PFLAG head, Huckaby, talks about allies, outings and his "biological clock" by Will O'Bryan. Published on *May 1, 2008* in Metro Weekly. http://www.metroweekly.com/gauge/?ak=3412
[1400] Family Research Council. See http://www.frc.org/about-frc
[1401] Family Research Council. See http://www.frc.org/about-frc
[1402] What Do We Mean When We Talk About Change?Jeff Johnston**http://www.citizenlink.org/FOSI/homosexuality/overcoming/A000007628.cfm**
[1403] Homosexuality and Gender. Courtesy of Focus on the Family's Issue Analysis. Hope in a World of Gender Confusion. Devon Williams and Jeff Johnston*Williams is an Associate Editor with* CitizenLink*; Johnston is a Gender Issues Analyst with* Love Won Out. http://www.citizenlink.org/FOSI/homosexuality/hgeducation/A000008402.cfm
[1404] Attempts To Change Sexual Orientation. From UC Davis. http://psychology.ucdavis.edu/rainbow/HTML/facts_changing.html
[1405] Ex-Gay Leader Confronted in Gay Bar. by Joel Lawson *Southern Voice,* Thursday, 21 September 2000 http://psychology.ucdavis.edu/rainbow/HTML/Paulk-Southern%20Voice.html
[1406] Ex-Gay Leader Confronted in Gay Bar. by Joel Lawson *Southern Voice,* Thursday, 21 September 2000 http://psychology.ucdavis.edu/rainbow/HTML/Paulk-Southern%20Voice.html
[1407] Ex-Gay Leader Confronted in Gay Bar. by Joel Lawson *Southern Voice,* Thursday, 21 September 2000 http://psychology.ucdavis.edu/rainbow/HTML/Paulk-Southern%20Voice.html
[1408] Ex-Gay Leader Confronted in Gay Bar. by Joel Lawson *Southern Voice,* Thursday, 21 September 2000 http://psychology.ucdavis.edu/rainbow/HTML/Paulk-Southern%20Voice.html
[1409] Ex-Gay Leader Confronted in Gay Bar. by Joel Lawson *Southern Voice,* Thursday, 21 September 2000 http://psychology.ucdavis.edu/rainbow/HTML/Paulk-Southern%20Voice.html
[1410] Ex-Gay Leader Confronted in Gay Bar. by Joel Lawson *Southern Voice,* Thursday, 21 September 2000 http://psychology.ucdavis.edu/rainbow/HTML/Paulk-Southern%20Voice.html
[1411] Ex-Gay Leader Confronted in Gay Bar. by Joel Lawson *Southern Voice,* Thursday, 21 September 2000 http://psychology.ucdavis.edu/rainbow/HTML/Paulk-Southern%20Voice.html
[1412] Ex-Gay Leader Confronted in Gay Bar. by Joel Lawson *Southern Voice,* Thursday, 21 September 2000 http://psychology.ucdavis.edu/rainbow/HTML/Paulk-Southern%20Voice.html
[1413] Image can be examined from http://psychology.ucdavis.edu/rainbow/assets/images/paulkbig.gif
[1414] Ex-Gay Leader Confronted in Gay Bar. by Joel Lawson *Southern Voice,* Thursday, 21 September 2000 http://psychology.ucdavis.edu/rainbow/HTML/Paulk-Southern%20Voice.html
[1415] Ex-Gay Leader Confronted in Gay Bar. by Joel Lawson *Southern Voice,* Thursday, 21 September 2000 http://psychology.ucdavis.edu/rainbow/HTML/Paulk-Southern%20Voice.html
[1416] Ex-Gay Leader Confronted in Gay Bar. by Joel Lawson *Southern Voice,* Thursday, 21 September 2000 http://psychology.ucdavis.edu/rainbow/HTML/Paulk-Southern%20Voice.html
[1417] Ex-Gay Leader Confronted in Gay Bar. by Joel Lawson *Southern Voice,* Thursday, 21 September 2000 http://psychology.ucdavis.edu/rainbow/HTML/Paulk-Southern%20Voice.html
[1418] Ex-Gay Leader Confronted in Gay Bar. by Joel Lawson *Southern Voice,* Thursday, 21 September 2000 http://psychology.ucdavis.edu/rainbow/HTML/Paulk-Southern%20Voice.html
[1419] Ex-Gay Leader Confronted in Gay Bar. by Joel Lawson *Southern Voice,* Thursday, 21 September 2000 http://psychology.ucdavis.edu/rainbow/HTML/Paulk-Southern%20Voice.html
[1420] Ex-Gay Leader Confronted in Gay Bar. by Joel Lawson *Southern Voice,* Thursday, 21 September 2000 http://psychology.ucdavis.edu/rainbow/HTML/Paulk-Southern%20Voice.html
[1421] **Reggie White rejects criticism for his remarks about homosexuality and race.** April 13, 1998 COPYRIGHT 1998 Johnson Publishing Co. COPYRIGHT 2008 Gale, Cengage Learning http://findarticles.com/p/articles/mi_m1355/is_n20_v93/ai_n27541905/print
[1422] Packers' White discusses 'sin' homosexuality in speech. CBS SportsLine wire reports. March 25, 1998. http://www.skeptictank.org/white.htm
[1423] Packers' White discusses 'sin' homosexuality in speech. CBS SportsLine wire reports. March 25, 1998. http://www.skeptictank.org/white.htm
[1424] Packers' White discusses 'sin' homosexuality in speech. CBS SportsLine wire reports. March 25, 1998. http://www.skeptictank.org/white.htm
[1425] Packers' White discusses 'sin' homosexuality in speech. CBS SportsLine wire reports. March 25, 1998. http://www.skeptictank.org/white.htm
[1426] **Reggie White rejects criticism for his remarks about homosexuality and race.** April 13, 1998 COPYRIGHT 1998 Johnson Publishing Co. COPYRIGHT 2008 Gale, Cengage Learning http://findarticles.com/p/articles/mi_m1355/is_n20_v93/ai_n27541905/print
[1427] **Reggie White rejects criticism for his remarks about homosexuality and race.** April 13, 1998 COPYRIGHT 1998 Johnson Publishing Co. COPYRIGHT 2008 Gale, Cengage Learning http://findarticles.com/p/articles/mi_m1355/is_n20_v93/ai_n27541905/print
[1428] Packers' White discusses 'sin' homosexuality in speech. CBS SportsLine wire reports. March 25, 1998. http://www.skeptictank.org/white.htm
[1429] Packers' White discusses 'sin' homosexuality in speech. CBS SportsLine wire reports. March 25, 1998. http://www.skeptictank.org/white.htm
[1430] Packers' White discusses 'sin' homosexuality in speech. CBS SportsLine wire reports. March 25, 1998. http://www.skeptictank.org/white.htm
[1431] **Reggie White rejects criticism for his remarks about homosexuality and race.** April 13, 1998 COPYRIGHT 1998 Johnson Publishing Co. COPYRIGHT 2008 Gale, Cengage Learning http://findarticles.com/p/articles/mi_m1355/is_n20_v93/ai_n27541905/print
[1432] Packers' White discusses 'sin' homosexuality in speech. CBS SportsLine wire reports. March 25, 1998. http://www.skeptictank.org/white.htm
[1433] Packers' White discusses 'sin' homosexuality in speech. CBS SportsLine wire reports. March 25, 1998. http://www.skeptictank.org/white.htm
[1434] Packers' White discusses 'sin' homosexuality in speech. CBS SportsLine wire reports. March 25, 1998. http://www.skeptictank.org/white.htm
[1435] Packers' White discusses 'sin' homosexuality in speech. CBS SportsLine wire reports. March 25, 1998. http://www.skeptictank.org/white.htm
[1436] Packers' White discusses 'sin' homosexuality in speech. CBS SportsLine wire reports. March 25, 1998. http://www.skeptictank.org/white.htm
[1437] Packers' White discusses 'sin' homosexuality in speech. CBS SportsLine wire reports. March 25, 1998. http://www.skeptictank.org/white.htm
[1438] Packers' White discusses 'sin' homosexuality in speech. CBS SportsLine wire reports. March 25, 1998. http://www.skeptictank.org/white.htm
[1439] Packers' White discusses 'sin' homosexuality in speech. CBS SportsLine wire reports. March 25, 1998. http://www.skeptictank.org/white.htm
[1440] **Reggie White rejects criticism for his remarks about homosexuality and race.** April 13, 1998 COPYRIGHT 1998 Johnson Publishing Co. COPYRIGHT 2008 Gale, Cengage Learning http://findarticles.com/p/articles/mi_m1355/is_n20_v93/ai_n27541905/print
[1441] **Reggie White rejects criticism for his remarks about homosexuality and race.** April 13, 1998 COPYRIGHT 1998 Johnson Publishing Co. COPYRIGHT 2008 Gale, Cengage Learning http://findarticles.com/p/articles/mi_m1355/is_n20_v93/ai_n27541905/print
[1442] Republicans Divided Over Lott Comments, GOP Wins, Loses Votes With Its Comments on Gays. By Marc Lacey, Times Staff Writer, *The Los Angeles Times.* June 17, 1998 http://www.lcrga.com/news/98061701.shtml
[1443] From June 1998 from Online Newshour. http://www.pbs.org/newshour/bb/congress/july-dec98/gop_7-22a.html
[1444] From June 1998 from Online Newshour. http://www.pbs.org/newshour/bb/congress/july-dec98/gop_7-22a.html
[1445] Republicans Divided Over Lott Comments, GOP Wins, Loses Votes With Its Comments on Gays. By Marc Lacey, Times Staff Writer, *The Los Angeles Times.* June 17, 1998 http://www.lcrga.com/news/98061701.shtml
[1446] Lott Comments an Insult to Gay Republican Officials, Activists. June 16, 1998 Copyright © 2008, Georgia Log Cabin Republicans, Inc/ http://www.lcrga.com/news/98061601.shtml.
[1447] Republicans Divided Over Lott Comments, GOP Wins, Loses Votes With Its Comments on Gays. By Marc Lacey, Times Staff Writer, *The Los Angeles Times.* June 17, 1998 http://www.lcrga.com/news/98061701.shtml
[1448] Republicans Divided Over Lott Comments, GOP Wins, Loses Votes With Its Comments on Gays. By Marc Lacey, Times Staff Writer, *The Los Angeles Times.* June 17, 1998 http://www.lcrga.com/news/98061701.shtml
[1449] Republicans Divided Over Lott Comments, GOP Wins, Loses Votes With Its Comments on Gays. By Marc Lacey, Times Staff Writer, *The Los Angeles Times.* June 17, 1998 http://www.lcrga.com/news/98061701.shtml
[1450] From June 1998 from Online Newshour. http://www.pbs.org/newshour/bb/congress/july-dec98/gop_7-22a.html
[1451] Are Gay Rumors The Real Reason Behind Trent Lott's Resignation? By *Julie.* Created *11/26/2007 - 8:26pm*http://www.clevelandleader.com/print/3917
[1452] ANGLES. The Policy Journal of the Institute for Gay and Lesbian Strategic Studies. **The Pseudo-science of Sexual Orientation Conversion Therapy.** Douglas C. Haldeman, Ph.D. http://drdoughaldeman.com/doc/Pseudo-Science.pdf
[1453] Attempts To Change Sexual Orientation. From UC Davis. http://psychology.ucdavis.edu/rainbow/HTML/facts_changing.html
[1454] Attempts To Change Sexual Orientation. From UC Davis. http://psychology.ucdavis.edu/rainbow/HTML/facts_changing.html
[1455] ANGLES. The Policy Journal of the Institute for Gay and Lesbian Strategic Studies. **The Pseudo-science of Sexual Orientation Conversion Therapy.** Douglas C. Haldeman, Ph.D. http://drdoughaldeman.com/doc/Pseudo-Science.pdf
[1456] Attempts To Change Sexual Orientation. From UC Davis. http://psychology.ucdavis.edu/rainbow/HTML/facts_changing.html
[1457] ANGLES. The Policy Journal of the Institute for Gay and Lesbian Strategic Studies. **The Pseudo-science of Sexual Orientation Conversion Therapy.** Douglas C. Haldeman, Ph.D. http://drdoughaldeman.com/doc/Pseudo-Science.pdf
[1458] Attempts To Change Sexual Orientation. From UC Davis. http://psychology.ucdavis.edu/rainbow/HTML/facts_changing.html
[1459] Attempts To Change Sexual Orientation. From UC Davis. http://psychology.ucdavis.edu/rainbow/HTML/facts_changing.html
[1460] ANGLES. The Policy Journal of the Institute for Gay and Lesbian Strategic Studies. **The Pseudo-science of Sexual Orientation Conversion Therapy.** Douglas C. Haldeman, Ph.D. http://drdoughaldeman.com/doc/Pseudo-Science.pdf
[1461] Child Molestation and Homosexuality/ By Paul Cameron, Ph. D. Copyright 1993, Family Research InstituteThis educational pamphlet has been produced by Family Research Institute.http://www.familyresearchinst.org/FRI_EduPamphlet2.html
[1462] Attempts To Change Sexual Orientation. From UC Davis. http://psychology.ucdavis.edu/rainbow/HTML/facts_changing.html
[1463] Attempts To Change Sexual Orientation. From UC Davis. http://psychology.ucdavis.edu/rainbow/HTML/facts_changing.html
[1464] APA quoted in Attempts To Change Sexual Orientation. From UC Davis. http://psychology.ucdavis.edu/rainbow/HTML/facts_changing.html
[1465] ANGLES. The Policy Journal of the Institute for Gay and Lesbian Strategic Studies. **The Pseudo-science of Sexual Orientation Conversion Therapy.** Douglas C. Haldeman, Ph.D. http://drdoughaldeman.com/doc/Pseudo-Science.pdf

[1466] Haldeman, D. (1994). "The Practice and Ethics of Sexual Orientation Conversion Therapy,"*Journal of Consulting and Clinical Psychology.*Vol. 62, 1994; Davison, G. "Constructionism and Morality in Therapy for Homosexuality." In J.Gonsiorek and J. Weinrich (see note 2). See ANGLES. The Policy Journal of the Institute for Gay and Lesbian Strategic Studies. **The Pseudo-science of Sexual Orientation Conversion Therapy.** Douglas C. Haldeman, Ph.D. http://drdoughaldeman.com/doc/Pseudo-Science.pdf
[1467] ANGLES. The Policy Journal of the Institute for Gay and Lesbian Strategic Studies. **The Pseudo-science of Sexual Orientation Conversion Therapy.** Douglas C. Haldeman, Ph.D. http://drdoughaldeman.com/doc/Pseudo-Science.pdf
[1468] ANGLES. The Policy Journal of the Institute for Gay and Lesbian Strategic Studies. **The Pseudo-science ofSexual Orientation Conversion Therapy.** Douglas C. Haldeman, Ph.D. http://drdoughaldeman.com/doc/Pseudo-Science.pdf
[1469] ANGLES. The Policy Journal of the Institute for Gay and Lesbian Strategic Studies. **The Pseudo-science of Sexual Orientation Conversion Therapy.** Douglas C. Haldeman, Ph.D. http://drdoughaldeman.com/doc/Pseudo-Science.pdf
[1470] Answers to Your Questions; For a Better Understanding of Sexual Orientation & Homosexuality http://www.apa.org/topics/sorientation.html;
[1471] ANGLES. The Policy Journal of the Institute for Gay and Lesbian Strategic Studies. **The Pseudo-science of Sexual Orientation Conversion Therapy.** Douglas C. Haldeman, Ph.D. http://drdoughaldeman.com/doc/Pseudo-Science.pdf
[1472] Answers to Your Questions; For a Better Understanding of Sexual Orientation & Homosexuality http://www.apa.org/topics/sorientation.html;
[1473] A Line in the Sand for Same-Sex Marriage Foes. By LAURIE GOODSTEIN. October 27, 2008. From http://www.nytimes.com/2008/10/27/us/27right.html?_r=1&oref=slogin&partner=rssnyt&emc=rss&pagewanted=print.
[1474] The Conservative Case for Gay Marriage. Time. **By Andrew Sullivan.** http://www.time.com/time/printout/0,8816,460232,00.html. **Sunday, Jun. 22, 2003**
[1475] The Conservative Case for Gay Marriage. Time. **By Andrew Sullivan.** http://www.time.com/time/printout/0,8816,460232,00.html. **Sunday, Jun. 22, 2003**
[1476] The Conservative Case For Gay Marriage (Again) 29 Dec 2007 06:09 pmhttp://andrewsullivan.theatlantic.com/the_daily_dish/2007/12/reihan-on-socia.html.
[1477] Monday, October 09, 2006. Why gay marriage is good conservative policyView my complete profile http://diogenesborealis.blogspot.com/2006/10/why-gay-marriage-is-good-conservative.html
[1478] Monday, October 09, 2006. Why gay marriage is good conservative policyView my complete profile http://diogenesborealis.blogspot.com/2006/10/why-gay-marriage-is-good-conservative.html
[1479] If It's Not a Crime to be Gay, Why Can't We Get Married? by Andrew Sullivan. *First published October 8, 2003, in The Wall Street Journal.* http://www.indegayforum.com/news/show/26930.html.
[1480] If It's Not a Crime to be Gay, Why Can't We Get Married? by Andrew Sullivan. *First published October 8, 2003, in The Wall Street Journal.* http://www.indegayforum.com/news/show/26930.html.
[1481] By Andrew Norton - posted Wednesday, 23 January 2008http://www.onlineopinion.com.au/view.asp?article=6907 First published in *Andrew Norton's* blog on March 19, 2007. The utilitarian conservative case against gay marriage.
[1482] **Power, Glory --and Politics.** By **RICHARD N. OSTLING.** Sunday, Jun. 24, 2001 Article from Time in the 1980s. http://www.time.com/time/magazine/article/0,9171,1101860217-143137,00.html
[1483] **Power, Glory --and Politics.** By **RICHARD N. OSTLING.** Sunday, Jun. 24, 2001 Article from Time in the 1980s. http://www.time.com/time/magazine/article/0,9171,1101860217-143137,00.html
[1484] **Forgiven: The Rise and Fall of Jim Bakker and the PTL Ministry. - book reviews**
Henry G. Brinton . COPYRIGHT 1990 Washington Monthly Company
[1485] **Forgiven: The Rise and Fall of Jim Bakker and the PTL Ministry. - book reviews**
Henry G. Brinton . COPYRIGHT 1990 Washington Monthly Company
[1486] **Power, Glory --and Politics.** By **RICHARD N. OSTLING.** Sunday, Jun. 24, 2001 Article from Time in the 1980s. http://www.time.com/time/magazine/article/0,9171,1101860217-143137,00.html
[1487] **Power, Glory --and Politics.** By **RICHARD N. OSTLING.** Sunday, Jun. 24, 2001 Article from Time in the 1980s. http://www.time.com/time/magazine/article/0,9171,1101860217-143137,00.html
[1488] **Power, Glory --and Politics.** By **RICHARD N. OSTLING.** Sunday, Jun. 24, 2001 Article from Time in the 1980s. http://www.time.com/time/magazine/article/0,9171,1101860217-143137,00.html
[1489] **Power, Glory --and Politics.** By **RICHARD N. OSTLING.** Sunday, Jun. 24, 2001 Article from Time in the 1980s. http://www.time.com/time/magazine/article/0,9171,1101860217-143137,00.html
[1490] **Enterprising Evangelism/ By Richard N. Ostling. Monday, Aug. 03, 1987** http://www.time.com/time/printout/0,8816,965155,00.html.
[1491] Timeline: A Half-Century of Falwell's Ministry. by Jeremy VanderKnyff http://www.npr.org/templates/story/story.php?storyId=10188427.
[1492] Timeline: A Half-Century of Falwell's Ministry. by Jeremy VanderKnyff http://www.npr.org/templates/story/story.php?storyId=10188427.
[1493] **Enterprising Evangelism/ By Richard N. Ostling. Monday, Aug. 03, 1987** http://www.time.com/time/printout/0,8816,965155,00.html.
[1494] **Enterprising Evangelism/ By Richard N. Ostling. Monday, Aug. 03, 1987** http://www.time.com/time/printout/0,8816,965155,00.html.
[1495] **Power, Glory --and Politics.** By **RICHARD N. OSTLING.** Sunday, Jun. 24, 2001 Article from Time in the 1980s. http://www.time.com/time/magazine/article/0,9171,1101860217-143137,00.html
[1496] **Power, Glory --and Politics.** By **RICHARD N. OSTLING.** Sunday, Jun. 24, 2001 Article from Time in the 1980s. http://www.time.com/time/magazine/article/0,9171,1101860217-143137,00.html
[1497] **Power, Glory --and Politics.** By **RICHARD N. OSTLING.** Sunday, Jun. 24, 2001 Article from Time in the 1980s. http://www.time.com/time/magazine/article/0,9171,1101860217-143137,00.html
[1498] PAT ROBERTSON. Founder and Chairman, The Christian Broadcasting Network. BIOGRAPHY http://www.patrobertson.com/Biography/index.asp.
[1499] PAT ROBERTSON. Founder and Chairman, The Christian Broadcasting Network. BIOGRAPHY http://www.patrobertson.com/Biography/index.asp.
[1500] PAT ROBERTSON. Founder and Chairman, The Christian Broadcasting Network. BIOGRAPHY http://www.patrobertson.com/Biography/index.asp.
[1501] PAT ROBERTSON. Founder and Chairman, The Christian Broadcasting Network. BIOGRAPHY http://www.patrobertson.com/Biography/index.asp.
[1502] **Power, Glory --and Politics.** By **RICHARD N. OSTLING.** Sunday, Jun. 24, 2001 Article from Time in the 1980s. http://www.time.com/time/magazine/article/0,9171,1101860217-143137,00.html
[1503] **Power, Glory --and Politics.** By **RICHARD N. OSTLING.** Sunday, Jun. 24, 2001 Article from Time in the 1980s. http://www.time.com/time/magazine/article/0,9171,1101860217-143137,00.html
[1504] **Power, Glory --and Politics.** By **RICHARD N. OSTLING.** Sunday, Jun. 24, 2001 Article from Time in the 1980s. http://www.time.com/time/magazine/article/0,9171,1101860217-143137,00.html
[1505] The Record of Pat Robertson On Religion and Government **December 27, 1987. By WAYNE KING** http://query.nytimes.com/gst/fullpage.html?res=9B0DEFD8163FF934A15751C1A961948260&sec=&spon=&pagewanted=print
[1506] The Record of Pat Robertson On Religion and Government **December 27, 1987. By WAYNE KING** http://query.nytimes.com/gst/fullpage.html?res=9B0DEFD8163FF934A15751C1A961948260&sec=&spon=&pagewanted=print
[1507] **Enterprising Evangelism/ By Richard N. Ostling. Monday, Aug. 03, 1987** http://www.time.com/time/printout/0,8816,965155,00.html.
[1508] The Record of Pat Robertson On Religion and Government **December 27, 1987. By WAYNE KING** http://query.nytimes.com/gst/fullpage.html?res=9B0DEFD8163FF934A15751C1A961948260&sec=&spon=&pagewanted=print.
[1509] The Record of Pat Robertson On Religion and Government **December 27, 1987. By WAYNE KING** http://query.nytimes.com/gst/fullpage.html?res=9B0DEFD8163FF934A15751C1A961948260&sec=&spon=&pagewanted=print
[1510] The Record of Pat Robertson On Religion and Government **December 27, 1987. By WAYNE KING** http://query.nytimes.com/gst/fullpage.html?res=9B0DEFD8163FF934A15751C1A961948260&sec=&spon=&pagewanted=print
[1511] The Record of Pat Robertson On Religion and Government **December 27, 1987. By WAYNE KING** http://query.nytimes.com/gst/fullpage.html?res=9B0DEFD8163FF934A15751C1A961948260&sec=&spon=&pagewanted=print
[1512] The Record of Pat Robertson On Religion and Government **December 27, 1987. By WAYNE KING** http://query.nytimes.com/gst/fullpage.html?res=9B0DEFD8163FF934A15751C1A961948260&sec=&spon=&pagewanted=print
[1513] The Record of Pat Robertson On Religion and Government **December 27, 1987. By WAYNE KING** http://query.nytimes.com/gst/fullpage.html?res=9B0DEFD8163FF934A15751C1A961948260&sec=&spon=&pagewanted=print
[1514] The Record of Pat Robertson On Religion and Government **December 27, 1987. By WAYNE KING** http://query.nytimes.com/gst/fullpage.html?res=9B0DEFD8163FF934A15751C1A961948260&sec=&spon=&pagewanted=print
[1515] The Record of Pat Robertson On Religion and Government **December 27, 1987. By WAYNE KING** http://query.nytimes.com/gst/fullpage.html?res=9B0DEFD8163FF934A15751C1A961948260&sec=&spon=&pagewanted=print
[1516] The Record of Pat Robertson On Religion and Government **December 27, 1987. By WAYNE KING** http://query.nytimes.com/gst/fullpage.html?res=9B0DEFD8163FF934A15751C1A961948260&sec=&spon=&pagewanted=print
[1517] The Record of Pat Robertson On Religion and Government **December 27, 1987. By WAYNE KING** http://query.nytimes.com/gst/fullpage.html?res=9B0DEFD8163FF934A15751C1A961948260&sec=&spon=&pagewanted=print
[1518] The Record of Pat Robertson On Religion and Government **December 27, 1987. By WAYNE KING** http://query.nytimes.com/gst/fullpage.html?res=9B0DEFD8163FF934A15751C1A961948260&sec=&spon=&pagewanted=print
[1519] BUSH ROUTS DOLE IN PRIMARIES AS DUKAKIS, JACKSON AND GORE MOVE FAR AHEAD OF GEPHARDT; RUNAWAY IN G.O.P. **By MICHAEL ORESKES March 9, 1988**http://query.nytimes.com/gst/fullpage.html?res=940DE2D81539F93AA35750C0A96E948260&sec=&spon=&pagewanted=print

[1520] BUSH ROUTS DOLE IN PRIMARIES AS DUKAKIS, JACKSON AND GORE MOVE FAR AHEAD OF GEPHARDT; RUNAWAY IN G.O.P. **By MICHAEL ORESKES March 9, 1988**http://query.nytimes.com/gst/fullpage.html?res=940DE2D81539F93AA35750C0A96E948260&sec=&spon=&pagewanted=print
[1521] BUSH ROUTS DOLE IN PRIMARIES AS DUKAKIS, JACKSON AND GORE MOVE FAR AHEAD OF GEPHARDT; RUNAWAY IN G.O.P. **By MICHAEL ORESKES March 9, 1988**http://query.nytimes.com/gst/fullpage.html?res=940DE2D81539F93AA35750C0A96E948260&sec=&spon=&pagewanted=print
[1522] BUSH ROUTS DOLE IN PRIMARIES AS DUKAKIS, JACKSON AND GORE MOVE FAR AHEAD OF GEPHARDT; RUNAWAY IN G.O.P. **By MICHAEL ORESKES March 9, 1988**http://query.nytimes.com/gst/fullpage.html?res=940DE2D81539F93AA35750C0A96E948260&sec=&spon=&pagewanted=print
[1523] Jerry Falwell quotes Jerry Falwell quotes from http://thinkexist.com/quotes/jerry_falwell/.
[1524] 1988: TV evangelist quits over sex scandal. BBC. http://news.bbc.co.uk/onthisday/hi/dates/stories/february/21/newsid_2565000/2565197.stm
[1525] The Record of Pat Robertson On Religion and Government **December 27, 1987. By WAYNE KING**
http://query.nytimes.com/gst/fullpage.html?res=9B0DEFD8163FF934A15751C1A961948260&sec=&spon=&pagewanted=print
[1526] The Record of Pat Robertson On Religion and Government **December 27, 1987. By WAYNE KING**
http://query.nytimes.com/gst/fullpage.html?res=9B0DEFD8163FF934A15751C1A961948260&sec=&spon=&pagewanted=print
[1527] The Record of Pat Robertson On Religion and Government **December 27, 1987. By WAYNE KING**
http://query.nytimes.com/gst/fullpage.html?res=9B0DEFD8163FF934A15751C1A961948260&sec=&spon=&pagewanted=print
[1528] The Record of Pat Robertson On Religion and Government **December 27, 1987. By WAYNE KING**
http://query.nytimes.com/gst/fullpage.html?res=9B0DEFD8163FF934A15751C1A961948260&sec=&spon=&pagewanted=print
[1529] The Record of Pat Robertson On Religion and Government **December 27, 1987. By WAYNE KING**
http://query.nytimes.com/gst/fullpage.html?res=9B0DEFD8163FF934A15751C1A961948260&sec=&spon=&pagewanted=print
[1530] **Pat Robertson warns of terrorist attack in '07.** Evangelist makes forecast as part of annual predictions. **The Associated Press.** Jan. 2, 2007URL: http://www.msnbc.msn.com/id/16442877/
[1531] God is warning of big storms, Robertson says. By The Associated Copyright © 2006 The Seattle Times CompanyPresshttp://seattletimes.nwsource.com/html/nationworld/2003004452_pat19.html. Friday, May 19, 2006
[1532] Pat Robertson warns of terrorist attack in '07. Evangelist makes forecast as part of annual predictions. The Associated Press. Jan. 2, 2007URL: http://www.msnbc.msn.com/id/16442877/
[1533] Pat Robertson warns of terrorist attack in '07. Evangelist makes forecast as part of annual predictions. The Associated Press. Jan. 2, 2007URL: http://www.msnbc.msn.com/id/16442877/
[1534] Pat Robertson warns of terrorist attack in '07. Evangelist makes forecast as part of annual predictions. The Associated Press. Jan. 2, 2007URL: http://www.msnbc.msn.com/id/16442877/
[1535] Pat Robertson Predicts Worldwide Violence, U.S. Recession in 2008. Wednesday, January 02, 2008. Associated Press. http://www.foxnews.com/story/0,2933,319728,00.html
[1536] What Quote » Celebrity Quotes » Quotes by Pat Robertson »http://www.whatquote.com/quotes/Pat-Robertson/31211-Feminism-encourages-.htm.
[1537] What Quote » Celebrity Quotes » Quotes by Pat Robertson »http://www.whatquote.com/quotes/Pat-Robertson/31211-Feminism-encourages-.htm.
[1538] What Quote » Celebrity Quotes » Quotes by Pat Robertson »http://www.whatquote.com/quotes/Pat-Robertson/31211-Feminism-encourages-.htm.
[1539] What Quote » Celebrity Quotes » Quotes by Pat Robertson »http://www.whatquote.com/quotes/Pat-Robertson/31211-Feminism-encourages-.htm.
[1540] TENNESSEE GUERILLA WOMEN .Tuesday, August 23, 2005, ABC Family TVs Pat Robertson Advocates Killing http://guerillawomentn.blogspot.com/2005/08/abc-family-tvs-pat-robertson-advocates.html.
[1541] TENNESSEE GUERILLA WOMEN .Tuesday, August 23, 2005, ABC Family TVs Pat Robertson Advocates Killing http://guerillawomentn.blogspot.com/2005/08/abc-family-tvs-pat-robertson-advocates.html.
[1542] TENNESSEE GUERILLA WOMEN .Tuesday, August 23, 2005, ABC Family TVs Pat Robertson Advocates Killing http://guerillawomentn.blogspot.com/2005/08/abc-family-tvs-pat-robertson-advocates.html.
[1543] Jerry Falwell, Evangelist, Political Activist, Dies (Update3). By Heather BurkeMay 15 (Bloomberg) – *Last Updated: May 15, 2007 21:23 EDT*
http://www.bloomberg.com/apps/news?pid=20601103&sid=auX3.SI9QH2M.
[1544] Timeline: A Half-Century of Falwell's Ministry. by Jeremy VanderKnyff http://www.npr.org/templates/story/story.php?storyId=10188427.
[1545] Timeline: A Half-Century of Falwell's Ministry. by Jeremy VanderKnyff http://www.npr.org/templates/story/story.php?storyId=10188427.
[1546] Jerry Falwell, Evangelist, Political Activist, Dies (Update3). By Heather BurkeMay 15 (Bloomberg) – *Last Updated: May 15, 2007 21:23 EDT*
http://www.bloomberg.com/apps/news?pid=20601103&sid=auX3.SI9QH2M.
[1547] Jerry Falwell, Evangelist, Political Activist, Dies (Update3). By Heather BurkeMay 15 (Bloomberg) – *Last Updated: May 15, 2007 21:23 EDT*
http://www.bloomberg.com/apps/news?pid=20601103&sid=auX3.SI9QH2M.
[1548] Jerry Falwell, Evangelist, Political Activist, Dies (Update3). By Heather BurkeMay 15 (Bloomberg) – *Last Updated: May 15, 2007 21:23 EDT*
http://www.bloomberg.com/apps/news?pid=20601103&sid=auX3.SI9QH2M.
[1549] **Power, Glory --and Politics.** By **RICHARD N. OSTLING.** Sunday, Jun. 24, 2001 Article from Time in the 1980s. http://www.time.com/time/magazine/article/0,9171,1101860217-143137,00.html
[1550] Televangelist, Christian Leader Jerry Falwell Dies. *All Things Considered,* May 15, 2007 by David Molpus. http://www.npr.org/templates/story/story.php?storyId=10188427
[1551] Televangelist, Christian Leader Jerry Falwell Dies. *All Things Considered,* May 15, 2007 by David Molpus. http://www.npr.org/templates/story/story.php?storyId=10188427
[1552] Jerry Falwell, Evangelist, Political Activist, Dies (Update3). By Heather BurkeMay 15 (Bloomberg) – *Last Updated: May 15, 2007 21:23 EDT*
http://www.bloomberg.com/apps/news?pid=20601103&sid=auX3.SI9QH2M.
[1553] Timeline: A Half-Century of Falwell's Ministry. by Jeremy VanderKnyff http://www.npr.org/templates/story/story.php?storyId=10188427.
[1554] Jerry Falwell, Evangelist, Political Activist, Dies (Update3). By Heather BurkeMay 15 (Bloomberg) – *Last Updated: May 15, 2007 21:23 EDT*
http://www.bloomberg.com/apps/news?pid=20601103&sid=auX3.SI9QH2M.
[1555] Jerry Falwell, Evangelist, Political Activist, Dies (Update3). By Heather BurkeMay 15 (Bloomberg) – *Last Updated: May 15, 2007 21:23 EDT*
http://www.bloomberg.com/apps/news?pid=20601103&sid=auX3.SI9QH2M.
[1556] Religiously-based conflicts, Controversial comments by leading fundamentalist Jerry Falwell: 1979 – 2006. About Jerry Falwell: http://www.religioustolerance.org/falwell.htm
[1557] Jerry Falwell, Evangelist, Political Activist, Dies (Update3). By Heather BurkeMay 15 (Bloomberg) – *Last Updated: May 15, 2007 21:23 EDT*
http://www.bloomberg.com/apps/news?pid=20601103&sid=auX3.SI9QH2M.
[1558] Televangelist, Christian Leader Jerry Falwell Dies. *All Things Considered,* May 15, 2007 by David Molpus. http://www.npr.org/templates/story/story.php?storyId=10188427
[1559] **Power, Glory --and Politics.** By **RICHARD N. OSTLING.** Sunday, Jun. 24, 2001 Article from Time in the 1980s. http://www.time.com/time/magazine/article/0,9171,1101860217-143137,00.html
[1560] Religiously-based conflicts, Controversial comments by leading fundamentalist Jerry Falwell: 1979 – 2006. About Jerry Falwell: http://www.religioustolerance.org/falwell.htm
[1561] Religiously-based conflicts, Controversial comments by leading fundamentalist Jerry Falwell: 1979 – 2006. About Jerry Falwell: http://www.religioustolerance.org/falwell.htm
[1562] Religiously-based conflicts, Controversial comments by leading fundamentalist Jerry Falwell: 1979 – 2006. About Jerry Falwell: http://www.religioustolerance.org/falwell.htm
[1563] Jerry Falwell, Evangelist, Political Activist, Dies (Update3). By Heather BurkeMay 15 (Bloomberg) – *Last Updated: May 15, 2007 21:23 EDT*
http://www.bloomberg.com/apps/news?pid=20601103&sid=auX3.SI9QH2M.
[1564] Gay Tinky Winky bad for children. Monday, 15 February 1999. http://news.bbc.co.uk/2/hi/entertainment/276677.stm
[1565] Gay Tinky Winky bad for children. Monday, 15 February 1999. http://news.bbc.co.uk/2/hi/entertainment/276677.stm
[1566] Gay Tinky Winky bad for children. Monday, 15 February 1999. http://news.bbc.co.uk/2/hi/entertainment/276677.stm
[1567] Gay Tinky Winky bad for children. Monday, 15 February 1999. http://news.bbc.co.uk/2/hi/entertainment/276677.stm
[1568] Gay Tinky Winky bad for children. Monday, 15 February 1999. http://news.bbc.co.uk/2/hi/entertainment/276677.stm
[1569] Gay Tinky Winky bad for children. Monday, 15 February 1999. http://news.bbc.co.uk/2/hi/entertainment/276677.stm
[1570] Gay Tinky Winky bad for children. Monday, 15 February 1999. http://news.bbc.co.uk/2/hi/entertainment/276677.stm
[1571] Jerry Falwell Quotes. The 10 Craziest Things Rev. Jerry Falwell Ever Said. By Daniel Kurtzman, About.comhttp://politicalhumor.about.com/od/stupidquotes/a/falwellquotes.htm
[1572] Jerry Falwell, Evangelist, Political Activist, Dies (Update3). By Heather BurkeMay 15 (Bloomberg) – *Last Updated: May 15, 2007 21:23 EDT*
http://www.bloomberg.com/apps/news?pid=20601103&sid=auX3.SI9QH2M.
[1573] **Rev. Jerry Falwell** (with Rev. Pat Robertson) **blames pagans, abortionists, feminists & gays and lesbians** for bringing on the terrorist attacks in New York and Washington. Partial transcript of comments from the September 13, 2001 telecast of the 700 Club. http://www.actupny.org/YELL/falwell.html
[1574] **Rev. Jerry Falwell** (with Rev. Pat Robertson) **blames pagans, abortionists, feminists & gays and lesbians** for bringing on the terrorist attacks in New York and Washington. Partial transcript of comments from the September 13, 2001 telecast of the 700 Club. http://www.actupny.org/YELL/falwell.html
[1575] **Rev. Jerry Falwell** (with Rev. Pat Robertson) **blames pagans, abortionists, feminists & gays and lesbians** for bringing on the terrorist attacks in New York and Washington. Partial transcript of comments from the September 13, 2001 telecast of the 700 Club. http://www.actupny.org/YELL/falwell.html
[1576] **Rev. Jerry Falwell** (with Rev. Pat Robertson) **blames pagans, abortionists, feminists & gays and lesbians** for bringing on the terrorist attacks in New York and Washington. Partial transcript of comments from the September 13, 2001 telecast of the 700 Club. http://www.actupny.org/YELL/falwell.html
[1577] Televangelist, Christian Leader Jerry Falwell Dies. *All Things Considered,* May 15, 2007 by David Molpus. http://www.npr.org/templates/story/story.php?storyId=10188427
[1578] Televangelist, Christian Leader Jerry Falwell Dies. *All Things Considered,* May 15, 2007 by David Molpus. http://www.npr.org/templates/story/story.php?storyId=10188427
[1579] Jerry Falwell quotes from http://thinkexist.com/quotation/aids_is_not_just_god-s_punishment_for_homosexuals/198214.html
[1580] Jerry Falwell quotes from http://thinkexist.com/quotes/jerry_falwell/2.html
[1581] Jerry Falwell Quotes. The 10 Craziest Things Rev. Jerry Falwell Ever Said. By Daniel Kurtzman, About.comhttp://politicalhumor.about.com/od/stupidquotes/a/falwellquotes.htm
[1582] Jerry Falwell Quotes. The 10 Craziest Things Rev. Jerry Falwell Ever Said. By Daniel Kurtzman, About.comhttp://politicalhumor.about.com/od/stupidquotes/a/falwellquotes.htm
[1583] Jerry Falwell Quotes. The 10 Craziest Things Rev. Jerry Falwell Ever Said. By Daniel Kurtzman, About.comhttp://politicalhumor.about.com/od/stupidquotes/a/falwellquotes.htm
[1584] Televangelist, Christian Leader Jerry Falwell Dies. *All Things Considered,* May 15, 2007 by David Molpus. http://www.npr.org/templates/story/story.php?storyId=10188427
[1585] Jerry Falwell Quotes. The 10 Craziest Things Rev. Jerry Falwell Ever Said. By Daniel Kurtzman, About.comhttp://politicalhumor.about.com/od/stupidquotes/a/falwellquotes.htm
[1586] Jerry Falwell quotes from http://thinkexist.com/quotation/aids_is_not_just_god-s_punishment_for_homosexuals/198214.html
[1587] Jerry Falwell quotes from http://thinkexist.com/quotation/aids_is_not_just_god-s_punishment_for_homosexuals/198214.html
[1588] Jerry Falwell quotes from http://thinkexist.com/quotation/aids_is_not_just_god-s_punishment_for_homosexuals/198214.html
[1589] Jerry Falwell quotes from http://thinkexist.com/quotation/aids_is_not_just_god-s_punishment_for_homosexuals/198214.html
[1590] 1988: TV evangelist quits over sex scandal. BBC. http://news.bbc.co.uk/onthisday/hi/dates/stories/february/21/newsid_2565000/2565197.stm
[1591] 1988: TV evangelist quits over sex scandal. BBC. http://news.bbc.co.uk/onthisday/hi/dates/stories/february/21/newsid_2565000/2565197.stm

[1592] SEX SCANDALS. ***March 07, 1988.*** *Vol. 29 . No. 9* The Fall of Jimmy Swaggart. By Joanne Kaufmanhttp://www.people.com/people/archive/article/0,,20098413,00.html
[1593] **Power, Glory --and Politics.** By **RICHARD N. OSTLING.** Sunday, Jun. 24, 2001 Article from Time in the 1980s. http://www.time.com/time/magazine/article/0,9171,1101860217-143137,00.html
[1594] SEX SCANDALS. ***March 07, 1988.*** *Vol. 29 . No. 9* The Fall of Jimmy Swaggart. By Joanne Kaufmanhttp://www.people.com/people/archive/article/0,,20098413,00.html
[1595] **Power, Glory --and Politics.** By **RICHARD N. OSTLING.** Sunday, Jun. 24, 2001 Article from Time in the 1980s. http://www.time.com/time/magazine/article/0,9171,1101860217-143137,00.html
[1596] **Enterprising Evangelism/ By Richard N. Ostling. Monday, Aug. 03, 1987** http://www.time.com/time/printout/0,8816,965155,00.html.
[1597] SEX SCANDALS. ***March 07, 1988.*** *Vol. 29 . No. 9* The Fall of Jimmy Swaggart. By Joanne Kaufmanhttp://www.people.com/people/archive/article/0,,20098413,00.html
[1598] SEX SCANDALS. ***March 07, 1988.*** *Vol. 29 . No. 9* The Fall of Jimmy Swaggart. By Joanne Kaufmanhttp://www.people.com/people/archive/article/0,,20098413,00.html
[1599] SEX SCANDALS. ***March 07, 1988.*** *Vol. 29 . No. 9* The Fall of Jimmy Swaggart. By Joanne Kaufmanhttp://www.people.com/people/archive/article/0,,20098413,00.html
[1600] SEX SCANDALS. ***March 07, 1988.*** *Vol. 29 . No. 9* The Fall of Jimmy Swaggart. By Joanne Kaufmanhttp://www.people.com/people/archive/article/0,,20098413,00.html
[1601] Jimmy Swaggart quotes from http://www.brainyquote.com/quotes/authors/j/jimmy_swaggart.html. Retrieved December 15, 2008.
[1602] Jimmy Swaggart quotes from http://www.brainyquote.com/quotes/authors/j/jimmy_swaggart.html. Retrieved December 15, 2008.
[1603] Jimmy Swaggart quotes from http://www.brainyquote.com/quotes/authors/j/jimmy_swaggart.html. Retrieved December 15, 2008.
[1604] **Power, Glory --and Politics.** By **RICHARD N. OSTLING.** Sunday, Jun. 24, 2001 Article from Time in the 1980s. http://www.time.com/time/magazine/article/0,9171,1101860217-143137,00.html
[1605] **Power, Glory --and Politics.** By **RICHARD N. OSTLING.** Sunday, Jun. 24, 2001 Article from Time in the 1980s. http://www.time.com/time/magazine/article/0,9171,1101860217-143137,00.html
[1606] Power, Glory --and Politics. By RICHARD N. OSTLING. Sunday, Jun. 24, 2001 Article from Time in the 1980s. http://www.time.com/time/magazine/article/0,9171,1101860217-143137,00.html
[1607] Enterprising Evangelism/ By Richard N. Ostling. Monday, Aug. 03, 1987 http://www.time.com/time/printout/0,8816,965155,00.html.
[1608] Enterprising Evangelism/ By Richard N. Ostling. Monday, Aug. 03, 1987 http://www.time.com/time/printout/0,8816,965155,00.html.
[1609] Enterprising Evangelism/ By Richard N. Ostling. Monday, Aug. 03, 1987 http://www.time.com/time/printout/0,8816,965155,00.html.
[1610] 1988: TV evangelist quits over sex scandal. BBC. http://news.bbc.co.uk/onthisday/hi/dates/stories/february/21/newsid_2565000/2565197.stm
[1611] 1988: TV evangelist quits over sex scandal. BBC. http://news.bbc.co.uk/onthisday/hi/dates/stories/february/21/newsid_2565000/2565197.stm
[1612] SEX SCANDALS. ***March 07, 1988.*** *Vol. 29 . No. 9* The Fall of Jimmy Swaggart. By Joanne Kaufmanhttp://www.people.com/people/archive/article/0,,20098413,00.html
[1613] 1988: TV evangelist quits over sex scandal. BBC. http://news.bbc.co.uk/onthisday/hi/dates/stories/february/21/newsid_2565000/2565197.stm
[1614] SEX SCANDALS. ***March 07, 1988.*** *Vol. 29 . No. 9* The Fall of Jimmy Swaggart. By Joanne Kaufmanhttp://www.people.com/people/archive/article/0,,20098413,00.html
[1615] **American Notes Scandals**Monday, Oct. 28, 1991http://www.time.com/time/magazine/article/0,9171,974120,00.html
[1616] 1988: TV evangelist quits over sex scandal. BBC. http://news.bbc.co.uk/onthisday/hi/dates/stories/february/21/newsid_2565000/2565197.stm
[1617] SEX SCANDALS. ***March 07, 1988.*** *Vol. 29 . No. 9* The Fall of Jimmy Swaggart. By Joanne Kaufmanhttp://www.people.com/people/archive/article/0,,20098413,00.html
[1618] SEX SCANDALS. ***March 07, 1988.*** *Vol. 29 . No. 9* The Fall of Jimmy Swaggart. By Joanne Kaufmanhttp://www.people.com/people/archive/article/0,,20098413,00.html
[1619] SEX SCANDALS. ***March 07, 1988.*** *Vol. 29 . No. 9* The Fall of Jimmy Swaggart. By Joanne Kaufmanhttp://www.people.com/people/archive/article/0,,20098413,00.html
[1620] **Enterprising Evangelism/ By Richard N. Ostling. Monday, Aug. 03, 1987** http://www.time.com/time/printout/0,8816,965155,00.html.
[1621] 1988: TV evangelist quits over sex scandal. BBC. http://news.bbc.co.uk/onthisday/hi/dates/stories/february/21/newsid_2565000/2565197.stm
[1622] 1988: TV evangelist quits over sex scandal. BBC. http://news.bbc.co.uk/onthisday/hi/dates/stories/february/21/newsid_2565000/2565197.stm
[1623] SEX SCANDALS. ***March 07, 1988.*** *Vol. 29 . No. 9* The Fall of Jimmy Swaggart. By Joanne Kaufmanhttp://www.people.com/people/archive/article/0,,20098413,00.html
[1624] **American Notes Scandals**Monday, Oct. 28, 1991http://www.time.com/time/magazine/article/0,9171,974120,00.html
[1625] SEX SCANDALS. ***March 07, 1988.*** *Vol. 29 . No. 9* The Fall of Jimmy Swaggart. By Joanne Kaufmanhttp://www.people.com/people/archive/article/0,,20098413,00.html
[1626] SEX SCANDALS. ***March 07, 1988.*** *Vol. 29 . No. 9* The Fall of Jimmy Swaggart. By Joanne Kaufmanhttp://www.people.com/people/archive/article/0,,20098413,00.html
[1627] SEX SCANDALS. ***March 07, 1988.*** *Vol. 29 . No. 9* The Fall of Jimmy Swaggart. By Joanne Kaufmanhttp://www.people.com/people/archive/article/0,,20098413,00.html
[1628] 1988: TV evangelist quits over sex scandal. BBC. http://news.bbc.co.uk/onthisday/hi/dates/stories/february/21/newsid_2565000/2565197.stm
[1629] 1988: TV evangelist quits over sex scandal. BBC. http://news.bbc.co.uk/onthisday/hi/dates/stories/february/21/newsid_2565000/2565197.stm
[1630] SEX SCANDALS. ***March 07, 1988.*** *Vol. 29 . No. 9* The Fall of Jimmy Swaggart. By Joanne Kaufmanhttp://www.people.com/people/archive/article/0,,20098413,00.html
[1631] **American Notes Scandals**Monday, Oct. 28, 1991http://www.time.com/time/magazine/article/0,9171,974120,00.html
[1632] SEX SCANDALS. ***March 07, 1988.*** *Vol. 29 . No. 9* The Fall of Jimmy Swaggart. By Joanne Kaufmanhttp://www.people.com/people/archive/article/0,,20098413,00.html
[1633] SEX SCANDALS. ***March 07, 1988.*** *Vol. 29 . No. 9* The Fall of Jimmy Swaggart. By Joanne Kaufmanhttp://www.people.com/people/archive/article/0,,20098413,00.html
[1634] 1988: TV evangelist quits over sex scandal. BBC. http://news.bbc.co.uk/onthisday/hi/dates/stories/february/21/newsid_2565000/2565197.stm
[1635] Reverend Jimmy Swaggart. *Apology Sermon.* delivered 21 February 1988, Family Worship Center, Baton Rouge, http://americanrhetoric.com/speeches/jswaggartapologysermon.html
[1636] 1988: TV evangelist quits over sex scandal. BBC. http://news.bbc.co.uk/onthisday/hi/dates/stories/february/21/newsid_2565000/2565197.stm
[1637] SEX SCANDALS. ***March 07, 1988.*** *Vol. 29 . No. 9* The Fall of Jimmy Swaggart. By Joanne Kaufmanhttp://www.people.com/people/archive/article/0,,20098413,00.html
[1638] Reverend Jimmy Swaggart. *Apology Sermon.* delivered 21 February 1988, Family Worship Center, Baton Rouge, http://americanrhetoric.com/speeches/jswaggartapologysermon.html
[1639] Reverend Jimmy Swaggart. *Apology Sermon.* delivered 21 February 1988, Family Worship Center, Baton Rouge, http://americanrhetoric.com/speeches/jswaggartapologysermon.html
[1640] SEX SCANDALS. ***March 07, 1988.*** *Vol. 29 . No. 9* The Fall of Jimmy Swaggart. By Joanne Kaufmanhttp://www.people.com/people/archive/article/0,,20098413,00.html
[1641] SEX SCANDALS. ***March 07, 1988.*** *Vol. 29 . No. 9* The Fall of Jimmy Swaggart. By Joanne Kaufmanhttp://www.people.com/people/archive/article/0,,20098413,00.html
[1642] SEX SCANDALS. ***March 07, 1988.*** *Vol. 29 . No. 9* The Fall of Jimmy Swaggart. By Joanne Kaufmanhttp://www.people.com/people/archive/article/0,,20098413,00.html
[1643] 1988: TV evangelist quits over sex scandal. BBC. http://news.bbc.co.uk/onthisday/hi/dates/stories/february/21/newsid_2565000/2565197.stm
[1644] 1988: TV evangelist quits over sex scandal. BBC. http://news.bbc.co.uk/onthisday/hi/dates/stories/february/21/newsid_2565000/2565197.stm
[1645] BUSH ROUTS DOLE IN PRIMARIES AS DUKAKIS, JACKSON AND GORE MOVE FAR AHEAD OF GEPHARDT; RUNAWAY IN G.O.P. **By MICHAEL ORESKES March 9, 1988**http://query.nytimes.com/gst/fullpage.html?res=940DE2D81539F93AA35750C0A96E948260&sec=&spon=&pagewanted=print
[1646] 1988: TV evangelist quits over sex scandal. BBC. http://news.bbc.co.uk/onthisday/hi/dates/stories/february/21/newsid_2565000/2565197.stm
[1647] SEX SCANDALS. ***March 07, 1988.*** *Vol. 29 . No. 9* The Fall of Jimmy Swaggart. By Joanne Kaufmanhttp://www.people.com/people/archive/article/0,,20098413,00.html
[1648] 1988: TV evangelist quits over sex scandal. BBC. http://news.bbc.co.uk/onthisday/hi/dates/stories/february/21/newsid_2565000/2565197.stm
[1649] Swaggart Plans to Step Down **October 15, The New York Times. 1991**
http://query.nytimes.com/gst/fullpage.html?res=9D0CE5DA1E3BF936A25753C1A967958260&sec=&spon=&pagewanted=print
[1650] Swaggart Plans to Step Down **October 15, The New York Times. 1991**
http://query.nytimes.com/gst/fullpage.html?res=9D0CE5DA1E3BF936A25753C1A967958260&sec=&spon=&pagewanted=print
[1651] Swaggart Plans to Step Down **October 15, The New York Times. 1991**
http://query.nytimes.com/gst/fullpage.html?res=9D0CE5DA1E3BF936A25753C1A967958260&sec=&spon=&pagewanted=print
[1652] **American Notes Scandals**Monday, Oct. 28, 1991http://www.time.com/time/magazine/article/0,9171,974120,00.html
[1653] **American Notes Scandals**Monday, Oct. 28, 1991http://www.time.com/time/magazine/article/0,9171,974120,00.html
[1654] Swaggart Plans to Step Down **October 15, The New York Times. 1991**
http://query.nytimes.com/gst/fullpage.html?res=9D0CE5DA1E3BF936A25753C1A967958260&sec=&spon=&pagewanted=print
[1655] SEX SCANDALS. ***March 07, 1988.*** *Vol. 29 . No. 9* The Fall of Jimmy Swaggart. By Joanne Kaufmanhttp://www.people.com/people/archive/article/0,,20098413,00.html
[1656] Jimmy Swaggart quotes from http://www.brainyquote.com/quotes/authors/j/jimmy_swaggart.html. Retrieved December 15, 2008.
[1657] Jimmy Swaggart quotes from http://www.brainyquote.com/quotes/authors/j/jimmy_swaggart.html. Retrieved December 15, 2008.
[1658] Jimmy Swaggart quotes from http://www.brainyquote.com/quotes/authors/j/jimmy_swaggart.html. Retrieved December 15, 2008.
[1659] Jimmy Swaggart quotes from http://www.brainyquote.com/quotes/authors/j/jimmy_swaggart.html. Retrieved December 15, 2008.
[1660] See http://www.jsm.org/explore.cfm/jimmyswaggart/; retrieved December 15, 2008.
[1661] See http://www.jsm.org/explore.cfm/jimmyswaggart/ retrieved December 15, 2008.
[1662] Forgiven: The Rise and Fall of Jim Bakker and the PTL Ministry. - book reviews
Henry G. Brinton . COPYRIGHT 1990 Washington Monthly Company
[1663] Forgiven: The Rise and Fall of Jim Bakker and the PTL Ministry. - book reviews
Henry G. Brinton . COPYRIGHT 1990 Washington Monthly Company
[1664] Ex-wife of evangelist Jim Bakker dies By William M. Welch, USA TODAY.http://www.usatoday.com/news/nation/2007-07-21-tammy-faye_N.htm
[1665] Ex-wife of evangelist Jim Bakker dies By William M. Welch, USA TODAY.http://www.usatoday.com/news/nation/2007-07-21-tammy-faye_N.htm
[1666] Tammy Faye Messner dies. CNN. http://www.cnn.com/2007/US/07/21/tammy.faye/index.html
[1667] Tammy Faye Messner dies. CNN. http://www.cnn.com/2007/US/07/21/tammy.faye/index.html
[1668] Ex-wife of evangelist Jim Bakker dies By William M. Welch, USA TODAY.http://www.usatoday.com/news/nation/2007-07-21-tammy-faye_N.htm
[1669] Tammy Faye Messner dies. CNN. http://www.cnn.com/2007/US/07/21/tammy.faye/index.html
[1670] Ex-wife of evangelist Jim Bakker dies By William M. Welch, USA TODAY. http://www.usatoday.com/news/nation/2007-07-21-tammy-faye_N.htm
[1671] Power, Glory --and Politics. By RICHARD N. OSTLING. Sunday, Jun. 24, 2001 Article from Time in the 1980s. http://www.time.com/time/magazine/article/0,9171,1101860217-143137,00.html
[1672] Ex-wife of evangelist Jim Bakker dies By William M. Welch, USA TODAY.http://www.usatoday.com/news/nation/2007-07-21-tammy-faye_N.htm
[1673] Power, Glory --and Politics. By RICHARD N. OSTLING. Sunday, Jun. 24, 2001 Article from Time in the 1980s. http://www.time.com/time/magazine/article/0,9171,1101860217-143137,00.html
[1674] Tammy Faye Bakker, 65, Emotive Evangelist, Dies By ANITA GATES. July 22, 2007 http://www.nytimes.com/2007/07/22/us/22bakker.html?_r=1&pagewanted=print.

[1675] [illegible]By William M. Welch, USA TODAY. http://www.usatoday.com/news/nation/2007-07-21-tammy-faye_N.htm
[1676] Tammy Faye Messner dies. CNN. http://www.cnn.com/2007/US/07/21/tammy.faye/index.html
[1677] Tammy Faye Messner dies. CNN. http://www.cnn.com/2007/US/07/21/tammy.faye/index.html
[1678] Tammy Faye Messner dies. CNN. http://www.cnn.com/2007/US/07/21/tammy.faye/index.html
[1679] Tammy Faye Bakker, 65, Emotive Evangelist, Dies By ANITA GATES. July 22, 2007 http://www.nytimes.com/2007/07/22/us/22bakker.html?_r=1&pagewanted=print.
[1680] Tammy Faye Messner dies. CNN. http://www.cnn.com/2007/US/07/21/tammy.faye/index.html
[1681] Tammy Faye Messner dies. CNN. http://www.cnn.com/2007/US/07/21/tammy.faye/index.html
[1682] Tammy Faye Messner dies. CNN. http://www.cnn.com/2007/US/07/21/tammy.faye/index.html
[1683] **Tammy Faye Bakker Messner.** July 23, 2007. Televangelist whose TV empire collapsed amid spectacular scandalhttp://www.timesonline.co.uk/tol/comment/obituaries/article2120961.ece
[1684] **Power, Glory --and Politics.** By **RICHARD N. OSTLING.** Sunday, Jun. 24, 2001 Article from Time in the 1980s. http://www.time.com/time/magazine/article/0,9171,1101860217-143137,00.html
[1685] **Tammy Faye Bakker Messner.** July 23, 2007. Televangelist whose TV empire collapsed amid spectacular scandalhttp://www.timesonline.co.uk/tol/comment/obituaries/article2120961.ece
[1686] Tammy Faye Bakker, 65, Emotive Evangelist, Dies By **ANITA GATES.** July 22, 2007 http://www.nytimes.com/2007/07/22/us/22bakker.html?_r=1&pagewanted=print.
[1687] **Tammy Faye Bakker Messner.** July 23, 2007. Televangelist whose TV empire collapsed amid spectacular scandalhttp://www.timesonline.co.uk/tol/comment/obituaries/article2120961.ece
[1688] **Tammy Faye Bakker Messner.** July 23, 2007. Televangelist whose TV empire collapsed amid spectacular scandalhttp://www.timesonline.co.uk/tol/comment/obituaries/article2120961.ece
[1689] **[illegible]By William M. Welch, USA TODAY.**http://www.usatoday.com/news/nation/2007-07-21-tammy-faye_N.htm
[1690] **Power, Glory --and Politics.** By **RICHARD N. OSTLING.** Sunday, Jun. 24, 2001 Article from Time in the 1980s. http://www.time.com/time/magazine/article/0,9171,1101860217-143137,00.html
[1691] **Power, Glory --and Politics.** By **RICHARD N. OSTLING.** Sunday, Jun. 24, 2001 Article from Time in the 1980s. http://www.time.com/time/magazine/article/0,9171,1101860217-143137,00.html
[1692] **Enterprising Evangelism/ By Richard N. Ostling. Monday, Aug. 03, 1987** http://www.time.com/time/printout/0,8816,965155,00.html.
[1693] Tammy Faye Bakker, 65, Emotive Evangelist, Dies By **ANITA GATES.** July 22, 2007 http://www.nytimes.com/2007/07/22/us/22bakker.html?_r=1&pagewanted=print.
[1694] **Enterprising Evangelism/ By Richard N. Ostling. Monday, Aug. 03, 1987** http://www.time.com/time/printout/0,8816,965155,00.html.
[1695] **Enterprising Evangelism/ By Richard N. Ostling. Monday, Aug. 03, 1987** http://www.time.com/time/printout/0,8816,965155,00.html.
[1696] **Enterprising Evangelism/ By Richard N. Ostling. Monday, Aug. 03, 1987** http://www.time.com/time/printout/0,8816,965155,00.html.
[1697] **Enterprising Evangelism/ By Richard N. Ostling. Monday, Aug. 03, 1987** http://www.time.com/time/printout/0,8816,965155,00.html.
[1698] **Enterprising Evangelism/ By Richard N. Ostling. Monday, Aug. 03, 1987** http://www.time.com/time/printout/0,8816,965155,00.html.
[1699] Tammy Faye Messner dies. CNN. http://www.cnn.com/2007/US/07/21/tammy.faye/index.html
[1700] Tammy Faye Messner dies. CNN. http://www.cnn.com/2007/US/07/21/tammy.faye/index.html
[1701] Tammy Faye Messner dies. CNN. http://www.cnn.com/2007/US/07/21/tammy.faye/index.html
[1702] **Monday, Aug. 03, 1987.God and Money. By David Brand**http://www.time.com/time/printout/0,8816,965156,00.html
[1703] **Jim Bakker's Crumbling World. By RICHARD N. OSTLING;JOSEPH J. KANE/ATLANTA Monday, Dec. 19, 1988 http://www.time.com/time/magazine/article/0,9171,956551,00.html.**
[1704] **Jim Bakker's Crumbling World. By RICHARD N. OSTLING;JOSEPH J. KANE/ATLANTA Monday, Dec. 19, 1988 http://www.time.com/time/magazine/article/0,9171,956551,00.html.**
[1705] **Jim Bakker's Crumbling World. By RICHARD N. OSTLING;JOSEPH J. KANE/ATLANTA Monday, Dec. 19, 1988 http://www.time.com/time/magazine/article/0,9171,956551,00.html.**
[1706] **Jim Bakker's Crumbling World. By RICHARD N. OSTLING;JOSEPH J. KANE/ATLANTA Monday, Dec. 19, 1988 http://www.time.com/time/magazine/article/0,9171,956551,00.html.**
[1707] Taking Command at Fort Mill. Monday, May. 11, 1987. By Richard N. Ostling http://www.time.com/time/magazine/article/0,9171,964322,00.html
[1708] **Jim Bakker's Crumbling World. By RICHARD N. OSTLING;JOSEPH J. KANE/ATLANTA Monday, Dec. 19, 1988 http://www.time.com/time/magazine/article/0,9171,956551,00.html.**
[1709] **Jim Bakker's Crumbling World. By RICHARD N. OSTLING;JOSEPH J. KANE/ATLANTA Monday, Dec. 19, 1988 http://www.time.com/time/magazine/article/0,9171,956551,00.html.**
[1710] Tammy Faye Bakker, 65, Emotive Evangelist, Dies By **ANITA GATES.** July 22, 2007 http://www.nytimes.com/2007/07/22/us/22bakker.html?_r=1&pagewanted=print.
[1711] **Forgiven: The Rise and Fall of Jim Bakker and the PTL Ministry. - book reviews**
Henry G. Brinton . COPYRIGHT 1990 Washington Monthly Company
[1712] **Forgiven: The Rise and Fall of Jim Bakker and the PTL Ministry. - book reviews**
Henry G. Brinton . COPYRIGHT 1990 Washington Monthly Company
[1713] **[illegible]By William M. Welch, USA TODAY.**http://www.usatoday.com/news/nation/2007-07-21-tammy-faye_N.htm
[1714] **Jim Bakker, with the PTL and prison behind him, dreams big in Missouri. By Todd C. Frankel • ST. LOUIS POST-DISPATCH.** 02/17/2008 **tfrankel@post-dispatch.com | 314-340-8110**http://www.stltoday.com/stltoday/news/stories.nsf/missouristatenews/story/9133CC5A10327DE7862573F2001D41BE?OpenDocument
[1715] **Tammy Faye Bakker Messner.** July 23, 2007. Televangelist whose TV empire collapsed amid spectacular scandalhttp://www.timesonline.co.uk/tol/comment/obituaries/article2120961.ece
[1716] **Tammy Faye Bakker Messner.** July 23, 2007. Televangelist whose TV empire collapsed amid spectacular scandalhttp://www.timesonline.co.uk/tol/comment/obituaries/article2120961.ece
[1717] Tammy Faye Messner dies. CNN. http://www.cnn.com/2007/US/07/21/tammy.faye/index.html
[1718] Tammy Faye Bakker, 65, Emotive Evangelist, Dies By **ANITA GATES.** July 22, 2007 http://www.nytimes.com/2007/07/22/us/22bakker.html?_r=1&pagewanted=print.
[1719] **[illegible]By William M. Welch, USA TODAY.**http://www.usatoday.com/news/nation/2007-07-21-tammy-faye_N.htm
[1720] **[illegible]By William M. Welch, USA TODAY.**
http://www.usatoday.com/news/nation/2007-07-21-tammy-faye_N.htm
[1721] **Enterprising Evangelism/ By Richard N. Ostling. Monday, Aug. 03, 1987** http://www.time.com/time/printout/0,8816,965155,00.html.
[1722] **[illegible]By William M. Welch, USA TODAY.**http://www.usatoday.com/news/nation/2007-07-21-tammy-faye_N.htm
[1723] Tammy Faye Messner dies. CNN. http://www.cnn.com/2007/US/07/21/tammy.faye/index.html
[1724] **[illegible]By William M. Welch, USA TODAY.**http://www.usatoday.com/news/nation/2007-07-21-tammy-faye_N.htm
[1725] Tammy Faye Messner dies. CNN. http://www.cnn.com/2007/US/07/21/tammy.faye/index.html
[1726] Tammy Faye Messner dies. CNN. http://www.cnn.com/2007/US/07/21/tammy.faye/index.html
[1727] Tammy Faye Messner dies. CNN. http://www.cnn.com/2007/US/07/21/tammy.faye/index.html
[1728] [illegible]By William M. Welch, USA TODAY.http://www.usatoday.com/news/nation/2007-07-21-tammy-faye_N.htm
[1729] Tammy Faye Bakker Messner. July 23, 2007. Televangelist whose TV empire collapsed amid spectacular scandalhttp://www.timesonline.co.uk/tol/comment/obituaries/article2120961.ece
[1730] Tammy Faye Messner dies. CNN. http://www.cnn.com/2007/US/07/21/tammy.faye/index.html
[1731] **Monday, Aug. 03, 1987.God and Money. By David Brand**http://www.time.com/time/printout/0,8816,965156,00.html
[1732] **Monday, Aug. 03, 1987.God and Money. By David Brand**http://www.time.com/time/printout/0,8816,965156,00.html
[1733] **Monday, Aug. 03, 1987.God and Money. By David Brand**http://www.time.com/time/printout/0,8816,965156,00.html
[1734] **Monday, Aug. 03, 1987.God and Money. By David Brand**http://www.time.com/time/printout/0,8816,965156,00.html
[1735] **Monday, Aug. 03, 1987.God and Money. By David Brand**http://www.time.com/time/printout/0,8816,965156,00.html
[1736] **Monday, Aug. 03, 1987.God and Money. By David Brand**http://www.time.com/time/printout/0,8816,965156,00.html
[1737] **Monday, Aug. 03, 1987.God and Money. By David Brand**http://www.time.com/time/printout/0,8816,965156,00.html
[1738] **Monday, Aug. 03, 1987.God and Money. By David Brand**http://www.time.com/time/printout/0,8816,965156,00.html
[1739] **Monday, Aug. 03, 1987.God and Money. By David Brand**http://www.time.com/time/printout/0,8816,965156,00.html
[1740] **Monday, Aug. 03, 1987.God and Money. By David Brand**http://www.time.com/time/printout/0,8816,965156,00.html
[1741] **Monday, Aug. 03, 1987.God and Money. By David Brand**http://www.time.com/time/printout/0,8816,965156,00.html
[1742] **Monday, Aug. 03, 1987.God and Money. By David Brand**http://www.time.com/time/printout/0,8816,965156,00.html
[1743] **Enterprising Evangelism/ By Richard N. Ostling. Monday, Aug. 03, 1987** http://www.time.com/time/printout/0,8816,965155,00.html.
[1744] **Preacher Scandals Strengthen TV Evangelism, Falwell Says. Washington Post.** Mar 19, 1988http://pqasb.pqarchiver.com/washingtonpost/access/73577139.html?dids=73577139:73577139&FMT=ABS&FMTS
[1745] **Tammy Faye Bakker Messner.** July 23, 2007. Televangelist whose TV empire collapsed amid spectacular scandalhttp://www.timesonline.co.uk/tol/comment/obituaries/article2120961.ece
[1746] **Tammy Faye Bakker Messner.** July 23, 2007. Televangelist whose TV empire collapsed amid spectacular scandalhttp://www.timesonline.co.uk/tol/comment/obituaries/article2120961.ece
[1747] Taking Command at Fort Mill. Monday, May. 11, 1987. By Richard N. Ostling http://www.time.com/time/magazine/article/0,9171,964322,00.html
[1748] Taking Command at Fort Mill. Monday, May. 11, 1987. By Richard N. Ostling http://www.time.com/time/magazine/article/0,9171,964322,00.html
[1749] Taking Command at Fort Mill. Monday, May. 11, 1987. By Richard N. Ostling http://www.time.com/time/magazine/article/0,9171,964322,00.html
[1750] **Jim Bakker's Crumbling World. By RICHARD N. OSTLING;JOSEPH J. KANE/ATLANTA Monday, Dec. 19, 1988 http://www.time.com/time/magazine/article/0,9171,956551,00.html.**
[1751] **Monday, Aug. 03, 1987.God and Money. By David Brand**http://www.time.com/time/printout/0,8816,965156,00.html
[1752] **Monday, Aug. 03, 1987.God and Money. By David Brand**http://www.time.com/time/printout/0,8816,965156,00.html
[1753] Tammy Faye Messner dies. CNN. http://www.cnn.com/2007/US/07/21/tammy.faye/index.html
[1754] Tammy Faye Messner dies. CNN. http://www.cnn.com/2007/US/07/21/tammy.faye/index.html
[1755] **[illegible]By William M. Welch, USA TODAY.**
http://www.usatoday.com/news/nation/2007-07-21-tammy-faye_N.htm

[1756] Tammy Faye Messner dies. CNN. http://www.cnn.com/2007/US/07/21/tammy.faye/index.html; and **Tammy Faye Bakker Messner.** July 23, 2007. Televangelist whose TV empire collapsed amid spectacular scandalhttp://www.timesonline.co.uk/tol/comment/obituaries/article2120961.ece

[1757] Tammy Faye Bakker, 65, Emotive Evangelist, Dies By **ANITA GATES**. July 22, 2007 http://www.nytimes.com/2007/07/22/us/22bakker.html?_r=1&pagewanted=print. And **Tammy Faye Bakker Messner.** July 23, 2007. Televangelist whose TV empire collapsed amid spectacular scandalhttp://www.timesonline.co.uk/tol/comment/obituaries/article2120961.ece

[1758] The Words of Tammy Faye. Interview with Tammy Faye Bakker-Messner. by Randy Shulman, Published on *June 6, 2002* http://www.metroweekly.com/feature/?ak=11

[1759] **[illegible]By William M. Welch, USA TODAY.**http://www.usatoday.com/news/nation/2007-07-21-tammy-faye_N.htm

[1760] **[illegible]By William M. Welch, USA TODAY.**http://www.usatoday.com/news/nation/2007-07-21-tammy-faye_N.htm

[1761] **Jim Bakker, with the PTL and prison behind him, dreams big in Missouri. By Todd C. Frankel • ST. LOUIS POST-DISPATCH.** 02/17/2008 **tfrankel@post-dispatch.com | 314-340-8110**http://www.stltoday.com/stltoday/news/stories.nsf/missouristatenews/story/9133CC5A10327DE7862573F2001D41BE?OpenDocument

[1762] **Jim Bakker, with the PTL and prison behind him, dreams big in Missouri. By Todd C. Frankel • ST. LOUIS POST-DISPATCH.** 02/17/2008 **tfrankel@post-dispatch.com | 314-340-8110**http://www.stltoday.com/stltoday/news/stories.nsf/missouristatenews/story/9133CC5A10327DE7862573F2001D41BE?OpenDocument

[1763] **Jim Bakker, with the PTL and prison behind him, dreams big in Missouri. By Todd C. Frankel • ST. LOUIS POST-DISPATCH.** 02/17/2008 **tfrankel@post-dispatch.com | 314-340-8110**http://www.stltoday.com/stltoday/news/stories.nsf/missouristatenews/story/9133CC5A10327DE7862573F2001D41BE?OpenDocument

[1764] **Jim Bakker, with the PTL and prison behind him, dreams big in Missouri. By Todd C. Frankel • ST. LOUIS POST-DISPATCH.** 02/17/2008 **tfrankel@post-dispatch.com | 314-340-8110**http://www.stltoday.com/stltoday/news/stories.nsf/missouristatenews/story/9133CC5A10327DE7862573F2001D41BE?OpenDocument

[1765] **Jim Bakker, with the PTL and prison behind him, dreams big in Missouri. By Todd C. Frankel • ST. LOUIS POST-DISPATCH.** 02/17/2008 **tfrankel@post-dispatch.com | 314-340-8110**http://www.stltoday.com/stltoday/news/stories.nsf/missouristatenews/story/9133CC5A10327DE7862573F2001D41BE?OpenDocument

[1766] **Jim Bakker, with the PTL and prison behind him, dreams big in Missouri. By Todd C. Frankel • ST. LOUIS POST-DISPATCH.** 02/17/2008 **tfrankel@post-dispatch.com | 314-340-8110**http://www.stltoday.com/stltoday/news/stories.nsf/missouristatenews/story/9133CC5A10327DE7862573F2001D41BE?OpenDocument

[1767] **[illegible]By William M. Welch, USA TODAY.**http://www.usatoday.com/news/nation/2007-07-21-tammy-faye_N.htm.

[1768] **Tammy Faye Bakker Messner.** July 23, 2007. Televangelist whose TV empire collapsed amid spectacular scandalhttp://www.timesonline.co.uk/tol/comment/obituaries/article2120961.ece

[1769] **Tammy Faye Bakker Messner.** July 23, 2007. Televangelist whose TV empire collapsed amid spectacular scandalhttp://www.timesonline.co.uk/tol/comment/obituaries/article2120961.ece

[1770] **[illegible]By William M. Welch, USA TODAY.**http://www.usatoday.com/news/nation/2007-07-21-tammy-faye_N.htm

[1771] Tammy Faye Messner dies. CNN. http://www.cnn.com/2007/US/07/21/tammy.faye/index.html

[1772] Tammy Faye Messner dies. CNN. http://www.cnn.com/2007/US/07/21/tammy.faye/index.html

[1773] Tammy Faye Messner dies. CNN. http://www.cnn.com/2007/US/07/21/tammy.faye/index.html

[1774] **Tammy Faye Bakker Messner.** July 23, 2007. Televangelist whose TV empire collapsed amid spectacular scandalhttp://www.timesonline.co.uk/tol/comment/obituaries/article2120961.ece

[1775] **Tammy Faye Bakker Messner.** July 23, 2007. Televangelist whose TV empire collapsed amid spectacular scandalhttp://www.timesonline.co.uk/tol/comment/obituaries/article2120961.ece

[1776] Tammy Faye Messner dies. CNN. http://www.cnn.com/2007/US/07/21/tammy.faye/index.html

[1777] The Words of Tammy Faye. Interview with Tammy Faye Bakker-Messner. by Randy Shulman. Published on *June 6, 2002* http://www.metroweekly.com/feature/?ak=11

[1778] The Words of Tammy Faye. Interview with Tammy Faye Bakker-Messner. by Randy Shulman. Published on *June 6, 2002* http://www.metroweekly.com/feature/?ak=11

[1779] The Words of Tammy Faye. Interview with Tammy Faye Bakker-Messner. by Randy Shulman. Published on *June 6, 2002* http://www.metroweekly.com/feature/?ak=11

[1780] The Words of Tammy Faye. Interview with Tammy Faye Bakker-Messner. by Randy Shulman. Published on *June 6, 2002* http://www.metroweekly.com/feature/?ak=11

[1781] The Words of Tammy Faye. Interview with Tammy Faye Bakker-Messner. by Randy Shulman. Published on *June 6, 2002* http://www.metroweekly.com/feature/?ak=11

[1782] The Words of Tammy Faye. Interview with Tammy Faye Bakker-Messner. by Randy Shulman. Published on *June 6, 2002* http://www.metroweekly.com/feature/?ak=11

[1783] The Re-Invention of Tammy Faye. **Former Christian Broadcasting Queen Has New Gay Following. June 20, 2002.** http://www.npr.org/programs/atc/features/2002/june/tammyfaye/

[1784] The Words of Tammy Faye. Interview with Tammy Faye Bakker-Messner. by Randy Shulman. Published on *June 6, 2002* http://www.metroweekly.com/feature/?ak=11

[1785] The Words of Tammy Faye. Interview with Tammy Faye Bakker-Messner. by Randy Shulman. Published on *June 6, 2002* http://www.metroweekly.com/feature/?ak=11

[1786] The Re-Invention of Tammy Faye. **Former Christian Broadcasting Queen Has New Gay Following. June 20, 2002.** http://www.npr.org/programs/atc/features/2002/june/tammyfaye/

[1787] **[illegible]By William M. Welch, USA TODAY.**http://www.usatoday.com/news/nation/2007-07-21-tammy-faye_N.htm.

[1788] Former Tammy Faye Bakker tells Larry King she has inoperable lung cancer. Associated Press/March 19, 2004 http://www.rickross.com/reference/bakker/bakker14.html

[1789] **[illegible]By William M. Welch, USA TODAY.**http://www.usatoday.com/news/nation/2007-07-21-tammy-faye_N.htm

[1790] Tammy Faye Messner dies. CNN. http://www.cnn.com/2007/US/07/21/tammy.faye/index.html

[1791] Tammy Faye Messner dies. CNN. http://www.cnn.com/2007/US/07/21/tammy.faye/index.html

[1792] **[illegible]By William M. Welch, USA TODAY.**http://www.usatoday.com/news/nation/2007-07-21-tammy-faye_N.htm. **Tammy Faye Bakker Messner.** July 23, 2007. Televangelist whose TV empire collapsed amid spectacular scandalhttp://www.timesonline.co.uk/tol/comment/obituaries/article2120961.ece

[1793] **[illegible]By William M. Welch, USA TODAY.**http://www.usatoday.com/news/nation/2007-07-21-tammy-faye_N.htm

[1794] Tammy Faye Messner dies. CNN. http://www.cnn.com/2007/US/07/21/tammy.faye/index.html

[1795] **Tammy Faye Bakker Messner.** July 23, 2007. Televangelist whose TV empire collapsed amid spectacular scandalhttp://www.timesonline.co.uk/tol/comment/obituaries/article2120961.ece

[1796] Tammy Faye Messner dies. CNN. http://www.cnn.com/2007/US/07/21/tammy.faye/index.html

[1797] Son of Jim and Tammy Faye Bakker takes on discrimination against homosexuals Sep 27, 2008. Asheville Citizen-Times. http://www.topix.com/who/tammy-faye-bakker/2008/09/son-of-jim-and-tammy-faye-bakker-takes-on-discrimination-against-homosexuals

[1798] **Son of Jim and Tammy Faye Bakker ministers to those who have given up on church. By Yonat Shimron. McClatchy Newspapers.** 10-04-2008http://www.annistonstar.com/religion/2008/as-churchnews-1004-0-8j03s5436.htm

[1799] **Son of Jim and Tammy Faye Bakker ministers to those who have given up on church. By Yonat Shimron. McClatchy Newspapers.** 10-04-2008http://www.annistonstar.com/religion/2008/as-churchnews-1004-0-8j03s5436.htm

[1800] **Son of Jim and Tammy Faye Bakker ministers to those who have given up on church. By Yonat Shimron. McClatchy Newspapers.** 10-04-2008http://www.annistonstar.com/religion/2008/as-churchnews-1004-0-8j03s5436.htm

[1801] **Son of Jim and Tammy Faye Bakker ministers to those who have given up on church. By Yonat Shimron. McClatchy Newspapers.** 10-04-2008http://www.annistonstar.com/religion/2008/as-churchnews-1004-0-8j03s5436.htm

[1802] **Son of Jim and Tammy Faye Bakker ministers to those who have given up on church. By Yonat Shimron. McClatchy Newspapers.** 10-04-2008http://www.annistonstar.com/religion/2008/as-churchnews-1004-0-8j03s5436.htm

[1803] **Son of Jim and Tammy Faye Bakker ministers to those who have given up on church. By Yonat Shimron. McClatchy Newspapers.** 10-04-2008http://www.annistonstar.com/religion/2008/as-churchnews-1004-0-8j03s5436.htm

[1804] **Son of Jim and Tammy Faye Bakker ministers to those who have given up on church. By Yonat Shimron. McClatchy Newspapers.** 10-04-2008http://www.annistonstar.com/religion/2008/as-churchnews-1004-0-8j03s5436.htm

[1805] **Haggard admits 'sexual immorality'.** Evangelical leader contrite after dismissal from Colorado megachurch. **The Associated Press.** updated 5:28 p.m. CT, Sun., Nov. 5, 2006 **MSNBC.com** http://www.msnbc.msn.com/id/15536263/.

[1806] Young-looking Haggard grows from Hoosier farm kid to power broker, Jean Torkelson, Rocky Mountain News. Published October 30, 2004. http://www.rockymountainnews.com/drmn/local/article/0,1299,DRMN_15_5114179,00.html#

[1807] State Of The Union: The Evangelical vote **By Tim Egan** In Montana http://news.bbc.co.uk/1/hi/programmes/3992067.stm The final episode of State Of The Union was broadcast on BBC Radio 4 on Friday, 5 November, 2004 and repeated on Sunday 7, November, 2004.

[1808] State Of The Union: The Evangelical vote **By Tim Egan** In Montana http://news.bbc.co.uk/1/hi/programmes/3992067.stm The final episode of State Of The Union was broadcast on BBC Radio 4 on Friday, 5 November, 2004 and repeated on Sunday 7, November, 2004.

[1809] **Haggard admits 'sexual immorality'.** Evangelical leader contrite after dismissal from Colorado megachurch. **The Associated Press.** updated 5:28 p.m. CT, Sun., Nov. 5, 2006 **MSNBC.com** http://www.msnbc.msn.com/id/15536263/.

[1810] TIME Names the 25 Most Influential EVANGELICALS in America. Sunday, Jan. 30, 2005 http://www.time.com/time/printout/0,8816,1022576,00.html

[1811] Young-looking Haggard grows from Hoosier farm kid to power broker, Jean Torkelson, Rocky Mountain News. Published October 30, 2004. http://www.rockymountainnews.com/drmn/local/article/0,1299,DRMN_15_5114179,00.html#

[1812] State Of The Union: The Evangelical vote **By Tim Egan** In Montana http://news.bbc.co.uk/1/hi/programmes/3992067.stm The final episode of State Of The Union was broadcast on BBC Radio 4 on Friday, 5 November, 2004 and repeated on Sunday 7, November, 2004.

[1813] Young-looking Haggard grows from Hoosier farm kid to power broker, Jean Torkelson, Rocky Mountain News. Published October 30, 2004. http://www.rockymountainnews.com/drmn/local/article/0,1299,DRMN_15_5114179,00.html#

[1814] Pastor will shut down controversial kids camp. By Religion News Service and The Associated Press. Wednesday, November 8, 2006http://www.google.com/search?hl=en&q=The+million-strong+United+Church+of+Christ+%28UCC%29+has+become+the+first+major+US+Christian+denomination+to+come+out+in+support+of+gay+marriage.&btnG=Search

[1815] State Of The Union: The Evangelical vote **By Tim Egan** In Montana http://news.bbc.co.uk/1/hi/programmes/3992067.stm The final episode of State Of The Union was broadcast on BBC Radio 4 on Friday, 5 November, 2004 and repeated on Sunday 7, November, 2004.

[1816] Pastor will shut down controversial kids camp. By Religion News Service and The Associated Press. Wednesday, November 8, 2006http://www.google.com/search?hl=en&q=The+million-strong+United+Church+of+Christ+%28UCC%29+has+become+the+first+major+US+Christian+denomination+to+come+out+in+support+of+gay+marriage.&btnG=Search

[1817] Young-looking Haggard grows from Hoosier farm kid to power broker, Jean Torkelson, Rocky Mountain News. Published October 30, 2004. http://www.rockymountainnews.com/drmn/local/article/0,1299,DRMN_15_5114179,00.html#.

[1818] State Of The Union: The Evangelical vote **By Tim Egan** In Montana http://news.bbc.co.uk/1/hi/programmes/3992067.stm The final episode of State Of The Union was broadcast on BBC Radio 4 on Friday, 5 November, 2004 and repeated on Sunday 7, November, 2004.

[1819] TIME Names the 25 Most Influential EVANGELICALS in America. Sunday, Jan. 30, 2005 http://www.time.com/time/printout/0,8816,1022576,00.html

[1820] TIME Names the 25 Most Influential EVANGELICALS in America. Sunday, Jan. 30, 2005 http://www.time.com/time/printout/0,8816,1022576,00.html

[1821] TIME Names the 25 Most Influential EVANGELICALS in America. Sunday, Jan. 30, 2005 http://www.time.com/time/printout/0,8816,1022576,00.html

[1822] State Of The Union: The Evangelical vote **By Tim Egan** In Montana http://news.bbc.co.uk/1/hi/programmes/3992067.stm The final episode of State Of The Union was broadcast on BBC Radio 4 on Friday, 5 November, 2004 and repeated on Sunday 7, November, 2004.
[1823] State Of The Union: The Evangelical vote **By Tim Egan** In Montana http://news.bbc.co.uk/1/hi/programmes/3992067.stm The final episode of State Of The Union was broadcast on BBC Radio 4 on Friday, 5 November, 2004 and repeated on Sunday 7, November, 2004.
[1824] **NAE Resolution On Homosexuality - Adopted In 1985 Re-Affirmed March, 2004.** http://www.nae.net/index.cfm?FUSEACTION=editor.page&pageID=46&IDcategory=9
[1825] Christianity Today Magazine. A Magazine of Evangelical Conviction. Ted Haggard: 'This isEvangelicalism's Finest Hour'. Posted June 2003 and retrieved November 18, 2008 fromhttp://www.christianitytoday.com/ct/2003/juneweb-only/6-2-21.0.html
[1826] Haggard Admits Buying Meth. Evangelical Leader Denies Accusation of Paying Former Gay Prostitute for Sex. By DAN HARRIS. **Nov. 3, 2006** Copyright © 2008 ABC News Internet Ventures. http://abcnews.go.com/print?id=2626067
[1827] NAE Resolution On Homosexuality - Adopted In 1985 Re-Affirmed March, 2004. http://www.nae.net/index.cfm?FUSEACTION=editor.page&pageID=46&IDcategory=9
[1828] Pastor will shut down controversial kids camp. By Religion News Service and The Associated Press. Wednesday, November 8, 2006http://www.google.com/search?hl=en&q=The+million-strong+United+Church+of+Christ+%28UCC%29+has+become+the+first+major+US+Christian+denomination+to+come+out+in+support+of+gay+marriage.&btnG=Search
[1829] Pastor will shut down controversial kids camp. By Religion News Service and The Associated Press. Wednesday, November 8, 2006http://www.google.com/search?hl=en&q=The+million-strong+United+Church+of+Christ+%28UCC%29+has+become+the+first+major+US+Christian+denomination+to+come+out+in+support+of+gay+marriage.&btnG=Search
[1830] Pastor will shut down controversial kids camp. By Religion News Service and The Associated Press. Wednesday, November 8, 2006http://www.google.com/search?hl=en&q=The+million-strong+United+Church+of+Christ+%28UCC%29+has+become+the+first+major+US+Christian+denomination+to+come+out+in+support+of+gay+marriage.&btnG=Search
[1831] Pastor will shut down controversial kids camp. By Religion News Service and The Associated Press. Wednesday, November 8, 2006http://www.google.com/search?hl=en&q=The+million-strong+United+Church+of+Christ+%28UCC%29+has+become+the+first+major+US+Christian+denomination+to+come+out+in+support+of+gay+marriage.&btnG=Search
[1832] Pastor will shut down controversial kids camp. By Religion News Service and The Associated Press. Wednesday, November 8, 2006http://www.google.com/search?hl=en&q=The+million-strong+United+Church+of+Christ+%28UCC%29+has+become+the+first+major+US+Christian+denomination+to+come+out+in+support+of+gay+marriage.&btnG=Search
[1833] Ted Haggard speaks out on 2006 scandal. **by Nick Cargo** http://pageoneq.com/news/2008/haggard111308.html.
[1834] Haggard Admits Buying Meth. Evangelical Leader Denies Accusation of Paying Former Gay Prostitute for Sex. By DAN HARRIS. **Nov. 3, 2006** Copyright © 2008 ABC News Internet Ventures. http://abcnews.go.com/print?id=2626067
[1835] Haggard Admits Buying Meth. Evangelical Leader Denies Accusation of Paying Former Gay Prostitute for Sex. By DAN HARRIS. **Nov. 3, 2006** Copyright © 2008 ABC News Internet Ventures. http://abcnews.go.com/print?id=2626067
[1836] Pastor will shut down controversial kids camp. By Religion News Service and The Associated Press. Wednesday, November 8, 2006http://www.google.com/search?hl=en&q=The+million-strong+United+Church+of+Christ+%28UCC%29+has+become+the+first+major+US+Christian+denomination+to+come+out+in+support+of+gay+marriage.&btnG=Search
[1837] Haggard Admits Buying Meth. Evangelical Leader Denies Accusation of Paying Former Gay Prostitute for Sex. By DAN HARRIS. **Nov. 3, 2006** Copyright © 2008 ABC News Internet Ventures. http://abcnews.go.com/print?id=2626067
[1838] Haggard Admits Buying Meth. Evangelical Leader Denies Accusation of Paying Former Gay Prostitute for Sex. By DAN HARRIS. **Nov. 3, 2006** Copyright © 2008 ABC News Internet Ventures. http://abcnews.go.com/print?id=2626067
[1839] Haggard Admits Buying Meth. Evangelical Leader Denies Accusation of Paying Former Gay Prostitute for Sex. By DAN HARRIS. **Nov. 3, 2006** Copyright © 2008 ABC News Internet Ventures. http://abcnews.go.com/print?id=2626067
[1840] **Haggard admits 'sexual immorality'.** Evangelical leader contrite after dismissal from Colorado megachurch. **The Associated Press.** updated 5:28 p.m. CT, Sun., Nov. 5, 2006 **MSNBC.com** http://www.msnbc.msn.com/id/15536263/.
[1841] Haggard Admits Buying Meth. Evangelical Leader Denies Accusation of Paying Former Gay Prostitute for Sex. By DAN HARRIS. **Nov. 3, 2006** Copyright © 2008 ABC News Internet Ventures. http://abcnews.go.com/print?id=2626067
[1842] **Haggard admits 'sexual immorality'.** Evangelical leader contrite after dismissal from Colorado megachurch. **The Associated Press.** updated 5:28 p.m. CT, Sun., Nov. 5, 2006 **MSNBC.com** http://www.msnbc.msn.com/id/15536263/.
[1843] Mike Jones still talking Haggard. One-man show takes expose to stage. By Lisa Bornstein, Rocky Mountain News (Contact). Published March 8, 2008 at 12:05 a.m. http://www.rockymountainnews.com/news/2008/Mar/08/out-growth/
[1844] Mike Jones still talking Haggard. One-man show takes expose to stage. By Lisa Bornstein, Rocky Mountain News (Contact). Published March 8, 2008 at 12:05 a.m. http://www.rockymountainnews.com/news/2008/Mar/08/out-growth/
[1845] Disgraced minister Ted Haggard moving to Phoenix, 07:34 PM CDT on Wednesday, April 18, 2007. Associated Press. http://www.dallasnews.com/sharedcontent/dws/dn/religion/stories/041907dnnathaggard.2acf8d8.html.
[1846] Disgraced minister Ted Haggard moving to Phoenix, 07:34 PM CDT on Wednesday, April 18, 2007. Associated Press. http://www.dallasnews.com/sharedcontent/dws/dn/religion/stories/041907dnnathaggard.2acf8d8.html.
[1847] Disgraced minister Ted Haggard moving to Phoenix, 07:34 PM CDT on Wednesday, April 18, 2007. Associated Press. http://www.dallasnews.com/sharedcontent/dws/dn/religion/stories/041907dnnathaggard.2acf8d8.html.
[1848] Ted Haggard speaks out on 2006 scandal. **by Nick Cargo** http://pageoneq.com/news/2008/haggard111308.html.
[1849] Pastor will shut down controversial kids camp. By Religion News Service and The Associated Press. Wednesday, November 8, 2006http://www.google.com/search?hl=en&q=The+million-strong+United+Church+of+Christ+%28UCC%29+has+become+the+first+major+US+Christian+denomination+to+come+out+in+support+of+gay+marriage.&btnG=Search
[1850] Haggard Admits Buying Meth. Evangelical Leader Denies Accusation of Paying Former Gay Prostitute for Sex. By DAN HARRIS. **Nov. 3, 2006** Copyright © 2008 ABC News Internet Ventures. http://abcnews.go.com/print?id=2626067
[1851] Haggard Admits Buying Meth. Evangelical Leader Denies Accusation of Paying Former Gay Prostitute for Sex. By DAN HARRIS. **Nov. 3, 2006** Copyright © 2008 ABC News Internet Ventures. http://abcnews.go.com/print?id=2626067
[1852] **Haggard admits 'sexual immorality'.** Evangelical leader contrite after dismissal from Colorado megachurch. **The Associated Press.** updated 5:28 p.m. CT, Sun., Nov. 5, 2006 **MSNBC.com** http://www.msnbc.msn.com/id/15536263/.
[1853] **Haggard admits 'sexual immorality'.** Evangelical leader contrite after dismissal from Colorado megachurch. **The Associated Press.** updated 5:28 p.m. CT, Sun., Nov. 5, 2006 **MSNBC.com** http://www.msnbc.msn.com/id/15536263/.
[1854] **Haggard admits 'sexual immorality'.** Evangelical leader contrite after dismissal from Colorado megachurch. **The Associated Press.** updated 5:28 p.m. CT, Sun., Nov. 5, 2006 **MSNBC.com** http://www.msnbc.msn.com/id/15536263/.
[1855] Haggard admits 'sexual immorality'. Evangelical leader contrite after dismissal from Colorado megachurch. The Associated Press. updated 5:28 p.m. CT, Sun., Nov. 5, 2006 MSNBC.com http://www.msnbc.msn.com/id/15536263/.
[1856] Haggard admits 'sexual immorality'. Evangelical leader contrite after dismissal from Colorado megachurch. The Associated Press. updated 5:28 p.m. CT, Sun., Nov. 5, 2006 MSNBC.com http://www.msnbc.msn.com/id/15536263/.
[1857] Disgraced minister Ted Haggard moving to Phoenix, 07:34 PM CDT on Wednesday, April 18, 2007. Associated Press. http://www.dallasnews.com/sharedcontent/dws/dn/religion/stories/041907dnnathaggard.2acf8d8.html.
[1858] Ted Haggard speaks out on 2006 scandal. **by Nick Cargo** http://pageoneq.com/news/2008/haggard111308.html.
[1859] Ted Haggard speaks out on 2006 scandal. **by Nick Cargo** http://pageoneq.com/news/2008/haggard111308.html.
[1860] Disgraced minister Ted Haggard moving to Phoenix, 07:34 PM CDT on Wednesday, April 18, 2007. Associated Press. http://www.dallasnews.com/sharedcontent/dws/dn/religion/stories/041907dnnathaggard.2acf8d8.html.
[1861] Disgraced minister Ted Haggard moving to Phoenix, 07:34 PM CDT on Wednesday, April 18, 2007. Associated Press. http://www.dallasnews.com/sharedcontent/dws/dn/religion/stories/041907dnnathaggard.2acf8d8.html.
[1862] Disgraced minister Ted Haggard moving to Phoenix, 07:34 PM CDT on Wednesday, April 18, 2007. Associated Press. http://www.dallasnews.com/sharedcontent/dws/dn/religion/stories/041907dnnathaggard.2acf8d8.html.
[1863] Disgraced minister Ted Haggard moving to Phoenix, 07:34 PM CDT on Wednesday, April 18, 2007. Associated Press. http://www.dallasnews.com/sharedcontent/dws/dn/religion/stories/041907dnnathaggard.2acf8d8.html.
[1864] Mike Jones responds to Ted Haggard's announcement of his heterosexuality. **by David Edwards and Michael Rogers** http://pageoneq.com/news/2006/haggard020706.html.
[1865] Mike Jones responds to Ted Haggard's announcement of his heterosexuality. **by David Edwards and Michael Rogers** http://pageoneq.com/news/2006/haggard020706.html.
[1866] Mike Jones responds to Ted Haggard's announcement of his heterosexuality. **by David Edwards and Michael Rogers** http://pageoneq.com/news/2006/haggard020706.html.
[1867] Former Pastor Ted Haggard Sexaholic, says Friend. June 25, 2008. By Tak Landrock http://www.krdo.com/Global/story.asp?S=8556903&nav=menu552_1
[1868] Former Pastor Ted Haggard Sexaholic, says Friend. June 25, 2008. By Tak Landrock http://www.krdo.com/Global/story.asp?S=8556903&nav=menu552_1.
[1869] Former Pastor Ted Haggard Sexaholic, says Friend. June 25, 2008. By Tak Landrock http://www.krdo.com/Global/story.asp?S=8556903&nav=menu552_1.
[1870] Former Pastor Ted Haggard Sexaholic, says Friend. June 25, 2008. By Tak Landrock http://www.krdo.com/Global/story.asp?S=8556903&nav=menu552_1.
[1871] Former Pastor Ted Haggard Sexaholic, says Friend. June 25, 2008. By Tak Landrock http://www.krdo.com/Global/story.asp?S=8556903&nav=menu552_1.
[1872] Former Pastor Ted Haggard Sexaholic, says Friend. June 25, 2008. By Tak Landrock.
[1873] Mike Jones still talking Haggard. One-man show takes expose to stage. By Lisa Bornstein, Rocky Mountain News (Contact). Published March 8, 2008 at 12:05 a.m. http://www.rockymountainnews.com/news/2008/Mar/08/out-growth/
[1874] Mike Jones still talking Haggard. One-man show takes expose to stage. By Lisa Bornstein, Rocky Mountain News (Contact). Published March 8, 2008 at 12:05 a.m. http://www.rockymountainnews.com/news/2008/Mar/08/out-growth/
[1875] Mike Jones still talking Haggard. One-man show takes expose to stage. By Lisa Bornstein, Rocky Mountain News (Contact). Published March 8, 2008 at 12:05 a.m. http://www.rockymountainnews.com/news/2008/Mar/08/out-growth/
[1876] Mike Jones still talking Haggard. One-man show takes expose to stage. By Lisa Bornstein, Rocky Mountain News (Contact). Published March 8, 2008 at 12:05 a.m. http://www.rockymountainnews.com/news/2008/Mar/08/out-growth/
[1877] More gay men describe sexual encounters with U.S. Sen. Craig December 03, 2007 Dan Popkey: 377-6438 http://www.idahostatesman.com/eyepiece/story/226703.html
[1878] Ted Haggard speaks out on 2006 scandal. **by Nick Cargo** http://pageoneq.com/news/2008/haggard111308.html.

[1879] Ted Haggard speaks out on 2006 scandal. **by Nick Cargo** http://pageoneq.com/news/2008/haggard111308.html.
[1880] Archive for Saturday, October 06, 2007. Oral Roberts' son, his wife face scandal at university - A lawsuit alleges lavish spending, political actions, other misdeeds. October 06, 2007 *in print edition A-18* http://articles.latimes.com/2007/oct/06/nation/na-roberts6
[1881] **Christian School Gay Alumni 'Coming Out'.** February 18, 2001 *in print edition A-15* http://articles.latimes.com/2001/feb/18/news/mn-27187
[1882] Archive for Saturday, October 06, 2007. Oral Roberts' son, his wife face scandal at university - A lawsuit alleges lavish spending, political actions, other misdeeds. October 06, 2007 *in print edition A-18* http://articles.latimes.com/2007/oct/06/nation/na-roberts6
[1883] Archive for Saturday, October 06, 2007. Oral Roberts' son, his wife face scandal at university - A lawsuit alleges lavish spending, political actions, other misdeeds. October 06, 2007 *in print edition A-18* http://articles.latimes.com/2007/oct/06/nation/na-roberts6
[1884] Archive for Saturday, November 24, 2007. **President of Oral Roberts steps down.** November 24, 2007 *in print edition A-15* http://articles.latimes.com/2007/nov/24/nation/na-roberts24
[1885] Archive for Saturday, November 24, 2007. **President of Oral Roberts steps down.** November 24, 2007 *in print edition A-15* http://articles.latimes.com/2007/nov/24/nation/na-roberts24
[1886] **Former Richard Roberts protege reacts to allegations**. By Staff Reports. Published: 10/9/2007.
[1887] **Former Richard Roberts protege reacts to allegations**. By Staff Reports. Published: 10/9/2007.
[1888] Archive for Saturday, November 24, 2007. **President of Oral Roberts steps down.** November 24, 2007 *in print edition A-15* http://articles.latimes.com/2007/nov/24/nation/na-roberts24
[1889] Archive for Saturday, October 06, 2007. Oral Roberts' son, his wife face scandal at university - A lawsuit alleges lavish spending, political actions, other misdeeds. October 06, 2007 *in print edition A-18* http://articles.latimes.com/2007/oct/06/nation/na-roberts6
[1890] Archive for Saturday, October 06, 2007. Oral Roberts' son, his wife face scandal at university - A lawsuit alleges lavish spending, political actions, other misdeeds. October 06, 2007 *in print edition A-18* http://articles.latimes.com/2007/oct/06/nation/na-roberts6
[1891] Archive for Saturday, October 06, 2007. Oral Roberts' son, his wife face scandal at university - A lawsuit alleges lavish spending, political actions, other misdeeds. October 06, 2007 *in print edition A-18* http://articles.latimes.com/2007/oct/06/nation/na-roberts6
[1892] Archive for Saturday, November 24, 2007. **President of Oral Roberts steps down.** November 24, 2007 *in print edition A-15* http://articles.latimes.com/2007/nov/24/nation/na-roberts24
[1893] Archive for Saturday, November 24, 2007. **President of Oral Roberts steps down.** November 24, 2007 *in print edition A-15* http://articles.latimes.com/2007/nov/24/nation/na-roberts24
[1894] ReligionNewsBlog.com • Item 1128 • Posted: Thursday November 7, 2002. The Oakland Tribune, Nov. 4, 2002. http://www.oaklandtribune.com/. By Melissa Evans. http://www.religionnewsblog.com/1128/kansas-anti-gay-church-embarrasses-topekans.
[1895] ReligionNewsBlog.com • Item 1128 • Posted: Thursday November 7, 2002. The Oakland Tribune, Nov. 4, 2002. http://www.oaklandtribune.com/. By Melissa Evans. http://www.religionnewsblog.com/1128/kansas-anti-gay-church-embarrasses-topekans.
[1896] ReligionNewsBlog.com • Item 1128 • Posted: Thursday November 7, 2002. The Oakland Tribune, Nov. 4, 2002. http://www.oaklandtribune.com/. By Melissa Evans. http://www.religionnewsblog.com/1128/kansas-anti-gay-church-embarrasses-topekans.
[1897] ReligionNewsBlog.com • Item 1128 • Posted: Thursday November 7, 2002. The Oakland Tribune, Nov. 4, 2002. http://www.oaklandtribune.com/. By Melissa Evans. http://www.religionnewsblog.com/1128/kansas-anti-gay-church-embarrasses-topekans.
[1898] ReligionNewsBlog.com • Item 1128 • Posted: Thursday November 7, 2002. The Oakland Tribune, Nov. 4, 2002. http://www.oaklandtribune.com/. By Melissa Evans. http://www.religionnewsblog.com/1128/kansas-anti-gay-church-embarrasses-topekans.
[1899] ReligionNewsBlog.com • Item 1128 • Posted: Thursday November 7, 2002. The Oakland Tribune, Nov. 4, 2002. http://www.oaklandtribune.com/. By Melissa Evans. http://www.religionnewsblog.com/1128/kansas-anti-gay-church-embarrasses-topekans.
[1900] Anti-gay church to participate in debate on gay marriage ban. Scott Travis, Sun-Sentinel. Originally published 10:19 p.m., October 15, 2008http://www.tcpalm.com/news/2008/oct/15/anti-gay-church-participate-debate-gay-marriage-ba/.
[1901] ReligionNewsBlog.com • Item 1128 • Posted: Thursday November 7, 2002. The Oakland Tribune, Nov. 4, 2002. http://www.oaklandtribune.com/. By Melissa Evans. http://www.religionnewsblog.com/1128/kansas-anti-gay-church-embarrasses-topekans.
[1902] Outrage at Funeral Protests Pushes Lawmakers to Act. April 17, 2006. By **LIZETTE ALVAREZ** http://www.nytimes.com/2006/04/17/us/17picket.html?pagewanted=print
[1903] Anti-gay church to participate in debate on gay marriage ban. Scott Travis, Sun-Sentinel. Originally published 10:19 p.m., October 15, 2008http://www.tcpalm.com/news/2008/oct/15/anti-gay-church-participate-debate-gay-marriage-ba/
[1904] ReligionNewsBlog.com • Item 1128 • Posted: Thursday November 7, 2002. The Oakland Tribune, Nov. 4, 2002. http://www.oaklandtribune.com/. By Melissa Evans. http://www.religionnewsblog.com/1128/kansas-anti-gay-church-embarrasses-topekans.
[1905] Sony tells Phelps to stop song. By CARL MANNING. The Associated Press. Sunday, Oct 26, 2008. http://www.kansascity.com/116/story/856873.html.
[1906] Sony tells Phelps to stop song. By CARL MANNING. The Associated Press. Sunday, Oct 26, 2008. http://www.kansascity.com/116/story/856873.html.
[1907] Sony tells Phelps to stop song. By CARL MANNING. The Associated Press. Sunday, Oct 26, 2008. http://www.kansascity.com/116/story/856873.html.
[1908] ReligionNewsBlog.com • Item 1128 • Posted: Thursday November 7, 2002. The Oakland Tribune, Nov. 4, 2002. http://www.oaklandtribune.com/. By Melissa Evans. http://www.religionnewsblog.com/1128/kansas-anti-gay-church-embarrasses-topekans.
[1909] ReligionNewsBlog.com • Item 1128 • Posted: Thursday November 7, 2002. The Oakland Tribune, Nov. 4, 2002. http://www.oaklandtribune.com/. By Melissa Evans. http://www.religionnewsblog.com/1128/kansas-anti-gay-church-embarrasses-topekans.
[1910] ReligionNewsBlog.com • Item 1128 • Posted: Thursday November 7, 2002. The Oakland Tribune, Nov. 4, 2002. http://www.oaklandtribune.com/. By Melissa Evans. http://www.religionnewsblog.com/1128/kansas-anti-gay-church-embarrasses-topekans.
[1911] Sony tells Phelps to stop song. By CARL MANNING. The Associated Press. Sunday, Oct 26, 2008. http://www.kansascity.com/116/story/856873.html.
[1912] Sony tells Phelps to stop song. By CARL MANNING. The Associated Press. Sunday, Oct 26, 2008. http://www.kansascity.com/116/story/856873.html.
[1913] Outrage at Funeral Protests Pushes Lawmakers to Act. April 17, 2006. By **LIZETTE ALVAREZ**http://www.nytimes.com/2006/04/17/us/17picket.html?pagewanted=print.
[1914] Outrage at Funeral Protests Pushes Lawmakers to Act. April 17, 2006. By **LIZETTE ALVAREZ**http://www.nytimes.com/2006/04/17/us/17picket.html?pagewanted=print.
[1915] Outrage at Funeral Protests Pushes Lawmakers to Act. April 17, 2006. By **LIZETTE ALVAREZ**http://www.nytimes.com/2006/04/17/us/17picket.html?pagewanted=print.
[1916] ReligionNewsBlog.com • Item 1128 • Posted: Thursday November 7, 2002. The Oakland Tribune, Nov. 4, 2002. http://www.oaklandtribune.com/. By Melissa Evans. http://www.religionnewsblog.com/1128/kansas-anti-gay-church-embarrasses-topekans.
[1917] Fred Phelps and the Westboro Baptist Church On Jews Anti-Defamation League http://www.adl.org/special_reports/wbc/wbc_on_jews.asp.
[1918] Fred Phelps and the Westboro Baptist Church On Jews Anti-Defamation League http://www.adl.org/special_reports/wbc/wbc_on_jews.asp.
[1919] The political affiliations of Fred Phelps: Saddam Hussein, Fidel Castro, and Al Gore.http://www.spiritus-temporis.com/fred-phelps/political-affiliations:-saddam-hussein,-fidel-castro,-al-gore,-and-the-democratic-party.html
[1920] The political affiliations of Fred Phelps: Saddam Hussein, Fidel Castro, and Al Gore.http://www.spiritus-temporis.com/fred-phelps/political-affiliations:-saddam-hussein,-fidel-castro,-al-gore,-and-the-democratic-party.html
[1921] The political affiliations of Fred Phelps: Saddam Hussein, Fidel Castro, and Al Gore.http://www.spiritus-temporis.com/fred-phelps/political-affiliations:-saddam-hussein,-fidel-castro,-al-gore,-and-the-democratic-party.html
[1922] Outrage at Funeral Protests Pushes Lawmakers to Act. April 17, 2006. By **LIZETTE ALVAREZ**http://www.nytimes.com/2006/04/17/us/17picket.html?pagewanted=print
[1923] Outrage at Funeral Protests Pushes Lawmakers to Act. April 17, 2006. By **LIZETTE ALVAREZ**http://www.nytimes.com/2006/04/17/us/17picket.html?pagewanted=print
[1924] Outrage at Funeral Protests Pushes Lawmakers to Act. April 17, 2006. By **LIZETTE ALVAREZ**http://www.nytimes.com/2006/04/17/us/17picket.html?pagewanted=print
[1925] Rep. Bachmann Holds Off the Blue Tidal Wave. ***Easha Anand*** *reports on a Minnesota House race.* November 5, 2008. http://blogs.wsj.com/washwire/2008/11/05/rep-bachmann-holds-off-the-blue-tidal-wave/
[1926] Rep. Bachmann Holds Off the Blue Tidal Wave. ***Easha Anand*** *reports on a Minnesota House race.* November 5, 2008. http://blogs.wsj.com/washwire/2008/11/05/rep-bachmann-holds-off-the-blue-tidal-wave/
[1927] Michelle Bachmann Denies Her Own Quote After It Is Read To Her. By Ben Cohenhttp://www.thedailybanter.com/tdb/2008/11/michelle-bachmann-denies-her-own-quote.html
[1928] Michelle Bachmann Denies Her Own Quote After It Is Read To Her. By Ben Cohenhttp://www.thedailybanter.com/tdb/2008/11/michelle-bachmann-denies-her-own-quote.html
[1929] Rep. Bachmann Holds Off the Blue Tidal Wave. ***Easha Anand*** *reports on a Minnesota House race.* November 5, 2008. http://blogs.wsj.com/washwire/2008/11/05/rep-bachmann-holds-off-the-blue-tidal-wave/
[1930] Tough talk helped Bachmann retain, win supporters.By **PAT DOYLE**, Star Tribune November 5, 2008 - http://www.startribune.com/politics/national/house/33902149.html?elr=KArksDyycyUtyycyUiD3aPc:_Yyc:aUU
[1931] Rep. Bachmann Holds Off the Blue Tidal Wave. ***Easha Anand*** *reports on a Minnesota House race.* November 5, 2008. http://blogs.wsj.com/washwire/2008/11/05/rep-bachmann-holds-off-the-blue-tidal-wave/
[1932] Tough talk helped Bachmann retain, win supporters.By **PAT DOYLE**, Star Tribune November 5, 2008 - http://www.startribune.com/politics/national/house/33902149.html?elr=KArksDyycyUtyycyUiD3aPc:_Yyc:aUU
[1933] Tough talk helped Bachmann retain, win supporters.By **PAT DOYLE**, Star Tribune November 5, 2008 - http://www.startribune.com/politics/national/house/33902149.html?elr=KArksDyycyUtyycyUiD3aPc:_Yyc:aUU

[1934] Somebody Say Oh Lord! Michele Bachmann heads an all-star cast of GOP Christian flat-earthers in the Sixth District. G.R. Anderson Jr. published: February 23, 2005. http://www.citypages.com/content/printVersion/15670

[1935] Somebody Say Oh Lord! Michele Bachmann heads an all-star cast of GOP Christian flat-earthers in the Sixth District. G.R. Anderson Jr. published: February 23, 2005. http://www.citypages.com/content/printVersion/15670

[1936] Somebody Say Oh Lord! Michele Bachmann heads an all-star cast of GOP Christian flat-earthers in the Sixth District. G.R. Anderson Jr. published: February 23, 2005. http://www.citypages.com/content/printVersion/15670

[1937] Somebody Say Oh Lord! Michele Bachmann heads an all-star cast of GOP Christian flat-earthers in the Sixth District. G.R. Anderson Jr. published: February 23, 2005. http://www.citypages.com/content/printVersion/15670

[1938] Tuesday, May 31, 2005. F a v o r i t e B a c h m a n n Q u o t e s Posted by lloydletta at 9:55 PM http://dumpbachmann.blogspot.com/2005/05/favorite-bachmann-quotes.html. Bachmann interviewing with Todd Fiel at KKMS as quoted in the Stillwater Gazette, September 29, 2003

[1939] Bachmann, appearing as guest on radio program "Prophetic Views Behind The News", hosted by Jan Markell, KKMS 980-AM, March 6, 2004. Issue: Bachmann quotes. Retrieved November 30, 2008 from http://www.thebachmannrecord.com/thebachmannrecod.html

[1940] Minnesota Monitor. **Michele Bachmann Speech at Church Could Cause Tax Troubles** *Sun Oct 15, 2006* by: **Andy Birkey**://www.minnesotamonitor.com/showDiary.do?diaryId=524

[1941] Somebody Say Oh Lord! Michele Bachmann heads an all-star cast of GOP Christian flat-earthers in the Sixth District. G.R. Anderson Jr. published: February 23, 2005. http://www.citypages.com/content/printVersion/15670

[1942] Somebody Say Oh Lord! Michele Bachmann heads an all-star cast of GOP Christian flat-earthers in the Sixth District. G.R. Anderson Jr. published: February 23, 2005. http://www.citypages.com/content/printVersion/15670

[1943] Somebody Say Oh Lord! Michele Bachmann heads an all-star cast of GOP Christian flat-earthers in the Sixth District. G.R. Anderson Jr. published: February 23, 2005. http://www.citypages.com/content/printVersion/15670

[1944] Somebody Say Oh Lord! Michele Bachmann heads an all-star cast of GOP Christian flat-earthers in the Sixth District. G.R. Anderson Jr. published: February 23, 2005. http://www.citypages.com/content/printVersion/15670

[1945] Somebody Say Oh Lord! Michele Bachmann heads an all-star cast of GOP Christian flat-earthers in the Sixth District. G.R. Anderson Jr. published: February 23, 2005. http://www.citypages.com/content/printVersion/15670

[1946] Somebody Say Oh Lord! Michele Bachmann heads an all-star cast of GOP Christian flat-earthers in the Sixth District. G.R. Anderson Jr. published: February 23, 2005. http://www.citypages.com/content/printVersion/15670

[1947] *Bachmann, appearing as guest on radio program "Prophetic Views Behind The News", hosted by Jan Markell, KKMS 980-AM, March 6, 2004* Issue: Bachmann quotes. Retrieved November 30, 2008 from http://www.thebachmannrecord.com/thebachmannrecod.html

[1948] *Bachmann, appearing as guest on radio program "Prophetic Views Behind The News", hosted by Jan Markell, KKMS 980-AM, March 20, 2004.*Issue: Bachmann quotes. Retrieved November 30, 2008 from http://www.thebachmannrecord.com/thebachmannrecod.html.

[1949]*Bachmann, appearing as guest on radio program "Prophetic Views Behind The News", hosted by Jan Markell, KKMS 980-AM, March 6, 2004.*Issue: Bachmann quotes. Retrieved November 30, 2008 from http://www.thebachmannrecord.com/thebachmannrecod.html.

[1950] *Bachmann, appearing as guest on radio program "Prophetic Views Behind The News", hosted by Jan Markell, KKMS 980-AM, March 20, 2004.* Issue: Bachmann quotes. Retrieved November 30, 2008 from http://www.thebachmannrecord.com/thebachmannrecod.html.

[1951] *Bachmann, appearing as guest on radio program "Prophetic Views Behind The News", hosted by Jan Markell, KKMS 980-AM, March 20, 2004.* Issue: Bachmann quotes. Retrieved November 30, 2008 from http://www.thebachmannrecord.com/thebachmannrecod.html.

[1952] *Bachmann, appearing as guest on radio program "Prophetic Views Behind The News", hosted by Jan Markell, KKMS 980-AM, March 6, 2004*Issue: Bachmann quotes. Retrieved November 30, 2008 from http://www.thebachmannrecord.com/thebachmannrecod.html.

[1953] *Bachmann, appearing as guest on radio program "Prophetic Views Behind The News", hosted by Jan Markell, KKMS 980-AM, March 20, 2004.*Issue: Bachmann quotes. Retrieved November 30, 2008 from http://www.thebachmannrecord.com/thebachmannrecod.html.

[1954] Bachmann, appearing as guest on radio program "Prophetic Views Behind The News", hosted by Jan Markell, KKMS 980-AM, March 20, 2004. Issue: Bachmann quotes. Retrieved November 30, 2008 from http://www.thebachmannrecord.com/thebachmannrecod.html.

[1955] Bachmann, appearing as guest on radio program "Prophetic Views Behind The News", hosted by Jan Markell, KKMS 980-AM, March 20, 2004. Issue: Bachmann quotes. Retrieved November 30, 2008 from http://www.thebachmannrecord.com/thebachmannrecod.html.

[1956] *Bachmann, speaking at EdWatch National Education Conference, November 6, 2004*Issue: Bachmann quotes. Retrieved November 30, 2008 from http://www.thebachmannrecord.com/thebachmannrecod.html.

[1957] *Michele Bachmann, speaking at EdWatch National Education Conference, November 6, 2004.* Issue: Bachmann quotes. Retrieved November 30, 2008 from http://www.thebachmannrecord.com/thebachmannrecod.html.

[1958] *Bachmann, appearing as guest on radio program "Prophetic Views Behind The News", hosted by Jan Markell, KKMS 980-AM, March 20, 2004* Issue: Bachmann quotes. Retrieved November 30, 2008 from http://www.thebachmannrecord.com/thebachmannrecod.html.

[1959] *Bachmann, appearing as guest on radio program "Prophetic Views Behind The News", hosted by Jan Markell, KKMS 980-AM, March 20, 2004.*Issue: Bachmann quotes. Retrieved November 30, 2008 from http://www.thebachmannrecord.com/thebachmannrecod.html.

[1960] *Senator Michele Bachmann, Tom Barnard Morning Show, KQRS, broadcast May 12, 2005.*Issue: Bachmann quotes. Retrieved November 30, 2008 from http://www.thebachmannrecord.com/thebachmannrecod.html.

[1961] *Michele Bachmann, speaking at EdWatch National Education Conference, November 6, 2004.* Issue: Bachmann quotes. Retrieved November 30, 2008 from http://www.thebachmannrecord.com/thebachmannrecod.html.

[1962] *Michele Bachmann, speaking at EdWatch National Education Conference, November 6, 2004.* Issue: Bachmann quotes. Retrieved November 30, 2008 from http://www.thebachmannrecord.com/thebachmannrecod.html.

[1963] *Bachmann, speaking at EdWatch National Education Conference, November 6, 2004.*Issue: Bachmann quotes. Retrieved November 30, 2008 from http://www.thebachmannrecord.com/thebachmannrecod.html.

[1964] *Bachmann, speaking at EdWatch National Education Conference, November 6, 2004.*Issue: Bachmann quotes. Retrieved November 30, 2008 from http://www.thebachmannrecord.com/thebachmannrecod.html.

[1965] *Michele Bachmann, speaking at EdWatch National Education Conference, November 6, 2004.* Issue: Bachmann quotes. Retrieved November 30, 2008 from http://www.thebachmannrecord.com/thebachmannrecod.html.

[1966] Tuesday, May 31, 2005. F a v o r i t e B a c h m a n n Q u o t e s Posted by lloydletta at 9:55 PM http://dumpbachmann.blogspot.com/2005/05/favorite-bachmann-quotes.html. Michele Bachmann email to supporters.

[1967] Mitt Romney's PAC. Retrieved November 31, 2008 from http://www.freestrongamerica.com/candidates/item/michele_bachman

[1968] About Gary Bauer. American Values. http://www.ouramericanvalues.org/aboutGaryBauer.php

[1969] About Gary Bauer. American Values. http://www.ouramericanvalues.org/aboutGaryBauer.php

[1970] About Gary Bauer. American Values. http://www.ouramericanvalues.org/aboutGaryBauer.php

[1971] See http://www.ouramericanvalues.org/aboutGaryBauer.php. The American Values webstite (October 2008; Gary Bauer president)

[1972] About Gary Bauer. American Values. http://www.ouramericanvalues.org/aboutGaryBauer.php

[1973] Bill Berkowitz, The Family Research Council's Tony Perkins is a rising star in a crowded universe of evangelical Christian leaders. http://www.mediatransparency.org/storyprinterfriendly.php?storyID=70. June 17, 2005.

[1974] (McNeely, Austin American-Statesman, 6/13). Call Senator Trent Lott and Register Your Opinion on His Recent Comments About Gays. June 16, 1998 Copyright © 2008, Georgia Log Cabin Republicans, Inc. http://www.lcrga.com/news/Trent+Lott+Gary+Bauer/98061602.shtml

[1975] (McNeely, Austin American-Statesman, 6/13). Call Senator Trent Lott and Register Your Opinion on His Recent Comments About Gays. June 16, 1998 Copyright © 2008, Georgia Log Cabin Republicans, Inc. http://www.lcrga.com/news/Trent+Lott+Gary+Bauer/98061602.shtml

[1976] (McNeely, Austin American-Statesman, 6/13). Call Senator Trent Lott and Register Your Opinion on His Recent Comments About Gays. June 16, 1998 Copyright © 2008, Georgia Log Cabin Republicans, Inc. http://www.lcrga.com/news/Trent+Lott+Gary+Bauer/98061602.shtml

[1977] About Gary Bauer. American Values. http://www.ouramericanvalues.org/aboutGaryBauer.php

[1978] Bauer officially jumps into 2000 race April 21, 1999 http://www.cnn.com/ALLPOLITICS/stories/1999/04/21/president.2000/bauer/

[1979] Gary Bauer Can't Go Home Again. *Internal survey at Family Research Council says 'partisan' leader unwelcome.*By Tony Carnes | posted 2/01/2000. Christianity Today magazine. http://www.christianitytoday.com/ct/2000/februaryweb-only/21.0.html

[1980] The Assault Of the Salonistas Published: February 20, 2000 Helen Thorpe. http://query.nytimes.com/gst/fullpage.html?res=9904E5DC1531F933A15751C0A9669C8B63&sec=&spon=&pagewanted=all

[1981] The Assault Of the Salonistas Published: February 20, 2000 Helen Thorpe. http://query.nytimes.com/gst/fullpage.html?res=9904E5DC1531F933A15751C0A9669C8B63&sec=&spon=&pagewanted=all

[1982] Stalking Gary Bauer, Sex columnist Dan Savage goes undercover, and hatches a plot, inside Bauer 2000 campaign headquarters in Des Moines. By Dan Savage ***Editor's note. 1.25.2000*** http://www.salon.com/politics2000/feature/2000/01/25/bauer/print.html

[1983] Stalking Gary Bauer, Sex columnist Dan Savage goes undercover, and hatches a plot, inside Bauer 2000 campaign headquarters in Des Moines. By Dan Savage ***Editor's note. 1.25.2000*** http://www.salon.com/politics2000/feature/2000/01/25/bauer/print.html

[1984] Stalking Gary Bauer, Sex columnist Dan Savage goes undercover, and hatches a plot, inside Bauer 2000 campaign headquarters in Des Moines. By Dan Savage ***Editor's note. 1.25.2000*** http://www.salon.com/politics2000/feature/2000/01/25/bauer/print.html

[1985] Stalking Gary Bauer, Sex columnist Dan Savage goes undercover, and hatches a plot, inside Bauer 2000 campaign headquarters in Des Moines. By Dan Savage ***Editor's note. 1.25.2000*** http://www.salon.com/politics2000/feature/2000/01/25/bauer/print.html

[1986] The Gary Bauer Scandal. *By William Saletan*Posted Friday, Oct. 1, 1999. http://www.slate.com/id/35836/
[1987] Gary Bauer Can't Go Home Again. *Internal survey at Family Research Council says 'partisan' leader unwelcome.*By Tony Carnes | posted 2/01/2000. Christianity Today magazine. http://www.christianitytoday.com/ct/2000/februaryweb-only/21.0.html
[1988] Bauer Says He Did Not Have Affair. 2 Ex-Aides Make Public Allegation. *By Thomas B. Edsall and Hanna Rosin*
Washington Post Staff Writers. Thursday, September 30, 1999; Page A14 http://www.washingtonpost.com/wp-srv/WPcap/1999-09/30/012r-093099-idx.html.
[1989] Bauer Says He Did Not Have Affair. 2 Ex-Aides Make Public Allegation. *By Thomas B. Edsall and Hanna Rosin*
Washington Post Staff Writers. Thursday, September 30, 1999; Page A14 http://www.washingtonpost.com/wp-srv/WPcap/1999-09/30/012r-093099-idx.html.
[1990] Bauer Says He Did Not Have Affair. 2 Ex-Aides Make Public Allegation. *By Thomas B. Edsall and Hanna Rosin*
Washington Post Staff Writers. Thursday, September 30, 1999; Page A14 http://www.washingtonpost.com/wp-srv/WPcap/1999-09/30/012r-093099-idx.html.
[1991] Bauer Says He Did Not Have Affair. 2 Ex-Aides Make Public Allegation. *By Thomas B. Edsall and Hanna Rosin*
Washington Post Staff Writers. Thursday, September 30, 1999; Page A14 http://www.washingtonpost.com/wp-srv/WPcap/1999-09/30/012r-093099-idx.html.
[1992] Bauer Says He Did Not Have Affair. 2 Ex-Aides Make Public Allegation. *By Thomas B. Edsall and Hanna Rosin*
Washington Post Staff Writers. Thursday, September 30, 1999; Page A14 http://www.washingtonpost.com/wp-srv/WPcap/1999-09/30/012r-093099-idx.html.
[1993] Special Event. Gary Bauer Endorses John McCain for President. Aired February 16, 2000 - 1:07 p.m. EThttp://transcripts.cnn.com/TRANSCRIPTS/0002/16/se.04.html
[1994] Gary Bauer Can't Go Home Again. *Internal survey at Family Research Council says 'partisan' leader unwelcome.*By Tony Carnes | posted 2/01/2000. Christianity Today magazine. http://www.christianitytoday.com/ct/2000/februaryweb-only/21.0.html.
[1995] American Values. http://www.ouramericanvalues.org/culture.php
[1996] **Bauer, Gary L.** *by James D'Entremont, from his web site* http://www.mediatransparency.org/personprofile.php?personID=18
[1997] Libby Copeland. Faith Based Initiative. Washington Post. Published June 7, 2006, C01. Retrieved June 16, 2006 from http://www.washingtonpost.com/wp-dyn/content/article/2006/06/06/AR2006060601616.html
[1998] Libby Copeland. Faith Based Initiative. Washington Post. Published June 7, 2006, C01. Retrieved June 16, 2006 from http://www.washingtonpost.com/wp-dyn/content/article/2006/06/06/AR2006060601616.html.
[1999] Libby Copeland. Faith Based Initiative. Washington Post. Published June 7, 2006, C01. Retrieved June 16, 2006 from http://www.washingtonpost.com/wp-dyn/content/article/2006/06/06/AR2006060601616.html.
[2000] Richard E. Cohen and Michael Barone. The Almanac of American Politics—2004. The National Journal Group. 2003, page 650
[2001] Bill Berkowitz. Brownback brands himself 'Full scale conservative' Media Transparency. Posted 1.4.07 and retrieved 1.13.07 from http://www.mediatransparency.org/storyprinterfriendly.php?storyID=170
[2002] Bill Berkowitz. Brownback brands himself 'Full scale conservative' Media Transparency. Posted 1.4.07 and retrieved 1.13.07 from http://www.mediatransparency.org/storyprinterfriendly.php?storyID=170
[2003] Sam Brownback. "Defining Marriage Down." National Review Online. Posted July 9, 2004 and retrieved November 10, 2005 from http://www.nationalreview.com/comment/brownback200407090921.asp.
[2004] Sam Brownback. "Defining Marriage Down." National Review Online. Posted July 9, 2004 and retrieved November 10, 2005 from http://www.nationalreview.com/comment/brownback200407090921.asp
[2005] **Defining Marriage Down** We need to protect marriage. By Senator Sam Brownback July 09, 2004, 9:21 a.m.. — *The Honorable Sam Brownback is a Republican senator from Kansas.* http://www.nationalreview.com/comment/brownback200407090921.asp.
[2006] **Defining Marriage Down** We need to protect marriage. By Senator Sam Brownback July 09, 2004, 9:21 a.m.. — *The Honorable Sam Brownback is a Republican senator from Kansas.* http://www.nationalreview.com/comment/brownback200407090921.asp.
[2007] **Defining Marriage Down** We need to protect marriage. By Senator Sam Brownback July 09, 2004, 9:21 a.m.. — *The Honorable Sam Brownback is a Republican senator from Kansas.* http://www.nationalreview.com/comment/brownback200407090921.asp.
[2008] **Defining Marriage Down** We need to protect marriage. By Senator Sam Brownback July 09, 2004, 9:21 a.m.. — *The Honorable Sam Brownback is a Republican senator from Kansas.* http://www.nationalreview.com/comment/brownback200407090921.asp
[2009] **Defining Marriage Down** We need to protect marriage. By Senator Sam Brownback July 09, 2004, 9:21 a.m.. — *The Honorable Sam Brownback is a Republican senator from Kansas.* http://www.nationalreview.com/comment/brownback200407090921.asp
[2010] **Defining Marriage Down** We need to protect marriage. By Senator Sam Brownback July 09, 2004, 9:21 a.m.. — *The Honorable Sam Brownback is a Republican senator from Kansas.* http://www.nationalreview.com/comment/brownback200407090921.asp.
[2011] **Defining Marriage Down** We need to protect marriage. By Senator Sam Brownback July 09, 2004, 9:21 a.m.. — *The Honorable Sam Brownback is a Republican senator from Kansas.* http://www.nationalreview.com/comment/brownback200407090921.asp.
[2012] AP. Same-sex ceremony delays nomination. MJS, Oct. 7, 2006, 8A. SB 8 p 10.
[2013] AP. Same-sex ceremony delays nomination. MJS, Oct. 7, 2006, 8A. SB 8 p 10.
[2014] Senator Sam Brownback. Brownback Comments on Senate Marriage Vote. Posted June 7, 2006 and retrieved June 16, 2006 from http://brownback.senate.gov/pressapp/record.cfm?id=256597.
[2015] **Defining Marriage Down** We need to protect marriage. By Senator Sam Brownback July 09, 2004, 9:21 a.m.. — *The Honorable Sam Brownback is a Republican senator from Kansas.* http://www.nationalreview.com/comment/brownback200407090921.asp.
[2016] PATRICK BUCHANAN: IN HIS OWN WORDS http://frank.mtsu.edu/~baustin/buchanan.html
[2017] **Pat Buchanan: In His Own Words**. Anti-Defamation League. *This report was originally issued in September 1999* **© 2000 Anti-Defamation League** http://www.adl.org/special_reports/buchanan_own_words/print.asp
[2018] (Right from the Beginning,Buchanan's 1988 autobiography, p. 131) Pat Buchanan, Antisemitism and the Holocaust http://frank.mtsu.edu/~baustin/buchanan.html
[2019] (New York Daily News, 10/1/90) Pat Buchanan, Antisemitism and the Holocaust http://frank.mtsu.edu/~baustin/buchanan.html
[2020] PATRICK BUCHANAN: IN HIS OWN WORDS http://frank.mtsu.edu/~baustin/buchanan.html
[2021] Boston Globe editorial, Derrick Z. Jackson, p. A23 Oct 1, 1999. 2000 Reform Candidate for President Pat Buchanan on Gay Rights. http://www.ontheissues.org/Celeb/Pat_Buchanan_Civil_Rights.htm
[2022] syndicated column, 2/25/89) Pat Buchanan, Antisemitism and the Holocaust http://frank.mtsu.edu/~baustin/buchanan.html
[2023] **Pat Buchanan: In His Own Words**. Anti-Defamation League. *This report was originally issued in September 1999* **© 2000 Anti-Defamation League** http://www.adl.org/special_reports/buchanan_own_words/print.asp
[2024] Pat Buchanan, Antisemitism and the Holocaust http://frank.mtsu.edu/~baustin/buchanan.html
[2025] (St. Louis Post Dispatch, 10/20/90) Pat Buchanan, Antisemitism and the Holocaust http://frank.mtsu.edu/~baustin/buchanan.html
[2026] (The Guardian, 1/14/92) Pat Buchanan, Antisemitism and the Holocaust http://frank.mtsu.edu/~baustin/buchanan.html
[2027] (New York Times, 4/21/87) Pat Buchanan, Antisemitism and the Holocaust http://frank.mtsu.edu/~baustin/buchanan.html
[2028] PATRICK BUCHANAN: IN HIS OWN WORDS http://frank.mtsu.edu/~baustin/buchanan.html
[2029] PATRICK BUCHANAN: IN HIS OWN WORDS http://frank.mtsu.edu/~baustin/buchanan.html
[2030] PATRICK BUCHANAN: IN HIS OWN WORDS http://frank.mtsu.edu/~baustin/buchanan.html
[2031] (New Republic, 10/22/90) Pat Buchanan, Antisemitism and the Holocaust http://frank.mtsu.edu/~baustin/buchanan.html
[2032] PATRICK BUCHANAN: IN HIS OWN WORDS http://frank.mtsu.edu/~baustin/buchanan.html
[2033] PATRICK BUCHANAN: IN HIS OWN WORDS http://frank.mtsu.edu/~baustin/buchanan.html
[2034] PATRICK BUCHANAN: IN HIS OWN WORDS http://frank.mtsu.edu/~baustin/buchanan.html
[2035] (ADLReport, 1994) Pat Buchanan, Antisemitism and the Holocaust http://frank.mtsu.edu/~baustin/buchanan.html
[2036] (syndicated column, 11/22/83) Pat Buchanan, Antisemitism and the Holocaust http://frank.mtsu.edu/~baustin/buchanan.html
[2037] (Right from the Pat Buchanan, Antisemitism and the Holocaust http://frank.mtsu.edu/~baustin/buchanan.html
Beginning, p. 149) Pat Buchanan, Antisemitism and the Holocaust http://frank.mtsu.edu/~baustin/buchanan.html
[2038] (Right from the Beginning, p. 341) 2000 Reform Candidate for President Pat Buchanan on Gay Rights. http://www.ontheissues.org/Celeb/Pat_Buchanan_Civil_Rights.htm.
[2039] Re-quoted from the *Washington Times*. November 18, 1983, **Pat Buchanan: In His Own Words**. Anti-Defamation League. *This report was originally issued in September 1999* **© 2000 Anti-Defamation League** http://www.adl.org/special_reports/buchanan_own_words/print.asp
[2040] Patrick Buchanan quotes. Retrieved January 5, 2009 from http://thinkexist.com/quotes/patrick_buchanan/.
[2041] CNN.com Aug 11, 2000. Pat Buchanan on Civil Rights. 2000 Reform Candidate for President Pat Buchanan on Gay Rights. http://www.ontheissues.org/Celeb/Pat_Buchanan_Civil_Rights.htm.
[2042] (Newsday,2/8/89) Pat Buchanan, Antisemitism and the Holocaust http://frank.mtsu.edu/~baustin/buchanan.html
[2043] Pat Buchanan, Antisemitism and the Holocaust http://frank.mtsu.edu/~baustin/buchanan.html
[2044] (Washington Post, 2/9/92) Pat Buchanan, Antisemitism and the Holocaust http://frank.mtsu.edu/~baustin/buchanan.html
[2045] (syndicated column, 9/3/89) Pat Buchanan, Antisemitism and the Holocaust http://frank.mtsu.edu/~baustin/buchanan.html
[2046] (New Republic, 3/30/92) Pat Buchanan, Antisemitism and the Holocaust http://frank.mtsu.edu/~baustin/buchanan.html
[2047] (Los Angeles Times, 11/28/86) Pat Buchanan, Antisemitism and the Holocaust http://frank.mtsu.edu/~baustin/buchanan.html
[2048] Seattle Times,7/31/93. Pat Buchanan, Antisemitism and the Holocaust http://frank.mtsu.edu/~baustin/buchanan.html
[2049] Pat Buchanan, Antisemitism and the Holocaust http://frank.mtsu.edu/~baustin/buchanan.html
[2050] (Buchanan column in Wall Street Journal, 1/21/93) Pat Buchanan, Antisemitism and the Holocaust http://frank.mtsu.edu/~baustin/buchanan.html
[2051] Buchanan wrote in 1990 Pat Buchanan, Antisemitism and the Holocaust http://frank.mtsu.edu/~baustin/buchanan.html
(syndicated column, 10/17/90). Pat Buchanan, Antisemitism and the Holocaust http://frank.mtsu.edu/~baustin/buchanan.html
[2052] PATRICK BUCHANAN: IN HIS OWN WORDS http://frank.mtsu.edu/~baustin/buchanan.html
[2053] Patrick Buchanan quotes. Retrieved January 5, 2009 from http://thinkexist.com/quotes/patrick_buchanan/.

[2054] **Pat Buchanan: In His Own Words**. Anti-Defamation League. *This report was originally issued in September 1999* © **2000 Anti-Defamation League** http://www.adl.org/special_reports/buchanan_own_words/print.asp

[2055] David Firestone, NY Times Sep 19, 20002000 Reform Candidate for President Pat Buchanan on Gay Rights. http://www.ontheissues.org/Celeb/Pat_Buchanan_Civil_Rights.htm

[2056] Source: National Public Radio interview, "Talk of the Nation" May 30, 2000 Pat Buchanan on Civil Rights. 2000 Reform Candidate for President Pat Buchanan on Gay Rights. http://www.ontheissues.org/Celeb/Pat_Buchanan_Civil_Rights.htm

[2057] Is Catholicism now 'unacceptable'?by Patrick Buchanan, Jun 20, 2006 http://www.theamericancause.org/print/062006_print.htm

[2058] National Public Radio interview, "Talk of the Nation" May 30, 2000. 2000 Reform Candidate for President Pat Buchanan on Gay Rights. http://www.ontheissues.org/Celeb/Pat_Buchanan_Civil_Rights.htm

[2059] Source: Nader-Buchanan debate on 'Meet the Press' Oct 1, 2000 Pat Buchanan on Civil Rights. 2000 Reform Candidate for President Pat Buchanan on Gay Rights. http://www.ontheissues.org/Celeb/Pat_Buchanan_Civil_Rights.htm

[2060] Interview on "Equal Time" Dec 21, 1999. 2000 Reform Candidate for President Pat Buchanan on Gay Rights. http://www.ontheissues.org/Celeb/Pat_Buchanan_Civil_Rights.htm

[2061] Interview on "Equal Time" Dec 21, 1999. 2000 Reform Candidate for President Pat Buchanan on Gay Rights. http://www.ontheissues.org/Celeb/Pat_Buchanan_Civil_Rights.htm

[2062] Source: The Associated Press May 4, 2000

[2063] National Public Radio interview, "Talk of the Nation" May 30, 2000. 2000 Reform Candidate for President Pat Buchanan on Gay Rights. http://www.ontheissues.org/Celeb/Pat_Buchanan_Civil_Rights.htm

[2064] Sen. Larry Craig to Join Idaho Hall of Fame, Despite Sex Sting Guilty Plea. Sunday, October 07, 2007. Assoociate Press. http://www.foxnews.com/story/0,2933,299919,00.html

[2065] Craig: I did nothing 'inappropriate' in airport bathroom. **(CNN)** CNN's Dana Bash and Jessica Yellin contributed to this report. http://www.cnn.com/2007/POLITICS/08/28/craig.arrest

[2066] Larry Edwin Craig. Retrieved November 25 @ http://bioguide.congress.gov/scripts/biodisplay.pl?index=C000858.

[2067] Men's room arrest reopens questions about Sen. Larry Craig. August 28, 2007 **Dan Popkey: 377-6400**. http://www.idahostatesman.com/eyepiece/story/143801.html.

[2068] Craig: I did nothing 'inappropriate' in airport bathroom. **(CNN)** CNN's Dana Bash and Jessica Yellin contributed to this report. http://www.cnn.com/2007/POLITICS/08/28/craig.arrest

[2069] Craig: I did nothing 'inappropriate' in airport bathroom. **(CNN)** CNN's Dana Bash and Jessica Yellin contributed to this report. http://www.cnn.com/2007/POLITICS/08/28/craig.arrest

[2070] Craig: I did nothing 'inappropriate' in airport bathroom. **(CNN)** CNN's Dana Bash and Jessica Yellin contributed to this report. http://www.cnn.com/2007/POLITICS/08/28/craig.arrest

[2071] Craig: I did nothing 'inappropriate' in airport bathroom. **(CNN)** CNN's Dana Bash and Jessica Yellin contributed to this report. http://www.cnn.com/2007/POLITICS/08/28/craig.arrest

[2072] Men's room arrest reopens questions about Sen. Larry Craig. August 28, 2007 **Dan Popkey: 377-6400**. http://www.idahostatesman.com/eyepiece/story/143801.html.

[2073] Men's room arrest reopens questions about Sen. Larry Craig. August 28, 2007 **Dan Popkey: 377-6400**. http://www.idahostatesman.com/eyepiece/story/143801.html.

[2074] Craig: I did nothing 'inappropriate' in airport bathroom. **(CNN)** CNN's Dana Bash and Jessica Yellin contributed to this report. http://www.cnn.com/2007/POLITICS/08/28/craig.arrest

[2075] Men's room arrest reopens questions about Sen. Larry Craig. August 28, 2007 **Dan Popkey: 377-6400**. http://www.idahostatesman.com/eyepiece/story/143801.html.

[2076] Craig: I did nothing 'inappropriate' in airport bathroom. **(CNN)** CNN's Dana Bash and Jessica Yellin contributed to this report. http://www.cnn.com/2007/POLITICS/08/28/craig.arrest

[2077] Craig: I did nothing 'inappropriate' in airport bathroom. **(CNN)** CNN's Dana Bash and Jessica Yellin contributed to this report. http://www.cnn.com/2007/POLITICS/08/28/craig.arrest

[2078] Craig: I did nothing 'inappropriate' in airport bathroom. **(CNN)** CNN's Dana Bash and Jessica Yellin contributed to this report. http://www.cnn.com/2007/POLITICS/08/28/craig.arrest

[2079] Idaho Senator Says He Regrets Guilty Plea in Restroom Incident. By PATTI MURPHY and DAVID STOUT Published: August 29, 2007 http://www.nytimes.com/2007/08/29/washington/29craig.html?_r=2&oref=slogin.

[2080] Craig: I did nothing 'inappropriate' in airport bathroom. **(CNN)** CNN's Dana Bash and Jessica Yellin contributed to this report. http://www.cnn.com/2007/POLITICS/08/28/craig.arrest

[2081] Craig: I did nothing 'inappropriate' in airport bathroom. **(CNN)** CNN's Dana Bash and Jessica Yellin contributed to this report. http://www.cnn.com/2007/POLITICS/08/28/craig.arrest

[2082] Idaho Senator Says He Regrets Guilty Plea in Restroom Incident. By PATTI MURPHY and DAVID STOUT Published: August 29, 2007 http://www.nytimes.com/2007/08/29/washington/29craig.html?_r=2&oref=slogin.

[2083] Craig: I did nothing 'inappropriate' in airport bathroom. **(CNN)** CNN's Dana Bash and Jessica Yellin contributed to this report. http://www.cnn.com/2007/POLITICS/08/28/craig.arrest

[2084] Officer's words paraphrasing Craig. Craig: I did nothing 'inappropriate' in airport bathroom. **(CNN)** CNN's Dana Bash and Jessica Yellin contributed to this report. http://www.cnn.com/2007/POLITICS/08/28/craig.arrest

[2085] Craig: I did nothing 'inappropriate' in airport bathroom. **(CNN)** CNN's Dana Bash and Jessica Yellin contributed to this report. http://www.cnn.com/2007/POLITICS/08/28/craig.arrest

[2086] Craig: I did nothing 'inappropriate' in airport bathroom. **(CNN)** CNN's Dana Bash and Jessica Yellin contributed to this report. http://www.cnn.com/2007/POLITICS/08/28/craig.arrest

[2087] Craig: I did nothing 'inappropriate' in airport bathroom. **(CNN)** CNN's Dana Bash and Jessica Yellin contributed to this report. http://www.cnn.com/2007/POLITICS/08/28/craig.arrest

[2088] Idaho Senator Says He Regrets Guilty Plea in Restroom Incident. By PATTI MURPHY and DAVID STOUT Published: August 29, 2007 http://www.nytimes.com/2007/08/29/washington/29craig.html?_r=2&oref=slogin.

[2089] Idaho Senator Says He Regrets Guilty Plea in Restroom Incident. By PATTI MURPHY and DAVID STOUT Published: August 29, 2007 http://www.nytimes.com/2007/08/29/washington/29craig.html?_r=2&oref=slogin.

[2090] Idaho Senator Says He Regrets Guilty Plea in Restroom Incident. By PATTI MURPHY and DAVID STOUT Published: August 29, 2007 http://www.nytimes.com/2007/08/29/washington/29craig.html?_r=2&oref=slogin.

[2091] Men's room arrest reopens questions about Sen. Larry Craig. August 28, 2007 **Dan Popkey: 377-6400**. http://www.idahostatesman.com/eyepiece/story/143801.html.

[2092] Men's room arrest reopens questions about Sen. Larry Craig. August 28, 2007 **Dan Popkey: 377-6400**. http://www.idahostatesman.com/eyepiece/story/143801.html.

[2093] More gay men describe sexual encounters with U.S. Sen. Craig December 03, 2007 Dan Popkey: 377-6438 http://www.idahostatesman.com/eyepiece/story/226703.html

[2094] Sen. Larry Craig's statement Tue August 28, 2007. Retrieved from CNN.com.

[2095] Craig: I did nothing 'inappropriate' in airport bathroom. **(CNN)** CNN's Dana Bash and Jessica Yellin contributed to this report. http://www.cnn.com/2007/POLITICS/08/28/craig.arrest

[2096] Craig: I did nothing 'inappropriate' in airport bathroom. **(CNN)** CNN's Dana Bash and Jessica Yellin contributed to this report. http://www.cnn.com/2007/POLITICS/08/28/craig.arrest

[2097] Idaho Senator Says He Regrets Guilty Plea in Restroom Incident. By PATTI MURPHY and DAVID STOUT Published: August 29, 2007 http://www.nytimes.com/2007/08/29/washington/29craig.html?_r=2&oref=slogin.

[2098] Craig: I did nothing 'inappropriate' in airport bathroom. **(CNN)** CNN's Dana Bash and Jessica Yellin contributed to this report. http://www.cnn.com/2007/POLITICS/08/28/craig.arrest

[2099] Idaho Senator Says He Regrets Guilty Plea in Restroom Incident. By PATTI MURPHY and DAVID STOUT Published: August 29, 2007 http://www.nytimes.com/2007/08/29/washington/29craig.html?_r=2&oref=slogin.

[2100] Craig: I did nothing 'inappropriate' in airport bathroom. **(CNN)** CNN's Dana Bash and Jessica Yellin contributed to this report. http://www.cnn.com/2007/POLITICS/08/28/craig.arrest

[2101] More gay men describe sexual encounters with U.S. Sen. Craig December 03, 2007 Dan Popkey: 377-6438 http://www.idahostatesman.com/eyepiece/story/226703.html

[2102] *Jokes on Larry Craig compiled by Daniel Kurtzman* @ http://politicalhumor.about.com/od/sexandpolitics/a/larrycraigjokes.htm

[2103] Craig: I did nothing 'inappropriate' in airport bathroom. **(CNN)** CNN's Dana Bash and Jessica Yellin contributed to this report. http://www.cnn.com/2007/POLITICS/08/28/craig.arrest

[2104] Craig: I did nothing 'inappropriate' in airport bathroom. **(CNN)** CNN's Dana Bash and Jessica Yellin contributed to this report. http://www.cnn.com/2007/POLITICS/08/28/craig.arrest

[2105] Idaho Senator Says He Regrets Guilty Plea in Restroom Incident. By PATTI MURPHY and DAVID STOUT Published: August 29, 2007 http://www.nytimes.com/2007/08/29/washington/29craig.html?_r=2&oref=slogin.

[2106] Idaho Senator Says He Regrets Guilty Plea in Restroom Incident. By PATTI MURPHY and DAVID STOUT Published: August 29, 2007 http://www.nytimes.com/2007/08/29/washington/29craig.html?_r=2&oref=slogin.

[2107] Craig: I did nothing 'inappropriate' in airport bathroom. **(CNN)** CNN's Dana Bash and Jessica Yellin contributed to this report. http://www.cnn.com/2007/POLITICS/08/28/craig.arrest

[2108] *Jokes on Larry Craig compiled by Daniel Kurtzman* @ http://politicalhumor.about.com/od/sexandpolitics/a/larrycraigjokes.htm

[2109] Craig: I did nothing 'inappropriate' in airport bathroom. **(CNN)** CNN's Dana Bash and Jessica Yellin contributed to this report. http://www.cnn.com/2007/POLITICS/08/28/craig.arrest

[2110] Craig: I did nothing 'inappropriate' in airport bathroom. **(CNN)** CNN's Dana Bash and Jessica Yellin contributed to this report. http://www.cnn.com/2007/POLITICS/08/28/craig.arrest

[2111] Men's room arrest reopens questions about Sen. Larry Craig. August 28, 2007 **Dan Popkey: 377-6400**. http://www.idahostatesman.com/eyepiece/story/143801.html.

[2112] Men's room arrest reopens questions about Sen. Larry Craig. August 28, 2007 **Dan Popkey: 377-6400**. http://www.idahostatesman.com/eyepiece/story/143801.html.

[2113] Men's room arrest reopens questions about Sen. Larry Craig. August 28, 2007 **Dan Popkey: 377-6400**. http://www.idahostatesman.com/eyepiece/story/143801.html.

[2114] Men's room arrest reopens questions about Sen. Larry Craig. August 28, 2007 **Dan Popkey: 377-6400**. http://www.idahostatesman.com/eyepiece/story/143801.html.

[2115] Men's room arrest reopens questions about Sen. Larry Craig. August 28, 2007 **Dan Popkey: 377-6400**. http://www.idahostatesman.com/eyepiece/story/143801.html.

[2116] Men's room arrest reopens questions about Sen. Larry Craig. August 28, 2007 **Dan Popkey: 377-6400**. http://www.idahostatesman.com/eyepiece/story/143801.html.

[2117] Men's room arrest reopens questions about Sen. Larry Craig. August 28, 2007 **Dan Popkey: 377-6400**. http://www.idahostatesman.com/eyepiece/story/143801.html.

[2118] Men's room arrest reopens questions about Sen. Larry Craig. August 28, 2007 **Dan Popkey: 377-6400**. http://www.idahostatesman.com/eyepiece/story/143801.html.

[2119] Men's room arrest reopens questions about Sen. Larry Craig. August 28, 2007 **Dan Popkey: 377-6400**. http://www.idahostatesman.com/eyepiece/story/143801.html.

[2120] Men's room arrest reopens questions about Sen. Larry Craig. August 28, 2007 **Dan Popkey: 377-6400**. http://www.idahostatesman.com/eyepiece/story/143801.html.

[2121] Men's room arrest reopens questions about Sen. Larry Craig. August 28, 2007 **Dan Popkey: 377-6400**. http://www.idahostatesman.com/eyepiece/story/143801.html.

[2122] Men's room arrest reopens questions about Sen. Larry Craig. August 28, 2007 **Dan Popkey: 377-6400**. http://www.idahostatesman.com/eyepiece/story/143801.html.

[2123] More gay men describe sexual encounters with U.S. Sen. Craig December 03, 2007 Dan Popkey: 377-6438 http://www.idahostatesman.com/eyepiece/story/226703.html

[2124] Men's room arrest reopens questions about Sen. Larry Craig. August 28, 2007 **Dan Popkey: 377-6400**. http://www.idahostatesman.com/eyepiece/story/143801.html.

[2125] More gay men describe sexual encounters with U.S. Sen. Craig December 03, 2007 Dan Popkey: 377-6438 http://www.idahostatesman.com/eyepiece/story/226703.html

[2126] Men's room arrest reopens questions about Sen. Larry Craig. August 28, 2007 **Dan Popkey: 377-6400**. http://www.idahostatesman.com/eyepiece/story/143801.html.

[2127] Men's room arrest reopens questions about Sen. Larry Craig. August 28, 2007 **Dan Popkey: 377-6400**. http://www.idahostatesman.com/eyepiece/story/143801.html.

[2128] Men's room arrest reopens questions about Sen. Larry Craig. August 28, 2007 **Dan Popkey: 377-6400**. http://www.idahostatesman.com/eyepiece/story/143801.html.

[2129] Men's room arrest reopens questions about Sen. Larry Craig. August 28, 2007 **Dan Popkey: 377-6400**. http://www.idahostatesman.com/eyepiece/story/143801.html.

[2130] Men's room arrest reopens questions about Sen. Larry Craig. August 28, 2007 **Dan Popkey: 377-6400**. http://www.idahostatesman.com/eyepiece/story/143801.html.

[2131] Craig: I did nothing 'inappropriate' in airport bathroom. **(CNN)** CNN's Dana Bash and Jessica Yellin contributed to this report. http://www.cnn.com/2007/POLITICS/08/28/craig.arrest

[2132] Men's room arrest reopens questions about Sen. Larry Craig. August 28, 2007 **Dan Popkey: 377-6400**. http://www.idahostatesman.com/eyepiece/story/143801.html.

[2133] Men's room arrest reopens questions about Sen. Larry Craig. August 28, 2007 **Dan Popkey: 377-6400**. http://www.idahostatesman.com/eyepiece/story/143801.html.

[2134] Men's room arrest reopens questions about Sen. Larry Craig. August 28, 2007 **Dan Popkey: 377-6400**. http://www.idahostatesman.com/eyepiece/story/143801.html.

[2135] Men's room arrest reopens questions about Sen. Larry Craig. August 28, 2007 **Dan Popkey: 377-6400**. http://www.idahostatesman.com/eyepiece/story/143801.html.

[2136] Craig: I did nothing 'inappropriate' in airport bathroom. **(CNN)** CNN's Dana Bash and Jessica Yellin contributed to this report. http://www.cnn.com/2007/POLITICS/08/28/craig.arrest
[2137] Men's room arrest reopens questions about Sen. Larry Craig. August 28, 2007 **Dan Popkey: 377-6400**. http://www.idahostatesman.com/eyepiece/story/143801.html.
[2138] Craig: I did nothing 'inappropriate' in airport bathroom. **(CNN)** CNN's Dana Bash and Jessica Yellin contributed to this report. http://www.cnn.com/2007/POLITICS/08/28/craig.arrest
[2139] Men's room arrest reopens questions about Sen. Larry Craig. August 28, 2007 **Dan Popkey: 377-6400**. http://www.idahostatesman.com/eyepiece/story/143801.html.
[2140] Men's room arrest reopens questions about Sen. Larry Craig. August 28, 2007 **Dan Popkey: 377-6400**. http://www.idahostatesman.com/eyepiece/story/143801.html.
[2141] Men's room arrest reopens questions about Sen. Larry Craig. August 28, 2007 **Dan Popkey: 377-6400**. http://www.idahostatesman.com/eyepiece/story/143801.html.
[2142] Men's room arrest reopens questions about Sen. Larry Craig. August 28, 2007 **Dan Popkey: 377-6400**. http://www.idahostatesman.com/eyepiece/story/143801.html.
[2143] Men's room arrest reopens questions about Sen. Larry Craig. August 28, 2007 **Dan Popkey: 377-6400**. http://www.idahostatesman.com/eyepiece/story/143801.html.
[2144] Men's room arrest reopens questions about Sen. Larry Craig. August 28, 2007 **Dan Popkey: 377-6400**. http://www.idahostatesman.com/eyepiece/story/143801.html.
[2145] Men's room arrest reopens questions about Sen. Larry Craig. August 28, 2007 **Dan Popkey: 377-6400**. http://www.idahostatesman.com/eyepiece/story/143801.html.
[2146] Men's room arrest reopens questions about Sen. Larry Craig. August 28, 2007 **Dan Popkey: 377-6400**. http://www.idahostatesman.com/eyepiece/story/143801.html.
[2147] More gay men describe sexual encounters with U.S. Sen. Craig December 03, 2007 Dan Popkey: 377-6438 http://www.idahostatesman.com/eyepiece/story/226703.html
[2148] More gay men describe sexual encounters with U.S. Sen. Craig December 03, 2007 Dan Popkey: 377-6438 http://www.idahostatesman.com/eyepiece/story/226703.html
[2149] More gay men describe sexual encounters with U.S. Sen. Craig December 03, 2007 Dan Popkey: 377-6438 http://www.idahostatesman.com/eyepiece/story/226703.html
[2150] Sen. Craig loses appeal in airport sex sting case *By STEVE KARNOWSKI, Associated Press Writer*. December 9, 2008. http://news.yahoo.com/s/ap/20081209/ap_on_re_us/craig_appeal
[2151] Men's room arrest reopens questions about Sen. Larry Craig. August 28, 2007 **Dan Popkey: 377-6400**. http://www.idahostatesman.com/eyepiece/story/143801.html.
[2152] Men's room arrest reopens questions about Sen. Larry Craig. August 28, 2007 **Dan Popkey: 377-6400**. http://www.idahostatesman.com/eyepiece/story/143801.html.
[2153] Men's room arrest reopens questions about Sen. Larry Craig. August 28, 2007 **Dan Popkey: 377-6400**. http://www.idahostatesman.com/eyepiece/story/143801.html.
[2154] Sen. Craig loses appeal in airport sex sting case *By STEVE KARNOWSKI, Associated Press Writer*. December 9, 2008. http://news.yahoo.com/s/ap/20081209/ap_on_re_us/craig_appeal
[2155] Sen. Craig loses appeal in airport sex sting case *By STEVE KARNOWSKI, Associated Press Writer*. December 9, 2008. http://news.yahoo.com/s/ap/20081209/ap_on_re_us/craig_appeal
[2156] Senate panel to Sen. Craig: You discredited the chamber Wed February 13, 2008 http://www.cnn.com/2008/POLITICS/02/13/larry.craig/index.html
[2157] Senate panel to Sen. Craig: You discredited the chamber Wed February 13, 2008 http://www.cnn.com/2008/POLITICS/02/13/larry.craig/index.html
[2158] Sen. Craig loses appeal in airport sex sting case *By STEVE KARNOWSKI, Associated Press Writer*. December 9, 2008. http://news.yahoo.com/s/ap/20081209/ap_on_re_us/craig_appeal
[2159] Sen. Craig loses appeal in airport sex sting case *By STEVE KARNOWSKI, Associated Press Writer*. December 9, 2008. http://news.yahoo.com/s/ap/20081209/ap_on_re_us/craig_appeal
[2160] Sen. Craig loses appeal in airport sex sting case *By STEVE KARNOWSKI, Associated Press Writer*. December 9, 2008. http://news.yahoo.com/s/ap/20081209/ap_on_re_us/craig_appeal
[2161] Sen. Craig loses appeal in airport sex sting case *By STEVE KARNOWSKI, Associated Press Writer*. December 9, 2008. http://news.yahoo.com/s/ap/20081209/ap_on_re_us/craig_appeal
[2162] Biography. Bill Frist, M.D. Retrieved July 28, 2006 from http://frist.senate.gov/index.cfm?FuseAction=AboutSenatorFrist.Biography.
[2163] Richard E. Cohen and Michael Barone. "The Almanac of American Politics—2004." Bill Frist. The National Journal Group. 2003, page 1480.
[2164] Tom Raum. Political junkies speculate on 2008 race. AP. The Arizona Daily Star. Retrieved December 15, 2004 from http://www.asstarnet.com/dailystar/relatedarticles/46526.php
[2165] Tom Raum. Political junkies speculate on 2008 race. AP. The Arizona Daily Star. Retrieved December 15, 2004 from http://www.asstarnet.com/dailystar/relatedarticles/46526.php
[2166] Biography. Bill Frist, M.D. Retrieved July 28, 2006 from http://frist.senate.gov/index.cfm?FuseAction=AboutSenatorFrist.Biography.
[2167] Biography of Majority Leader Bill Frist, M.D. PDF file was obtained through http://frist.senate.gov/index.cfm?FuseAction=AboutSenatorFrist.Biography, retrieved July 28, 2006.
[2168] Biography of Majority Leader Bill Frist, M.D. PDF file was obtained through http://frist.senate.gov/index.cfm?FuseAction=AboutSenatorFrist.Biography, retrieved July 28, 2006.
[2169] [illegible] Posted 6/29/2003. AP**http://www.usatoday.com/news/washington/2003-06-29-frist-gay-marriage_x.htm**
[2170] [illegible] **Posted 6/29/2003. APhttp://www.usatoday.com/news/washington/2003-06-29-frist-gay-marriage_x.htm**
[2171] [illegible] **Posted 6/29/2003. APhttp://www.usatoday.com/news/washington/2003-06-29-frist-gay-marriage_x.htm**
[2172] [illegible] **Posted 6/29/2003. APhttp://www.usatoday.com/news/washington/2003-06-29-frist-gay-marriage_x.htm**
[2173] [illegible] **Posted 6/29/2003. APhttp://www.usatoday.com/news/washington/2003-06-29-frist-gay-marriage_x.htm**
[2174] [illegible] **Posted 6/29/2003. APhttp://www.usatoday.com/news/washington/2003-06-29-frist-gay-marriage_x.htm**
[2175] **On The Issues. Bill Frist on Civil Rights. Republican Senate Majority Leader (TN, retiring 2006). Retrieved January 13, 2009 @ http://ontheissues.org/Domestic/Bill_Frist_Civil_Rights.htm**
[2176] **Frist plans June vote on gay marriage. From Ed Henry. CNN. Monday, February 13, 2006. http://www.cnn.com/2006/POLITICS/02/13/gay.marriage/index.html.**
[2177] **Bill Frist**. Quotes. Retrieved January 12, 2009 from **http://www.brainyquote.com/quotes/authors/b/bill_frist.html. See also http://thinkexist.com/quotes/bill_frist/.**
[2178] **Some Abstinence Programs Mislead Teens, Report Says.** ***By Ceci Connolly.*** **Washington Post Staff Writer. Thursday, December 2, 2004; Page A01 http://www.washingtonpost.com/ac2/wp-dyn/A26623-2004Dec1?language=printer**
[2179] **Health Organizations and AIDS Organizations Denounce Sen. Frist's Inaccurate and Harmful Comments about HIV Transmission, Condom Effectiveness. December 10, 2004 Center for Health and Gender Equity (CHANGE) http://www.planetwire.org/details/5153**
[2180] **Some Abstinence Programs Mislead Teens, Report Says.** ***By Ceci Connolly.*** **Washington Post Staff Writer. Thursday, December 2, 2004; Page A01 http://www.washingtonpost.com/ac2/wp-dyn/A26623-2004Dec1?language=printer**
[2181] **Some Abstinence Programs Mislead Teens, Report Says.** ***By Ceci Connolly.*** **Washington Post Staff Writer. Thursday, December 2, 2004; Page A01 http://www.washingtonpost.com/ac2/wp-dyn/A26623-2004Dec1?language=printer**
[2182] **Some Abstinence Programs Mislead Teens, Report Says.** ***By Ceci Connolly.*** **Washington Post Staff Writer. Thursday, December 2, 2004; Page A01 http://www.washingtonpost.com/ac2/wp-dyn/A26623-2004Dec1?language=printer**
[2183] **Some Abstinence Programs Mislead Teens, Report Says.** ***By Ceci Connolly.*** **Washington Post Staff Writer. Thursday, December 2, 2004; Page A01 http://www.washingtonpost.com/ac2/wp-dyn/A26623-2004Dec1?language=printer**
[2184] **Health Organizations and AIDS Organizations Denounce Sen. Frist's Inaccurate and Harmful Comments about HIV Transmission, Condom Effectiveness.** December 10, 2004 Center for Health and Gender Equity (CHANGE) http://www.planetwire.org/details/5153
[2185] **Health Organizations and AIDS Organizations Denounce Sen. Frist's Inaccurate and Harmful Comments about HIV Transmission, Condom Effectiveness.** December 10, 2004 Center for Health and Gender Equity (CHANGE) http://www.planetwire.org/details/5153
[2186] **Health Organizations and AIDS Organizations Denounce Sen. Frist's Inaccurate and Harmful Comments about HIV Transmission, Condom Effectiveness.** December 10, 2004 Center for Health and Gender Equity (CHANGE) http://www.planetwire.org/details/5153
[2187] **Health Organizations and AIDS Organizations Denounce Sen. Frist's Inaccurate and Harmful Comments about HIV Transmission, Condom Effectiveness.** December 10, 2004 Center for Health and Gender Equity (CHANGE) http://www.planetwire.org/details/5153
[2188] **Health Organizations and AIDS Organizations Denounce Sen. Frist's Inaccurate and Harmful Comments about HIV Transmission, Condom Effectiveness.** December 10, 2004 Center for Health and Gender Equity (CHANGE) http://www.planetwire.org/details/5153
[2189] **Health Organizations and AIDS Organizations Denounce Sen. Frist's Inaccurate and Harmful Comments about HIV Transmission, Condom Effectiveness.** December 10, 2004 Center for Health and Gender Equity (CHANGE) http://www.planetwire.org/details/5153
[2190] **Health Organizations and AIDS Organizations Denounce Sen. Frist's Inaccurate and Harmful Comments about HIV Transmission, Condom Effectiveness.** December 10, 2004 Center for Health and Gender Equity (CHANGE) http://www.planetwire.org/details/5153
[2191] **Health Organizations and AIDS Organizations Denounce Sen. Frist's Inaccurate and Harmful Comments about HIV Transmission, Condom Effectiveness.** December 10, 2004 Center for Health and Gender Equity (CHANGE) http://www.planetwire.org/details/5153
[2192] **Health Organizations and AIDS Organizations Denounce Sen. Frist's Inaccurate and Harmful Comments about HIV Transmission, Condom Effectiveness.** December 10, 2004 Center for Health and Gender Equity (CHANGE) http://www.planetwire.org/details/5153
[2193] **Health Organizations and AIDS Organizations Denounce Sen. Frist's Inaccurate and Harmful Comments about HIV Transmission, Condom Effectiveness.** December 10, 2004 Center for Health and Gender Equity (CHANGE) http://www.planetwire.org/details/5153
[2194] **Health Organizations and AIDS Organizations Denounce Sen. Frist's Inaccurate and Harmful Comments about HIV Transmission, Condom Effectiveness.** December 10, 2004 Center for Health and Gender Equity (CHANGE) http://www.planetwire.org/details/5153
[2195] **Health Organizations and AIDS Organizations Denounce Sen. Frist's Inaccurate and Harmful Comments about HIV Transmission, Condom Effectiveness.** December 10, 2004 Center for Health and Gender Equity (CHANGE) http://www.planetwire.org/details/5153
[2196] **Health Organizations and AIDS Organizations Denounce Sen. Frist's Inaccurate and Harmful Comments about HIV Transmission, Condom Effectiveness.** December 10, 2004 Center for Health and Gender Equity (CHANGE) http://www.planetwire.org/details/5153
[2197] Bill Frist Says It Won't Happen If You Do It Standing Up. December 2004. ***http://wonkette.com/26962/bill-frist-says-it-wont-happen-if-you-do-it-standing-up.***
[2198] Bill Frist Says It Won't Happen If You Do It Standing Up. December 2004. ***http://wonkette.com/26962/bill-frist-says-it-wont-happen-if-you-do-it-standing-up.***
[2199] Fox News Sunday. "Transcript: Sen. Martinez on 'FNS'." Posted and retrieved March 20, 2005, from http://www.foxnews.com_printer_friendly_story/0,3566,150959,00.html.
[2200] Fox News Sunday. "Transcript: Sen. Martinez on 'FNS'." Posted and retrieved March 20, 2005, from http://www.foxnews.com_printer_friendly_story/0,3566,150959,00.html.
[2201] Fox News Sunday. "Transcript: Sen. Martinez on 'FNS'." Posted and retrieved March 20, 2005, from http://www.foxnews.com_printer_friendly_story/0,3566,150959,00.html.
[2202] Congress prepares to intervene in feeding tube case. Knight Ridder News Service and AP, the Milwaukee Journal Sentinel, March 20, 2005 1A.
[2203] Bush enters fray in right-to-die case dividing the US. David Teather and Richard Luscombe. The Guardian. Posted and retrieved March 21, 2005 from http://www.guardian.co.uk/usa/story/0,12271,1442416,00.html.
[2204] "Poll: No Role for Government in Schiavo Case." Analyzed by Gary Langer. ABC News. Posted March 21, 2005 and retrieved March 31 from http://abcnews.go.com/Politics/PollVault/story?id=599622&page=1.
[2205] Bill Frist's balancing Act. U.S. News and World Report for the week of 4/4/05. Retrieved 3.28.05 from http://www.usnews.com/usnews/news/articles/050404/4culture.b.htm.
[2206] Congress prepares to intervene in feeding tube case. Knight Ridder News Service and AP, the Milwaukee Journal Sentinel, March 20, 2005 1A.
[2207] Out of context, videos showed only one side of Schiavo story. Tim Cuprisin. The Milwaukee Journal Sentinel. April 1, 2005.
[2208] Out of context, videos showed only one side of Schiavo story. Tim Cuprisin. The Milwaukee Journal Sentinel. April 1, 2005.
[2209] Out of context, videos showed only one side of Schiavo story. Tim Cuprisin. The Milwaukee Journal Sentinel. April 1, 2005.

[2210] EJ Dionne Jr. "Where's the Apology?" The Washington Post. Posted and retrieved June 17, 2005 from http://www.washingtonpost.com/wp-dyn/content/article/2005/06/16/AR2005061601375.html
[2211] EJ Dionne Jr. "Where's the Apology?" The Washington Post. Posted and retrieved June 17, 2005 from http://www.washingtonpost.com/wp-dyn/content/article/2005/06/16/AR2005061601375.html
[2212] Joanne Kenen. Sen. Frist defends role in Schiavo case. Reuters. Posted June 16, 2005 and retrieved June 24, 2005 from http://www.alertnet.org/thenews/newsdesk/N1636368.htm.
[2213] Joanne Kenen. Sen. Frist defends role in Schiavo case. Reuters. Posted June 16, 2005 and retrieved June 24, 2005 from http://www.alertnet.org/thenews/newsdesk/N1636368.htm.
[2214] Joanne Kenen. Sen. Frist defends role in Schiavo case. Reuters. Posted June 16, 2005 and retrieved June 24, 2005 from http://www.alertnet.org/thenews/newsdesk/N1636368.htm.
[2215] Joanne Kenen. Sen. Frist defends role in Schiavo case. Reuters. Posted June 16, 2005 and retrieved June 24, 2005 from http://www.alertnet.org/thenews/newsdesk/N1636368.htm.
[2216] Janet Hook. Frist Plagued again by comments on Schiavo. LA Times. Posted June 17, 2005 and retrieved June 24 from http://www.latimes.com/news/nationworld/nation/la-na-frist17jun17,0,1567488.story?coll=la-home-nation.
[2217] Janet Hook. Frist Plagued again by comments on Schiavo. LA Times. Posted June 17, 2005 and retrieved June 24 from http://www.latimes.com/news/nationworld/nation/la-na-frist17jun17,0,1567488.story?coll=la-home-nation
[2218] EJ Dionne Jr. "Where's the Apology?" The Washington Post. Posted and retrieved June 17, 2005 from http://www.washingtonpost.com/wp-dyn/content/article/2005/06/16/AR2005061601375.html.
[2219] Newsweek. Lindsay Graham Expresses Concern over Bill Frist's Involvement in Prayer Service About easing Senate Filibuster Debate rule. Posted April 17, 2005 and retrieved April 18, 2005 from http://www.finance.lycos.com/qc/news/story.aspx?story=200504171422_PRN__NYSU013&symbols=QCNEWS:0.
[2220] His American Dream. John Heilemann. New York Magazine. Posted 12.11 and retrieved 12.14.06 from http://nymag.com/news/politics/25015/. 4 /11.
[2221] Bill Frist. Chattanoogan. Bill Frist Will Not Run for President in 2008. Breaking News. Posted 11.29.06 and retrieved 12.3.06 from http://www.chattanoogan.com/articles/article_97469.asp/.
[2222] Kate Zerniki. Frist Announces He'll Forgo a Run for the White House. Published Nov.30, 2006 in the New York Times, and retrieved 12.3.06 from http://ww.nytimes.com/2006/11/30/us/politics/30frist.html?...
[2223] Kate Zerniki. Frist Announces He'll Forgo a Run for the White House. Published Nov.30, 2006 in the New York Times, and retrieved 12.3.06 from http://ww.nytimes.com/2006/11/30/us/politics/30frist.html? ...
[2224] LA Times. Frist won't run for President in 2008, small boost for McCain and others. The China Post. Posted 12.1.06 and retrieved 12.3.06 from http://www.chinapost.com.tw/p_detail.asp?id=96520&GRP=D&onNews=.
[2225] Washington Post/AP. Senator will not seek White House. Washington Post/AP. Milwaukee Journal Sentinel. 11.30.06. 3A.
[2226] John Nichols. Farewell to Senator Bill Frist, R-Frist Family. Posted 11.29 and retrieved 12.3.06 from http://www.thenation.com/blogs/thebeat?bid=1&pid=144105. 1/4.
[2227] John Nichols. Farewell to Senator Bill Frist, R-Frist Family. Posted 11.29.06 and retrieved 12.3.06 from http://www.thenation.com/blogs/thebeat?bid=1&pid=144105. 2/4.
[2228] CNN.com. Late Edition with Wolf Blitzer, aired April 2, 2006. Retrieved April 3, 2006 from http://transcripts.cnn.com/TRANSCRIPTS/0604/02/le.01.html 14/20.
[2229] Hardball with Chris Matthews for May 10. MSNBC.com. Retrieved May 22, 2006 from http://www.msnbc.msn..com/id/12756628/
[2230] H. Josef Hebert. Frist Breaks With Bush on Stem-Cell Bill. Posted 7.29.05 and retrieved 7.29.05 from http://abcnews.go.com/Health/pint?id=990152.
[2231] Meet the Press. NBC News. Transcript for July 31 (2005). Retrieved 8.2.05 from http://www.msnbc.msn.com/id/8714260/print/1/displaymode/1098/.
[2232] LA Times. Frist won't run for President in 2008, small boost for McCain and others. The China Post. Posted 12.1.06 and retrieved 12.3.06 from http://www.chinapost.com.tw/p_detail.asp?id=96520&GRP=D&onNews=.
[2233] LA Times. Frist won't run for President in 2008, small boost for McCain and others. The China Post. Posted 12.1.06 and retrieved 12.3.06 from http://www.chinapost.com.tw/p_detail.asp?id=96520&GRP=D&onNews=.
[2234] Republicans Divided Over Lott Comments, GOP Wins, Loses Votes With Its Comments on Gays. By Marc Lacey, Times Staff Writer, *The Los Angeles Times.* June 17, 1998 http://www.lcrga.com/news/98061701.shtml
[2235] From June 1998 from Online Newshour. http://www.pbs.org/newshour/bb/congress/july-dec98/gop_7-22a.html
[2236] Republicans Divided Over Lott Comments, GOP Wins, Loses Votes With Its Comments on Gays. By Marc Lacey, Times Staff Writer, *The Los Angeles Times.* June 17, 1998 http://www.lcrga.com/news/98061701.shtml
[2237] Lott Comments an Insult to Gay Republican Officials, Activists. June 16, 1998 Copyright © 2008, Georgia Log Cabin Republicans, Inc/ http://www.lcrga.com/news/98061601.shtml.
[2238] Republicans Divided Over Lott Comments, GOP Wins, Loses Votes With Its Comments on Gays. By Marc Lacey, Times Staff Writer, *The Los Angeles Times.* June 17, 1998 http://www.lcrga.com/news/98061701.shtml
[2239] Republicans Divided Over Lott Comments, GOP Wins, Loses Votes With Its Comments on Gays. By Marc Lacey, Times Staff Writer, *The Los Angeles Times.* June 17, 1998 http://www.lcrga.com/news/98061701.shtml
[2240] Republicans Divided Over Lott Comments, GOP Wins, Loses Votes With Its Comments on Gays. By Marc Lacey, Times Staff Writer, *The Los Angeles Times.* June 17, 1998 http://www.lcrga.com/news/98061701.shtml
[2241] From June 1998 from Online Newshour. http://www.pbs.org/newshour/bb/congress/july-dec98/gop_7-22a.html
[2242] Are Gay Rumors The Real Reason Behind Trent Lott's Resignation? By *Julie.* Created *11/26/2007 - 8:26pm*http://www.clevelandleader.com/print/3917
[2243] **Race for the Presidency. Alan Keyes. Knight Ridder** http://graphics.boston.com/news/politics/campaign2000/candidates/keyes/bio/html/print.htm
[2244] **Race for the Presidency. Alan Keyes. Knight Ridder** http://graphics.boston.com/news/politics/campaign2000/candidates/keyes/bio/html/print.htm
[2245] America's wake-up call? Alan Keyes strikes a chord with Iowa voters. **By Anthony York** http://archive.salon.com/politics2000/feature/2000/01/25/keyes/index.html
[2246] **Race for the Presidency. Alan Keyes. Knight Ridder** http://graphics.boston.com/news/politics/campaign2000/candidates/keyes/bio/html/print.htm
[2247] **Race for the Presidency. Alan Keyes. Knight Ridder** http://graphics.boston.com/news/politics/campaign2000/candidates/keyes/bio/html/print.htm
[2248] **Race for the Presidency. Alan Keyes. Knight Ridder** http://graphics.boston.com/news/politics/campaign2000/candidates/keyes/bio/html/print.htm
[2249] Dem. & GOP Presidential Primaries: Utah. See http://www.cnn.com/ELECTION/2000/primaries/UT/results.html.
[2250] Top News. Alan Keyes joins GOP '08 field. Published: Sept. 15, 2007. UPI http://www.upi.com/Top_News/2007/09/15/Alan_Keyes_joins_GOP_08_field/UPI-49271189900180/.
[2251] **Mr. Keyes the Carpetbagger.** Monday, August 9, 2004; Page A14 http://www.washingtonpost.com/wp-dyn/articles/A50885-2004Aug8.html
[2252] **Mr. Keyes the Carpetbagger.** Monday, August 9, 2004; Page A14 http://www.washingtonpost.com/wp-dyn/articles/A50885-2004Aug8.html
[2253] the BBC's paraphrasing. Republicans' gay debate By Daniel Griffiths BBC News, Washington http://news.bbc.co.uk/2/hi/americas/3600134.stm.
[2254] The BBC's paraphrasing. Republicans' gay debate. By Daniel Griffiths BBC News, Washington http://news.bbc.co.uk/2/hi/americas/3600134.stm.
[2255] Alan Keyes teaches sex education lesson to homosexual interviewer. Mary Mostert. September 4, 2004. Retrieved @ http://www.renewamerica.us/columns/mostert/040904
[2256] Alan Keyes teaches sex education lesson to homosexual interviewer. Mary Mostert. September 4, 2004. Retrieved @ http://www.renewamerica.us/columns/mostert/040904
[2257] Alan Keyes teaches sex education lesson to homosexual interviewer. Mary Mostert. September 4, 2004. Retrieved @ http://www.renewamerica.us/columns/mostert/040904
[2258] Alan Keyes teaches sex education lesson to homosexual interviewer. Mary Mostert. September 4, 2004. Retrieved @ http://www.renewamerica.us/columns/mostert/040904
[2259] Alan Keyes teaches sex education lesson to homosexual interviewer. Mary Mostert. September 4, 2004. Retrieved @ http://www.renewamerica.us/columns/mostert/040904
[2260] Alan Keyes teaches sex education lesson to homosexual interviewer. Mary Mostert. September 4, 2004. Retrieved @ http://www.renewamerica.us/columns/mostert/040904
[2261] Alan Keyes teaches sex education lesson to homosexual interviewer. Mary Mostert. September 4, 2004. Retrieved @ http://www.renewamerica.us/columns/mostert/040904
[2262] Alan Keyes teaches sex education lesson to homosexual interviewer. Mary Mostert. September 4, 2004. Retrieved @ http://www.renewamerica.us/columns/mostert/040904
[2263] Alan Keyes teaches sex education lesson to homosexual interviewer. Mary Mostert. September 4, 2004. Retrieved @ http://www.renewamerica.us/columns/mostert/040904
[2264] Alan Keyes teaches sex education lesson to homosexual interviewer. Mary Mostert. September 4, 2004. Retrieved @ http://www.renewamerica.us/columns/mostert/040904
[2265] Alan Keyes teaches sex education lesson to homosexual interviewer. Mary Mostert. September 4, 2004. Retrieved @ http://www.renewamerica.us/columns/mostert/040904
[2266] Alan Keyes teaches sex education lesson to homosexual interviewer. Mary Mostert. September 4, 2004. Retrieved @ http://www.renewamerica.us/columns/mostert/040904
[2267] Alan Keyes teaches sex education lesson to homosexual interviewer. Mary Mostert. September 4, 2004. Retrieved @ http://www.renewamerica.us/columns/mostert/040904
[2268] Alan Keyes teaches sex education lesson to homosexual interviewer. Mary Mostert. September 4, 2004. Retrieved @ http://www.renewamerica.us/columns/mostert/040904
[2269] Alan Keyes teaches sex education lesson to homosexual interviewer. Mary Mostert. September 4, 2004. Retrieved @ http://www.renewamerica.us/columns/mostert/040904
[2270] Alan Keyes teaches sex education lesson to homosexual interviewer. Mary Mostert. September 4, 2004. Retrieved @ http://www.renewamerica.us/columns/mostert/040904
[2271] Conservative parent adjust to gay kids, Keyes story is latest in a series JOE CREA. Friday, October 15, 2004 http://www.washingtonblade.com/2004/10-15/news/national/conkids.cfm.
[2272] Conservative parent adjust to gay kids, Keyes story is latest in a series JOE CREA. Friday, October 15, 2004 http://www.washingtonblade.com/2004/10-15/news/national/conkids.cfm.
[2273] Conservative parent adjust to gay kids, Keyes story is latest in a series JOE CREA. Friday, October 15, 2004 http://www.washingtonblade.com/2004/10-15/news/national/conkids.cfm.
[2274] Conservative parent adjust to gay kids, Keyes story is latest in a series JOE CREA. Friday, October 15, 2004 http://www.washingtonblade.com/2004/10-15/news/national/conkids.cfm.
[2275] **When Sexuality Undercuts A Family's Ties.** By Marc Fisher. Sunday, February 13, 2005; Page C01 © 2005 The Washington Post Company http://www.washingtonpost.com/ac2/wp-dyn/A20005-2005Feb12?language=printer
[2276] **When Sexuality Undercuts A Family's Ties.** By Marc Fisher. Sunday, February 13, 2005; Page C01 © 2005 The Washington Post Company http://www.washingtonpost.com/ac2/wp-dyn/A20005-2005Feb12?language=printer
[2277] **When Sexuality Undercuts A Family's Ties.** By Marc Fisher. Sunday, February 13, 2005; Page C01 © 2005 The Washington Post Company http://www.washingtonpost.com/ac2/wp-dyn/A20005-2005Feb12?language=printer
[2278] **When Sexuality Undercuts A Family's Ties.** By Marc Fisher. Sunday, February 13, 2005; Page C01 © 2005 The Washington Post Company http://www.washingtonpost.com/ac2/wp-dyn/A20005-2005Feb12?language=printer
[2279] **When Sexuality Undercuts A Family's Ties.** By Marc Fisher. Sunday, February 13, 2005; Page C01 © 2005 The Washington Post Company http://www.washingtonpost.com/ac2/wp-dyn/A20005-2005Feb12?language=printer
[2280] **When Sexuality Undercuts A Family's Ties.** By Marc Fisher. Sunday, February 13, 2005; Page C01 © 2005 The Washington Post Company http://www.washingtonpost.com/ac2/wp-dyn/A20005-2005Feb12?language=printer
[2281] **When Sexuality Undercuts A Family's Ties.** By Marc Fisher. Sunday, February 13, 2005; Page C01 © 2005 The Washington Post Company http://www.washingtonpost.com/ac2/wp-dyn/A20005-2005Feb12?language=printer
[2282] Alan Keyes' Daughter Coming Out. Conservative's Daughter Making 1st Public Appearance As Lesbian.
Feb. 13, 2005 **(CBS)** http://www.cbsnews.com/stories/2005/02/13/politics/main673732.shtml.

[2283] Alan Keyes' Daughter Coming Out. Conservative's Daughter Making 1st Public Appearance As Lesbian. Feb. 13, 2005 **(CBS)** http://www.cbsnews.com/stories/2005/02/13/politics/main673732.shtml.

[2284] Alan Keyes' Daughter Coming Out. Conservative's Daughter Making 1st Public Appearance As Lesbian. Feb. 13, 2005 **(CBS)** http://www.cbsnews.com/stories/2005/02/13/politics/main673732.shtml.

[2285] Alan Keyes' Daughter Coming Out. Conservative's Daughter Making 1st Public Appearance As Lesbian. Feb. 13, 2005 **(CBS)** http://www.cbsnews.com/stories/2005/02/13/politics/main673732.shtml.

[2286] Alan Keyes' Daughter Coming Out. Conservative's Daughter Making 1st Public Appearance As Lesbian. Feb. 13, 2005 **(CBS)** http://www.cbsnews.com/stories/2005/02/13/politics/main673732.shtml.

[2287] Alan Keyes' Daughter Coming Out. Conservative's Daughter Making 1st Public Appearance As Lesbian. Feb. 13, 2005 **(CBS)** http://www.cbsnews.com/stories/2005/02/13/politics/main673732.shtml.

[2288] Top News. Alan Keyes joins GOP '08 field. Published: Sept. 15, 2007. UPI http://www.upi.com/Top_News/2007/09/15/Alan_Keyes_joins_GOP_08_field/UPI-49271189900180/.

[2289] [illegible] Updated 5/5/2008. (AP) http://www.usatoday.com/news/politics/2008-04-16-keyes_N.htm

[2290] Constitution Party stunner: Chuck Baldwin KOs firebrand Alan KeyesBlog from Kerwin 4.27.2008. http://primebuzz.kcstar.com/?q=node/11314.

[2291] The 2008 Election: A Winnowing Season. By Alan Keyes. Nov. 3, 2008. http://www.alankeyes.com/

[2292] Brian McGrory. In sanctum Santorum. Boston Globe. Posted July 12, 2005 and retrieved July 15, 2005 from http://www.boston.com/news/local/articles/2005/07/12/in/_sanctum_santorum/

[2293] Brian McGrory. In sanctum Santorum. Boston Globe. Posted July 12, 2005 and retrieved July 15, 2005 from http://www.boston.com/news/local/articles/2005/07/12/in/_sanctum_santorum/

[2294] Anand Vaishnav. Romney begs to differ with Santorum remark. Boston Globe. Posted July 15, 2005 and retrieved July 15, 2005 from http://www.boston.com/news/local/massachusetts/articles/2005/07/15/romney_begs_to_differ_with_santorum_remark/.

[2295] Anand Vaishnav. Romney begs to differ with Santorum remark. Boston Globe. Posted July 15, 2005 and retrieved July 15, 2005 from http://www.boston.com/news/local/massachusetts/articles/2005/07/15/romney_begs_to_differ_with_santorum_remark/

[2296] The Kansas City Star. The BUZZ: Boston basher. Posted 7.14.05 and retrieved 7.15.05 from http://www.kansascity.com/mld/kansascitystar/news/politics/12127067.htm.

[2297] Brett Lieberman. Santorum hits back at Kennedy. Pennlive.com. The Patriot News. Posted July 15, 2005 and retrieved July 15, 2005 from http://www.pennlive.com/news/patriotnews/index.ssf?/base/news/1121419422185420.xml&coll=1.

[2298] Brett Lieberman. Santorum hits back at Kennedy. Pennlive.com. The Patriot News. Posted July 15, 2005 and retrieved July 15, 2005 from http://www.pennlive.com/news/patriotnews/index.ssf?/base/news/1121419422185420.xml&coll=1.

[2299] (quote was reported by Brett Lieberman of the Harrisburg Patriot-News) Found in James O' Toole. "It takes a controversy: Santorum book could be asset after initial hit, strategist says." The Pittsburgh Post-Gazette. Posted July 17, 2005 and retrieved July 22, 2005 from http://www.post-gazette.com/pg/05198/539270.stm.

[2300] Michael Kranish, Santorum blasts Mass. Senators over church scandals. The Boston Globe/ Boston.com. Posted August 1, 2005 and retrieved August 5, 2005 from http://www.boston.com/news/nation/articles/2005/08/01/santorum_blasts_mass_senators_over_church_scandal/.

[2301] Michael Kranish, Santorum blasts Mass. Senators over church scandals. The Boston Globe/ Boston.com. Posted August 1, 2005 and retrieved August 5, 2005 from http://www.boston.com/news/nation/articles/2005/08/01/santorum_blasts_mass_senators_over_church_scandal/

[2302] AP. Philadelphia Archdiocese hid years of abuse by priests, grand jury say. The Milwaukee Journal Sentinel, September 22, 2005, 9A.

[2303] Santorum under fire for comments on homosexuality. By Sean Loughlin. CNN Washington Bureau Tuesday, April 22, 2003. http://www.cnn.com/2003/ALLPOLITICS/04/22/santorum.gays/

[2304] Santorum under fire for comments on homosexuality. By Sean Loughlin. CNN Washington Bureau Tuesday, April 22, 2003. http://www.cnn.com/2003/ALLPOLITICS/04/22/santorum.gays/.

[2305] Santorum is right. Posted: April 28, 2003. by Joseph Farah. © 2008 WorldNetDaily.com. April 2003.

[2306] USA Today. Posted 4/23/2003. Excerpt from Santorum interview. The Associated Press. Unedited. Taped April 7, 2003. http://www.usatoday.com/news/washington/2003-04-23-santorum-excerpt_x.htm

[2307] Santorum defends comments on homosexuality-White House maintains silence on issue. Wednesday, April 23, 2003. -- Written by CNN.Com Producer Sean Loughlin in Washington. http://www.cnn.com/2003/ALLPOLITICS/04/23/santorum.gays/index.html

[2308] Santorum and gays. Apr 26, 2003 . Salon. http://dir.salon.com/story/news/feature/2003/04/26/santorum_quotes/

[2309] Santorum and gays. Apr 26, 2003 . Salon. http://dir.salon.com/story/news/feature/2003/04/26/santorum_quotes/

[2310] Santorum and gays. Apr 26, 2003 . Salon. http://dir.salon.com/story/news/feature/2003/04/26/santorum_quotes/

[2311] Santorum and gays. Apr 26, 2003 . Salon. http://dir.salon.com/story/news/feature/2003/04/26/santorum_quotes/

[2312] Santorum and gays. Apr 26, 2003 . Salon. http://dir.salon.com/story/news/feature/2003/04/26/santorum_quotes/

[2313] Santorum and gays. Apr 26, 2003 . Salon. http://dir.salon.com/story/news/feature/2003/04/26/santorum_quotes/

[2314] STEWART VS. SANTORUM: "NOT BAD DUDES"?The Daily Show with John Stewart. http://towleroad.typepad.com/towleroad/2005/07/can_y9ou_confus.html.

[2315] Rick Santorum Quotes. Retrieved 6.29.07 from http://www.brainyquote.com/quotes/authors/r/rick_santorum.html.

[2316] STEWART VS. SANTORUM: "NOT BAD DUDES"?The Daily Show with John Stewart. http://towleroad.typepad.com/towleroad/2005/07/can_y9ou_confus.html.

[2317] STEWART VS. SANTORUM: "NOT BAD DUDES"?The Daily Show with John Stewart. http://towleroad.typepad.com/towleroad/2005/07/can_y9ou_confus.html.

[2318] STEWART VS. SANTORUM: "NOT BAD DUDES"?The Daily Show with John Stewart. http://towleroad.typepad.com/towleroad/2005/07/can_y9ou_confus.html.

[2319] STEWART VS. SANTORUM: "NOT BAD DUDES"?The Daily Show with John Stewart. http://towleroad.typepad.com/towleroad/2005/07/can_y9ou_confus.html.

[2320] STEWART VS. SANTORUM: "NOT BAD DUDES"?The Daily Show with John Stewart. http://towleroad.typepad.com/towleroad/2005/07/can_y9ou_confus.html.

[2321] USA Today. Posted 4/23/2003. Excerpt from Santorum interview. The Associated Press. Unedited. Taped April 7, 2003. http://www.usatoday.com/news/washington/2003-04-23-santorum-excerpt_x.htm.

[2322] USA Today. Posted 4/23/2003. Excerpt from Santorum interview. The Associated Press. Unedited. Taped April 7, 2003. http://www.usatoday.com/news/washington/2003-04-23-santorum-excerpt_x.htm.

[2323] USA Today. Posted 4/23/2003. Excerpt from Santorum interview. The Associated Press. Unedited. Taped April 7, 2003. http://www.usatoday.com/news/washington/2003-04-23-santorum-excerpt_x.htm

[2324] Richard E. Cohen and Michael Barone. The Almanac of American Politics—2004. The National Journal Group. 2003, page 130.

[2325] Fergus Cullen. "Will Mike Huckabee follow the same path as Bill Clinton?" The Union Leader and New Hampshire Sunday News. Posted August 31, 2005 and retrieved September 8, 2005 from http://www.theunionleader.com/articles_showfast.html?article=59781.

[2326] Fergus Cullen. "Will Mike Huckabee follow the same path as Bill Clinton?" The Union Leader and New Hampshire Sunday News. Posted August 31, 2005 and retrieved September 8, 2005 from http://www.theunionleader.com/articles_showfast.html?article=59781

[2327] Arkansas Gov. Mike Huckabee: Ban Gay Foster Parents. NEwsmax.com. June 30, 2006 and retrieved July 28, 2006 from http://newsmax.com/archives/ic/2006/6/30/131101.shtml.

[2328] Arkansas Gov. Mike Huckabee: Ban Gay Foster Parents. NEwsmax.com. June 30, 2006 and retrieved July 28, 2006 from http://newsmax.com/archives/ic/2006/6/30/131101.shtml.

[2329] Mike Glover. Huckabee Optimistic of Gay Parents Ban. AP. Posted July 8, 2006 and retrieved July 28, 2006 from http://www.examiner.com/a-170906~Huckabee_Optimistic_of_Gay_Parents_Ban.html.

[2330] Mike Glover. Huckabee Optimistic of Gay Parents Ban. AP. Posted July 8, 2006 and retrieved July 28, 2006 from http://www.examiner.com/a-170906~Huckabee_Optimistic_of_Gay_Parents_Ban.html

[2331] Mike Glover. Huckabee Optimistic of Gay Parents Ban. AP. Posted July 8, 2006 and retrieved July 28, 2006 from http://www.examiner.com/a-170906~Huckabee_Optimistic_of_Gay_Parents_Ban.html.

[2332] Arkansas Gov. Mike Huckabee: Ban Gay Foster Parents. NEwsmax.com. June 30, 2006 and retrieved July 28, 2006 from http://newsmax.com/archives/ic/2006/6/30/131101.shtml.

[2333] FOX 16 of Little Rock. Gay Foster Parent Ban. Posted July 9, 2006 and retrieved July 28, 2006 from http://www.fox16.com/news/story.aspx?content_id=09302117-4F41-4125-9367-AE2F674E99D3.

[2334] Mike Glover. Huckabee Optimistic of Gay Parents Ban. AP. Posted July 8, 2006 and retrieved July 28, 2006 from http://www.examiner.com/a-170906~Huckabee_Optimistic_of_Gay_Parents_Ban.html

[2335] Mike Glover. Huckabee Optimistic of Gay Parents Ban. AP. Posted July 8, 2006 and retrieved July 28, 2006 from http://www.examiner.com/a-170906~Huckabee_Optimistic_of_Gay_Parents_Ban.html

[2336] **Ali Frick** on Dec 10th, 2008 at 9:53 am. **Stewart Grills Huckabee On Gay Marriage: 'At What Age Did You Choose Not To Be Gay?' Retrieved October 30, 2009 @ http://thinkprogress.org/2008/12/10/stewart-grills-huckabee/.**

[2337] **Ali Frick** on Dec 10th, 2008 at 9:53 am. **Stewart Grills Huckabee On Gay Marriage: 'At What Age Did You Choose Not To Be Gay?' Retrieved October 30, 2009 @ http://thinkprogress.org/2008/12/10/stewart-grills-huckabee/.**

[2338] **Ali Frick** on Dec 10th, 2008 at 9:53 am. **Stewart Grills Huckabee On Gay Marriage: 'At What Age Did You Choose Not To Be Gay?' Retrieved October 30, 2009 @ http://thinkprogress.org/2008/12/10/stewart-grills-huckabee/.**

[2339] **Ali Frick** on Dec 10th, 2008 at 9:53 am. **Stewart Grills Huckabee On Gay Marriage: 'At What Age Did You Choose Not To Be Gay?' Retrieved October 30, 2009 @ http://thinkprogress.org/2008/12/10/stewart-grills-huckabee/.**

[2340] **Ali Frick** on Dec 10th, 2008 at 9:53 am. **Stewart Grills Huckabee On Gay Marriage: 'At What Age Did You Choose Not To Be Gay?' Retrieved October 30, 2009 @ http://thinkprogress.org/2008/12/10/stewart-grills-huckabee/.**

[2341] **Matt Corley** on Dec 30th, 2007 at 1:41 pm. **Huckabee: 'I Don't Know' If People Are 'Born' Gay, But It's A 'Choice' To Act Gay. Retrieved October 30, 2009 @ http://thinkprogress.org/2007/12/30/huckabee-gay-choice.**

[2342] **Matt Corley** on Dec 30th, 2007 at 1:41 pm. **Huckabee: 'I Don't Know' If People Are 'Born' Gay, But It's A 'Choice' To Act Gay. Retrieved October 30, 2009 @ http://thinkprogress.org/2007/12/30/huckabee-gay-choice.**

[2343] **Matt Corley** on Dec 30th, 2007 at 1:41 pm. **Huckabee: 'I Don't Know' If People Are 'Born' Gay, But It's A 'Choice' To Act Gay. Retrieved October 30, 2009 @ http://thinkprogress.org/2007/12/30/huckabee-gay-choice.**

[2344] *—Steve Benen. Washington Monthly.com. Posted December 30, 2007 @ http://www.washingtonmonthly.com/archives/individual/2007_12/012806.php.*

[2345] High Infidelity. Steve Benen. Washington Monthly. July/August 2006. Retrieved June 30, 2006 from http://www.washingtonmonthly.com/features/2006/0607.benen.html.
[2346] High Infidelity. Steve Benen. Washington Monthly. July/August 2006. Retrieved June 30, 2006 from http://www.washingtonmonthly.com/features/2006/0607.benen.html. 2/4.
[2347] Jake Tapper. Gingrich Admits to Affair During Clinton Impeachment. ABC News. 3.9.07 and retrieved 6.29.07 from http://abcnews.go.com/print?id=2937633.
[2348] Jake Tapper. Gingrich Admits to Affair During Clinton Impeachment. ABC News. 3.9.07 and retrieved 6.29.07 from http://abcnews.go.com/print?id=2937633.
[2349] Jake Tapper. Gingrich Admits to Affair During Clinton Impeachment. ABC News. 3.9.07 and retrieved 6.29.07 from http://abcnews.go.com/print?id=2937633.
[2350] High Infidelity. Steve Benen. Washington Monthly. July/August 2006. Retrieved June 30, 2006 from http://www.washingtonmonthly.com/features/2006/0607.benen.html. 2/4.
[2351] High Infidelity. Steve Benen. Washington Monthly. July/August 2006. Retrieved June 30, 2006 from http://www.washingtonmonthly.com/features/2006/0607.benen.html. 2/4.
[2352]Bill Schneider. CNN Senior Political Analyst. Gingrich confession: Clearing the way for a 2008 run? CNN.com. Posted 3.9.07 and retrieved 6.29.07 from http://www.cnn.com/2007/POLITICS/03/09/gingrich.schneider/index.html.
[2353] Janet Hook. LA Times. Gingrich Writes Act 2 of his Political Life. Posted 1.16.05 and retrieved 7.20.07 from http://www.newt.org/backpage.sp?art=1463.
[2354] Jake Tapper. Gingrich Admits to Affair During Clinton Impeachment. ABC News. 3.9.07 and retrieved 6.29.07 from http://abcnews.go.com/print?id=2937633.
[2355] Dave Bohon. WDC MEDIA. "Newt Gingrich Signs as Columnist for Church Report. Posted December 13, 2005 and retrieved December 15, 2005 form http://www.michnews.com/artman/publish/article_10805.shtml See also http://www.newt.org/backpage.asp?art=2567.
[2356] Dave Bohon. WDC MEDIA. Newt Gingrich Signs as Columnist for Church Report. Posted December 13, 2005 and retrieved December 15, 2005 form http://www.michnews.com/artman/publish/article_10805.shtml
[2357] John M. Broder. Gingrich sees a higher calling. New York Times. Milwaukee Journal Sentinel. Dec.17, 2006, 5A.
[2358] John M. Broder. Gingrich sees a higher calling. New York Times. Milwaukee Journal Sentinel. Dec.17, 2006, 5A.
[2359] AP. Huckabee: Character issues apply to GOP, too. MSNBC.com. Posted 4.6.07 and retrieved 8.1.07 from http://www.msnbc.msn.com/id/17980177/print/1/displaymode/1098/.
[2360] Tahman Bradley. Romney Boasts His 'Right' Record. Dec. 14, 2006, Retrieved 12.14.06 from http://blogs.abcnews.com/politicalradar/2006/12/romney_boasts_h.html.
[2361] Tahman Bradley. Romney Boasts His 'Right' Record. Dec. 14, 2006, Retrieved 12.14.06 from http://blogs.abcnews.com/politicalradar/2006/12/romney_boasts_h.html.
[2362] Rick Klein. Kennedy rethinks support for a Kerry presidential run in '08. Globe. Posted Dec.11 and retrieved 12.14.06 from http://www.boston.com/news/nation/washington/articles/2006/12/11/kennedy_drops_support_for_a_kerry_presidential_run_in_08/ see Kennedy ditching of Kerry.
[2363] Two Contrasting views. Retrieved 12.14.06 from http://www.ovaloffice2008.com/.
[2364] Two Contrasting views. Retrieved 12.14.06 from http://www.ovaloffice2008.com/.
[2365] Two Contrasting views. Retrieved 12.14.06 from http://www.ovaloffice2008.com/.
[2366] National Journal Group Inc. White House 2008 Rankings. Jan. 11. 2007. Retrieved 1.13.07 from http://nationaljournal.com/racerankings/wh08/republicans/.
[2367] Washington Post/AP. Which Romney will Run? MJS, Dec.23, 2006, 3A. SB 9 p 13.
[2368] Washington Post/AP. Which Romney will Run? MJS, Dec.23, 2006, 3A. SB 9 p 13.
[2369] Washington Post/AP. Which Romney will Run? MJS, Dec.23, 2006, 3A. SB 9 p 13.
[2370] Steve LeBlanc. Report blasts Romney's political record. 1.12 and retrieved 1.13.07 from http://www.newsone.ca/westfallweeklynews/ViewArticle.aspx?id=43392&source=2.
[2371] Steve LeBlanc. Report blasts Romney's political record. 1.12 and retrieved 1.13.07 from http://www.newsone.ca/westfallweeklynews/ViewArticle.aspx?id=43392&source=2.
[2372] Kathyrn Jean Lopez. National Review Online. 1.13.07 and posted 1.10 @ http://article.nationalreview.com/?q=YTUxMTViMDAxZGNhYiO0NiA0ODBlZiRhMWVmOGIwNWU=/.
[2373] Kathyrn Jean Lopez. National Review Online. 1.13.07 and posted 1.10 @ http://article.nationalreview.com/?q=YTUxMTViMDAxZGNhYiO0NiA0ODBlZiRhMWVmOGIwNWU=/.
[2374] Kathyrn Jean Lopez. National Review Online. 1.13.07 and posted 1.10 @ http://article.nationalreview.com/?q=YTUxMTViMDAxZGNhYiO0NiA0ODBlZiRhMWVmOGIwNWU=/.
[2375] Yvonne Abraham. Romney: gay outsiders can't marry in Mass. Posted April25, 2006. and retrieved 1.13.07 from http://www.boston.com/news/local/articles/2004/04/25/romney_gay_outsiders_can't_marry_in_mass?.
[2376] Kathyrn Jean Lopez. National Review Online. 1.13.07 and posted 1.10 @ http://article.nationalreview.com/?q=YTUxMTViMDAxZGNhYiO0NiA0ODBlZiRhMWVmOGIwNWU=/.
[2377] Peter LaBarbera. Americans for Truth Calls on Mitt Romney to Apologize for Attacking Pro-Family Hero Brian Camenker.Posted and Retrieved 1.13.07 from http://www.christiannewswire.com/news/201361936.html.
[2378] Selwyn Duke. American Chronicle. Mitt Romney: A Massachusetss Liberal for President. Posted 1.11 and retrieved 1.13 from http://www.americanchronicle.com/articles/viewArticle.asp?articleID=189980.
[2379] Peter Cassels. Log Cabin President Seeks Explanation from Romney. Dec.19, 2006 and Retrieved 1.13.07 from http://www.edgeboston.com/index.php?ci=108&ch=news&sc=glbt&sc2=news&sc3_id=circumstance.
[2380] Peter Cassels. Log Cabin President Seeks Explanation from Romney. Dec.19, 2006 and Retrieved 1.13.07 from http://www.edgeboston.com/index.php?ci=108&ch=news&sc=glbt&sc2=news&sc3_id=circumstance.
[2381] Andy Humm. Log Cabin Promotes From Within. Posted 12.21.06 and retrieved 1.13.07 from http://www.gaycitynews.com/site/news.cfm?newsid=17621528&BRD=2729&PAG=461&...
[2382] NY Times. Letter may hurt Romney in /08. Dec. 10, 2006 17A. SB 9 p 17A.
[2383] NY Times. Letter may hurt Romney in /08. Dec. 10, 2006 17A. SB 9 p 17A
[2384] Rick Klein. Old Romney debate clip is now a hit on the Web. Posted Jan.11, 2007 and retrieved 1.13.07 from http://www.boston.com/news/local/articles/2007/01/11/old_romney_debate_clip_is_now_a_hit_on_the_web.
[2385] Rick Klein. Old Romney debate clip is now a hit on the Web. Posted Jan.11, 2007 and retrieved 1.13.07 from http://www.boston.com/news/local/articles/2007/01/11/old_romney_debate_clip_is_now_a_hit_on_the_web
[2386] Selwyn Duke. American Chronicle. Mitt Romney: A Massachusetss Liberal for President. Posted 1.11 and retrieved 1.13 from http://www.americanchronicle.com/articles/viewArticle.asp?articleID=189980.
[2387] Rick Klein. Old Romney debate clip is now a hit on the Web. Posted Jan.11, 2007 and retrieved 1.13.07 from http://www.boston.com/news/local/articles/2007/01/11/old_romney_debate_clip_is_now_a_hit_on_the_web
[2388] Retrieved 1.13.07 from Quote of the Day. http.//politicalwire.com/archives/2008_campaign/.
[2389] Rick Klein. Old Romney debate clip is now a hit on the Web. Posted Jan.11, 2007 and retrieved 1.13.07 from http://www.boston.com/news/local/articles/2007/01/11/old_romney_debate_clip_is_now_a_hit_on_the_web
[2390] Rick Klein. Old Romney debate clip is now a hit on the Web. Posted Jan.11, 2007 and retrieved 1.13.07 from http://www.boston.com/news/local/articles/2007/01/11/old_romney_debate_clip_is_now_a_hit_on_the_web
[2391] James Kirchick: Mitt Romney's pomp and circumstance. Posted 1.11.07 and retrieve d1.13.07 from http://www.examiner.com/a-522561~James_Kirchick__Mitt_Romney_s_pomp_and_circumstance.
[2392] James Kirchick: Mitt Romney's pomp and circumstance. Posted 1.11.07 and retrieve d1.13.07 from http://www.examiner.com/a-522561~James_Kirchick__Mitt_Romney_s_pomp_and_circumstance.
[2393] Liz Soditi. John McCain a Target for All Sides. Examiner.com. AP. Poted Jan. 4, 2007 and retrieed 1.13.07 from http://www.examiner.com/a-489685~John_McCain_a_Target_for_All_Sides.html.
[2394] Liz Soditi. John McCain a Target for All Sides. Examiner.com. AP. Poted Jan. 4, 2007 and retrieed 1.13.07 from http://www.examiner.com/a-489685~John_McCain_a_Target_for_All_Sides.html.
[2395] Liz Soditi. John McCain a Target for All Sides. Examiner.com. AP. Poted Jan. 4, 2007 and retrieed 1.13.07 from http://www.examiner.com/a-489685~John_McCain_a_Target_for_All_Sides.html.
[2396] Liz Soditi. John McCain a Target for All Sides. Examiner.com. AP. Poted Jan. 4, 2007 and retrieed 1.13.07 from http://www.examiner.com/a-489685~John_McCain_a_Target_for_All_Sides.html.
[2397] ***Bankruptcy, ill will plague Bryant. Thomas C. Tobin. St. Petersburg Times. 4.28.2002.*** http://www.stpetersburgtimes.com/2002/04/28/State/Bankruptcy__ill_will_.shtml

[2398] Belated curtain call http://www.tulsaworld.com/news/article.aspx?articleID=070419_1_A2_hNote80156.
By KAREN SHADE World Scene Writer 4/19/2007.
[2399] ***Bankruptcy, ill will plague Bryant. Thomas C. Tobin. St. Petersburg Times. 4.28.2002.*** http://www.stpetersburgtimes.com/2002/04/28/State/Bankruptcy__ill_will_.shtml
[2400] ***Bankruptcy, ill will plague Bryant. Thomas C. Tobin. St. Petersburg Times. 4.28.2002.*** http://www.stpetersburgtimes.com/2002/04/28/State/Bankruptcy__ill_will_.shtml.
[2401] **Anita Bryant** retrieved from http://www.nndb.com/people/177/000024105/.
[2402] ***Bankruptcy, ill will plague Bryant. Thomas C. Tobin. St. Petersburg Times. 4.28.2002.*** http://www.stpetersburgtimes.com/2002/04/28/State/Bankruptcy__ill_will_.shtml
[2403] ***Bankruptcy, ill will plague Bryant. Thomas C. Tobin. St. Petersburg Times. 4.28.2002.*** http://www.stpetersburgtimes.com/2002/04/28/State/Bankruptcy__ill_will_.shtml.
[2404] ***Bankruptcy, ill will plague Bryant. Thomas C. Tobin. St. Petersburg Times. 4.28.2002.*** http://www.stpetersburgtimes.com/2002/04/28/State/Bankruptcy__ill_will_.shtml.
[2405] **Anita Bryant** retrieved from http://www.nndb.com/people/177/000024105/.
[2406] **Anita Bryant** retrieved from http://www.nndb.com/people/177/000024105/.
[2407] **Anita Bryant** retrieved from http://www.nndb.com/people/177/000024105/.
[2408] **Anita Bryant** retrieved from http://www.nndb.com/people/177/000024105/.
[2409] **Anita Bryant** retrieved from http://www.nndb.com/people/177/000024105/.
[2410] "Playboy Interview: Anita Bryant," *Playboy* (May 1978), pp. 73-96 in Williams and Retter, pp. 143-144. Originally retrieved in an article by Joseph Corsetti @ http://teachers.yale.edu/curriculum/search/viewer.php?id=initiative_09.02.07_u.
[2411] **Anita Bryant** retrieved from http://www.nndb.com/people/177/000024105/.
[2412] **Anita Bryant** retrieved from http://www.nndb.com/people/177/000024105/.
[2413] ***Bankruptcy, ill will plague Bryant. Thomas C. Tobin. St. Petersburg Times. 4.28.2002.*** http://www.stpetersburgtimes.com/2002/04/28/State/Bankruptcy__ill_will_.shtml.
[2414] **Anita Bryant** retrieved from http://www.nndb.com/people/177/000024105/.
[2415] **Anita Bryant** retrieved from http://www.nndb.com/people/177/000024105/.
[2416] ***Bankruptcy, ill will plague Bryant. Thomas C. Tobin. St. Petersburg Times. 4.28.2002.*** http://www.stpetersburgtimes.com/2002/04/28/State/Bankruptcy__ill_will_.shtml.
[2417] ***Bankruptcy, ill will plague Bryant. Thomas C. Tobin. St. Petersburg Times. 4.28.2002.*** http://www.stpetersburgtimes.com/2002/04/28/State/Bankruptcy__ill_will_.shtml.
[2418] ***Bankruptcy, ill will plague Bryant. Thomas C. Tobin. St. Petersburg Times. 4.28.2002.*** http://www.stpetersburgtimes.com/2002/04/28/State/Bankruptcy__ill_will_.shtml.

[2419] ***Bankruptcy, ill will plague Bryant. Thomas C. Tobin. St. Petersburg Times. 4.28.2002.*** http://www.stpetersburgtimes.com/2002/04/28/State/Bankruptcy__ill_will_.shtml.
[2420] ***Bankruptcy, ill will plague Bryant. Thomas C. Tobin. St. Petersburg Times. 4.28.2002.*** http://www.stpetersburgtimes.com/2002/04/28/State/Bankruptcy__ill_will_.shtml.
[2421] ***Bankruptcy, ill will plague Bryant. Thomas C. Tobin. St. Petersburg Times. 4.28.2002.*** http://www.stpetersburgtimes.com/2002/04/28/State/Bankruptcy__ill_will_.shtml.
[2422] ***Bankruptcy, ill will plague Bryant. Thomas C. Tobin. St. Petersburg Times. 4.28.2002.*** http://www.stpetersburgtimes.com/2002/04/28/State/Bankruptcy__ill_will_.shtml.
[2423] ***Bankruptcy, ill will plague Bryant. Thomas C. Tobin. St. Petersburg Times. 4.28.2002.*** http://www.stpetersburgtimes.com/2002/04/28/State/Bankruptcy__ill_will_.shtml.
[2424] Belated curtain call http://www.tulsaworld.com/news/article.aspx?articleID=070419_1_A2_hNote80156.
By KAREN SHADE World Scene Writer 4/19/2007
[2425] Belated curtain call http://www.tulsaworld.com/news/article.aspx?articleID=070419_1_A2_hNote80156.
By KAREN SHADE World Scene Writer 4/19/2007
[2426] ***Bankruptcy, ill will plague Bryant. Thomas C. Tobin. St. Petersburg Times. 4.28.2002.*** http://www.stpetersburgtimes.com/2002/04/28/State/Bankruptcy__ill_will_.shtml
[2427] ***Bankruptcy, ill will plague Bryant. Thomas C. Tobin. St. Petersburg Times. 4.28.2002.*** http://www.stpetersburgtimes.com/2002/04/28/State/Bankruptcy__ill_will_.shtml

[2428] Belated curtain call http://www.tulsaworld.com/news/article.aspx?articleID=070419_1_A2_hNote80156.
By KAREN SHADE World Scene Writer 4/19/2007
[2429] WorldNetDaily News Article :: Anita Bryant Was Right :: March 11, 2008 :: Janet Folger Posted: March 11, 2008 1:00 am Eastern © 2008 http://www.baptistpress.org/bpnews.asp?id=11448.
[2430] **Anita Bryant** retrieved from http://www.nndb.com/people/177/000024105/.
[2431] **Anita Bryant** retrieved from http://www.nndb.com/people/177/000024105/.
[2432] **Anita Bryant** retrieved from http://www.nndb.com/people/177/000024105/.
[2433] Tue, Nov 9, 2004. Limbaugh: Openly gay students are "trumpeting" their sexuality, "inviting dissent"http://mediamatters.org/items/200411090003.
[2434] Tue, Nov 9, 2004. Limbaugh: Openly gay students are "trumpeting" their sexuality, "inviting dissent"http://mediamatters.org/items/200411090003.
[2435] Tue, Nov 9, 2004. Limbaugh: Openly gay students are "trumpeting" their sexuality, "inviting dissent"http://mediamatters.org/items/200411090003.
[2436] Tue, Nov 9, 2004. Limbaugh: Openly gay students are "trumpeting" their sexuality, "inviting dissent"http://mediamatters.org/items/200411090003.
[2437] Tue, Nov 9, 2004. Limbaugh: Openly gay students are "trumpeting" their sexuality, "inviting dissent"http://mediamatters.org/items/200411090003.
[2438] Tue, Nov 9, 2004. Limbaugh: Openly gay students are "trumpeting" their sexuality, "inviting dissent"http://mediamatters.org/items/200411090003.
[2439] The "Truth" according to Limbaugh: Feminism established "to allow unattractive women easier access to the mainstream of society"—J.K August 2005.
http://mediamatters.org/items/200508160001
[2440] The "Truth" according to Limbaugh: Feminism established "to allow unattractive women easier access to the mainstream of society"—J.K August 2005.
http://mediamatters.org/items/200508160001
[2441] Limbaugh defended his use of term "feminazi" as "right" [2441] and "accurate" Fri, Jun 24, 2005. http://mediamatters.org/items/200506240002.
[2442] Limbaugh defended his use of term "feminazi" as "right" [2442] and "accurate" Fri, Jun 24, 2005. http://mediamatters.org/items/200506240002.
[2443] Limbaugh defended his use of term "feminazi" as "right" [2443] and "accurate" Fri, Jun 24, 2005. http://mediamatters.org/items/200506240002.
[2444] THE 2004 CAMPAIGN: EVANGELICAL CHRISTIANS; Warily, a Religious Leader Lifts His Voice in Politics May 13, 2004, By DAVID D. KIRKPATRICK
http://query.nytimes.com/gst/fullpage.html?res=9E02EED9113CF930A25756C0A9629C8B63&sec=&spon=&pagewanted=print
[2445] THE 2004 CAMPAIGN: EVANGELICAL CHRISTIANS; Warily, a Religious Leader Lifts His Voice in Politics May 13, 2004, By DAVID D. KIRKPATRICK
http://query.nytimes.com/gst/fullpage.html?res=9E02EED9113CF930A25756C0A9629C8B63&sec=&spon=&pagewanted=print
[2446] THE 2004 CAMPAIGN: EVANGELICAL CHRISTIANS; Warily, a Religious Leader Lifts His Voice in Politics May 13, 2004, By DAVID D. KIRKPATRICK
http://query.nytimes.com/gst/fullpage.html?res=9E02EED9113CF930A25756C0A9629C8B63&sec=&spon=&pagewanted=print
[2447] THE 2004 CAMPAIGN: EVANGELICAL CHRISTIANS; Warily, a Religious Leader Lifts His Voice in Politics May 13, 2004, By DAVID D. KIRKPATRICK
http://query.nytimes.com/gst/fullpage.html?res=9E02EED9113CF930A25756C0A9629C8B63&sec=&spon=&pagewanted=print
[2448] TIME Names the 25 Most Influential EVANGELICALS in America. Sunday, Jan. 30, 2005
http://www.time.com/time/printout/0,8816,1022576,00.html
[2449] THE 2004 CAMPAIGN: EVANGELICAL CHRISTIANS; Warily, a Religious Leader Lifts His Voice in Politics May 13, 2004, By DAVID D. KIRKPATRICK
http://query.nytimes.com/gst/fullpage.html?res=9E02EED9113CF930A25756C0A9629C8B63&sec=&spon=&pagewanted=print
[2450] TIME Names the 25 Most Influential EVANGELICALS in America. Sunday, Jan. 30, 2005 http://www.time.com/time/printout/0,8816,1022576,00.html
[2451] Reviews. **The Wizard of Colorado Springs**. *Reviewed by Randall Balmer*
Book Review: *The Jesus Machine: How James Dobson, Focus on the Family, and Evangelical America are Winning the Culture War* by Dan Gigoff.
http://www.sojo.net/index.cfm?action=magazine.article&issue=soj0708&article=070833a
[2452] Reviews. **The Wizard of Colorado Springs**. *Reviewed by Randall Balmer*
Book Review: *The Jesus Machine: How James Dobson, Focus on the Family, and Evangelical America are Winning the Culture War* by Dan Gigoff.
http://www.sojo.net/index.cfm?action=magazine.article&issue=soj0708&article=070833a
[2453] Reviews. **The Wizard of Colorado Springs**. *Reviewed by Randall Balmer*
Book Review: *The Jesus Machine: How James Dobson, Focus on the Family, and Evangelical America are Winning the Culture War* by Dan Gigoff.
http://www.sojo.net/index.cfm?action=magazine.article&issue=soj0708&article=070833a
[2454] Reviews. **The Wizard of Colorado Springs**. *Reviewed by Randall Balmer*
Book Review: *The Jesus Machine: How James Dobson, Focus on the Family, and Evangelical America are Winning the Culture War* by Dan Gigoff.
http://www.sojo.net/index.cfm?action=magazine.article&issue=soj0708&article=070833a
[2455] THE 2004 CAMPAIGN: EVANGELICAL CHRISTIANS; Warily, a Religious Leader Lifts His Voice in Politics May 13, 2004, By DAVID D. KIRKPATRICK
http://query.nytimes.com/gst/fullpage.html?res=9E02EED9113CF930A25756C0A9629C8B63&sec=&spon=&pagewanted=print
[2456] THE 2004 CAMPAIGN: EVANGELICAL CHRISTIANS; Warily, a Religious Leader Lifts His Voice in Politics May 13, 2004, By DAVID D. KIRKPATRICK
http://query.nytimes.com/gst/fullpage.html?res=9E02EED9113CF930A25756C0A9629C8B63&sec=&spon=&pagewanted=print
[2457] THE 2004 CAMPAIGN: EVANGELICAL CHRISTIANS; Warily, a Religious Leader Lifts His Voice in Politics May 13, 2004, By DAVID D. KIRKPATRICK
http://query.nytimes.com/gst/fullpage.html?res=9E02EED9113CF930A25756C0A9629C8B63&sec=&spon=&pagewanted=print
[2458] What Will a New Bush Term Mean for the American Family? Monday, November 15, 2004. Fox News. Hannity and Colmes.
[2459] What Will a New Bush Term Mean for the American Family? Monday, November 15, 2004. Fox News. Hannity and Colmes.
[2460] Reviews. **The Wizard of Colorado Springs**. *Reviewed by Randall Balmer*
Book Review: *The Jesus Machine: How James Dobson, Focus on the Family, and Evangelical America are Winning the Culture War* by Dan Gigoff.
http://www.sojo.net/index.cfm?action=magazine.article&issue=soj0708&article=070833a
[2461] Reviews. **The Wizard of Colorado Springs**. *Reviewed by Randall Balmer*
Book Review: *The Jesus Machine: How James Dobson, Focus on the Family, and Evangelical America are Winning the Culture War* by Dan Gigoff.
http://www.sojo.net/index.cfm?action=magazine.article&issue=soj0708&article=070833a
[2462] What Will a New Bush Term Mean for the American Family? Monday, November 15, 2004. Fox News. Hannity and Colmes.
[2463] **Dobson, James C.** Talking Points Memo. Josh Marshall Nov 9, 2004. ...exchange [Nov 7, 2004] between George Stephanopoulos and James Dobson on ABC's *This Week*:
http://www.mediatransparency.org/personprofile.php?personID=19
[2464] **Dobson, James C.** Talking Points Memo. Josh Marshall Nov 9, 2004. ...exchange [Nov 7, 2004] between George Stephanopoulos and James Dobson on ABC's *This Week*:
http://www.mediatransparency.org/personprofile.php?personID=19
[2465] **Dobson, James C.** Talking Points Memo. Josh Marshall Nov 9, 2004. ...exchange [Nov 7, 2004] between George Stephanopoulos and James Dobson on ABC's *This Week*:
http://www.mediatransparency.org/personprofile.php?personID=19
[2466] **Dobson, James C.** Talking Points Memo. Josh Marshall Nov 9, 2004. ...exchange [Nov 7, 2004] between George Stephanopoulos and James Dobson on ABC's *This Week*:
http://www.mediatransparency.org/personprofile.php?personID=19
[2467] **Dobson, James C.** Talking Points Memo. Josh Marshall Nov 9, 2004. ...exchange [Nov 7, 2004] between George Stephanopoulos and James Dobson on ABC's *This Week*:
http://www.mediatransparency.org/personprofile.php?personID=19
[2468] **Dobson, James C.** Talking Points Memo. Josh Marshall Nov 9, 2004. ...exchange [Nov 7, 2004] between George Stephanopoulos and James Dobson on ABC's *This Week*:
http://www.mediatransparency.org/personprofile.php?personID=19
[2469] THE 2004 CAMPAIGN: EVANGELICAL CHRISTIANS; Warily, a Religious Leader Lifts His Voice in Politics May 13, 2004, By DAVID D. KIRKPATRICK
http://query.nytimes.com/gst/fullpage.html?res=9E02EED9113CF930A25756C0A9629C8B63&sec=&spon=&pagewanted=print
[2470] Conservative leader targets Specter. Tuesday, November 9, 2004. http://www.cnn.com/2004/ALLPOLITICS/11/07/specter.judiciary/index.html
[2471] What Will a New Bush Term Mean for the American Family? Monday, November 15, 2004. Fox News. Hannity and Colmes.
[2472] What Will a New Bush Term Mean for the American Family? Monday, November 15, 2004. Fox News. Hannity and Colmes.
[2473] The Boy Scouts Controversy. **Mike Haley's Letter**. Mike Haley is on the staff of Focus on the Family; Haley gave permission to Bridges Across to use his letter along with a response.
http://www.bridges-across.org/ba/scouts.htm (Mike Haley is the Youth and Gender Specialist at Focus on the Family.
[2474] The Boy Scouts Controversy. **Mike Haley's Letter**. Mike Haley is on the staff of Focus on the Family; Haley gave permission to Bridges Across to use his letter along with a response.
http://www.bridges-across.org/ba/scouts.htm (Mike Haley is the Youth and Gender Specialist at Focus on the Family.
[2475] Homosexuality and Gender. Courtesy of Focus on the Family's Issue Analysis. Hope in a World of Gender Confusion. Devon Williams and Jeff Johnston*Williams is an Associate Editor with* CitizenLink*; Johnston is a Gender Issues Analyst with* Love Won Out. http://www.citizenlink.org/FOSI/homosexuality/hgeducation/A000008402.cfm
[2476] James Dobson Identifies Cause of Homosexuality. **Posted on Nov 25, 2006. Transcript from Crooks and Liars:**
http://www.truthdig.com/avbooth/item/20061125_james_dobson_identifies_homosexuality/
[2477] James Dobson Identifies Cause of Homosexuality. **Posted on Nov 25, 2006. Transcript from Crooks and Liars:**
http://www.truthdig.com/avbooth/item/20061125_james_dobson_identifies_homosexuality/

[2478] James Dobson Identifies Cause of Homosexuality. **Posted on Nov 25, 2006. Transcript from Crooks and Liars:** http://www.truthdig.com/avbooth/item/20061125_james_dobson_identifies_homosexuality/
[2479] Homosexuality and Gender. Courtesy of Focus on the Family's Issue Analysis. Hope in a World of Gender Confusion. Devon Williams and Jeff Johnston*Williams is an Associate Editor with* CitizenLink*; Johnston is a Gender Issues Analyst with* Love Won Out. http://www.citizenlink.org/FOSI/homosexuality/hgeducation/A000008402.cfm
[2480] Homosexuality and Gender. Courtesy of Focus on the Family's Issue Analysis. Hope in a World of Gender Confusion. Devon Williams and Jeff Johnston*Williams is an Associate Editor with* CitizenLink*; Johnston is a Gender Issues Analyst with* Love Won Out. http://www.citizenlink.org/FOSI/homosexuality/hgeducation/A000008402.cfm
[2481] Eleven Arguments Against Same-Sex Marriage.Dr. James C. Dobson. *Dr James Dobson present eleven key arguments against same-sex marriage.*
[2482] Eleven Arguments Against Same-Sex Marriage.Dr. James C. Dobson. *Dr James Dobson present eleven key arguments against same-sex marriage.*
[2483] Eleven Arguments Against Same-Sex Marriage.Dr. James C. Dobson. *Dr James Dobson present eleven key arguments against same-sex marriage.*
[2484] Eleven Arguments Against Same-Sex Marriage.Dr. James C. Dobson. *Dr James Dobson present eleven key arguments against same-sex marriage.*
[2485] Eleven Arguments Against Same-Sex Marriage.Dr. James C. Dobson. *Dr James Dobson present eleven key arguments against same-sex marriage.*
[2486] Eleven Arguments Against Same-Sex Marriage.Dr. James C. Dobson. *Dr James Dobson present eleven key arguments against same-sex marriage*
[2487] Eleven Arguments Against Same-Sex Marriage.Dr. James C. Dobson. *Dr James Dobson present eleven key arguments against same-sex marriage*
[2488] James Dobson Identifies Cause of Homosexuality. **Posted on Nov 25, 2006. Transcript from Crooks and Liars:** http://www.truthdig.com/avbooth/item/20061125_james_dobson_identifies_homosexuality/
[2489] James Dobson Identifies Cause of Homosexuality. **Posted on Nov 25, 2006. Transcript from Crooks and Liars:** http://www.truthdig.com/avbooth/item/20061125_james_dobson_identifies_homosexuality/
[2490] Justice Sunday Preachers. By *Max Blumenthal.* April 26, 2005. The Nation. http://www.thenation.com/doc/20050509/blumenthal
[2491] Biography. **Tony Perkins. President. Retrieved December 20, 2008 @** http://www.frc.org/get.cfm?i=by03h27.
[2492] Biography. **Tony Perkins. President. Retrieved December 20, 2008 @** http://www.frc.org/get.cfm?i=by03h27.
[2493] Biography. **Tony Perkins. President. Retrieved December 20, 2008 @** http://www.frc.org/get.cfm?i=by03h27.
[2494] Biography. **Tony Perkins. President. Retrieved December 20, 2008 @** http://www.frc.org/get.cfm?i=by03h27.
[2495] Biography. **Tony Perkins. President. Retrieved December 20, 2008 @** http://www.frc.org/get.cfm?i=by03h27.
[2496] Biography. **Tony Perkins. President. Retrieved December 20, 2008 @** http://www.frc.org/get.cfm?i=by03h27.
[2497] Reviews. **The Wizard of Colorado Springs.** *Reviewed by Randall Balmer*
Book Review: *The Jesus Machine: How James Dobson, Focus on the Family, and Evangelical America are Winning the Culture War* by Dan Gigoff. http://www.sojo.net/index.cfm?action=magazine.article&issue=soj0708&article=070833a
[2498] Biography. **Tony Perkins. President. Retrieved December 20, 2008 @** http://www.frc.org/get.cfm?i=by03h27.
[2499] Family Research Council. See http://www.frc.org/about-frc
[2500] About FRC. Retrieved December 20, 2008 @ http://www.frc.org/about-frc.
[2501] Bill Berkowitz, The Family Research Council's Tony Perkins is a rising star in a crowded universe of evangelical Christian leaders. http://www.mediatransparency.org/storyprinterfriendly.php?storyID=70. June 17, 2005.
[2502] Bill Berkowitz, The Family Research Council's Tony Perkins is a rising star in a crowded universe of evangelical Christian leaders. http://www.mediatransparency.org/storyprinterfriendly.php?storyID=70. June 17, 2005.
[2503] Bill Berkowitz, The Family Research Council's Tony Perkins is a rising star in a crowded universe of evangelical Christian leaders. http://www.mediatransparency.org/storyprinterfriendly.php?storyID=70. June 17, 2005.
[2504] Bill Berkowitz, The Family Research Council's Tony Perkins is a rising star in a crowded universe of evangelical Christian leaders. http://www.mediatransparency.org/storyprinterfriendly.php?storyID=70. June 17, 2005.
[2505] Bill Berkowitz, The Family Research Council's Tony Perkins is a rising star in a crowded universe of evangelical Christian leaders. http://www.mediatransparency.org/storyprinterfriendly.php?storyID=70. June 17, 2005.
[2506] Bill Berkowitz, The Family Research Council's Tony Perkins is a rising star in a crowded universe of evangelical Christian leaders. http://www.mediatransparency.org/storyprinterfriendly.php?storyID=70. June 17, 2005.
[2507] Bill Berkowitz, The Family Research Council's Tony Perkins is a rising star in a crowded universe of evangelical Christian leaders. http://www.mediatransparency.org/storyprinterfriendly.php?storyID=70. June 17, 2005.
[2508] Justice Sunday Preachers. By *Max Blumenthal.* April 26, 2005. The Nation. http://www.thenation.com/doc/20050509/blumenthal/2
[2509] Justice Sunday Preachers. By *Max Blumenthal.* April 26, 2005. The Nation. http://www.thenation.com/doc/20050509/blumenthal/2
[2510] Justice Sunday Preachers. By *Max Blumenthal.* April 26, 2005. The Nation. http://www.thenation.com/doc/20050509/blumenthal/2
[2511] Justice Sunday Preachers. By *Max Blumenthal.* April 26, 2005. The Nation. http://www.thenation.com/doc/20050509/blumenthal/2
[2512] Justice Sunday Preachers. By *Max Blumenthal.* April 26, 2005. The Nation. http://www.thenation.com/doc/20050509/blumenthal/2
[2513] Justice Sunday Preachers. By *Max Blumenthal.* April 26, 2005. The Nation. http://www.thenation.com/doc/20050509/blumenthal
[2514] Justice Sunday Preachers. By *Max Blumenthal.* April 26, 2005. The Nation. http://www.thenation.com/doc/20050509/blumenthal
[2515] Justice Sunday Preachers. By *Max Blumenthal.* April 26, 2005. The Nation. http://www.thenation.com/doc/20050509/blumenthal/2
[2516] Special Publication. **A Response to False Claims made by *The Nation*.** June 15, 2005. http://www.frc.org/get.cfm?i=LH05F09
[2517] Justice Sunday Preachers. By *Max Blumenthal.* April 26, 2005. The Nation. http://www.thenation.com/doc/20050509/blumenthal
[2518] Justice Sunday Preachers. By *Max Blumenthal.* April 26, 2005. The Nation. http://www.thenation.com/doc/20050509/blumenthal
[2519] FRC attacks "bigoted bloggers"; media have ignored the FRC's own history of bigotry. http://mediamatters.org/items/200702100003.
[2520] FRC attacks "bigoted bloggers"; media have ignored the FRC's own history of bigotry. http://mediamatters.org/items/200702100003.
[2521] FRC attacks "bigoted bloggers"; media have ignored the FRC's own history of bigotry. http://mediamatters.org/items/200702100003.
[2522] FRC attacks "bigoted bloggers"; media have ignored the FRC's own history of bigotry. http://mediamatters.org/items/200702100003.
[2523] FRC attacks "bigoted bloggers"; media have ignored the FRC's own history of bigotry. http://mediamatters.org/items/200702100003.
[2524] FRC attacks "bigoted bloggers"; media have ignored the FRC's own history of bigotry. http://mediamatters.org/items/200702100003.
[2525] FRC attacks "bigoted bloggers"; media have ignored the FRC's own history of bigotry. http://mediamatters.org/items/200702100003
[2526] Justice Sunday Preachers. By *Max Blumenthal.* April 26, 2005. The Nation. http://www.thenation.com/doc/20050509/blumenthal/2
[2527] Justice Sunday Preachers. By *Max Blumenthal.* April 26, 2005. The Nation. http://www.thenation.com/doc/20050509/blumenthal/2
[2528] Justice Sunday Preachers. By *Max Blumenthal.* April 26, 2005. The Nation. http://www.thenation.com/doc/20050509/blumenthal/2
[2529] Justice Sunday Preachers. By *Max Blumenthal.* April 26, 2005. The Nation. http://www.thenation.com/doc/20050509/blumenthal/2
[2530] Justice Sunday Preachers. By *Max Blumenthal.* April 26, 2005. The Nation. http://www.thenation.com/doc/20050509/blumenthal/2
[2531] Justice Sunday Preachers. By *Max Blumenthal.* April 26, 2005. The Nation. http://www.thenation.com/doc/20050509/blumenthal/2
[2532] Justice Sunday Preachers. By *Max Blumenthal.* April 26, 2005. The Nation. http://www.thenation.com/doc/20050509/blumenthal/2
[2533] Justice Sunday Preachers. By *Max Blumenthal.* April 26, 2005. The Nation. http://www.thenation.com/doc/20050509/blumenthal
[2534] Justice Sunday Preachers. By *Max Blumenthal.* April 26, 2005. The Nation. http://www.thenation.com/doc/20050509/blumenthal
[2535] Justice Sunday Preachers. By *Max Blumenthal.* April 26, 2005. The Nation. http://www.thenation.com/doc/20050509/blumenthal
[2536] FRC attacks "bigoted bloggers"; media have ignored the FRC's own history of bigotry. http://mediamatters.org/items/200702100003.
[2537] Justice Sunday Preachers. By *Max Blumenthal.* April 26, 2005. The Nation. http://www.thenation.com/doc/20050509/blumenthal
[2538] Justice Sunday Preachers. By *Max Blumenthal.* April 26, 2005. The Nation. http://www.thenation.com/doc/20050509/blumenthal
[2539]Justice Sunday Preachers. By *Max Blumenthal.* April 26, 2005. The Nation. http://www.thenation.com/doc/20050509/blumenthal
[2540] Justice Sunday Preachers. By *Max Blumenthal.* April 26, 2005. The Nation. http://www.thenation.com/doc/20050509/blumenthal/2
[2541] Justice Sunday Preachers. By *Max Blumenthal.* April 26, 2005. The Nation. http://www.thenation.com/doc/20050509/blumenthal/2
[2542] Justice Sunday Preachers. By *Max Blumenthal.* April 26, 2005. The Nation. http://www.thenation.com/doc/20050509/blumenthal
[2543] Justice Sunday Preachers. By *Max Blumenthal.* April 26, 2005. The Nation. http://www.thenation.com/doc/20050509/blumenthal
[2544] Justice Sunday Preachers. By *Max Blumenthal.* April 26, 2005. The Nation. http://www.thenation.com/doc/20050509/blumenthal
[2545] Justice Sunday Preachers. By *Max Blumenthal.* April 26, 2005. The Nation. http://www.thenation.com/doc/20050509/blumenthal
[2546] Justice Sunday Preachers. By *Max Blumenthal.* April 26, 2005. The Nation. http://www.thenation.com/doc/20050509/blumenthal
[2547] Justice Sunday Preachers. By *Max Blumenthal.* April 26, 2005. The Nation. http://www.thenation.com/doc/20050509/blumenthal
[2548] Justice Sunday Preachers. By *Max Blumenthal.* April 26, 2005. The Nation. http://www.thenation.com/doc/20050509/blumenthal
[2549] FRC attacks "bigoted bloggers"; media have ignored the FRC's own history of bigotry. http://mediamatters.org/items/200702100003.
[2550] Bill Berkowitz, The Family Research Council's Tony Perkins is a rising star in a crowded universe of evangelical Christian leaders. http://www.mediatransparency.org/storyprinterfriendly.php?storyID=70. June 17, 2005.
[2551] Bill Berkowitz, The Family Research Council's Tony Perkins is a rising star in a crowded universe of evangelical Christian leaders. http://www.mediatransparency.org/storyprinterfriendly.php?storyID=70. June 17, 2005.
[2552] Bill Berkowitz, The Family Research Council's Tony Perkins is a rising star in a crowded universe of evangelical Christian leaders. http://www.mediatransparency.org/storyprinterfriendly.php?storyID=70. June 17, 2005.
[2553] Bill Berkowitz, The Family Research Council's Tony Perkins is a rising star in a crowded universe of evangelical Christian leaders. http://www.mediatransparency.org/storyprinterfriendly.php?storyID=70. June 17, 2005.
[2554] Bill Berkowitz, The Family Research Council's Tony Perkins is a rising star in a crowded universe of evangelical Christian leaders. http://www.mediatransparency.org/storyprinterfriendly.php?storyID=70. June 17, 2005.
[2555] Tony Perkins: "liberals," like (military volunteer) Kerry, "don't have an understanding" of why Americans "would volunteer." http://mediamatters.org/items/200611030008.

[2556]Human Sexuality. Including Abstinence & Health, and homosexuality. Retrieved December 20, 2008 http://www.frc.org/human-sexuality#homosexuality.
[2557] FRC attacks "bigoted bloggers"; media have ignored the FRC's own history of bigotry. http://mediamatters.org/items/200702100003.
[2558] Matthews, Perkins forgot Bush's 17 proclamations of national days of prayer Fri, Mar 31, 2006 2:14pm EThttp://mediamatters.org/items/200603310006
[2559] Matthews, Perkins forgot Bush's 17 proclamations of national days of prayer Fri, Mar 31, 2006 2:14pm EThttp://mediamatters.org/items/200603310006
[2560] Tue, Mar 14, 2006 12:42pm ET, Family Research Council's Perkins: Feingold's call for censure is "borderline treasonous behavior"http://mediamatters.org/items/200603140006
[2561] Human Sexuality. Including Abstinence & Health, and homosexuality. Retrieved December 20, 2008 http://www.frc.org/human-sexuality#homosexuality.
[2562] Human Sexuality. Including Abstinence & Health, and homosexuality. Retrieved December 20, 2008 http://www.frc.org/human-sexuality#homosexuality.
[2563] Human Sexuality. Including Abstinence & Health, and homosexuality. Retrieved December 20, 2008 http://www.frc.org/human-sexuality#homosexuality.
[2564] AC360: Dan Savage Takes On Tony Perkins Over Prop 8. By Heather Thursday Nov 13, 2008 2:00pm http://videocafe.crooksandliars.com/heather/ac360-dan-savage-takes-tony-perkins-over-p
[2565] Tony Perkins Claims Gay Marriage Ban Is 'Totally Different' Than Interracial Marriage Ban. http://thinkprogress.org/2008/11/13/savage-perkins-prop8/
[2566] Tony Perkins Claims Gay Marriage Ban Is 'Totally Different' Than Interracial Marriage Ban. http://thinkprogress.org/2008/11/13/savage-perkins-prop8/
[2567] Tony Perkins Claims Gay Marriage Ban Is 'Totally Different' Than Interracial Marriage Ban. http://thinkprogress.org/2008/11/13/savage-perkins-prop8/
[2568] Tony Perkins Claims Gay Marriage Ban Is 'Totally Different' Than Interracial Marriage Ban. http://thinkprogress.org/2008/11/13/savage-perkins-prop8/
[2569] AC360: Dan Savage Takes On Tony Perkins Over Prop 8. By Heather Thursday Nov 13, 2008 2:00pm http://videocafe.crooksandliars.com/heather/ac360-dan-savage-takes-tony-perkins-over-p
[2570] AC360: Dan Savage Takes On Tony Perkins Over Prop 8. By Heather Thursday Nov 13, 2008 2:00pm http://videocafe.crooksandliars.com/heather/ac360-dan-savage-takes-tony-perkins-over-p
[2571] ANDERSON COOPER 360. Extreme Challenges for Obama; Sarah Palin Fires Back; The Fight for Same-Sex Marriage. Aired November 7, 2008.
http://transcripts.cnn.com/TRANSCRIPTS/0811/07/acd.02.html
[2572] ANDERSON COOPER 360. Extreme Challenges for Obama; Sarah Palin Fires Back; The Fight for Same-Sex Marriage. Aired November 7, 2008.
http://transcripts.cnn.com/TRANSCRIPTS/0811/07/acd.02.html
[2573] ANDERSON COOPER 360. Extreme Challenges for Obama; Sarah Palin Fires Back; The Fight for Same-Sex Marriage. Aired November 7, 2008.
http://transcripts.cnn.com/TRANSCRIPTS/0811/07/acd.02.html
[2574] ANDERSON COOPER 360. Extreme Challenges for Obama; Sarah Palin Fires Back; The Fight for Same-Sex Marriage. Aired November 7, 2008.
http://transcripts.cnn.com/TRANSCRIPTS/0811/07/acd.02.html
[2575] **Conservative parent adjust to gay kids [illegible]** NATIONAL | washingtonblade.com, By JOE CREA. Oct. 15, 2004http://www.washblade.com/print.cfm?content_id=4038.
[2576] Family Research Council. See http://www.frc.org/about-frc
[2577] Family Research Council. See http://www.frc.org/about-frc
[2578] Family Research Council. See http://www.frc.org/about-frc
[2579] Wisconsin Family Council Pushes Punishment Under 1915 Law. By Chris | July 11, 2008 http://www.rightwingwatch.org/2008/07/wisconsin_famil.html
[2580] See About WFC http://www.wifamilycouncil.org/about.html (November 2008).
[2581] Professor challenges amendment banning gay marriage, **Lawsuit contends it wasn't properly presented to voters**. By Stacy Forster of the Journal Sentinel. Dec. 30, 2007http://www.jsonline.com/news/wisconsin/29386344.html
[2582] See About WFC http://www.wifamilycouncil.org/about.html (November 2008).
[2583] **Just Say No Katie McKy - Raw Story Columnist** Published: Monday September 4, 2006 http://www.rawstory.com/news/2006/Just_Say_No_0904.html
[2584] **Just Say No Katie McKy - Raw Story Columnist** Published: Monday September 4, 2006 http://www.rawstory.com/news/2006/Just_Say_No_0904.html
[2585] State Politics. Marriage measure backer savors win. By Bill Glauber and Bill Glauber of the Journal Sentinel
Posted: Nov. 9, 2006 http://www.jsonline.com/news/statepolitics/29180609.html

[2586] GAY WED FOE: CHURCH-STATE WALL IS FICTION AMENDMENT BACKER, OPPONENT SPAR.(METRO) The Capital Times (Madison, WI) October 13, 2006 . by Davidoff, Judith http://www.highbeam.com/doc/1G1-152930596.html
[2587] AS THE FAMILY, SO THE STATE. Speech given Friday, April 4, 2008
as part of THE FUTURE WISCONSIN CONFERENCE 2008. Julaine K. Appling, CEO WISCONSIN FAMILY COUNCIL. http://wifamilycouncil.org/materials/As_the_Family_040408_web.pdf
[2588] TESTIMONY OF JULAINE K. APPLING. EXECUTIVE DIRECTOR, THE FAMILY RESEARCH INSTITUTE OF WISCONSIN. SENATE JOINT RESOLUTION 63 - "DEFENSE OF MARRIAGE CONSTITUTIONAL AMENDMENT." PUBLIC HEARING OF THE SENATE COMMITTEE ON JUDICIARY, CORRECTIONS AND PRIVACY. MONDAY, MARCH 1, 2004 http://www.wifamilycouncil.org/testimony/Testimony_Appling_030104.pdf
[2589] TESTIMONY OF JULAINE K. APPLING. EXECUTIVE DIRECTOR, THE FAMILY RESEARCH INSTITUTE OF WISCONSIN. SENATE JOINT RESOLUTION 63 - "DEFENSE OF MARRIAGE CONSTITUTIONAL AMENDMENT." PUBLIC HEARING OF THE SENATE COMMITTEE ON JUDICIARY, CORRECTIONS AND PRIVACY. MONDAY, MARCH 1, 2004 http://www.wifamilycouncil.org/testimony/Testimony_Appling_030104.pdf
[2590] TESTIMONY OF JULAINE K. APPLING. EXECUTIVE DIRECTOR, THE FAMILY RESEARCH INSTITUTE OF WISCONSIN. SENATE JOINT RESOLUTION 63 - "DEFENSE OF MARRIAGE CONSTITUTIONAL AMENDMENT." PUBLIC HEARING OF THE SENATE COMMITTEE ON JUDICIARY, CORRECTIONS AND PRIVACY. MONDAY, MARCH 1, 2004 http://www.wifamilycouncil.org/testimony/Testimony_Appling_030104.pdf
[2591] TESTIMONY OF JULAINE K. APPLING. EXECUTIVE DIRECTOR, THE FAMILY RESEARCH INSTITUTE OF WISCONSIN. SENATE JOINT RESOLUTION 63 - "DEFENSE OF MARRIAGE CONSTITUTIONAL AMENDMENT." PUBLIC HEARING OF THE SENATE COMMITTEE ON JUDICIARY, CORRECTIONS AND PRIVACY. MONDAY, MARCH 1, 2004 http://www.wifamilycouncil.org/testimony/Testimony_Appling_030104.pdf
[2592] TESTIMONY OF JULAINE K. APPLING. EXECUTIVE DIRECTOR, THE FAMILY RESEARCH INSTITUTE OF WISCONSIN. SENATE JOINT RESOLUTION 63 - "DEFENSE OF MARRIAGE CONSTITUTIONAL AMENDMENT." PUBLIC HEARING OF THE SENATE COMMITTEE ON JUDICIARY, CORRECTIONS AND PRIVACY. MONDAY, MARCH 1, 2004 http://www.wifamilycouncil.org/testimony/Testimony_Appling_030104.pdf
[2593] TESTIMONY OF JULAINE K. APPLING. EXECUTIVE DIRECTOR, THE FAMILY RESEARCH INSTITUTE OF WISCONSIN. SENATE JOINT RESOLUTION 63 - "DEFENSE OF MARRIAGE CONSTITUTIONAL AMENDMENT." PUBLIC HEARING OF THE SENATE COMMITTEE ON JUDICIARY, CORRECTIONS AND PRIVACY. MONDAY, MARCH 1, 2004 http://www.wifamilycouncil.org/testimony/Testimony_Appling_030104.pdf
[2594] TESTIMONY OF JULAINE K. APPLING. EXECUTIVE DIRECTOR, THE FAMILY RESEARCH INSTITUTE OF WISCONSIN. SENATE JOINT RESOLUTION 63 - "DEFENSE OF MARRIAGE CONSTITUTIONAL AMENDMENT." PUBLIC HEARING OF THE SENATE COMMITTEE ON JUDICIARY, CORRECTIONS AND PRIVACY. MONDAY, MARCH 1, 2004 http://www.wifamilycouncil.org/testimony/Testimony_Appling_030104.pdf
[2595] TESTIMONY OF JULAINE K. APPLING. EXECUTIVE DIRECTOR, THE FAMILY RESEARCH INSTITUTE OF WISCONSIN. SENATE JOINT RESOLUTION 63 - "DEFENSE OF MARRIAGE CONSTITUTIONAL AMENDMENT." PUBLIC HEARING OF THE SENATE COMMITTEE ON JUDICIARY, CORRECTIONS AND PRIVACY. MONDAY, MARCH 1, 2004 http://www.wifamilycouncil.org/testimony/Testimony_Appling_030104.pdf
[2596] Thursday, September 14, 2006, Julaine Appling Knows Best http://noontheamendment.blogspot.com/2006/09/julaine-appling-knows-best.html
[2597] Wisconsin bill to legalize gay-marriage proposal. by **Abby Peterson.** Thursday, February 12, 2004http://badgerherald.com/news/2004/02/12/wisconsin_bill_to_le.php
[2598] State Politics. Marriage measure backer savors win. By Bill Glauber and Bill Glauber of the Journal Sentinel Posted: Nov. 9, 2006http://www.jsonline.com/news/statepolitics/29180609.html
[2599] State Politics. Marriage measure backer savors win. By Bill Glauber and Bill Glauber of the Journal Sentinel Posted: Nov. 9, 2006http://www.jsonline.com/news/statepolitics/29180609.html
[2600] State Politics. Marriage measure backer savors win. By Bill Glauber and Bill Glauber of the Journal Sentinel Posted: Nov. 9, 2006http://www.jsonline.com/news/statepolitics/29180609.html
[2601] State Politics. Marriage measure backer savors win. By Bill Glauber and Bill Glauber of the Journal Sentinel Posted: Nov. 9, 2006http://www.jsonline.com/news/statepolitics/29180609.html
[2602] ***Wisconsin Family Connection. Week of April 14, 2008 - # 725/ "Counting the Cost of Family Fragmentation"*** http://www.house.leg.state.mn.us/fiscal/files/ibgf1006.pdf, accessed 04/14/08. http://wifamilycouncil.org/Media/Radio%20transcripts/2008/725.htm
[2603] ***Wisconsin Family Connection. Week of April 14, 2008 - # 725/ "Counting the Cost of Family Fragmentation"*** http://www.house.leg.state.mn.us/fiscal/files/ibgf1006.pdf, accessed 04/14/08. http://wifamilycouncil.org/Media/Radio%20transcripts/2008/725.htm
[2604] AS THE FAMILY, SO THE STATE. Speech given Friday, April 4, 2008
as part of THE FUTURE WISCONSIN CONFERENCE 2008. Julaine K. Appling, CEO WISCONSIN FAMILY COUNCIL. http://wifamilycouncil.org/materials/As_the_Family_040408_web.pdf
[2605] Michael Savage. Retrieved October 25, 2008 from http://www.nndb.com/people/588/000044456/.
[2606] Michael Savage. Retrieved October 25, 2008 from http://www.nndb.com/people/588/000044456/.
[2607] Michael Savage. Retrieved October 25, 2008 from http://www.nndb.com/people/588/000044456/.
[2608] Michael Savage. Retrieved October 25, 2008 from http://www.nndb.com/people/588/000044456/.
[2609] Know Your Right-Wing Speakers: Michael Savage, By Andrew Bean, Wesleyan University. Wednesday June 28, 2006http://www.campusprogress.org/tools/974/know-your-right-wing-speakers-michael-savage
[2610] Michael Savage. Retrieved October 25, 2008 from http://www.nndb.com/people/588/000044456/.
[2611] Michael Savage. Retrieved October 25, 2008 from http://www.nndb.com/people/588/000044456/.
[2612] Savage again called gay parenting "child abuse" Mon, Jun 11, 2007 11:48am ET *Michael Maio is an intern at Media Matters for America.* http://mediamatters.org/items/200706110001.
[2613] Savage: "[P]eople wonder why" JFK Jr. "died in a plane crash and then suddenly, enter from ... stage left, the carpetbagger Hillary Clinton" **Wednesday, December 17, 2008 at 01:06 PM ET** http://mediamatters.org/items/printable/200812170008
[2614] Know Your Right-Wing Speakers: Michael Savage, By Andrew Bean, Wesleyan University. Wednesday June 28, 2006http://www.campusprogress.org/tools/974/know-your-right-wing-speakers-michael-savage
[2615] Know Your Right-Wing Speakers: Michael Savage, By Andrew Bean, Wesleyan University. Wednesday June 28, 2006http://www.campusprogress.org/tools/974/know-your-right-wing-speakers-michael-savage
[2616] Know Your Right-Wing Speakers: Michael Savage, By Andrew Bean, Wesleyan University. Wednesday June 28, 2006http://www.campusprogress.org/tools/974/know-your-right-wing-speakers-michael-savage
[2617] **[illegible]** NEW YORK (AP) Posted 7/8.2003, http://www.usatoday.com/news/nation/2003-07-07-talk-host-fired_x.htm.
[2618] **[illegible]** NEW YORK (AP) Posted 7/8.2003, http://www.usatoday.com/news/nation/2003-07-07-talk-host-fired_x.htm.
[2619] MSNBC Fires Michael Savage for Anti-Gay Comments. By Jeralyn, Section Media Posted on Mon Jul 07, 2003 at 05:02:49 PM ESThttp://www.talkleft.com/story/2003/07/07/139/14303.

[2620] MSNBC Fires Michael Savage for Anti-Gay Comments. By Jeralyn, Section Media Posted on Mon Jul 07, 2003 at 05:02:49 PM ESThttp://www.talkleft.com/story/2003/07/07/139/14303.
[2621] Savage again called gay parenting "child abuse" Mon, Jun 11, 2007 11:48am ET *Michael Maio is an intern at Media Matters for America.* http://mediamatters.org/items/200706110001.
[2622] Savage again called gay parenting "child abuse" Mon, Jun 11, 2007 11:48am ET *Michael Maio is an intern at Media Matters for America.* http://mediamatters.org/items/200706110001.
[2623] Savage again called gay parenting "child abuse" Mon, Jun 11, 2007 11:48am ET *Michael Maio is an intern at Media Matters for America.* http://mediamatters.org/items/200706110001.
[2624] Savage again called gay parenting "child abuse" Mon, Jun 11, 2007 11:48am ET *Michael Maio is an intern at Media Matters for America.* http://mediamatters.org/items/200706110001.
[2625] Know Your Right-Wing Speakers: Michael Savage, By Andrew Bean, Wesleyan University. Wednesday June 28, 2006http://www.campusprogress.org/tools/974/know-your-right-wing-speakers-michael-savage
[2626] Michael Savage. Retrieved October 25, 2008 from http://www.nndb.com/people/588/000044456/.
[2627] Know Your Right-Wing Speakers: Michael Savage, By Andrew Bean, Wesleyan University. Wednesday June 28, 2006http://www.campusprogress.org/tools/974/know-your-right-wing-speakers-michael-savage
[2628] Savage: "When you hear 'human rights,' think gays. ... [T]hink only one thing: someone who wants to rape your son"http://mediamatters.org/items/200408050004
[2629] Know Your Right-Wing Speakers: Michael Savage, By Andrew Bean, Wesleyan University. Wednesday June 28, 2006http://www.campusprogress.org/tools/974/know-your-right-wing-speakers-michael-savage
[2630] At 80, Schlafly is still a conservative force. By Yvonne Abraham, Globe Staff. September 2, 2004
http://www.boston.com/news/nation/articles/2004/09/02/at_80_schlafly_is_still_a_conservative_force?mode=PF.
[2631] Conservative leader Schlafly says `outing' of son was `strike at me'. By Mary Voboril. Knight-Ridder Newspapers http://www.qrd.org/qrd/misc/text/schlafly.outing.reaction-KNIGHT.RIDDER
[2632] At 80, Schlafly is still a conservative force. By Yvonne Abraham, Globe Staff. September 2,
2004http://www.boston.com/news/nation/articles/2004/09/02/at_80_schlafly_is_still_a_conservative_force?mode=PF.
[2633] According to an article in *The Sun Journal.* From Scott Jaschik. May 2008; http://www.insidehighered.com/news/2008/05/05/schlafly.
[2634] According to an article in *The Sun Journal.* From Scott Jaschik. May 2008; http://www.insidehighered.com/news/2008/05/05/schlafly.
[2635] **Gay Agenda Targets Free Speech**. by **Phyllis Schlafly**. Posted http://www.humanevents.com/article.php?print=yes&id=17883
[2636] **Gay Agenda Targets Free Speech**. by **Phyllis Schlafly**. Posted http://www.humanevents.com/article.php?print=yes&id=17883
[2637] **Battle over Pro-Gay Curriculum Heats Up. June 8, 2005. By Phyllis Schlafly.**
http://www.eagleforum.org/column/2005/june05/05-06-08.html
[2638] At 80, Schlafly is still a conservative force. By Yvonne Abraham, Globe Staff. September 2,
2004http://www.boston.com/news/nation/articles/2004/09/02/at_80_schlafly_is_still_a_conservative_force?mode=PF.
[2639] At 80, Schlafly is still a conservative force. By Yvonne Abraham, Globe Staff. September 2,
2004http://www.boston.com/news/nation/articles/2004/09/02/at_80_schlafly_is_still_a_conservative_force?mode=PF.
[2640] At 80, Schlafly is still a conservative force. By Yvonne Abraham, Globe Staff. September 2,
2004http://www.boston.com/news/nation/articles/2004/09/02/at_80_schlafly_is_still_a_conservative_force?mode=PF.
[2641] At 80, Schlafly is still a conservative force. By Yvonne Abraham, Globe Staff. September 2,
2004http://www.boston.com/news/nation/articles/2004/09/02/at_80_schlafly_is_still_a_conservative_force?mode=PF.
[2642] At 80, Schlafly is still a conservative force. By Yvonne Abraham, Globe Staff. September 2,
2004http://www.boston.com/news/nation/articles/2004/09/02/at_80_schlafly_is_still_a_conservative_force?mode=PF.
[2643] At 80, Schlafly is still a conservative force. By Yvonne Abraham, Globe Staff. September 2,
2004http://www.boston.com/news/nation/articles/2004/09/02/at_80_schlafly_is_still_a_conservative_force?mode=PF.
[2644] Conservative leader Schlafly says `outing' of son was `strike at me'. By Mary Voboril. Knight-Ridder Newspapers http://www.qrd.org/qrd/misc/text/schlafly.outing.reaction-KNIGHT.RIDDER
[2645] Conservative leader Schlafly says `outing' of son was `strike at me'. By Mary Voboril. Knight-Ridder Newspapers http://www.qrd.org/qrd/misc/text/schlafly.outing.reaction-KNIGHT.RIDDER
[2646] Schlafly's Son, Out of the Closet; Homosexual Backs Mother's Views, Attacks `Screechy Gay Activists'**The Washington Post. September 19, 1992 . Laura Blumenfeld.**
http://www.highbeam.com/doc/1P2-1025819.html.
[2647] Schlafly's Son, Out of the Closet; Homosexual Backs Mother's Views, Attacks `Screechy Gay Activists'**The Washington Post. September 19, 1992 . Laura Blumenfeld.**
http://www.highbeam.com/doc/1P2-1025819.html.
[2648] At 80, Schlafly is still a conservative force. By Yvonne Abraham, Globe Staff. September 2,
2004http://www.boston.com/news/nation/articles/2004/09/02/at_80_schlafly_is_still_a_conservative_force?mode=PF.
[2649] Conservative leader Schlafly says `outing' of son was `strike at me'. By Mary Voboril. Knight-Ridder Newspapers http://www.qrd.org/qrd/misc/text/schlafly.outing.reaction-KNIGHT.RIDDER
[2650] Conservative leader Schlafly says `outing' of son was `strike at me'. By Mary Voboril. Knight-Ridder Newspapers http://www.qrd.org/qrd/misc/text/schlafly.outing.reaction-KNIGHT.RIDDER
[2651] Conservative leader Schlafly says `outing' of son was `strike at me'. By Mary Voboril. Knight-Ridder Newspapers http://www.qrd.org/qrd/misc/text/schlafly.outing.reaction-KNIGHT.RIDDER
[2652] Conservative leader Schlafly says `outing' of son was `strike at me'. By Mary Voboril. Knight-Ridder Newspapers http://www.qrd.org/qrd/misc/text/schlafly.outing.reaction-KNIGHT.RIDDER
[2653] Conservative leader Schlafly says `outing' of son was `strike at me'. By Mary Voboril. Knight-Ridder Newspapers http://www.qrd.org/qrd/misc/text/schlafly.outing.reaction-KNIGHT.RIDDER
[2654] Conservative leader Schlafly says `outing' of son was `strike at me'. By Mary Voboril. Knight-Ridder Newspapers http://www.qrd.org/qrd/misc/text/schlafly.outing.reaction-KNIGHT.RIDDER
[2655] Conservative leader Schlafly says `outing' of son was `strike at me'. By Mary Voboril. Knight-Ridder Newspapers http://www.qrd.org/qrd/misc/text/schlafly.outing.reaction-KNIGHT.RIDDER
[2656] Conservative leader Schlafly says `outing' of son was `strike at me'. By Mary Voboril. Knight-Ridder Newspapers http://www.qrd.org/qrd/misc/text/schlafly.outing.reaction-KNIGHT.RIDDER
[2657] Conservative leader Schlafly says `outing' of son was `strike at me'. By Mary Voboril. Knight-Ridder Newspapers http://www.qrd.org/qrd/misc/text/schlafly.outing.reaction-KNIGHT.RIDDER
[2658] Conservative leader Schlafly says `outing' of son was `strike at me'. By Mary Voboril. Knight-Ridder Newspapers http://www.qrd.org/qrd/misc/text/schlafly.outing.reaction-KNIGHT.RIDDER
[2659] Conservative leader Schlafly says `outing' of son was `strike at me'. By Mary Voboril. Knight-Ridder Newspapers http://www.qrd.org/qrd/misc/text/schlafly.outing.reaction-KNIGHT.RIDDER
[2660] Conservative leader Schlafly says `outing' of son was `strike at me'. By Mary Voboril. Knight-Ridder Newspapers http://www.qrd.org/qrd/misc/text/schlafly.outing.reaction-KNIGHT.RIDDER
[2661] Conservative leader Schlafly says `outing' of son was `strike at me'. By Mary Voboril. Knight-Ridder Newspapers http://www.qrd.org/qrd/misc/text/schlafly.outing.reaction-KNIGHT.RIDDER
[2662] Conservative leader Schlafly says `outing' of son was `strike at me'. By Mary Voboril. Knight-Ridder Newspapers http://www.qrd.org/qrd/misc/text/schlafly.outing.reaction-KNIGHT.RIDDER
[2663] At 80, Schlafly is still a conservative force. By Yvonne Abraham, Globe Staff. September 2,
2004http://www.boston.com/news/nation/articles/2004/09/02/at_80_schlafly_is_still_a_conservative_force?mode=PF.
[2664] The History Behind the Equal Rights Amendment.by Roberta W. Francis, Co-Chair, ERA Task Force, National Council of Women's Organizations
http://www.equalrightsamendment.org/era.htm.
[2665] **ERA battle enters new era**,By: Carrie Sheffield April 24, 2007 05:02 PM EST http://www.politico.com/news/stories/0407/3670.html
[2666] The History Behind the Equal Rights Amendment.by Roberta W. Francis, Co-Chair, ERA Task Force, National Council of Women's Organizations
http://www.equalrightsamendment.org/era.htm.
[2667] The History Behind the Equal Rights Amendment.by Roberta W. Francis, Co-Chair, ERA Task Force, National Council of Women's Organizations
http://www.equalrightsamendment.org/era.htm.
[2668] The History Behind the Equal Rights Amendment.by Roberta W. Francis, Co-Chair, ERA Task Force, National Council of Women's Organizations
http://www.equalrightsamendment.org/era.htm.
[2669] National Right to Life Committee. Letter sent 3.28.2007; http://www.nrlc.org/Federal/era/ERAHouseLetter032807.html.
[2670] At 82, Schlafly still a strong voice of conservatism. Associated Press, Apr. 03, 2007 Wednesday, April 04, 2007 http://eagleforum.org/blog/2007/04/at-82-schlafly-still-strong-voice-of.html.
[2671] 'Equal rights' for women: wrong then, wrong now EQUAL RIGHTS REDUX, April 8, 2007 By Phyllis Schlaflyhttp://www.latimes.com/news/opinion/la-op-schafly8apr08,0,6143259.story
[2672] 'Equal rights' for women: wrong then, wrong now EQUAL RIGHTS REDUX, April 8, 2007 By Phyllis Schlaflyhttp://www.latimes.com/news/opinion/la-op-schafly8apr08,0,6143259.story
[2673] 'Equal rights' for women: wrong then, wrong now EQUAL RIGHTS REDUX, April 8, 2007 By Phyllis Schlaflyhttp://www.latimes.com/news/opinion/la-op-schafly8apr08,0,6143259.story
[2674] 'Equal rights' for women: wrong then, wrong now EQUAL RIGHTS REDUX, April 8, 2007 By Phyllis Schlaflyhttp://www.latimes.com/news/opinion/la-op-schafly8apr08,0,6143259.story
[2675] 'Equal rights' for women: wrong then, wrong now EQUAL RIGHTS REDUX, April 8, 2007 By Phyllis Schlaflyhttp://www.latimes.com/news/opinion/la-op-schafly8apr08,0,6143259.story
[2676] 'Equal rights' for women: wrong then, wrong now EQUAL RIGHTS REDUX, April 8, 2007 By Phyllis Schlaflyhttp://www.latimes.com/news/opinion/la-op-schafly8apr08,0,6143259.story
[2677] 'Equal rights' for women: wrong then, wrong now EQUAL RIGHTS REDUX, April 8, 2007 By Phyllis Schlaflyhttp://www.latimes.com/news/opinion/la-op-schafly8apr08,0,6143259.story
[2678] 'Equal rights' for women: wrong then, wrong now EQUAL RIGHTS REDUX, April 8, 2007 By Phyllis Schlaflyhttp://www.latimes.com/news/opinion/la-op-schafly8apr08,0,6143259.story
[2679] 'Equal rights' for women: wrong then, wrong now EQUAL RIGHTS REDUX, April 8, 2007 By Phyllis Schlaflyhttp://www.latimes.com/news/opinion/la-op-schafly8apr08,0,6143259.story
[2680] A letter to the people of Illinois courtesy of Phyllis Schlafly; February 2008 @ http://www.eagleforum.org/era/pdf/ERA-Letter.pdf
[2681] **ERA battle enters new era**,By: Carrie Sheffield April 24, 2007 05:02 PM EST http://www.politico.com/news/stories/0407/3670.html
[2682] **ERA battle enters new era**,By: Carrie Sheffield April 24, 2007 05:02 PM EST http://www.politico.com/news/stories/0407/3670.html
[2683] A letter to the people of Illinois courtesy of Phyllis Schlafly; February 2008 @ http://www.eagleforum.org/era/pdf/ERA-Letter.pdf
[2684] A letter to the people of Illinois courtesy of Phyllis Schlafly; February 2008 @ http://www.eagleforum.org/era/pdf/ERA-Letter.pdf
[2685] National Right to Life Committee. Letter sent 3.28.2007; http://www.nrlc.org/Federal/era/ERAHouseLetter032807.html.
[2686] **ERA battle enters new era**,By: Carrie Sheffield April 24, 2007 05:02 PM EST http://www.politico.com/news/stories/0407/3670.html
[2687] ERA battle enters new era. By Carrrie Sheffield. April 24, 2007. http://www.politico.com/news/stories/0407/3670.html.
[2688] A letter to the people of Illinois courtesy of Phyllis Schlafly; February 2008 @ http://www.eagleforum.org/era/pdf/ERA-Letter.pdf
[2689] A letter to the people of Illinois courtesy of Phyllis Schlafly; February 2008 @ http://www.eagleforum.org/era/pdf/ERA-Letter.pdf
[2690] McCain Poised to Flip on GOP Abortion Platform. In '00 and '07, McCain Called for Exceptions in GOP's Platform on Abortion for Rape, Incest, Mother's Life. By TEDDY DAVIS. **May 9, 2008.** *ABC News' Talal Al-Khatib contributed to this report.* Copyright © 2008 ABC News Internet Ventureshttp://abcnews.go.com/print?id=4824779
[2691] Jerry Falwell quotes from http://thinkexist.com/quotation/aids_is_not_just_god-s_punishment_for_homosexuals/198214.html
[2692] Jerry Falwell quotes from http://thinkexist.com/quotation/aids_is_not_just_god-s_punishment_for_homosexuals/198214.html
[2693] "*Falwell called NOW 'the National Order of Witches'*," Media Matters for America, 2004-NOV-23, at: http://mediamatters.org/ in Religiously-based conflicts, Controversial comments by leading fundamentalist Jerry Falwell: 1979 – 2006. About Jerry Falwell: http://www.religioustolerance.org/falwell.htm.
[2694] What Quote » Celebrity Quotes » Quotes by Pat Robertson »http://www.whatquote.com/quotes/Pat-Robertson/31211-Feminism-encourages-.htm.

[2695] Can Anything Be Done to Stop Gay Rights? The Family Research Institute. Retrieved October 2008 from http://www.familyresearchinst.org/Default.aspx?tabid=145.
[2696] AC360: Dan Savage Takes On Tony Perkins Over Prop 8. By Heather Thursday Nov 13, 2008 2:00pm http://videocafe.crooksandliars.com/heather/ac360-dan-savage-takes-tony-perkins-over-p
[2697] Loving v. Virginia. See @ http://www.law.umkc.edu/faculty/projects/ftrials/conlaw/loving.html
[2698] Loving v. Virginia. See @ http://www.law.umkc.edu/faculty/projects/ftrials/conlaw/loving.html
[2699] Groundbreaking Interracial Marriage. Mildred Loving Never Expected Her Marriage Would End Up at the Supreme Court. By MELIA PATRIA. **June 14, 2007 — http://abcnews.go.com/**. http://www.abcnews.go.com/print?id=3277875
[2700] Groundbreaking Interracial Marriage. Mildred Loving Never Expected Her Marriage Would End Up at the Supreme Court. By MELIA PATRIA. **June 14, 2007 — http://abcnews.go.com/**. http://www.abcnews.go.com/print?id=3277875
[2701] Court Nominee Advised Group on Gay Rights. August 5, 2005. By **SHERYL GAY STOLBERG** and **DAVID D. KIRKPATRICK**. http://www.nytimes.com/2005/08/05/politics/politicsspecial1/05roberts.html?pagewanted=print.
[2702] Court Nominee Advised Group on Gay Rights. August 5, 2005. By **SHERYL GAY STOLBERG** and **DAVID D. KIRKPATRICK**. http://www.nytimes.com/2005/08/05/politics/politicsspecial1/05roberts.html?pagewanted=print.
[2703] Court Nominee Advised Group on Gay Rights. August 5, 2005. By **SHERYL GAY STOLBERG** and **DAVID D. KIRKPATRICK**. http://www.nytimes.com/2005/08/05/politics/politicsspecial1/05roberts.html?pagewanted=print.
[2704] Court Nominee Advised Group on Gay Rights. August 5, 2005. By **SHERYL GAY STOLBERG** and **DAVID D. KIRKPATRICK**. http://www.nytimes.com/2005/08/05/politics/politicsspecial1/05roberts.html?pagewanted=print.
[2705] Court Nominee Advised Group on Gay Rights. August 5, 2005. By **SHERYL GAY STOLBERG** and **DAVID D. KIRKPATRICK**. http://www.nytimes.com/2005/08/05/politics/politicsspecial1/05roberts.html?pagewanted=print.
[2706] Court Nominee Advised Group on Gay Rights. August 5, 2005. By **SHERYL GAY STOLBERG** and **DAVID D. KIRKPATRICK**. http://www.nytimes.com/2005/08/05/politics/politicsspecial1/05roberts.html?pagewanted=print.
[2707] Court Nominee Advised Group on Gay Rights. August 5, 2005. By **SHERYL GAY STOLBERG** and **DAVID D. KIRKPATRICK**. http://www.nytimes.com/2005/08/05/politics/politicsspecial1/05roberts.html?pagewanted=print.
[2708] Court Nominee Advised Group on Gay Rights. August 5, 2005. By **SHERYL GAY STOLBERG** and **DAVID D. KIRKPATRICK**. http://www.nytimes.com/2005/08/05/politics/politicsspecial1/05roberts.html?pagewanted=print.
[2709] Court Nominee Advised Group on Gay Rights. August 5, 2005. By **SHERYL GAY STOLBERG** and **DAVID D. KIRKPATRICK**. http://www.nytimes.com/2005/08/05/politics/politicsspecial1/05roberts.html?pagewanted=print.
[2710] Court Nominee Advised Group on Gay Rights. August 5, 2005. By **SHERYL GAY STOLBERG** and **DAVID D. KIRKPATRICK**. http://www.nytimes.com/2005/08/05/politics/politicsspecial1/05roberts.html?pagewanted=print.
[2711] Duke Law. Erwin Chemerinsky Lawrence v. Texas. Retrieved http://www.law.duke.edu/publiclaw/supremecourtonline/commentary/lawvtex.html.
[2712] The Conservative Case for Gay Marriage. Time. **By Andrew Sullivan**. http://www.time.com/time/printout/0,8816,460232,00.html. **Sunday, Jun. 22, 2003**
[2713] If It's Not a Crime to be Gay, Why Can't We Get Married? by Andrew Sullivan. *First published October 8, 2003, in The Wall Street Journal.* http://www.indegayforum.com/news/show/26930.html
[2714] The Strange History of Sodomy Laws. By Margot Canaday, The Nation. Posted on September 16, 2008, Printed on October 12, 2008 *http://www.alternet.org/story/99092/* Alternet.
[2715] Duke Law. Erwin Chemerinsky Lawrence v. Texas. Retrieved http://www.law.duke.edu/publiclaw/supremecourtonline/commentary/lawvtex.html.
[2716] Duke Law. Erwin Chemerinsky Lawrence v. Texas. Retrieved http://www.law.duke.edu/publiclaw/supremecourtonline/commentary/lawvtex.html.
[2717] The Strange History of Sodomy Laws. By Margot Canaday, The Nation. Posted on September 16, 2008, Printed on October 12, 2008*http://www.alternet.org/story/99092/* Alternet.
[2718] The Strange History of Sodomy Laws. By Margot Canaday, The Nation. Posted on September 16, 2008, Printed on October 12, 2008*http://www.alternet.org/story/99092/* Alternet.
[2719] Court to Weigh Texas' Ban on Gay Sodomy. By David G. Savage
December 03, 2002 *in print edition A-21* http://articles.latimes.com/2002/dec/03/nation/na-gays3
[2720] Court to Weigh Texas' Ban on Gay Sodomy. By David G. Savage
December 03, 2002 *in print edition A-21* http://articles.latimes.com/2002/dec/03/nation/na-gays3
[2721] Duke Law. Erwin Chemerinsky Lawrence v. Texas. Retrieved http://www.law.duke.edu/publiclaw/supremecourtonline/commentary/lawvtex.html.
[2722] Duke Law. Erwin Chemerinsky Lawrence v. Texas. Retrieved http://www.law.duke.edu/publiclaw/supremecourtonline/commentary/lawvtex.html.
[2723] Duke Law. Erwin Chemerinsky Lawrence v. Texas. Retrieved http://www.law.duke.edu/publiclaw/supremecourtonline/commentary/lawvtex.html.
[2724] Duke Law. Erwin Chemerinsky Lawrence v. Texas. Retrieved http://www.law.duke.edu/publiclaw/supremecourtonline/commentary/lawvtex.html.
[2725] Duke Law. Erwin Chemerinsky Lawrence v. Texas. Retrieved http://www.law.duke.edu/publiclaw/supremecourtonline/commentary/lawvtex.html.
[2726] The Strange History of Sodomy Laws. By Margot Canaday, The Nation. Posted on September 16, 2008, Printed on October 12, 2008*http://www.alternet.org/story/99092/* Alternet.
[2727] Professor challenges amendment banning gay marriage, **Lawsuit contends it wasn't properly presented to voters**. By Stacy Forster of the Journal Sentinel. Dec. 30, 2007http://www.jsonline.com/news/wisconsin/29386344.html
[2728] State Politics. Marriage measure backer savors win. By Bill Glauber and Bill Glauber of the Journal Sentinel
Posted: Nov. 9, 2006http://www.jsonline.com/news/statepolitics/29180609.html
[2729] Referendum - 1 Same-Sex Marriage Ban http://hosted.ap.org/dynamic/files/elections/2006/general/by_county/ballot_other/WI.html?SITE=WIMILELN&SECTION=POLITICS
[2730] Marriage amendment strategy backfires on GOP, Posted: Nov. 9, 2006 *Cary Spivak and Dan Bice* http://www.jsonline.com/news/statepolitics/29188669.html
[2731] Marriage amendment strategy backfires on GOP, Posted: Nov. 9, 2006 *Cary Spivak and Dan Bice* http://www.jsonline.com/news/statepolitics/29188669.html
[2732] Marriage amendment strategy backfires on GOP, Posted: Nov. 9, 2006 *Cary Spivak and Dan Bice* http://www.jsonline.com/news/statepolitics/29188669.html
[2733] Marriage amendment strategy backfires on GOP, Posted: Nov. 9, 2006 *Cary Spivak and Dan Bice* http://www.jsonline.com/news/statepolitics/29188669.html
[2734] Marriage amendment strategy backfires on GOP, Posted: Nov. 9, 2006 *Cary Spivak and Dan Bice* http://www.jsonline.com/news/statepolitics/29188669.html
[2735] Marriage amendment strategy backfires on GOP, Posted: Nov. 9, 2006 *Cary Spivak and Dan Bice* http://www.jsonline.com/news/statepolitics/29188669.html
[2736] The will of the people should be respected, By JULAINE K. APPLING. *Julaine K. Appling is CEO of Wisconsin Family Council Inc.* Posted: Nov. 27, 2007http://www.jsonline.com/news/opinion/29332774.html
[2737] [WI] Judge Upholds Constitutional Ban on Gay Marriage (Yes!) May 30, 2008 | Judith Davidoff Posted on Friday, May 30, 2008 2:34:55 PM by Diana in Wisconsin
[2738] Marriage debate rages on. by **Carolyn Smith.** Wednesday, March 30, 2005http://badgerherald.com/news/2005/03/30/marriage_debate_rage.php
[2739] State voters say 'I do' to marriage amendment. Civil unions may be banned; lawsuits could follow/ By Bill Glauber of the Journal Sentinel Posted: Nov. 8, 2006
[2740] Professor challenges amendment banning gay marriage, **Lawsuit contends it wasn't properly presented to voters**. By Stacy Forster of the Journal Sentinel. Dec. 30, 2007http://www.jsonline.com/news/wisconsin/29386344.html
[2741] **Wisconsinites support gay-marriage ban, uncertain on civil unions.** by **Abby Peterson.** Tuesday, April 13,2004http://badgerherald.com/news/2004/04/13/wisconsinites_suppor.php The Badger Poll was conducted between March 23 and 31 by the University of Wisconsin Survey Center. The poll has a margin of error of plus or minus 4 percent.
[2742] Professor challenges amendment banning gay marriage, **Lawsuit contends it wasn't properly presented to voters**. By Stacy Forster of the Journal Sentinel. Dec. 30, 2007http://www.jsonline.com/news/wisconsin/29386344.html
[2743] [WI] Judge Upholds Constitutional Ban on Gay Marriage (Yes!) May 30, 2008 | Judith Davidoff Posted on Friday, May 30, 2008 2:34:55 PM by Diana in Wisconsin
[2744] [WI] Judge Upholds Constitutional Ban on Gay Marriage (Yes!) May 30, 2008 | Judith Davidoff Posted on Friday, May 30, 2008 2:34:55 PM by Diana in Wisconsin
[2745] [WI] Judge Upholds Constitutional Ban on Gay Marriage (Yes!) May 30, 2008 | Judith Davidoff Posted on Friday, May 30, 2008 2:34:55 PM by Diana in Wisconsin
[2746] Quotes on homosexuality retrieved October 2008 from http://www.quotegarden.com/homosexuality.html
[2747] Jerry Falwell quotes from http://thinkexist.com/quotation/aids_is_not_just_god-s_punishment_for_homosexuals/198214.html
[2748] Desmond Tutu: ***By staff writer*** "Homophobia equals apartheid" **afrol News**, 7 July.
[2749] Desmond Tutu: ***By staff writer*** "Homophobia equals apartheid" **afrol News**, 7 July.
[2750] **Bakker, Brown: What the hell happened to Christianity? POSTED: 6:01 p.m. EST, December 18, 2006.** By Jay Bakker and Marc Brown. Special to CNNhttp://www.cnn.com/2006/US/12/13/bakker.brown.commentary/index.html
[2751] CNN. Matthew Shepard News Articles. http://uwacadweb.uwyo.edu/spectrum/mattnews.htm
[2752] 10 Years Later, Shepard Case Haunts Reporters by Peter O'Dowd *Weekend Edition Sunday*, October 12, 2008 · http://www.npr.org/templates/story/story.php?storyId=95553578
[2753] **Mon Oct 12, 1998 - Gay Wyoming College Student Dies After Beating** Reuters. Matthew Shepard News Articles. http://uwacadweb.uwyo.edu/spectrum/mattnews.htm
[2754] New Details Emerge in Matthew Shepard Murder.Killers Talk About Crime That Shocked the Nation. Nov. 26, 2004. http://abcnews.go.com/2020/Story?id=277685&page=1
[2755] New Details Emerge in Matthew Shepard Murder.Killers Talk About Crime That Shocked the Nation. Nov. 26, 2004. http://abcnews.go.com/2020/Story?id=277685&page=1
[2756] **Fri Oct 9, 1998 - 6:10PM EDT - FAMILY RESEARCH COUNCIL OPPOSES HATE CRIME LAWS** Matthew Shepard News Articles. http://uwacadweb.uwyo.edu/spectrum/mattnews.htm
[2757] **Northeastern University criminologist who studies hate crime.**[illegible]**By Steve Mitchell for USA TODAY by Marisol Bello, USA TODAY Updated 10/21/2008http://www.usatoday.com/news/nation/2008-10-20-hategroups_N.htm**
[2758] [illegible]**By Steve Mitchell for USA TODAY by Marisol Bello, USA TODAY Updated 10/21/2008http://www.usatoday.com/news/nation/2008-10-20-hategroups_N.htm**
[2759] [illegible]**By Steve Mitchell for USA TODAY by Marisol Bello, USA TODAY Updated 10/21/2008http://www.usatoday.com/news/nation/2008-10-20-hategroups_N.htm**
[2760] [illegible]**By Steve Mitchell for USA TODAY by Marisol Bello, USA TODAY Updated 10/21/2008http://www.usatoday.com/news/nation/2008-10-20-hategroups_N.htm**
[2761] [illegible]**By Steve Mitchell for USA TODAY by Marisol Bello, USA TODAY Updated 10/21/2008http://www.usatoday.com/news/nation/2008-10-20-hategroups_N.htm**
[2762] [illegible]**By Steve Mitchell for USA TODAY by Marisol Bello, USA TODAY Updated 10/21/2008http://www.usatoday.com/news/nation/2008-10-20-hategroups_N.htm**
[2763] [illegible]**By Steve Mitchell for USA TODAY by Marisol Bello, USA TODAY Updated 10/21/2008http://www.usatoday.com/news/nation/2008-10-20-hategroups_N.htm**
[2764] [illegible]**By Steve Mitchell for USA TODAY by Marisol Bello, USA TODAY Updated 10/21/2008http://www.usatoday.com/news/nation/2008-10-20-hategroups_N.htm**
[2765] [illegible]**By Steve Mitchell for USA TODAY by Marisol Bello, USA TODAY Updated 10/21/2008http://www.usatoday.com/news/nation/2008-10-20-hategroups_N.htm**
[2766] [illegible]**By Steve Mitchell for USA TODAY by Marisol Bello, USA TODAY Updated 10/21/2008http://www.usatoday.com/news/nation/2008-10-20-hategroups_N.htm**
[2767] The Express-Times. Holland Township man names son after Adolf Hitler Sunday, December 14, 2008

By DOUGLAS B. BRILL http://www.lehighvalleylive.com/printer/printer.ssf?/base/news-0/122923112231930.xml&coll=3
[2768] The Express-Times. Holland Township man names son after Adolf Hitler Sunday, December 14, 2008
By DOUGLAS B. BRILL http://www.lehighvalleylive.com/printer/printer.ssf?/base/news-0/122923112231930.xml&coll=3
[2769] The Express-Times. Holland Township man names son after Adolf Hitler Sunday, December 14, 2008
By DOUGLAS B. BRILL http://www.lehighvalleylive.com/printer/printer.ssf?/base/news-0/122923112231930.xml&coll=3
[2770] The Express-Times. Holland Township man names son after Adolf Hitler Sunday, December 14, 2008
By DOUGLAS B. BRILL http://www.lehighvalleylive.com/printer/printer.ssf?/base/news-0/122923112231930.xml&coll=3
[2771] The Express-Times. Holland Township man names son after Adolf Hitler Sunday, December 14, 2008
By DOUGLAS B. BRILL http://www.lehighvalleylive.com/printer/printer.ssf?/base/news-0/122923112231930.xml&coll=3
[2772] The Express-Times. Holland Township man names son after Adolf Hitler Sunday, December 14, 2008
By DOUGLAS B. BRILL http://www.lehighvalleylive.com/printer/printer.ssf?/base/news-0/122923112231930.xml&coll=3
[2773] The Express-Times. Holland Township man names son after Adolf Hitler Sunday, December 14, 2008
By DOUGLAS B. BRILL http://www.lehighvalleylive.com/printer/printer.ssf?/base/news-0/122923112231930.xml&coll=3
[2774] Federal Agents Foil Skinhead Plot To Kill Obama Oct 28, 2008 12:24 am US/Pacific
http://cbs5.com/campaign08/obama.assasination.plot.2.849858.html
[2775] Federal Agents Foil Skinhead Plot To Kill Obama Oct 28, 2008 12:24 am US/Pacific
http://cbs5.com/campaign08/obama.assasination.plot.2.849858.html
[2776] Two held over Obama 'murder plot' Tuesday, 28 October 2008 http://news.bbc.co.uk/1/hi/world/americas/7694254.stm.
[2777] Two held over Obama 'murder plot' Tuesday, 28 October 2008 http://news.bbc.co.uk/1/hi/world/americas/7694254.stm.
[2778] Federal Agents Foil Skinhead Plot To Kill Obama Oct 28, 2008 12:24 am US/Pacific http://cbs5.com/campaign08/obama.assasination.plot.2.849858.html
[2779] Federal Agents Foil Skinhead Plot To Kill Obama Oct 28, 2008 12:24 am US/Pacific http://cbs5.com/campaign08/obama.assasination.plot.2.849858.html
[2780] Federal Agents Foil Skinhead Plot To Kill Obama Oct 28, 2008 12:24 am US/Pacific http://cbs5.com/campaign08/obama.assasination.plot.2.849858.html
[2781] Federal Agents Foil Skinhead Plot To Kill Obama Oct 28, 2008 12:24 am US/Pacific
http://cbs5.com/campaign08/obama.assasination.plot.2.849858.html
[2782] Federal Agents Foil Skinhead Plot To Kill Obama Oct 28, 2008 12:24 am US/Pacific
http://cbs5.com/campaign08/obama.assasination.plot.2.849858.html
[2783] Anti semitism from http://www.ushmm.org/outreach/asemit.htm.
[2784] Rio float depicting Hitler, dead Jews banned. AP
Judge orders removal of mannequins, bars dancers dressed as Nazi leader/ Thurs., Jan. 31, 2008 http://www.msnbc.msn.com/id/22934625
[2785] Matt Hale, in a press release e-mailed to his followers. ANTI-SEMITISM ON THE INTERNET thru the ADL @ http://www.adl.org/backgrounders/Anti_Semitism_us.asp.
[2786] ANTI-SEMITISM ON THE INTERNET thru the ADL @ http://www.adl.org/backgrounders/Anti_Semitism_us.asp.
[2787] ANTI-SEMITISM ON THE INTERNET thru the ADL @ http://www.adl.org/backgrounders/Anti_Semitism_us.asp.
[2788] **Anti-Semitism on the Rise in America -- ADL Survey on Anti-Semitic Attitudes Reveals 17 Percent of Americans Hold "Hardcore" Beliefs** New York, NY, June 11, 2002. Anti Defamation League. http://www.adl.org/PresRele/ASUS_12/4109_12.htm
[2789] **Anti-Semitism on the Rise in America -- ADL Survey on Anti-Semitic Attitudes Reveals 17 Percent of Americans Hold "Hardcore" Beliefs** New York, NY, June 11, 2002. Anti Defamation League. http://www.adl.org/PresRele/ASUS_12/4109_12.htm
[2790] (Neiwert, D., *The Eliminationists*, PoliPoint Press, LLC.,2009, pp.2-3.)
[2791]
[2792] Neiwert, D., *The Eliminationists*, PoliPoint Press, LLC.,2009, p.19)
[2793] Every 72 seconds someone in America develops Alzheimer's. Alzheimer's Disease Facts and Figures. Alzheimer's Association.
http://www.alz.org/national/documents/report_alzfactsfigures2007.pdf.
[2794] Alzheimer's Facts and Figures. Retrieved 11.16.07 from http://www.alz.org/alzheimers_disease_alzheimer_statistics.asp.
[2795] Every 72 seconds someone in America develops Alzheimer's. Alzheimer's Disease Facts and Figures. Alzheimer's Association.
http://www.alz.org/national/documents/report_alzfactsfigures2007.pdf. Page 10.
[2796] Every 72 seconds someone in America develops Alzheimer's. Alzheimer's Disease Facts and Figures. Alzheimer's Association.
http://www.alz.org/national/documents/report_alzfactsfigures2007.pdf. Page 10.
[2797] Every 72 seconds someone in America develops Alzheimer's. Alzheimer's Disease Facts and Figures. Alzheimer's Association.
http://www.alz.org/national/documents/report_alzfactsfigures2007.pdf. Page 11.
[2798] Every 72 seconds someone in America develops Alzheimer's. Alzheimer's Disease Facts and Figures. Alzheimer's Association.
http://www.alz.org/national/documents/report_alzfactsfigures2007.pdf. Page 11.
[2799] Every 72 seconds someone in America develops Alzheimer's. Alzheimer's Disease Facts and Figures. Alzheimer's Association.
http://www.alz.org/national/documents/report_alzfactsfigures2007.pdf. Page 13.
[2800] Every 72 seconds someone in America develops Alzheimer's. Alzheimer's Disease Facts and Figures. Alzheimer's Association.
http://www.alz.org/national/documents/report_alzfactsfigures2007.pdf. Page 15.
[2801] Every 72 seconds someone in America develops Alzheimer's. Alzheimer's Disease Facts and Figures. Alzheimer's Association.
http://www.alz.org/national/documents/report_alzfactsfigures2007.pdf. Page 13.
[2802] Every 72 seconds someone in America develops Alzheimer's. Alzheimer's Disease Facts and Figures. Alzheimer's Association.
http://www.alz.org/national/documents/report_alzfactsfigures2007.pdf. Page 13.
[2803] Ann Coulter, February 26, 2002, (The Democratic Underground, Sept. 16, 2009)
[2804] Answers to Your Questions; For a Better Understanding of Sexual Orientation & Homosexuality http://www.apa.org/topics/sorientation.html;
[2805] Retrieved from http://www.quotegarden.com/homosexuality.html.
[2806] When Your Child Is Gay. The odds are good that you or someone you know will raise a gay child. Are you ready? by Ted Hesson InTown Westchester • April 24, 2008http://www.lohud.com/article/20080424/CUSTOM02/804240550/1276/CUSTOM0301
[2807] When Your Child Is Gay. The odds are good that you or someone you know will raise a gay child. Are you ready? by Ted Hesson InTown Westchester • April 24, 2008http://www.lohud.com/article/20080424/CUSTOM02/804240550/1276/CUSTOM0301
[2808] When Your Child Is Gay. The odds are good that you or someone you know will raise a gay child. Are you ready? by Ted Hesson InTown Westchester • April 24, 2008http://www.lohud.com/article/20080424/CUSTOM02/804240550/1276/CUSTOM0301
[2809] When Your Child Is Gay. The odds are good that you or someone you know will raise a gay child. Are you ready? by Ted Hesson InTown Westchester • April 24, 2008http://www.lohud.com/article/20080424/CUSTOM02/804240550/1276/CUSTOM0301
[2810] When Your Child Is Gay. The odds are good that you or someone you know will raise a gay child. Are you ready? by Ted Hesson InTown Westchester • April 24, 2008http://www.lohud.com/article/20080424/CUSTOM02/804240550/1276/CUSTOM0301.
[2811] When Your Child Comes Out: Lesbian, Bisexual, Gay or Trans. What Do You Do? By Kathy Belge, About.comhttp://lesbianlife.about.com/od/families/a/LesbianDaughter.htm.
[2812] Quentin Crisp, *The Naked Civil Servant*, 1978 http://www.quotegarden.com/homosexuality.html
[2813] Memorable Quotes from Mississippi Burning @ http://www.imdb.com/title/tt0095647/quotes.
[2814] American Social Health Association http://www.ashastd.org/parents/parents_overview.cfm
[2815] American Social Health Association http://www.ashastd.org/parents/parents_overview.cfm
[2816] American Social Health Association http://www.ashastd.org/parents/parents_overview.cfm
[2817] American Social Health Association http://www.ashastd.org/parents/parents_overview.cfm
[2818] When Your Child Is Gay. The odds are good that you or someone you know will raise a gay child. Are you ready? by Ted Hesson InTown Westchester • April 24, 2008http://www.lohud.com/article/20080424/CUSTOM02/804240550/1276/CUSTOM0301
[2819] When Your Child Comes Out: Lesbian, Bisexual, Gay or Trans. What Do You Do? By Kathy Belge, About.com http://lesbianlife.about.com/od/families/a/LesbianDaughter.htm.
[2820] When Your Child Is Gay. The odds are good that you or someone you know will raise a gay child. Are you ready? by Ted Hesson InTown Westchester • April 24, 2008http://www.lohud.com/article/20080424/CUSTOM02/804240550/1276/CUSTOM0301.
[2821] When Your Child Is Gay. The odds are good that you or someone you know will raise a gay child. Are you ready? by Ted Hesson InTown Westchester • April 24, 2008http://www.lohud.com/article/20080424/CUSTOM02/804240550/1276/CUSTOM0301.
[2822] When Your Child Is Gay. The odds are good that you or someone you know will raise a gay child. Are you ready? by Ted Hesson InTown Westchester • April 24, 2008http://www.lohud.com/article/20080424/CUSTOM02/804240550/1276/CUSTOM0301.
[2823] When Your Child Is Gay. The odds are good that you or someone you know will raise a gay child. Are you ready? by Ted Hesson InTown Westchester • April 24, 2008http://www.lohud.com/article/20080424/CUSTOM02/804240550/1276/CUSTOM0301.
[2824] When Your Child Is Gay. The odds are good that you or someone you know will raise a gay child. Are you ready? by Ted Hesson InTown Westchester • April 24, 2008http://www.lohud.com/article/20080424/CUSTOM02/804240550/1276/CUSTOM0301.
[2825] When Your Child Is Gay. The odds are good that you or someone you know will raise a gay child. Are you ready? by Ted Hesson InTown Westchester • April 24, 2008http://www.lohud.com/article/20080424/CUSTOM02/804240550/1276/CUSTOM0301
[2826] When Your Child Is Gay. The odds are good that you or someone you know will raise a gay child. Are you ready? by Ted Hesson InTown Westchester • April 24, 2008http://www.lohud.com/article/20080424/CUSTOM02/804240550/1276/CUSTOM0301
[2827] When Your Child Is Gay. The odds are good that you or someone you know will raise a gay child. Are you ready? by Ted Hesson InTown Westchester • April 24, 2008http://www.lohud.com/article/20080424/CUSTOM02/804240550/1276/CUSTOM0301

[2828] When Your Child Is Gay. The odds are good that you or someone you know will raise a gay child. Are you ready? by Ted Hesson InTown Westchester • April 24, 2008http://www.lohud.com/article/20080424/CUSTOM02/804240550/1276/CUSTOM0301

[2829] When Your Child Is Gay. The odds are good that you or someone you know will raise a gay child. Are you ready? by Ted Hesson InTown Westchester • April 24, 2008http://www.lohud.com/article/20080424/CUSTOM02/804240550/1276/CUSTOM0301.

[2830] From the issue dated March 31, 2008. Personal Experience Guides Leader of Group for Families of Gay People. By Peter Panepento. The Chronicle of Philanthropy Managing. http://philanthropy.com/free/articles/v17/i12/12005001.htm

[2831] Jody's Family Affair. PFLAG head, Huckaby, talks about allies, outings and his "biological clock" by Will O'Bryan. Published on *May 1, 2008* in Metro Weekly. http://www.metroweekly.com/gauge/?ak=3412

[2832] Jody's Family Affair. PFLAG head, Huckaby, talks about allies, outings and his "biological clock" by Will O'Bryan. Published on *May 1, 2008* in Metro Weekly. http://www.metroweekly.com/gauge/?ak=3412

[2833] From the issue dated March 31, 2008. Personal Experience Guides Leader of Group for Families of Gay People. By Peter Panepento. The Chronicle of Philanthropy Managing. http://philanthropy.com/free/articles/v17/i12/12005001.htm

[2834]Does and Don'ts retrieved from PFLAG in November 2008. http://www.gayfamilysupport.com/pflag.html

[2835] Does and Don'ts retrieved from PFLAG in November 2008. http://www.gayfamilysupport.com/pflag.html

[2836] Does and Don'ts retrieved from PFLAG in November 2008. http://www.gayfamilysupport.com/pflag.html

[2837] Does and Don'ts retrieved from PFLAG in November 2008. http://www.gayfamilysupport.com/pflag.html

[2838] Answers to Your Questions; For a Better Understanding of Sexual Orientation & Homosexuality http://www.apa.org/topics/sorientation.html;

[2839] Gay Marriage Is Back On The Radar For Republicans, Evangelicals. But Overall Opposition to Gay Marriage is Less Than in 2004. June 12, 2008. PEW RESEARCH CENTER FOR THE PEOPLE & THE PRES. http://pewresearch.org/pubs/868/gay-marriage.

[2840] See http://www.vancouversun.com/news/Pope+Benedict+named+twist+German+pedophile+priest+furor/2676995/story.html.

LaVergne, TN USA
19 May 2010
183227LV00003B/2/P